Praise for *Masters of the Air*

"Donald L. Miller's *Masters of the Air* is a st[...] pound effect of the book's narrative vitality a[...] terrific in all the meanings of the word—terri[...] mirable. What a story it is!"

—David McCullough

"[A] searching, thoroughly engrossing history of the American air war against Nazi Germany. . . . vividly recreates the day-to-day life of the men who flew the missions and their comrades on the ground. . . . unflinchingly describes the devastation wrought by the civilian bombing campaign and tackles the moral issues head-on. . . . Mr. Miller has a fluid way of moving from discussion of theory and tactics to the personal stories that give them human weight."

—William Grimes, *The New York Times*

"Over the first years of World War II, the only American casualties on European soil were flyboys shot out of the sky. Long before Normandy, America's bomber boys waged the Allies' longest WWII campaign and brought the war to Hitler. Now we are fortunate that the incomparable Donald Miller has brought the memory of these Masters of the Air back to us."

—James Bradley, author of *Flags of Our Fathers* and *Flyboys*

"Miller's work is always extraordinary but this large volume is especially remarkable for its valuable recovery of details, like all the psychiatric ruin of the many bomber boys assigned to kill German civilians. This is a rare account of the American Eighth Air Force, and with so many readers hoodwinked by fantasies of The Good War, it deserves wide acceptance and ultimate enshrinement as a classic."

—Paul Fussell, author of *The Great War* and *Modern Memory*

"Absorbing and exhaustive. . . . Miller leaves no doubt as to the contribution of the Eighth Air Force to defeating the Germans and helping end what could have been a much longer war."

—Stephen J. Lyons, *Chicago Tribune*

"*Masters of the Air* sucks the wind out of the reader. . . . It is a piece of history that accurately and comprehensively tells the story of the Eighth Air Force going *mano a mano* against a tough and determined foe. The incredible cost to both sides is recounted in riveting detail. It left me shaken."

—Lt. Gen. Bernard E. Trainor, USMC (Ret.) and coauthor of *Cobra II: The Inside Story of the Invasion and Occupation of Iraq*

"For sixty years we have waited for a history to equal the epic saga of the Eighth Air Force's struggle with fighters, flak and weather on a battlefield moving at three miles per minute five miles above the earth's crust. Now it is here. With brilliant artistry, Don Miller paints the story from the palette of the voices of the men who manned the planes or waited them out."

—Richard B. Frank, author of
Downfall: The End of the Imperial Japanese Empire

"Miller's book works on many levels: strategic critique, operational analysis and testimonial to the brave 'bomber boys' who brought war home to Germany at a time when no other American force could. *Masters of the Air* is a terrific read, and I hereby designate it 'Book of the Year.'"

—Robert Citino, *World War II* Magazine

"A superlative chronicle. . . . a wonderful history. . . . Awesomely researched and written."

—*Library Journal*

"*Masters of the Air* is masterful narrative history, the elegantly interwoven story of the men and boys who first took the war to the heart of Germany. Vivid and meticulous, judicious but not judgmental, Donald L. Miller chronicles the air war over Europe in all its heroism and horror."

—Geoffrey C. Ward, author of
Unforgivable Blackness: The Rise and Fall of Jack Johnson

"A first-rate one-volume treatment of a vast subject, and one that's sure to satisfy."

—Bruce Heydt, *America in WWII* Magazine

"When I learned that Don Miller had written a history of the air war against Germany, I knew that readers would be transported as virtual eyewitnesses to this aerial battlefield. His gripping reconstruction of what was happening in the planes is matched by the best account yet of what the bombings were doing to Germans on the ground. This book bears the Miller trademark: a strong narrative supported by solid history."

—Joseph E. Persico, author of
Eleventh Month, Eleventh Day, Eleventh Hour: Armistice Day 1918

"Miller's massive, readable volume may prove to be the standard history of the Eighth Air Force."

—*Booklist*

"Absorbing and comprehensive. . . . *Masters of the Air* covers a lot of ground, both figuratively and literally. . . . Miller and his research assistants have read through a vast amount of the specialist literature as well as a lot of primary sources, and they have conducted numerous interviews with veterans. . . . [Miller] is admirably sane and clear about what the air war cost, on all sides, and also about what it achieved."

—Fredric Smoler, *American Heritage*

Also by Donald L. Miller

D-Days in the Pacific

The Story of World War II

City of the Century: The Epic of Chicago and the Making of America

Lewis Mumford, A Life

The Lewis Mumford Reader

*The Kingdom of Coal: Work, Enterprise, and
Ethnic Communities in the Mine Fields*
(with Richard Sharpless)

The New American Radicalism

MASTERS
OF THE
AIR

America's Bomber Boys Who Fought the Air War

Against Nazi Germany

Donald L. Miller

SIMON & SCHUSTER PAPERBACKS

New York   London   Toronto   Sydney

SIMON & SCHUSTER PAPERBACKS
A Division of Simon & Schuster, Inc.
1230 Avenue of the Americas
New York, NY 10020

First Simon & Schuster trade paperback edition October 2007

SIMON & SCHUSTER PAPERBACKS and colophon are registered trademarks
of Simon & Schuster, Inc.

For information about special discounts for bulk purchases,
please contact Simon & Schuster Special Sales at
1-800-456-6798 or business@simonandschuster.com

Designed by Jaime Putorti

Maps by Paul Pugliese

Manufactured in the United States of America

1   3   5   7   9   10   8   6   4   2

The Library of Congress has cataloged the hardcover edition as follows:
Miller, Donald L., date.
Masters of the air : America's bomber boys who fought the air war against Nazi
Germany / Donald L. Miller.
p.   cm.
Includes bibliographical references and index.
1. World War, 1939–1945—Aerial operations, American.   2. United States.
Army Air Forces. Air Force, 8th—History.   3. World War, 1939–1945—Campaigns—
Western Front.   4. Bomber pilots—United States—Biography.   I. Title.
D790.228th.M55   2006
940.54'4973—dc22   2006050461
ISBN-13: 978-0-7432-3544-0
ISBN-10:   0-7432-3544-4
ISBN-13: 978-0-7432-3545-7 (pbk)
ISBN-10:   0-7432-3545-2 (pbk)

Photo Credits
Hundredth Bomb Group Archives, Historian, Michael Faley: 4, 5. Louis Loevsky: 44.
Mighty Eighth Air Force Museum, Savannah, Georgia: 3, 7, 8, 9, 10, 13, 14, 18, 22, 28,
29, 30, 33, 34, 35, 36, 37, 38, 40, 41, 45, 46. National Archives and Record
Administration, College Park, Maryland: 1, 2, 6, 11, 12, 15, 16, 17, 19, 20, 21, 23, 24, 25,
26, 27, 31, 32, 39, 42, 43.

To the gang at the Black Cat Bar:
Alyssa, Alexis, Ashlee, Devin,
Austin, and Mason

Contents

In the spring of 1944 . . . we were masters in the air. The bitterness of the struggle had thrown a greater strain on the Luftwaffe than it was able to bear. . . . For our air superiority, which by the end of 1944 was to become air supremacy, full tribute must be paid to the United States Eighth Air Force.

WINSTON CHURCHILL, *Closing the Ring*

There was a consciousness always of the presence of his comrades about him. He felt the subtle battle brotherhood more potent even than the cause for which they were fighting. It was a mysterious fraternity born of the smoke and danger of death.

STEPHEN CRANE, *The Red Badge of Courage*

U. S. Eighth Air Force Bases

△1 First Air Division Stations

②2 Second Air Division Stations

▢3 Third Air Division Stations

✛ Special Operations
(Carpetbaggers)

Eighth Air Force
Heavy Bombardment Groups
as of June 6, 1944

34: Mendlesham, B-24	392: Wendling, B-24
44: Shipdham, B-24	398: Nuthampstead, B-17
91: Bassingbourn, B-17	401: Deenethorpe, B-17
92: Podington, B-17	445: Tibenham, B-24
93: Hardwick, B-24	446: Bungay, B-24
94: Bury St. Edmunds, B-17	447: Rattlesden, B-17
95: Horham, B-17	448: Seething, B-24
96: Snetterton Heath, B-17	452: Deopham Green, B-17
100: Thorpe Abbotts, B-17	453: Old Buckenham, B-24
303: Molesworth, B-17	457: Glatton, B-17
305: Chelveston, B-17	458: Horsham St. Faith, B-24
306: Thurleigh, B-17	466: Attlebridge, B-24
351: Polebrook, B-17	467: Rackheath, B-24
379: Kimbolton, B-17	486: Sudbury, B-24
381: Ridgewell, B-17	487: Lavenham, B-24
384: Grafton Underwood, B-17	489: Halesworth, B-24
385: Great Ashfield, B-17	490: Eye, B-24
388: Knettishall, B-17	491: Metfield, B-24
389: Hethel, B-24	492: North Pickenham, B-24
390: Framlingham, B-17	493: Debach, B-24

Headquarters

Bushy Park: HQ, United States Strategic Air Forces
in Europe (USSTAF). Code name: Widewing

High Wycombe: HQ Eighth AF. Code name: Pinetree

Bushey Hall: HQ, Eighth AF Fighter Command

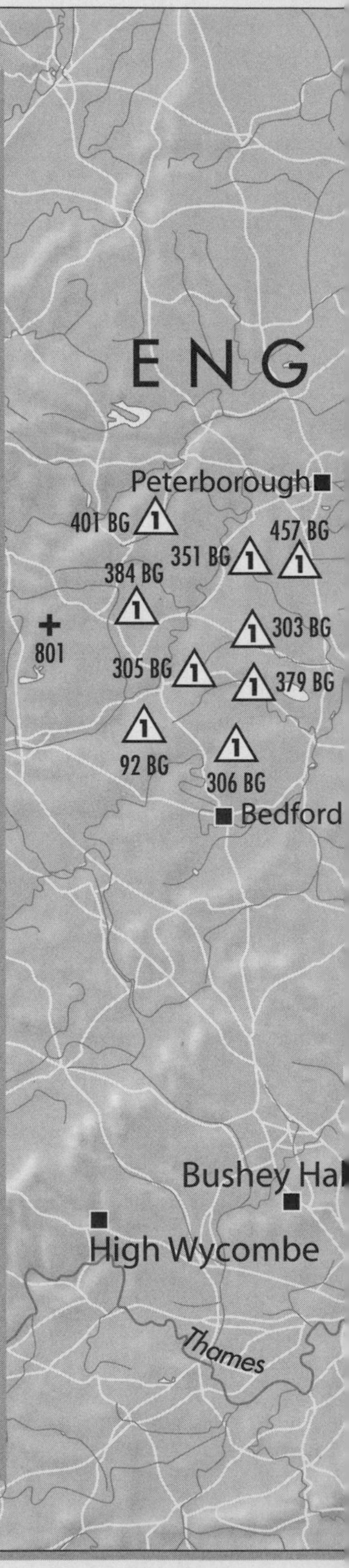

ENG

Peterborough ■

401 BG △1
457 BG △1
351 BG △1
384 BG △1
303 BG △1
✛ 801
305 BG △1
379 BG △1
92 BG △1
306 BG △1

■ Bedford

Bushey Ha

■

High Wycombe

Thames

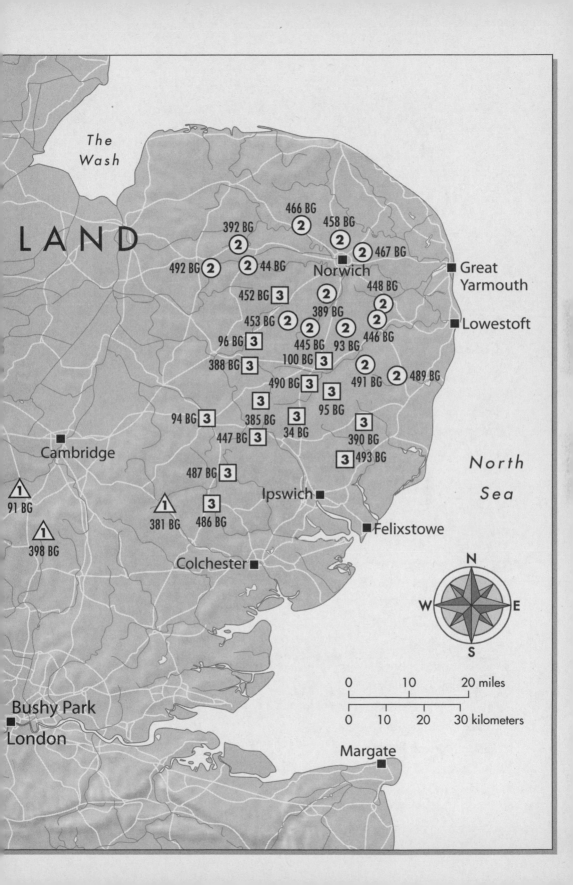

The Wash

LAND

466 BG ②
392 BG ②   458 BG ②
                    ② 467 BG
492 BG ②   ② 44 BG
                Norwich
452 BG ③   ② 389 BG   448 BG
453 BG ②   ② 446 BG
96 BG ③   ② 445 BG 93 BG
388 BG ③   100 BG ③
490 BG ③
            ③ 95 BG   ② 491 BG ② 489 BG
94 BG ③   385 BG ③
447 BG ③   ③ 34 BG
                    ③ 390 BG
                    ③ 493 BG
487 BG ③
Ipswich
① 91 BG
            ① 381 BG   ③ 486 BG
① 398 BG
Colchester

Cambridge

Great Yarmouth

Lowestoft

North Sea

Felixstowe

Bushy Park
London

Margate

N
W   E
S

0   10   20 miles
0   10   20   30 kilometers

North
Sea

IRELAND

GREAT
BRITAIN

WALES   *ENGLAND*
                              Norwich
Bassingbourn   ● Cambridge
(8th AF base) ●

NETH.

May 1943:
Spitfire (U.K.),
range 175 miles

● Amsterdam

High Wycombe ●
(8th AF Headquarters)   ● London
                    Thames

● Rotterdam

June
1943:
P-47 Thunderbolt
(U.S.) range
230 miles

● Dover

*Atlantic
Ocean*

● Essen

English Channel

Pas-de-Calais ●   ● Dunkirk
                                  ● Antwerp

● Lille

● Cologne
● Bonn

● Abbeville

Brussels ●

BELGIUM

St. Lô ●

● Rouen
● Caen   *Seine*

LUX.

Luxembourg ●

Brest ●

Falaise ●

Paris ●
        Marne

● Saarbrücken

Lorient ●

● Le Mans

Loire

St. Nazaire ●

● Nantes

Rhine

FRANCE

*Bay of
Biscay*

● La Rochelle

SWITZ.

Allier

● Bordeaux

175 miles
230 miles

Key

 U-boat
installation

 Railway
center

⚓ Shipbuilding
or naval base

⌇ Missile
launch
site

🏭 War industry

🛢 Oil refinery

✈ Aircraft factory

Other sites

✗ German fighter field

N

W   E

S

*Mediterranean
Sea*

Selected Targets of the Eighth Air Force

SWEDEN

DENMARK

Baltic Sea

Flensburg

Kiel

Vegesack

Hamburg

Bremen

Weser

GERMANY

Hanover

Münster

Hamm

Dortmund

Kassel

August 1943:
P-47 Thunderbolt
with belly tank,
range 375 miles

Gotha

Buchenwald

November 1943:
P-38 Lightning (U.S.),
range 520 miles

Frankfurt

Schweinfurt

Mainz

Nuremberg

Stuttgart

March 1944:
P-51 Mustang
with drop tanks (U.S.),
range more than 600 miles

Regensburg

Munich

Friedrichshafen

Zurich

Berchtesgaden

Peenemünde

Anklam

Stettin (Pölitz)

Berlin

Brunswick

Oschersleben

Dessau

Merseburg/Leuna

Leipzig

Dresden

Liegnitz

Prague

Pilsen

Braunau

Linz

Krems

Vienna

Gdynia

Danzig

Marienburg

EAST PRUSSIA (GERMANY)

POLAND

Oder

Warta

SOVIET UNION

SLOVAKIA

Danube

HUNGARY

Budapest

Trieste

YUGOSLAVIA

SERBIA

ROMANIA

Ploesti

ITALY

Adriatic Sea

Rome

Anzio

Foggia
(15th AF Headquarters)

Naples

AUSTRIA

BULGARIA

ALBANIA

375 miles

520 miles

600 miles

Elbe

0   100   200 miles

0   100   200   300 kilometers

The Bloody Hundredth

The Eighth Air Force was one of the great fighting forces in
the history of warfare. It had the best equipment and the
best men, all but a handful of whom were civilian
Americans, educated and willing to fight for their country
and a cause they understood was in danger—freedom. It's
what made World War II special.

ANDY ROONEY, *My War*

London, October 9, 1943

Maj. John Egan's private war began at breakfast in a London hotel.
Egan was on a two-day leave from Thorpe Abbotts, an American bomber base some ninety miles north of London and a
short stroll from the Norfolk hamlet that gave it its name. Station #139, as
it was officially designated, with its 3,500 fliers and support personnel, was
built on a nobleman's estate lands, and the crews flew to war over furrowed
fields worked by Sir Rupert Mann's tenant farmers, who lived nearby in
crumbling stone cottages heated by open hearths.

Thorpe Abbotts is in East Anglia, a history-haunted region of ancient
farms, curving rivers, and low flat marshland. It stretches northward from
the spires of Cambridge, to the high-sitting cathedral town of Norwich, and
eastward to Great Yarmouth, an industrial port on the black waters of the

North Sea. With its drainage ditches, wooden windmills, and sweeping fens, this low-lying slice of England brings to mind nearby Holland, just across the water.

It is a haunch of land that sticks out into the sea, pointed, in the war years, like a raised hatchet at the enemy. And its drained fields made good airbases from which to strike deep into the German Reich. A century or so behind London in its pace and personality, it had been transformed by the war into one of the great battlefronts of the world, a war front unlike any other in history.

This was an air front. From recently built bases in East Anglia, a new kind of warfare was being waged—high-altitude strategic bombing. It was a singular event in the history of warfare, unprecedented and never to be repeated. The technology needed to fight a prolonged, full-scale bomber war was not available until the early 1940s and, by the closing days of that first-ever bomber war, was already being rendered obsolete by jet engine aircraft, rocket-powered missiles, and atomic bombs. In the thin, freezing air over northwestern Europe, airmen bled and died in an environment that no warriors had ever experienced. It was air war fought not at 12,000 feet, as in World War I, but at altitudes two and three times that, up near the stratosphere where the elements were even more dangerous than the enemy. In this brilliantly blue battlefield, the cold killed, the air was unbreathable, and the sun exposed bombers to swift violence from German fighter planes and ground guns. This endless, unfamiliar killing space added a new dimension to the ordeal of combat, causing many emotional and physical problems that fighting men experienced for the first time ever.

For most airmen, flying was as strange as fighting. Before enlisting, thousands of American fliers had never set foot in an airplane or fired a shot at anything more threatening than a squirrel. A new type of warfare, it gave birth to a new type of medicine—air medicine. Its pioneering psychiatrists and surgeons worked in hospitals and clinics not far from the bomber bases, places where men were sent when frostbite mauled their faces and fingers or when trauma and terror brought them down.

Bomber warfare was intermittent warfare. Bouts of inactivity and boredom were followed by short bursts of fury and fear; and men returned from sky fights to clean sheets, hot food, and adoring English girls. In this incredible war, a boy of nineteen or twenty could be fighting for his life over Berlin at eleven o'clock in the morning and be at a London hotel with the date of his dreams at nine that evening. Some infantrymen envied the airmen's comforts, but as a character in an American navigator's novel asks, "How many infantry guys do you think would be heading for the front lines if you gave them a plane with full gas tanks?" Sold to the American public as a quicker, more decisive way of winning than slogging it out on the ground, the air war became a slow, brutal battle of attrition.

John Egan was commander of a squadron of B-17 Flying Fortresses, one of the most fearsome killing machines in the world at that time. He was a bomber boy; destruction was his occupation. And like most other bomber crewmen, he went about his work without a quiver of conscience, convinced he was fighting for a noble cause. He also killed in order not to be killed.

Egan had been flying combat missions for five months in the most dangerous air theater of the war, the "Big Leagues," the men called it; and this was his first extended leave from the fight—although it hardly felt like a reprieve. That night, the German air force, the Luftwaffe, plastered the city, setting off fires all around his hotel. It was his first time under the bombs and he found it impossible to sleep, with the screaming sirens and the thundering concussions.

Egan was attached to the Eighth Air Force, a bomber command formed at Savannah Army Air Base in Georgia in the month after Pearl Harbor to deliver America's first blow against the Nazi homeland. From its unpromising beginnings, it was fast becoming one of the greatest striking forces in history. Egan had arrived in England in the spring of 1943, a year after the first men and machines of the Eighth had begun occupying bases handed over to them by the RAF—the Royal Air Force—whose bombers had been hammering German cities since 1940. Each numbered Bombardment Group (BG)—his was the 100th—was made up of four squadrons of eight to twelve four-engine bombers, called "heavies," and occupied its own air station, either in East Anglia or the Midlands, directly north of London, around the town of Bedford.*

For a time in 1943, the Eighth was assigned four Bomb Groups equipped with twin-engine B-26 Marauders, which were used primarily for low- and medium-level bombing, with mixed results. But in October of that year, these small Marauder units were transferred to another British-based American air command—the Ninth Air Force, which was being built up to provide close air support for the cross-Channel invasion of Nazi-occupied Europe. From this point until the end of the war, all Eighth Air Force bombers were either Fortresses or B-24 Liberators, the only Ameri-

---

* The fliers commonly referred to their Bombardment Group as their Bomb Group, the term I have used throughout the text.

can bombers designed for long-range, high-altitude strikes. But the Eighth did retain its own Fighter Command to provide escort aircraft for its bombers on shallow-penetration missions into Northern Europe. Its pilots flew single-engine P-47 Thunderbolts and twin-engine P-38 Lightnings, and operated from bases located in the vicinity of the bomber stations.

When the 100th Bomb Group flew into combat, it was usually accompanied by two other bomb groups from nearby bases, the 390th and the 95th, the three groups forming the 13th Combat Wing. A combat wing was one small part of a formation of many hundreds of bombers and fighter escorts that shook the earth under the English villagers who spilled out of their cottages at dawn to watch the Americans head out "to hit the Hun."

"No one . . . could fail to thrill at the sight of the great phalanxes streaming away from their East Anglian airfields," wrote the historian John Keegan, a boy growing up in England during the war. "Squadron after squadron, they rose to circle into groups and wings and then set off southeastward for the sea passage to their targets, a shimmering and winking constellation of aerial grace and military power, trailing a cirrus of pure white condensation from 600 wing tips against the deep blue of English summer skies. Three thousand of America's best and brightest airmen were cast aloft by each mission, ten to a 'ship,' every ship with a characteristic nickname, often based on a song title, like *My Prayer*; or a line from a film, like 'I am Tondelayo.' "

On the flight to the coast, "we turned on the BBC to listen to all the sentimental songs of the day," recalled co-pilot Bernard R. Jacobs of Napa, California. Passing over the eternally green English countryside, it seemed strange to Jacobs that such a tranquil-looking land was the staging area for a campaign of unimaginable slaughter, destruction such as the world had never seen.

Although President Franklin D. Roosevelt had recently ended all voluntary enlistments, the Eighth Air Force was still an elite outfit, made up almost entirely of volunteers, men who had signed up before the president's order or highly qualified men who were snapped up by Air Force recruiters after they were drafted by the Army but before they were given a specific assignment. Eighth Air Force bomber crews were made up of men from every part of America and nearly every station in life. There were Harvard history majors and West Virginia coal miners, Wall Street lawyers and Oklahoma cow punchers, Hollywood idols and football heroes. The actor Jimmy Stewart was a bomber boy and so was the "King of Hollywood," Clark Gable. Both served beside men and boys who had washed office windows in Manhattan or loaded coal cars in Pennsylvania—Poles and Italians, Swedes and Germans, Greeks and Lithuanians, Native Americans and Spanish-Americans, but not African-Americans, for official Air Force policy prevented blacks from flying in combat units of the Eighth Air Force. In the claustrophobic compartments of the heavy bombers, in the crucible of combat, Catholics and Jews, Englishmen and Irishmen, became brothers in spirit, melded together by a desire not to die. In bomber warfare, the ability to survive, and to fight off fear, depended as much on the character of the crew as on the personality of the individual. "Perhaps at no time in the history of warfare," wrote Starr Smith, former Eighth Air Force intelligence officer, "has there been such a relationship among fighting men as existed with the combat crews of heavy bombardment aircraft."

The Eighth Air Force had arrived in England at the lowest moment of the war for the nations aligned against the Axis Powers: Germany, Italy, Japan, and their allies. The Far Eastern and Pacific empires of the English, the Dutch, and the French had recently fallen to the Japanese, as had the American-occupied Philippines. By May 1942, when Maj. Gen. Carl A. "Tooey" Spaatz arrived in London to take command of American air operations in Europe, Japan controlled a far-reaching territorial empire. The Royal Air Force's fighter boys had won the Battle of Britain the previous summer, and England had stood up to the Blitz, the first long-term bombing campaign of the war, but since the evacuation of the British army at Dunkirk in May 1940, and the fall of France soon thereafter, Germany had been the absolute master of Western Europe. In the spring of 1942, Great Britain stood alone and vulnerable, the last surviving European democracy at war with the Nazis. And the question became, How to hit back at the enemy?

"We have no Continental Army which can defeat the German military power," Prime Minister Winston Churchill declared. "But there is one thing that will bring him . . . down, and that is an absolutely devastating, exterminating attack by very heavy bombers from this country upon the Nazi homeland." Beginning in 1940, the RAF's Bomber Command went after industrial targets in the Rhineland and the Ruhr, centers of Nazi material might. The first RAF raids of the war had been flown in daylight, but after taking murderous losses, the RAF was forced to bomb at night and to alter its targeting. Since industrial plants could not be sighted, let alone hit, on moonless nights, the RAF began bombing entire cities—city busting, the crews correctly called it. The purpose was to set annihilating fires that killed thousands and that would break German civilian morale. The bombing was wildly inaccurate and crew losses were appalling. But killing Germans was wonderful for British morale—payback for the bombing of Coventry and London, and England had no other way to directly hurt Germany. Until Allied armies entered Germany in the final months of the war, strategic bombing would be the only battle fought inside the Nazi homeland.

The Eighth Air Force had been sent to England to join this ever accelerating bombing campaign, which would be the longest battle of World War II. It had begun combat operations in August 1942, in support of the British effort but with a different plan and purpose. The key to it was the top secret Norden bombsight, developed by Navy scientists in the early 1930s. Pilots like Johnny Egan had tested it in the high, sparkling skies of the American West and put their bombs on sand targets with spectacular accuracy, some bombardiers claiming they could place a single bomb in a pickle barrel from 20,000 feet. The Norden bombsight would make high-altitude bombing both more effective and more humane, Air Force leaders insisted. Cities could now be hit with surgical precision, their munitions mills destroyed with minimal damage to civilian lives and property.

The Eighth Air Force was the proving instrument of "pickle-barrel" bombing. With death-dealing machines like the Flying Fortress and the equally formidable Consolidated B-24 Liberator, the war could be won, the theorists of bomber warfare argued, without a World War I–style massacre on the ground or great loss of life in the air. This untested idea appealed to an American public that was wary of long wars, but less aware that combat always confounds theory.

Daylight strategic bombing could be done by bombers alone, without fighter planes to shield them. This was the unshakable conviction of Brig. Gen. Ira C. Eaker, the former fighter pilot that Carl Spaatz had picked to head the Eighth Air Force's bomber operations. Flying in tight formations—forming self-defending "combat boxes"—the bombers, Eaker believed, would have the massed firepower to muscle their way to the target.

Johnny Egan believed in strategic bombing, but he didn't believe this. He had entered the air war when Ira Eaker began sending his bomber fleets deep into Germany, without fighter escorts, for at that time no single-engine plane had the range to accompany the heavies all the way to these distant targets and back. In the summer of 1943, Johnny Egan lost a lot of friends to the Luftwaffe.

There were ten men in the crew of an Eighth Air Force heavy bomber. The pilot and his co-pilot sat in the cockpit, side by side; the navigator and bombardier were just below, in the plane's transparent Plexiglas nose; and directly behind the pilot was the flight engineer, who doubled as the top turret gunner. Further back in the plane, in a separate compartment, was the radio operator, who manned a top-side machine gun; and at mid-ship there were two waist gunners and a ball turret gunner, who sat in a revolving Plexiglas bubble that hung—fearfully vulnerable—from the underside of the fuselage. In an isolated compartment in the back of the plane was the tail gunner, perched on an oversized bicycle seat. Every position in the plane was vulnerable; there were no foxholes in the sky. Along with German and American submarine crews and the Luftwaffe pilots they met in combat, American and British bomber boys had the most dangerous job in the war. In October 1943, fewer than one out of four Eighth Air Force crew members could expect to complete his tour of duty: twenty-five combat missions. The statistics were discomforting. Two-thirds of the men could expect to die in combat or be captured by the enemy. And 17 percent would either be wounded seriously, suffer a disabling mental breakdown, or die in a violent air accident over English soil. Only 14 percent of fliers assigned to Major Egan's Bomb Group when it arrived in England in May 1943 made it to their twenty-fifth mission. By the end of the war, the Eighth Air Force would have more fatal casualties—26,000—than the entire United States Marine Corps. Seventy-seven percent of the Americans who flew against the Reich before D-Day would wind up as casualties.

As commander of the Hundredth's 418th Squadron, Johnny Egan flew with his men on all the tough missions. When his boys went into danger, he wanted to face it with them. "Anyone who flies operationally is crazy," Egan confided to Sgt. Saul Levitt, a radioman in his squadron who was later injured in a base accident and transferred to the staff of *Yank* magazine, an army publication. "And then," says Levitt, "he proceeded to be crazy and fly operationally. And no milk runs. . . .

When his "boy-men," as Egan called them, went down in flaming planes, he wrote home to their wives and mothers. "These were not file letters," Levitt remembered. "It was the Major's idea they should be written in long-hand to indicate a personal touch, and there are no copies of these letters. He never said anything much about that. The letters were between him and the families involved."

Major Egan was short and skinny as a stick, barely 140 pounds, with thick black hair, combed into a pompadour, black eyes, and a pencil-thin mustache. His trademarks were a white fleece-lined flying jacket and an idiomatic manner of speaking, a street-wise style borrowed from writer Damon Runyon. At twenty-seven, he was one of the "ancients" of the outfit, but "I can out-drink any of you children," he would tease the fresh-faced members of his squadron. On nights that he wasn't scheduled to fly the next day, he would jump into a jeep and head for his "local," where he'd gather at the bar with a gang of Irish laborers and sing ballads until the taps ran dry or the tired publican tossed them out.

When Egan was carousing, his best friend was usually in the sack. Major Gale W. Cleven's pleasures were simple. He liked ice cream, cantaloupe, and English war movies; and he was loyal to a girl back home named Marge. He lived to fly and, with Egan, was one of the "House of Lords of flying men." His boyhood friends had called him "Cleve," but Egan, his inseparable pal since their days together in flight training in the States, renamed him "Buck" because he looked like a kid named Buck that Egan knew back in Manitowoc, Wisconsin. The name stuck. "I never liked it, but I've been Buck ever since," Cleven said sixty years later, after he earned an MBA from Harvard Business School and a Ph.D. in interplanetary physics.

Lean, stoop-shouldered Gale Cleven grew up in the hardscrabble oil country north of Casper, Wyoming, and worked his way through the University of Wyoming as a roughneck on a drilling crew. With his officer's cap cocked on the side of his head and a toothpick dangling from his mouth, he looked like a tough guy, but "he had a heart as big as Texas and was all for his men," one of his fliers described him. He was extravagantly alive and was easily the best storyteller on the base.

A squadron commander at age twenty-four, he became a home-front hero when he was featured in a *Saturday Evening Post* story of the Regensburg Raid by Lt. Col. Beirne Lay, Jr., later the co-author, with Sy Bartlett, of *Twelve O'Clock High!,* the finest novel and movie to come out of the European air war. The Regensburg-Schweinfurt mission of August 17, 1943, was the biggest, most disastrous American air operation up to that time. Sixty bombers and nearly 600 men were lost. It was a "double strike" against the aircraft factories of Regensburg and the ball bearing plants of Schweinfurt, both industrial powerhouses protected by one of the most formidable aerial defense systems in the world. Beirne Lay was flying with the Hundredth that day as an observer in a Fortress called *Piccadilly Lilly,* and in the fire and chaos of battle he saw Cleven, in the vulnerable low squadron—the so-called Coffin Corner, the last and lowest group in the bomber stream—"living through his finest hour." With his plane being shredded by enemy fighters, Cleven's co-pilot panicked and prepared to bail out. "Confronted with structure damage, partial loss of control, fire in the air and serious injuries to personnel, and faced with fresh waves of fighters still rising to the attack, [Cleven] was justified in abandoning ship," Lay wrote. But he ordered his co-pilot to stay put. "His words were heard over the interphone and had a magical effect on the crew. They stuck to their guns. The B-17 kept on."

Beirne Lay recommended Cleven for the Medal of Honor. "I didn't get it and I didn't deserve it," Cleven said. He did receive the Distinguished Service Cross but never went to London to pick it up. "Medal, hell, I needed an aspirin," he commented long afterward. "So I remain undecorated."

The story of Cleven on the Regensburg raid "electrified the base," recalled Harry H. Crosby, a navigator in Egan's 418th Squadron. Johnny Egan had also fought well that day. Asked how he survived, he quipped, "I carried two rosaries, two good luck medals, and a $2 bill off of which I had chewed a corner for each of my missions. I also wore my sweater backwards and my good luck jacket." Others were not so fortunate. The Hundredth lost ninety men.

Casualties piled up at an alarming rate that summer, too fast for the men to keep track of them. One replacement crewman arrived at Thorpe Abbotts in time for a late meal, went to bed in his new bunk, and was lost the next morning over Germany. No one got his name. He was thereafter known as "the man who came to dinner."

With so many of their friends dying, the men of the Hundredth badly needed heroes. At the officers club, young fliers gathered around Cleven and Egan and "watched the two fly missions with their hands," Crosby wrote in his memoir of the air war. "Enlisted men adored them," and pilots wanted to fly the way they did. With their dashing white scarves and crushed "fifty-mission caps," they were characters right out of *I Wanted Wings,* another Beirne Lay book, and the Hollywood film based on it, which inspired thousands of young men to join the Army Air Corps. They even talked like Hollywood. The first time Crosby set eyes on Cleven was at the officers club. "For some reason he wanted to talk to me, and he said, 'Taxi over here Lootenant.' "

Cleven liked the young replacements but worried about their untested bravado. "Their fear wasn't as great as ours, and therefore was more dangerous. They feared the unknown. We feared the known."

On the morning of October 8, 1943, an hour of so before Johnny Egan stepped on the train that brought him to London on his first leave from Thorpe Abbotts, Buck Cleven took off for Bremen and didn't return. Three Luftwaffe fighters flew out of the sun and tore into his Fortress, knocking out three engines, blowing holes in the tail and nose, sheering off a good part of the left wing, and setting the cockpit on fire. The situation hopeless, Cleven ordered the crew to jump. He was the last man out of the plane. When he jumped, the bomber was only about 2,000 feet from the ground.

This was at 3:15 P.M., about the time Johnny Egan would have been checking into his London hotel. Hanging from his parachute, Cleven saw he was going to land near a small farmhouse "and faster than I wanted to." Swinging in his chute to avoid the house, he spun out of control and went flying through the open back door and into the kitchen, knocking over furniture and a small iron stove. The farmer's wife and daughter began screaming hysterically, and in a flash, the farmer had a pitchfork pressed against Cleven's chest. "In my pitiful high school German, I tried to convince him I was a good guy. He wasn't buying it."

That night, some of the men in Cleven's squadron who had survived the Bremen mission walked to a village pub and got extravagantly drunk. "None of them could believe he was gone," said Sgt. Jack Sheridan, another member of Cleven's squadron. If Cleven "the invincible" couldn't make it, who could? But as Sheridan noted, "missing men don't stop a war."

The next morning, over a hotel breakfast of fried eggs and a double Scotch, Johnny Egan read the headlines in the London *Times,* "Eighth Air Force Loses 30 Fortresses Over Bremen." He sprang out of his chair and rushed to a phone to call the base. With wartime security tight, the conversation was in code. "How did the game go," he asked. Cleven had gone down swinging, he was told. Silence. Pulling himself together, Egan asked, "Does the team have a game scheduled for tomorrow?"

"Yes," came the reply.

"I want to pitch."

He was back at Thorpe Abbotts that afternoon in time to "sweat out" a long mission the group flew to Marienburg, a combat strike led by the Hundredth's Commander, Col. Neil B. "Chick" Harding, a former West Point football hero. As soon as the squadrons returned, Egan got Harding's permission to lead the Hundredth's formation on the next day's mission. At dawn, he went to one of the crew huts and woke up pilot John D. Brady, a former saxophone player in one of the country's big bands. Harry Crosby, whose bed was directly across from Captain Brady's, overheard the conversation. "John, I am flying with you. . . . We are going to get the bastards that got Buck." Then the two men left for the pre-flight briefing.

"The target for today is Munster," the intelligence officer, Maj. Miner Shaw, informed the sleepy crews as he pulled back the curtain that covered a wall-size map of Northern Europe. A red string of yarn stretched from

Thorpe Abbotts across the Netherlands to a small railroad juncture just over the Dutch border. It would be a short raid, and P-47 Thunderbolts—the best Allied fighter planes available—would escort the bombers to the limit of their range, nearly all the way to the target. It looked routine—except for one thing. The Aiming Point was the heart of the old walled city, a marshaling yard, and an adjacent neighborhood of workers' homes. Nearby, was a magnificent cathedral whose bishop was known to be a strident opponent of the Nazis. "Practically all of the railroad workers in the [Ruhr] valley [are] billeted in Munster," Shaw droned on in a low monotone. If the bombardiers hit their target accurately, the entire German rail system in this heavily trafficked area would, he said, be seriously disrupted.

This was a radical change in American bombing practice. Later, the Eighth Air Force would officially deny it, but the Münster raid was a city-busting operation. Declassified mission reports and flight records clearly list the "center of town" as the Aiming Point; one report, that of the 94th Bomb Group, describes the Aiming Point as, "Built up section of North East tip of Marshalling yards."

When Shaw announced that "we were going to sock a residential district. . . . I find [sic] myself on my feet, cheering," Egan said later. "Others, who had lost close friends in [previous] . . . raids joined in the cheering 'cause here is a chance to kill Germans, the spawners of race hatred and minority oppression. It was a dream mission to avenge the death of a buddy."

Some of the fliers who were in the briefing room that morning do not recall any cheering. One of them, Capt. Frank Murphy, was at the time a twenty-two-year-old jazz musician from Atlanta, Georgia, who had left Emory University to become an Air Force navigator. Murphy has no recollection of Egan jumping up and swearing revenge, but he does say that no one in the room openly protested the targeting of civilians, not even those like himself who had relatives born in Germany. Perhaps some of the men remembered the warning that their first commander, Col. Darr H. "Pappy" Alkire, had given them back in the States, right after they completed flight training and received their wings. "Don't get the notion that your job is going to be glorious or glamorous. You've got dirty work to do, and you might as well face the facts. You're going to be baby-killers and women-killers."

Not everybody in the Hundredth saw himself in the murder business, but most of the men trusted their leaders. "I felt I was there to help win the war, if possible," said Lt. Howard "Hambone" Hamilton, Captain Brady's bombardier. "The basic problem in trying to bomb a railway system is that, if sufficient labor is available, railroad tracks can be repaired in a short time. We were told that the idea of bombing these railroad worker's homes was to deprive the Germans of the people to do the repair work."

But at briefings that same morning at neighboring bomber bases, there was some grumbling about the target selection. "It was a Sunday, and many crewmen . . . had deep reservations about bombing anywhere near churches," recalled Lt. Robert Sabel, a pilot with the 390th Bomb Group. Capt. Ellis Scripture, a navigator who would be flying in the 95th Bomb Group's lead Fortress, *The Zootsuiters,* later described his reaction. "I'd been raised in a strict Protestant home. My parents were God-oriented people. . . . I was shocked to learn that we were to bomb civilians as our primary target for the first time in the war." Ellis Scripture went to his group commander after the briefing and told him he didn't want to fly that day. Col. John Gerhart exploded: "Look Captain, this [is] war, spelled W-A-R. We're in an all-out fight; the Germans have been killing innocent people all over Europe for years. We're here to beat the hell out of them . . . and we're going to do it. . . . Now—I'm leading this mission and you're my navigator. . . . If you don't fly, I'll have to court-martial you. Any questions?"

Scripture said "no sir" and headed for the flight line. "I made up my mind there and then that war isn't a gentleman's duel," he said later. "I never again had any doubts about the strategy of our leaders. They had tough decisions to make—and they made them."

Another flier from Scripture's bomb group, Lt. Theodore Bozarth, described most accurately how most of the men in the 13th Combat Wing felt about this mission. It would be the wing's third mission in three days: Bremen, Marienburg, and now Münster. "We were just too tired to care much one way or the other."

Harry Crosby was not slated to fly to Münster. He and his pilot, Capt. Everett Blakely, were recovering from a spectacular crash landing on the English coast on their return from Bremen. The morning of the Münster mission they decided to commandeer a war-damaged plane and fly down to the resort town of Bournemouth for a brief seaside break from the war. Before taking off, Crosby called the base weatherman, Capt. Cliff Frye, and arranged a code for Crosby to receive a telephone report of the Münster strike.

At four that afternoon he called Frye. "Did all my friends get back from pass?"

No answer.

"Did some of them have a permanent change of station?"

"Yes, all but one."

Then, losing his composure, Frye broke the code. "Egan's gone. Your old crew is gone. The whole group is gone. The only one who came back was that new crew in the 418th [Squadron]. They call [their pilot] Rosie."

Lt. Robert "Rosie" Rosenthal had not trained with the Hundredth's original crews. He and his crew had been assigned to the group that August from a replacement pool in England, to fill in for men lost on the Regensburg raid. "When I arrived, the group was not well organized," Rosenthal recalled. "They were a rowdy outfit, filled with characters. Chick Harding was a wonderful guy, but he didn't enforce tight discipline on the ground or in the air." Rosenthal didn't fly a mission for thirty days. "No one came around to check me out and approve me for combat duty. Finally, my squadron commander, John Egan, had me fly a practice formation. I flew to the right of his plane. I had done a lot of formation flying in training and I was frustrated; I desperately wanted to get into the war. I put the wing of my plane right up against Egan's, and wherever he went, I went. When we landed, Egan told me he wanted me to be his wing man."

Rosenthal had gone to Brooklyn College, not far from his Flatbush home. An outstanding athlete, he had been captain of the football and baseball teams, and later was inducted into the college's athletic hall of fame. After graduating summa cum laude from Brooklyn Law School, he went to work for a leading Manhattan law firm. He was just getting started in his new job when the Japanese bombed Pearl Harbor. The next morning he joined the Army Air Corps.

He was twenty-six years old, with broad shoulders, sharply cut features, and dark curly hair. A big-city boy who loved hot jazz, he walked, incongruously, with the shambling gait of a farmer, his toes turned inward—and there wasn't an ounce of New York cynicism in him. He was shy and easily embarrassed, but he burned with determination. "I had read *Mein Kampf* in college and had seen the newsreels of the big Nazi rallies in Nuremberg, with Hitler riding in an open car and the crowds cheering wildly. It was the faces in the crowd that struck me, the looks of adoration. It wasn't just Hitler. The entire nation had gone mad; it had to be stopped.

"I'm a Jew, but it wasn't just that. Hitler was a menace to decent people everywhere. I was also tremendously proud of the English. They stood alone against the Nazis during the Battle of Britain and the Blitz. I read the papers avidly for war news and listened to Edward R. Murrow's live radio broadcasts of the bombing of London. I couldn't wait to get over there.

"When I finally arrived, I thought I was at the center of the world, the place where the democracies were gathering to defeat the Nazis. I was right where I wanted to be."

Rosie Rosenthal didn't share these thoughts with his crewmates, simple guys who distrusted what they called deep thinking. They never learned what was inside him, what made him fly and fight with blazing resolve. Later in the war, when he became one of the most decorated and famous fliers in the Eighth, word spread around Thorpe Abbotts that his family was in a German concentration camp. But when someone asked him directly, he said "that was a lot of hooey." His family—mother, sister, brother-in-law, and niece (his father had recently died)—were all back in Brooklyn. "I have no personal reasons. Everything I've done or hope to do is strictly because I hate persecution. . . . A human being has to look out for other human beings or else there's no civilization."

At the briefing for Münster, Rosie remembered the target being the city's marshaling yard, not workers' housing. "It was near the center of the town; innocent people would die, as they did in all wars."

On that hazy October morning, Rosie's plane was third on the runway, lined up with the rest of the thirty-ton destruction machines, engines thundering, ready to take off at half-minute intervals. He and his crew were flying in a new plane, *Royal Flush.* Their regular plane, *Rosie's Riveters,* had suffered heavy battle damage on the missions to Bremen and Marienburg. The men were superstitious, apprehensive about flying in a strange bomber. Gathering them together in a huddle under one of the wings, Rosie calmed them down.

"The doors to the bomb bays close behind you, and you know that you are a prisoner of this ship," *Yank* correspondent Denton Scott described the fear many airmen felt on the flight line that morning. "That imprisonment can be broken only by three factors, and they are, in order: Disaster by explosion and parachuting to another prison, death, or a safe return."

At 11:11 A.M., the wheels of Brady's lead plane, *M'lle Zig Zig,* with Major Egan in the co-pilot's seat and Lt. John Hoerr, Brady's co-pilot, in the jump seat, touched off the ground, and with its belly full of bombs, barely cleared the high trees at the end of the runway. It was Brady's first time in the lead position, and he felt unprepared. Egan was uneasy as well. He had left his lucky white flying jacket behind. Buck Cleven, the friend he was revenging, never liked it because it wasn't clean.

The fifty-three bombers of the 13th Combat Wing assembled over Great Yarmouth, the Hundredth forming behind the leading 95th, and flew southwest to join the other Combat Wings, 275 B-17s making up the bomber formation. Over the North Sea, four bombers turned back, claiming mechanical difficulties. The depleted formation would have thirty-six fewer .50 caliber machine guns. This could mean a lot in an air fight, but it didn't seem to concern anyone. "We felt pretty easy about the trip," recalled Lt. Douglas Gordon-Forbes, bombardier of the 390th Bomb Group's *Cabin in the Sky.* "It was the first time we had fighter escort any distance into Germany, and our confidence overflowed."

The Germans had a chain of radar stations that stretched from Norway to northern France, and they knew the Americans were coming from the time the planes began stacking up over East Anglia. As the bombers crossed the Dutch border and passed over the neatly defined towns of Westphalia, they began to run into intense antiaircraft fire, "flak," as it was called, a contraction of *Fliegerabwehrkanonen,* antiaircraft artillery. Looking over at Brady, Egan saw him make the sign of the cross. Seconds later, one of their waist gunners was killed by a piece of shrapnel from a Nazi antiaircraft gun.

As the Hundredth's formation approached the Initial Point (IP)—the place where the heavies lined up for the bomb run—Egan called out to the group that the Thunderbolts were "heading back to the barn," having reached the limit of their range. After turning to his right to watch them dip their wings to signal good luck, Egan looked straight ahead and shouted, "Jesus Christ! Pursuits at twelve o'clock high! Looks like they're on us!" Some 200 German fighters attacked head-on not breaking off contact until they were within a split second of colliding with the bombers.

Brady's lead plane was hit first. Flying in the glass-enclosed nose of *Aw-R-Go,* directly behind *M'lle Zig Zig,* Frank Murphy saw "a horrendous fiery explosion" directly underneath Brady's plane, and watched in silent horror as the wounded Fortress went into a sickening dive, trailing black smoke and fuel. "[Our bombardier] came up from the nose looking quite messy to tell us that we have to leave the formation because 'Hambone' Hamilton had numerous holes in him and wanted to go home," Egan later described the scene in the stricken plane. "I assured him that we'd left the formation."

While Brady struggled to keep his ship level so the crew would have a "platform" from which to jump, Egan supervised the "abandon ship" maneuver. As he began speaking on the interphone, the plane burst into flames. At that moment he sent John Hoerr down to help nineteen-year-old "Hambone" Hamilton make it to the forward escape hatch, in the floor of the plane. Then Egan and Brady put the bomber on automatic pilot and scrambled back to the open bomb bay. Standing on the precariously narrow catwalk that separated the two main compartments of the bomb bay, Egan looked down at the ground and shouted, "Go ahead, Brady . . . I'm the senior man on board." But Brady wanted to be last; it was his ship and crew. "We prattled some more," said Egan, "when the nicest spaced holes you ever did see, a row about six inches below our feet, appeared along the entire length of the bomb bay door. They were thirty caliber punctuation marks, and I say, 'I'll see you Brady,' step out, count one, and pull the rip-cord about the time I go by the ball turret. The chute opened without a jar and the family jewels were safe."

Seconds later, Egan saw three German fighters break away from the bombers and zero in on him. Cannons blazing, they nicked him and filled his chute with holes; they disappeared, he said, only when they thought "I [was] very dead, not knowing that I'm Irish." When he hit the ground, Egan spotted some enemy soldiers heading toward him. Shedding his chute and his cumbersome winter flying equipment, he disappeared into a patch of woods.

"Hambone" Hamilton landed less than a mile away, although the two men never made contact. Hamilton was lying alone on the ground, still bleeding badly. But this, he believed, was not his day to die; minutes earlier he had made a near miraculous escape from the jaws of death.

When Lieutenant Hoerr had gone to the nose of the plane to help Hamilton, he found the wounded bombardier hanging on the escape door, outside the plane, with nothing but 20,000 feet of air between his dangling feet and a ghastly end. With his punctured lung, Hamilton did not have the strength to push open the escape hatch with his hands. So he stood on it and twisted the release handle. When the door dropped open, he fell through, but the right shoulder strap of his parachute caught on the handle, and he hung outside the bomber with the inboard propeller only inches from his head.

After a tense struggle, Hoerr was able to free Hamilton from the exit door, and both men dropped to earth in their parachutes, where they were captured by German soldiers. An ambulance was called for, and Hamilton was driven into Münster. The driver's grandson, a boy about fifteen, pointed a long hunting rifle at Hamilton's head during the entire thirty-minute trip.

At about that time, the crew of Rosenthal's *Royal Flush* was in the final minutes of what one air commander called "the single most vicious air battle of that war, or of all time." It lasted only forty-five minutes, but almost nothing in the European war matched it in focused fury. That afternoon the Eighth Air Force confronted what Lt. Gordon-Forbes called "the greatest concentration of Nazi fighters ever hurled at an American bomber formation."

The Luftwaffe employed new tactics and weapons. It attacked only a few bomb groups in order to maximize the number of kills and fired air-to-air missiles into the tightly massed combat boxes. The Hundredth, flying in the dangerous low position in its combat wing, took the brunt of the attack. Seconds after Brady's plane was hit, the Hundredth's entire formation was broken up and scattered by swarms of single-engine planes, and by rockets launched by twin-engine planes that flew parallel to the bombers, out of range of their powerful machine guns. "Red balls of fire, trailing long white plumes of smoke, came lobbing toward us, then passed swiftly in great swishes," Douglas Gordon-Forbes described these terrifying rocket attacks. "Several narrowly missed our ship, one passing four feet under the Plexiglas nose in which I was sitting."

Flying alone, the bombers of the Hundredth were easy prey for determined enemy pilots, some of them flying above the Westphalia homes of their families. "The German fighters came after the 100th in wave after wave," recalled Frank Murphy. "Several times I turned my head sideways and squinted, expecting a head-on collision." This was Murphy's twenty-first mission, but he had never seen so many fighters at one time, not even over Regensburg. The Luftwaffe had never repulsed an Eighth Air Force strike. "I think this attack was aimed at turning us back for the first time," Rosie Rosenthal said later.

In seven minutes the Hundredth ceased to exist as an organized fighting unit. But a few of its planes, including Murphy's and Rosenthal's, fought their way to the target and dropped their ordnance. The 500-pound bombs began falling in the center of the city just as the bells of the cathedral began tolling the call for afternoon vespers. "We go four miles high," a young pilot would write, "and let them go, and haven't the faintest idea what happens when they connect."

The fighters broke off their attack when the bombers went into the heavy flak field directly over the target, but when the remaining planes of the Hundredth made a wide sweeping turn to their rallying point with the 95th and 390th Bomb Groups, the Luftwaffe reappeared in force. "Almost as soon as we turned there was an explosion behind me and I was knocked to the floor," Murphy remembered. "It felt as though someone had hit me with a baseball bat and thrown a bucket of hot water on me. It was an absolutely terrifying moment. I didn't know how badly I was hit and I wondered if I was going to die." Lying on top of a three-inch-high bed of hot shell casings from his Browning machine gun, slipping and sliding uncontrollably, Murphy looked up and spotted co-pilot Glenn Graham, with his oxygen mask pulled off, motioning with his hand to follow him. Graham pulled the emergency release of the forward crew door in the nose of the plane, kicked it open, and jumped out. Murphy paused, looked down at the earth, which seemed "a hundred miles away," and slowly lowered himself by his arms through the opening. "Suddenly, it [was] deathly quiet. There was no more battle noise, no guns firing, no smell of cordite, no engines straining and groaning, no intercom chatter." Then, as the planes of the 390th Bomb Group flew into sight, directly above Murphy, the sky erupted with fire and exploding metal. The flak batteries that ringed the city opened up on the 390th and fighter planes swooped in for the kill. "I was at my gun now, and didn't have to look for fighters," recalled bombardier Gordon-Forbes. "They were everywhere."

The entire sky was "a fantastic panorama of black flak bursts, burning and exploding B-17s, spinning and tumbling crazily," said Lt. William Overstreet, co-pilot of the inaptly named *Situation Normal.* "It was like flying through an aerial junkyard," observed a Fortress gunner. There were so many parachutes it looked to Gordon-Forbes like an airborne invasion. And men who had been blown out of their planes before they had time to put on their chutes were falling to the ground, tumbling and twisting in the whipping wind. "What happens to your body when you fall 25,000 feet?" a flier asked himself as he watched men he knew drop through the clouds. "Do you die on the way down, or are you conscious . . . screaming all the way down?"

Prewar strategists foresaw the bomber war as a battle of machines against machines, with little human contact. But with every Eighth Air Force mission an invasion of the Reich, downed airmen like "Hambone" Hamilton met the enemy face-to-face on his own soil before a single American infantryman crossed into Germany; and air fights often approached the grim intimacy of close-quarter fighting on the ground. At one point in the furious battle over Münster, a German fighter plane streaked past the nose section of *Cabin in the Sky.* "In that split second he was so close I remember sitting there staring him in the face while he stared back," recalled Douglas Gordon-Forbes. "He looked scared too."

That afternoon, fifteen-year-old Otto Schuett was attending a horse show on the outskirts of Münster. An apprentice printer, he was born in Brooklyn, New York, perhaps not far from Rosenthal's old neighborhood. His parents had returned to Germany in 1931, moving from Lübeck to Münster in 1939, where his father became a leading figure in the Nazi Party. Shortly after the war broke out, Otto joined the Hitler Youth, proudly rising to the position of group leader.

From Münster's Show Ground, three miles from the city center, Otto

Schuett heard the bombers coming, but they were hard to spot because they blended so beautifully into the high autumn sky. "From our position, we saw smoke, in dense clouds, erupting . . . [from] the town center. . . . As the bombs dropped closer and closer . . . we suddenly realized that our lives were at stake. We all started to scatter and race for cover as the bomb explosions and anti-aircraft fire reached a crescendo. I simply sprawled face-down on the ground."

During a lull in the bombing, Schuett ran for better cover; as he did, he saw the falling wing of a B-17, its propellers still spinning, heading straight for him. The wing crashed to the earth just ahead of him, "burning fiercely and sending up clouds of black, oily smoke. . . . I lay there in the dirt, expecting death at any minute."

Inside the walled city, Hildegard Kosters, a fourteen-year-old schoolgirl, clung to life in an air raid shelter built under the railroad station. "The earth shook, vibrated, shuddered and heaved from the impact of the concussions. The solid concrete bunker trembled and shook to its very foundations. The railway junction and marshalling yards must have been the target.

"Suddenly all the lights went out. The people—mostly women and children—huddled together like sheep in the slaughterhouse, praying, crying and shrieking in terror. Some were mute with fear."

"It was an inferno," recalled a German soldier who happened to be changing trains at Münster. "All around me I could hear injured people screaming who were trapped under demolished and burning houses. Almost all of the city center had been flattened to the ground and the main railway station had been heavily damaged."

Looking up, the soldier watched the bombers passing through the enormous smoke clouds they had created, heading back to England. Some of them, he could tell, were badly damaged.

"We had a big rocket hole through the starboard wing, two engines were out, my two waist gunners were seriously injured, and my tail gunner had also been hit," Rosenthal later described the situation in *Royal Flush*. "After we left the target, we were attacked again by fighters. Our gunners could not shoot an enemy plane down unless they had a stable platform, but if I had kept the plane level and stable we would have been shot down. So I went into a series of maneuvers, every kind of evasive action. The plane was all over the sky. I guess the German pilots eventually got frustrated and decided to go for an easier target."

The crew began barking over the interphone that the oxygen system had been shot out and that they were having trouble drawing air. Rosenthal told them to cut the chatter, that they were sinking so fast they would not need the plane's oxygen in a few seconds. At that moment, co-pilot Winfrey "Pappy" Lewis turned around and asked the flight engineer for a report on their gas supply. He got no answer; the man's eyeballs were floating in their sockets, a symptom of oxygen deprivation. He didn't come around until they dropped to below 12,000 feet.

"In a situation like that you don't think about dying," said Rosenthal. "You focus on what you have to do to save the plane and crew. You drive everything else out of your mind. You're frightened, but there's a difference between fear and panic. Panic paralyzes; fear energizes. You sweat— even at 50 degrees below zero—your heart pumps, you act. Truthfully, the only fear I ever experienced in the war was the fear that I would let my crew down.

"People talk about courage, but that's a bunch of baloney. I wasn't courageous on the Münster mission. I had a job to do, to deliver those bombs, and I did it. After that, my only concern was the nine other men in my plane. How would I get them home?"

As suddenly as the battle began, it ended. "Directly ahead, lone white vapor trails signaled our reprieve from death," Gordon-Forbes recalled. "Thunderbolts! The Nazis banked away, hightailing it."

Col. Hubert "Hub" Zemke's 56th Fighter Group—Zemke's Wolf Pack— had taken off from their Suffolk air station in miserable weather to rendezvous with the withdrawing bombers. They and other Thunderbolt outfits fought off the German fighters, most of them low on fuel and ammunition, and then escorted their "big friends" across the North Sea. Rosenthal's badly crippled plane was unable to keep up with the rest of the formation. It had to go it alone.

With *Royal Flush* flying dangerously low over the North Sea, navigator Ronald Bailey had trouble sighting the English coast through the fastgathering evening mist, and an even more difficult time finding Thorpe Abbotts, which looked exactly like the other American bomber bases that had been built nearby. As *Royal Flush* approached the field through low-hanging black clouds, its crew fired red flares to signal "wounded aboard," and nearly everyone on the base raced to the runway to watch the distressed bomber come in. Anxious eyes searched the skies for more Fortresses—hopefully all thirteen—but there was only one. After Rosie nosed his chewed-up ship into its hardstand, the concrete circular pad on which the bomber was parked, he climbed down through the bomb bay, turned to the intelligence officer, and asked: "Are they all this tough?" Then he jumped into an ambulance with his two wounded gunners and accompanied them to the base hospital. "I didn't feel relieved," he said years later. "I felt guilty. Why had I lived when all those other good men died?"

Air gunner Loren Darling recovered quickly, but his friend John Shaffer had to be sent home to have shrapnel removed from near his heart. Later, Rosenthal learned from the ground crews that there had been an unexploded cannon shell rolling around in one of *Royal Flush*'s wing tanks. A member of his crew speculated that a slave laborer, working in a Nazi munitions factory, had sabotaged the shell.

There were two sets of victims in the European bomber war: those who were bombed and the men who bombed them. Nearly 700 civilians were killed in Münster on October 10, 1943, most of them residents of medieval town houses in the vicinity of the marshaling yard. Münster Cathedral was only slightly damaged and two schools that took direct hits were mercifully unoccupied. When Otto Schuett returned to his neighborhood, a few hundred yards from the cathedral, only the front wall of his house was standing, and bomb-shocked survivors, including his family, were climbing out of basement shelters, carrying the dead with them. For people on the ground, it had been forty-five minutes of unrelieved terror. In those same forty-five minutes the 13th Combat Wing alone lost twenty-five of the thirty Fortresses destroyed that day, 300 boys who didn't make it back to their bunks.*

Cold figures fail to convey the unimaginable trauma inside the bombers that went down, or inside battle-damaged planes like *Royal Flush* that flew out of Germany with crewmen holding the hands of butchered friends who feared they would not make it back in time for doctors to save them. There were no medics at 25,000 feet, no men wearing Red Cross brassards to rush to the aid of shot-up comrades. Fliers who knew almost nothing about first aid had to take care of each other, and themselves. Lt. Paul Vance, pilot

---

* Although German records indicate that only 22 fighters were lost, many of them, surely, to Zemke's Thunderbolts, Eighth Air Force gunners claimed 183 enemy fighters destroyed. The 13th Combat Wing alone was credited with 105 "victories." Air Force leaders realized that in this battle, as in others, the claims by air gunners of German fighters destroyed were wildly optimistic. Throughout the war, measures were taken to scale down the number of claims, but they would always remain inaccurate on the high side. Some gunners may have exaggerated their success, but most believed their claims were accurate. There is the suspicion, as well, that the Luftwaffe may have suppressed evidence of large losses. No one will ever know how many German planes were lost on October 10, but reliable historians put the number between 60 and 90.

of *Miss Carry,* had a leg almost severed by flak on the Münster mission. He bandaged the wound himself, using his interphone cord for a tourniquet, and then coached his co-pilot though the bomb run and the trip back to England. Lt. Robert Sabel, the 390th BG pilot who had reservations about bombing a city on Sunday, brought home *Rusty Lode* with over 750 flak and shell holes in her, and only two minutes of gas left in her tanks. Three of his despairing crewmen had parachuted out over Germany when the situation seemed hopeless, yet Sabel got *Rusty Lode* back on two engines, making a blind landing at Thorpe Abbotts, miles from his home base, with four of his crewmen lying dead in a spreading pool of blood in the radio room.

The evening of the Münster raid, the personal belongings of bomber boys who failed to return were hastily stuffed into bags and their bunks stripped. Within an hour, there was no sign that they had existed. Unable to sleep, Robert Rosenthal walked to the officers club. He didn't drink, but he badly needed companionship. The place was almost empty, and the men who were there were sitting in silence, not knowing how to react. Neither did Rosie.

Later that night, Harry Crosby looked over at John Brady's empty bunk and did some counting. Of the 140 officers who had begun operations at Thorpe Abbotts just four months before, there were only three left on flying status. In the last week alone, the Hundredth had lost over 200 men, including two squadron leaders—Cleven and Egan. That was almost half of its airmen. The group had earned its nom de guerre, "The Bloody Hundredth." How, Crosby wondered, had he survived?

That night, Frank Murphy was asking himself the same question. His right arm was filled with small pieces of shrapnel, his ankle was throbbing from his hard fall to the ground in his parachute, but he was alive, sitting in the small holding area of a Luftwaffe fighter base with thirty or so other American airmen captured that day. The Americans were talking quietly with some of the German pilots who had shot them down. "They were fairly complimentary of us and I think we were rightfully complimentary of them." The Germans seemed particularly interested in talking with one prisoner, Lt. John Winant, a pilot in the 390th Bomb Group and the son of the United States ambassador to Great Britain, John G. Winant, Sr.

When the Luftwaffe pilots left, the American prisoners began debating how long they were likely to be "guests" of the Germans. No one doubted that the Allies would win the war, but every flier in the room knew that the Eighth Air Force was losing the air war. They could be prisoners for up to ten years, one airman said. "My God, ten years!" Murphy cried out. "I'll be an old man before I get home."

The next morning, John Winant was taken to a facility for special prisoners. Murphy and the other downed airmen were driven to Münster and marched through the streets, past angry crowds that lined the sidewalks all the way to the train station the prisoners had bombed. Their destination was Dulag Luft, the Luftwaffe's interrogation center, just outside Frankfurt. On arrival, the officers were put in solitary confinement and kept isolated from one another throughout their interrogation. So Frank Murphy had no idea that John Egan and Gale Cleven were at Dulag Luft at that time; and neither Egan nor Cleven knew the other was there.

Egan, who had evaded the Germans for a few days before being captured, was in a cramped, unheated cell not far from Cleven's, his only companions "about a million fleas." After nine days in solitary confinement and incessant rounds of interrogation, Cleven was released and sent with a "purge" of other prisoners to Stalag Luft III, a prison camp for American and British air force officers in German-occupied Silesia, a former region of Poland. The men traveled in vile boxcars that had been used to haul livestock, and the smell of fresh manure was overwhelming. Since the transport of prisoners was given low priority, the cars were attached to one freight train after another and were often shunted off to railroad sidings. The 300-mile trip took three days.

Stalag Luft III was in a thick pine forest just outside the small town of Sagan, about ninety miles southeast of Berlin. When Cleven arrived there on Sunday morning, October 23, there was a reunion of the Hundredth, which by the end of the war would have nearly a thousand of its fliers in German prison camps. Half of Cleven's original squadron were prisoners at Sagan; Frank Murphy and John Brady were also there. Howard "Hambone" Hamilton, Brady's bombardier, was in a German hospital. When he was released after a long recuperation, he was sent to another officers camp, Stalag Luft I, at Barth, on the Baltic Sea.

Three days after Cleven arrived, the camp guards announced that another group of American fliers was at the front gate. Cleven watched them file into a neighboring stockade. Spotting Johnny Egan, he called out to him, "What the hell took you so long?"

"Well, that's what you get for being sentimental," Egan shouted back.

At first, they were kept in separate compounds, cordoned off by barbed wire and guard towers, but four months later they were united in West Compound, where the senior American officer was their old blunt-speaking leader, Col. Darr "Pappy" Alkire. He had been stripped of the command of the Hundredth before it left for England and had recently been shot down while commanding a Liberator outfit in the Mediterranean Theater of Operations. Cleven and Egan were roommates again, as they had been in training, but were fighting a different war, a war against boredom and despair—and toward its end, in the punishing winter of 1945, a desperate fight for survival, as the entire Nazi edifice came crashing down around them.

"It was good to see Egan and some of the boys from my squadron," Cleven remembered his first days at Sagan. "We had been through some tough times together. I also met some of the guys from the first American bomb groups to arrive in England. As bad as the war was going against us, these guys had suffered more. We were in training in the States when they were flying suicide missions. No one knew a thing. There had been no time; the war came on the country so quickly. There were navigators who couldn't navigate, bombardiers who couldn't hit their targets, gunners who couldn't shoot straight. And their commanders had no idea how to beat the German air force or stop losing so many men.

"There weren't many of these guys at Sagan, but then again there weren't many of them in England in the summer before we showed up."

One of the Eighth Air Force pioneers was Lt. Walt Kelley, a bartender's son from Norristown, Pennsylvania. He was a pilot in the 97th Bomb Group, the first Eighth Air Force heavy bombardment group to reach England. "When we got to England, the RAF told us we would get our butts blown off if we . . . [did] daylight bombing," he recalled. But "we were ready for action and wanted to prove ourselves in combat. . . . We were impatient for the big day to come. We didn't have to wait long. August 17, 1942, turned out to be a beautiful sunlit day."

CHAPTER ONE

The Bomber Mafia

"The bomber will always get through."

BRITISH PRIME MINISTER STANLEY BALDWIN

Grafton Underwood, August 17, 1942

The first of the dozen Fortresses to clear the runway was *Butcher Shop,* piloted by twenty-seven-year-old Paul W. Tibbets, Jr., of Miami, Florida. The finest flier in the 97th Bombardment Group, Major Tibbets was leading the opening assault of what would become the biggest American bombing offensive of the war. Three years later, on August 6, 1945, he would fly from a remote island in the Western Pacific to Hiroshima, Japan, and drop a single bomb that would help bring to a terrible climax a six-year-long war that destroyed the lives of sixty million people worldwide.

Eighth Air Force commander Maj. Gen. Carl "Tooey" Spaatz was on hand to watch the 97th take off, along with skeptical observers from the Royal Air Force and almost three dozen British and American reporters. "It would have been a hell of a time to blow a mission," Tibbets said later. Tibbets was not flying his regular airplane, *Red Gremlin,* or with his regular crew, which included two of the men who would accompany him to Hiroshima on the *Enola Gay:* bombardier Thomas Ferebee and navigator Theodore "Dutch" Van Kirk. His pickup crew had been chosen by the man sitting across from him in the cockpit of *Butcher Shop,* Col. Frank A. Armstrong, Jr., the 97th's iron-willed commander. Armstrong's crushing discipline had sharpened the fighting efficiency of the hastily trained crews that had been rushed to England the previous month. After the war, his friend Lt. Col. Beirne Lay, Jr., the air commander and popular writer who would make Buck Cleven famous for his courage under fire on the Regensburg mission, used Armstrong as his model for the lead character in *Twelve O' Clock High!,* Gen. Frank Savage. In the novel and in the Hollywood film based on it, Savage, played by Gregory Peck, eventually cracks under the strain of command, but Armstrong never did. The men of the 97th both feared and idolized him. They called him "Butcher" and the truculent commander turned this into a compliment, naming his plane after his reputation.

At the briefing for the mission, Armstrong had told his crews that they were beginning a daylight bombing offensive that would steadily build in strength until it shattered the enemy's will and ability to make war. This must have struck British observers in the room as empty bravado. At the time, the Eighth had fewer than a hundred bombers in England and their entry into the war had been delayed for seven weeks until Armstrong, under mounting pressure from Washington to get Americans into the fight, had finally pronounced his crews ready. They were not, and he knew it, but they would have to go. The Luftwaffe had been dropping taunting messages on the Eighth's two tiny aerodromes at Grafton Underwood and nearby Polebrook, asking: "Where are the American bombers?" "Now they will find out," Armstrong had told his fliers before sending them to their planes. "Stay close together up there and right on my tail and I assure you we'll hurt the Hun and get back safely." No one in the room doubted him.

Butcher Shop lifted off the runway at about three-thirty in the afternoon. Right behind it, in the lead plane of the second element of six Fortresses was *Yankee Doodle.* Seated in the plane's radio cabin was Brig. Gen. Ira Eaker, head of the Eighth Air Force Bomber Command. A sharp-featured Texan with a winning smile, he had set a fistful of aviation records as a fighter pilot in the peacetime Army Air Corps but had never seen combat. His old friend and poker pal Tooey Spaatz had wanted to lead this historic mission, but he had been briefed on ULTRA, the code word used to identify the highly secret intelligence produced by decrypting enemy communications, and the Allied high command thought it too risky to send him over enemy territory, especially after what had happened the previous month.

On July 4, six crews from the Eighth Air Force's 15th Bomb Squadron, a light-bomber outfit that had been sent to England in May to train on British planes, had joined an equal number of RAF crews on a low-level sweep of heavily defended German airfields in Holland. The raid had been ordered by Lt. Gen. Henry H. "Hap" Arnold, commander of the U.S. Army Air Forces, and had the enthusiastic support of President Franklin D. Roosevelt.* Arnold thought the Glorious Fourth would be an ideal day for America to strike its first blow against the Nazis, but Spaatz had no planes in England in the first week of July. The Independence Day crews had flown American-made Douglas A-20s that had been sold to the RAF and renamed Bostons. Two of the twelve Bostons with American crews, and one with a British crew, had failed to return, and USAAF Capt. Charles C. Kegelman had barely made it back in his badly shot-up aircraft.

Although this had technically been the Eighth's first combat strike, it was, in Spaatz's view, a propaganda stunt triggered by pressure exerted by the American and British press, who believed the home front in both countries needed a psychological boost. "The cameramen and newspapermen finally got what they wanted—and everybody seemed contented," Spaatz had written sourly in his diary after pinning the Distinguished Service Cross, the nation's second highest award for gallantry, on Kegelman.

The Tibbets mission was different and far more important. The four-engine heavies, the heart of the Eighth's bomber force, were going out for the first time, and at high altitude. This would be the initial test of the new form of warfare that Arnold, Spaatz, and Eaker had helped to develop. Air Corps strategists had been plotting and planning for years, and practice missions had been flown in the States, but now "[our] theory that day bombardment is feasible is about to be tested when men's lives are put at stake," Eaker wrote Arnold before the mission.

The target was a railroad marshaling yard near Rouen, the city in northwestern France where Joan of Arc was burned at the stake. It was a "milk run," a shallow penetration mission with fighter cover from British Spitfires going in and coming back, but Spaatz was concerned. Churchill had been pressuring Roosevelt to disband the newly established Eighth and have its bombers join the RAF in its night raids on the factory cities of the Ruhr. If the bombing was not good and Armstrong lost planes, the prime minister might get his way.

---

* On June 20, 1941, the U.S. Army Air Corps (USAAC) had become the U.S. Army Air Forces (USAAF). To avoid awkward and sometimes confusing phrasing, I have generally used the term "Air Force" instead of the correct term, Air Forces. If it's the formal full name, Army Air Forces, I of course leave it plural.

Standing with Spaatz on the observation deck of the control tower at Grafton Underwood, RAF officers looked on apprehensively. Flying in daylight on earlier strikes, their Wellington and Blenheim bombers had been shredded by German fighters. And the twenty Fortresses the Americans had sent the British the previous year had performed abysmally in combat. Spaatz, however, thought this an unfair test of a potentially war-winning weapon. For security reasons, the British Fortresses had not been equipped with the highly secret Norden bombsights, nor did they have the defensive firepower of the newest model B-17. And the British had flown them at excessively high altitudes to avoid flak, guaranteeing poor bombing accuracy and mechanical problems in the paralyzing cold above 30,000 feet. Still, the British remained unconvinced of the plane's combat potential. As the twelve American Fortresses disappeared into the clouds above Grafton Underwood, an RAF flight lieutenant, a portly Scotsman, turned to the American officer standing next to him and said, "Laddie, ye'll be bloody lucky if ye get one of them back!"

It was a smooth run to the big marshaling yard on the Seine, cloudless skies and no German fighters. On the return, the Fortresses ran into a few Messerschmitts, Me 109s, fast, powerfully armed single-seat fighter planes, but the Spitfires, their equals in combat, drove them off. Only one Me 109 came within range of the Forts and was nicked by a spray of machine gun fire from *Birmingham Blitzkrieg*. The enemy fighters "evidently had been reluctant to engage our Fortresses at close quarters," Eaker would tell a credulous correspondent from *Life* magazine. "I can understand why. They had never seen our new B-17s before and the sight of big guns bristling from every angle probably gave the Nazis ample reason to be wary."

Back at Grafton Underwood, Spaatz searched the skies for the returning planes. Any losses would be a setback, but the loss of one or both of his top commanders, Eaker and Armstrong, would be calamitous. Shortly before seven o'clock, black specks could be seen in the distance. Spaatz counted them: there were only eleven—but then a twelfth came suddenly into view. They were all back.

As the bombers swept low over the tiny, box-shaped control tower where the brass had regathered, the bombers' freshly painted names were clearly visible on their nose sections: *Baby Doll, Peggy D, Heidi Ho, Johnny Reb*—great names for great planes. The high-spirited language matched the confidence of the crews, American boys too young and untested to be afraid. When the Fortresses touched down, the ground crews of the 97th rushed onto the field to greet the Rouen raiders. "Everyone was yelling, jumping like kids, slapping everybody else on the back," recalled Air Force public relations officer William R. Laidlaw. Even the Scots RAF officer fell into the mood. "By God, what'd I tell ye!" he shouted from his perch on the tower. "No boogery Yank'll ever miss his deener!"

When *Yankee Doodle* nosed onto its hardstand, Eaker slipped out of his flying clothes, lit a cigar, and went to meet the press. "One swallow does not make a summer," he declared, but the big grin on his face told it all. He was clearly pleased with the results and happy, as well, to finally fly a combat mission. "Why, I never got such a kick out of anything in my life!" After reviewing the aerial photographs of the damage, he pronounced the bombing "exceptionally good" for untried crews. Colonel Armstrong was more exuberant. "We ruined Rouen," he told reporters, thereby setting a standard of exaggeration that would mark official Air Force bombing reports for the remainder of the war.

Only one Fortress suffered flak damage and there were only two casualties, both of them caused by a single pigeon. It collided with the Plexiglas nose of a Fortress from a small formation of bombers sent out that same afternoon to divert German fighters from the main force. The impact shattered the Plexiglas nose, slightly injuring the navigator and the bombardier. Their surface cuts were the first blood spilled by American heavy-bomber crews in a campaign of nearly a thousand days that would result in the deaths of some 26,000 Eighth Air Force crewmen.

After their intelligence debriefing, the crews, still wearing their heavy flying clothing, met with reporters, reliving the mission "like a happy football team." That night there was a " 'Saturday after the big game' atmosphere on the base," with the hero of the hour Staff Sergeant Kent West, the ball turret gunner of *Birmingham Blitzkrieg,* who was given credit for shooting down a German fighter. His claim was later changed to "damaged," but Eaker would still send for his twin guns and mount them, like a deer's antlers, on the wall of his headquarters at Wycombe Abbey, a converted girls school on an old estate in the town of High Wycombe, just west of London.

"It was a cakewalk," said tavern keeper's son Walt Kelley, who flew in *Heidi Ho*. "We were cocky when we took off and more so when we landed. There was lots of hoopla and queries from the press. Several planes buzzed the runway before landing."

It would never be the same. A month later, when the Americans pushed beyond the range of the protecting Spitfires, enemy fighter pilots would begin blowing Eaker's bombers out of the sky with alarming regularity. And some of the exuberant boys who had stood in the slop of "Grafton Undermud," as they called their miserably drained base, toasting their first success, lay cold in their graves. Exactly a year to the day after the Rouen mission, five times as many American bombers and airmen would fall from the skies over Regensburg and Schweinfurt as had flown on that first strike from Grafton Underwood, the small airfield named after its neighbor, a Midland village of ninety-nine souls.

But in one important way, Rouen did turn out to be a harbinger. With this raid, the young men in the planes took over the burden of the American bomber war from the generals and their support staffs on the ground, the brass who picked the targets and plotted the missions. Before every raid, aircrews were exactingly briefed on the weather, on enemy defenses, and on the location of the targets, but once in the air the crews were in another world, on their own. "The most perfect plan could not succeed in the face of their failure," said William Laidlaw.

Beginning in the early fall of 1942, American bomber crews learned to fight the air war by experience and experiment, every mission a learning exercise. It was a special kind of experience, different from that of the ground forces. Once sent into combat, bomber boys could not report back to headquarters with intelligence that might reconfigure the battle plan. The killing was too quick for that and too distant from central command. And there were no reinforcements; almost every mission was a maximum effort. The men who went in had to fight their way out. In the air the crews were alone, forced to make their own decisions if the mission's master plan broke down, as it almost always did in the blinding chaos of combat. As Colonel Laidlaw wrote, "In a strategic air campaign, no military man—not even the most experienced air commanders with the best air staff on earth—could mark out the targets alone." The weather, the mechanical condition of the planes, the weight of the opposition, the training and mental stability of the crews, and at least a dozen other variables determined what would be bombed and who would die, on the ground and in the air.

The infantry and Navy had centuries of accumulated experience to draw from in plotting battle strategy. Although primitive bomber aircraft had been employed by both sides in World War I, and although Japan, Germany, and Italy had used dive-bombers to terrorize cities and villages in China, Spain, and North Africa in the 1930s, no nation had ever fought a full-scale bomber war prior to World War II. As the novelist John Steinbeck wrote in 1942, "Of all branches of the Service, the Air Force must act with the least precedent, the least tradition."

Col. Budd J. Peaslee, one of the legendary commanders of the Eighth, has argued that few great air leaders are recognized by historians because they rarely exercised command once their forces were airborne, and because a general's decision never produced a decisive victory. In the Air

Force, it was the skill and courage of small combat teams that made the difference in battle. "They had," Peaslee wrote, "power and authority far beyond their age, rank and experience."

"The attack on Rouen," Gen. Hap Arnold announced the very next day, "verifies the soundness of our policy of precision bombing of strategic objectives rather than the mass (blitz) bombing of large, city-size areas." He was getting ahead of himself. Daylight precision bombing would have to be proved on tougher missions, in vile weather and against determined opposition. The history of the American air war against Germany is the story of an experiment: the testing of a new idea of warfare that had been spun into dogma long before Paul Tibbets arrived in the United Kingdom. "The first bomb mission was little more than a gesture," Budd Peaslee remarked, "yet it carried with it the hopes and dreams of two decades of American airmen."

Command of the Air

In modern warfare there are two main types of aerial bombing—strategic and tactical. "Strategic bombing," as defined by the Air Force, "strikes at the economy of the enemy; it attempts to cripple its war potential by blows at industrial production, civilian morale, and communications. Tactical bombardment is immediate air support of movements of air, land, or sea forces." The Eighth Air Force would conduct both kinds of bombing, but at the start of the war its leaders hoped to commit it almost exclusively to strategic bombing.

Arnold, Eaker, and Spaatz were disciples of the late William "Billy" Mitchell, the founding father of American airpower. In 1927, when twelve-year-old Paul Tibbets made his maiden flight in an open-cockpit biplane piloted by a stuntman wearing a dashing white silk scarf and a tight-fitting leather helmet, Billy Mitchell was writing and lecturing about a terrifying, world-changing idea—bomber warfare. It was an idea that would lead to the theory of strategic bombing that Major Tibbets would first test in the skies over Rouen.

American airpower was born in World War I and Billy Mitchell was its prophet. He was the first American airman to arrive at the Western Front and fly over enemy lines, and the first of his countrymen to fully appreciate the destructive potential of bomber warfare. The son of a United States senator from Wisconsin and the grandson of a Gilded Age railroad king, Mitchell was a press agent's dream—handsome, fearless, and flamboyant, a championship polo player who spoke flawless French and wore high cavalry boots and expensively tailored uniforms. He had quit college at age eighteen to fight in the Spanish-American War, and a decade later was writing exuberant reports urging the horse-drawn army he had served with in Cuba to develop a modern air arm. In 1916, the year he learned to fly at the late age of thirty-six, he was appointed chief of the U.S. Army Signal Corps' tiny Aviation Section, the first American air force. Two years later, as a brigadier general, he organized and led the overseas section of the U.S. Army's new Air Service, the larger organization that replaced the Aviation Section and was the predecessor of the even larger Army Air Corps, formed in 1926. In France, Mitchell would become a crack combat leader, audacious and innovative—and idolized by young fliers like Carl Spaatz, whom Mitchell would recommend for the Military Cross after he downed three enemy planes. But it was as an advocate of new ideas about airpower that Mitchell would achieve his greatest fame.

His first experience in the war was the transforming event of his life. Living in the trenches with the infantry, he had an opportunity to fly over the enemy's positions with a French pilot. "We could cross the lines of these contending armies in a few minutes in our airplane," he wrote, "whereas the armies had been locked in the struggle, immobile, powerless to advance, for three years." As Mitchell saw it, "the art of war had departed. Attrition, or the gradual killing off of the enemy, was all the ground armies were capable of."

When Gen. John J. "Black Jack" Pershing arrived in France as commander of the American Expeditionary Forces, Mitchell approached him with a daring proposal: use airpower to strike the Germans behind their lines, knocking out airfields and sources of supply. Here was a way to use "the airplane for the [William Tecumseh] Sherman strategy of carrying war to the enemy's economy and people," wrote historian Russell F. Weigley. At first, Mitchell got nowhere with Pershing, who saw the infantry as the Queen of Battle and his pitifully small air force as a scouting and support arm of minimal military value. But in the last months of the war, when American airpower had been built up from nothing to something of consequence—750 planes, fully 10 percent of the Allied effort—Pershing allowed him to use massed Allied fighter and bomber forces to support two major infantry offenses at St. Mihiel and the Meuse-Argonne. "The air offensive which Mitchell laid on in the Meuse-Argonne in September [1918] was the greatest thing of its kind seen in the war," Hap Arnold wrote in his memoirs. "Until then, the air fighting had been chiefly between individual pilots. . . . [This] was the first massed air striking power ever."

Arnold only wished he could have been there to see his friend pull it off. He had desperately wanted to be in the war. A West Point graduate, he was one of the Army's first four licensed pilots, having been taught to fly by the Wright brothers, Orville and Wilbur, at their Dayton, Ohio, flying school; and in 1912 he had won the highly prized Mackay Trophy for the outstanding military flight of the year. But as part of the Air Service's headquarters staff, he had been considered too valuable as a war planner to send overseas. Friends called him "Hap," short for Happy, because he had an enigmatic smile permanently fixed on his face, but that benign countenance hid a volcanic temper and a crusading desire to advance the cause of American military aviation. He was one of the first and most enthusiastic of Billy Mitchell's supporters.

Arnold and Mitchell were both strongly influenced by Air Marshal Hugh Trenchard, the Royal Air Force's founding father and first commander. World War I was preeminently a fighter pilot's war, but Trenchard was a deep believer in bomber warfare, which he perceived as the future. When the Germans bombed London first with dirigibles (Zeppelins), then, in 1917, with twin-engine Gotha bombers, killing almost 1,400 people, Trenchard sent four-engine Handley Page bombers to attack Rhineland cities. In conversations with Trenchard at the front, Mitchell became convinced that America should have what the British had created after the bombing of London—an autonomous air force, equal in stature and power to the two other military services.

When the Armistice was signed on November 11, 1918, two days after the first squadron of American night bombers appeared at the front, Mitchell was laying plans for strategic assaults on the German homeland, using incendiary bombs and poison gas to destroy crops, forests, and livestock. "I was sure that if the war lasted, air power would decide it," he wrote later.

Mitchell drew his ideas from many sources. One of them was the Italian air commander Gen. Giulio Douhet. Three years after Mitchell returned from the war, Douhet published his masterwork, *The Command of the Air,* a book that established him as the world's leading proponent of airpower. Mitchell never read the book, but he may have read translated excerpts prepared by the War Department, and he corresponded with one of Douhet's friends and countrymen, Gianni Caproni, a designer of bomber aircraft. Whatever the nature of the connection, Mitchell shared with Douhet a number of core assumptions about airpower. The experience of World War I was paramount; both sought to end long wars of attrition and close-quarter slaughter. They proposed to shorten war by returning the advantage to the offensive. Advances in the technology of killing–the machine gun, poison gas, and rifled artillery–had made infantry attacks on dug-in positions suicidal. The solution they arrived at independently was airpower–Winged Victory. Just as technology had swung the advantage to the defense, now it would favor the offense. The airplane, the greatest offensive weapon yet developed, would break the hegemony of the defense. At a time when German strategists, in reaction to the static war they had just lost, were secretly developing a new form of warfare based on quick-striking tanks and armored vehicles, Mitchell and Douhet were advancing ideas for blitzkrieg warfare from the skies.

Douhet insisted that future wars would be short, total, and "violent to a superlative degree." They would be won from the skies with vast fleets of long-range bombers, with the winning side the one that attacked first and without cease, gaining command of the air, not primarily by destroying the enemy's air force in combat but by destroying its airbases, communications, and centers of production. In Douhet's words, "It is not enough to shoot down all birds in flight if you want to wipe out the species; there remain the eggs and the nests." Destroying the eggs and the nests was strategic bombing, the only type of bombing Douhet favored.

Once command of the air was achieved by marauding bombers, not fighter planes, which, in Douhet's view would be annihilated by new-age bombers, the main targets would be the enemy's key industrial cities, not its armies in the field. Attacks on these vital centers would shatter civilian morale, destroy the enemy's war-making capability, and produce a mercifully quick capitulation, without the need for either armies or navies. In the new warfare "the entire nation is or may be considered a combatant force," Mitchell echoed Douhet. "War," Douhet wrote, "is no longer a clash between armies, but is a clash between nations, between whole populations. Any distinction between belligerents and non-belligerents is no longer admissible . . . because when nations are at war, everyone takes a part in it: the soldier carrying his gun, the woman loading shells in a factory, the farmer growing wheat, the scientist in his laboratory."

Douhet, a passionate fascist, put the case for total warfare in more implacable terms than Mitchell ever would. There was no place for morality in the new warfare; it would be swift slaughter without mercy or sentimentality. "The limitations applied to the so-called inhuman and atrocious means of war are nothing but international demagogic hypocrisies. . . . War," he wrote, "has to be regarded unemotionally as a science, regardless of how terrible a science." As a modern historian has written, "One senses [in Douhet's work], the final and frightening abandonment by the soldier of any sense of responsibility for the political and social consequences of his military acts."

For the first time in the history of modern armed conflict, civilians were singled out as deliberate military targets, not only because they were valuable producers, but also because they were easy to intimidate. Both Douhet and Mitchell were convinced that civilians lacked the fortitude to stand up to vertical warfare waged with high explosives, incendiaries, and poisonous gases, that generation's equivalent, in terror-generating capacity, of atomic warfare. The evidence they had before them was the mass panic and terror in London and Cologne caused by World War I bombing attacks, air strikes far smaller than either of them envisioned in future wars. The new wars will be decided swiftly, Douhet argued, precisely because "the decisive blows will be directed at civilians, that element of the countries at war least able to sustain them."

In one of Mitchell's hair-raising scenarios—the bombing of New York City—deadly gases released by bombs fill the air and seep into the subways, triggering a massive evacuation of the city. When the refugees of New York and other large American cities that have been bombed are unable to obtain the essentials of life, the government is forced to capitulate.

To Douhet and Mitchell, quick wars meant reduced casualties. In becoming more terrible, warfare would actually become more humane. Better to decide a war by terrorizing the population with "a few gas bombs," Mitchell wrote, than "the present methods of blowing people to bits by cannon projectiles or butchering them with bayonets." Mitchell even suggested that future wars might be fought, not by large armies, but an elite cadre of aerial warriors, the modern equivalent of "the armored knights in the Middle Ages." This, too, would save lives. And the very threat of total annihilation, he argued in anticipation of the Cold War proponents of nuclear deterrence, would prevent war from breaking out. "Air power has brought with it a new doctrine of war . . . and a new doctrine of peace."

On this point, Douhet and Mitchell parted company. Douhet cast his arguments in dark Darwinian language. Warfare was in our blood and bones, part of our evolutionary makeup; peace was a pipe dream. Douhet advocated the "merciless pounding from the air [of] . . . very large centers of civilian population," with the aim of destroying, not just factories and communications systems but all "social organization."

For over a century, military theorists in the Western world had been under the spell of the Prussian writer Carl von Clausewitz, who argued that the supreme objective of warfare is the destruction of the enemy's armed forces. Mitchell and Douhet challenged this iron dictum. A contemporary military observer has nicely encapsulated their thinking. "The history of civilized mankind shows us but three . . . revolutionary military inventions, or discoveries: discipline, gunpowder, and the airplane. . . . The airplane for the first time in the . . . history of human conflict, has given to warfare the means of striking . . . directly at the seat and source of [the enemy's] power—at his citizenry, at his capital city, at his industrial, commercial, and political centers—without first having to overthrow the armed forces with which he seeks to protect them."

Mitchell predicted that a nation prepared to build a massive bomber force to strike hard, continuous blows at an enemy's economy and people would end the next war before its infantry or the Navy had an opportunity to enter the fight. He did not, however, envision precision bombing. High-altitude bombing would be highly inaccurate. To hit industrial targets, bombers would have to "drop their eggs well into the center of the towns," in Air Marshal Trenchard's phrase, killing not just factories but innocent civilians.

Mitchell promoted his ideas with crusading fervor, inside the military bureaucracy, as assistant chief of the Air Service, and outside it, in a stream of books, articles, and public lectures. Standing at a podium, he would use his gold-headed swagger stick to drive home his points; the "Napoleon of the Air," the humorist Will Rogers called him. When Mitchell was opposed by the brass hats of both the Army and the Navy, who saw airpower—power in the third dimension—as a mere adjunct to traditional surface warfare, he attacked them with rancor, alienating the very powers he hoped to persuade.

Mitchell's ideas on warfare ran ahead of their enabling technology; no bomber in planning, production, or use was capable of carrying out long-range strategic bombing. As one military expert explained in 1925, a bomber "can hit a town from ten thousand feet—if the town is big enough." But Mitchell was a modern man, a technological enthusiast; American science and engineering, he was convinced, would soon develop the bomber that would make him a prophet.

Mitchell's ideas ran into another obstacle, what one writer has called a "moral blockade." Toward the end of World War I, Secretary of War Newton D. Baker had ordered the Air Service not to undertake an air assault that "has as its objective, promiscuous bombing upon industry, commerce or population." Warring on civilians, Baker believed, violated long-standing religious and humanitarian ideals. Opinion polls conducted later showed the public in broad agreement. Most Americans were also weary of war and unwilling to support large government outlays for the military.

So Mitchell had to shrewdly cast his arguments for an independent Air Force in the language of fiscal restraint and national defense. A large, land-based Air Force could defend the nation's shores and its far-off bases in Alaska, Hawaii, and the Philippines more effectively and less expensively than the Navy, he claimed—the cost of one battleship equaling that of a thousand planes.

At the time, the prevailing military orthodoxy was that an airplane could not sink a battleship. Seeing this as archaic nonsense, Mitchell pressured his supporters in Congress to force the Navy to conduct a series of tests. In the most spectacular one, in July 1921, his small air fleet used six 2,000-pound bombs to send the captured German battleship *Ostfriesland* to the bottom of the waters off the Virginia Capes. The Navy called the test unfair; the anchored ship, with its guns muffled, was a sitting duck. And with General Pershing heading the fight against an independent Air Force, Mitchell got nowhere with the Army. Nonetheless, he continued to press his case with such vehemence that the Army refused to reappoint him as assistant chief of the Air Service, and in 1925, transferred him to a base in out-of-the-way San Antonio, where one wall of his office was an open latrine for clerks. "Mitchell's stay in Texas," wrote one historian, "was a little like Napoleon's exile to Elba. He plotted and planned to continue the fight." But unlike the little emperor, he could not keep quiet, "even out in the sagebrush." When he blamed two terrible military air accidents on the incompetence and "criminal negligence" of the Navy and War Departments, he provoked the court-martial that would serve as a national forum for his ideas. "He wouldn't rest, until he became a martyr," said Hap Arnold, who had recently become the Air Service's chief public relations officer.

At the sensational seven-week-long trial, Spaatz and Arnold put their careers on the line by testifying on Mitchell's behalf; and Ira Eaker, who had some legal training, helped shape the defense. All three of them revered the vainglorious air commander, despite his excesses. Airmen further down the chain of command supported Mitchell's ideas about airpower, although a few, like Lt. James H. Doolittle, felt his stridency hurt his cause. "Like all zealots, he was intolerant of any view other than his own," Doolittle wrote later.

Mitchell was convicted of making insubordinate public statements and was suspended from duty for five years. But his ideas meant more to him than his military career. He resigned his commission to continue his public fight for an independent, offensive-minded Air Force. Inside the corridors of power he depended on loyalists like Hap Arnold to continue to lead the "battle of ideas" that pitted younger flying officers against the entrenched powers in the War Department.

Arnold and his band of mavericks–the Bomber Mafia, as they have been called–were bound together by their devotion to Mitchell and their pure love of the air. They were aerial pioneers who made a succession of record-setting flights, widely publicized exploits that did as much as Mitchell's writings to prove the potential of the military airplane. In 1929, Spaatz and Eaker were half of the crew of a Trimotor plane, *Question Mark*, which used the revolutionary technique of midair refueling to set a world endurance record, remaining airborne for over 150 hours. Seven years later, flying with a hood over his cockpit, Ira Eaker was the first pilot to make a transcontinental flight on instruments alone. This experience would make him a better bomber commander in the coming war, when his planes were forced to fly in one of the most capricious weather systems in the world.

Not to be outdone by his younger friends, Hap Arnold, at age forty-eight, led ten two-engine bombers on a 1934 nonstop flight from Washington state to Alaska and back, an astonishing feat at a time when there were almost no air routes over the trackless subarctic mountains. The next year he was promoted to brigadier general and command of the Air Corps' chief combat outfit, the 1st Bombardment Wing, at March Field, California. All the while, he and Eaker, who had taken courses in journalism at the University of Southern California, co-authored three books on airpower, which bore the strong stamp of Mitchell's influence. As a newspaper had predicted at the time of Mitchell's court-martial, " 'Mitchellism' will remain after . . . Mitchell has gone."

The Bomber Mafia

When Billy Mitchell died in 1936, his reputation lived on in the lectures of the instructors at the Air Corps Tactical School at Maxwell Field, in Montgomery, Alabama. This was the first professional school for aviators and aviation planners in the world, and it became a nurturing center for the newest thinking about strategic bombing. "We are not concerned with fighting the past war," Lt. Col. Harold L. George, the faculty's leading bomber theorist, described the school's mission to his students. "We are concerned . . . in determining how air power will be employed in the next war." In their dealings with the War Department, air commanders continued to speak of the bomber as a defensive weapon, but at Maxwell Field the ideas of the offense prevailed. It was Mitchellism with a difference. Colonel George and his colleagues rejected Mitchell's and Douhet's idea that bombing would have a greater impact on morale than production. And while Mitchell and Douhet called for the destruction of the enemy's pivotal economic centers, the only target they had precisely identified was a country's aircraft industry. What were the critical strong points in a modern industrial nation's infrastructure, and how could they be taken out? The air visionaries at Maxwell Field addressed these questions directly. In doing so, they came up with something new and expressly American: daylight precision bombing.

They fashioned their new "philosophy" of warfare even before the Air Corps began secretly testing the invention that made it possible. This was the Norden bombsight, America's most important secret weapon before the Manhattan Project. It was first developed in 1931 for sea-based naval aircraft by a reclusive Dutch engineer, Carl L. Norden. His wife teased him, calling him a "merchant of death," but Norden claimed he was trying to save lives by making bombing more precise. Two years after the Navy began testing the bombsight, the Army ordered it for aircraft engaged in coastal defense, eventually spending approximately $1.5 billion—65 percent of the cost of the Manhattan Project—to purchase 90,000 of them. When air crews of Hap Arnold's 1st Bombardment Wing tested it in the clear, dry skies over California's Mojave Desert, they were amazed by its accuracy.

Here was the technological breakthrough the faculty at Maxwell Field had been hoping for. Carl Norden's gyroscope-stabilized instrument, which computed drift and dropping angle, would make high-altitude bombing both more effective and more humane, they began arguing in 1935, the year they learned of it. But there was a problem. The War Department envisioned the Norden bombsight as a defensive weapon; it was to be installed solely in bombers guarding the North American coastline from a naval-based invasion. The Bomber Mafia had other ideas. Cities could now be bombed with surgical precision, they argued, targeting only key economic sites such as electric power plants and oil refineries. This upended Billy Mitchell's argument that high-altitude bombing would have to be indiscriminate. "The idea of killing thousands of men, women, and children [is] basically repugnant to American mores," wrote Major Haywood S. Hansell, one of the bright lights at Maxwell—and later a bomber strategist and combat commander in the war. Hansell added tellingly, however, that killing civilians was also militarily ineffective. People were poor targets for bombs because they had, contrary to Douhet and Mitchell, stoic staying power. They could also be evacuated from cities or find protection in public bomb shelters, whereas industries were fragile, immobile, and virtually indefensible.* This was warfare suited to the American character. "[It] combined moral scruples, historical optimism, and technological pioneering, all three distinctly American characteristics," wrote historian John Keegan.

Forbidden by the War Department from studying the economies of other nations, and prevented by their budget from hiring trained economists, the ascendant theorists at Maxwell—Donald Wilson, Kenneth Walker, Harold George, Muir Fairchild, and Haywood Hansell—did their own close-in analysis of the American industrial system. This led to an Air Plan based on the idea of "industrial webs," a strategy they would later have the opportunity to implement as members of Hap Arnold's wartime planning staff.

Modern industrial states, they theorized, were highly vulnerable to air attack because their economies formed a delicate, interconnected fabric or web. A relentless precision bombing campaign needed to hit only those industries that made products, or supplied services, essential to almost all other industries. Destroy an enemy's "choke points"—its steel, electric power, ball bearing, oil, and railroad industries—and its entire war economy would collapse, making continued military resistance untenable.

Japan and Germany were expected to be America's enemies in the next war, so it was important, the Bomber Mafia argued, to find bases in countries of likely allies, like China and England, from which to launch a strategic bombing campaign. This campaign would begin in the earliest months of the war and build to full strength within two years, the time it would take to fully mobilize America's prodigious productive power. In early 1935, without a plane—or a war—to test it, the theory was pure vision and speculation. Later that year, the Air Corps got its plane. Six years later, it got its war.

In 1927, General Douhet had written that "the true combat plane, able to impose its will upon the enemy, had not yet been invented; nor does it seem likely it will be soon." In the 1930s the Air Corps had set out to prove him wrong. Under contract with the Army, the Boeing Airplane Company of Seattle, Washington, took on a project that many aviation engineers thought unfeasible: developing an all-metal monoplane that was both large and fast, one that proved that size does not necessarily compromise aerodynamic efficiency. Boeing's answer was the B-17 Flying Fortress (model 299). While previous American bombers had two engines, the prototype

---

* By 1943, German industry was resilient, mobile, and powerfully defended.

Fortress of 1935 had four 750 horsepower radial engines, which made it faster than any American fighter plane. The final production model, the B-17G, introduced in the war in 1943, had four 1,200 horsepower engines, carried a normal bomb load of 4,000 pounds, flew, fully loaded, at between 150 and 250 miles per hour at 25,000 feet, and had a combat radius of 650 to 800 miles, depending on the size of the bomb load. It was an elegantly engineered aircraft, suggesting both power and movement. Menacing-looking on the ground, it was beautiful to watch in the air.

The first silver Fortresses arrived at the Air Corps' bombardier training group at Langley Field, Virginia, not far from the capital, in early 1937, a year after Hap Arnold returned to Washington as assistant to the chief of the Air Corps. A flexible man, more a fixer than an ideologue, Arnold's stormy days with Billy Mitchell had taught him to be more diplomatic in his relations with the War Department, where he had built friendships with superiors, who had helped him get this position. The first time Arnold flew the new bomber, he fell in love with it. Unlike the "abstract science at the Air Corps Tactical School," this was "air power that you could put your hand on." In its later combat-developed form, with up to thirteen .50 caliber Browning machine guns, eight of them mounted in movable turrets, it was a fearsome war machine. Equipped with the Norden bombsight and a new automatic pilot system developed in the 1930s, it was the plane that could give weight to the Bomber Mafia's ideas. But only if they could convince the War Department to use it offensively, and not strictly to protect America's airspace and sea approaches.

The introduction of the B-17 solidified the idea of the bomber's impregnability, which had been a central tenet of Douhet's work. But what if the enemy developed an air defense system capable of inflicting unacceptable punishment on the unescorted Fortresses? Why didn't Air Corps planners push for the development of a long-range fighter escort? One reason was a failure of imagination. The Bomber Mafia failed to foresee that radar, then being developed by eight countries, including the United States, as a means of early warning against air attack, would soon be widely employed for military detection. Their thinking on fighter escorts went like this: with the entire ether to fly through, bombers would be almost impossible to detect before they reached their target; and near the target they would be flying at altitudes above the range of enemy ground guns, and in self-protecting formations that would be too formidable for enemy fighters to penetrate. "A well-planned and well-conducted air attack, once launched, cannot be stopped," declared Air Corps Tactical School instructor Kenneth Walker. Haywood Hansell took a more realistic approach, at least admitting the possibility that an enemy's air defenses might prove successful against a bomber invasion. If that happened, those defenses, he argued, would have to be broken by direct air combat and by air attacks on fighter bases, aircraft factories, and sources of aviation fuel. That meant knocking out the Luftwaffe in a brutal head-to-head confrontation, with the bombers bearing the burden of the fight, "seeking attrition through air combat." In the contested skies over Germany, the Flying Fortress would have to live up to its name.

The bomber enthusiasts had another argument against developing long-range escorts. Since the B-17 was faster than any fighter plane in operation in 1935, equipping fighters with additional gas tanks for long-range escort duty would reduce their speed and maneuverability, making them incapable of keeping up with the bombers and leaving them unable to defend themselves against lighter, faster fighter planes. Developing a high-speed fighter with the range of a bomber was considered an engineering impossibility. "We just closed our minds to [long-range escorts]; we couldn't be stopped; the bomber was invincible," Gen. Laurence S. Kuter observed in a refreshingly candid postwar interview.

Money was another factor. With Congress and the War Department initially willing to order only thirteen B-17s, to push for pursuit planes would have jeopardized the bomber program that the Air Corps counted on as "an excuse for existence," in Maj. Donald Wilson's apt phrase.

If airpower theorists like Wilson and Kuter had studied the life and work of Billy Mitchell more closely, they might have paid more attention to the role of fighter aircraft in bomber warfare, not only as escorts but also in pursuit. In World War I, Mitchell and other air commanders at the front realized that no aerial operation—tactical, strategic, or reconnaissance—was possible without mastery of the air. "For Mitchell an air force's first task," historian Williamson Murray pointed out, "should be destruction of the enemy's air force, particularly his pursuit aircraft; not until one had achieved that goal could an air force turn against other targets. Thus, the enemy fighter force was the essential target." Accordingly, Mitchell called for a balanced air force made up of at least 60 percent fighter aircraft.

Air supremacy achieved by fighter aircraft was the prerequisite for a successful bombing offensive. In the coming European war, it would take American Air Force leaders more than a year and near paralyzing loss rates to absorb this lesson. But the Bomber Mafia did work mightily in the late 1930s to encourage the development of something overlooked by both Mitchell and Douhet—a military-industrial complex committed to the production of staggering numbers of warplanes.

Clouds of Planes

In the summer of 1937 the Air Corps was fighting desperately, often despairingly, for funds to buy greater numbers of B-17s. At the time it had only seven B-17s on the runway at Langley under the command of Carl Spaatz. One year later, Munich changed everything.

After Hitler annexed Austria, he demanded the ethnically German province of the Sudetenland from Czechoslovakia. At the Munich conference of September 29–30, 1938, Britain and France abandoned Czechoslovakia to her fate. "[I bring you] peace with honor," Prime Minister Neville Chamberlain said famously upon his return to London. "I believe it is peace for our time."

Less than two months later, Franklin Roosevelt, a devoted Navy man, came out for a stupendous expansion of American airpower, urging immediate action to increase production of every type of warplane, for America's own use as well as for shipment to threatened France and England. Only thousands of bombers, he was convinced, would impress Hitler and shield America's shores and strategic possessions, including the Panama Canal and the Philippines, from air- and sea-based attacks from Japan and bases in the Western hemisphere that Germany might seize in the near future. After the Munich capitulation, Roosevelt was "sure . . . that we were going to get into the war" and "that air power would win it," said Harry Hopkins, his chief aide. But like most Americans, Roosevelt insisted that air war should be conducted with moral restraint. When war finally broke out in Europe in 1939, he would appeal to both sides to refrain from "ruthless bombing from the air of civilians in unfortified centers of population." Churchill agreed, and so, treacherously, did Hitler, even as his Luftwaffe was about to begin bombing the center of Warsaw.

In the month of the Munich crisis, Hap Arnold became chief of the Army Air Corps and immediately elevated Spaatz and Eaker to positions of influence at headquarters. They had won the "battle of the White House," he told his planning staff; now they had to win the battle of production. Arnold headed this fight with vigor and imagination. He was a fine leader "in an inspiring sense," recalls Robert A. Lovett, the Wall Street financier who became the new secretary of war for air. "There was something flamboyant, almost boyish, about his enthusiasms." Arnold's guiding dictum was carved in a wooden plaque that sat prominently on his desk. "The difficult we do today. The impossible takes a little longer." He had learned this, he told people, from the Wright brothers.

A smooth and smiling diplomat with his superiors, Arnold could be distant and brutally difficult with those who served under him. He was a driven man, "ruthlessly" impatient with failure, like his stern father, an Ardmore, Pennsylvania, physician. Arnold was famous for his withering harangues. The target at one staff meeting was Steve Ferson, a lower-level staff officer. Ferson turned crimson and began to sweat profusely as Arnold screamed in his face. Grabbing his chest, he dropped dead of a massive heart attack on the carpet in front of the general's desk. After he was carried off, Arnold told everyone to go home for the rest of the day, but he stayed at his desk, working alone. "Most of the rest of us," said Laurence Kuter, "went to our desks also."

Arnold would suffer five heart attacks himself, the last of them fatal. Some his staff called their fast-acting boss a "slave driver," but those closest to him understood his urgency. The Air Corps had "to be built in time to forestall disaster in Europe and the Pacific," said Kuter. "As the leader, no-one worked under the pressure he did. He took the brunt of the demands of the president, Harry Hopkins, and the White House staff, as well as other high outside agencies."

To win these battles Arnold developed alliances in the business and scientific communities, in Hollywood, in Congress, and in the White House, where his old friend Gen. George C. Marshall was put in charge of building a large, modern army to meet the Axis threat. And it was comforting to him to have Carl Spaatz at his elbow, as his chief of staff. Spaatz was born and raised in Boyertown, Pennsylvania, not far from Arnold's hometown. Though the two men remained lifelong friends, they were polar opposites. Lt. Gen. Elwood R. "Pete" Quesada, who served under both of them in World War II, compared them: "Spaatz was a . . . plotter [and] planner. . . . He wouldn't get into trouble. Arnold, on the other hand, was a dynamic doer . . . always trying something new. . . . He had some new project every day. . . . Spaatz was a thoughtful guy, whereas Arnold was the agitating guy and that's what made him such a marvelous chief. [Without him] we would never have had the Air Force." But without Spaatz as a counterbalance, Arnold might never have gotten as far as he did. "Spaatz got along with people better than Arnold." A "modest" man, "he engendered confidence because he was so damn stable."

Spaatz loved poker, bridge, Cuban cigars, and Kentucky whiskey. At bright-spirited parties at Arnold's home, he would get out his guitar and launch into his bottomless repertoire of risqué songs. When he was finished, he would go off in a corner and puff on his stogie. "I never learned anything when I was talking," he would tell people. Arnold and Spaatz "adored each other," said Quesada. "They matched each other and were a real team, even though Arnold [would] exaggerate . . . the potential of air-power, whereas Spaatz was not inclined toward exaggerating anything." But the real difference between them, Quesada shrewdly noted, was that Spaatz "was more wise than decisive. Arnold was more decisive than wise."

In 1938, the Army Air Corps had "plans but not planes." In May 1940, with France about to fall to the Nazis, Roosevelt called for an annual output of 50,000 planes, imploring the aircraft industry to expand its normal capacity of 2,000 a year to more than 4,000 a month. Congress quickly provided the funding. In Arnold's words, "In forty-five minutes I was given $1,500,000,000 and told to get an air force." At the time of the Munich crisis, the American air force, with 1,200 combat aircraft and 22,700 officers and enlisted men, was twentieth in size in the world. By December 1941, it had almost 340,000 officers and enlisted personnel and almost 3,000 combat planes. The newest of them was the B-24 Liberator, which flew faster, further, and carried a larger bomb load than the more rugged and maneuverable B-17. By 1944, mass production and mass education—areas in which this country had long led the world—would give the United States the greatest air force on earth, with 80,000 planes and 2.4 million fliers and support personnel, 31 percent of total Army strength. It was a force larger than the entire combat army that General Pershing had commanded in World War I. In March 1944, American factories poured out over 9,000 military planes, over twice the number Roosevelt had requested in 1940, an estimate that was considered "fantastically impossible" at the time by both Hitler and most of the president's advisors. "Never before or since," wrote one of Arnold's biographers, "has a military machine of such size and technological complexity been created in so short a period"; and it was built through a close partnership between business and government that was not possible in the highly militarized Nazi state. Arnold "provided the leadership, the fire, the push behind it all," said Lovett. But the pace of production was not quick enough to manufacture a sizable bomber fleet by 1942. And with the first burst of expansion, from 1938 to 1942, came an unavoidable watering down of production and training standards that would affect crew and plane performance in the first year of combat operations.

On June 20, 1941, Secretary of War Henry L. Stimson officially established the Army Air Forces; and with Arnold eventually serving on both the U.S. Joint Chiefs of Staff and the British-American Combined Chiefs of Staff, the Air Force acquired a good measure of independence from the ground forces. With this came presidential authority to draw up its own production blueprint for the fast approaching war. In August 1941, during nine days of furious effort, four former Maxwell Field instructors—Harold George, Kenneth Walker, Laurence Kuter, and Haywood Hansell—drafted a document, Air War Plans Division-1, which "read like a Tactical School lecture." AWPD-1 forecast with uncanny accuracy the number of men and machines it would take to win an air war against Germany, and it went beyond production planning to boldly establish the Air Force's supreme mission in the war: "to conduct a sustained and unremitting air offensive against Germany and Italy, to destroy their will and capability to continue the war, and to make an invasion either unnecessary or feasible without excessive cost." Predictably, Harold George and his planning team gave the development of a long-range fighter escort low priority. The escort they called for, moreover, was the wrong type—a large, heavily armed war ship, a Flying Fortress without the bombs.

When Marshall and Stimson endorsed the plan, the Army Air Forces finally gained official acceptance of strategic bombing. It had achieved what Arnold called its "Magna Carta."

There were problems ahead, however. Air Force planners based their war-winning strategy on practice bombing runs flown in cloudless weather, at low altitudes, and without even simulated resistance. In *Command Decision,* his brilliant post-war novel about the Eighth Air Force, William Wister Haines, who served as a staff officer with the Eighth, wrote that precision bombing, as envisioned in 1941, "could no more end wars than a doctor can confer immortality." It was, at best, an unproven "therapy." More than that, it had become dogma, not just untested but unquestioned orthodoxy, a doctrine that would lead to unnecessary losses of men and planes in the first year and a half of bombing operations over the Reich, when American bomber crews experienced a type of air war unforeseen by the Bomber Mafia.

CHAPTER TWO

Eaker's Amateurs

"It is summer and there is war all over the world."

BERT STILES, PILOT, EIGHTH AIR FORCE

Washington, D.C., December 1941

The Japanese attack on Pearl Harbor "shook the United States as nothing had since the firing on Fort Sumter," wrote historian Samuel Eliot Morison. Republicans and Democrats, interventionists and isolationists, labor and capital, closed ranks, and the nation moved from peace to war with a unity that it had never known before in time of crisis. On December 8, President Roosevelt appeared before a joint session of the Congress to ask for a declaration of war against Japan. Congress responded with only a single dissenting vote. Three days later, Germany declared war on the United States, a decision more calamitous for its cause than its invasion of Russia the previous June.

At the Arcadia Conference, a high-level Anglo-American meeting convened at the White House that December, Churchill and Roosevelt endorsed the "defeat Germany first" strategy they had tentatively agreed to earlier and called for an immediate buildup of American airpower in Britain. The following month, Hap Arnold created the Eighth Air Force and appointed Spaatz to head it and Eaker to command its bombardment force. The three friends would run the European bomber war that they had been preparing for since the Munich crisis.

Spaatz—a West Point graduate, decorated combat flier, and Arnold's closest friend—was a predictable choice. Eaker was a surprise. The son of struggling Texas sharecroppers, he had entered the Signal Corps in 1917 after graduating from Southeastern Normal School in Durant, Oklahoma, too late to see combat. Although he had flown a number of record-smashing Air Corps test flights in the 1930s, his experience was solely with fighter planes. But he was Arnold's protégé and co-author, and Arnold knew he would strike at the enemy like a pit viper. "I want . . . the fighter spirit in bombardment," he told Eaker on giving him his new command.

A short, square-jawed, balding man, Eaker spoke so softly he could barely be heard, but he was ferociously ambitious and had advanced on his own merits in the smothering culture of West Point favoritism. He was an accomplished writer and speaker; and with his courtly manner and soft Texas accent, he was a born-to-the-saddle diplomat, a skill he would need in sensitive dealings with the Royal Air Force. The British had seen their own, and Germany's, daylight bombing effort fail, and wanted either to absorb the Eighth Air Force into their Bomber Command's night force or have the Americans send them bombers to be flown by England's own battle-seasoned crews. Eaker had served briefly in England in 1941 as an observer of RAF operations against the Luftwaffe and had built close friendships with British flight officers and government ministers. He knew how persuasive the British could be, but he was sworn to keep the Eighth an independent command.

Haywood Hansell and his fellow air war planners had warned General Arnold that America would not have the planes and personnel needed to begin sustained strategic bombing until late 1943. And Spaatz cautioned Gen. George Marshall, America's chief war strategist, not to commit the force Eaker would be building in England before it was able to deliver decisive blows. But in early 1942, with Japan sweeping through Southeast Asia and the lightning-quick German army driving deeply into Russia and across North Africa toward the Suez Canal, it "looked," Arnold wrote later, "as if the Allies were losing the war." So Marshall ordered Arnold to immediately send what heavy bombers he had available to Britain. They were not expected to undertake the all-out assault on the German war machine that the Bomber Mafia envisioned. Their mission was to help prepare the way for a cross-Channel invasion of Nazi-occupied France. This was to occur in the fall of 1942, if Russia collapsed, but more likely the following spring. General Marshall, the most passionate proponent of an Anglo-

American invasion of northern France—"our shortest route to the heart of Germany"—told Eaker that his bombers and fighter escorts had one year to achieve air supremacy over Northern Europe. "I do not believe a cross-Channel invasion of Europe will ever be possible until the Luftwaffe is destroyed," he said. "Do your plans provide that?" Eaker assured him that they did and that the skies over the invasion beaches would be swept clean of German planes if he was given men and machines sufficient to the task.

On February 4, 1942, Ira Eaker and six staff officers left for their new assignment in England. Carl Spaatz stayed behind in Washington to oversee the preparation and dispatch of the first planes and crews of the Eighth, including its Fighter Command, headed by Brig. Gen. Frank "Monk" Hunter, a decorated World War I ace. When they were ready to be shipped out he would accompany them to England. This left the task of building an entire air force on foreign soil to a newly minted forty-five-year-old general whose largest command up to then was a fighter unit of 1,500 men. Eaker's charge was daunting: to establish a headquarters operation, secure airbases and work closely with the RAF to assemble the airpower infrastructure essential to Eighth Air Force bombing operations. Eaker would increase the size of the Eighth Air Force in England from seven men and no planes in February 1942 to 185,000 men and 4,000 planes by December 1943.

In 1942, the largest American corporation was General Motors, with 314,000 employees in 112 production plants. Eaker's job was comparable to building this gargantuan automobile enterprise from scratch in less than two years. "Few men who are thought of as industrial giants ever put a major organization together as fast as the Eighth was formed," wrote Eaker's aide, James Parton. "And there was the added element of inspiring the crews to risk their lives; it was not just getting a large factory ready to make and sell automobiles."

Hap Arnold didn't make Eaker's task any easier, keeping the best minds in the Air Force on his own Washington-based staff. "You assemble some bright young civilians . . . and train them and I will commission them in any grade you ask," he told Eaker. "You can take a smart executive and make a fair Army officer out of him in a few months. You can never take a dumb Army officer and make a good combat leader out of him."

Only two of Eaker's initial staff was regular Army: Lt. William S. Cowart, Jr., a young fighter pilot who had served under him in the 20th Pursuit Squadron, and Col. Frank Armstrong, Jr., an old and trusted friend who became Eaker's executive officer. Three staff members were plucked from the Army reserves: Beirne Lay, Jr., a Yale graduate who had retired from the Army Air Corps in the 1930s to pursue a full-time career as a writer, and two executives from the Sperry Gyroscope Corporation, Harris B. Hull and Hull's friend Frederick W. Castle, a West Point graduate and, like Hull, an experienced pilot. The final member of the staff was a freshly commissioned Major, Peter Beasley, a Lockheed Aircraft executive.

Later, Hull and Castle did some recruiting of their own, almost entirely from civilian ranks: journalists, lawyers, businessmen, editors, and newspaper and publishing executives, among them Eaker's editor at *Harper's*, an editor at the *Saturday Evening Post*, and Parton, a *Time* magazine editor and executive who would join Eaker in England that spring. Dubbed "Eaker's Amateurs" by their doubting RAF hosts, they formed a surprisingly capable headquarters staff, and two of them, Armstrong and Castle, became excellent combat commanders.

The original seven almost didn't make it to England. With no Air Force planes available, they flew first to Portugal, a neutral country, on the Pan American Clipper, a four-engine Boeing flying boat. From there they planned to travel to England on a transport operated by the Dutch airline, KLM, now under the control of the Netherlands government in exile in London. Landing in Lisbon, they saw Luftwaffe planes parked wingtip to wingtip on the runway, and the city was swarming with Nazi undercover agents. "We had been warned [about this]," Eaker recalls. "We were sent in civilian clothes and told to carry no papers of any kind. . . . All of our directives were in our heads." Before leaving the Metropole hotel for dinner, Eaker's group rearranged the contents of their suitcases. When they returned to their rooms that evening, they discovered that their luggage had been searched, probably by Gestapo agents. Two days later, at five o'clock in the morning, a Dutch pilot led them aboard a KLM DC-3 transport. Everyone was on edge, knowing that the waters of the Bay of Biscay were being heavily patrolled by German warplanes. The Gestapo knew they were in Lisbon, heading for London. Would Hermann Göring's airmen be ordered to shoot them down?

A half-hour after takeoff, the Dutch pilot made an unscheduled landing at Porto, in northern Portugal. Calling Eaker to the cabin, he informed him that a German plane had been shadowing them. After waiting an hour or so, he took off. Flying far out on the Bay of Biscay to avoid detection, he again summoned Eaker forward and pointed to a German bomber bearing in on them. The Dutch pilot "jockeyed slightly from one side to the other in an effort to throw off the aim of the German if he opened up on us," Frank Armstrong recalls. "At that opportune time Lady Luck took a hand in the affair. One engine of the German plane belched a blob of smoke," and when the pilot cut off the engine he was thrown off course. "The fighter bomber passed under us at about 800 yards and headed for land and a place of safety. Our pilot came out of his compartment, turned his coat collar up high under his eyes and peeped at the passengers. For the next few seconds everyone was silent—silent in prayer of thanksgiving."

Later that day, they reached England. The aircraft log read, "Arrived at destination: flight uneventful." A year later, the Germans shot down a commercial plane over the Bay of Biscay, the second reported attack the Luftwaffe had made on airliners flying out of Lisbon. The plane was carrying thirteen passengers, among them the English actor Leslie Howard. There were no survivors.

On arriving in London, Eaker's party was taken on a drive through the battered but defiant metropolis. The German Blitz, eight months of fire and fear in 1940 and '41, had killed some 30,000 Londoners and left another 50,000 injured. And on far fronts, the war was going disastrously for the Allies. In Libya, British forces had been soundly defeated by Field Marshal Erwin Rommel's desert army; in Russia, the Red Army had been pushed back to Moscow and Leningrad; and in the Philippines, a starving, undermanned American force under Lt. Gen. Douglas C. MacArthur was making its final stand in the mountain jungles of Bataan. On February 15, five days before Eaker arrived in London, Singapore, the bastion of Occidental power in the Far East, fell to the Japanese.

For Britain, these were the bleakest months of the war. Even America's entry into the conflict, which Churchill happily saw as an assurance that "England would live" and that Germany and Japan "would be ground to powder," had failed to excite English public opinion. Londoners scorned America for being caught napping at Pearl Harbor and carped about it coming into the war so late.

For Eaker and his group, it was a shock to be in a country under siege; none of them had realized how pinched life had become in Great Britain. Meat, fish, vegetables, jam, margarine, eggs, condensed milk, breakfast cereal, cheese, and biscuits were severely rationed, along with clothing, soap, and coal for home heating. No one was starving, but rationing had reduced everyone to a monotonous, starchy diet that sapped vitality.

Eaker and his tiny staff had left an America that was not yet prepared for total war. England was fully mobilized, almost a garrison state. Ablebodied men and women between the ages of eighteen and sixty were required to perform national service of some kind. Childless women between the ages of twenty and thirty were conscripted for home-front military service or jobs in munitions industries, the first time this had been done in any Western nation. In no combatant country except Russia were civilians subjected to a greater degree of government regulation and compulsory mobilization. Women operated antiaircraft batteries in London, and factories all over the country worked around the clock, seven days a week, with workers putting in ten-to-twelve-hour shifts.

England had the look of a country fighting for survival. Hundreds of thousands of working-class families, 60 percent of them in London, had had their places of residence damaged or destroyed by Nazi warplanes and countless thousands of them were still mourning the loss of family and friends. German air raids had already killed nearly 43,000 British civilians. Not until the fourth year of the war would the Germans kill more British soldiers than British women and children. "This is a war of the unknown warriors," Churchill declared. "The whole of the warring nations are engaged, not only soldiers, but the entire population, men, women and children."

It was a people's war, but the people were weary. "What a different London from last year, when people were keyed up by raids and threats and filled with recklessness, very gay and smart," a British woman wrote in her diary. Families went to bed early because of crippling cuts in electrical service and coal deliveries, and at night the streetlights were left unlit and windows were covered with blackout curtains. Even when the sun occasionally showed its face, "people rarely smile."

On the dreary Sunday that Ira Eaker and his staff made their way through London in an RAF staff car, they passed through bombed-out neighborhoods in the East End, near the city's major docks. The American newspaperman Harrison Salisbury "didn't understand how air power worked," he wrote in his journal, until he took a bus to a street fair in this neighborhood, the most heavily bombed area of the city. "All around [was] the desert left by the bombers." Salisbury had met General Spaatz in Washington and had gone to house parties where he and other Air Force generals talked far into the night about war-winning airpower. This was Salisbury's first face-to-face confrontation with "successful bomb warfare. I understood now what Tooey Spaatz was talking about. This is what they wanted to do to Germany."

More accurately, this is what Britain decided it must do to Germany. At first, the only thing the RAF had dropped on German civilians were leaflets urging them to rise up against their tyrannical rulers. Bombing operations were severely limited and confined largely to airfields and maritime shipping. And they were conducted in daylight by small numbers of obsolete twin-engine bombers. British leaders feared that terror bombing German cities would provoke Luftwaffe reprisal raids on London and concerned, as well, that the RAF did not yet possess sufficient bombers and crews to damage German production or morale. Better to build and conserve the bomber force for more decisive operations.

Then in mid-May 1940, when the German army overran the Netherlands with shocking ease and bombed Rotterdam, killing 980 civilians, Churchill and the War Cabinet authorized Bomber Command to attack marshaling yards and synthetic oil plants in the Ruhr and the Rhineland. Their hope was that these raids would damage the sources of German military might and give Allied armies massed in northern France a chance of holding on against the Nazi juggernaut. The raids were to be conducted under the cover of darkness, since German fighters and flak were decimating the RAF's small air fleets.

The RAF raid on the night of May 15–16, 1940, was the beginning of the world's first large-scale strategic bombing war. Although terror was not the objective, Churchill knew that there would be civilian casualties and that the Luftwaffe would probably strike back at London, but he expected the RAF's new radar-guided fighters to defeat the German bombers. Then in retaliation for an accidental Luftwaffe raid on London on the night of August 24–25, 1940, part of a German air campaign to soften up Britain for invasion, Churchill ordered a reprisal raid on Berlin the very next night. Damage was minimal, but Hitler was furious. Beginning on September 7, he launched a devastating bomber Blitz on London, which soon extended to other British cities with the primary aim of destroying factories and terrorizing the civilian population to the point where its support for the war collapsed. As payback for the massive bombing of Coventry the night of November 14–15, Britain's new chief of the Air Staff, Sir Charles Portal, ordered a terror raid on Mannheim in mid-December 1940, which was largely ineffective, with bombs dispersed all over the countryside around the city.

The bomber war that airpower theorists Giulio Douhet and Billy Mitchell had predicted was beginning to materialize. But for a time Britain showed more restraint. Throughout the Blitz, German attacks on British cities were continuous, night after night, and almost wholly indiscriminate. The main British bombing effort was directed at military targets, and only a small number of German civilians living within the target areas were killed. There was also a difference in intent. Germany's aim was conquest, England's survival. After the evacuation of its army at Dunkirk, Britain had no other way to hit back directly at Germany. In 1940, "[bombing] represented a clear example of making war as Britain must, rather than as Britain might have wished," writes historian Max Hastings.

The results of these attacks were discouraging: both losses and inaccuracy remained high. In the summer of 1941, an alarming government study of bombing accuracy was released. Its author, a civil servant named D. M. Butt, claimed that only one-third of British planes that reached their targets that June and July had dropped their bombs within five miles of the Aiming Point. In the heavily defended Ruhr, with its permanent cloud of industrial smoke, the number was only in ten.

The Butt report led to a marked change in bombing strategy. With precision bombing impossible at night, England would now do what Churchill had sworn it would never do: deliberately bomb noncombatants. The targets of the new British air campaign were the built-up areas of German cities, the residential centers where most of the workforce lived. Fifty-eight cities of over 100,000 people were put in the target list. The objective: to destroy "the morale of the enemy civil population and in particular, of the industrial workers." It was to be terror bombing, a fulfillment of the ideas of Douhet and Mitchell. Only it was an act of desperation, not of original military purpose.

The new bombing policy was endorsed by Churchill, who also approved the man appointed to carry it out, Air Marshal Arthur Harris, an earthy, blunt-speaking career officer who had been serving as head of an RAF delegation to Washington. There Harris had met Ira Eaker at a dinner just before both men were scheduled to leave for England, at almost the same time but on separate planes, for their new and exactly parallel commands. On February 22, the day after Eaker's arrival in London, Harris became commander in chief of Bomber Command. Harris had not instituted the new bombing directive but he enthusiastically supported it, with one salient exception. He considered one of the goals of morale bombing—social revolution—a chimera. Douhet had predicted that a people subjected to unrelenting terror bombing would eventually rise up and force an end to the war. But even if the spirit of the German people was eventually broken by bombing, how would the suffering millions rise against the Nazi regime, with its ruthlessly efficient system of spying, torture, and repression? Harris's paramount aim was to employ area bombing to slow down German production by destroying industrial sites and killing industrial workers. Good workers, he would tell Eaker, took longer to produce than good machines, and "in short supply would affect war production as much as loss of their factory." Destroying workers' housing would also disrupt production by creating anxiety and high rates of absenteeism. Retreating to euphemism, a British official called the new initiative "de-housing," but the aggressively outspoken "Bomber" Harris, as the press began calling him, never denied that it was terror bombing.

Harris inherited a small, obsolete bomber force of fewer than 400 serviceable planes, only sixty-nine of them heavy bombers. But Bomber Command was already in the process of becoming greatly larger and more technically proficient. That March, British bombers began using a new navigational aid, code-named Gee (Ground electronics engineering) to guide them to targets on nonmoonlit nights, and British factories were beginning to mass-produce the four-engine Stirlings, Halifaxes, and Lancasters that would be the delivering instruments of Harris's "city-busting" campaigns, a succession of "bomber battles" that would, Harris believed, bring Germany to its knees before a land invasion was undertaken. "I was convinced," he wrote later, "that a bomber offensive of adequate weight and the right kind of bombs would, if continued for long enough, be something that no country could endure."

Churchill did not share Harris's confidence that bombing alone would bring down Nazi Germany, but in the absence of alternatives, he endorsed a bombing program of ruthless resolve, carried out by the man he called—half in admiration, half in abhorrence—the Buccaneer. (Harris's adoring crews, whom he supported unreservedly, called him Butcher, Butch, for short.) And the prime minister had no moral reservation, then or later, about unrestricted air warfare. After the war, he wrote to a former officer in Bomber Command: "We should never allow ourselves to apologize for what we did to Germany."

After a three-day stay in London, Eaker and his staff went out to Bomber Command headquarters in High Wycombe, a suburb in the Chiltern Hills, about twenty-five miles west of London. They were greeted warmly by Harris—now Sir Arthur—who invited them to share living and working space with Bomber Command until they established their own headquarters. Harris insisted that Eaker live in the interim with his family—his radiant wife, Lady Jill, and their two-year-old daughter—who had taken up residence in a magnificent country estate with horse barns and tree-shaded riding paths.

Eaker and Harris shared a birthday and both had faced physical hardship earlier in their lives, Harris spending part of his youth in the harsh Rhodesian bush, driving horse teams, clearing mosquito-infested land, and managing a tobacco farm. But in almost every other way, they were opposites. Raymond Daniell, a *New York Times* correspondent, deftly sketched them. "Harris, who had been a gold miner and tobacco planter in Rhodesia, is a hulking giant of a man—tall with shoulders to match—having a lusty, mordant sense of humor. He is bluff and hearty for an Englishman— a provocative, stimulating conversationalist. . . . Eaker is a soft-spoken Texan with an agile, athletic body. His features, like those of so many men who have devoted most of their lives to flying, have set themselves into sharp, firm lines that make one think of an eagle. He is modest and retiring almost to the point of shyness, and he has that unconsciously thoughtful courtesy usually associated with the antebellum South."

Harris read military history and books on farming in his spare moments; Eaker exercised with religious regularity. Harris enjoyed cocktails in the evening, mixing and serving the drinks in his velvet smoking jacket; Eaker drank sparingly—some sherry, now and then—but loved poker, cigars, and hearty male companionship. Harris had "a dry, cutting, often vulgar wit," and was outrageously, often savagely, direct. Eaker kept his passions under tight rein and, in social company, was eager to please. While Harris, the son of a Foreign Service officer, liked to poke fun at the "monocled" class, he was rigidly aloof with his staff, a cold and exacting commander. Eaker had a more relaxed style. He worked closely and informally with his staff, played volleyball, softball, and poker with them, and sought their advice. He was a man totally without pretense. Riding in the back of his limousine, he would ask his driver to stop and pick up British soldiers who were hitchhiking, heading home on leave. "British officers would never do this," one soldier told him. And when Eaker went into town for a haircut, he would sit patiently in the barbershop with the other villagers, waiting his turn. When asked by the mayor to give an impromptu speech before a group of High Wycombe citizens, he said only this: "We won't do much talking until we've done more fighting. We hope that when we leave, you'll be glad we came."

A ruthless taskmaster on the job, Arthur Harris was a cordial and relaxed host in his home, a completely different person than he was in the underground Operations Room at Bomber Command headquarters. He and Eaker liked each other immensely and convened every evening in Harris's famous "conversation room," a leather and wood study where Harris had set up a stereopticon machine that displayed three-dimensional aerial photographs of the enemy cities his crews were destroying. But their instant friendship never bridged the gap between their philosophies of bombing. Harris wished Eaker well in his upcoming experiment with daylight bombing, and did everything in his power to prepare him to succeed, sharing information on intelligence, operations, weather forecasting, and target selection. Even so, Harris was convinced that the American experiment would fail and that Eaker would eventually be forced to retrain his crews, reequip his bombers, and join the RAF in its night raids. "God knows, I hope you can do it," he told Eaker, "but I don't think you can. Come join us at night. Together we'll lick them."

In his memoirs, James Parton recounts a famous story about Harris to illuminate a moral divide between the two commanders. Driving his Bentley at breakneck speed on one of his regular runs between London and High Wycombe, Harris was stopped by a motor policeman, who politely reprimanded him. "You might have killed someone, sir."

"Young man," Harris snapped, "I kill thousands of people every night!"

Far from being squeamish about killing civilians, "he relished it," writes Parton. That may have been so, but the implication is misleading. Ira Eaker never opposed Harris's raids out of concern for people under the bombs. "I don't believe there was any moral consideration among military men [in World War II]," he remarked after the war. "When I watched bombs falling and hitting houses and churches I had a distaste for the whole business, but they were shooting at us." If the atomic bomb had been available in 1942, and he had had authorization to use it, he would have dropped it on Germany with no reservations, he said.

Eaker's objections to area bombing were founded entirely upon military considerations—it was not the most efficient way of finishing off the enemy. Yet he did believe that area bombing, in conjunction with American precision bombing, would put Germany under intolerable, round-the-clock pressure, hastening its demise. He saw Harris's operations as complementary to his own and considered him a partner, not a rival.

Harris was helpful in procuring a permanent headquarters for Eaker and his staff, which was growing by the week. Returning from one of their scouting missions through the Chiltern Hills, Eaker's aides reported that they had found the perfect spot, the Wycombe Abbey School for Girls, a crenellated manor house on a parklike campus, its walkways lined with linden trees. With Harris's and Eaker's insistent lobbying, the Air Ministry was pressured to remove the students to Oxford and hand over the school to the Eighth Air Force. On the April day that Eaker and twenty other American officers moved in, they laid out a softball diamond and set up volleyball nets. That night, the duty officer heard bells begin suddenly ringing all over the manor house. Some checking revealed that beside each bed was a bell labeled, "If you need a mistress in the night, ring twice."

Wycombe Abbey, code-named Pinetree, was only four miles from Harris's headquarters. This facilitated communication and liaison. Work-

ing with Harris, Eaker secured eight former RAF airbases in Huntingdonshire, in the Midlands, the great central plain of England just north of London. Over a hundred additional American bases—bomber and fighter
bases as well as supply, training, and repair stations—would soon be built,
most of them in Norfolk and Suffolk, in neighboring East Anglia. By late
1943, the Eighth would transform these lands of tall churches and small villages into a great land-based aircraft carrier. East Anglia would become a
"distinct American bomber zone," with the RAF concentrating its bomber
bases further to the north.

In May, while British construction crews were completing work on the
first two Eighth Air Force bases—Polebrook and neighboring Grafton Underwood—General Hap Arnold arrived in England. On May 30, Churchill
invited him and his delegation, along with Eaker and Ambassador Winant,
to dinner at Chequers, his Buckinghamshire retreat. As his guests sat down
to dinner, the prime minister rose and made a dramatic announcement: at
that very minute, he said, the RAF was taking off on the greatest air strike
in history, a 1,000-plane raid on Cologne.

Harris had already burned to cinder the historic cores of two combustible medieval cities, Lübeck and Rostock, but he needed a bigger,
more convincing demonstration of carpet bombing. Late that evening, as
the guests sat in the drawing room sipping port and puffing on cigars, the
prime minister announced that Operation Millennium had been a staggering success. The entire center of the Rhineland city was a sea of flames.
Later, it was learned that in less than two hours, nearly 500 people were
killed, 45,000 left homeless, and 12,000 buildings destroyed, at a cost of
only forty-one British aircraft. It had been a publicity grab as much as a
military operation. Harris had been able to marshal a force of 1,046
"bombers" only by sending out 400 obsolete planes from training units,
but with this raid, he became a national hero and the darling of the British
press.

That night at Chequers, Hap Arnold warmly congratulated the prime
minister, but in the British success, he saw a lost American opportunity. He
had arrived at Chequers to sell Churchill and his RAF advisors on the future of American daylight bombing. "Of all the moments of history. . . . I
had picked the night when they were selling their own kind of bombardment to the world. . . . It was plain that now there would be renewed pressure from the British to get our four-engine bombers for the R.A.F."

The night of the Cologne raid, the Eighth Air Force had only 1,871 men
in England—almost all of them ground staff—and not a single warplane. The
next day, Ambassador Winant sent an urgent message to President Roo-

sevelt. "England is the place to win the war. Get planes and troops over here as soon as possible."

The first combat group was already on its way. On the morning of June 10, the stately *Queen Elizabeth,* refitted as a troopship, docked in the Firth of Clyde. On board, along with thousands of American infantrymen, were air gunners of the 97th Bomb Group; the pilots and navigators would join them a month later, after having experienced a journey over the Atlantic nearly as harrowing as Charles Lindbergh's crossing fifteen years before.

A B-17 was a far more reliable machine than the *Spirit of St. Louis,* but Lindbergh was a magnificent aviator. The pilots of the Eighth flew their bombers across the same ocean with only a few months of flight training, relying on the reports of radio operators who had trouble translating dots and dashes and on the guidance of navigators who had an insecure grasp of their complex art. Soaring off the coast of Maine, fliers from heartland towns looked down on the first ocean they had ever seen. Their destination was Prestwick, Scotland, the eastern terminus of what was called the "great circle" route. Their "stepping-stones" were four large landmasses: Newfoundland, Labrador, Greenland, and Iceland. Although later groups flew nonstop to Scotland—a distance of some 2,000 miles—the first groups would find these stations indispensable, for they flew through some of the foulest weather on earth.

On the first leg of the crossing, airmen headed for one of two possible destinations: Goose Bay, Labrador, or Gander Lake in southern Newfoundland, both about 700 miles from the northern coast of Maine. Next was a perilous 700-to-1,000-mile over-water run to one of the two bases on Greenland that the United States had recently built, under agreement with Denmark. The first planes of the 97th Bomb Group, led by Paul Tibbets, made it to Greenland with ease. Then the trouble began. Flying over the island's jagged coastal mountains, Tibbets could see an endless icecap sparkling in the sun. This was his warning that he was approaching Bluie West One, one of the most dangerous landing fields anywhere. Tibbets maneuvered his bomber into a precariously narrow fjord, twenty miles long, flanked by high, serrated cliffs, which were just off his wingtips. There were, he remembered, "several tricky turns. A number of canyons branched off from the main fjord, and I had to watch our map closely to avoid following one of them. . . . to a dead end with no way of escape."

When a pilot entered the fjord, he had to know what the weather was at the airfield at the end of it. There was no room to turn around, and no B-17 could climb fast enough to avoid crashing into the immense wall of stone and ice just behind the landing strip. The weather was high and clear, and Tibbets brought in his bomber flawlessly. But later American airmen would crash and burn when fog or rapidly moving storms closed in on them.

BW-1 was a forbidding place, just south of the Arctic Circle. There was a mess hall, a weather shack, a scattering of drafty huts for sleeping, and across the fjord, an isolated Eskimo village. There was no temptation to linger there. After refueling, Tibbets flew to Iceland and then on to Prestwick, 846 miles to the east. A Royal Air Force navigator met his squadron there and guided the bombers to Polebrook, where they landed on a runway that had recently been a potato patch. When the last plane of the 97th touched down weeks later, Tibbets learned how fortunate his Group had been. They had lost five aircraft, but not a single man. "These youthful crews and their aircraft proved that they had what it takes to win a war," Tibbets wrote later.

Gen. Carl Spaatz had arrived in England a month earlier in a B-24 Liberator, and had already set up his headquarters in Bushy Park, close to London and the headquarters of the new commander of the European Theater of Operations, Maj. Gen. Dwight David Eisenhower. With the arrival of the 97th, the Eighth Air Force was ready to go to war.

It was made up of four commands. In addition to the Bomber and Fighter Commands, there was the Ground-Air Support Command, to be equipped, a year later, with twin-engine B-26 Marauder bombers, and the Air Service Command, responsible for supply and maintenance. Gen. Frank "Monk" Hunter set up Fighter Command headquarters at Bushey Hall, a country mansion in Hertfordshire, on the outskirts of northwest London, close to RAF Fighter Command. By August there would be four American fighter groups in the U.K., two of them flying British Spitfires and two flying American P-38 Lightnings.

For the planning and direction of combat operations, the Eighth's Bomber Command was organized into combat wings. Each wing was comprised of three bomb groups, which met in the skies over their neighboring bases and flew into battle together. Each combat wing, in turn, belonged to one or another larger organization, called, initially, a bombardment wing, and later an air division. These were the equivalent of infantry divisions, big organizations to fight big battles. In 1942, there were only two bombardment wings, the 1st and the 2nd. Each had its own commander and headquarters building, where bombing strikes requiring close coordination were plotted and organized.

ORGANIZATION CHART
8ᵀᴴ AIR FORCE

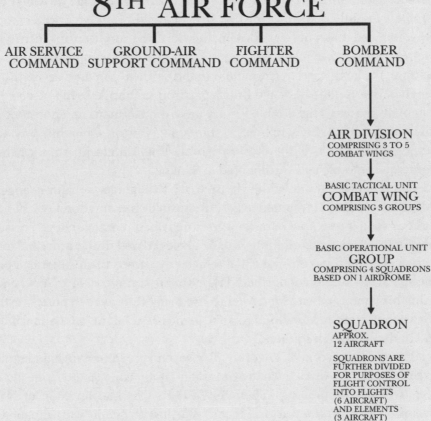

AIR SERVICE
COMMAND

GROUND-AIR
SUPPORT COMMAND

FIGHTER
COMMAND

BOMBER
COMMAND

AIR DIVISION
COMPRISING 3 TO 5
COMBAT WINGS

BASIC TACTICAL UNIT
COMBAT WING
COMPRISING 3 GROUPS

BASIC OPERATIONAL UNIT
GROUP
COMPRISING 4 SQUADRONS
BASED ON 1 AIRDROME

SQUADRON
APPROX.
12 AIRCRAFT

SQUADRONS ARE
FURTHER DIVIDED
FOR PURPOSES OF
FLIGHT CONTROL
INTO FLIGHTS
(6 AIRCRAFT)
AND ELEMENTS
(3 AIRCRAFT)

This organizational pattern was incomprehensible to most English farm families who resided in ancient places recently designated and renamed for wartime purposes. These tradition-bound local folk would soon have the young American fliers ignoring military terminology and calling their bomber stations, not by their Air Force numbers, but by the names of the ancient hamlets the new airfields were built near: Seething and Snetterton Heath, Wendling and Wattisham, Alconbury and Attlebridge, Thorpe Abbotts and Thurleigh.

The vast majority of American GIs who began pouring into England in the late summer of 1942 came to train for the invasion. The airmen would begin their battle at once. But as the crews of the 97th Bomb Group prepared for their first mission there occurred a major change in Allied war strategy. On July 1, the day the first B-17 manned by an American combat crew touched down in Great Britain, the German army won an electrifying victory, breaking the 245-day-long siege of the mighty naval base of Sevastopol, the final Russian stronghold in the Crimea. Ten days earlier Rommel had overrun the besieged British garrison at Tobruk, in Libya, near the Egyptian border. This double victory gave the Germans an enormous injection of confidence, while in Washington, Winston Churchill privately confessed that he was the most miserable Englishman in America since General Burgoyne had surrendered at Saratoga.

Churchill was at the White House to try to engineer a major change in Allied war policy. He wanted to get American troops and bombers into the fight as soon as possible in order to restore Allied morale, relieve pressure on the Russians, and reinforce Britain's beleaguered desert army in North Africa. The previous April, he had reluctantly agreed to an American plan for an Allied invasion of northern France in the spring of 1943. Now he was using his famous persuasive powers to try to get Roosevelt to postpone that invasion. Recalling Dunkirk, he spoke to the president of "a Channel full of the bodies of British soldiers."

The strategy worked. That July, Roosevelt agreed to an Allied landing in French North Africa, a controversial and hotly contested change in policy. It meant postponing indefinitely a cross-Channel invasion of Nazi-occupied France, the "second front" that Joseph Stalin was impatiently demanding. George Marshall and his protégé, Dwight Eisenhower, the untested general Roosevelt picked to command Operation Torch, as the North African campaign was code-named, bitterly opposed the plan, but Churchill was right. An adequate invasion fleet had not yet been built; German U-boats were inflicting heavy damage on Atlantic convoys; and the Luftwaffe owned the skies over Northern Europe. For Roosevelt, there were also political considerations. With congressional elections approaching in November, he was under pressure to get American ground forces into action against the Germans. And North Africa, with British assistance, was the only place the still mobilizing Americans were strong enough to take on the fearsome German war machine.

Arnold was furious. As part of the invasion plan, he was ordered to strip the fledgling Eighth to support upcoming operations in the Mediterranean, and he was not yet authorized to tell Spaatz and Eaker of these changes.

The 97th and the 301st, which had just arrived in England, were to be reassigned in the early fall to North Africa, and other bombers were to be sent there directly from training bases in the States. This meant that the Air Force plan to have a thousand heavy bombers over Germany by April 1943 would have to wait—how long, Arnold did not know.

It was more than a matter of delay. Arnold saw Operation Torch as a threat to the very existence of the Eighth Air Force. Before it was completed, the depleted Eighth might be absorbed into the Royal Air Force's night campaign.

This is the reason Arnold pressured Spaatz and Eaker to get their crews into combat before they were properly trained. The weeks prior to the November invasion of North Africa might be the American Air Force's only opportunity in the war to prove its doctrine of daylight strategic bombing. When informed after the Rouen mission of Operation Torch, Eaker and Spaatz also became convinced that the future of Air Force operations in Europe "rode upon the outcome" of the next dozen or so missions.

"We didn't know quite how we were going to make that offensive work at first," Arnold admitted later. "All we knew was that we *would* make it work." But Eaker and Spaatz had faith in their planes, faith in their crews, and above all, faith in the doctrine of strategic bombing. So in the late summer of the third year of the war, from small airfields in England, American boys flew into danger to test an idea about airpower that went back to the time when Billy Mitchell soared over the trenches in a flimsy two-winger built of fiber and wood.

CHAPTER THREE

The Dangerous Sky

Those who flew in late 1942 and early 1943 fought a very different war from those who came later.

RUSSELL STRONG, *First over Germany*

Polebrook, September 6, 1942

The target was an aircraft factory in northern France, with Paul Tibbets again leading the Eighth. There had been no losses up to now but today the Luftwaffe would be out in force. "On September 6," wrote Eighth Air Force commander Budd Peaslee, "the Americans got their first taste of air war as it was to be."

Göring's fighters waited until the bombers began returning from their targets, then tore past the Spitfire escorts and swarmed on them like a nest of angry hornets. Two Forts, one of them piloted by Tibbets's friend, Lt. Paul Lipsky, erupted in flames and sank sickingly out of sight, disintegrating piece by fiery piece as they dropped through the empty air. "He was a wonderful kid," Tibbets wrote later, "and his death shook me up. Up to now, the war was a game to us; we took off, dropped our bombs, and always returned safely. We thought we were supermen and that we were beating the odds with our skill in the sky. That was how stupidly inflated our confidence was until we watched Paul's plane spin out of control, [and] burst into a ball of flame." In Tibbets's plane, no one said a word on the interphone. Everyone silently pictured himself in Paul's shoes. "The very next mission we nearly made that same dive to eternity," Tibbets recalled. "It was . . . the most frightening brush with death that I was to experience in all my wartime missions over Germany, Africa, and the Pacific."

Messerschmitt Bf 109s (Me 109s), the most numerous fighter plane in the Luftwaffe air defense fleet, jumped on Tibbets's formation as soon as it completed its bomb run. "The guns from all our planes were spitting fire like mad as the enemy planes dived at us from three directions, ripping holes in the wings and fuselages of our B17s." Just as the worst seemed over, an enemy interceptor came straight out of the sun at Tibbets's bomber. A cannon shell smashed through the cockpit's right-hand window and part of the instrument panel disappeared. "At that moment, I felt the sting of flying metal, several fragments imbedding themselves in my right side," Tibbets recalled.

The co-pilot, Lt. Gene Lockhart, took the brunt of the hit. Part of his right hand was blown off and blood sprayed all over the shattered cabin. Tibbets, lean and hard-muscled, managed to keep the plane on course while it shuddered and shook from repeated hits. This was when a crew had to be disciplined. Panic erupted, but it came from an unlikely source: Col. Newton D. Longfellow, the new commander of the 2nd Bombardment Wing, who was flying with Tibbets on a combat orientation run. "[Longfellow] had a tough-guy reputation among his subordinates. Half the outfit was scared to death of him," said Tibbets. "In the frenzied moments that followed, all of the . . . bravado that had struck fear into the hearts of Newt's subordinates suddenly left him. Reacting with blind frenzy, he reached over my shoulder and grabbed a handful of throttles and turbo controls, sapping the power of our engines at 25,000 feet.

"There was chaos in the cabin. I was trying to fly the plane with one hand and keep Lockhart from bleeding to death with the other. While he held his shattered hand above his head, I grasped his wrist tightly with my right hand and tried to maintain level flight at the same time."

Tibbets shouted at Longfellow to get his hands off the controls, but with freezing air tearing through a hole in the instrument panel, Longfellow failed to hear him. Tibbets then gave him a "backhand shot" to the chin with his left elbow, knocking him out. Seconds later, a machine gun bullet creased the skull of one of the gunners, who fell in a heap on Longfellow. When Longfellow regained consciousness, he grabbed a first aid kit, put a tourniquet on Lockhart's hand, and bandaged the head of the unconscious turret gunner.

Tibbets regained control of the plane, and with Longfellow as his co-pilot, brought it home. Longfellow turned to Tibbets as they climbed out of the battered bomber. "Paul, you did the right thing."

The two badly injured men recovered and, along with Tibbets, received the Purple Heart. Standing beside the heavily bandaged Lockhart at the ceremony, posing for pictures for *Life* magazine, Tibbets was visibly embarrassed. He had suffered only minor puncture wounds and didn't have time for "parades and ceremonies," he had protested to Air Force publicists. That day, he was helping to plan what would be the biggest Eighth Air Force operation up to then.

Lille

On October 9, the Eighth would be flying to Lille, a French steel and rail center that fed Hitler's expanding war machine. With more bomb groups available, Ira Eaker was finally able to mount a considerable force of 108 heavies, including twenty-four twin-tailed B-24 Liberators from the newly operational 93rd Bomb Group, commanded by Col. Edward J. "Ted" Timberlake, who would become one of the finest air leaders of the war. It would be the B-24's first combat mission with the Eighth. Over 400 fighters were dispatched to cover the bombers. Among them were three dozen P-38 Lightnings and an equal number of Spitfires flown by pilots of the famed Eagle Squadrons, air groups made up of Americans who had joined the Royal Air Force before Pearl Harbor and had recently been absorbed into the Eighth's nascent Fighter Command as the 4th Fighter Group.

Lille was Lt. J. Kemp McLaughlin's maiden mission. A twenty-three-year-old graduate of West Virginia University, he was a product of the Great Depression. This was his first steady job and it was for a cause he cared for: he was being paid $250 a month, plus $90 flight pay, to help bring down the most dangerous man in the world. As he and his crewmates from the 92nd Bomb Group, a Fortress outfit that had just arrived in England, filed into the briefing room at Bovingdon aerodrome on this raw October morning, McLaughlin noticed that he was wasn't the only one who was nervous; everyone looked pale and drawn. Some men let out groans when the commanding officer, Col. James S. Sutton, warned them to expect an ugly reception from the Luftwaffe.

Then Maj. Gardiner "Gordy" Fiske, the group's chief intelligence officer, briefed the crews on expected enemy opposition. Fiske was from a top-tier Boston family and had been a member of the famed Lafayette Escadrille in the last war. He had reenlisted in the Air Force after Pearl Harbor with little knowledge of how far military aviation had progressed since he had fought over the trenches in his twin-winged fighter. When he completed his briefing, a flier asked him about antiaircraft defenses along the French coast. "He looked puzzled," recalled McLaughlin, "and finally said, 'Well, there weren't any there when I was there in World War I.' " At that point, Colonel Sutton jumped out of his seat and shouted, " 'Gordy, for God's sake, sit down!' " Only a few men laughed.

McLaughlin was flying co-pilot, with his squadron commander, Maj. Robert Keck, and Keck's presence steadied his nerves. As the bombers approached Lille, a heavy layer of haze began to form and Keck's bombardier could not get a proper sighting on the target. Keck ordered the squadron to head for the secondary target, an airfield at St. Omer, where they ran into a thick field of antiaircraft fire. McLaughlin watched in horror as a flak burst hit the left wing, where half of the plane's gas tanks were located, setting the entire wing on fire. Another flak burst threw hot shrapnel through the fuselage, wounding the radio operator, "who began screaming over the interphone, blocking all other communication." Major Keck signaled McLaughlin to take over and went down to the nose compartment to help fight the fire—or so McLaughlin thought. After the hostile fighters left and the fire burned out, Keck climbed back into the cockpit and took over the controls. Later, McLaughlin learned from the navigator what Keck had been doing below. He had strapped on his chute and sat on the lower escape hatch, shivering with fear, prepared to be the first to bail out if the plane exploded or lost its wing. "Though it would take a year to catch up with him, that incident," said McLaughlin, "eventually ended his military career."

After returning to base, McLaughlin climbed on his bicycle and headed back to his quarters. As he passed one of his old flying school classmates who had been on the mission, he hailed him, but got no reply. Later he learned that his friend was on his way to group headquarters to turn in his wings. He would never fly again.

The mission left Kemp McLaughlin with the feeling that neither he nor the leaders he had trusted were ready to fight an air war. His chances of survival, he surmised, were slim to none.

Lille was the Eighth's "first real brawl." Four bombers went down, the first losses the Eighth suffered since September 6, and forty-six other bombers were damaged by fighter attacks "unprecedented in ferocity and duration." No gunner in the Eighth had been prepared for what he met in the skies over Lille and St. Omer. As waves of enemy fighters wove in and out of the bomber formations, trigger-happy gunners had sprayed machine gun fire all over the sky, hitting their own bombers, their fighter escorts, and only occasionally the enemy. After the battle, Air Force publicists boasted that the gunners had a "field day." The official claims were fantastic: fifty-six German fighters destroyed and forty-six "probably destroyed" or badly damaged, the total of 102 being more fighters than the Luftwaffe put in the air that day. German records, on the other hand, showed only two losses. "We were living in a fool's paradise," one commander commented.

The gunners were inexperienced, miserably trained, and anxious to prove themselves—a catastrophic combination. Most of them did not set out to deceive. In the fog of battle, as many as a dozen gunners might be firing on a single German fighter plane. If that enemy aircraft was shot down, five or six gunners might make individual claims, each believing his claim was legitimate. Another factor led to inaccurate claims. German pilots, boring in on the gunners' sights at closing speeds of over 500 miles an hour, flipped their planes belly-up after firing a burst, and as they plunged straight down, their exhausts emitted trails of thick black smoke. Many gunners mistook the smoke and evasion maneuvers for fatal damage inflicted by their .50 caliber machine guns.

Navigators and bombardiers had an equally difficult time. For some of them, it was their first bomb run at an altitude over 10,000 feet. Every bomber was equipped with a $10,000 Norden bombsight. Asked if bombardiers using his sight could actually drop a bomb into a pickle barrel from 20,000 feet, Carl Norden had replied, "Which pickle would you like to hit?" But his sensitive bombsight was difficult to operate, even in practice runs on cloudless days back in the States. In Western Europe, cloud or industrial haze was present two days out of every three, and when a bombardier was able to see clearly, the enemy could easily spot him. With hot slugs and pieces of jagged shrapnel smashing into his glass-enclosed work station, he had to remain calm and focused as he entered data into the instrument on ground speed, rate of closure, wind drift, and the estimated air resistance and time of fall of the bombs. Pilots were supposed to keep the plane as level and steady as possible on the bomb run, but as a classified Air Force report noted, excitable pilots often took violent evasive action under fire, unsetting the sensitive gyroscopes on the Norden bombsights. Some bombardiers became so nervous that they forgot to open the bomb bay doors.

To bomb accurately, inexperienced bombardiers had to depend on equally inexperienced navigators to locate the target, navigators who had trouble finding their own English bases returning from training missions. "When a new crew is turned loose over England with a map," reported an Air Force investigator, "they can be expected to be lost in between five and ten minutes." Average bombing accuracy over the course of the war, "expressed as a circular error probable," was approximately three-quarters of a mile, hardly the circumference of a pickle barrel. A secret Air Force report on the Lille mission disclosed that bombing errors were "so large and so recurrent that unless we can drastically reduce them we shall derive very little advantage from our excellent Norden sight." General Eaker knew the bombing had been poor, but misrepresented the results to reporters.

The crews that flew to Lille had been informed that their targets were "in the thick" of a densely populated area. "As we came above . . . a church . . . which was the guide for our target, it came over me that if we missed the target we would hurt a lot of people," Tibbets told a reporter after the mission. "We don't want to kill French people. . . . My anxiety is for the women and kids. . . . You see, I have a three-year-old baby of my own at home. I hate to think of him playing near a bombed factory. That makes me careful." But in the confusion of aerial combat, with the wind blowing fiercely at bombing altitude, no amount of care could ensure that innocent people were spared. The crews were also being asked to do the impossible by commanders seduced by a deep-driven faith in pinpoint bombing. These blind believers had enough sense, however, to cover their tails. Two days before the Lille raid, they had the British Broadcasting Corporation warn Frenchmen living within two kilometers of a factory or rail yard in the northern part of the country to evacuate their homes.

Eighth Air Force crews were never told that their bombs had killed at least forty civilians in Lille, 150 Frenchmen on a later raid on the port of Lorient, and 140 more on a second raid on Rouen. The damage at Rouen, the cultural center of Normandy, would have been far greater had not dozens of bombs been duds, among them one that went through the roof of a hospital.

But nothing eroded Eighth Air Force enthusiasm.

Ira Eaker saw Lille as a turning point—the successful conclusion of the first phase of America's daylight strategic bombing campaign. The Lille mission proved conclusively, he wrote Hap Arnold, that bombers "in strong formation can be employed effectively and successfully without fighter support." Arnold had been relaying Eaker's reports to President Roosevelt, who, under continuing pressure from Churchill, was beginning to doubt that these raids were doing any harm to the Germans. "I assured him that there was no reason for being concerned," Arnold wrote Spaatz. "I hope we are right."

Roosevelt may have been skeptical, but Eaker's sunny reports were not directly challenged by American war correspondents in Britain, who either believed them outright or felt it important, with the war going badly, for the American public to believe them. That October, *Life* magazine sent its star photojournalist, Margaret Bourke-White, to do a lavish photo spread on the Eighth Air Force, the only American fighting force engaging the Nazis at the time. "All the raids have been tremendously successful," *Life* reported. The Eighth's Bomber Command was admittedly small, but it "would grow and grow," and as it grew tremendously, "the intensity and terribleness of the attack on Germany [will] grow with it, until the skies of Europe [are] blackened and its earth furrowed with American bombs."

The expansion of destruction did not occur as fast as *Life* anticipated. Over the next six months, the Eighth Air Force was never able to put as many bombers over Hitler's Fortress Europe on a single day as it had on the Lille raid. Eaker had been right; Lille was a turning point, but not in the way he had sanguinely envisioned.

In hindsight, however, the appearance of the Eighth over Northwestern Europe in the fall of 1942 was "the most critical event in the strategic bombing war," wrote Horst Boog, the outstanding German historian of the air war. The creation of a daytime offensive, in conjunction with the British night campaign, would put demands on German air defenses "round the clock, and the superiority of the Allies became oppressive." But in 1942, both the German and Allied high commands saw the early Eighth Air Force campaign as pathetically ineffective. And that fall Anglo-American global strategy would further weaken the Eighth, putting its very survival in jeopardy.

The Pens of Biscay

In late October 1942, Paul Tibbets received orders to assemble five Fortresses for a top secret airlift to Gibraltar. The passengers would be the American and British commanders of Operation Torch, the invasion of North Africa. His passenger in the *Red Gremlin* would be General Eisenhower, the supreme commander of the operation. On November 2, Tibbets's small fleet flew from Polebrook to an airport near Bournemouth, a popular seaside resort on the English Channel. The following day, Eisenhower and his command staff arrived from London on a special train, packed and prepared to transfer their headquarters to Gibraltar. The weather was miserable, drizzle and fog so thick "even the birds were walking," as the fliers used to joke. After several postponements, Eisenhower decided to fly just as the weather turned worse. Standing on the flight line with part of his staff, taking shelter underneath one of *Red Gremlin*'s wings, he turned to Tibbets and said, "Son, I've got a war about to begin down there and that's where I have to be." Tibbets could barely see the wingtips of his plane as it sped down the runway in the blinding fog and rain.

Three days later, at 3:00 A.M. on November 8, two vast troop and supply convoys, one sailing from the United States, the other from Britain, converged with machine precision on their main objectives. An American force, part of the greatest war fleet ever to sail from home waters, landed at Casablanca, on the Atlantic coast of Morocco, and two other task forces made up of British and American troops landed at Oran and Algiers on the Mediterranean coast of Algeria. Altogether, 65,000 troops were put ashore. It was the largest American amphibious operation up to that point. Later that month, Tibbets was sent to North Africa to command a squadron of American bombers in the newly created Twelfth Air Force.

The Twelfth was aptly code-named Junior. Spaatz and his staff were ordered to strip the air force they had just begun creating in England for strategic bombing in order to build another air force, whose operations would be primarily tactical, supporting infantry and interdicting enemy supply lines. "You can't have that; it's for Junior," became a standing joke at Park House, Spaatz's residence on Wimbledon Common, just up the Thames from London and not far from Eighth Air Force headquarters in Bushy Park, code-named Widewing. At Park House, a simple but cozy Victorian residence, Spaatz lived and worked with his top advisors and held daily staff meetings, preferring the atmosphere here to Widewing, a group of drab one-story cinder block buildings. It was an around-the-clock operation. "I can remember being there at two o'clock in the morning," one officer recalled, "rushing over to General Spaatz's house; General [Frederick] Anderson [Spaatz's chief advisor on operational matters] came out in his bathrobe, and General Spaatz served us tea. During a big night we were up all night." As the general's biographer noted, "living and working together fit in with Spaatz's philosophy of leadership." He hated to work in an office, at a desk piled with papers and stacks of harassing memos. "Tooey, like some literary characters, was inclined to get up very late and work very late," a friend recalled. Like Churchill, he did the lion's share of his work in the late morning, propped up in bed dressed in pajamas. He worked best alone or with three or four men he trusted completely, men he often mapped strategy with over late night poker games. Orders were rarely given; Spaatz assumed that the men at the table sipping his bourbon and trying to take his money understood what he wanted from them.

Eisenhower had instructed Spaatz to contribute to Torch his two most experienced heavy-bombardment groups, the 97th and the 301st, and all but one of his fighter groups, the Fourth, stationed at Debden, directly north of London. By the beginning of November, the Eighth had siphoned off to Junior over 27,000 men and 1,200 aircraft. The Eighth also lost Brig. Gen. Jimmy Doolittle, the first American air hero of the war. After his Tokyo Raid, for which he was awarded the Medal of Honor, he had been assigned to take over one of the Eighth's bombardment wings, but instead was given command of the Twelfth Air Force. "What is left of the Eighth Air Force after the impact of Torch? We find we haven't much left," Spaatz remarked at a staff meeting. And with English weather grounding his bombers for entire weeks that October, Spaatz feared that as Allied forces took territory in the Mediterranean, the Eighth would be completely dismantled, its bombers dispatched to bases in Southern Europe, where weather was less of an impediment.

As it turned out, it was its commander, not the entire Eighth, who was sent to North Africa. On the eve of the invasion, Eisenhower appointed Spaatz to head Air Force operations in the Mediterranean Theater. Ira Eaker was elevated to command of the diminished Eighth, and Newton Longfellow succeeded him as head of the Eighth's Bomber Command. The Eighth was left with only four Fortress groups—the 91st, 303rd, 305th, and 306th—and two Liberator groups—the 44th and Ted Timberlake's 93rd. Both of them, however, would be sent to North Africa on special temporary assignments in the coming year, leaving the Fortresses to carry out most of the bombing from England from November 1942 into the following summer. Yet after being depleted by Torch, the Eighth was given its toughest assignment yet by the commander of Torch: to hit Nazi U-boat pens in France's Bay of Biscay in an effort to keep the Atlantic supply lines open to Allied forces in North Africa.

The purpose of the first missions that the Eighth had flown from England had been less to hurt the enemy than to prove that the Americans could do daylight bombing without prohibitive losses. Fearing that dangerous missions and large losses would doom the entire bombing experiment, Spaatz and Eaker had mounted relatively safe shallow penetration raids against industrial targets in France and Holland, targets well within the range of fighter escorts. In the next phase of the air war, when the heavies were sent out against targets their bombs couldn't destroy and their escorts were unable to reach, many of the friends Paul Tibbets left behind in England would die.

When Ira Eaker took over the Eighth, he moved from High Wycombe to Bushy Park, leaving behind the tightly knit staff of 150 officers he had welded into a deeply devoted operational team. Spaatz offered him Park House, but Eaker, expecting a steady stream of visitors, wanted a larger residence. "Elaborate entertaining at a time when the bitter war was far from won may sound rather like Nero fiddling while Rome burned," Parton wrote in his memoirs, but Eaker had two important diplomatic and propaganda campaigns to wage. "He had to maintain close and cordial relations with the British at all levels from the king down. And he had to keep on persuading the river of high-level visitors that the still unproven concept of high-level precision bombardment by day would work beyond the fringes of France."

His friends in the RAF found him the perfect place, a handsomely appointed Tudor house called Castle Coombe, not far from Bushy Park. It had two acres of gardens, a tennis court, twelve bedrooms, a spacious reception area, and a gate that opened onto Coombe Hill golf course, where Eaker would often sneak in nine holes in Britain's long summer twilight. The RAF furnished the house and Parton decorated the walls with fifty paintings and prints on loan from the bombproof storage areas of the Tate Gallery. While Castle Combe was being readied, Eaker lived at Park House, directing the first phase of the bombing operation that would come closer than Torch to destroying the Eighth Air Force as an independent command.

The greatest naval confrontation of World War II was the Battle of the Atlantic, a mortal struggle to prevent enemy U-boats from severing the oceanic lifeline between Britain and her allies, as well her fighting forces around the world. "The Battle of the Atlantic," said Churchill, "was the dominating factor all through the war. . . . Everything happening elsewhere, on land, at sea, or in the air, depended ultimately on its outcome." For Great Britain, it was also a fight for survival. A vulnerable island economy, despite its immense industrial capacity, Britain imported much of its nonferrous metal, half its food, and all its oil. If blockaded successfully by the undersea fleet of Adm. Karl Dönitz, commander of the German submarine service, it would be starved into submission. The blockade also threatened to cut off the shipment from Britain to Russia of warplanes and tanks needed to stop the German advance on Moscow and Leningrad, of avia-

tion gasoline, airplanes, and air personnel from America to England, and
of men and supplies to North Africa. "The only thing that really frightened
me during the war," Churchill said later, "was the U-boat peril."

In 1942, it looked like the Allies might lose the Battle of the Atlantic, as
U-boat production soared and Dönitz's boats began attacking convoys in
wolf packs, teams of marauding underwater killers. In that year alone,
U-boats sank over a thousand Allied ships in the North Atlantic. For the Allies, the worst month of this maritime massacre was November 1942, when
116 ships were sent to the bottom by Dönitz's gray wolves, losses that menaced the North African invasion. Churchill pleaded with Roosevelt to send
him long-range B-24 Liberators to hunt down the wolf packs in the sea
lanes of the far North Atlantic, but production delays, demands of American theater commanders in the Pacific, and Hap Arnold's insistent pleas to
the president that the daylight raids from England continue, delayed the
delivery of all but a token number of bombers for long-range air patrol. So
against all common sense, American bombers were sent against targets less
vital and vulnerable than submarines at sea.

The British would help, but air attacks on U-boat operations would be
mainly an American effort. Harris's bombers would hit submarine production facilities in northern Germany, while the Eighth went after five U-boat
bases on the western coast of France: Lorient, St. Nazaire, Brest, La Pallice,
and Bordeaux. Along with Paris, these Biscay ports had been the chief
prizes of the Nazi conquest of France. With them under German control,
U-boats no longer had to make the treacherous week-long trip from bases
at Kiel and Wilhelmshaven, across the North Sea, and around the top of
the British Isles to their hunting grounds in the North Atlantic. They could
remain at sea longer and range farther while staying closer to their sources
of supply, command, maintenance, and intelligence. In 1942, twelve
U-boats based along the Bay of Biscay each sank more than 100,000 tons of
shipping. No American submarine in the Pacific sank more tonnage than
that during the entire war.

Dönitz made these ports the U-boats' main operational base and set up
his headquarters in a château outside Lorient, at the head of a long peninsula that sheltered what had formerly been a lazy fishing port. Standing on
his sweeping terrace, he could see the largest of the concrete pens that Nazi
engineering crews were building to shelter his boats. Fifteen thousand
slave laborers were working on three colossal enclosures, each with a
twenty-five-foot-thick reinforced-concrete roof. When completed in January 1943, these were among the most imposing defensive fortifications in
the history of armed conflict, and the entire project was one of the greatest

construction feats of World War II, requiring three-quarters of the concrete used to build the Hoover Dam.

An Eighth Air Force study described the sub pens at Lorient and other Biscay ports. "From four miles up, these shelters resembled cardboard shoeboxes. From the ground they looked like enormous square-jawed railroad tunnels. They squatted on dry land with ramps leading down to water. Entering U-boats were hauled up in cradles and shunted into any one of twelve individual pens." In deep tunnels beneath the pens, German engineers had built elaborate repair and service facilities, along with living arrangements that included dormitories, dental clinics, hospitals, bakeries, kitchens, and air raid shelters.

Allied intelligence considered the pens virtually bombproof. They would be, in General Spaatz's words, "hard, maybe impossible nuts to crack," but he and Eaker believed that high-altitude bombing could do heavy damage to the floating docks, rail yards, torpedo sheds, power stations, and foundries that surrounded and serviced the pens. Disrupting these facilities would, it was hoped, extend the turnaround time of U-boats in port, reducing the number of submarines patrolling the Atlantic sea lanes at any one time. The defeat of the U-boat "[is] one of the basic requirements to the winning of the war," Eisenhower told the commanders of the Eighth. Eaker assured Ike that his heavies could do it. He didn't like the job he was given, seeing it as a diversion from true strategic bombing, but for the next ten months U-boat facilities would be "first priority" for his airmen.

Eaker opened the assault on October 21, 1942, sending ninety bombers to Lorient. Thick overcast forced all but fifteen to turn back before reaching the target, but the cocky veterans of the 97th Bomb Group, on their last mission before being sent to North Africa, found a hole in the clouds and descended to 17,500 feet. Their aim was excellent, but their one-ton bombs bounced off the roofs of the U-boat shelters "like ping-pong balls." The attacking planes, flying an all-water route to avoid enemy fighters, had caught the Lorient flak crews napping, but the Americans met fierce fighter resistance on their way out and lost three bombers.

Forty Frenchmen died in the raid, but agents of the Resistance reported that the people of Lorient stood in the streets applauding the accuracy of the American bombers and commenting that their countrymen who were killed had "asked for their fate" by working for the Germans on the naval base.

The next mission was to St. Nazaire. This time, Eaker purposely sent his bombers in at dangerously low altitude, where they met heavy resistance. Bad weather had grounded the Eighth for eighteen days, enough time for the Germans to rim the port with flak batteries, most of them armed with 88 millimeter cannons that delivered 20-pound explosive shells. Over half the Fortresses executing the bomb run were damaged, and the last group to attack, the 306th, was horribly mauled; almost all of its Fortresses were damaged and three were lost to antiaircraft fire. For the rest of the war, St. Nazaire would be known to crewmen of the Eighth as Flak City. "You always get good trouble over St. Nazaire," said one gunner. "They got post graduates at them flak guns."

In the remaining months of 1942, the Eighth flew six additional missions against the U-boat lairs. The bombers did their heaviest damage at St. Nazaire, the most important of the bases, but repair crews had this and other bombed bases operating at full tilt within weeks, sometimes days. The Eighth also hit Rouen and Lille again, and German air force installations in France. On almost every one of these missions, the heaviest opposition, unlike the first St. Nazaire strike, was from German fighters.

In the early winter of 1942, former fighter ace Lt. Gen. Adolf Galland, head of the Luftwaffe's fighter arm, and at age thirty, the youngest general in the German forces, became exceedingly worried about the Reich's air defenses in northwestern Europe. The RAF was already plastering German cities, and once the Americans began mass-producing bombers they, too, would be invading German airspace, threatening the war industries of the Reich. Galland had fewer than 200 battle-ready aircraft as his front line of defense in France and the Low Countries against the American daylight raiders. Most of them were organized into two Jagdgeschwader, or Fighter Wings—JG 2 and JG 26, the latter known to American fliers as the "Abbeville Kids," for their main base in northern France. These were both elite units, with crack pilots and the finest fighter planes German industry was producing, but Galland's pilots, he later admitted, were "insufficiently prepared" to engage the American bombers, with their "colossal defensive armament"; even a wounded bomber was considered a deadly threat. When four German fighters pounced on a B-17 limping back to the Channel on three engines, three of the inexperienced attackers were shot down. "As a result," reported a leading German fighter pilot, "It was said that Fortresses were not to be attacked, as no fighter can shoot them down." As Galland observed, "Not only had our pilots to overcome the psychological barrier, but absolutely new tactics had to be devised." Unless his fighter outfits were built up, and unless they developed new ways of attacking the Fortresses, "these birds will one day fly all the way to Berlin," he told a doubting Göring, who, remembering the unfortunate British experience with them, dismissed them as "flying coffins." Göring also ridiculed Roosevelt's plans to produce overwhelming numbers of war planes, insisting that the soft, materialistic Americans were capable of making only "cars and refrigerators."

In late 1942, the German supreme leadership considered the air war over the Western Reich a secondary theater, "a side show," in the words of historian Horst Boog. The true fight was on the Eastern Front, and that is where German fighter aircraft were most heavily concentrated. As for the homeland, Hitler believed unreasonably that flak guns, in combination with a few hundred pursuit planes, would be sufficient deterrence to Allied bombers. And the Luftwaffe high command arrogantly assumed that the Allied bomber offensive would fail, just as Germany's bombing campaign against Britain in 1940 and 1941 had failed.

Both Hitler and Gen. Hans Jeschonnek, chief of the Luftwaffe General Staff, ignored Galland's pleas for an emergency program of fighter production. Since the late 1930s, Luftwaffe doctrine had stressed attack over defense, a strategy that gave bomber production priority over fighter production. To this, Hitler added his own consuming concern with vengeance weapons—bombers and new rockets under development at secret research sites, "wonder weapons" that would make England pay in blood for its pitiless pounding of German cities. But for Germany, the problem was that Anglo-American airpower strategy also stressed offensive action, and the RAF and the Eighth Air Force had a secure base in England from which to launch attacks by bombers in greater numbers and with greater range and destructive capacity than the Luftwaffe's twin-engine bombers. By giving low priority to Galland's fighter force, the Nazi leadership opened "a dangerous gap" in Germany's air defenses, a gap into which Allied bombers would strike with awesome effectiveness once America and England had decisively won the first and most important battle of the bomber war, the production war.

Even if Hitler had wanted to move more fighters to the west in late 1942, it could only have been done at extreme risk to the Wehrmacht, which was fighting for its life, and losing badly, on two battlefronts: Russia and North Africa. The overstretched Luftwaffe simply did not have enough aircraft to fight the wide-spreading war Hitler had initiated. With the führer unwilling to massively increase fighter production, Galland's defensive force in the west had to come up with new tactics to meet and defeat the fearsomely armed Fortresses that Galland's pilots called the "Boeings."

Up to now, the Germans had attacked the bombers singly and from the rear, putting themselves under withering fire for periods of up to one minute. When the Eighth returned to St. Nazaire on November 23, the Luftwaffe sprang a surprise. Thirty Focke-Wulf 190s (Fw 190s), Germany's newest and fastest fighter plane, lined up to attack the Forts head-on. These Fw 190s were from JG 2, led by Oberstleutnant Egon Mayer, one of the storied fighter aces of the war. Mayer had closely studied previous American raids and noticed that the Fortresses and Liberators had a weak spot in their defenses in the nose section. Some Forts had only one handheld .30 caliber machine gun, fired through an eyelet in the Plexiglas nose of the plane, while others had twin .50 caliber nose guns, mounted on swivels just aft of the nose. The Liberators were equipped with similar frontal defenses, leaving both bombers with a blind spot that the other gunners could not cover.

Mayer and his pilots flew level with the bombers, just out of range of their machine guns, but close enough for the nervous American gunners to see them. Then they moved a mile ahead, made an abrupt turn, and tore into the lead bomber in the formation in waves of two to four planes, flying wingtip to wingtip. Each pilot held his fire until he could see the spinning propellers of the bomber he was attacking and then fired "from all buttonholes," diving away an instant before ramming the nose of the bomber.

A German fighter pilot later explained the effectiveness of these frontal attacks. Because of the concentration of fire from the massed bombers and the density of the cone of fire, the most dangerous distance for the attacker was between 1,000 and 600 meters. "Once you are nearer than that . . . the smallest [aiming] error . . . will cause the whole cone of fire to miss you . . . and you have a chance of bringing them down. . . . You can kill the crew straight away [or hit] the engines and the [fuel] tanks."

On subsequent missions, as German fighters pressed their nerve-rattling attacks to within a hundred yards of the bombers, and as losses to fighters continued to mount, some forward-facing crewmen began to develop nearly disabling fears that a Focke-Wulf carrying a dead pilot would smash directly into them. Of the original crews assigned to the 306th Bomb Group, which flew its first mission in early October 1942, 30 percent of the pilots and co-pilots were killed in action. A morale-building poster was put up on a bomber base in East Anglia. Under the face of a grinning pilot was the challenge, "Who's afraid of the new Focke-Wulf?" An airman pinned a piece of paper on it, with the words, "Sign here." Every flying officer in the group, including the group commander, put his signature on it.

Pilots would often have to settle down their crews before takeoff. This was done on the flight line, after the men arrived at their planes in an Army jeep or truck. For many crewmen, that short ride to the waiting planes was the most agonizing part of the mission. "If it's going to hit you, it's going to hit you then—whatever peak of fear, anxiety, or urge to turn back, that you're going to feel," recalled Capt. Robert Morgan, pilot of the *Memphis Belle* of the 91st Bomb Group, the most famous American bomber of the European war. "Being under way is actually a relief. It's that damn ride to the planes that nearly kills you." The airmen had an expression, "You die on the runway, not after you're hit."

Just before boarding the plane on the airstrip at Bassingbourn, Morgan, a hard-drinking hell-raiser from Asheville, North Carolina, would call his crew together and have them huddle up like a football team. He would talk to his men quietly for a few minutes. What was said was unimportant. "The important thing," Morgan recalled, "was that this was *our* huddle, our moment to come together among ourselves. To hear one another's breathing, feel one another's hands on our shoulders. To experience that instant when we stopped being ten separate entities, and became one." These wisecracking American boys who seemed to take nothing seriously would suddenly have "the solemnity and level gazes of men twice their age. . . . It was ten minds coming into acute focus."

A Mission

The *Memphis Belle*'s first mission was on November 7, against the submarine pens at Brest. Morgan prepared for it by writing to his fiancée, Margaret Polk, the Memphis belle he had met in training in Walla Walla, Washington, and had named his plane after. "You must always have faith that I'll be back one of these days. You and I have a wonderful life ahead of us."

The night before the raid, the officers dined together in near silence, and turned in early. No one was interested in a pub crawl. "We'd heard all the stories about the losses the RAF had taken . . . [but] none of us had any idea, really, what to expect, no concept of what it would be like to be shot at." Lying quietly in their beds, their eyes still open, the men could hear Harris's bombers rumbling overhead, headed across to the Ruhr.

There was no such thing as a typical mission. Every mission was unique, a singular experience, but there was a recognizable pattern in all of them. For the flight crews, a mission usually began with the sound of a jeep stopping outside their Nissen huts around 4:00 A.M. "A courtly staff sergeant would come in and go to the officers' bunks who were scheduled to fly," recalled co-pilot Bernard Jacobs of the 384th Bomb Group, stationed at Grafton Underwood. "The enlisted men were billeted in another area. We would feign sleep until he stopped at our bunk and gave a tug on the arm. He would then say, 'Good morning, sir. You and your [crew] will be flying number 6 in the low squadron, low group today. Breakfast at 4:30, briefing at 5:15, takeoff at 6:15.' "

The sergeant gunners were awakened with less propriety. "Drop your cocks and grab your socks, boys, you're flying today," an orderly would bellow, banging the heel of his hand on the hut's low, corrugated steel roof.

Outside, there were no ground lights on; the base was blacked out in the event of a surprise night attack by the German air force. Walking to the mess hall with their flashlights to guide them, the men could see searchlight beams crisscrossing the sky, beacons to guide the RAF home.

At the briefing for Morgan's first mission, Col. Stanley Wray, the 91st's commander, paced in front of a wall-size map of Europe, a wooden pointer in his hand. On the map, a colored piece of yarn ran from Bassingbourn, located not far from the college spires of Cambridge, straight to the target, the submarine pens at Brest. "Bombardiers, if you can't see the first target, go to the second. If you can't see the second, go to the third. But don't drop your bombs indiscriminately. If you can't bomb any targets, don't jettison on open cities. Bring your bombs home." Later, when the Eighth began flying missions into Germany, these precautions were often not observed.

"All you men—this is your first mission. I expect you to do a good job. . . . That's it. Synchronize your watches."

As the fliers began filing out of the room, Catholic boys stopped near

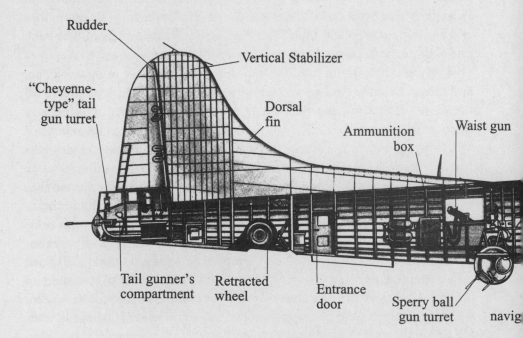

Rudder

Vertical Stabilizer

"Cheyenne-type" tail gun turret

Dorsal fin

Ammunition box

Waist gun

Tail gunner's compartment

Retracted wheel

Entrance door

Sperry ball gun turret

navig

the door, knelt, and received absolution and communion from their chaplain. Protestants stood with bowed heads before their chaplain, reciting the Lord's Prayer. Jewish boys had to go it alone. Some base commanders preferred that the chaplains not be at the briefings, or out at the flight line, blessing the bombers as their engines coughed and sputtered in the damp English air. "Don't like my boys to be reminded that they are liable to need anything more than luck and guts to get home," said one commander.

The crews were taken by truck to pick up their parachutes and gear. From there they were driven to their planes. On a brilliant autumn day these wide-winged war birds were a sight to see, big and brown against the green shade trees of the surrounding farms. The smell of gasoline mixed with that of farm animals in the field, and from the low wire fence that marked the borders of the base, farm families shouted encouragement to the Americans, some of whom they had accepted into their homes as their "adopted" sons. The men lounged on the grass or sat in tight circles, cross-legged, smoking and talking quietly. Then, one after the other, they boarded their machines.

"The interior of a B-17 was like a lightweight aluminum cigar tube," observed waist gunner Jack Novey. The plane's closely spaced aluminum ribs, held in place by thousands of rivets, gave it aerodynamic strength and durability, but the aluminum skin the ribs supported was so thin that you

CROSS SECTION OF A BOEING B-17

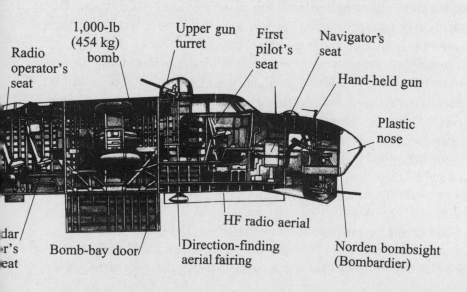

Radio operator's seat

1,000-lb (454 kg) bomb

Upper gun turret

First pilot's seat

Navigator's seat

Hand-held gun

Plastic nose

dar r's eat

Bomb-bay door

Direction-finding aerial fairing

HF radio aerial

Norden bombsight (Bombardier)

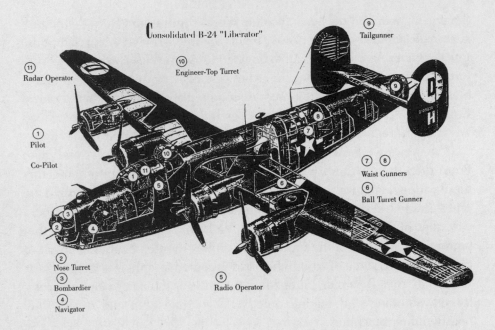

Consolidated B-24 "Liberator"

⑨ Tailgunner

⑪ Radar Operator

⑩ Engineer-Top Turret

① Pilot

Co-Pilot

⑦ ⑧ Waist Gunners

⑥ Ball Turret Gunner

② Nose Turret

③ Bombardier

④ Navigator

⑤ Radio Operator

could poke a hole through it with a screwdriver. The Fort's hundred-foot wingspan made the plane look large, but the ten-man crew was crowded together in a claustrophobic space that was tighter than the inside of a submarine. The backs of the waist gunners nearly touched when they stood and fired through their open port windows, fighting each other for maneuvering room as they fought the enemy. Behind them—and out of their sight—the tail gunner hunched, facing backward, in his torturously cramped compartment underneath the plane's soaring tail section. His windowed space was so tight that his twin guns had to be fed by a track that led to a storage magazine in the middle of the ship.

Just forward of the waist gunners was the hydraulic mounting for the ball turret. When the plane was in flight, the Plexiglas belly turret, only thirty inches in diameter, was turned, guns pointing straight down, hatch open, and the gunner slipped into it. In flight, he curled against the contour of the glass ball like an embryo in the egg, his twin machine guns resting just outside his spread legs, the tiny hatch above him locked tight. His only angle of sight was between his knees, and the ball was so small that there was no room for his parachute. That he kept inside the plane, near the access hatch.

Forward of the entrance to the ball turret, a bulkhead door led to the radio room. This was the only sealed and self-contained cabin on the bomber. The radio operator sat at a small desk facing the front of the plane.

Above him, in an open slot, was his handheld .50 caliber machine gun, pointing rearward. In later model B-17s equipped with radar guidance systems for bombing through overcast, the radar navigator sat just forward of the radio operator.

The bomb bay, the belly of the whale, was just ahead, through the radio room's other bulkhead. Bombs were stacked in racks from floor to ceiling on both sides, "hung like huge black fish fixed on skewers." To cross this area a crewman had to negotiate an eighteen-inch-wide catwalk. After takeoff, the bombardier or top turret gunner would go into the bomb bay and remove a pin from each bomb. These pins prevented the bombs from detonating prematurely when loaded onto the bomber.

If bombs got stuck in their racks on the bomb run, a crewman had to balance himself on the catwalk as he tried to release them by hand. And if the bomb bay doors were hit by flak and failed to shut, he and another member of the crew had to crank them shut by hand, standing on the catwalk and steadying themselves against the fierce winds and "against that terrible nothingness," as one crewman put it, "that spreads between you and the indifferent distant earth."

Immediately forward, directly behind the cockpit, was the hydraulically controlled top turret, with twin .50 caliber guns "that could spin around the sky, their arc cut out only enough to keep the engineer from blasting the plane's tail." In air combat, the technical sergeant who manned the guns placed his head and shoulders inside the revolving dome. He was also the plane's engineer and chief mechanic in flight. When not firing his guns, he stood behind the pilot, looking over his shoulder at the gauges "that monitored the health and functioning of four engines."

An opening in the flight deck led to the nose compartment. The navigator sat on the port side behind a shelflike desk containing his charts and instruments. His space was lit by two pairs of windows, one pair on each side of the fuselage, by an astrodome above him, and by the green-tinted Plexiglas nose. As navigator Elmer Bendiner explained, the astrodome allowed "[me] to determine the relationship of the stars to earth, and so deduce our position."

The bombardier's perch was ahead of the navigator, in the most exposed position in the plane. In front of him was the Norden bombsight and to his left were the release handle and switch that controlled the doors of the bomb bay. On the bomb run he would crouch over his aiming instrument like an eagle eyeing its prey from a lofty perch, seemingly suspended in air. At that moment, he looked like and was one of the most dangerous men in the world, a destroyer in charge of 5,000 pounds of explosives.

In later models, the bombardier was responsible for two handheld guns, one poking through the tip of the glass nose "like an insect's sting," the other in the left side of the nose section. The navigator's gun was positioned in a large window on the right side of the nose.

The pilot and co-pilot sat at the top of the bomber, riding "as on the bridge of a ship," able to see "the sky and the curve of the far horizon but not the swell of the sea or the rich details of the earth." They were "embedded in instruments": over 150 switches, dials, cranks, handles, and gauges, any one of which might save or doom the entire plane and crew. An air surgeon described the difficulty of flying one of these fully loaded 60,000-pound Goliaths: "The coordinated operations of all these gadgets would be difficult in the swivel-chair comfort of your office. But reduce your office to a five-foot cube size, engulf it in the constant roar of engines, and increase your height to around five miles. . . . That will give you an idea of the normal conditions under which these men worked out the higher mathematical relationships of engine revolutions, manifold and fuel pressures, aerodynamics, barometric pressure, altitude, wind drift, airspeed, ground speed, position and direction."

No one had ever designed a more splendid-looking plane, but inside it smelled of grease, stale sweat, cordite, dried blood, and urine; and before takeoff it was thick with cigarette smoke. Even airmen who had never smoked before found relief in tobacco. When the final checks were performed, the crew, a few of them munching on apples and dried candy, waited for the green flare from the tower, the signal that they might die that day.

The runways were short and "it was nip and tuck as to whether we would have enough airspeed to get airborne and stay there when we ran out of runway," Bernard Jacobs remembered. "The engineer called out the speed, '60-70-90-110.' When the end of the runway came in sight we pulled it off the ground and prayed."

Cloud cover sometimes extended to 23,000 feet, forcing most planes to fly blind—on instruments—to that altitude. Ascending in darkness, some pilots lost their horizon, became hopelessly disoriented, and crashed into other bombers.

"Breaking out of the overcast revealed a breathtaking scene" that co-pilot Jacobs described poetically. "The sun was just coming up and we were now above a carpet of reddish orange cotton as far as the eye could see. Other airplanes were breaking out of the overcast and looked like fish coming up out of their element." Each bomber fell into its assigned slot in the formation, three groups of eighteen planes comprising a combat wing.

Then the formation "headed for the final radio beacon on the coast to fall in train with the other wings that made up the strike force."

Over the North Sea the sergeants cleared their guns; when they fired together, the entire plane shook and the noise was ear-splitting, the smell of cordite overpowering. Then it became quiet as the men readied their minds for combat, the only sound the low monotonous roar of the engines. Everyone was prepared. The crew wore inflatable Mae West jackets in case they had to ditch in the water, and parachute harnesses. The parachutes themselves were placed near every crew station, although some men did not know how to use them properly, and no one on board had ever jumped out of an airplane; that had not been part of their training. Some men tied an extra pair of GI boots to their belts in case they had to bail out and survive on the ground in Nazi-infested France. Every man carried a small escape kit in his pocket: folding money, first aid, a waterproof silk map, a small compass, and some rations.

As they ascended into the substratosphere they entered a profoundly alien world. The crew's first battle was with the cold, an invisible enemy waiting for them at 20,000 feet. Some crewmembers wore electrically heated suits, gloves, and boots, but early in the war there were enough for only two or three crewmembers on each bomber. Only the front part of the plane—the cockpit, nose, and radio room—was heated, albeit inadequately. Most of the crew shivered and shook in their alpaca coats and pants and sheepskin flying boots.

The tension heightened when the "little friends"—the fighter escorts—tipped their wings, the signal that they were at the end of their range. Then every eye searched the sky for "bandits." Morgan and his men saw only one enemy fighter on their first mission, but that would change. "Those frontal assaults by German fighter planes put the fear of God in you," Morgan recalled. "It was bad in the cockpit, but it was far worse in the nose. The bombardier and navigator were sitting in a big bay window, open to the sky, with nothing but a peashooter to defend themselves. And sometimes that peashooter got so hot in combat that it bent. Up on the flight deck, my co-pilot and I were completely preoccupied with flying the plane." Fighting as many as four of Hitler's best at a time, the pilots had no time to think. It took every ounce of concentration and physical strength to hold the shivering planes steady and in formation. Some bombers flew so close together that they put dents in each other's fuselages.

In the rear, the waist gunners, standing on the plane's smooth, curved floor, slid like donkeys on ice on piles of spent shells, the boreal wind blasting in their faces. Exertion and fear would cause gunners to breathe heavily and their hot breath would escape into their oxygen masks, fogging their goggles, and solidifying into ice. Gunner John H. Morris recalled how he responded when this happened. "Once or twice I let go of the gun with one hand to reach up and scrape a hole in the goggle ice with my fingertip and peeked out and saw up-close German fighters that had begun to fly through our formation. But the ice would start to form again right away, so I didn't see much. . . . A blinded gunner! But I survived." He survived with German fighters putting cannon holes in his plane big enough to shove sheep through.

Often the flak was so thick the men could smell it through their oxygen masks; and the concentrated barrages exploded with such force that the concussions would have driven the pilots through the roofs of their planes had they not been strapped in. On some planes, men sat on armor plate to protect their genitals. Helpless in the flak field, all they could do was sit and take it. This was when pilots and crewmen alike learned that it was possible to sweat at 40 degrees below zero.

Bombardier Theodore Hallock was not a praying man, but when he was in a tight spot over the target he would whisper to himself, "God, you gotta. You gotta get me back. God, listen, you gotta." Many of the men promised the Almighty that if they got through they'd swear off liquor and women. Hallock said he never promised that "because I figured that if God was really God he'd be bound to understand how men feel about liquor and women."

When Robert Morgan took the *Memphis Belle* over the submarine pens of Brest on its maiden mission, the lead bombardier of the formation, flying in a plane just ahead, had a hard time calibrating his Norden bombsight in the soupy cloud cover and released the bombs at the wrong time. All the other planes in formation made the same mistake, and most of the bombs fell outside the city. The Fortresses of the 91st then dipped below the bursting clouds of flak, turned slowly, and headed home through peaceful skies.

But for many planes on other missions it was "a hard and terrible transition to come back." Heading across the North Sea, as fog rolled in over their island home, men knew that they could still crash and die after swallowing their hearts in combat. When the *Memphis Belle* touched down at Bassingbourn after the Brest mission and the crew stood on the airstrip, feet fixed to the ground, no one smiled, but every face indicated that it was good to be on firm earth.

On landing, some men who had just flown their first mission became disoriented. It was as if they had returned from another world "devoid of all reasoning except the primary will to live. . . . We had been to a battlefield, not of this earth and not of the men in it," wrote Denton Scott, a *Yank* reporter who flew with the Eighth to the submarine pens. "There is a chasm greater than 25,000 feet of bright blue altitude between those two worlds." There was a sudden release from fear and strain, but deeper than that was a powerfully felt affinity with every other man on the plane and with the plane itself, the crews' only protection against flak fragments and shells the size of brass knuckles. "The swearing and the violence in the sky had only brought ten men closer together in eight hours than eight years might have in that other, more normal world, such being the inevitable bonds between men who have suffered fear together and fought against it. This is perhaps the strongest of all ties among men," said Scott.

Men felt suddenly and excruciatingly tired, but their job was not done. There was the post-mission interrogation. "There you must go through it all over again, remembering everything in detail. . . . The coffee and sand-wiches help, but you miss familiar faces."

At the debriefing, the crews were treated to shots of whiskey. "After a couple of those we would be half crocked . . . and we would hit the sack," recalled Bernard Jacobs. Men shivered noticeably as they entered their quarters and looked at the stripped beds of men they would never see again. The survivors never talked about the fallen; this was the unstated conspiracy. "When a crewman was killed but his plane returned, most of us decided that funerals were not for survivors," a navigator recalled. "I never attended a funeral. . . . We memorialized them by painting the names of those we lost on the barracks walls, with their hometown and the name and date of their last mission."

No one who survived considered himself a hero. To draw attention to one-self was another violation of the unwritten crewmen's code. It was hard to spot the real heroes. Men who carried out unimaginable acts of courage in the air would scream with fear in their sleep, or when awake, complain in-cessantly about the "chickenshit" Army, or announce to their friends, in beer-soaked conversations, that the only reason they flew and fought was to get a "ticket home." Technical Sergeant Arizona T. Harris, a ranch hand from the desert town of Tempe, Arizona, hated almost everything about Air Force life, but he was a different man in the plane.

Harris was a crew engineer and top turret gunner on a Flying Fortress and knew his aircraft better than anyone except its ground crew chief. When *Sons of Fury* taxied down the runway, the boys standing on the perimeter could easily spot it. A red head and a strong arm would poke out of the window next to the pilot. It was Harris giving the windshield one last wipe. "Them specks on the windshield get to look like Me 109s" in the air, he'd say.

Harris met his end on the way back from St. Nazaire on January 3, 1943. Sgt. P. D. Small, a tail gunner in another of the 306th's bombers, observed Harris's final minutes. Small saw four white parachutes snap open just before *Sons of Fury* hit the water. The gunners who remained on the ship must have gone to the radio room, the safest place to be in a crash. But two guns were still blazing, Harris's twin .50s. Then *Sons of Fury* made a perfect belly landing in the freezing waters of the Bay of Biscay. As sheets of white water rolled over the wings and the plane began to drop out of sight, the top turret guns were still spitting flame "as fast as the feeding arms would pull the shells into the guns." Arizona Harris was trying to protect the pilot and co-pilot, who were in the water and under fire from Fw 190s, "the steel gray sea boiling under the rain of bullets." Harris must have felt the winter water fill his turret and climb to where it began to cut off his breath, yet he kept firing until the sea swallowed the hot muzzles of his guns.

When reports like this reached home, the American public began to realize that its boys in England were fighting an air war entirely different from that of World War I, or even from the Battle of Britain. The first one to tell them was the reporter Ernie Pyle, who spent the fall of 1942 touring American airbases in England before heading off to North Africa to cover Operation Torch. "The men who fight our wars in the air have always seemed, somehow, more glorious than those who fight in the mud," he wrote in one of his dispatches from the "air front." But in the epoch of aerial warfare now beginning, "the era of the giant battleship of the air—the lone, gay-hearted, swashbuckling hero of the sky is likely to become more and more rare," he wrote. The Eighth Air Force would certainly have its share of heroes, Pyle predicted, but most them would fight and die in teams, to protect each other, as Arizona Harris had. "Even planes fight as teams. Our bombers go to France in great formations, following their leader. Running in a pack is their protection."

In the Air Force, officers and noncommissioned officers were closer than they were in the infantry. Everyone who flew in a bomber had the rank of sergeant or above, and it helped that only a tiny percentage of the officers were regular Army. Almost all were volunteers, just like the sergeants. Spit-and-polish discipline was a rarity; there was not a lot of saluting on American airbases in England.

Dr. Malcolm C. Grow, the Eighth Air Force's chief surgeon, told air intelligence investigators: "[These men] are not interested in democracy or freedom; they are interested in their buddies or [their] team. The teams are the closest knit things that you have ever seen." As Fortress gunner Jack Novey recalled: "I can't explain why we bomber crews, without any gung ho attitude at all, would put our lives on the line mission after mission against the terrible odds of those days. . . . Even when my fears were about to overwhelm me, even when I was physically sick, I kept flying my missions. I didn't want to let my crewmates down. I would rather have been dead."

The equipment of survival both tightened and symbolized this bond. Ten men were linked to the ship and to one another by hose lines and wires, hoses to keep them breathing, wires to keep them in touch with one another.

The crews were amazingly diverse. On one plane, *Hell's Angels,* there was a car salesman, a rancher, a government farm inspector, a gas attendant, a rodeo rider, a window dresser, a dance-band trumpeter, a merchant marine sailor, a college student, and a professional traveler. Yet none of these men had joined the Air Force before Pearl Harbor and only three had ever flown in an airplane before flight training in the States.

"We never worried about this not-coming-back business," their captain noted after their twenty-eighth mission. "Our attitude is that we will have to die sometime and when that might be never bothered me, or any of the rest of the men." This was said for the benefit of the reporters. No one in a bomber flew without fear, scornful of his fate. "Flying men are scared, just as you and I are," wrote Ernie Pyle. Many of them were as frightened of the air they flew through as they were of the Luftwaffe.

Into Thin Air

In its first year of operations the Eighth Air Force's greatest enemy was not flak or fighters, but weather and the elements. Good weather was a prerequisite for successful daylight bombing, but in the fall and winter of 1942, the weather over Northern Europe was unusually bad. As the official Air Force history notes, "By early October it was seriously debated whether it was feasible to conduct a full-scale offense of this sort from British bases." At most, there were five to eight days a month when it was possible to launch sizable strikes, and the weather over the Continent made visual bombing possible only between 20 and 30 percent of the time. Only in Alaska and the Aleutian Islands was the weather more unfavorable for large-scale operations by the American Air Force.

Bad weather was hazardous for a single plane, flying alone. It could be catastrophic for large, tightly grouped formations. Long-range formation flying required favorable weather at least five different times during the mission: at takeoff, on assembly, on the way to the target, over the target, and on return to base. A mission could not be sent out in fair skies at 8:00 A.M. if the weather over England was expected to turn wretched when the bombers were scheduled to return six hours later. As it was, the English countryside began to be littered with the wreckage of American bombers that failed to make it home through the island's fast-forming fog and cloud cover.

Just as a good ground commander must know the terrain his army fights on, so an air commander had to know the atmospheric "terrain," or weather, his men would have to contend with. But Northern European weather was as difficult to predict as it was to fly through; and meteorology was still a crude science. Throughout the war, weather reduced operations by 45 percent, and 10 percent of the planes that were sent into combat over Northern Europe aborted or were recalled because of weather. These unwanted reprieves from combat created a festering morale problem. A recall or abort over enemy territory failed to count toward the assigned number of combat missions a crewman had to fly before being sent home. Repeated cancellations meant repeating the experience of preflight trauma and tension, whose symptoms included uncontrollable vomiting and diarrhea. With men forced to fly "eight missions on the ground for every one in the air," combat crews reported nearly unanimously that the letdown and depression that followed these cancellations was "far worse than actual participation in a combat flight." Even missions that were weather-delayed, but not scrubbed, tested the mental stamina of the most stable men.

Unlike infantry, airmen could not get to the fight or stay in it without a highly complex technological support system—the bomber and its life-giving oxygen equipment. If it failed to function, which was often, they were helpless. Flying in the withering cold caused windows and gun sights to blur, bomb bay doors to ice over, and essential mechanical equipment to freeze and malfunction. Men also froze up and broke down. Flying in temperatures experienced on the ground only in the Arctic and Antarctic or on the peaks of immense mountains, frostbite did more damage than the enemy. In the Eighth's first year of operations, 1,634 men were removed from flying duty for frostbite, over 400 more than were removed for combat wounds. Capt. William F. Sheeley, an Eighth Air Force flight surgeon, studied the problem. Arctic explorers, he reported, had long warned that a wet foot is a frozen foot. "Men who walked through the rain to their aircraft; who slept in heated suits; who played sweaty games in their flying clothes were wet when they took off. They were casualties when they came back."

When available, the new electrical suits were notoriously undependable. They shorted out and sent electric shocks through the hands, feet, and testicles; and after a few missions, they tended to burn out, usually because the men were not told how to take proper care of them. After a mission, exhausted men wrapped them in a ball with their other flying clothing and stuffed them into lockers or barracks bags, damaging the fragile heat elements.

The whip-crack cold found most of its victims at exposed positions in the bombers: waist gunners at open windows, breasting heavy winds, and tail gunners who removed frozen canvas covers that impeded the movement of their guns. Ball turret gunners who were forced to remain in their turrets for hours over enemy territory urinated in their clothing, freezing their backs, buttocks, and thighs "so badly muscles sloughed and bones were exposed." Ball turret gunner George E. Moffat of the 482nd BG observed that "by the time you reach your objective you are so miserably fed up you don't particularly give a damn whether you 'get it' or not." On one mission, just after the "bombs away," there was a tremendous explosion of flak just below Moffat's turret. Within seconds, he began to feel his fingers and feet growing numb. "I looked around and found a small hole in the Plexiglas and my wire connection between my glove and suit was severed." The electric suits were wired in series, like Christmas tree lights, and when one glove went out, other parts of the suit went out as well. Moffat knew he couldn't stay in the turret long without freezing, but if he left his guns with fighters still in the area he would put the lives of the crew in jeopardy. "So I stayed." He pounded his fist against his guns and his feet on the floor of the turret to quicken the movement of his blood. "The pain was maddening and almost unbearable. Tears streamed down my face over my oxygen mask and froze. . . . I was nearly ready to quit and welcome death." A minute or so later, the enemy fighters disappeared and he was able to crawl out of his turret. When the pilot dropped the bomber down to 20,000 feet, a buddy offered Moffat one of his electrically heated gloves. "The heat made my feet and hands ache so that I had to shut my eyes and grit my teeth to keep from screaming."

When a gun jammed in combat, some men would panic and pull off their thick gloves to try to clear it. Their cold hands would stick to the bare metal, and to pull them away they had to tear off long strips of flesh. Occasionally, wounds were self-inflicted by men overcome with the fear that they would soon die in combat. When the bomber reached maximum altitude, they would pull off their gloves, ensuring a long, painful hospital stay but a temporary reprieve from a fate possibly far worse.

Men wounded in combat were especially vulnerable to frostbite. Their electric suits were often shorted out by the same piece of steel that pierced their flesh. As they lay unconscious on the freezing floor of the plane, their extremities would go numb, despite attempts by crewmates to keep them warm with the few thin blankets available. Dr. Sheeley described the excruciating ordeal of a navigator whose oxygen mask was perforated by a flak blast that blew open the nose of the plane. With his oxygen supply impaired, he lay unconscious for a full hour. "Six weeks later, his hands, feet, ears, nose were amputated, his frozen eyeballs had been [removed], necrotic tissue was dropping from his cheekbones. He is still alive."

Unknown numbers of men died because their crewmates lacked either the medical knowledge or equipment to save them. When a tail gunner on a B-17 had both cheeks of his buttocks blown off by cannon fire, his fellow gunners dressed the wound as best they could. The bleeding continued, so "we put a 140-pound ammunition box directly over the wound," one of the gunners recalled. "The pressure seemed to stop the bleeding. He rested comfortably but was almost frozen because his heated suit was torn and we had no blankets available." This stricken boy awaited his death in a place alien to normal mortals. "That's the thing that doubles the strain on your nerves—the environment in which your guts have to digest danger is unnatural," said an Air Force officer.

At the end of every mission, men were hauled off planes with inflamed and swollen hands, feet, and faces. The wounds turned purple within a day or two, then a lurid black. One-third of the frostbite victims required hospitalization; mild cases kept men on the ground for up to two weeks. "This is a real emergency," Dr. Sheeley warned his colleagues early in Eighth Air Force operations. "Many men seen in the hospital will not return to duty for months—if ever."

Unable to fight frostbite once it struck, inexperienced flight surgeons fell back on an old Russian cure: "wait for everything to drop off that is going to drop off and then see what you can do with what is left." Prevention was the only adequate treatment. By midwinter of 1942–43, flight surgeons—at least one assigned to every base—had begun to take action, giving lectures and demonstrations to crews on the dangers of frostbite, placing urine tubes in ball turrets, and issuing thin silk gloves to be worn under heavier, heated gloves. But in the first year of operations the effort was never commensurate with the problem. Nor was a cure ever found for aerotitis media, a chronic inflammation of the middle ear caused by multiple descents from high altitude in a nonpressurized cabin. It reached epidemic proportions among bomber crews as operations increased, accounting for two-thirds of the cases of temporary removal from flying status.

Anoxia, or oxygen deprivation, was part of the "aero-medical nightmare" that afflicted the Eighth. Saliva or vomit from airsickness would get into the men's molded rubber face masks and freeze, blocking the hose and causing men to pass out or even die. Throughout a mission, the navigator would call out oxygen checks every few minutes on the plane's interphone. If a crewman failed to answer, another was sent to investigate, and, if needed, perform artificial respiration or administer oxygen from a portable walk-around bottle. "It's altogether too easy to have a leak in your mask or hose, or anywhere else in the line, and to be totally unaware of the problem," a navigator described a typical mission at 25,000 feet. "Without oxygen at this altitude, you're unconscious in thirty seconds. After two minutes you're dead."

Although fewer than 100 men died from anoxia—most of them in the Eighth's first year in England—between 50 and 60 percent of fliers experienced some form of it on combat missions. This was the inexcusable result of poor planning. "We did not contemplate operating at such extreme heights," Dr. Malcolm Grow lamely admitted to Air Force interrogators after the first year of operations. "There are apparently little things that one doesn't think about prior to getting into operations." But part of the blame must be placed on air planners more concerned with bombing strategy than with preparing crews to survive in atmospheric conditions necessary to execute that strategy. In trying to destroy the enemy, poorly prepared American boys were inadvertently destroying themselves.

Anoxia was a hidden killer; men rarely knew when their oxygen supply failed. The oxygen equipment did have an indicator—a small ball-like valve in a transparent tube—showing whether oxygen was flowing. The ball bounced up and down as a man breathed. If the ball was hopping the airman was all right, but crewmen fighting the Luftwaffe had no time to pay attention to the ball, and if a problem developed, they were often dead before anyone spotted the condition.

The tail gunner, at his isolated post, was the most likely victim of anoxia. After a savage fight with enemy fighters, the navigator on George Moffat's Fortress called on the interphone to see if anyone had been hit. Bill Galba, the tail gunner, failed to answer. When a crewmember checked, he found Galba slumped over his guns, his oxygen tube disconnected. The crewman tried unsuccessfully to revive him. When they headed out over the North Sea, the pilot dove for the water and breathable air, but Galba remained unresponsive. At that point, Moffat climbed out of his ball turret and carefully laid out his friend on the floor of the plane. "I crawled along the narrow passage and up over his body. My face came to a stop about six inches from his. His face was as white as snow with frozen mucous in his nose and mouth and his eyes were staring wide open into mine, all covered with frost. . . . I knew then that he was dead."

Moffat lit a cigarette for himself and another gunner and they "sat in silence and smoked." When the plane landed, "I watched as they rolled his body out onto the stretcher and took him into the ambulance and a tear rolled down my cheek. I wasn't ashamed. He was my buddy.

"It had been a rough day and our ship was full of holes. I left for bed but couldn't sleep." Galba's bed was next to Moffat's. The quartermaster had taken Galba's clothes and stripped his bed. Moffat rolled over so he would not have to look at it.

They buried William Galba in a cemetery not far from the base. Whenever he could, George Moffat went there to place flowers on his grave.

Aviation Medicine

High-altitude aerial combat subjected bomber crews to emotional and physical stresses that human beings had never confronted before. Strange things happened to the human body when it entered the earth's upper air. Men's ears clogged up painfully, their minds and movements slowed down, and their stomachs and intestines expanded inordinately, a condition exacerbated by the gaseous food they had been fed at breakfast.

This new kind of warfare demanded a new kind of medicine—for the mind as well as the body. Col. Malcolm Grow's Eighth Air Force medical staff had no precedents to fall back on. Aviation medicine, then in its infancy, had yet to address the problems flight surgeons encountered in England. Like the bomber commanders of the Eighth, their early efforts were entirely experimental, and physicians, too, suffered grievous shortages of equipment and personnel.

Every bomber base had a small dispensary run by a flight surgeon, with beds for a few dozen men who were mildly sick or slightly wounded. Seriously wounded men were evacuated by ambulance to an Army hospital at Oxford. This was a rough three-to-four-hour journey, over rutted roads and often in the middle of the night, under total blackout conditions, with even the headlights of the ambulances shaded. Battle-torn men died on these long late-night runs and some suffered additional injuries in road ac-

cidents in the English hedgerows. So Grow requisitioned a C-47 troop carrier and turned it into the Eighth's permanent flying ambulance. All the
while, he pressured headquarters to build hospitals closer to the fields from
which his men flew. In the first year of bombing operations, medical supplies and equipment remained dangerously scarce and nearly half of
Eighth Air Force personnel were virtually isolated from all medical facilities, except their primitive base hospitals. Yet by 1944, thanks largely to
Grow's efforts, all but one bomber base was within thirty miles of a fully
staffed Army hospital. Grow also lobbied strenuously for better trained
medical personnel. In 1942, three-quarters of the flight surgeons assigned
to England had no aero-medical training and only 10 percent of the medics
had any medical training at all. When flight surgeons arrived at bomber
bases they found that wounded airmen had died because they had not
been promptly and properly treated.

Grow and Col. Harry G. Armstrong, his chief assistant in England, were
pioneers in the new field of aviation medicine. In 1934 they had founded
the Aero Medical Research Laboratory at Wright Field, near Dayton,
Ohio, to study the effect of manned flight on the human organism. Shortly
after the Eighth Air Force arrived in England, they established a small research center near High Wycombe, called the Central Medical Establishment. Headed by Armstrong, its mission was to develop training
techniques and equipment to allow airmen to survive and perform to maximum efficiency in the first high-altitude war ever fought. They were dedicated to a single, all-consuming task: "the care of the flyer."

In its first year of existence, CME, working in coordination with Wright
Field, Harvard's School of Public Health, and American private industry
launched sixty separate research efforts to develop better oxygen equipment, flying clothing, and air-sea rescue operations. In addition to CME's
research functions, it conducted courses on survival techniques for both
crewmen and flight surgeons. And almost on his own, Armstrong, a
ruggedly handsome man with a dashing, upturned mustache, established
the Psychiatric Unit, dedicated to the practice of preventive psychiatry and
to the diagnosis and rehabilitation of airmen suffering from emotional illnesses.

The staff of CME was small—never more than eighteen doctors—but superbly qualified. Armstrong personally picked his staff from the upper
ranks of the best medical colleges, research centers, and psychiatric insti-
tutes in the United States. "They all came from civilian life," he recalled
years later, "and almost without exception eventually returned to civilian
life and every one of them later became outstanding in the medical profes-

sion." By the fall of 1943, their research would begin to pay dividends: new preventive equipment and treatment greatly reduced suffering and death from frostbite, oxygen deprivation, and enemy fire. Unfortunately, there was no relief available for the men who flew in the first year of combat operations. The few hard-pressed pioneers who managed to survive their tours of duty finished them as they had begun them, flying and fighting without proper oxygen equipment, armor, warmth, or rest.

CHAPTER FOUR

Airman Down!

We were gaining experience and we were having experiences too, not all of them good.

CURTIS E. LEMAY

North Sea, October 9, 1942

That afternoon Lt. Donald Swenson was in the worst trouble of his young life. Flying on the historic Lille mission, his Fortress was raked by cannon fire from Focke-Wulf 190s and lost two engines. Struggling to make it back to England, Swenson's plane was dropping through the sky at over a thousand feet per minute. The radio operator sent out a distress signal but shore stations failed to pick it up. With the interphone knocked out, Swenson turned over the controls to his co-pilot and crawled to the rear of the plane to alert the gunners that he was going to belly-land at sea. Leaving the pilot and co-pilot alone in the front of the plane, the rest of the crew assembled in the radio room, where there was a forward bulkhead against which they could brace themselves. Before hunkering down, his head between his knees, his hands clasped behind his neck, the radio operator ate the rice paper containing the plane's secret call letters and frequencies.

"The water looked cold, and I remember thinking it also looked hard," Swenson recalled. There were fifteen-to-twenty-foot-tall whitecaps, "and I had heard that when you land on water and hit a wave the effect is very much like flying into a stone wall.

"It was. We laid her in a belly landing, as slowly as we could, with the tail well down. But even at that we hit so hard that it threw the crew all over the ship."

Swenson crawled out of the narrow cockpit window on his side of the plane. When he came up for air, he saw his injured co-pilot drifting under one of the wings. He swam over to him and began pulling him back toward the rest of the crew. They had climbed out of the radio room gun hatch and were struggling to reach the plane's two self-inflating rubber rafts. One of the rafts was riddled with bullet holes and men were shouting that it would not inflate properly.

The bomber sank in less than two minutes. The pilot ordered three of the gunners into the undamaged raft. The rest of the men hung on to the edges of the partially inflated one, stripping off their heavy sheepskin flying clothes. One of the gunners tried to drown himself. "He'd go down and then come up and spit sea water and then go down again; but he kept trying to make us let him go. It took a direct order to make him behave. He thought he was hurting our chances of survival. Then came the worst part: waiting for help to get there and wondering if any help was going to come."

At that moment, the men in the water could not have known that they were as good as rescued. Seconds before their plane went into the sea, the machinery of the RAF's Air/Sea Rescue service had gone into high gear. One of the bomber's escorting Spitfires had radioed the plane's approximate position, a mile or so from North Foreland, at the top of the Strait of Dover, and another friendly fighter circled overhead to give its exact location, which was not far from land. "Soon a small boat with a rescue crew on deck came foaming up to us."

It was the first rescue at sea of an Eighth Air Force crew.

If a bomber was in distress over Northern Europe, the crews usually preferred to try to limp back to England, rather than crash-land or parachute into German-occupied Northern Europe. Many of the bombers that failed to make it home ditched in the North Sea or in the English Channel. "Unless you have heard a man talk on the radio when he is really scared, you would not know that high-pitched vibration that edges into his voice, until he seems on the point of screaming," an Air/Sea rescue pilot described a typical distress call. These rescue pilots knew that there was "nothing more terrifying than the sound of a man's fear."

The Swenson crew had been lucky. In its first year of operations, the

Eighth had neither an air-sea rescue system nor a training program in ditching procedures. The inflatable dinghies and markers in its bombers were inadequate for the rigors of open sea survival, and the flares, K rations, and first aid packs all lacked waterproof protection. Nor were its bombers designed for easy egress in forced sea landings. The Eighth relied entirely on the RAF and the Royal Navy for air-sea rescue, yet failed to work closely with their deeply dedicated personnel. The result: 99 percent of its fliers who went into the sea were lost. (During this same period, approximately one-third of ditched RAF bomber crews, all of them flying night missions, were rescued.) A year later, still relying on the British, but working in unison with them, the Eighth upped its survival rate to 44 percent—and to 66 percent by the war's end.

More than one in ten of these survivors suffered psychological damage that required professional treatment and forced them off flying status. These were generally men who had to survive for long stretches of time at sea, without food or fresh water, burying their dead in storm-tossed waters with improvised religious services. "We all said the Lord's prayer together. And I let him over the side as gently as I could," Sgt. Eugene Dworaczyk remembered the last time he looked at the face of a friend who died in his arms while whispering the name of his wife.

Escape and Evasion

Allied airmen who successfully crash-landed in Northern Europe or parachuted to the ground had only one chance of avoiding capture: the help of foreign friends. The Dutch, the Belgians, and the French all ran elaborate, highly secret escape operations for Allied fliers. Ordinary citizens, not trained Underground operators, controlled most of the escape lines. The risks were enormous. The penalty for hiding or aiding a downed Allied flier was death by firing squad for men, and concentration camp imprisonment for women, usually the equivalent of a death sentence. A British intelligence agent estimated that for every downed flier who was evacuated, one French, Belgian, or Dutch helper was shot or died under torture.

Most of these courageous partisans worked in close collaboration with British and American intelligence agents in London, but the most successful of the escape routes, the Comet Line, was entirely independent. Early in the war, it was run by hundreds of Belgian volunteers organized in Brussels under the leadership of a petite twenty-five-year-old commercial artist named Andrée de Jongh. Her code name was "Dédée."

The Comet Line stretched for 1,200 miles, from Brussels to Gibraltar, through Nazi-occupied France and fascist, but officially neutral, Spain, areas under the jurisdiction of the most ruthless secret police in Europe. Dédée began the line without financial backing and with the assistance of only her schoolteacher father, Frédéric, and a young fellow Belgian, Arnold Depée. Escaping airmen were hidden in safe houses in and around Brussels, and were taken by train to Paris, the central collection point for escaping airmen. From there the men were sent in small, discrete groups, first by rail, then by bicycle, and finally on foot, to a farmhouse at the foothills of the Pyrenees. After a hardy meal and cups of strong Spanish coffee, they began their grueling climb, led by experienced Basque smugglers that Dédée had recruited. When the mountain parties reached San Sebastian, in northern Spain, they were handed over to British diplomat Michael Creswell and taken by car to Gibraltar, then by sea or air to England.

Dédée provided escapees—known as "parcels"—with false passports and identity cards, bought them civilian clothing and black-market food, and established a chain of halfway houses on the route to Spain. One of her co-conspirators, Ann Brusselmans, sheltered over fifty airmen at a time in various safe houses in Brussels. "No one of our extended family knew of my mother's activities in the Underground," wrote her daughter, Yvonne Daley-Brusselmans. "On the outside, we were just a normal family going through the daily hardship of enemy occupation, minding our own business." The Germans had warned the Allies that airmen captured wearing civilian clothing or without military identification would be treated as spies, and would be shot or sent to concentration camps. This presented a dilemma for downed fliers. Instructed by their commanders that their sworn duty was to try to escape, they found out escape was possible only in civilian clothing. Ann Brusselmans tried to solve the problem by sewing the American airmen's dog tags inside the cuffs of their pants. She provided street clothing for them—berets, long jackets, and high-topped European shoes—and sent them on their way with the warning to be careful not to act too "American" by chewing gum or jingling loose change in their pockets. If they smoked, they were told to grip their cigarettes from the burned end, as the Europeans did, using their fingertips and thumbs.

To raise the money to start the Comet Line, Dédée had sold her small collection of jewelry. In thirty-two separate journeys, she personally escorted over a hundred airmen across France and over the Pyrenees. When British intelligence services came to her with an offer of assistance, she refused. The line must be entirely independent, she told them, run by Belgians she knew intimately. She did not want it taken over by trained intelligence agents who might also be working with groups in the Resistance engaged in acts of sabotage or spying. That might make it easier for double agents to penetrate the line. To help her identify moles—Gestapo agents posing as downed airmen—she had the owners of her Brussels safe houses interrogate airmen who approached them for help. If a flier arriving at Ann Brusselmans's apartment claimed to be from New York, he was asked the name of the current center fielder of the New York Yankees. If he answered wrong, Brusselmans had members of the Belgian underground army take him for "a long walk in the woods."

The Gestapo infiltrated but was never able to shut down the Comet Line. When Dédée was arrested with several escaping airmen in January 1943, the Comet Line was apparently broken, but in twenty-one separate interrogations at Mauthausen and Ravensbrück concentration camps, she refused to reveal the identities of those she worked with. In her absence, her father took over the line. After he and his chief assistants were betrayed by an informer, and he was executed, a new leader emerged, a fiery twenty-three-year-old Belgian, Jean-François Nothomb, whose code name was "Franco." Run-down and in failing health, Nothomb reluctantly took a British-trained Belgian agent into the organization, and with his help, continued to evacuate downed airmen. The Comet Line aided approximately 700 of the 5,000 to 6,000 downed Allied airmen—3,000 of them Americans—who eventually made it back to England.

The Comet Line closed down two days before D-Day. In the spring of 1944, Allied bombing of French railroads in support of the upcoming Normandy invasion made it almost impossible to run rescue missions. Downed Allied airmen were now hidden on farms and in forests and supplied by parachute drops until they were liberated late that summer by advancing Anglo-American armies. After being freed from Ravensbrük in 1945, Dédée went to work in a leper colony in the Belgian Congo. An airman she guided to freedom said of her, "Andrée de Jongh was one of those rare beings who felt the misery of the world and would not let it rest."

Nothing did more to boost the morale of airmen in England than the return of men who had been considered lost forever. They were greeted with shouts of joy and recognition and were given an opportunity to spend a few days with old friends before being sent home for reassignment. It was considered too risky to have them fly again in the European Theater. If captured and tortured, they might reveal the existence of escape routes that fliers continued to depend upon until Northern Europe was liberated. In lectures at their old bases, evaders gave their fellow fliers essential information about surviving behind enemy lines. "[The men] eat up the stories of the escaped fliers," an Air Force chaplain wrote in his diary. "They cling to the accounts like men to a life raft." These heroic storytellers were living proof that lost fliers could return from the dead.

LeMay

Airmen did not have to go down in the numbers they did. They could bomb accurately and with fewer losses. That was the belief of Maj. Curtis E. LeMay, the man who arrived in England in October 1942 and changed the way the American bomber war was fought.

Lt. Ralph H. Nutter of the 305th Bomb Group worshipped Curtis LeMay, the former navigator who was now his group commander. Nutter had left Harvard Law School to join the Army Air Force the day after Pearl Harbor. On the flight over to England, he navigated his crew's plane *Royal Flush* to Gander Lake, Newfoundland, without trouble, but upon landing the crew learned that they would be flying into an Arctic storm moving in from the north. At the Gander aerodrome, a forbidding outpost surrounded by a dense evergreen forest, Major LeMay called his nervous crews together. He knew this route intimately. Before Pearl Harbor, he had flown it many times, ferrying planes fresh from the factory to America's future European allies. Icing could be a serious problem, he told his crews, and the storm might prevent navigators from checking their course with celestial readings. If they allowed their pilots to drift too far south, he cautioned the navigators, they would either run out of fuel over open ocean or run into Nazi fighters over the coast of France. "You can't rely on radio aids or directional finders. The Nazis have set up a false beam with a frequency identical with the RAF radio beam in England. Don't be fooled. . . . In the States you relied on your pilots and radio aids. Now the pilots and crews are relying on you. Don't let them down."

Ralph Nutter, who had just turned twenty-two, had taken his first ride in an airplane two months before. That was in the Mojave Desert. Later that night, speeding down the runway, *Royal Flush*'s only life raft flew out the top hatch. At first, Nutter was able to take celestial fixes through holes in the clouds, but within an hour the sky closed in on them and blinding snow covered the Plexiglas nose and his small astrodome. Minutes later, the propellers of a faltering engine stopped spinning. An hour later, another engine went out, and *Royal Flush* began to lose altitude. Nutter asked the pilot to level off just above the storm-tossed sea and turn on the landing lights. If he could see the whitecaps, he might be able to compute their wind drift with his drift meter and correct their course by dead reckoning, flying a compass course the way Charles Lindbergh had in the *Spirit of St. Louis*. "Finally, just before dawn, I was able to take three celestial shots through holes in the cloud cover. 'We're on course,' I announced on the interphone." Then the clouds broke, and in the distance they could see the green hills of Ireland. Flying over Belfast, Nutter gave the pilot a direct course to Prestwick. As they climbed out of the plane, friendly townspeople surrounded them. "What took you so long?" a Scotsman shouted. "We've been waiting for you Yanks for nearly two years!"

The next day they flew to Grafton Underwood. They wouldn't stay long, but the mud, fog, and chill they found there would accompany them for the rest of their tour. Nutter's barracks was a corrugated metal Quonset hut shaped in a half-circle and heated by a single coal stove. There were twenty-two bunks for officers. After checking in, the men hit the sack. Nutter looked around the room before dozing off. He couldn't believe they had all made it. A year later, only two of the original group he had trained with in California would be alive.

The next morning, LeMay called a group meeting. "You are all confined to base until further notice. Our first combat mission will be against the German submarine bases on the French coast. It'll be on-the-job training."

Curtis LeMay is one of the most controversial figures in American military history. A stern-jawed disciplinarian, "he was," says Rosie Rosenthal, "the greatest air leader in the history of airpower." Yet in later years, even Rosenthal found LeMay's behavior troubling. His old air division commander became "Bombs Away" LeMay, the model for the crackpot, cigar-chomping Gen. Jack D. Ripper in director Stanley Kubrick's raucous Cold War satire, *Dr. Strangelove*. As the immensely capable but truculent head of the Strategic Air Command (SAC) in the 1950s, LeMay was a belligerent advocate of nuclear deterrence, and in 1962, as Chief of Staff of the U.S. Air Force during the Cuban Missile Crisis, he pressed President John F. Kennedy to authorize the bombing of all suspected nuclear sites in Cuba. When the crisis was over, he proposed invading the island. Two years later, he urged President Lyndon Johnson to launch an annihilating bombing campaign against North Vietnam, and in 1968, he ran for vice president on the George Wallace ticket, embarrassing even the extremist Alabama governor with his stridency.

He was a man in the mold of Gen. William Tecumseh Sherman and

George S. Patton, warriors ill-suited for peacetime. A Midwesterner from a footloose family that had been buffeted by hardship, LeMay rose entirely on his own abilities. Lacking the influence to gain entrance to West Point, he enrolled at the Ohio State University in his hometown of Columbus, majoring in engineering and taking ROTC classes while working nine hours a night, six days a week, in a local foundry. "The work was hard," he recalled, "but I liked it."

LeMay began his Army career in 1929 as a fighter pilot and transferred to bombers eight years later when he was put in charge of the navigation school at Langley Field for the Second Bomb Group, the first Army Air Corps unit equipped with B-17s. Although he had attended the Air Corps Tactical School at Maxwell Field, he believed more in the airplane he flew than in the airpower doctrine its instructors preached to him. He was only thirty-five when he took over the 305th Bomb Group in April 1942, but he knew more about the bomber that would carry the early burden of the air war than anyone in the world.

He was a big, beefy man with coal black eyes and a blocklike face frozen permanently in a scowl. No one who served with him ever saw him break into a smile. It wasn't that he was humorless; he suffered from a mild form of Bell's palsy, which partially paralyzed the facial muscles at the corners of his mouth. His exterior toughness hid his ferocious dedication to his men. He was a fanatic about discipline, certain that it saved lives. LeMay was a brilliant air tactician, courageous as well as creative. He flew with his men on some of the toughest missions of the war. He wanted to set an example for them, but more importantly, to learn firsthand the problems they were confronting.

LeMay did not need to scream and shout to move men. He spoke so softly that he could hardly be heard; and he was unemotional, a self-enclosed man with the instincts of an alley-fighter. "We were more afraid of him," said Gale Cleven, "than Hitler." Hard-crusted and brutally frank, he had a reputation for fairness. "I can forgive a mistake—once anyway," he told his men. "But God help you if you ever lie to me."

For LeMay, performance was everything; he ranked men entirely by what they did. "He doesn't want to hear any bullshit," a fellow officer told Ralph Nutter, when Nutter first reported to the 305th. "I hear you went to law school. He doesn't like lawyers, he thinks they're talkers, not doers." On their arrival in England, the 305th was nothing but a gang of "civilians in uniform," Nutter recalled. "We needed a leader like LeMay if we were going to survive fighting the Nazis."

LeMay knew that he headed a pathetically ill-prepared outfit. His bombardiers had never dropped live bombs, and in training in the Mojave Desert, his gunners' only experience with moving targets had been shooting rattlesnakes with pistols. But he wondered if he himself was prepared to meet the Luftwaffe. This was his first combat command and he had no precedent to fall back on. The Army Air Force's bomber command had wonderful theories about high-altitude bombing but had developed no combat tactics to make them work. A pure pragmatist, LeMay would do more than anyone else to give the dangerously deceptive ideas of Mitchell and Douhet, Hansell and Eaker a greatly needed grounding in reality. Distrustful of theory, combat was his school. This was the secret to his narrow genius. "It was LeMay," Andy Rooney wrote, "who . . . changed the way the bombers flew."

A single incident altered the trajectory of his career. When LeMay first arrived at Prestwick airport with the 305th, he looked across the room and spotted Col. Frank Armstrong, who was about to catch a flight back to the States. "He had *been* in combat. He had been shot at," LeMay remembered thinking at the time. "Maybe he could tell us about it," and maybe some of his knowledge "would rub off on us. We felt almost that we should bow from the waist when we shook his hand."

LeMay and his rookie flight officers peppered Armstrong with questions. What was it like on a bomb run? How bad was the opposition? "The flak is murder," Armstrong told them. "If you fly straight and level through it for more than ten seconds, you're a dead duck." LeMay believed him, thinking he had heard "the word of God." But in the days ahead, he began to have doubts. "Hell's bells, I said to myself, if you cannot fly straight and level for more than ten seconds, how are you going to get bombs on the target?" In their understandable concern for survival, Armstrong and his pilots had routinely taken evasive action on the bomb run, making sudden changes in direction and altitude to avoid enemy flak. In saving themselves, they had saved the enemy by scattering their bombs all over creation; and saving the enemy meant going back after him again and again. That was a waste of men and planes.

Tossing in his bed one evening, unable to sleep, LeMay had an idea. He flicked on the light, went to his footlocker, and pulled out a dog-eared artillery manual he had kept from his ROTC days. Sitting upright in bed with pencil and paper, he did some crude calculations. It would take 272 rounds of ammunition, on average, to hit a target the size of a B-17 flying dead level, straight into the target. Those "were pretty good odds."

That was it! On the group's first mission, he was going to have the men fly straight as a pool stick on the bomb run, and fly a much longer bomb run as well. It would be risky, but if the American Air Force could not put bombs on its targets "we might as well all stay at home." On the morning of November 23, LeMay briefed the 305th for its first battle strike of the war. "If we're going to St. Nazaire we're going to get some bombs on that target, by God. And this is the only way I can see to do it." Fly straight and steady, he told the men, and put dying out of your minds. "Losses go with the territory." The destruction of the enemy was the main matter. "If any of you don't have the stomach for this, maybe you'll be happier in the infantry. See the adjutant if you want a transfer. . . . Any questions?" There was a lot of "howling," LeMay admits, but the room calmed down when he announced that he would lead the mission.

The 305th made the bomb run over St. Nazaire exactly as LeMay plotted it, flying straight and level, not for ten, but for 420 seconds. The group did not lose a single plane to flak. The only losses—two bombers—were to Egon Mayer's swift-hitting Fw 190s. Aerial photography showed that the 305th had put twice the number of bombs on St. Nazaire as the other groups on the mission. From then on, with the endorsement of wing commander Laurence Kuter, LeMay's bombing tactics became standard operating procedure for all groups.

LeMay's 305th had been lucky on November 23. Losses shot up over the next three months from 3.7 percent to 8 percent of the attacking bombers, and with no replacements in the pipeline because of operations in the Mediterranean, there were more empty chairs in the mess halls. "When I went to the officers club after a mission, there would usually be a few faces missing," recalled Robert Morgan. "I would concentrate on the scotch in front of me. That scotch was my instrument panel through those nighttime navigations." Drink ruined a lot of good airmen, and it came close to ruining Bob Morgan. But scotch, he said, "was the only antidote I had for all those exploding B-17s that haunted my dreams."

By this time, the men of Morgan's 91st BG had begun to realize that they were "pawns in a great experiment being tried by the Army Air Forces. . . . The members of the group even referred to themselves as 'guinea pigs,' " wrote their official historian. This was an experiment in blood, not a theoretical debate, as it had been in the 1930s. "Is anyone scared?" a commander barked at his men. "If not, there is something wrong with you. I'll give you a little clue how to fight this war—make believe you're dead already; the rest comes easy."

While LeMay's tactics did improve bombing accuracy, results were still abysmal. No more than 3 percent of the bombs were landing within a thousand feet of the Aiming Point. Bombardiers were not hitting targets properly because they didn't have time to study them, LeMay was convinced. The first time a bombardier learned the location of the target of the day was at the morning briefing, when he was "sleepy and groggy and homesick." And when the curtain was pulled from the big wall map, he knew "nothing whatsoever" about the factory he was expected to hit through haze and exploding flak. All the information he would receive about it came through some slides he would be shown at a preflight briefing for bombardiers and navigators after the general briefing, an experience LeMay likened to cramming for a semester exam in five minutes.

LeMay's solution was to identify the best navigators and bombardiers in the group, school them thoroughly on the targets, and position these "lead crews" in planes at the head of the formation. From this point on, only lead bombardiers in LeMay's group would have Norden bombsights. The other bombardiers would release their bombs with a toggle switch the moment they saw bombs dropping from the lead planes. At one stroke, LeMay improved the accuracy of the entire formation from "the common denominator" to the skill of his best men. One of the first of the finest was Ralph Nutter, who was ordered by LeMay to set up a school for lead bombardiers.

But as the Americans improved their offensive tactics, the German defenses grew stronger. On January 3, 1943, German gunners cut the Eighth Air Force to pieces over St. Nazaire. Previously, they had tracked and fired at individual bombers or formations. On this day, they used a "predicted barrage," a lethal box of explosives through which the entire American formation had to fly. Three bombers were lost and thirty-nine others were hit in a gigantic flak field 500 feet wide and 1,000 feet high and deep. "Air discipline," says an Air Force report, "was poor and navigation sloppy."

After this, things changed, and the unlikely agent was the prewar theorist of bomber warfare, Brig. Gen. Haywood Hansell. On January 1, 1943, Hansell replaced Laurence Kuter, Spaatz's newly appointed chief aide in North Africa, as commander of the Eighth Air Force's 1st Bombardment Wing.

Three years older than LeMay, Hansell came from an old Southern military family and was a close student of the history of warfare, a great admirer of Robert E. Lee, a general, unlike Sherman, who waged war only on combatants. Hansell was a warm, genial man with an even disposition who was known to his friends as "Possum" because of his scoop nose and clever mind. Everyone who worked with him considered him one of the brightest heads in the Army Air Forces. This was his first combat command, the opportunity he had been thirsting for, a chance to test the airpower theory he had helped to fashion.

Big things were expected of him, but he quickly found himself at odds with a blood-and-guts major who was his exact opposite in temperament and upbringing, and who had been one of his students at the Air Corps Tactical School. LeMay came on like a storm, bringing in turbulence with him. Hansell's classroom theories were being smashed to dust, LeMay told him directly, by the finest antiaircraft defenses in the world. America's bombers could not fly above enemy flak or outrun enemy fighters, as Hansell and the Bomber Mafia had argued; nor could they bomb as precisely as they had in the high desert skies of the American Southwest. And the bombers desperately needed the long-range fighter escorts that Hansell and his fellow war planners had considered both unnecessary and impossible to build.

At wing meetings, LeMay tore into Hansell with tough questions. Who was the sad sack who put .30 caliber peashooters in the nose of the bombers? Who was the "pickle barrel" theorist who said we could bomb accurately and decisively without fighter cover? Hansell, a smooth consensus builder, was shaken by LeMay's pugnacious probing and would try to politely shift the subject. Hansell's saving element, however, was his lack of interest in the nuts and bolts of military tactics and his eventual willingness to concede tactical matters to his group commanders while he focused on target priorities, a subject no one in the Air Force knew better.

In the end, they formed an effective, if less than amicable, team: the dreamer and the doer. The thing that cut the friction between them was that they were both deeply courageous men. It was only when Hansell flew with the 305th and took a hard beating over St. Nazaire that he implemented his junior officer's tactics throughout the entire 1st Wing.

By the following summer, the entire Eighth would be bombing "on the leader." During his seven to ten minutes over the target, the lead bombardier became, for those few moments, the Eighth Air Force. The other bombardiers complained of being reduced to button pushers, but bombing accuracy, while still erratic, tripled. Using newly developed Air Force equipment, Nutter also helped set up an automatic flight control system. This allowed the bombardier to actually fly the plane through the Norden bombsight in the final minutes of the bomb run, providing a steadier "platform" than could be achieved by the best pilots. "The Automatic Flight Control Equipment held you so straight and rigid you thought you were on railroad tracks," said pilot Craig Harris.

Hansell and other air commanders adopted this tactic as well, along with a variant of the wedge-shaped "combat box" that LeMay experimented with on his first missions from Grafton Underwood. LeMay stacked the planes so that a lead formation—the point of the wedge—was followed by two other formations, one slightly higher than the leader, the other slightly lower. This compressed formation of eighteen to twenty-one bombers, flying with one or two other combat boxes to form a combat wing, was arranged so that the concentrated cones of fire from the .50 caliber machine guns covered the sky for a thousand yards in every direction. It was too large a unit, however, for "point precision bombing," the bombing pattern being the approximate width of the combat box, up to 2,500 feet wide. Bombing by individual planes was far more accurate than bombing as a group, but the ferocity of fighter opposition during the bomb run forced the Eighth into group bombing, which kept the combat box intact. That left the bombers more exposed to flak, "but the fighter opposition was so much the worst of the two that we had to take the anti-aircraft fire and stay together," Hansell explained to his superiors when he returned to Washington in the late summer of 1943.

The Eighth Air Force would never find a way to bomb with maximum precision and maximum protection. This threw it into a conundrum that led irrevocably to carpet bombing, with some bombs hitting the target and the rest spilling all over the place. It was combat realities, not prewar theory, that led the Eighth inexorably in the direction of Bomber Harris's indiscriminate area attacks. In their writings, Douhet and Mitchell had tried to swing the advantage to the attackers, but as long as the Luftwaffe's flak and fighters remained formidable, the defenders always compromised bombing accuracy. "It would be . . . more desirable to go back to individual bombing if we could," Hansell informed his superiors, "but the cost is too high."

Giulio Douhet had prophesied a new form of warfare based on annihilation rather than attrition. He failed to foresee the kind of warfare—close-fought, brutal, and prolonged—that would be necessary to gain command of the air. LeMay never read him. That was fortunate for the Army Air Forces in England.

Curtis LeMay—"Old Iron Ass," to his men—knew something about visionaries. His father, an incurable dreamer, had moved from job to job, all across the country, in a fruitless search for satisfaction, a search that turned his disgruntled son, in bitter reaction, into a hard-eyed pragmatist. LeMay's deep skepticism, his narrow and necessary focus on combat oper-

ations and tactics, made him the right man for command when the Eighth
Air Force was losing the war that Hansell and the planners had already
won in their lectures.

In December 1942, Curtis LeMay's 305th Bomb Group received orders to
move from Grafton Underwood to a new and better-equipped base at
Chelveston, named after an old Norman family that had settled in the area
between Cambridge and Northampton. By this time, his improving crews
were calling themselves proudly the "Can Do" boys. They would need that
confidence. The next target was Germany.

CHAPTER FIVE

The Anatomy of Courage

The thing in the world I am most afraid of is fear.

MONTAIGNE

Casablanca, January 1943

The decision that would eventually turn the Eighth Air Force into a true machine of mass destruction was made in January 1943 at a meeting between Roosevelt and Churchill at Casablanca, on the Atlantic coast of French Morocco. After the Anglo-American Allies completed the defeat of the Wehrmacht, the German army, in North Africa, their next great offensive, the two world leaders agreed, would be in the Mediterranean the following summer, most likely against Sicily. The invasion of Northern Europe was pushed back another year, a clear victory for Churchill. In anticipation of that invasion, Roosevelt and Churchill announced plans for a Combined Bomber Offensive. Its primary purpose would be the defeat of the Luftwaffe in both air-to-air combat and by smashing its production facilities. The British would continue to bomb at night, the Americans by day.

It could have turned out differently. As the conference was about to convene, Gen. Ira Eaker received an urgent message from Hap Arnold to meet him the following day in Casablanca. Eaker called headquarters and told them to have a B-17 ready for him that evening; twelve hours later the

Fortress lifted off from a small airfield on Land's End, the peninsula on the coast of Cornwall. Upon arriving in North Africa, Eaker and his aide, James Parton, were taken to the Anfa hotel, a cluster of sun-baked villas on a high bluff overlooking the turquoise sea. "Ira, I've got bad news for you." Arnold told Eaker. "President Roosevelt has agreed, at Mr. Churchill's request, that your Eighth Air Force will cease daylight bombing and join the RAF in night bombing."

Eaker exploded. It was a "stupid" decision, he told Arnold. "I won't play, [and] I reserve the right to tell our people why I won't." Within an hour, Arnold arranged for Eaker to see Churchill the following morning. Eaker had less than twenty-four hours to prepare a case to save the Eighth Air Force from extinction. "Only you can save us," Arnold told him.

Eaker and Parton drafted a succinct one-page memorandum to be presented to the prime minister and a longer report that Arnold and his staff could use in their own high-level discussions with the British. The next day, Eaker showed up at Churchill's wide-windowed villa at ten o'clock sharp. The prime minister came down the stairs, resplendent in his air commodore's uniform. "I had been told that when he was receiving a naval person, he wore his navy uniform—the same for the other services—but this was the first time I had seen him in Royal Air Force uniform," Eaker recalled. "This struck me then as a good omen."

Churchill got right to the point. "Young man, I am half American; my mother was a U.S. citizen. The tragic losses of so many of our gallant crews tears my heart." Eaker then handed him his memorandum and Churchill motioned for the general to sit down on the couch beside him while he read it in an audible whisper. The memo's commanding point was an argument for "round the clock bombing." If the RAF continued bombing at night and the Eighth greatly accelerated its day campaign, the German defenses would get no rest. Hitler would be forced to double, perhaps triple, the size of his air defenses, ordering tens of thousands of factory workers to hand in their hammers for helmets and move from vitally important war mills to antiaircraft emplacements. "Be patient, give us our chance and your reward will be ample—a successful day bombing offense to combine and conspire with the admirable night bombing of the RAF to wreck German industry, transportation and morale—soften the Hun for land invasion and the kill." Eaker's memo concluded with a promise that the Eighth would begin attacking Germany before the end of the month and would increase the size and frequency of these attacks as it was strengthened tremendously with planes and crews from expanding factories and training facilities in the United States.

"You have not entirely converted me to your view," Churchill remarked after putting down the memorandum. But the prime minister did like the ring and intent of the phrase "round the clock bombing." "He rolled the words off his tongue as if they were tasty morsels," Eaker recalled. "When I see your president at lunch today, I shall tell him that I withdraw my suggestion that you discontinue your daylight bombing and join us in the night bombing effort." The Allies would try round-the-clock bombing, but only "for a time," Churchill added emphatically.

Churchill remembered coming to a more decisive decision. "I decided to back Eaker and his theme and I turned round completely and withdrew all my opposition to the daylight bombing by the fortresses," he wrote in his history of the war. Eaker, however, left the meeting in Casablanca convinced that the survival of the Eighth was still in question.

This son of a Texas sharecropper had been brilliantly persuasive, but there were other voices in the PM's ear. Churchill's air advisors, led by RAF Chief Sir Charles Portal, had been cautioning him to temper his opposition to the American bombing effort. A cessation of daylight bombing from England might cause war planners in Washington to reassign the bombers stationed there to other theaters. Both Churchill and Roosevelt were convinced, moreover, that the planned invasion of northern France would fail unless the Allies achieved air superiority from the English Channel to the Rhine. The most "economical method of reducing German air strength," Eaker had pointed out in his memorandum, was daylight bombing: the enemy "has to fight our bombers when we hit his vital targets." In this air brawl between German fighters and unescorted American bombers, Eaker was confident that the Eighth would prevail. It was one of the largest mistakes of the war.

At Casablanca, British and American air commanders assured Churchill and Roosevelt that the skies over Northern Europe would be swept clean of German aircraft by the time the Allied armada left England's shores for northern France. Unlike George Marshall and Ira Eaker, however, Air Marshal Arthur Harris and Gen. Carl Spaatz were convinced that an all-out bomber offensive would bring Germany to its knees before a land invasion was attempted. With the invasion tentatively scheduled for the spring of 1944, they had only a year and a few months to make good on their extravagant claim that airpower alone would bring down the Reich.

The Writing 69th

The Combined Bomber Offensive would not officially begin for another six months. That winter and spring the submarine menace remained the highest priority of Allied target planners. Eighth Air Force attacks on the operating bases of the U-boats continued to be ineffective, so the Eighth was also called upon to aid Bomber Harris's efforts to destroy the sources of supply: the sprawling submarine-building yards inside Germany at Wilhelmshaven, Bremen, Vegesack, and Kiel. On January 27, 1943, the Eighth Air Force made its first penetration of German airspace, hitting the submarine yards at Wilhelmshaven, on the North Sea. Ira Eaker gave the 306th Bomb Group and its newly promoted commander, Gen. Frank Armstrong, the honor of being "First Over Germany." This was Armstrong's reward for taking over the decimated 306th earlier that month and restoring discipline and morale, the central story of the novel *Twelve O'Clock High!* The Germans were caught off guard and there was little opposition, but clouds obscured the target and bomb damage was minimal. Nonetheless, with this modest beginning, America, with its tremendous productive power, joined Britain in what would build to become the greatest campaign of urban and economic devastation in the history of warfare.

On February 26, after a long weather delay, the Eighth struck Wilhelmshaven again, and this time American reporters went along. One of them was Andy Rooney. A graduate of Colgate University, he was lead correspondent for the London-based, GI-run paper, *Stars and Stripes*. "The Eighth Air Force was the best story in the European war at that time," Rooney recalled, "and we were tired of going up to those airbases and interviewing young guys our age that lost friends in battle and returning to the comforts of London that night. But we didn't realize until the top boys in the Eighth cleared the idea that we'd have to attend gunnery school for a week. If we were going to be on a bomber in battle, we were told, we'd better know how to shoot a gun in case we got into trouble."

Eight reporters were granted permission to fly. Among them were Walter Cronkite of United Press; Gladwin Hill of the Associated Press; Denton Scott of the Army weekly, *Yank;* Bob Post of the *New York Times;* and the *New York Herald-Tribune*'s Homer Bigart, one the most respected war correspondents of his time. (Scott missed the Wilhelmshaven mission, but flew later to Lorient.) An Air Force public relations officer called them "The Writing 69th," a parody of World War I's Fighting 69th. The American press dubbed them "The Flying Typewriters"; they called themselves "The Legion of the Doomed." "I was not happy about it," Cronkite's boss, Harrison Salisbury, recalled, "but a dozen elephants could not have kept Walter out of the B-17."

After learning how to strip a gun blindfolded and how to tell a Focke-Wulf from a British Hurricane at 1,000 yards—no easy thing—they were taken out to the range for some target practice with shotguns and Thompson submachine guns. Five days later, they all passed a written test. "God help Hitler," Denton Scott shouted when he received his score.

At this point, they split up. Rooney went to Thurleigh with the 306th; Cronkite went to Molesworth with the 303rd; and two reporters flew with LeMay's 305th. Apprehension ran high on the morning of the raid, for on the Eighth's previous penetration into Germany, Robert Morgan's group had been the target of a new Luftwaffe tactic: the American bombers were themselves bombed. Flying 2,000 feet above the bomber stream, twin-engine German planes had dropped time-release bombs into their formations. No bombers were hit, but these air-to-air attacks signaled a new Nazi determination.

On the Wilhelmshaven mission, Andy Rooney was assigned to Lt. Bill Casey's *Banshee,* whose crew had watched Arizona Harris fire his final round of bullets as the sea closed over him. Although a regular visitor to bomber bases, Rooney had never been to a preflight briefing. "I remember thinking how good, how all-American, the young fliers looked in their leather jackets, open shirt collars, and jaunty, leather-peaked caps set on their heads at a casually rakish angle. There were a few who wore neckties, Yale, perhaps." When the briefing officer told them the target for the day was in Germany, Rooney thought seriously for the first time about his own demise. At twenty-four, with a wife at home waiting for him, he felt he had made a colossal mistake, but there was no turning back.

"Everything was quiet—almost monotonous—for an hour after we left the English coast," Rooney wrote in the story his paper published the next day. "Then the trouble began." Silver fighter planes came diving out of the sun and disappeared into a cloudbank as quickly as they had appeared. "They seemed tiny, hardly a machine of destruction, and an impossible target." Sitting in the cramped nose compartment, Rooney was almost knocked into the lap of the bombardier when the navigator spun his hand-held gun around to fire at a Messerchmitt as it streaked past them. For the next two hours, German fighters filled the sights of the gunners, and before the bombers were far into Germany, they began to fly through dense fields of floating metal. On the bomb run, there was an ear-splitting explosion and the Plexiglas nose seemed about to break off from the fuselage. The bombardier pulled back in shock and covered his eyes with his hands, thinking he was blinded. He was unhurt, however, and "what appeared to be the nose being ripped off actually was only a small hole the size of a man's fist." When the bombardier ripped off his gloves and tried to close the hole with them, his hands froze instantly and "chips of flesh broke off his fingers as they caught on the jagged edges of the plastic."

On the bomb run, Rooney noticed that the navigator was having trouble with his oxygen supply. Suddenly the man turned purple and his head dropped on top of his gun. With the help of the bombardier, Rooney fitted the mask to the man's face. Then, as he went up to the flight deck for some emergency equipment, Rooney mistakenly unhooked his own mask and began to lose his legs. "Lt. Casey almost yawned at what I was sure was a major crisis of my life. He fixed me up with oxygen and the remainder of my brief first glimpse at the war was from the pit behind the pilot."

The six correspondents who flew that day had planned to meet afterward in a windowless room at Molesworth. There they would write their stories, have them cleared by the censors, and transmit them back to London. They straggled in, pale and exhausted, yet eager to talk. Everyone was there but Bob Post. The night before, he had told friends he was going to die the next day. After what seemed like hours, an Air Force representative burst into the room. It was the worst possible news. Someone would have to notify Post's wife. She had just arrived from London to spend the rest of the war with him.

Hollywood Joins the Eighth

Capt. Robert Morgan remembered first seeing him at Bassingbourn a month or so before the Wilhelmshaven mission: a trim, assertive man in a gunner's flight jacket and billed leather cap "waving his arms in the air, a cigarette burning from the middle of his lips and a couple of cameramen dogging his footsteps. He wore a major's uniform, and had a crisp way of ordering everyone around, so I figured he must be quite the VIP."

He was the Hollywood director William Wyler. His 1942 film, *Mrs. Miniver,* the story of a British family trying to hold itself together during the Nazi Blitz, was still packing the theaters in both England and America and would win six Academy Awards, including one for Wyler as Best Director. Wyler and his film crews had been in England for five months shooting a documentary about strategic bombing for the War Department.

Carl Spaatz had met the director at a party in Washington just after Pearl Harbor and arranged for his appointment as a major and the opportunity to do some on-the-spot war reporting for the Air Force in England. Wyler received his commission in an hour. "No training, nothing," Wyler recalled. "I was sent someplace to buy a uniform. Next thing, I put on this uniform that didn't fit and walk down the street with my cigarette, my briefcase, and here comes a general. Jeez, what do I do? Swallow the cigarette, throw the briefcase away? I threw away the cigarette and saluted. The general saw me and laughed."

A U-boat sank the ship carrying Wyler's expensive 35mm cameras, leaving the film crews with the handheld 16mm cameras they had packed in their suitcases. They handed these out to fliers to shoot film on their missions, but Wyler was unsatisfied with this. He insisted on flying with the crews; he wanted to make a film of power and authenticity, not a piece of facile propaganda. He got his wish, but only after attending gunnery school with Rooney, Cronkite, and the rest of the Writing 69th.

At Bassingbourn, his team of photographers shot most of their color footage of a bomber called *Invasion II*. One day it failed to return from a raid. "So we got in a jeep," one of the cameramen recalled, "and started driving around the base looking planes over." Wyler saw a Fortress with a leggy redhead in a bathing suit painted on its nose, and beside her the evocative name *Memphis Belle*. "Willy pointed his finger at the name and said, 'That's it.'"

The nose art on the bombers was one of the first things that had caught his attention on arriving at Bassingbourn. Neither the Nazis nor the British had anything like it, and Marine Corps and Navy regulations forbade it. It seemed so expressive of the exuberant spirit of the boy crews. "It was a way of holding on to our individuality, or sense of humor, in a war that was overwhelmingly vast, mechanized, and brutal," Robert Morgan would observe later. There were cartoon icons like Mickey Mouse and ferocious fire-breathing dragons but the favorite subjects of the amateur nose cone artists were voluptuous girls in pinup poses popularized by the work of commercial artists George Petty, Gil Elvgren, and the Peruvian Alberto Vargas. Coyly seductive and impossibly beautiful, they were more than idealized versions of girls back home; they were brazen symbols of life on a war front where death was on everyone's mind.

When Morgan picked a name for his plane, just before flying to England, he phoned George Petty and asked if he could use one of his *Esquire* magazine pinup girls on his bomber. Petty sent him a drawing and Morgan had an artist in his squadron paint two copies on his plane, one on each side of the nose. The crew loved them; the girl fit their youthful dash and homesick, sexual longing. "To the German fighter pilots homing in our American bombers, it must have looked sometimes as though they were being attacked by a wave of flying underwear catalogues," Morgan said later.

When Morgan met Wyler at the officers club, he told Wyler his plane was named after his real-life sweetheart and that he planned to marry her in Memphis as soon as he returned home. At that moment Wyler knew his film would be the story of the *Memphis Belle*. Wyler told Morgan he wanted to fly with him. "I told him, O.K.," recalled Morgan, "if he didn't get in the way and get all of us killed. I got to like the guy; he had guts and passion, but he did get in the way." Whenever the *Belle* came under fire, Wyler would erupt, scurrying around the plane, a portable oxygen bottle in one hand, a small camera in the other, pointing excitedly at flak bursts or incoming fighters. Once, when he missed getting a film shot of exploding flak, he begged Morgan to steer the bomber into the thick of the shrapnel field.

Wyler was a Jew from Alsace who wanted to play a part in bringing down Hitler. When General Eaker ordered him grounded, fearing that the Nazis would turn his capture into a major propaganda victory, Wyler went on another mission anyway. Told by Eaker's aide Beirne Lay, Jr. that he could be court-martialed for directly violating an order, Wyler shot back, "I've got to get the film." Lay never informed Eaker that Wyler had refused to be grounded. Wyler put "his own skin on the line," Lay later explained his decision, "because he wanted the picture to be right."

Once, Wyler nearly died when his oxygen supply was cut off, and on another mission, he risked his life to get a spectacular shot of a Flying Fortress lifting off the runway by sitting in the ball turret on takeoff, something that no gunner was permitted to do. When one of his cameras would freeze up at 25,000 feet, he would slip it inside his heavy flight jacket and reach for another one that had been thawing out. Nothing was going to stop him from making his film.

Capt. Clark Gable had an equal passion for his work and took as many chances as Willy Wyler. The "King of Hollywood" had arrived in April 1943 at neighboring Polebrook to serve with the newly operational 351st Bomb Group. He had been personally recruited by Hap Arnold to help produce a short training film on aerial gunnery called *Combat America*.

Gable had enlisted in the Air Force the previous summer, following the death of his wife, the glamorous actress Carole Lombard. A passionate patriot, she had been pressing him to enlist and seek a commission, and he had been tempted. Touring the country on a war bond drive, she sent him teasing telegrams saying, "Hey, Pappy. You better get into this man's Army." Coming home in January 1942, she was killed in a plane crash.

The day after her funeral, Hap Arnold, who knew Gable casually, had sent him a telegram offering him a "highly important assignment." Not wanting to lose its star, MGM told Arnold he was unavailable and the telegram was never delivered. But that August, Gable, on his own, enlisted as a private. He wanted to be a machine gunner, he told a reporter, "where the going is really hot," but Arnold refused to give him a regular combat assignment. Gable was not disappointed. He knew that filming the air war would be nearly as dangerous as fighting it. "It's murder up there," he told one of his film crew. "They're falling like moths. Like dying moths."

The men didn't accept him at first, seeing him as a pampered Hollywood hotshot, but Gable set out to prove them wrong. His overseas flying pay was $320 a month; he had made a hundred times that playing Rhett Butler in *Gone With the Wind*. And he surprised everyone by going out with the crews on some of the toughest hauls. When he left with the 351st on its maiden mission, his close friend and chief writer, John Lee Mahin, was in the tower. "I hear Gable's up there," he said for everyone to hear. The men in the tower said that was "a lot of bullshit. Gable wasn't going on any missions." When he returned, they said it was "a milk run." It wasn't. Gable had been nearly killed when a shell tore through the plane, blew the heel off his boot, and exited the fuselage inches from his head. "After his second mission, though, which was a tough one, the kids adored him," says Mahin. "They couldn't stay away from him."

It was difficult, but Gable tried to fit in. When Bob Hope brought his USO show to Polebrook, he looked out at the sea of faces and asked for Rhett Butler, calling on him to stand up and be recognized. Gable remained seated and the boys around him wouldn't point him out. Even Hitler knew Gable was in England. Hermann Göring offered his fliers a reward equaling $5,000 to bring him down. Gable, fearing Hitler would put him in a cage "like a gorilla" and exhibit him all over Germany, told Jack Mahin he would never bail out of his plane if it got into trouble. "How could I hide this face? If the plane goes, I'll just go with the son of a bitch."

Never Saw Such Kids

The film William Wyler was making "will deal with the ultimate destruction of Germany from the air," an Air Force publicist told a *Stars and Stripes* reporter. As the Eighth's losses went up so did the volume of its publicity campaign. After a May 18 pinpoint precision raid on the submarine construction yards at Vegesack on the Weser River near Bremen, General Eaker called a press conference and announced that the experimental days were over. "Today a new chapter begins. We have proved beyond doubt that our bombers can penetrate in daylight to any target in Germany; that they can go alone, without benefit of fighter protection . . . without suffering prohibitive losses. All that remains is for us to concentrate enough bombers for this vital task." The last line is telling. Eaker knew he did not have the bombers to do the job.

That winter, Hap Arnold kept promising Eaker that more planes and crews were on the way, all the while demanding additional and larger raids, raids that, with Eaker's thinned-out fleet, were becoming sacrificial. Vegesack *was* an accurate strike, but the Eighth Air Force massively exaggerated its effect on German submarine production. The continuing raids on the U-boat pens along the Bay of Biscay were equally ineffective. The strike photographs that Eaker showed reporters were impressive. St. Nazaire and Lorient had ceased to exist as habitable human communities. As Admiral Dönitz noted in a report to the German high command: "No dog nor cat is left in these towns. Nothing but the submarine shelters remain." They were, however, the only facilities that the admiral cared about. Dönitz had recently moved the essential equipment for servicing his U-boats inside their impregnable pens.

Looking back at these operations years later, lead navigator Ralph Nutter saw a numbers game at work, not unlike the one Washington would play during the Vietnam War. "Instead of a bogus body count, Army Air Forces headquarters released grossly exaggerated reports of Nazi fighter losses and the tonnage of our bombs that hit German targets. . . . American air leaders had promised the American people dramatic results and victory through airpower." Desperate for results, they bent the truth to get the money and men to finish the job.

"The Eighth Air Force," reporter Harrison Salisbury wrote in his memoirs, "was a high-octane outfit. It was run by ambitious men and backed by an ambitious command in Washington. It had set up a large public relations staff—men from newspapers, publicity firms, advertising agencies—and made use of Hollywood celebrities." Eaker worked wonderfully with the press, inviting notables like columnist Walter Lippmann and *New York Times* publisher Arthur Sulzberger to dinner and private poker games at Eighth Air Force headquarters. The Eighth's public relations office in London's Grosvenor Square was run by people of persuasive power and influence, among them John "Tex" McCrary, a popular columnist for the *New York Mirror,* John Hay "Jock" Whitney, a Hollywood mogul and playboy who would later become U.S. ambassador to Great Britain, and Ben Lyon, a former silent screen idol. Lyon and his wife, the actress Bebe Daniels, hosted sparkling parties at their London town house with guest lists that included Eaker and his staff, British lords and admirals, visiting dignitaries, and influential members of the press. McCrary, whom Andy Rooney called "one of the great public relations experts and con artists of all time," would show up with his radiant wife, Jinx Falkenberg, and make sure that no one of importance left without an earful of statistics about the staggering strength and success of the Mighty Eighth.

An obliging press, understandably more angry with the Nazis than eager to be objective, went along with the rosy reviews of the bomber barons. "We were all on the same side, then," Walter Cronkite explained later, "and most of us newsmen abandoned any thought of impartiality as we reported on the heroism of our boys and bestiality of the hated Nazis." As Andy Rooney noted, "the worst kind of censorship has always been the kind that newspaper people impose on themselves."

Rooney's paper, *Stars and Stripes,* was written and edited by uniformed soldiers and was in 1943 a self-admitted "Air Force trade journal" because there was no fighting close to England except in the skies. General Eisenhower, however, had ordered Army censors not to make it an obsequious house organ. Under the eccentric but clear-eyed direction of S. Sgt. Robert Moora, formerly of the *New York Herald Tribune,* and Cpl. Bud Hutton, onetime editor of the *Buffalo Evening News,* it was a solidly written and unbiased paper, the daily sheet of the American soldier overseas. Two military censors were stationed in the paper's London offices, but "they rarely stopped us from publishing anything. And when they tried to, we could argue with them and sometimes talk them into letting us run the story," Rooney recalled. "Like them, we knew what the rules were; and the rules, designed to keep the Nazis in the dark about coming operations, made perfect sense."

A bred-in-the-bones skeptic, Rooney ignored the fantastic claims of enemy damage and focused instead on the boys in the bombers. It was his job, he thought, to tell their story, a story "buried under the damnably cold heap of statistics the Allies are trying to pile higher than Axis statistics." But there were, he conceded later, stories that were "too sad" to report. One in particular lived in his mind.

While Rooney and some other reporters were waiting in front of a control tower for a squadron of bombers to return, word spread that a ball turret gunner was trapped in his plastic bubble underneath the plane. "The gears that rotated the ball to put the gunner in position to shoot and then return him to the position that enabled him to climb out and back up into the aircraft had been hit and were jammed. The ball-turret gunner was caught in a plastic cage."

Just before landing, the Fortress's hydraulic system, which was riddled with shell holes, malfunctioned, making it impossible for the pilot to put down the wheels. The emergency hand crank for operating the main landing gear has also been destroyed by enemy fire. The pilot would have to make a belly landing. "There were eight minutes of gut-wrenching talk among the tower, the pilot, and the man trapped in the ball turret. He knew what comes down first when there are no wheels. We all watched in horror as it happened. We watched as this man's life ended, mashed between the concrete pavement of the runway and the belly of the bomber."

Rooney returned to London that evening, unable to write the most dramatic and ghastly story he had ever witnessed.

"The boys in the Forts over Germany have the toughest time of all—with the possible exception of the guys who go down in submarines," Tex McCrary wrote to his son, a fighter pilot on a carrier in the Pacific. "Never saw such kids." Years later, Tom Brokaw would call the young Americans who battled the Axis Powers "The Greatest Generation," but in the first year of the war some people questioned their commitment. In 1942, the social critic Philip Wylie published a widely influential book about the youth culture of his time, *Generation of Vipers*. In the late 1930s, while the armies of Hitler and Hirohito threatened freedom everywhere, American teenage boys hid their heads in the sand, Wylie charged, riding souped-up cars, reading cheap comic books, and listening to Sinatra records. They performed shoddily in math and science and had a horribly deficient knowledge of history and the world they lived in, 59 percent of them having failed to locate China on a map. But after flying on several missions with them, Tex McCrary found them "the best that ever came out of America; they are the richest harvest of all American history," he told a friend in a wartime letter from England. "The challenge of total war revealed the same high qualities that have always been beneath the skin of the American people when the time of great testing has stripped them lean." In a book published during the war, McCrary offered the story of the Mathis brothers from San Angelo, Texas, as a counter to Wylie's acid indictment.

Mark Mathis and his brother Jack joined the Air Force in 1941, vowing to serve together. Both were assigned to bombardier school, but at different sites. Jack became a bombardier in heavies, Mark in twin-engine bombers. When Jack flew on the first American raid on Germany with the 303rd

Bomb Group, Mark was still back in the States. A little while later, Jack got a telegram from his brother; he was in England. Jack requisitioned a jeep and brought Mark back to his station. That night, they started an impromptu reunion party at the officers club, which was cut short by the warning that "the deal" was on for tomorrow. On his way out, Mark asked his brother's squadron commander, Bill Calhoun, if he could go along on the raid. That was impossible, Calhoun told him. He'd have to go all the way to Roosevelt to get permission.

It was March 11 and the target for the following day was Vegesack. Mark accompanied his brother to the plane. "See you boys at 6 o'clock," he shouted as Jack and his crew climbed aboard *The Duchess,* one of the lead planes in the largest contingent of American bombers sent against Germany up to that time.

Later in the day, Mark was at the tower to watch the Forts come in. *The Duchess* landed first, but on the wrong runway and after firing a flare that signaled wounded aboard. Mark got to the plane after the ambulance had been loaded and was told his brother had been wounded. At the infirmary, the chaplain took him aside and said Jack was dead.

Jessie H. Elliott, the navigator, had been with Mathis in the nose of *The Duchess* when he was hit. His story is recorded in the deposition accompanying the citation of Jack Mathis for the Congressional Medal of Honor, the first to go to a flier in the Eighth.

Just seconds before the bomb-release point, a shell had burst directly in front of the nose. "A hunk of flak came tearing through the side of the nose. It shattered the glass on the right side and broke through with a loud crash. I saw Jack falling back toward me and threw up my arm to ward off the fall. By that time both of us were way back in the rear of the nose—blown back there I guess by the flak flying in." Dressed in their thick, confining flight clothing, Calhoun didn't know that Mathis's arm was nearly severed below the elbow and that the right side of his body was full of shrapnel. On his own, Mathis pulled himself back to the bombsight, knelt over it, and pulled the lever, releasing the bombs. Calhoun heard him call out on the interphone, "Bombs . . ."—and slump on his bombsight before he could complete the sentence. His bombs fell directly on the aiming point. The target photographs proved it.

Back at the base hospital, Mark Mathis looked at his brother's shattered body and broke down. They had planned to finish their reunion bash that night; instead he would have to notify his parents. Turning to leave, he told the chaplain he would kill the killers of his brother. Calhoun got him a transfer in "record time" and allowed him to take Jack's place on the crew of *The Duchess*. Mark even slept in his brother's bed.

His first mission was Bremen. When he crawled into his position in the front of the nose, he looked down and saw that the bombsight was scarred by the flak burst that had taken his brother.

Three missions later, McCrary interviewed him. A lot of fliers were saying that they found it hard to hate the Germans, that they'd rather be getting revenge against the Japanese. What did he think about that? "You don't start hating till you been hurt," Mark said. "Me, well, I've been hurt. So I hate the Germans. I wish we bombed their cities instead of just their factories."

Mark Mathis was killed leaning over his bombsight on his next mission.

Dark Days

"Our morale got down to a . . . low ebb late in the winter," recalled Curtis LeMay. With deeper penetration raids into enemy airspace, casualties rose, and with no replacements on the horizon, men began to see their situation as hopeless. Even when fully trained crews became available, foul weather closed the North Atlantic air ferrying route, and there was not enough shipping to transport them to England. Many airmen began to feel conflicted about their country: willing to fight for it, they also felt abandoned by it. Men grumbled but they flew; and bone-weary maintenance crews worked through the nights stripping parts from "hanger queens"—bombers too damaged to fly—to keep their beat-up but flyable bombers in the fight.

By the late winter of 1943, LeMay's 305th had lost nearly half its crews, and the other three pioneer Fortress groups were down to 20 percent of their original personnel. This made every mission a maximum effort; sick and wounded men were pulled out of base hospitals to fill the crews. After a tough run over Lorient or Wilhelmshaven, boys who had aged six years in six months would sit around in reading rooms and mess halls and play "a new morbid game," reported Haywood Hansell, plotting their chances of survival on a graph. In his memoirs, Harrison Salisbury reported that "to fly in the Eighth Force then was to hold a ticket to a funeral. Your own."

That winter there were distressing reports from flight surgeons and Air Force psychiatrists of abnormal behavior among crewmen, as combat insidiously shook the moorings of the airmen's self-control. Great numbers of fliers began to experience one or more of the symptoms of emotional disintegration: insomnia, irritability, sudden temper flashes, inability to concentrate, withdrawal from friends, nausea, weight loss, dizziness, blurring of vision, heart palpitations, Parkinson-like tremors, sexual impotence and aggressiveness, binge drinking, and terrifying battle dreams, nightmares so alarmingly vivid that men screamed and shook, and a few of them fell out of their top bunks and shattered legs and arms. "The monthly dances held at operational groups have been marked by numbers of violent fights," reported a research team headed by Donald W. Hastings, chief psychiatrist of the Central Medical Establishment. "On one occasion two squadron commanders, quite close friends, riding back to the post after an evening of moderate drinking . . . decided they 'needed a fight,' and . . . got out of the car and fought violently until one broke a metacarpal bone, after which they amicably climbed back in the car and drove home." At night, it was not unusual for men to put out the lights in their barracks "with a burst from a 'Tommy gun' or shoot their initials into the walls with pistols." Airmen confided to flight surgeons and chaplains that they had "seduced women, in quantity, not for sexual satisfaction, but for the sake of subduing and conquering" their unrelieved anxiety. And some men feared that they were slowly slipping into insanity.

A later CME study found that virtually every flier who completed a tour of combat duty suffered from one or more of the symptoms of combat fatigue. Most of these men suppressed their anxiety and continued to fly, admitting their fear and talking shamelessly about it with crewmates, joking that they were "flak-happy" or had the " 'Focke-Wulf Jitters.' . . . To the airmen such an admission carried no implication of being 'yellow,' or a coward," Hastings reported. Most frightened airmen among the approximately 25 percent that beat the odds and lived achieved enough mastery over stress to continue to fight resolutely, even heroically. However, when the symptoms piled up over a short stretch of time, that man became a danger to both himself and his crewmates.

On combat runs, some airmen experienced hysteria reactions: shakes and tremors, fainting spells, temporary blindness, and catatonia. When pilot Clint Hammond flew into murderous enemy fire on his maiden mission, his co-pilot passed out cold and Hammond had to revive him with a wild punch to the head.

One co-pilot from a distinguished military family went temporarily blind every time he crossed into Holland. When the plane passed over the North Sea on its return to England, he would suddenly regain his sight. LeMay grounded him, and Ralph Nutter was one of the few officers who would speak to him. But when Nutter's own bombardier suffered temporary blindness on the bomb run, Nutter slapped his fear-filled face and forced him to sight the target.

Other men experienced a delayed reaction to extreme stress, breaking down hours, sometimes weeks, after a traumatic experience. On a practice mission over England, the bomb bay doors of a Fortress broke loose and one of the doors sliced off the tail of the plane. The trapped gunner tried frantically to punch his way through the heavy glass of his gun station as the entire tail section went hurtling to earth, end over end. He managed to kick a small hole through the aluminum skin of the tail section and tried to wiggle through it, but his shoulders became wedged. Just when he thought he was finished he was blown free, dropping to the ground several hundred feet below without a parachute. Miraculously, he was unhurt. Seconds after he hit the ground, the rest of the fuselage crashed and exploded less than a hundred yards from him, burning his crewmates beyond recognition.

The tail gunner said he was okay and continued to fly, but began to have dreams of ghastly crashes and was unable to tolerate whistling and whining noises, which reminded him of the wind tearing through the severed tail section as it fell from the sky. He would not ask for help, not wanting to be considered "yellow" or a "quitter," but on his next five missions he was a wreck, "listening to the creaking of the plane, waiting for the tail section to break off again." A few days later, he broke down and his squadron surgeon grounded him.

Hastings and his colleagues had a difficult time convincing bomb group commanders that a growing number of their fliers were not just tired— suffering from what the Air Force called "flying fatigue"—but truly sick. These men needed rest, not medical treatment, their commanders insisted. Squadron COs showed no compassion for another and vastly smaller group of fliers—those who broke down after only a few missions in which their planes and crews suffered little or no battle damage. These men were treated as cowards, lacking a quality the British called moral fiber. They were believed to have a predisposition to breakdown—a deep character flaw that had not been detected by Air Force doctors before they were admitted into the flying service. Convinced that mental disorders were "as contagious as measles," base commanders tried to get rid of these men before they "infected" others.

Men charged as "lacking in moral fiber" were handled by administrative, not medical, procedures. Officers were sent to an Army reclassification board, where they were given the opportunity to resign "for the good of the service." Those not choosing this option were charged with "lack of intestinal fortitude" and discharged without honor. Enlisted men were treated differently. They were reduced to the grade of private, removed from flying status, and sent to a replacement pool for reassignment. (Cases of men refusing to fly were rare; for the entire war, fewer than a hundred officers were referred to a reclassification board.)

It was different for fliers who *had* shown intestinal fortitude in combat but broke down near the end of their tour of duty or after a traumatic experience in the air. Many commanders hid problems like this from CME doctors; they didn't want solid men "stigmatized," in LeMay's phrase, by "head shrinkers."

"Bomber bases were damn depressing places to visit," Andy Rooney recalled. "Death was always in the air, even though the guys were trying hard to laugh and forget." Men were willing to face death, but no one knew how many times they would have to do it. Were they expected to keep flying until they were killed, wounded, captured, or crazy? It seemed so.

Late that winter, Dr. Malcolm Grow, the Eighth's chief medical officer, brought news to Eaker of an alarming increase in both flight fatigue and mental breakdown, with seventy-three crews diagnosed as "war weary." He pleaded with Eaker to limit the number of missions to fifteen. Eaker refused. There was no morale problem, he insisted. The men were simply exhausted. But believing that flight crews had to have an end in sight, he agreed to set the required number of missions at twenty-five. After completing their twenty-five, airmen would be sent home for reassignment or given ground duties in England. (In March 1944, the number increased to thirty, and in July 1944, to thirty-five.) The chances of completing the new combat tour were, at the time only one in five. Hardly encouraging, but a sliver of hope.

Still, every operation brought with it more psychiatric casualties. Most of the men suffered from anxiety states that Air Force psychiatrists placed into two broad categories. One was "flying fatigue," a mild form of emotional anxiety that arose from insufficient rest and the "nervous strain of flying." The other was "operational fatigue," emotional, not physical, fatigue caused by accumulating stress or harrowing experiences in the air, and exhibiting itself as "chronic fear and chronic psychic conflict." A few days' rest, doctors believed, could cure the first condition; the second condition called for both rest and extensive psychiatric treatment, and had a far lower recovery rate.

Dr. Grow knew that his figure of seventy-three war-weary crews was conservative. Most men who had been temporarily removed from flying by their commanders never appeared in Air Force statistics. Their bomb group or squadron commanders grounded them, usually on the advice of flight surgeons, and when they "recovered" after a brief period of rest and treatment on the base, they were returned to flying status. Only the most severe cases were referred to the CME psychiatrists for treatment, and, as a result, became statistics.

Of the estimated 225,000 airmen who flew combat missions for the Eighth during the entire war, only a small number, between 4,000 and 5,000, were treated as emotional casualties; and only about 2,100 of these men were permanently grounded for neuro-psychiatric disorders. This does not include men removed from flying duty or discharged for "lack of moral fiber," which was considered a character, not a mental, problem. These figures, however, are incomplete and highly problematic. With the exception of the Central Medical Establishment, the Eighth Air Force did not keep reliable statistics on emotional casualties, nor did Air Force doctors ever establish a clear and consistent definition of a psychiatric casualty. In addition, many men were grounded by their squadron flight surgeons for physical symptoms that pointed to an incipient mental breakdown; and some men judged to be "lacking moral fiber" by their commanders were suffering from undiagnosed emotional problems. There is also strong circumstantial evidence that bomb group commanders suppressed evidence of mental breakdowns. And there is indisputable evidence from personal testimonies that many fliers experiencing excruciating anxiety hid their condition from both their commanders and their crewmates to avoid punishment or censure—or because they wanted to complete their tours of duty as rapidly as possible. Flight surgeons reported that great numbers of men did not show up for medical treatment until they had completed their final mission. We will never know how many Eighth Air Force fliers suffered emotional problems severe enough to ground them, but the number is surely greater than official statistics indicate.

The Anatomy of Courage

The experience of the American infantry in North Africa and Italy helped convince Hap Arnold and the command structure of the Eighth Air Force to take a more understanding attitude toward emotional casualties. In the Mediterranean Theater, where green American troops first met the feared Wehrmacht, psychiatric disorders were the leading cause of medical evacuation from combat areas and medical discharges from the Army. Fully one-third of nonfatal casualties were psychiatric. To gain a better understanding of this medical disaster, the Army sent one of its top physicians, John W. Appel, to conduct a study of men under fire. His conclusions were sobering.

Appel insisted that there was no such thing as " 'getting used to combat.' Each moment of it imposes a strain so great that men will break in direct relation to the intensity and duration of their exposure. Thus psychiatric casualties are as inevitable as gun shot wounds in warfare." In the infantry, this breakdown usually occurred after about a hundred days of exposure to combat. By that time, the body's fight-or-flight mechanism—designed by nature for sudden emergencies—became dangerously overextended.

Early studies by Eighth Air Force psychiatrists yielded similar conclusions. Beginning in the winter of 1943, "emotional disorders" were the most frequent cause of long-term removals from flying, and the number of emotional casualties bore a direct relationship to aircraft loss rates—one flesh-and-blood breakdown for every two heavy bombers that failed to return. Actual danger in the air, not any inherent flaw in the individual's character or psychic makeup, "has been by far the most important single cause of emotional breakdowns in this theater," Hastings and his colleagues reported.

Hap Arnold understood this connection between danger and breakdown. As one of the U.S. Army's first test pilots, he had been involved in a near-fatal air accident that left him with a paralyzing fear of flying. "My nervous system is in such a condition that I will not get in any machine," he had written to his commanding officer. It took Arnold four years to overcome this deep-seated phobia, an experience that may have eventually made him sympathetic to fliers who suffered similar trauma in the air war over the Reich.

Overwhelming fear of death and dismemberment—combat stress—was the leading cause of emotional casualties in the Eighth Air Force, Hastings concluded after an exhaustive medical study of the first year of combat operations. Given sufficient stress, even the best men broke down. A fighting man's reservoir of courage, his ability to adapt to fear, was limited. Unknown to Hastings, this conclusion was reached years earlier by World War I combat surgeons, most prominent among them England's Lord Moran—later Churchill's personal physician. "How is courage spent in war?" Moran asked in *The Anatomy of Courage,* his classic treatise on the subject, which was not available in print until 1967. "Courage is will-power, whereof no man has an unlimited stock; and when in war it is used up, he is finished. A man's courage is his capital and he is always spending."

Moran mainly studied the infantry, and there were, to be sure, enormous differences between air and ground combat. The physical strain of air combat was not as prolonged or debilitating as ground fighting. The airman's battles were short and sharp, and when not flying, he did not have to endure the animal-like existence of the ground soldier—fighting and living in the mud, sleet, and rain without bathing or toilet facilities.

Air Force bomber crews endured stress of a different order. It was intermittent rather than continuous, and therefore less debilitating. Among aviators, there was a lower incidence of incapacitating trauma requiring long-term hospitalization, fewer cases where the soldier's entire ego was shattered and he spun into a stupor, suffering amnesia and exhibiting wildly bizarre behavior. "True psychoses were conspicuously absent" in the Eighth Air Force, Hastings concluded. But fliers suffered their own unique forms of combat neurosis, along with far higher casualty rates than the infantry. The sharp contrast between the soft civilian-like security of the base and the moments of desperate peril in the air added to their troubles "by keeping alive the idea of another way of life—the chronic danger of an alternative in war." And unlike infantry, airmen were thoroughly briefed about the danger they were about to enter, which excited the mind dangerously. "You leave your imagination behind you or it will do you harm," Moran wrote.

Crewmen on heavy bombers were susceptible to a special kind of fear. They experienced what psychiatrists called phobic states, where disabling anxiety showed itself only when they were exposed to a particular situation, whether it be foul weather or a fighter attack. When put in these circumstances, some men's "narcissistic defenses," the ego mechanisms that allowed them to deny their biological vulnerability, disintegrated. From believing that "nothing can happen to me," these airmen became convinced that "some disaster *must* happen to me." From feeling that they were spectators, they came to consider themselves sitting targets. Short of being hit by enemy fire, the most frightening experience in the air was the feeling of helplessness over the target—the utter inability to evade danger. And when disaster struck, it came with terrifying suddenness, the monotonous, sleep-inducing hum of the engines interrupted by a violent explosion that sent bone and blood flying everywhere. A characteristic of technological war, this was akin to the shock suffered by disaster victims, or by infantrymen under intense shelling, or by the enemy civilians these airmen bombed, deliberately or not. On the bomb run, an experience akin to a German mother and her children cowering in their coal cellar with the air raid sirens screaming, random luck alone determined who lived and who died. All that the bomber crews could do was hunker down and take it; there was no way to relieve the rising tension. In the exploding flak, airmen stood alone in the face of fear. As Freud wrote, "the essence of the traumatic situation is the experience of helplessness."

"In the presence of danger," Lord Moran observed, "man often finds salvation in action." There was no such salvation in a flak field. "I can still see and hear the flak bursts as clearly as when I was in the plane," Eighth Air Force tail gunner Sherman Small admitted sixty years after the war. "At the time, I successfully blocked out the fear by pretending that I was an actor in a Hollywood action movie. That fiction ended with the end of the war. Then the excruciating memories of the fear pulled me down and I had to be sent to an Air Force mental hospital."

Chance was the all-determining force in an airman's life. It determined the composition and character of his crew, his plane's position in the combat formation, the weather his formation flew into, the intensity of enemy opposition, and ultimately whether he lived or died. Having little or no control over any of these things, some fliers went to pieces, often without knowing why. "I have a yellow streak up my back a yard wide and I don't know where I got it," said one airman. "I never used to be yellow."

In most of these cases the anxiety was directly related to the plane itself—to flying—and disappeared when men were grounded. Air Force psychiatrists cautioned commanders not to send mentally fragile men back into action. "It is not difficult to force men with crippling anxiety to fly, but very often it is impossible to force them to fly effectively." It was this—the danger that anxiety-torn men posed to themselves and other fliers—that finally caused air commanders to ground them.

Eighth Air Force psychiatrists were also beginning to prove that some emotionally damaged men *could* be salvaged and returned to flying. With expensively trained airmen in short supply, this was yet another reason for commanders to work more closely with CME psychiatrists and their own flight surgeons.

The key person in the Air Force's medical chain of command was the flight surgeon, one of them serving each squadron on a bomber base. When a man broke in combat or showed dangerous signs of cracking, he was initially diagnosed and treated by his flight surgeon, whose only psychiatric training might have been a short course at CME headquarters in High Wycombe. Flight surgeons had to perform a nearly impossible balancing act. On the one hand, they were trained healers who tried to get as close to the men as a chaplain would to his flock, making themselves available for counseling and medical treatment at all hours of the day and night.

On the other hand, they were military officers whose principal duty was to keep men healthy and sane enough to kill for their country. Emotionally sick men looked to the surgeon for relief from war, temporarily or permanently, yet the surgeon's duty was to return as many of these men as possible to the very scenes of terror and suffering that had incapacitated them.

The Central Medical Establishment's handful of overworked psychiatrists went out to the bomber bases and helped flight surgeons deal with this dilemma. They also flew with the crews "to get to know what happened in a man's head" during aerial combat. CME psychiatrist Lt. David G. Wright spent four months as a field consultant in psychiatry with Curtis LeMay's 305th Bomb Group. He flew on five combat missions, experiences that helped him to write a number of pioneering reports that have become classics in the field of military psychology.

Wright also flew with the men to gain their trust. "[Airmen] seldom will talk freely, particularly if they are emotionally disturbed, with anyone who has not experienced the rigors of combat," he wrote in a report the Air Force distributed as required reading to its flight surgeons. In 1943 alone, fifty-three flight surgeons went on ninety-one combat missions. None were lost, although some were wounded.

In order to do "positive, preventive psychotherapy" you must make the men feel that you "are with them and for them anytime, anywhere," Wright advised combat surgeons. Yet it was more important, he cautioned, to be respected than loved. A good flight surgeon had to be tough-minded, as committed to winning the war as he was to the care of his men. That meant supporting and encouraging their latent drives to continue to fly in spite of the trauma and terror they had to endure.

Capt. Wendell C. "Smoky" Stover of the Bloody Hundredth fit this description excellently. "He was with us all back in the States, and got to know us all by our first names" wrote Stars and Stripes reporter Sgt. Saul Levitt, an original member of the 100th Bomb Group, "and [at Thorpe Abbotts] when the missions first began to bring back their wounded and shocked gunners, 'Smoky' was there as the red flare went up over the field." A husky, slow-talking thirty-three-year-old from Boonville, Indiana, where most of his patients were coal miners, Smoky Stover did not coddle his men. The story around the base was "that you'd have to be pretty near dead before he'd ground you." Even so, airmen with troubles talked to him as though he was the base chaplain and he made himself available to everybody, "the nearest closest thing in the Army to a family doctor."

Stover realized that the burden of detecting combat fatigue fell primarily on him, and that to spot it and diagnose its severity, he had to know his men. He kept them under unnoticeable scrutiny, observed their behavior in briefings, on the flight line, in the planes, in the barracks, and at the local drinking holes. Yet excellent flight surgeons like Stover, who were at one time or another "Doctor, Chaplain, Lawyer, Mother, Father, Brother and Friend" to the men, were also "under the thumb" of the bomber group's commanding officer. A surgeon's recommendation to ground a man carried no binding power. For this reason, David Wright advised surgeons to develop a close relationship with their commanding officers and not be perceived as weak or excessively tolerant with the men.

The iron rule of Eighth Air Force psychiatry was to treat as many men as possible on the base, where they were known, rather than sending them to hospital facilities administered by CME. If the flight surgeon detected mild emotional distress, he could send a war-weary airman for a week's rest at one of the country estates that the Air Force had begun turning into recovery centers for its fliers. Men exhibiting more severe mental symptoms were kept on base and given doses of sodium amytal, which put them into a deep sleep for up to two days. Dr. Hastings explained the Army's widespread use of sleep treatment: "It is . . . much easier to adjust to a terrifying experience with the attitude 'it happened two days ago' than to have to immediately face the situation with all its recent memories and impressions."

Sleep therapy was followed by sympathetic talk treatment. In the majority of cases, rest alone—relief from combat—was enough to produce what the Air Force loosely called a "cure"—making the man well enough to return to combat. Fliers who continued to suffer crippling anxiety were sent to an Army hospital equipped by the CME with a special narcosis, or sleep therapy, ward. Here the patient was put into a more prolonged sleep, often up to seventy-two hours. This was, at the time, the standard treatment in civilian practice for manic depression.

In addition to sodium amytal, the Air Force used Sodium Pentothal, a so-called truth serum, to produce a state of dreamy semiconsciousness, during which doctors, in a semidarkened room, aggressively probed and provoked the patient, trying to induce him to relive the traumatic experience that had sent him into an emotional descent. The theory was that this drug-induced lowering of the patient's defenses would allow him to face, and eventually surmount, his most dreaded fears by strengthening his ego in its battle with overwhelming anxiety. The "cure" had a single aim: to get the patient back into the war.

Air Force doctors Roy Grinker and John P. Spiegel described the ag-

gressive treatment they pioneered in North Africa: "The therapist can play
the role of a fellow crewmate, calling out fighters or flak in various positions, warning of an imminent ditching or asking for help with a wounded
buddy. . . . In some men the situation is relived with such intensity that [the
patient] . . . may wander about the room as if about the plane, or, using the
pillow or bedclothes as armor plate . . . may wince and cower at flak and
cannon bursts. . . . The terror exhibited in moments of supreme danger,
such as during explosions within the plane, the falling of a plane, the muti-
lation or death of a friend before the flier's eyes, is electrifying to watch. As
the event approaches, the body becomes increasingly tense and rigid. The
eyes widen and the pupils dilate, while the skin becomes covered with fine
perspiration. The hands move about convulsively, seeking a support, a
protection, a weapon or a friend to share the danger. Breathing becomes
incredibly rapid and shallow. The intensity of the emotion sometimes becomes more than can be borne and frequently at the height of the reaction,
there is a collapse. . . . In such cases, more than one pentothal treatment
may be required, each one bringing out new pieces of repressed material."

Later in the war, when Dr. Douglas Bond replaced Hastings—who used
the same therapy as Lieutenant Colonel Grinker and Major Spiegel—as
head of CME's Psychiatric Unit, he discontinued Pentothal therapy, arguing that it produced hysterical simulations that terrified the patient, actually
worsening his anxiety. He also abandoned deep narcosis therapy with
sodium amytal after he and a colleague performed additional studies, using
as their criterion of success not the number of men who returned to combat, as Hastings had done, but the number that returned and performed
reasonably well for at least four missions. When these new criteria were
employed, the percentage of successful drug-induced treatments plummeted from 70 to 13.

When a patient completed his treatment at CME, the director of psychiatry made a recommendation—either to keep him flying or ground him—to
the Central Medical Board, made up of Air Force doctors. After the board
made its own finding, the flier was sent back to his bomber base, where his
fate was in the hands of the group commander. Of the sixty-nine men given
narcosis treatment by Hastings and his colleagues in early 1943, sixty-two
recovered or improved somewhat. But only thirty-eight of the sixty-two
were put back in the air. Most of the rest were assigned to ground duty. Patients who failed to respond to any type of therapy at CME were sent to Air
Force hospitals in the States for prolonged treatment. Here, the cure rate
improved, but only when patients were assured that they would never

again have to fly combat missions. True healing, Air Force doctors would eventually discover, only occurred "in an atmosphere of safety."

What stands out in Eighth Air Force history is not the number of men who broke in combat but the overwhelmingly larger number who did not. The most puzzling question in warfare is how fighting men stay the course. What inspires them to fight when every core instinct calls upon them to flee? What possesses rational men to act so irrationally?

If this ability to hold together in the face of peril can be called courage, what exactly is courage? "Courage," Lord Moran shrewdly observed, "is a moral quality; it is not a chance gift of nature like an aptitude for games. It is a cold choice between two alternatives, the fixed resolve not to quit; an act of renunciation which must be made not once but many times, by the power of the will. Courage is will power."

But what sustains willpower? For most Americans fighting in the air against Germany it was not deep hatred of the enemy. Studies have shown that the preponderance of airmen had only a slim comprehension of the pervasive evil of the Nazi state, and that their hatred was powerfully aroused only when friends were killed. "It was love more than hate that propelled these men," concluded Air Force psychiatrist Herbert Spiegel, who treated both fliers and infantrymen in North Africa—the love of comrades "who shared the same dangers." The group was supremely important because, initially, a fighting man confronted terror alone. As the war correspondent Eric Sevareid observed, "War happens inside a man. It happens to one man alone." Because he was alone in his fear, the man needed to be sustained by friends fighting the same inner battle.

The World War II experience of four Flying Fortress gunners illustrates the tightness of these bonds. Before going into combat, the four sergeants made a pact that if one of them got into a tight spot the others would not abandon him, "no matter what." Weeks later, when their plane was shredded by flak, the pilot ordered everyone to bail out. The top turret gunner, who had not entered the pact, parachuted out of the plane and later reported what happened before he jumped. Enemy shrapnel had jammed the release mechanism of the ball turret, trapping the gunner in his Plexiglas bubble. Unable to extricate him, the other three gunners, all of them uninjured, told their trapped friend that they would die with him. And they did.

In the plane, a collective personality, or "group ego" was formed, and if strong enough, every crewman felt emotionally sustained and protected. When it was weak, the incidence of neurotic symptoms skyrocketed. But there had to be inspired leadership to buttress morale, the most important of all the war-winning qualities. On almost every plane, the acknowledged leader was the pilot, the raft to which the rest of the crew "clung for support and for hope." How he reacted in desperate circumstances reverberated through the plane. If he was afraid, and said so, it did not matter, for all fighting men knew that fear is not cowardice. Cowardice is "something a man does. What passes though his mind is his own affair," Lord Moran wrote.

The bomb group itself performed the same integrating function as the pilot, but tribal-like loyalty rarely extended to other bomb groups. "If another group across the road suffers a big loss, the personnel say that's too bad, but it doesn't particularly shake them. They rationalize that that's what happens to groups that don't keep their heads where they belong," reported Lt. Col. John C. Flanagan, an Air Force officer who investigated morale on American air stations in England and elsewhere. Flanagan was having lunch one day with the men of an unidentified bomb group when the conversation turned to the high losses that two of the groups in its combat wing had recently suffered. One man then speculated on the effect these losses might have on his own team's chances in an Eighth Air Force basketball league. "If one more group gets hit like these other two have, we might win the [championship]."

Gallows humor was common among men living on the brink, but it did express a hard reality. War had become too personal for these men to respond to political lectures and Army morale films on fighting for freedom and country. The only speeches that mattered to men on a bomber base were the words of reassurance that pilots shared with their crews on the flight line at dawn. Men listened there, for nothing mattered more to them than the coming test in the sky.

Nothing, that is, except going home. Why do you fight? an airman was asked by Air Force psychiatrists. "So I can go home!" he shot back. In early 1943, thoughts of home could have been emotionally incapacitating to Eighth Air Force airmen had it not been for the newly established tour of duty. To some fliers, the "25" was the "single factor that bolstered their nerve," but for the "25" to really mean anything, some bomber crews had to reach that number. In the winter of 1943 none of them did.

An Unkept Promise

"Last winter was a very critical time for [the Eighth]," Haywood Hansell told Air Force intelligence officers who debriefed him on his return to

Washington in August 1943. "It looked for a while as though it might pass out of existence altogether." Living conditions magnified the gloom. "The mud was atmosphere," recalled LeMay, "you breathed it even if you didn't want to, it was under your nails, it was in the grooves of your hands." Coal, the only source of fuel, was rationed by the British government; and with merchant marine losses still running high, the food was monotonously bad, with Brussels sprouts and powdered eggs as standard fare.

On black drizzly days when they were not flying, some men stayed in bed all day, smoking, writing letters, reading, or staring at the metal ceilings of their Nissen huts. Others rode their bicycles into the local villages, to pubs where the beer was warm, the whiskey watered, but the company good. At first, mothers kept their daughters away from the brazen Yanks, but there were Land Girls everywhere, young women drafted to work on the farms of Britain. Curtis LeMay remembered his men hanging on the fences around the base, trying to strike up conversations with uniformed girls pushing wheelbarrows through the fields. "A lot of them struck up more than conversation." It didn't take long for venereal disease rates to skyrocket on the bases and in the surrounding towns. Mothers marched in protest.

Then there was London. Blacked out, bombed out, expensive, and hard to get around in, it was still magnificent—the Paris of World War II, filled with servicemen, diplomats, and reporters from every place on earth that was menaced by fascism. Worn down by losses and depression, most fliers who visited in early 1943 saw London as a release, not a city to be explored. London would be a different, more varied, place for the fliers who came after them, when the number of American soldiers increased tremendously, making the city more familiar and inviting. The men of '43 had neither the time nor the inclination to take in the sights. They were there to drink and forget, almost always in the company of women.

"If it hadn't been for London, we'd all have gone crazy," said Robert Morgan. Morgan traveled with the other officers in his crew; the enlisted men went their separate way. "This had nothing to do with rank or our feelings for one another; it was just that we were billeted separately." Eighth Air Force officers spent most of their time in the city's grand hotels, and the grandest of them all was the Savoy, the favorite watering hole of Noel Coward and Evelyn Waugh. "Tea dances were a tradition at the Savoy, and the management kept them up during wartime, even given [the] lopsided ratio of ladies to men. [We] did our best to even up that ratio," says Morgan.

They would also hit the smaller bottle clubs where patrons brought their own liquor. Liquor was hard to get in wartime Britain, but Morgan found a way. "One of our officers had a connection with the Coca-Cola company and whenever a supply of Coke was sent to Bassingbourn, he'd see to it that some Scotch was included. It went down easy, and it got you girls. Our money got 'em, too. We were paid three times what a British soldier got, and they had to resent that, especially since we used that overage to steal their women."

Eric Westman, a British serviceman during the war, remembered the first wave of the American invasion of London. "The Yanks were the most joyful thing that ever happened to British womanhood. They had *every-thing*—money in particular, glamour, boldness, cigarettes, chocolate, nylons, Jeeps—and genitalia. The Yanks were sex-mad and countless British women who had virtually no experience in this line were completely bowled off their feet (and on their back, I suppose I should add). . . . Almost every working girl aspired to 'have a Yank.'

"I think never in history has there been such a conquest of women by men as was won by the American army in Britain in World War II."

Morgan had a string of girlfriends in London whom he slept with. That he had his Memphis belle waiting at home did not bother him in the least. This was wartime and "to lie in another girl's arms for a few nights didn't strike me like the worst sin in the world."

On their trips to London, Morgan and his fellow officers occasionally had Capt. Clark Gable with them. "Everywhere we went we were mobbed by women, but Gable took it all in stride, tried to act more like an airman on leave than a Hollywood idol. That was impossible. When we'd enter a club, the bandleader, seeing Gable, would strike up a rendition of 'Wild Blue Yonder,' and beautiful girls—English, French, Belgian—would crowd around our table. It was great just being in Gable's wake—picking up the leftovers."

Some of the women were better-looking than the ones that Gable went after. Gable liked beautiful women, "but he was a sucker for anything," said his friend Jack Mahin. "[He] seemed to think he got into less trouble with the ugly ones."

When they weren't with Gable, Morgan and his three crewmates did London by themselves, even if the small train cars that took them there were packed with other GIs. "We didn't want to make friends. Having more friends was risky. With so many guys getting killed, you tried to keep down the suffering you'd have to endure. And we never talked about the folks back home, not even our wives and lovers. We talked about the plane, the engine problems we might be having, not about the problems we were having in combat. Someone listening in would have thought we were a gang of truck drivers."

The reporters had the same code. As Walter Cronkite told Harrison Salisbury when he first took him on a bomber base: "Don't make friends with the kids. . . . It's too much when they are lost, and most of them, you know, will be."

As the Eighth began flying deeper into Germany, into the massively defended Ruhr Valley, it met ever stronger fighter resistance. Göring, finally awakening to the American threat, began a shift of planes and pilots from the Eastern to the Western Front that would increase Luftwaffe fighter strength in Northern Europe from 260 in the fall of 1942 to double that number by the spring of 1943. On April 17, at Bremen, the Eighth fought the fiercest air-to-air fight of the war up to then, losing fifteen bombers to enemy fighters, twice that of any previous mission. Men who had been fine before Bremen would have laughing fits for no apparent reason. Late night drinking increased dangerously, but commanders were hesitant to shut down the base clubs; the men might mutiny. Even Clark Gable, who flew only occasionally, came close to breaking down. He would drink himself to sleep, and every now and then disappear from the base for a day or two to find refuge in a cottage near Windsor Castle owned by his friend, the actor David Niven.

When visiting a badly wounded comrade at an Air Force hospital he lost control, putting himself close to a court-martial. The ball turret gunner had been hit in nearly every part of his body and was wrapped up like a mummy. The doctor in charge, an Army colonel, told Gable the boy had only hours to live and was so numbed by morphine he would not know the actor was in the room. The surgeon described the injuries with clinical precision, pointing to each of them: lung gone, spine severed, ribs broken. Gable noticed the gunner's eyes getting moist. He grabbed the doctor's arm, pulled him into the hall, and pinned him against the wall. "If you ever do anything like that again, I'll kill you," he said.

Late that spring, Ira Eaker sent a blistering report to Hap Arnold. Eaker had been promised new crews and planes and had not received them, and his impatience boiled over into a potentially career-breaking communiqué. "The current position of the Eighth Air Force is not a credit to the American Army. After sixteen months in the war, we are not yet able to dispatch more than 123 bombers toward an enemy target. Many of the crews who fly this pitiful number have been on battle duty for eight months. They understand the law of averages. They have seen it work on their friends." The Eighth Air Force was still, he concluded, "an unkept promise."

Round-the-clock bombing, he told Arnold, was a fiction. The division of work between the Eighth and the RAF was geographical, not chronological. With a few exceptions, "they bomb Germany and we bomb France." That was because the Eighth did not yet have the strength to conduct "sustained operations over Germany." This had given Germany time to build up its fighter defenses. The enemy, he warned, may have already achieved the aerial supremacy over Northern Europe that the Allies needed to make the invasion succeed.

Eaker also worried about his crews, the 1,500 or so men who were the "blood and guts" of the Eighth Air Force. These "pioneers," the four Fortress groups that had been carrying the burden of the bombing war since November 1942—the men of the 91st, 303rd, 305th, and 306th—were desperately in need of relief. "They are battle tested. . . . They have made mistakes and overcome them. . . . [They] should be returning now, to pass on the lessons and bring back squadrons trained in our bloodily bought experience. Instead they will have to remain in dwindling numbers, until replacements as green as they once were arrive to relieve them. This is the most serious intrinsic consequence of our failure to receive the promised replacements."

Arnold had his own problems. It was not his fault, he told a colleague back in Washington, that bombers were being diverted to North Africa. In his official response to Eaker, Arnold reminded him that he had "eight mouths to feed, and that we are pushing airplanes out to all eight theaters [of the war] as fast as they are ready." Every one of these theater commanders thought the boil on his back was the biggest. Things would get better in England soon, he promised.

With morale sinking badly, Air Force public relations officers begged reporters stationed in London to come up to the bases and do more stories on the boys. "The crews wanted someone to know they were fighting and dying, and it was the PROs' job," Rooney said, "to get their names in a newspaper somewhere, anywhere." That suited Rooney, who wanted a break from writing depressing stories about men killed in combat. That spring, the most stirring story of survival in the Eighth was of a pint-sized, troublemaking sergeant in the 306th Bomb Group named "Snuffy" Smith.

Maynard Harrison Smith was with the first group of replacements to arrive that spring; and at age thirty-two, he was one of the oldest. The son of a small-town judge, he styled himself a debater and frequented the pubs around the base arguing politics with the locals. Back on base, he was forever in trouble, known to his hut mates as "a real fuckup."

Smith went on his first raid on May 1, 1943. His veteran pilot was Lt. Lewis Page Johnson, and Smith, filling in for another man, was assigned to the ball turret, even though he had never before flown in the glass bubble. Coming back from St. Nazaire the group sighted land and started to descend. "The visibility was lousy, but we were pretty happy," the co-pilot later described the scene in the plane. "All of a sudden, there was a terrific crossfire of flak, wham wham wham wham, and we were in the middle of it." They were not over England. A navigator's error had brought them over the U-boat base at Brest. Moments later, they were attacked by a swarm of Fw 190s that came ripping through the haze.

William Fahrenhold, the top turret gunner, came down and said there was "a helluva fire in the back of the ship." The interphone was shot out, so Johnson ordered him to go back and appraise the damage. When Johnson opened the forward radio compartment door, a solid wall of fire stopped him in his tracks. "The ammunition was exploding and I saw Smith walking through the fire with shell casing bouncing off his [parachute] harness."

Just before this, Smith had crawled out of his turret and found himself bestride two angry fires, both closing in on him. Sheets of flame were coming out of the radio room and there was another fire in the rear section. "Suddenly, the radio operator came staggering out of the flames," Smith later told Rooney. "He made a bee line for the gun hatch and dived out. I glanced out and watched him hit the horizontal stabilizer [the plane's tail], bounce off, and open his chute." Seconds later, the two waist gunners bailed out. Interviewed later, the pilot said he couldn't understand "why Smith stayed."

With the smoke and gas fumes making it almost impossible for him to breathe, Smith wrapped a sweater around his face, grabbed a fire extinguisher, and went to attack the fire in the radio room. "Glancing over my shoulder at the tail fire, I thought I saw something coming, and ran back. It was [Roy H.] Gibson, the tail gunner, painfully crawling back, wounded. He had blood all over him. Looking him over, I saw that he had been hit in the back and that it had probably gone through his left lung. I laid him down on his left side so the blood would not drain into the right lung, [and] gave him a shot of morphine." The first aid kits on American bombers were equipped with single-injection morphine vials. Crewmen were taught to break off the glass casing and feed the morphine into the nerve system of a wounded man by squeezing the tiny tube. It was difficult for Smith to do this with fire and freezing wind filling the plane and with the wounded man wearing heavy clothing.

After stabilizing Gibson, Smith "went back to the fires." Just then a Focke-Wulf returned to finish off his Fortress. "I jumped for one of the waist guns and fired at him . . . [then] went back to the radio room fire again. I got into the room this time and began throwing out burning debris. The fire had burned holes so large in the side of the ship that I just tossed the stuff out through them. Gas from a burning extinguisher was choking me, so I went back to the tail fire. I took off my chute so I could move easier. I'm glad I didn't take if off sooner, because later I found that it had stopped a .30 caliber bullet."

After emptying the last extinguisher, Smith urinated on the fire and tried to smother it with his hands and feet until his gloves and boots began to smolder. "That FW came around again and I let him have it. That time he left us for good. The fire was under control, more or less, and we were in sight of land."

Smith knelt down and tried to comfort the wounded tail gunner. He told him they were home clear, but he knew the tail wheel was gone and feared the shock of landing would break the Fort in half. The stubby gunner had fought the fire and the enemy alone for an hour and fifteen minutes. The full ammunition cans he tossed out of the plane weighed a hundred pounds, just thirty pounds less than he did.

With the bombers flying in close formation, the crew of the ship on Johnson's left wing, piloted by Capt. Raymond J. Check, had witnessed the scene. "We saw Smith going past the open waist through the flames to help the tail gunner. We could see the ammunition inside his ship exploding through the openings above and at the side of the radio compartment. We could see him fighting the fire and then stopping to fight off attacking enemy pilots. All this was done with the wind blowing the flames over him. That he did not lose his life by these actions is a matter entirely with his Creator."

When the battle-tough Fort landed on an emergency field near Land's End the fuselage held. "It was a miracle she didn't break in two," Smith told Air Force investigators. "I wish I could shake hands personally with the people who built her."

Snuffy's story was "a dream-come-true for public relations officers and his exploits were played up to the press to the hilt," wrote the 306th's historian. Usually, a Medal of Honor recipient was sent home to receive his award from the president, but Secretary of War Stimson was touring the airbases, and the men, it was thought, would get a boost from seeing one of the sergeants receive the nation's highest award for bravery in combat.

The day Stimson arrived in an eight-car caravan Smith was nowhere in sight. A search was quickly organized and he was found in the mess kitchen peeling potatoes. He had been assigned to KP duty for coming in late after a pass and had forgotten what time he was expected to show up for the ceremony. "He was," said his citation, "an inspiration to the armed forces of the United States." But the boys who knew him, said Rooney, never stopped thinking of him as a "fuckup." Maybe so, but this dour screw-up from Caro, Michigan, had performed what his pilot called an act of "complete self-sacrifice."

Finishing

That May more crews arrived from the States, and morale began to improve. The replacements came at exactly the right time, when losses peaked and the Eighth made its deepest penetration into northern Germany, a radius of some 460 miles, against Kiel, the raid on which Mark Mathis was killed. On May 13, with the arrival of a batch of reinforcements, the Eighth's operational strength more than doubled, from 100 to 215 crews. The pioneer groups paid a heavy price to keep the Eighth in business. In its first ten months of operations, the Eighth lost 188 heavy bombers and approximately 1,900 crewmen, not counting those dead and wounded who returned to England in their battered ships. Approximately 73 percent of the combat fliers who had arrived in England in the summer and fall of 1942 failed to complete their tour of duty. Fifty-seven percent were killed or missing in action, and another 16 percent had either been seriously wounded, killed in crashes in England, or permanently grounded by a serious physical or mental disability.

On May 29, the Eighth Air Force flew mission number 61, putting 279 heavies into the air. This ended what Eaker called the Eighth's testing period. He now had the force, he believed, to carry out his share of the round-the-clock devastation he had promised Churchill at Casablanca. That he continued to think he could do this without long-range fighter escorts is, perhaps, a testament to his hardened belief in prewar air doctrine. It was also a confidence born out of necessity, for such planes were not yet available, nor would they be arriving soon.

But at least the Air Force was finally beginning to recognize that they were necessary. Even Haywood Hansell was now pushing for the development of a long-range fighter escort. After the war, Hansell would admit that he and the other Maxwell Field air planners had been wrong to insist that the development of an effective long-range fighter was technologically unfeasible. "People like me who didn't know enough about the technical factors were weighing the technical features when we shouldn't have been. But [later] it was explained to us by engineers that it could be done, and it sounded perfectly sensible." When Robert Lovett, assistant secretary of war for air, returned from a tour of English bases in June 1943, he urged Hap Arnold, who had just returned to duty following a heart attack in May, his second that year, to give immediate attention to the production of a long-range escort. Arnold then wrote what one historian has called his most important memo of the entire war. It was to his chief of staff, Maj. Gen. Barney Giles. Lovett's report, Arnold wrote, underlined "the absolute necessity for building a fighter airplane that can go in and out with the bombers. Moreover, this fighter has got to go into Germany. . . . About six months remain before deep penetration of Germany begins. Within the next six months, you have to get a fighter that can protect our bombers. Whether you use an existing type or have to start from scratch is your problem. Get to work on this right away."

Arnold's urgency was commendable; his projected timing lamentable. Eaker would have his unprotected bombers over German cities that summer.

In his memorandum, Arnold did not even mention the P-51 Mustang, the fighter plane that would turn the tide of the air war, nor did he sufficiently prod the production teams in charge of the fighter escort project. It was Giles who began riding herd on engineers and aircraft designers who began attacking the problem. Giles was told, however, that the Mustang would not be ready until the end of the year. Until then, the bombers would have to rely on the new barrel-nosed P-47 Thunderbolts that began escorting them that May, replacing the Spitfires. The 56th Fighter Group, led by Maj. Hubert "Hub" Zemke, the group that would escort the bombers back from the Münster mission the following October, was a crack unit, highly trained and motivated. However, its heavily armed Thunderbolts, each equipped with eight .50 caliber guns—could cover the bombers only to the German border.

Back in the 1930s, Harold George, the chief theorist of bomber warfare, had told his students, men who would fight the next air war: "The spectacle of huge air forces meeting in the air is the figment of imagination of the uninitiated." Beginning in the early summer of 1943, the American heavies

Ira C. Eaker, head of the Eighth Air Force Bomber Command, meets with reporters on August 17, 1942, after flying as an observer on the Eighth's first heavy bombing mission of the war.

Carl Spaatz, senior U.S. air officer in Europe, speaks to Eighth Air Force commanders. On his left is Jimmy Doolittle, Eighth Air Force Commander, and William E. Kepner, Eighth Air Force Fighter Commander. On Spaatz's right is Frederick L. Anderson, his deputy for operations.

Gen. Henry "Hap" Arnold, Commanding General of the Army Air Forces (right), meets with Jimmy Doolittle in England.

Squadron leaders and inseparable friends John "Bucky" Egan (left) and Gale "Buck" Cleven of the Hundredth Bomb Group.

The Hundredth's inspirational leader, Robert "Rosie" Rosenthal, recovers from injuries sustained when he was shot down over France.

Members of the 826th Aviation Engineer Battalion use a paving machine to construct an airfield in East Anglia. By 1944, there were over 12,000 African-American Air Force personnel in England.

Most Eighth Air Force bases were built on farmland in eastern England.

Luftwaffe ace Klaus Mietusch, commander of a squadron of JG 26, one of the Reich's front line defensive units against the Eighth Air Force. He was shot down and killed on September 17, 1944.

Adolf Galland, head of the German Fighter Arm.

Haywood "Possum" Hansell, Jr. (left), one of the Air Force's key prewar planners, with Curtis E. LeMay, an air leader distrustful of classroom theory.

A B-17 bombardier at his position above the chin turret, his Norden bombsight in front of him.

Hundreds of crippled bombers were forced down in the North Sea. The crew of the Liberator *Lorelei* (458th Bomb Group) wears their inflatable "Mae West" life preservers.

Ball turret gunner Maynard H. "Snuffy" Smith saved his crew on his very first mission. He received the Congressional Medal of Honor from Secretary of War Henry L. Stimson.

Clark Gable, Hollywood actor and Eighth Air Force gunner, with the crew of *Delta Rebel No. 2* (91st Bomb Group) after returning from a mission.

Sgt. Benedict B. Borostowski tests the equipment in his ball turret underneath the Fortress.

The crew of the *Memphis Belle,* led by Capt. Robert Morgan (front, left), return from their twenty-fifth mission on May 17, 1943. They were the first Eighth Air Force crew to complete their required twenty-five missions and return to the United States. Hollywood director William Wyler flew with them and produced the famous film documentary *The Memphis Belle.*

would meet the greatly augmented Luftwaffe in massed aerial battles "never before equaled—and, it seems probable, never to be equaled again."

In April 1943, just as the buildup for this new air war began, twenty-year-old radio gunner Michael Roscovich, who had flown with the crews of several planes, became the first flier to complete twenty-five missions. He had planned to bail out over the field, but high winds and angry orders from the tower stopped him. When his ship came to a stop on the runway, the crew tore off his clothes and painted "25 MISSIONS" in large letters on his back. "Rosky" then grabbed the nearest bike and rode around the base in his underwear.

By early May, a number of Fortresses and their regular crews were closing in on "25." *Hell's Angels, Delta Rebel II, Jersey Bounce, Connecticut Yankee,* and *Memphis Belle*. The first of these to do it was *Hell's Angels,* on May 14. But Willy Wyler, with connections to the top, made sure that the *Memphis Belle* got the most notice when its crew finished its tour of duty three days later.

Morgan's crew flew that final raid, a run to Lorient, as though it was "just another day at the office," but when they reached the Channel and spotted the White Cliffs of Dover, the men "went crazy." They were all over the plane, hugging and slapping one another on the back, shouting and singing. Colonel Wray, the group commander, radioed the other planes to land before the *Belle,* so it could have the Hollywood finale Wyler wanted. Coming in, Morgan buzzed the field. "I gave it a grass-cutting you couldn't get these days with a Lawnboy."

"The whole base was going wild when the *Belle* finally taxied up to its mark and I cut the engines. Men were cheering, throwing their hats in the air, rushing toward us. Somebody with a movie camera got a great shot of waist gunner Bill Winchell looking out his window, a grin plastered all over his skinny face, making that little spiral motion with his hand to signal that he'd knocked down a fighter." One of the crew jumped out and kissed the ground, and Morgan was lifted up so he could plant a kiss on the sexy lady on the *Belle*'s nose. Wyler fought his way through the crowd and congratulated Morgan. Turning to him, Morgan asked what he would have done if the *Belle* had crashed. "No problem," Wyler said. "We have plenty of film on *Hell's Angels.*"

The next month, Morgan and nine other crewmen, not the original crew, but men picked by the Eighth Air Force from the larger group that had flown on the *Belle,* returned to the United States for a barnstorming tour of thirty-one cities. Eaker and Arnold saw the tour as a way of boosting home support for the beefed-up bombing campaign the Eighth was about to launch that summer. In a deftly deceptive publicity release, Air Force public relations writers failed to make it clear that the *Belle* was not the first bomber in the Eighth to complete twenty-five missions, or that all the men on tour had not flown on all twenty-five missions. Few crewmen in the Eighth flew all their missions on the same plane.

When the tour was completed in December, Bob Morgan got married, but not to Margaret Polk, his Memphis belle. Their relationship was torn apart by the pressing demands of the Air Force's public relations tour. Morgan's new wife was Dotty Johnson, a hometown girl he met on his war bond tour. After the wedding, Morgan was sent to Pratt Army Air Base in Kansas to train on the new B-29 Superfortresses the Air Force planned to send to the Pacific the following year. Transferred to the Mariana Islands in the fall of 1944, Morgan's first commander would be Haywood Hansell; his next, Curtis LeMay. And the plane he would fly from Saipan on the first B-29 raid on Tokyo was called *Dauntless Dotty.*

After completing his filming at Bassingbourn, William Wyler flew one more mission, his fifth, which he needed to qualify for an Air Medal. "I almost didn't come back," he told an interviewer. "It was a stupid thing to go on." Friends said he was more proud of that decoration than of any of the movie awards he received.

That summer, Clark Gable continued to fly missions and shoot film for his documentary. In late October, he returned to the States to edit his 5,000 feet of film. The Air Force was relieved to see him go. "He's scaring the hell out of us," one of his commanders had told the director Frank Capra, in London on a film assignment. "He's trying to get himself killed." When he returned to Washington, Arnold told him there was no reason to finish the film. The Air Force now had all the gunners it needed, thanks to a massive recruiting drive, aided by Gable's own example. Gable went ahead and completed the film anyway. He showed it on the war bond drives he continually volunteered for until he was discharged from the Army after D-Day, still disappointed that he had not been given another front-line assignment. *Combat America* is a clumsily edited effort, but it is the only film on the Eighth in which the sergeant gunners speak for themselves and it has some of the finest action footage of the air war.

William Wyler, on the other hand, crafted a masterwork of war reportage and propaganda. After completing the forty-one-minute documentary in April 1944, he arranged for a White House viewing. The president sat next to him in a wheelchair during the showing. When the lights were turned on, Roosevelt leaned over and said to Wyler, "This has to be shown right away, everywhere." Paramount Pictures distributed it to theaters across the country and it received sensational reviews. One of them appeared on the front page of the *New York Times,* a first for the newspaper. The *Times* film critic, Bosley Crowther, called it "a story that every American should know."

Wyler didn't get all the facts right. The film is about a raid on Wilhelmshaven on May 15, when actually the *Memphis Belle*'s target that day was Heligoland, a tiny island off the north German coast; and there were not, as Wyler's narrator claims, a thousand Allied planes in the air that day. But in every other way, the film is absolutely authentic in its portrayal of bomber warfare.

After being nearly drummed out of the Army for slugging a bellman who made an anti-Semitic remark in his presence, Wyler made another film for the Air Force, *Thunderbolt.* In 1946, he rounded out his film coverage of the war with his masterwork, *The Best Years of Our Lives,* a depiction of three servicemen's traumatic collision with peacetime America. One of them, played by Dana Andrews, is a returning bombardier. It is a film Wyler could never have made had he not seen warfare up close in the skies over Europe. For him, the war had been, as he once said, "an escape to reality." On an airbase in England, "the only thing that mattered were human relationships; not money, not position, not even family. Only relationships with people who might be dead tomorrow were important. It is a sort of wonderful state of mind. It's too bad it takes a war to create such a condition among men."

As the pioneers headed home in the early summer of 1943, they sailed through seas largely cleared of the U-boat menace they had tried to eliminate. That spring, the U-boat had been defeated in one of the most sudden and dramatic turnarounds of World War II. In May, the Allies gained supremacy in the Atlantic, sinking forty-one U-boats, more than they had sunk in the first three years of the war. The Nazis would call it Black May, and at the end of the month Admiral Dönitz pulled his boats from the North Atlantic and put them in safer waters. "We had lost the Battle of the Atlantic," he privately admitted.

In the next several months, sixty-two convoys of merchant ships crossed the Atlantic without losing a single ship. That, and a tremendous increase in American production of merchant ships, had a huge impact on the air war. Bomber crews continued to fly across the Atlantic, many of them taking a new southern route in midwinter that took them over the tip of Brazil and the Azores, but ships carrying air gunners, repair crews, control tower operators, intelligence experts, and tens of thousands of other service personnel arrived safely over sea routes that had been hugely dangerous earlier in the year. Liberty Ships, their holds bursting with aviation fuel, airplane parts, and fighter planes, nosed into Britain's ports every week. Churchill and Roosevelt both breathed a little easier as one of the two great menaces to an amphibious invasion had been all but eliminated. Now the Allied air forces could focus entirely on the Luftwaffe and the industries that supported it.

The U-boat had been defeated not by the bombing of its lairs and assembly plants, but by new advances in the technology and tactics of antisubmarine warfare, among them the interception and decoding of German naval message traffic and the assembly of enormous convoys protected by fast destroyers equipped with underwater detection and killing equipment. It was the airplane, however, that became the U-boat's deadliest foe. B-24 Liberators hunted down the wolf packs far out at sea, and lighter aircraft, flying from escort carriers, finished them off.

Bombing the U-boat pens had been a wasteful exercise. In the first quarter of 1943, over 63 percent of the bombs dropped by the Eighth, and 30 percent by the RAF, had been directed at U-boat facilities. Allied air commanders knew they were not destroying the concrete pens, but incomplete intelligence led them to grossly overestimate the effect of the damage they inflicted on support services outside the pens, and on submarine construction facilities inside Germany. This led Adm. Ernest King, the American naval chief, to continue to put heavy pressure on both Marshall and Roosevelt to keep hitting the Biscay bases.

Ira Eaker tried to put the best face on these misguided missions, arguing that the Eighth first learned how to fight a war at high altitude over Lorient and St. Nazaire, and that crews coming later would profit from the experience of these men. "Maybe so," Robert Morgan observed years later, "but we could have been hitting other targets and learning the same lessons."

Interviewed after the war, Gen. Laurence Kuter, who directed these operations in late 1942, called them "an inexcusable waste of strategic air strength. . . . We wasted men, great numbers of fine men, and lots of talent, and accomplished nothing. We sprayed bombs all over . . . the Brest peninsula where we killed more French than Germans." The Luftwaffe did "their fighter training around those submarine pens. They moved in squadron after squadron and had over a hundred batteries of antiaircraft artillery. It was target practice for the Germans; we were the targets. . . .

"I did what I could to point out those facts and correct this misuse of the 1st Bombardment Wing with no success at all, due, I am sure, to the persuasive nature of Admiral King's position and the cold fact that we might lose the war to the submarines." Looking back, Kuter felt he could have tried harder to stop these raids, and to redirect the bombing toward Hamburg, a major submarine manufacturing center. "I got told I was 'crying.' I was supposed to perform a mission."

In his final report before leaving England for North Africa, Kuter had pointed out that the Eighth was "not picking war-winning objectives," but when the Eighth did focus on Hamburg that summer with far greater force than it was able to mount in late 1942, the Germans rebuilt their U-boat yards in an astonishingly short period of time. The fact is that the Eighth Air Force did not have sufficient bombers in its first year of operations to seriously hurt Germany, no matter where it struck.

An argument can be made that the Eighth should not have begun operations until it had the strength to strike a telling blow, overwhelming the German air defenses before they were able to recover from the initial surprise. But nearly every commander in the Eighth would have opposed such a strategy in the fall of 1942, fearing that delay threatened the very existence of the depleted Eighth. And these men were soldiers, after all, men bred to believe that wars are lost by waiting.

Laurence Kuter's sympathies went out to the crews. "It was a heartbreaking job" flying missions "they knew would be failures. They couldn't hit their damn targets. And if they hit their targets, they wouldn't hurt them. And still, they'd take off on every mission. That is the greatest example of leadership that I can attribute to any military organization at any time."

The first men were going home and new men were coming in, but some of those who completed their "25" never got an opportunity to see their families. Dissatisfied with his work as a gunnery instructor, Mike Roscovich of Fayette City, Pennsylvania, joined another aircrew and was killed in a crash landing. And then there was Capt. Raymond Check of Minot, North Dakota, and the 306th Bomb Group, the pilot who had seen Snuffy Smith putting out the fires in his Fortress. His story is further proof, as Andy Rooney wrote, that "happy endings were rare" on air stations in England.

On June 26, 1943, Captain Check took off on his twenty-fifth mission, in the Fortress *Chennault's Pappy III*. It was to be a milk-run, a quick jump over the Channel to an airfield in France, and his squadron mates had planned a big party for him that evening. On this special day, Check was the co-pilot. Lt. Col. James W. Wilson, Check's original squadron commander, was in the left seat. He had come back to Thurleigh to fly with his friend on his last haul. Lt. William Cassedy, Check's regular co-pilot and his good buddy, flew as a waist gunner.

On the final seconds of the bomb run, German fighters came straight out of the sun and the crew failed to see them until it was too late. A 20mm cannon shell hit Check in the neck and exploded, killing him instantly. A fire started in the cockpit and Wilson tried but failed to put it out with his hands. Just before they were hit, he had been having problems with the engines and had taken off his gloves to make an adjustment. With oxygen leaking from punctured oxygen tanks, the fire turned into an inferno. Another crewman got the fire under control with an extinguisher. Wilson tried to control the Fort "with his arms above the elbow." He was in terrible pain; the rubber on his oxygen mask was melting on his badly scorched face, and his hands were almost without skin.

Just then, a machine gun bullet hit the box behind the pilot's seat where the flares were stored. The flares exploded and the concussion blew open the bomb bay doors and started another fire. Someone rang the alarm bell, the signal to bail out. Lt. Lionel Drew, the bombardier, bailed out, but Cassedy told the men in the rear to wait until he investigated. The plane was holding altitude and there appeared to be no engine damage. Cassedy crawled to the cockpit and pulled back in horror when he saw Check's head dangling from his neck by a few strands of bloody sinew, and Wilson flying the plane with his elbows, with black pieces of flesh hanging from his hands. When Wilson pulled the oxygen mask off his burned face, he went below for medical assistance. A visiting flight surgeon, Maj. George L. Peck, had "hitched a ride" to get some combat experience.

No one was manning the guns. Everyone was hurt except Cassedy and Peck. There were flak holes all over the fuselage and there was a hole in the dorsal fin.

After Major Peck dressed and bandaged Wilson's hands, Wilson went back to the cockpit but was in too much pain to help. With the assistance of the navigator, Lt. Milton P. Blanchette, who was also on his twenty-fifth mission, Lieutenant Cassedy brought the ship home. He stared straight ahead, trying not to look at the bloody stump where his friend's head should have been.

Without its flares, and with the radio shot out, the plane was unable to signal that there were wounded and dead aboard.

Cassedy was supposed to land the plane into the wind. Instead, he landed downwind and against incoming traffic, a dangerous maneuver. It was an entirely personal decision. He knew that Check's girlfriend, an

American nurse, would be waiting for him in a jeep at the end of the main runway. They were to be married the next day. "We couldn't bring her in that way with his head blown off," Blanchette told Andy Rooney late in both their lives, "so we come in with the wind on our tail. She never saw him. Good thing."

CHAPTER SIX

Teach Them to Kill

"All wars are . . . fought by boys."

HERMAN MELVILLE, "THE MARCH INTO VIRGINIA"

Firth of Clyde, August 17, 1942

On this bright northern morning, as Paul Tibbets and the crews at Grafton Underwood were preparing for the Eighth's first bombing strike of the war, a tremendous troop convoy was steaming across the Irish Sea toward the Firth of Clyde, the entranceway to the port of Glasgow. It was in calm, protected waters now, after twelve tension-crowded days on the stormy, U-boat-infested North Atlantic. By now, the marathon poker and dice games had ended, along with the daily debates among the men about where they were headed—to Greenland or Iceland, to Russia or North Africa. It was England, they had been told that morning.

One of the lead ships of the convoy was the *Monterey,* a converted pleasure liner stripped of its luxuries and painted a drab military gray. When it reached the Firth of Clyde, Sgt. Robert S. Arbib, Jr., sneaked up unnoticed to the sundeck, reserved for officers only. As the ship made its way toward the narrow waters that ran into the heart of Glasgow, Arbib hung on the rail, transfixed. Just ahead, high in the sky, were enormous barrage balloons, tied by threadlike cables to barges in the river, and in the distance was a rusty freighter with a gaping torpedo hole at its waterline. Everything in the harbor was camouflaged in faded shades of green—the factories, workshops, and water tanks that lined the river, even the warships resting at anchor. And everywhere there was bomb damage, blasted and black-ened buildings and shattered bricks and paving stones piled as high as houses. The Americans had entered a war zone and suddenly it got strangely quiet on the open deck of the *Monterey,* 4,000 men trying to peer ahead into their uncertain future in this strange northern land, in the im-mense war they knew so little about.

As they passed a wall of red-faced factories near the harbor town of Greenock, whistles shrieked and workers poured out and began waving at them. The Americans hung over the decks and out the portholes, tossing oranges, apples, and cigarettes to British soldiers standing below.

"Where are we?" a GI cried out to a British sergeant.

"Glazzga," answered the native.

"When does the next boat sail for America?" shouted Arbib's friend, Johnny Ludwig.

"Canna taell ye thot," answered another Scotsman, his hands cupped around his mouth. "Bu' ah can taell ye thus . . . yew'll no' be on ut!"

And with that, the debarkation order was given and the GIs marched down the gangplank with their eighty-pound packs and headed through the cobblestone streets to a spacious park, where they were to spend the night in tents. As the battalions paraded through the city in disorderly fash-ion, waving to the young girls on the sidewalks, a group of excited children followed them, giving the "V" sign and begging for candy and chewing gum. "Got any gum, chum?"

When the column swung around a corner, Arbib stumbled and dropped a large bundle he was carrying, bound with cord, containing cartons of cigarettes and packets of pipe tobacco. Determined not to lose the last American tobacco he might see for a while, he kicked the boxes out of the way of the marching columns and stepped out of line. As he crouched in the street, picking up his "scattered prizes," his equipment—rifle, gas mask, pack, blanket, and overcoat—began falling all over the place. "The Scottish audience," he recalled, "was polite but amused." The world-saving Americans had arrived, and they looked and acted like a gang of boys.

Most of them were regular Army, and thousands would be shipped out to North Africa that November as part of the invasion armada of Operation Torch. But Arbib's 820th Engineer Aviation Battalion had come to Britain not to prepare to fight, but to prepare the airfields for the bomber boys who would begin arriving in greatly increasing numbers in the late spring of

1943. It was then that the American Air Force began the staggering buildup that would put nearly half a million of its personnel—two-thirds of its combat strength worldwide—in the United Kingdom on the eve of the Normandy invasion. By then there would be forty heavy bombardment groups in England, a total combat fleet of 3,000 Forts and Liberators, most of them based in the adjoining East Anglian counties of Norfolk and Suffolk.

When the first large group of Eighth Air Force replacements began arriving in May and June of 1943, the months that Robert Morgan and Raymond Check flew their final missions, almost all of them would be stationed on new bases built by civilian workers employed by the British Ministry of Works. But with the arrival of Robert Arbib's unit, American engineering battalions would begin constructing ten additional air stations, to be completed later that year. One of them was at Debach (pronounced Deb'-itch), a short distance from the North Sea. It was there that Robert Arbib's battalion was headed by rail on the morning after it arrived at Glasgow, prepared to join the biggest civil works project in the history of Great Britain. It was a project that had none of the glory and gore of the air war, but one that would help reverse the course of that war within a war and forever change the lives and land in a largely undisturbed corner of England—a place of rural splendor and welcoming pubs, greatly loved by Keats.

"Our official welcome to England did not come until our third night at Debach . . . when we decided to wander, against strict regulations, into the countryside, and see what this England was like," Robert Arbib wrote in the observant book of memories he composed during the war. At the time, his battalion was camped in tents on the site of the aerodrome they had been sent to build—a flat, rounded hilltop with narrow roads that wound down from it in all directions. The curving lanes cut between high hedgerows and ran past fields of wheat, sugar beets, and potatoes, perfectly defined squares bordered by hedges and split-rail fences. Hidden behind the hedges were thatched-roof cottages draped with rose vines. Standing at their low front gates—set between the hedges—farmers and their wives nodded to Arbib and six of his mates as they made their way down to the village of Grundisburgh. Reaching the village center, built around a handsome triangular green, they crossed a wooden bridge that led to the door of the local public house, the Dog.

Entering the dark, wood-beamed pub, they found it nearly empty. The only customers were some ancient-looking regulars in the back room smoking their pipes and speaking slowly in an incomprehensible local dialect. To Robert Arbib, a fast-talking New Yorker, "the conversation bordered on paralysis in social intercourse." One of his friends whispered, "I thought these people were supposed to speak English."

After a quick look around, the soldiers bellied up to the bar and ordered some beers. "Is this American money any good?" the red-faced publican, a pleasant fellow named Watson, inquired. They discussed this and Watson, after some counsel from his wife, offered them an exchange rate of four shillings to the dollar, agreeing to repay them later if the exchange was higher. When they put the bulky coins in their pockets they felt as if they were listing leeward.

They tried the bitter, the brown ale, and the stout, before settling on the drink of the evening, a light ale that was the only variety that put a head on the glass. "They're all about the same now," Watson commented dryly. "War-time quality, you know, pretty weak."

It was Saturday evening, and around seven the pub began to fill up. A girl named Molly began playing an antiquated upright piano, and the beer began to disappear faster and "with less philosophy." Word had spread through the village that some Americans were in the Dog and by eight o'clock the place was packed and the air was thick with pipe smoke and lies. "Everyone was shouting, everyone was singing and milling about, holding hands full of glasses over their heads as they pushed through the crowd. The word 'Yanks' was on everyone's lips," Arbib recalled. Most of the conversation was about the airfield, which would bring yet more Americans to Grudisburgh, bomber boys to pay back the Jerries for smashing great sections of Ipswich, a port center a few miles to the south.

Late in the evening, Johnny Ludwig, a wild boy from Philadelphia, began grinning at a tall, cross-eyed girl sitting across the room, who smiled back at him invitingly. An old village woman sitting next to Johnny spotted the exchange and leaned into his ear. "Stay away from that hussy. . . . She's got a bad name and a bad reputation. Went bad almost the day her husband went away to the Middle East. I know. I'm her mother-in-law."

Johnny and his mates were buying for everybody. The last order they put in was for forty-seven drinks. That, Watson announced, was a record for the Dog. At that point, tall, skinny Tom Stinson, the battalion's chief surveyor, climbed up on an oak table, called for silence, and launched into a boozy speech, starting off, incredibly, with "Friends, Britons, and countrymen!" He staggered and swayed and knocked over a few of Watson's closely guarded beer glasses but somehow managed to finish. As he did, a sonorous voice cut through the din. "Time, please, Gentlemen!" Watson announced. "Hurry up, please, it's Time!"

Positioning themselves at the door of the Dog, Arbib and his mates said so long to their new friends. The next morning, none of them remembered how they got back, through the pitch-dark country lanes, to their tent city on the hill.

The following Tuesday, when they returned to the Dog, there was a sign on the door—"No Beer." The inn was closed for the night, the first time in its 450-year history.

Gypsy-Builders

Building a bomber base was a prodigious undertaking. It involved constructing miles of concrete runways, scores of brick and wooden buildings, hundreds of corrugated iron Quonset huts, and steel hangars the size of football fields. As a historian of the region noted, the construction of a heavy bomber base typically meant "clearing eight miles of hedgerow and 1,500 trees, excavating 400,000 cubic yards of soil, and then laying down ten miles of roads, twenty miles of drains, ten miles of conduit, six miles of water mains and four miles of sewers. The runways required 175,000 cubic yards of concrete, the buildings four and half million bricks, and the circulating areas 32,000 square yards of tarmac." At Debach, the war-rushed project of the American engineers came at a heavy cost: the destruction of a splendid stretch of countryside that Arbib, a former biology student, loved to explore on foot. There was no time to work around nature; everything in an area surveyed and staked had to yield to earth-leveling machines that would clear the way for the city-leveling bombers. Centuries-old cottages that stood in the way of the advancing ribbons of concrete were pulled down with chains and crushed into powder by thundering American machines bigger and noisier than any land vehicles the locals had ever seen before. "It was as if a flood had risen and hidden a beautiful landscape, and then subsided, leaving a desolate waste land where there was no life and no motion," Arbib wrote in his diary.

The farmers protested, some of them chasing Army surveyors away with shotguns, but were powerless to stop the Yankee juggernaut that put the soil they drew their living from under eight inches of concrete. "They didn't take kindly to us Americans moving in and tearing up their countryside," observed Bill Ong of the 862nd Engineers, who were building a base at the same time at Glatton, in the neighboring county of Huntingdonshire. What Arbib wanted to tell the protesting farmers at Debach—but never managed to—was that the forward crush of the battalion's work was going to turn the Allied wheel of war from defense to offense, help crush the Germans, and bring their sons home from fields afar.

Work went forward on the Debach airfield through the wet, bitterly cold winter. Here, and at over a hundred other war-related construction sites north and east of London, it was a battle against the mud. "English mud," wrote Air Force historians, "is infinite in its variety and ranges from watery slop to a gelatinous mass with all the properties of quick-setting cement." With the trees stripped of their leaves, the land scraped raw, and the days short and sunless, some of the men wondered "why the Germans wanted England at all!"

The American papers lauded the building of the bases as a fabulous war-winning exercise. "Across the green fields of England, from before dawn to late at night, U.S. engineers are pouring concrete and steel and sweat into one of the most gigantic building projects ever undertaken anywhere," reported *Stars and Stripes*. But there was no romance in the hard, dispiriting work, and morale was difficult to sustain. The Americans lived in tents or in Nissen huts heated by coal fires that were always inadequate. They worked in two ten-hour shifts, with their meals brought to them in the field to save time. Work began before it was "light enough to see," and all through the day "a constant stream of trucks, driven by civilians, and loaded with gravel, sand, cement, [and] rubble from bombed cities . . . rumbled along the narrow lanes and deposited their loads in the stockpiles that rose like small hills on the landscape." Cranes as tall as local church steeples loaded the battalion's trucks, which dumped their loads into an enormous paving machine. Crews were able to lay a half-mile of runway a day. By D-Day, one engineering unit in England had poured enough concrete to build a two-lane highway across the Channel and had laid enough brick to build the tallest skyscraper in the world.

The hardest assignment was the cement gang. Men stood all day on a wooden platform and emptied hundred-pound bags of cement into trucks that passed by, one every monotonous minute. Billowing cement dust blew in their faces, penetrated their clothing, and burrowed deep into their skin, turning the men into "gray-green, ghostly automatons." Some soldiers grew long, bushy beards to keep the dust off their faces. Asked by a reporter from *Yank* to describe his work, an enlisted man spat out: "Call us mules and you got the story."

Late one afternoon at Glatton, as the black-booted crews were laying a runway, a shot-up Fortress flying on one engine came into view, looking for a place to crash-land. "We watched him go down behind the trees, and everybody started running as the plane disappeared," Bill Ong remembered. When Ong arrived at the smoking wreckage, every member of the crew was soaked in blood. "The meat wagon and fire trucks all came . . . and everything went quiet as all those poor guys were taken to sick bay. Suddenly all the mud and cold and rain and damp that we had had to endure seemed pretty small beer."

By June 1943, the month the crew of *Memphis Belle* left Bassingbourn for home, 13,500 American troops were working at construction sites all over eastern England. They were joined by 32,000 civilian workers—a number of them women—recruited from as far as Wales, Scotland, and Northern Ireland. The men lived in special camps; the women were recruited from local homes.

Like servicemen everywhere, the engineering battalions lived for their leave time. On Saturdays they shed their muddy work fatigues, slipped into clean dress uniforms, and descended on Ipswich in a long line of trucks for "an evening of come-what-may." Even on less raucous evenings back at Debach, they were not an easy bunch for the local sheriff—known to all as Mr. Moody—to handle, a rowdy gang of 700 men, many of them recruited by the Army from the most dangerous jobs in America. There were ironworkers who had hoisted steel for the silver towers of Manhattan and lumberjacks who had felled towering pines in the Michigan wilderness. "There were incidents in the meadows and behind the hay-stacks at night, and angry parents and sad girls to be somehow straightened out," Arbib recalled. "There were the big speedy American trucks careening over the narrow one-way lanes, and that meant accidents. There were the men who went down the hill to 'The Dog,' or 'The Crown,' or 'The Turk's Head,' and who could not quite find their way home. But Mr. Moody carried on, and brought his soft-spoken, polite patience to bear, and somehow things went more smoothly for it."

In time, most of the people in the community embraced the boys on the hill. Families invited them into their homes for Sunday dinner and a few fathers allowed them to date their unmarried daughters. Some of the Yanks, in turn, came to like England. "We couldn't help it," says Arbib.

At other construction sites, special gestures helped to appease the locals. Bill Ong's outfit threw a big Christmas bash for the children of the village and, by special invitation, their big sisters. Two huts were turned into a dance hall, an Air Force band was brought in, parachutes were hung from the ceiling, the cookhouse boys made ice cream, and boxes of candy were ordered from central supply. It was at this party that the local girls found out that the grimy engineers they would watch in the fields could dance like the Americans they had seen in the movies. "Jitterbugging was something strange to these country girls," Bill Ong recalled, "but, hell, they soon learned to spin and turn and leap along with the best of them. Earlier we had sat down 200 kids and they had a real Christmas party—with Father Christmas arriving on a bulldozer decorated for the occasion. They all had presents. It was quite a sight to see married guys, who were separated from their own kids by the war, squatting down and helping these British youngsters unwrap their presents. Friendships started on that day which were to last long after the war ended, and when the trucks queued up outside the huts to take everybody home it was as though all the bad feelings of before had never existed."

There would be more problems, most of them sexual, and some of them handled clumsily by Army officials. Several weeks after the Christmas party at Glatton, a few local girls showed up at the office of the commanding officer. They had gotten drunk and pregnant at the party and couldn't remember "what had happened—or with whom." The commanding officer organized a relief fund, with each soldier in camp ordered to contribute $10 a week until the guilty parties came forward. The men eventually turned themselves in to the battalion chaplain, who somehow talked them into agreeing to marry the girls. "No dice," declared the commanding officer. "Those guys were drunk and didn't know they were going to make themselves fathers—better that they're moved out of sight." The guilty parties were transferred to another post, and the girls, one of them barely sixteen, never saw them again.

"The Army engineer," wrote *Yank* correspondent Saul Levitt, "is a gypsybuilder. He builds and then he moves." In April 1943, when winter finally released its grip, Robert Arbib's battalion was transferred to nearby Wattisham to convert a Royal Air Force facility into an American fighter base. An African-American engineering battalion was brought in to finish the work at Debach. By then, the Eighth Air Force had nearly fifty air stations, enough to handle the new bomb groups, reconnaisance outfits, and supply units that had begun to flow into England. In mid-June, there were over 100,000 American airmen in the United Kingdom, up from 30,000 the previous December. By D-Day there would be an airbase every eight miles, on average, in East Anglia. This friendly invasion was the largest influx of foreigners that Britain had experienced until then; with the exception of London and large ports like Liverpool, there were no sizable groups of foreign immigrants anywhere in homogeneous Britain.

"We went to our local pub, the Green Man, and there they all were," an Englishwoman remembered. "If they'd dropped from Mars we couldn't

have been more surprised." Some proper Britons were scandalized by
their appearance. "The motley crew that descended had to be seen to be
believed," a British soldier described a group of American airmen who arrived at Buttonwood, a big supply and maintenance center. "They had all
manner of clothes on . . . topped with all sorts of hats [and] caps . . . and
what shocked us was the array of sports gear they had brought with them.
There were golf clubs, baseball bats, fishing tackle, footballs, and all manner of things guaranteed to make any sportsman blissfully happy. One
couldn't help wondering, in our fun-starved island, which they had come
to do, help with a war or compete in a World's Sports Competition?"

Their numbers were overwhelming. East Anglia was a self-contained
province of just 1.7 million people, with only four urban centers, Norwich,
Ipswich, Cambridge, and Colchester, the oldest town in England. Soon,
the Americans came to outnumber the villagers who lived by their bases
by as much as a hundred to one, and in no time changed the character and
color of these once unhurried places. "Nothing in their lives causes them to
examine their established habits and beliefs," a prewar observer described
the inward-looking character of East Anglia's people. With the departure
of the construction battalions and the arrival of tens of thousands of American flyboys, settled ways were threatened. Americans packed the trains,
the pubs, and the movie houses, the pace of life quickened, and people's
expectations were no longer as meager as their income. "Even the sky
ceased to be peaceful," wrote Roger A. Freeman, a schoolboy at the time
who would spend much of the rest of his life producing books about the
Eighth Air Force.

Pointblank

On June 10, 1943, the European air war entered a new phase. It was the official beginning of the Combined Bomber Offensive, code-named Pointblank. This was to be the fulfillment of the pledge made at Casablanca by
Roosevelt and Churchill to launch a "round-the-clock" Anglo-American
bombing effort to pave the way for the great invasion. In May 1943, at the
Trident Conference in Washington, the Combined Chiefs of Staff—made
up of the top military leaders in Britain and the United States—had provi-
sionally scheduled the cross-Channel invasion of Hitler's Fortress Europe
for May 1, 1944, and linked the Allied bomber campaign directly to that invasion, code-named Overlord. The Pointblank directive made the German
air force—its combat aircraft as well as the industries that produced them—

the single most important target of the CBO. Only when the German air force was weakened to the point where it posed no threat to the land invasion would the Anglo-American air forces be released to begin the systematic bombing of Germany's other essential industries.

Some of the bomber barons had an agenda of their own. Arthur Harris, an impossible man for the British Air Ministry to control because he was doing so much apparent—and applauded—damage to the enemy, would continue his "city-busting" campaign, virtually ignoring Pointblank until Eisenhower finally brought him into line in the months before D-Day. Nor would Harris closely coordinate his efforts with the Eighth Air Force. As the term CBO unwittingly indicated, it would be a combined, not an integrated, bombing offense.

Spaatz, too, had his own agenda but was not as insistent in pursuing it. Although he was still in the Mediterranean Theater, he had Arnold's ear, and hence influence on air operations all over Europe. He continued to believe that a land invasion could be avoided if Allied bombers were sent in force against vital industries like oil and steel upon which the German war economy depended. But unlike Harris, he fell in line with the decision of the Combined Chiefs without public complaint, feeling he had no other option. Ira Eaker, on the other hand, was enthusiastic about the new Pointblank directive. It accorded with his conviction that only a combined air, ground, and sea campaign could bring down the Nazi regime. A full-scale program of daylight bombing aimed at disabling the German economy could not be undertaken, he was further convinced, until the Luftwaffe was broken and beaten. He had learned from Billy Mitchell that the destruction of the enemy's air force was the prerequisite for a successful bomber offensive. Yet, armed with additional heavies and crews at the time of the Pointblank directive, he remained confident that he could win air supremacy without long-range fighter coverage for his bombers.

But first he had to straighten out some problems with Hap Arnold, who had begun pressuring Eaker to put more of his fighter planes on escort duty. The handsome, swashbuckling commander of the Eighth's small fighter force, Gen. Frank "Monk" Hunter, was sending his Thunderbolts on cross-Channel sweeps, hoping to lure the Luftwaffe into plane-to-plane combat, but Göring ordered his fighter pilots to concentrate on the bombers. It was on escort duty, not on sweeps, Arnold argued, that the Luftwaffe was to be found, fought, and destroyed.

Arnold was right about this but failed to see that he himself was part of the problem, which went well beyond tactics. Arnold was unrealistically optimistic about the combat capabilities of the B-17. Back in Washington he was "making wild statements about what the B-17 could do," according to later testimony by Air Secretary Robert Lovett. Even after agreeing to push a program for the production of long-range escorts, he was not pressing it hard enough. In Lovett's opinion, "his hands were tied by his mouth. He said our only need was Flying Fortresses, that's all; very few fighters could keep up with them." But as Lovett added sourly, "the Messerschmitts had no difficulty at all."

The Eighth might need long-range escorts, Arnold told his Washington staff, but Eaker was not getting results because he was not putting enough bombers on missions, even after being reinforced in the spring. Arnold showed no appreciation of the service problem the Eighth Air Force was saddled with. Eaker, a recklessly aggressive commander, did not have enough maintenance and repair crews to keep his combat fleet in the air at maximum strength, and one of the reasons was due to sloppy planning in Washington. Impulsive, impatient, plagued by heart problems, and out of touch with the situation on the ground in England, Arnold was, nonetheless, unyielding. He pressed Eaker to fire both his fighter and bomber commanders, who were both "playing safe," he charged, unwilling to take big losses by sending larger formations of bombers and escorts against the enemy. With intemperate cables flying back and forth across the Atlantic, "it began to look," recalled Eaker's aide, James Parton, "as if generals Arnold and Eaker were devoting more time to fighting each other than to defeating the Germans."

On July 1, Eaker relieved Newton Longfellow as Eighth Air Force bomber commander, replacing him with thirty-seven-year-old Maj. Gen. Frederick Anderson, a fiercely aggressive air leader. The following month, Maj. Gen. William E. Kepner, an old friend and test-flying mate of Eaker's, took over the Eighth Air Force Fighter Command. Eaker had yielded to his boss, but in a smoldering letter he warned him: "I am [not] a horse which needs to be ridden with spurs." A friendship and professional bond that had been forged twenty years before was unraveling under the pressures of total war.

Eaker had other concerns. He feared that the greater losses his enhanced forces would suffer might lead to public and official pressure to dismantle the Eighth, which was consuming an ever-larger slice of American war resources, without showing commensurate results. "One of my principal worries now," he confided to Arnold, "is that our official supporters in the highest levels, and our supporting public, may not be able to stand our losses in combat." He then made a dead-on prediction. "We may as well frankly admit that it is going to be a bloody battle. The side will win which can make good its losses. In other words, the side which has the most reserve strength."

The butcher's bill would be higher than he imagined. That summer and fall of 1943, the Eighth Air Force would sustain losses that would dangerously deplete its men and machines, shake the morale of its surviving crews, cost Eaker his command, and throw in doubt the feasibility of defeating Germany from the air. These would be the darkest months in the history of the American air arm. An American flying in a heavy bomber over Germany in these months would have the approximate chance of surviving as the victim of "a deep-seated cancer."

Training

The 381st Bomb Group was one of the units rushed to England to join Ira Eaker's great summer offensive. Thirty-nine summers later, as John Comer approached the weed-choked site of the 381st's station at Ridgewell, just south and east of Cambridge, he felt the pull of the past. "I could hear the raucous roar of Flying Fortress engines revving up for takeoff in the damp pre-dawn cold of an English morning. I could smell that mixture of oil and gasoline that filled the air when engines coughed and started." But his sharpest memories were of his old crewmates, men with whom he had forged unbreakable bonds of friendship at training bases in the States.

John Comer's journey to wartime England began on a wind-swept November day, eleven months after Pearl Harbor. A hard-featured major, his pants pressed with knife-edge precision, strode to an elevated speaker's stand on a remote airfield in Texas and paused for a moment to survey his audience—a group of raw recruits with Army buzz cuts assembled on the parade ground. After a few seconds the major launched into a fiery speech describing the action-packed life of an aerial gunner. When he finished he asked the men who had the guts for the job to step forward and volunteer. Fifty of them did, including thirty-two-year-old John Comer.

An hour later Comer was sitting in the base hospital waiting for his physical. Ten years earlier he had been turned down by the Air Corps for defective depth perception. This time the examining officer told him his results were "close enough." The Air Force badly needed flight engineers—airborne mechanics who also operated the top gun turret of a heavy bomber. Did he want to be a flight engineer, the doctor asked him? Nine months later, John Comer, a recently married machine tool salesman with a degree from the University of Texas, was in the gun turret of a Flying Fortress fighting for his life.

In 1938, the Army Air Corps had only 21,000 officers and enlisted men. In the period of its greatest growth, from the day after Pearl Harbor to the beginning of Pointblank, it grew from 354,000 to over 2.1 million men, an increase of 520 percent. Classifying, assigning, and training these vast numbers of men—1.8 million in eighteen months—was a staggering undertaking. To accomplish it, the Air Force fell back on the belt line production methods of Henry Ford. Fresh recruits who had read the Air Force's official recruiting manual knew what lay ahead. "AAF training," the guide noted, "may be compared to assembly line production."

Bomber boys like John Comer were trained first as individuals and then as parts of a closely coordinated team, and throughout this training process the greatest enemy was time. To get men overseas as rapidly as possible the Air Force lowered its stringent prewar requirements. In January 1942, the minimum age for officer candidates was dropped from twenty to eighteen and recruits no longer needed two years of college; passing a rigorous written exam was sufficient. In the first two years of the war crews at hastily assembled training centers, some of them tent cities, took off from fields that were only half-completed and in aircraft that were dangerously obsolete. Medical and physical requirements—although still high by Army standards—were also reduced. The Air Force prided itself on being an all-volunteer outfit, but that ended in December 1942 when President Roosevelt terminated all voluntary enlistments. Even then, however, an Army draftee could apply for voluntary induction into the Army Air Force. This allowed the Air Force's aggressive recruiters to cream off what novelist John Steinbeck called "the best physical and mental specimens the country produces."

Men volunteered for an endless range of reasons, from unsullied patriotism to a desire to escape the infantry. Young men who were still jobless and psychologically scarred by the Great Depression were lured by the prospect of steady work at decent pay. Freshly minted second lieutenants made $1,800 a year, plus a 50 percent supplement for flight pay, seemingly a pittance, but not at a time when the base salary of a four-star general was $8,000. But a remarkably large number of volunteers were attracted to the Air Force as a result of a youthful romance with flying. Growing up in the Golden Age of Aviation, they had whittled balsa wood into airplane models, followed the storied career of Charles Lindbergh, and thrilled to the aerial exploits of barnstorming stunt pilots who showed up at their local airports. When Paul Tibbets was twelve years old he was taken up in the sky for the first time by a flamboyant barnstormer named Doug Davis, who piloted an open-cockpit biplane with a wooden propeller and fabric-covered wings. Davis worked for the Curtiss Candy Company and he gave Tibbets a job dropping cartons of Baby Ruth candy bars, tied to tiny parachutes, out of the rear seat of his plane. After that experience, Tibbets knew, he said later, that "nothing else would satisfy me."

For candidates who wanted to become flying officers, training usually began at an Air Force classification center staffed by Army doctors and psychologists. Its purpose was to determine if a man should be allowed in a combat plane and in what capacity. Recruits were given a battery of tests to check eyesight, mental aptitude, motor coordination, and psychological stability. Their scores, together with their personal preferences and the Air Force's needs, determined the training school to which they were assigned: pilot, navigator, or bombardier. The tests were demanding. More than half the men failed. Most of these unfairly labeled "washouts" either volunteered for aerial gunnery training or were shipped off to the infantry.

Graduates were called "mister" and "every time we turn around they tell us that we are the cream of the country," an air cadet wrote to his mother. Their training usually began with a one-to-two-month-long military orientation course, where the prospective flier "learned to be a soldier." There was physical training and close-order drill, along with instruction in marksmanship, chemical warfare, military procedure, and map interpretation. The physical training was intense: cross-country runs, obstacle courses, calisthenics, and weightlifting sessions. Cadets marched in formation, singing cadence songs and the Army Air Corps anthem, and there were formal parades for the entire cadet corps, with saber saluting and close review, exercises that imparted a sense of "drama and a feeling of common endeavor."

It was the beginning of the most mentally demanding training program in the American military. For pilots especially, selection and training had to be rigorous. They would not be handling a rifle, but a huge, highly complex weapon of immense cost and destructive capability. Before a pilot received his wings and his commission as a second lieutenant, he went through three flight training schools—Primary, Basic, and Advanced—at three separate bases, each course of instruction lasting about nine weeks (ten weeks later in the war). After that there was a ten-week postgraduate course. At this last level pilots learned to fly the machines they would take into combat and were taught "to kill, maim, burn, destroy . . . without emotion."

In Primary, cadets flew a two-seater biplane called a Stearman, with a civilian instructor in the rear seat. (There were not enough military pilots for the job.) For Richard C. Baynes, a star high school athlete from Mansfield, Pennsylvania, who had never been in a plane before, it was the tensest experience of his life up to that point. But he took to flying with surprising ease, and was soon doing "acrobatics, lazy eights, the loop, and the snap roll. . . . It all got to be great fun." Less exciting than this new experience in the third dimension was the classroom instruction. Cadets took courses in Morse code, navigation, meteorology, aircraft engines and parts, fuel and lubrication procedures, and maintenance and repair. They also spent hours in Link trainers, simulated airplane cockpits designed to teach pilots to fly blind with the aid of instruments.

On the next step of the ladder, Basic Flying School, trainees learned to fly slow prewar fighters under the guidance of experienced Army pilots. After seventy hours of flight time, and more classroom instruction, students were assigned to either single-engine training—fighters—or twin-engine training—bombers. Here the atmosphere was "more relaxed," Richard Baynes recalled. The cadets still drilled and marched to classes but there was less academic work and "the chances of our washing out were minimal now, and we could concentrate on the finer points of flying and navigation." They made cross-country flights and were taught how to land a bomber on a single engine. That made things more dangerous. In 1943, there were over 20,000 major accidents at Army Air Forces bases in the continental United States, with 5,603 airmen killed. Over the course of the war, some 15,000 airmen became fatal casualties at training bases in the States and abroad. At MacDill Air Force Base in Florida the bomber crews in training came up with a grim couplet to describe the situation: "One a day in Tampa Bay."

The week after Thanksgiving 1943, Richard Baynes completed his training and was commissioned a second lieutenant in the Army Air Forces. When he received his silver wings, Lieutenant Baynes had every right to feel both proud and lucky. Almost 40 percent of the cadets who entered the pilot instruction program during the war—over 124,000 men—washed out or were killed in training exercises. Baynes was part of what was fast becoming the best-trained air force in the world.

Men who graduated from navigator and bombardier school were just as proud as the newly minted pilots. Elmer Bendiner, a Jewish kid from Brooklyn, New York, celebrated his graduation from navigation school by buying a fashionable tan trench coat and a pair of "pinks," the rakish-looking dress pants of an Army Air Forces officer. "I was presented with a set of calling cards inscribed with my name and rank. . . . I was ready for war."

Bendiner, who graduated a year earlier than Baynes, had been sent in the early winter of 1943 to Sioux City, Iowa, where he filled the last vacancy of the last crew of the freshly formed 379th Bombardment Group, which was hastily preparing to be sent overseas. He was assigned to a plane called *Tondelayo,* named for a character played by ravishing Hedy Lamarr in the film *White Cargo.* By the time he and his crewmates left for England, they had become a family. "It was around *Tondelayo,*" Bendiner would write, "that we spun our loyalties."

Richard Baynes entered the war a year later. As casualties began to rise alarmingly in the summer and fall of 1943 increasing numbers of aircrews began pouring into England not as members of bomb groups formed in the States, but as replacements for decimated groups like Bendiner's 379th, which would fly more missions and drop more bombs than any other group in the Eighth. After landing in western England, these individual crews reported to a replacement depot, where they were assigned to bomb groups bled down by losses.

Bomb groups like Bendiner's had undergone their final training together in the States as a unit—ground crews and flight personnel—and on arrival in England they took possession of airbases specially prepared for them. The bombers of the 379th began touching down at Kimbolton airfield, in Cambridgeshire, in late May 1943, the month before the first planes of another new group, the Hundredth, landed at Thorpe Abbotts, the eighth bomb group sent to Great Britain by the Eighth Air Force. The Air Force had already marked the Hundredth as a wild, undisciplined outfit, trouble for Col. Curtis LeMay, who had just been given command of the new 4th Bombardment Wing, which the Hundredth would fly with.

The Hundredth

One week after Japan bombed Pearl Harbor, Harry Crosby left the Master of Arts program in writing at the University of Iowa and joined the Army Air Corps, leaving behind a girl he had fallen in love with but who had shown little long-term interest in him. A few weeks later, Crosby washed out as a pilot and was sent off to become a navigator. When he was awarded his gold bars and wings, he was assigned to the Hundredth Bomb Group and told he would fly B-17s. The first time he saw one land, it crashed, killing everyone on board.

His pilots were John Brady and John Hoerr, and the bombardier was Howard "Hambone" Hamilton, an oval-faced country boy from Augusta,

Kansas. It was a polyglot group in the back of the bomber. The engineer, Adolf Blum, was a farmer from upstate New York who spoke with a heavy German accent. The ball turret gunner, Roland Gangwer, was Polish Catholic. One of the waist gunners, Harold Clanton, was part American Indian, the other waist gunner, George Petrohelos, was a Greek from Chicago. The radio operator, Saul Levitt, was a Jew from New York City, a former reporter who had covered the famous gangland investigations of Thomas Dewey, and the tail gunner, Crosby recalled, seemed to be a new guy every week.

When John Brady first set eyes on his crew in the early morning darkness he smiled and told them he was not impressed. "Then he smiled again, and we liked him on the spot," Crosby remembered. "Before the war he was a saxophone player in one of Bunny Berrigan's bands."

The Hundredth, commanded by Col. Darr "Pappy" Alkire, a veteran B-17 man, trained briefly at Boise, Idaho, and Walla Walla, Washington, before being sent to the desolate salt beds of Wendover, Utah, in December 1942. It arrived there with only four banged-up, out-of-commission B-17s and with several hastily trained ground crews "who approached the monsters in eager ignorance," wrote one of their group's chronicles. Some of the men had never seen a B-17 before, but luckily a few of them had experience as mechanics. Kenneth Lemmons, a nineteen-year-old volunteer from Pocahontas, Arkansas, had quit school in the ninth grade to help his father run the family farm. "We did all of our own mechanical work around the farm . . . so mechanics came quite naturally to me." Sergeant Lemmons, a flight chief in charge of fifteen men, helped his less-experienced crew keep the Hundredth's tiny allotment of planes flying. "Men of the ground crews are the backbone of this outfit," Colonel Alkire lectured his new men. "Without [them], the flying prima donnas aren't worth a damn."

More bombers and aircrews arrived within the week, and soon squadrons were in the air on training exercises. Every crewman needed work because their training at Wendover, Utah, had been so inadequate that the Hundredth almost didn't make it into the war.

On New Year's Day, the Hundredth was moved from Wendover to Sioux City, Iowa. The ground personnel, traveling on troop trains, arrived before the fliers, who had been delayed by what they called a "tour of airfields," most of them conveniently located in the hometowns of crewmen. Flying over his old neighborhood in Minneapolis, one gunner decided to send a note to his parents. He tied it to a monkey wrench and dropped it from

10,000 feet. Military censors returned it to Alkire, commenting that the country would be safer when the Hundredth was in Europe.

Sioux City was to be the final stage of Stateside training for the Hundredth, but the group received the bad news that it had not been certified as ready for overseas combat. The Air Force briefly considered breaking up the Hundredth. The aircrews were dispatched for additional training to eight separate bases all over the western United States. They would remain scattered for three months, while the ground crews encamped at Kearney Army Air Base in western Nebraska.

At the end of March, Alkire received the order he was praying for, instructing him to reassemble his group for an overseas assignment. On April 20, all of the original crews were at Kearney, eager to begin a final checkout run to San Francisco. It was a disaster. Fourteen of the thirty-seven planes failed to make it to their destination. Some of the pilots, claiming engine problems, landed at the homes of their girlfriends. One crew wound up in Smyrna, Tennessee. The flight cost Alkire his command, and Maj. Johnny Egan was demoted from air executive to squadron commander. Col. Howard Turner, an assistant to Hap Arnold, became the temporary commander of the Hundredth. His sole job was to get the group to England without incident.

Under Turner, the aircrews received new B-17Fs, the latest model of the Fortress, and were sent to Wendover, Utah, for additional training. Back at Kearney, when an announcement went out that all passes were canceled, and unit commanders allowed their charges to get stinking drunk in the barracks, the men knew this was it: "the flight to war." Records were checked, new flight clothing was issued, and on May 27, with Turner in the lead plane, the four squadrons of the Hundredth, one of them led by Gale Cleven, took off for Bangor, Maine, the staging point for the flight across the Atlantic.

A number of the boys left behind new brides. Harry Crosby married the girl he had been chasing in Iowa City, after she had written him expressing an upsurge of interest. While he was in England she would share an apartment with two of the brides of his squadron mates, Lt. Howard Hamilton and Capt. Everett "Ev" Blakely. Returning home to Pocahontas, Arkansas, for his final furlough, Sgt. Ken Lemmons had married his fiancée, Fonda, and had brought her back to Kearney, putting her up in a hotel for the little time they had left together. When he got his orders to go overseas, he sent her back to northeastern Arkansas, where she lived with her parents for the next two and half years. "It was," he says, "a difficult farewell for two young newlyweds."

The 1,500 or so men of the earthbound echelon had already left Kearney earlier in the month, headed by rail for Camp Kilmer, New Jersey, which was within sight of the skyscrapers of Manhattan. Then, one drizzly morning in late May, the gates of the base were locked, the world was shut out, and after only seven months of training, the ground personnel of the Hundredth boarded stale-smelling troop trains for Hoboken, New Jersey. From there they were ferried across the Hudson River, past endless lines of warships at anchor, to a long pier with a vast, vaulted roof. Waiting for them in silent grandeur was the Cunard White Star liner *Queen Elizabeth,* now one of His Majesty's ships, wearing its drab uniform of war. "There was so much of her," one of the men remembered, "that all you could see were her slate gray sides."

The following afternoon, harbor tugs nudged her out of her slip and she turned and pointed her majestic prow to the sea, with a cargo of souls that equaled the size of a small city. But all that the nearly 15,000 soldiers on board experienced was the powerful movement of the great ship. The men were confined to their musty quarters below deck, unaware of their destination.

Out on the open sea, sailors began covering the portholes and windows as protection against U-boat detection, and the great ship "became a part of the night around her," wrote Jack Sheridan, an orderly with the Hundredth. The *Queen* took eight days to make the crossing, changing course every three minutes, the eyes of watchmen glued to their binoculars as they searched the dark waves for periscopes. The ship's zigzagging movement caused eruptions of seasickness in the cramped, foul-smelling quarters below, where the enlisted men were assigned two to a hammock, each man spending twelve hours in and twelve hours out. The officers slept in bunks that were three tiers high and placed right next to one another, eighteen men crammed into a cabin made for two. With little else to do, the men played blackjack, craps, and faro; and soon, says Sheridan, "the whole of the ship was gripped in a gambling wave. It was impossible to walk around the boat and not run into a game of some sort in every alley and room."

The ship reached the stony shores of Scotland and moored at Greenock on the morning of June 3, 1943. As the men came down the gangplanks of the river tenders that brought them to shore they were greeted by a sad-looking pier-side band playing "Take Me Back to New York." After a snack of tea and donuts provided by Scottish ladies, the ground personnel of the Hundredth were taken by train to a station stop called Diss. "The wits of the outfit," wrote the group's official historians, "lost no time in taking up the cry of 'Dis is Diss,' " which would soon become the men's trademark refrain on trips back from London.

At the station they piled into trucks, which took them past a pub called the King's Head, to a hamlet tucked behind the base, a former RAF station that was still being built. From the cornfields of Nebraska to the "doorstep of the Nazis" in a few fast weeks; it was, said Sheridan, "a pretty big jump."

That first night at Thorpe Abbotts, someone in Lemmons's hut turned on the radio and the men listened to a broadcast from Berlin. It was Axis Sally, the infamous Nazi propagandist, and she was speaking directly to the men of the Hundredth, welcoming them to England. "You've made a mistake. This isn't your war. Why die for England? Go home."

On June 9, the bomber crews arrived, circling the field and roaring in. "The whole family was all together again," said Sheridan. "And this time, for action."

The arrival of the bombers created a sensation in the local community. "One day I was cycling back from school and they started coming in, landing thick and fast and at close intervals," recalled Gordon E. Deben, then a twelve-year-old who lived on a farm right by the runway. "I was near the end of the main runway and started to get goose bumps and wanted to go home but was afraid to pass beneath them, they were so close to the ground."

All the planes of the Hundredth landed except one, the Fortress piloted by John Brady. On the final leg of its flight over the Atlantic, Harry Crosby made a navigation error and they missed England. After nearly flying over Nazi-occupied France they changed course and found the big island, but the landing gear froze and they crash-landed on a runway on England's rugged western coast. No one was hurt, not even the crew's new mascot, Meatball, a Husky they had kidnapped in Iceland. "The countryside looked peaceful," recalled radioman Saul Levitt, "but we knew this was the gateway to a troubled continent."

Wasting no time, the crew took a train to Diss. The men were sitting in the back of a truck when it pulled up to two white-helmeted MPs guarding what looked like the gate to a cattle compound. The guards saluted them and asked for their papers. Looking around, Crosby could see that they were on a farm, with a strange fellow out in the field with a team of horses. He thought for a moment that this was the wrong place until he saw a group of GIs playing catch in front of a long row of Nissen huts. This was it; they were in the war.

Their living quarters were standard Nissen huts—prefabricated plates of corrugated iron, bolted together in the shape of a half-cylinder and painted a drab olive-brown. The floors were concrete slabs, and the huts were heated by small coal stoves, with flue pipes extending up through the roofs. A few low-watt light bulbs hung from each ceiling. The huts were scattered in small clusters, called sites, organized by squadron, and their round roofs made the entire base look like "a colony of mound builders." Each officers hut housed eight men, the officers of two bomber crews, each man having his own cot; sergeant gunners slept on bunk beds in larger huts capable of handling up to three dozen men. So both officers and enlisted men lived with the physical closeness of a submarine crew, in a half-tube that smelled of cigarette smoke, sweat, and unlaundered clothing.

Crosby's crew shared a hut with navigator Frank D. Murphy and the other officers of that crew, which was commanded by Capt. Charles B. Cruikshank, a slim, straight-to-the-point New Englander who carried himself with unaffected assurance.

None of the huts had plumbing. There was a building with latrines and wash basins in each squadron living area, but the ones for the mechanics had no hot water. That caused resentment, as did the squadron leaders' desire to conduct inspections of the enlisted men's barracks. As Ken Lemmons recalled: "All of us master sergeants got together and told them to stay out of our barracks. We were subject to work anytime day or night. We had to work many a night all night . . . so we didn't allow anyone else in our barracks. When you got a chance to sleep you grabbed it, and the officers were wise enough not to press the issue. . . . The officers and enlisted men were like brothers. There was no such thing as rank . . . in the combat zone."

There were three intersecting runways at Thorpe Abbotts, with concrete hardstands off to the side, one for each parked plane. The mechanics set up canvas tents next to the hardstands, unheated shelters for when they worked on the planes in the early hours of the morning, before the crews were awakened. Close by, at the top of a drainage ditch, Ken Lemmons and the mechanics built "one-holers" out of bomb boxes to relieve themselves. One of five crew chiefs, Lemmons was in charge of five bombers, which sat on eight-by-eleven hardstands right next to the boxlike control tower. "The hardstands were our office, our focus, and our life's work while we were at Thorpe Abbotts."

The hardstands were miles away from the living sites of the mechanics, for the base and the planes were widely dispersed to minimize damage from occasional Luftwaffe raids. Soon the men began riding locally purchased bicycles to work. To do almost anything at Thorpe Abbotts—from taking a shower to eating a meal—you had to climb on your bicycle.

•   •   •

An entire little community, Upper Billingford, lay within the perimeter of the base, which never had a fence around it. On the first Sunday, hundreds of local folk came on foot or bike, with mothers pushing prams, to see the great Fortresses, many of them parked a few feet from an approach lane to the base, their high tail sections hanging over the road. Some village boys sneaked into a roadside ditch situated under the rear of one of the Forts to get a look at the bomber's belly guns. A ground crewman spotted them and let them sit at the controls. From then on, the boys would pedal out to the base every day after school and play in the planes that weren't flying. On days when ice cream was served for dessert, the mechanics would sneak them into their mess hall and the boys would eat at long tables with the Americans.

Most of the local farm people were tenants of Sir Rupert Mann, whose titled family had owned vast tracts of land in the area for centuries. They mingled with the men, inviting their favorites to dimly lit cottages for soup and stew. On some evenings, lonely boys in their flying hats would knock on farmhouse doors and ask to be let in for a bit of conversation, sharing a pipe in the kitchen with the man of the house.

When the rains stopped and the mist lifted, men toured the area on bikes in their free time, looking for pubs and girls. This could be dangerous, for American boys were unfamiliar with English handle brakes. As Andy Rooney observed: "the number of American airmen who have tried to put on nonexistent brakes with their pedals . . . is exactly equal to the number of American airmen who have come to England." Ken Everett, who lived by the base, swears that as many airmen at Thorpe Abbotts were hurt on bicycles as in warplanes. "They rode like wild men and had spectacular accidents. Every day, it seemed, there was an ambulance taking one of them away to hospital. You'd see 'em in the pubs, entire gangs of them, banged up and with splints, and you thought they'd been on a mission."

The airmen had no trouble meeting and impressing the local farm girls, but the men from the villages found it harder to get close to the Americans. "They had tons of money," recalled John Goldsmith, a young hotel porter, "and their smart, well-cut uniforms made them stand out. Our fathers wore mud-splattered, lace-up boots, loose trousers, and old bowlers, keeping their Sunday clothes packed away in boxes by their beds for weddings and funerals. Even our soldiers, with their heavy, ill-fitting wool uniforms, looked shabby by comparison with the Americans. Naturally the Yanks got all the best girls."

The American's casual military deportment offended some of the

British, whose military services were rigidly stratified, with officers rarely seen socializing with their men. "Fancy going to fight a war and treating your officers as 'buddies,' " an Englishman commented caustically.

"What bothered a lot of us," recalled John Goldsmith was that most of the Yanks used talcum powder and we thought that was a little bit sissy. And they were so awfully loud. But after a while you couldn't help liking them. They were so friendly, always ready for a chat, and what impressed us was that they never talked about their missions.

"In a way, though, we really didn't take to them until they started dying. We'd miss the lads that didn't come back and feel sorry for their mates, knowing their chances of surviving were so slim. You had to feel for them. I was fifteen years old in 1943, and a lot of the Yanks were only three and four years older than I was, and some of them didn't even look my age."

The men of the Hundredth trained nearly every day and some of them drank nearly every night. Those, like Gale Cleven, who didn't go to the pubs would stay in their dimly lit huts talking about the girls they left behind and the war just ahead of them. Everyone wondered how it would be. "I hear the Krauts will blow holes through the chutes," said one of Brady's crew. "Even if you get into the chute they'll shoot it full of holes so you ain't got a chance."

While men smoked and talked under ceilings plastered with cutouts of Hollywood dreamboats, the war birds on the runways waited "like so many beasts" for the first day of action.

CHAPTER SEVEN

The Bells of Hell

The sun will not be seen today;
The sky doth frown and lower upon our army.

WILLIAM SHAKESPEARE, *RICHARD III*,
ACT V, SCENE 3

Thorpe Abbotts, June 25, 1943

Just after midnight, Ken Lemmons got word that this was the day: the Hundredth's first chance to deliver a blow.

The mechanics were at their hardstands by 3:00 A.M., just as the flight crews were being awakened. The ordnance men and armorers had begun their work even earlier. Roused from their bunks minutes after the mission order was received, they headed out to the bomb dump to begin loading that day's allotment of destruction—500 1,000-pound bombs neatly stacked in pyramidal piles in a fenced-off enclosure the men called boom city. The bombs were placed on long, low trailers, hauled to the planes, hoisted into their empty bellies with hand-operated winches, and hung on horizontal racks in the bomb bay. After the armorers inserted the fuses, they attached a cotter pin to the fuse mechanism of each bomb to prevent the propeller in its tail from spinning—as it would on descent, when it was armed. This prevented the bomb from detonating on board a plane.

It was dangerous work, especially if the bomb handlers, in their haste, fused the bombs before loading them on the plane. At Ridgewell, home of the 381st Bombardment Group, which arrived in England at the same time as the Hundredth, eleven bombs exploded under a Fortress. "Hearing the explosion, I hastened to the scene and was appalled," the group's chaplain, James Good Brown, wrote in his diary. Where there had been a Flying Fortress and twenty-three men, there was nothing but splinters of metal and bone.

While the bombs were being loaded at Thorpe Abbotts, armaments experts hauled wooden crates stacked with belts of 50 caliber shells into the planes, placing a box at each gunner's station. Then they inspected the power-operated gun turrets, tearing them apart, making sure everything was exactly right. Men's lives depended on their scrutiny.

When they had finished, the ground mechanics—three to each plane, a crew chief and his two assistants—took over, making the final mechanical checks: engine, hydraulics, brakes, tires, and oxygen system. The most physically demanding job was hand-pulling the propeller blades to turn the engine and remove any oil that had built up in the cylinders. The crew chief then climbed into the cockpit and engaged the engines, testing them, along with the plane's sensitive electrical and hydraulic functions. If everything checked out, the engines were shut down and the gas tanks topped up. The ground crews were never told where their machines were going. They did know that a full tank meant a long and dangerous day for the air crews.

The mechanics were just completing their work when the gunners arrived, an hour or so before takeoff. They mounted and secured their guns, which were usually stored in the armament shop beside the hardstand, where they were wrapped in oil-soaked rags to prevent rust. This heavy oil coating had to be removed. At high altitude it might absorb moisture, causing the guns to freeze.

When the four flying officers arrived from their briefing, the pilot handed out emergency kits to the crew and did a "walk-around" with the ground crew chief, the final visual inspection before takeoff. While they circled the plane, running through a long checklist, the gunners slipped into their electrically heated flying suits, which they had carried out to the hardstand in zippered equipment bags.

Most of the gunners had already put on the rest of their cumbersome flying clothing in the Flight Equipment Room, but some men preferred to dress for war right at the plane. The men wore detachable parachute harnesses, inflatable life preservers, fleece-lined leather jackets and pants, heavy leather flying boots, and lined leather gloves. The gunners wore fleece-lined flight caps, and by this time, some crewmen had available to them flak helmets and body armor, which they donned when they entered enemy airspace. Each officer was issued a .45 caliber Colt automatic pistol and most men carried talismans: St. Christopher medals, letters from wives or sweethearts, lucky socks or scarves—anything to ward off the devils of war.

Most of the crew entered the bomber through the rear fuselage door, behind one of the waist gunners' open windows. Some officers preferred to pull themselves up—like chinning oneself—through the nose hatch, a more athletic way of getting to their stations. When the entire crew was on board, the pilot opened his side window, shouted "All clear left," and started the propeller of his number one engine. "With a big belching cough the Wright Cyclone engine started," Ken Lemmons recalled the morning of the Hundredth's first strike. "One by one, beginning with the left outboard engine, they roared to life, sending a billow of smoke out the rear. The back draft from those engines could easily blow a man over."

The pilots motioned for the ground crews to remove the wheel chocks so they could begin taxiing down the perimeter track. Like wary mothers, the ground crews walked beside their "babies" to the main runway. The pilots could not see the ground ahead of them over the high nose sections of the Forts and needed their guidance. A green light flashed from a van parked at the end of the runway and within minutes the Hundredth was battle-bound, off to hit Bremen. When the bombers disappeared into the low heavy clouds, hardly a sound could be heard on the base. After clearing their tools off the hardstands, the ground crews headed to the mess hall and from there straight to bed. But it was hard for them to sleep with their planes out there in danger. After a few restless hours in the sack, some men played cards or craps, others wrote letters home, and a few sneaked into the village for a pint of ale or a morning delight with a young British war widow. "We couldn't completely relax," said Ken Lemmons, "until they were home."

About an hour before noon, word went out: they were coming back. Men poured out of kitchens and offices, machine shops and huts. Within minutes every "ground pounder" was out on the flight line prepared to "count them in." At about 11:15 they were over Thorpe Abbotts and started to land one at a time. There were fourteen bombers, but there were supposed to be seventeen. The ground crews of the missing planes waited by the runway, hoping for a miracle. When they learned that the three bombers had been officially listed as missing, they gathered their equipment and walked back in silence to their dispersal tents. Thirty men they had shaken hands with that promising morning were gone.

There was no time to mourn. Ken Lemmons was a flight chief in charge of five bombers and fifteen mechanics and the flight chiefs had to have their planes ready for the next day. Mechanics cleaned out plugged oil sumps, checked spark plugs and cylinders, inspected superchargers and electrical lines. When the "gassers" arrived in their enormous tank trucks, the mechanics crawled out on the wings, opened the fuel doors, and helped them fill the self-sealing tanks, six on each Fortress. On late model B-17s these tanks held over 2,800 gallons of gasoline, nearly a quarter of the plane's weight at takeoff. As the mechanics went about their work, ex-changing friendly insults, the sheet metal crews patched the battle damage, securing the patches with rivets from a noisy air gun. Major structural dam-age was usually repaired at special Air Force depots, but in the rush of com-bat, Ken Lemmons's crews would sometimes be called on to change a propeller or to pull off a wing in order to replace a punctured gas tank. That kind of work went on far into the night.

The mechanics worked in an environment of perpetual mud and grease. When filth built up on their clothing, some of the men washed their coveralls and Class-A uniforms in big tubs of gasoline, drying them on clotheslines they strung up outside their huts. Air Force personnel were re-quired to wear their dress uniforms off the base, but if a man drew a pass before his Class-A uniform dried, he would rather wear it damp than spend the night alone on base. "It's a wonder," said Lemmons, "the [men] didn't explode when they lit a cigarette."

There was no glory in their work and virtually no recognition; no medals were handed out for changing spark plugs. And mechanics had no blood-and-thunder stories to tell at the pubs. But everyone on base knew they were helping to win the war by "keeping 'em up there." When the Nazis started this war of machines—of fast-moving tanks and planes—they forgot that the United States was "a nation of mechanics," where boys were "teethed on erector sets" and where farm kids like Ken Lemmons could re-pair the family Chevy before they were sixteen. It was these "soldier-mechanics," a reporter from *Yank* wrote, who were repairing the bombers that would knock the Nazi supermen back into their beer cellars.

With the crews rotating through on their twenty-five mission tours, and with so many of them lost in combat, the ground crews—whose tours of op-eration were "for the duration plus"—could not get to know all of them. But "we loved them," says Ken Lemmons. "They were fighting the war for us."

Combat and Craziness

Having arrived in England with a reputation for ill discipline, the Hundredth came under the cold scrutiny of Col. Curtis LeMay. When LeMay came to Thorpe Abbotts for an inspection, a rowdy corporal sped by him in a truck pulling a bomb trailer, nearly hitting him. Minutes later, a jeep driven by a crew chief slammed into the side of the colonel's command car. LeMay found the men's quarters in wild disarray, with beds unmade, empty rum bottles littering the floor, and laundry piled in rank-smelling heaps. When he asked to see Gale Cleven, having heard that he and John Egan were the source of the group's "raunchy discipline," a sergeant told him that the squadron leader was nowhere to be found.

The group's easygoing commander, Col. Neil "Chick" Harding, a former football coach at West Point, drank with his fliers and did little to enforce discipline on the base. As missions got tougher, he saw liquor and fistfights as acceptable forms of release. His men, he would say, were made of "flesh and brain," not unfeeling iron. After watching friends die in exploding planes, they should be allowed to get crazy once in a while.

Craziness, however, came in different packages, and at least once it resulted in an excellent decision. Later that summer, Harry Crosby was unable to sight his primary target through a thick cloudbank. Both backup targets were socked in as well, freeing the squadrons to bomb a "target of opportunity," an Air Force euphemism for anyplace that could be conveniently creamed. Sighting a large German city through a clearing in the clouds, Crosby gave the OK sign to the pilot. Just as he heard the bomb doors opening, he looked down at his map and discovered that the city was Bonn.

He immediately hit his mike button. "All positions from navigator, I have another target. We can't bomb Bonn."

"Command to navigator. Why not?"

"That is where Beethoven went to school."

Crosby happened to know this because he had read it on the cover of the phonograph record he had played in his room the night before the raid, Beethoven's 5th, a fitting musical prelude, he thought, for a mission into Germany. He had also read on the cover that Bonn was a university town, one of the most picturesque places in Europe.

After an outburst of "Oh, shits" from the crew, the pilot went along with Crosby and sixty-three Forts passed over the city, some of them with their bomb doors open. Minutes later, they found a marshaling yard in the Ruhr and obliterated it.

Hamburg

Hamburg was not so fortunate. A port city of nearly two million people, it was nearly annihilated by the first man-made firestorm in recorded history. The crews of Bomber Harris did the burden of the destruction, but the Eighth contributed. This was part of the first sustained American bombing offensive beyond the Rhine, the opening of the summer offensive that Ira Eaker had been building toward for almost six months. It began in the last week of July 1943. The Air Force called it Blitz Week.

Blitz Week was made possible by a sudden break in the weather. The Eighth's operations had been hampered by a three-month-long period of cloudy weather over German targets. When the sky cleared spectacularly on July 24, the Eighth, joined by the RAF, launched what official Air Force historians called "the heaviest and most continuous attacks in the history of aerial warfare to that date." This was the real beginning of Pointblank.

That week, Harris's Lancasters, Halifaxes, Stirlings, and Wellingtons dropped record amounts of explosives on Germany, and the Eighth set its own tonnage records in daylight raids that took its bombers further into Germany than they had dared to go before. The week began with the Eighth hitting economic targets in Norway, its longest mission to date. On the following two days, July 25 and 26, Eaker's bombers teamed up with the RAF on coordinated daylight and night raids on Hamburg, the biggest port on the European continent and Germany's second largest city.

The Eighth concentrated on the city's aircraft engine plants and its immense U-boat construction yards, while Harris's men gutted the center of the city in a succession of apocalyptic night raids. On the evening of July 24–25, the RAF set ferocious fires that were still burning when the Eighth arrived over the city the next day. "Smoke lies over the town like an enormous thundercloud, through which one sees the sun like a red disc," wrote one German observer. "Now, at 8 o'clock in the morning it is nearly dark, as in the middle of the night." The worst came two days later.

July 27 was a beautiful summer night in Hamburg. The city was quiet—no flak, no sirens. Perhaps it was over, the optimists speculated. Then at 1:00 A.M. the British bombers—over 700 of them—could be heard approaching. "Suddenly there came a rain of fire from heaven," recalled a Hamburg firefighter. "The air was actually filled with fire. . . . Then a storm started, a shrill howling in the street. It grew into a hurricane so that we had to abandon all hope of fighting the fire." Hamburg, already attacked numerous times by the RAF, had a formidable antiaircraft network of flak and fighters, but this time the British employed an ingenious new defensive tactic, code-named Window. Thousands of bundles of aluminum foil strips, resembling Christmas tree tinsel, were dropped from planes, creating a blizzard of false echoes on the radar screens of air and ground defenders.

The weather, unusually hot and dry for this part of Germany, provided near perfect atmospheric conditions for what turned into a city-consuming cyclone of fire. Within twenty minutes after the raid began, a column of turbulent, heated air rose more than two and a half miles into the night sky. Superheated air raced through the city at speeds in excess of 150 miles per hour, sending terrified people scurrying to air raid cellars, their shirts and dresses lit up like torches. Inside the shelters, thousands suffocated as the voracious fire sucked oxygen out of the atmosphere. The bodies of other victims were baked and reduced to ashes by radiant heat. "It was as though they had been placed in a crematorium, which was indeed what each shelter proved to be," said a secret German report. "The fortunate were those who jumped into the canals and waterways and remained swimming or standing up to their necks in water for hours until the heat should die down." Later that night, the oily water in the industrial canals caught fire and people trapped there "became insane," said one witness.

In shelters hit by fire sticks—small, highly lethal incendiary bombs—children "yelled like animals," reported another witness. "One woman next to me took a knife and cut her child's wrists. Then she cut her own, and slipped down on her, calling out: 'Darling, my darling, we shall soon see Daddy now.' "

The brains of fire victims fell from their burst temples and tiny children "lay like fried eels on the pavement. Even in death," said a witness, "they showed signs of how they must have suffered—their hands and arms stretched out as if to protect themselves from that pitiless heat." When survivors found dead family members, everything around them was gone—home, photographs, all possessions. "Nothing to remember them by."

After the final RAF attack on August 2, relief workers were called in to clear streets littered with charred corpses. "We stacked the bodies in 30 to 35 layers on top of each other," reported a member of the local Hitler Youth. "We stacked them all, and if you went past two or three days later you could only go with cellophane over your eyes because everything was smokey. The air was absolutely still. We didn't have any sun at all for three or four days; it was completely dark out. . . . The dead were piled in the entrances of houses. And when you went by you just saw a heap of feet, some barefoot, some with burned soles. The corpses were beyond identification.

We would dig entire families out of their basements . . . they'd fit into a bathtub. Even adults were very small. They were completely mummified, burned, and melted together by the heat."

Looters picking around in the ruins were shot on the spot by police and Gestapo agents. Victims fleeing collapsing bunkers, their bodies on fire, "rushed into the next air-raid shelter and were shot in order not to spread the flames," reported a Hamburg woman.

The fire storm, the first ever created by bombing, was a deliberate act, achieved by a lethal combination of high-explosive and incendiary bombs. Enormous 4,000-pound blast bombs were then dropped into the inferno to blow craters in the roads in order to impede the firefighters. "A wave of terror radiated from the suffering city and spread throughout Germany. Appalling details of the great fires were recounted and their glow could be seen for days from a distance of a hundred and twenty miles," reported a German air commander. "[News of] . . . the Terror of Hamburg spread rapidly to the remotest villages of the Reich," the horrific details carried by over a million people who escaped the city, many of them in a wild stampede.

Traveling with other fire victims on a train to Berlin, a German housewife witnessed a scene beyond human belief. A young woman, her face blackened by soot and ash, was staring out the window of the car, frozen in a trancelike state. Resting on her knees was a small suitcase. Another woman who had lost all her belongings turned to her and commented coldly, "Well, at any rate *you* managed to save something out of it. You've been luckier than some of us, haven't you?"

The young woman said, yes, she had. "I've saved the dearest thing in the world to me. Do you want to see it?"

She opened the suitcase. Inside was what looked like the blackened shrunken body of a baby. The woman began laughing hysterically. "That's my daughter. Isn't she sweet: She has such beautiful fair curls and blue eyes, hasn't she. . . . She's grown a lot this last year. She's just twelve years old. But now she's shriveled. I can carry her in my suitcase now."

It was suffering and loss never seen before in a bombing raid. Forty-five thousand bodies—mostly women, children, and the elderly—were recovered from the ruins, and at least 10,000 more bodies remained buried or were obliterated by the flames, according to Hamburg fire authorities. Nearly 60 percent of the city—an area of almost thirteen square miles—was totally burned out, leaving hundreds of thousands of people homeless. In ten days, more civilians were killed in Hamburg than were lost in Great Britain during the entire Blitz. RAF losses were heavy—eighty-seven aircraft—but Bomber Harris was satisfied with Operation Gomorrah, as the raid was aptly code-named. His crews nearly silenced a city.

Fritz Reck, whose vocal opposition to the Nazis would land him in Dachau, where he would be silenced forever, wrote despairingly in his diary that there was "no possible way . . . back to the world of yesterday." Germany had brought this on itself and would suffer as it never had in its history.

For the first time in the war, the RAF had profoundly shaken the Nazi leadership. "Psychologically the war . . . reached its most critical point," wrote commander of fighters Adolf Galland. "Stalingrad had been worse, but Hamburg was not hundreds of miles away on the Volga but on the Elbe, right in the heart of Germany."

"Hamburg . . . put the fear of God in me," wrote Albert Speer, Hitler's minister of armaments. "At a meeting of Central Planning on July 29 I pointed out: 'If the air raids continue on the present scale, within three months we shall be relieved of a number of questions we are at present discussing. . . . We might just as well hold the final meeting of Central Planning.'" Three days later, Speer warned a shaken Hitler—who refused to visit Hamburg or even receive a delegation of emergency workers that had performed heroic service in the stricken city—that "a series of attacks of this sort, extended to six more major cities, would bring German armaments production to a total halt." Hitler waved off the warning. "You'll straighten all that out again," he said to Speer.

Indeed, Harris had vastly underestimated the recuperative powers of the Reich economy. Within five months, Hamburg had regained 80 percent of its former productivity. An organizational genius, Speer directed the recovery, but Hamburg was saved as a center of Nazi war production because it was never hit again with such vehemence. Harris moved on to other cities, principally Berlin. In the months ahead, British bombing "took on almost an aimless quality, piling up vast rubble, yet too dispersed in time and space to apply a decisive shock to either morale or production," wrote historian Michael Sherry. "Its bombing was stark testimony to the ease with which men equated the destructiveness of air power with its decisiveness." Fearing massive retaliation from the Luftwaffe, Harris found it preferable, as historian Max Hastings has argued, "to strike a target at intervals of some weeks rather than to return immediately."

The Battle of Hamburg exposed the fraudulence of round-the-clock bombing, the central idea of Pointblank. The independently planned raids by the Eighth were too small to do permanent damage to Hamburg's docks, aircraft factories, and U-boat facilities. And swirling smoke from the

inferno that the RAF created hampered efforts by American crews to locate their precision targets.

On July 28, Eighth Air Force gunner Jack Novey's Fortress flew over
Hamburg after bad weather prevented it from finding its main target.
"Even at 17,000 feet the heat was so intense that my face was prickling as if
I were standing in front of an open fireplace." Only a tiny percentage of the
estimated 46,000 people who were killed in Hamburg were victims of
American bombs, but Novey and a number of other crewmen of his 96th
Bomb Group were shocked that the Eighth Air Force had participated in
what they saw as an indiscriminate slaughter. "I couldn't help picturing
children down below," Novey wrote later. But even silent dissenters like
Novey remained convinced of the correctness of their cause. The "Mad
Dictator" had brought this down on himself, and, for supporting him, the
German people would have to accept even the death of innocents. And
while the airmen never thought of themselves as innocents, they, too, were
suffering.

Red Morgan

To "Red" Morgan and his crew, the mission to Hanover during Blitz Week
was about all the war any ten men could bear. Lt. John Morgan of the 92nd
Bomb Group was a B-17 co-pilot from Amarillo, Texas. Impatient to get
into the fight, he had flown with the Royal Canadian Air Force before the
Japanese attack on Pearl Harbor. That had taken courage. What he did
over Hanover on July 26, 1943, made him a legend in the Eighth.

On the way to the target, Morgan took over the controls of his battered
Fortress from his mortally wounded pilot, Robert Campbell. The delirious
man, the back of his head sheared off by a 20mm shell, was slumped over
the steering column, his arms clasped around it in a death grip. For two
hours he instinctively fought Morgan for control of the gyrating ship. Morgan could easily have ended Campbell's life by pulling off his oxygen
mask, but he wanted to try to get his friend back alive. With the plane's
communication system shot out, he was unable to call for assistance. Help
would have been hard to get anyway. The top turret gunner, S. Sgt. Tyre C.
Weaver, had just had his arm blown off by cannon fire and was lying unconscious on the freezing floor of the plane. The navigator, Lt. Keith
Koske, tore the white scarf from his neck and tried to wrap it around the
stump of Weaver's arm, but the arm had been shot off too close to the

shoulder for Koske to apply enough pressure to stop the bleeding. "I tried to apply morphine," Koske told Andy Rooney later, "but the needle was bent. I couldn't get it in."

The bomber was four hours from England and Koske knew Weaver could not hold on that long. He put a parachute on Weaver's harness, placed the ripcord in his remaining hand, and lowered him through an escape hatch. His hope was that the subzero cold would stop the bleeding and that a German doctor would get to him in time to save his life. While Koske was tending to Weaver, the rear gunners, unknown to Morgan, were unconscious. Their oxygen hoses had been cut by cannon fire.

Piloting the Fortress with one hand, while fighting off the dying pilot with the other, Morgan, a six-foot-two powerhouse, got *Ruthie II* to the target and bombed a Hanover rubber factory. Later, with the help of Koske and one of the revived gunners, he pulled Campbell from his seat, placed him on the floor of the cockpit, and covered him with a blanket. They would have prayed over him if they had had the time.

Morgan made an emergency landing at an RAF field in Norfolk with his fuel gauges on zero and with the windshield shattered so badly he had to guide the plane from his side window. The pilot died an hour or so later. That December, S. Sgt. Tyre Weaver of Riverview, Alabama, sent a letter to a friend informing him that he was "safe" in Stalag 17B, a German prison camp in Austria. A few days later, Morgan was awarded the Congressional Medal of Honor. He thought it should have gone to Koske.

Zero Raiders

Despite good weather, Gen. Ira Eaker ordered a stand-down on July 31. The Eighth would not resume full operations for almost two weeks. It had lost ninety-seven Forts during Blitz Week, 10 percent of the planes that attacked the targets, and the exhausted and shaken fliers needed time to recuperate. Eaker also needed to replenish his supply of bombers for a highly secret raid that had been in the planning stage for almost six months.

This was an attack on the ball bearing factories at Schweinfurt, which a Luftwaffe commander called the "Achilles' heel" of German industry. No war machine moves without friction-reducing bearings, and Schweinfurt, a handsome town of 43,000 residents on the River Main, just northwest of Nuremberg, had three plants that together produced 57 percent of Germany's antifriction bearings. This was to be a dual raid, with another fleet of bombers striking a Messerschmitt assembly plant at Regensburg–also in Bavaria–that produced 30 percent of Germany's single-engine fighter planes. The Regensburg force would then fly to American bases in North Africa, while the Schweinfurt contingent would head back to England. This "shuttle" mission would be the Eighth's deepest penetration yet of German airspace, and the bombers would have no escorts from the time they crossed the German border. But by dividing and confusing the enemy's defenses, the double strike would allow both armadas to deliver heavy blows without taking prohibitive losses. That was the plan.

Eaker would have to execute this mission without three of his Liberator groups. The previous June they had been sent to the recently conquered Libyan desert to train for another top secret operation against another of the Reich's "choke points": the gigantic oil refinery complex at Ploesti, Romania, source of 60 percent of Hitler's crude oil. This attack on what Churchill called "the taproot of German might" was scheduled for August 1, 1943, the day after Eaker grounded his Fortresses.

Both missions were undertaken to deliver a knockout blow, a sign of Hap Arnold's rising impatience with the progress of the European air war. As Curtis LeMay would say later, these operations were "the outgrowth of a search by those intellectual souls in Plans and Intelligence to find an easy way of winning the war in Europe. That's just about like searching for the Fountain of Youth–there *is* no such thing; never was." The three main targets–oil, ball bearings, and aircraft plants–had been recommended by a panel of civilian experts that Arnold convened in December 1942. The Committee of Operations Analysts (COA) had a glittering membership. It included Wall Street financiers Thomas W. Lamont of J. P. Morgan and Co. and Elihu Root, Jr., son of Theodore Roosevelt's secretary of state, attorney George W. Ball, Princeton military historian Edward Mead Earle, Judge John Marshall Harlan, later a Supreme Court justice, and Col. Guido R. Perera, who had left his prestigious Boston law practice to serve with Arnold in Washington. The following March, after a close study of the German economy, the committee urged the Eighth Air Force to focus on a select number of target systems. "It is better to cause a high degree of destruction in a few really essential industries or services than to cause a small degree of destruction in many industries." By hitting these "bottleneck" targets repeatedly and "with relentless determination," the American air arm could, it was hoped, "paralyze the Western Axis war effort," particularly the Luftwaffe, a heavy user of both oil and ball bearings.

The Schweinfurt-Regensburg raid was risky; Ploesti was suicide.

·   ·   ·

Germany, a country without major sources of crude oil, had gone to war with meager reserve stocks of aviation and motor gasoline and never recovered from this precarious position. It had made up for its paucity of natural supplies by a two-fold process of conquest and creativity. By 1943, it had the largest synthetic oil industry in the world and enormous supplies of crude oil were being imported from subject states, chiefly Romania. The Romanian refineries had become doubly important to the German war effort because of the Wehrmacht's failure to capture Russian oilfields in the Caucasus, one of the major aims of the German invasion of the Soviet Union.

Germany's synthetic plants were located deep inside the Reich and were cleverly camouflaged and stoutly defended. But with the Allied conquest of North Africa, Ploesti, lying on a broad plain at the foot of the Transylvanian Alps, thirty-five miles north of the capital city of Bucharest, could be reached by long-range bombers flying from desert fields that had been used to chase Erwin Rommel from the sand seas of Libya. Allied ground intelligence reported that Ploesti was lightly defended, mostly by Romanians who despised their Nazi masters and were unlikely to put up resistance. But a captured Romanian flier reported that Ploesti was one of the most heavily fortified targets in Europe. No reconnaissance missions were flown over the site to confirm this, for fear of alerting the enemy. It was one of the biggest intelligence blunders of the war.

Operation Tidal Wave, as the Ploesti mission was code-named, was the brainchild of Col. Jacob E. Smart, a staff advisor to Hap Arnold. The keys to it were surprise and razor-sharp timing. The Germans knew that the American Air Force was completely committed to high-altitude precision bombing and they had set up their defenses at Ploesti with this in mind after a small, unsuccessful high-altitude raid by the Americans in the spring of 1942. Smart proposed to go in low, at treetop level, at recklessly high speeds of up to 200 miles per hour. The attacking planes would observe radio silence all the way to the target, across a broad stretch of the Mediterranean and over the rugged mountains of Albania and Yugoslavia. After climbing over the 9,000-foot summits of the Pindus Range, they would drop to zero level and thunder up the Danube plain, arriving simultaneously and in massed numbers at the target, overwhelming their unprepared defenders and turning Ploesti into a boiling inferno.

Flying low, under enemy radar, would allow the bombers to hit their targets with pinpoint precision—from 200 to 800 feet—and would give enemy flak gunners and fighters difficult targets to sight and hit. It would also reduce civilian casualties and give battle-ravaged bombers a better chance of surviving crash landings.

Flying Fortresses lacked the range for this mission—an unprecedented 2,400-mile round trip, so Smart was forced to use Liberators, with the knowledge that this would make the mission even riskier. The B-24s were difficult to maneuver (just moving the yoke required great physical strength), a disabling disadvantage on a mission that called for close formation flying and almost inhuman aerial agility. The bomber's aerodynamically advanced wing, the so-called Davis wing, was also less resilient than that of the B-17, another critical disadvantage on an operation in which the bombers would fly directly into the sights of the enemy's ground gunners.

Five bomb groups were selected to carry out the strike. Two were from Lt. Gen. Lewis Brereton's Ninth Air Force, a small tactical outfit stationed on the desert wastes near the coastal city of Benghazi, Libya, and three were on loan from the Eighth Air Force. Two of the outfits from the Eighth—the 44th, "The Flying Eightballs," and the 93rd—had combat experience against Nazi submarine pens on the coast of France, and the 93rd had just finished a winter tour in North Africa in support of Operation Torch. On their return from Africa, they had dubbed themselves "Ted's Traveling Circus," after their crusty commander, Col. Edward "Ted" Timberlake, a former football star at West Point. The third group, the 389th—"The Sky Scorpions"—was just completing training in the States.

Ira Eaker opposed the mission. It would deprive him of desperately needed bombers and crews. But that May, with Arnold's backing, Colonel Smart received approval from the combined Chiefs of Staff, who wanted to relieve pressure on the Russians, still locked in a death duel with a German army heavily dependent on Romanian oil.

When Philip Ardery of Bourbon County, Kentucky, arrived in England in June 1943 he was told not to unpack. There were rumors that a detachment from his outfit, the Sky Scorpions, was to be sent to North Africa on a highly dangerous secret mission. Less than two weeks later, the Sky Scorpions were in the Libyan Desert with four other bomb groups practicing low-altitude formation flying under General Brereton's direction. Living and flying conditions were abysmal. Fierce sandstorms impeded operations, swarms of lizards and desert rats invaded the men's tents, and most of the fliers came down with dysentery. The crews were not told the objective of their desert exercises. When they were not on practice maneuvers they flew with the Ninth Air Force in support of the invasion of Sicily. After bombing Rome on July 19, they began intensive training for their ground-hugging raid, dropping wooden bombs on a full-scale mock-up of the Ploesti oil complex that engineers had laid out on the desert sand with whitewash and oil cans. "This was the type of flying every hot pilot had dreamed of all his life," wrote Ardery, at the time a recent graduate of Harvard Law School. "When you go 200 miles per hour at an altitude of eight hundred feet, you really know you're going 200 miles per hour."

At the mission briefing, the fliers were warned to expect losses of up to 50 percent, tolerable casualties, Brereton insisted, for a strike that could shorten the war by six months. Gunners were told they would be flying so low they could expect to engage enemy gun batteries in close-quarter firefights. Co-pilots were given submachine guns and told how to fire them out of their cockpit windows. "When we walked out of that briefing, each of us knew that coming back was secondary on this job," said one pilot.

The evening before the mission, Father Gerald Beck, the Flying Scorpions' Catholic chaplain, went from tent to tent hearing confession and trying to settle the men's nerves. An impressively tall Irishman with blue eyes and iron gray hair, he was the most beloved member of the group. When he wasn't ministering to his men he was playing poker with them. When he won, which was almost always, he gave his winnings to boys who needed it.

The night before the mission, each flier was told to write a letter home and place it on his bed in the morning. It would be mailed if he failed to return. Unknown to most of the fliers, their commanders were at odds about the raid. The mission leader, Maj. Gen. Uzal Ent, of the Ninth Air Force, had drafted a petition to General Brereton—which he wanted all bomb group leaders to sign—requesting that the planes bomb from high altitude. Col. John "Killer" Kane, commander of the 98th Bomb Group, joined him in dissent, complaining that "some idiot armchair warrior in Washington" had to have planned this raid. When Ent's petition nearly cost him his command, he withdrew his opposition.

At first light, on August 1, after twelve days of grueling training, a task force of 178 Liberators equipped with auxiliary wing tanks and additional forward armor and guns fired up their engines. Out on the runway was Father Beck, blessing the bombers. A co-pilot shouted to him, "You got good connections up there, Chappie?" Beck yelled back over the roar of the propellers, "I pray through channels." The men in the bombers gave him the thumbs-up sign and began taxiing out to the end of the runway, their whirling propellers raising tremendous clouds of dust. A baby-faced sergeant leaned out of his gun portal and bade farewell to Father Beck, "Make contact for us, Padre."

It took an hour for the Zero Raiders to assemble in the air for the seven-hour run to the target and less time to suffer their first loss. A Liberator named *Kickapoo* crashed and burned minutes after takeoff. Three hours later another bomber flipped over and dropped into the Ionian Sea. Tension in the remaining planes would have been even higher had the fliers known that the Germans had a signal station in Greece that had broken the American code, making radio silence unnecessary. Ploesti's early warning system was alerted and would track the Liberators all the way to Bucharest.

Approaching the mountains of Albania, the bombers flew into a towering cloud formation, rising to a height of 17,000 feet. "Our success and our salvation depended not only on surprise, but also on a simultaneous sweep across our various targets," Eighth Air Force pilot William R. Cameron wrote later. "We must arrive together, attack together, and depart together." When the bombers became separated in the clouds, this kind of coordination became impossible.

One problem followed another. On the approach to the target, the command pilot of the lead group, Col. Keith Compton, with General Ent riding in the co-pilot's seat, made a wrong turn and took the 376th Bomb Group—with the ships from the Traveling Circus right behind them—south toward Bucharest. Other navigators broke radio silence and sent out urgent warnings—"Mistake! Mistake!" When the church domes of Bucharest came into sight, Compton abruptly changed course but his navigational mistake shattered the last hope of carrying out a tightly massed attack.

Before the mission, each group had been assigned a specific target in the refinery and an exact time to hit it. Now orders went out to the pilots in Compton's formation to fly in from any convenient direction and bomb at will. It was a recipe for chaos.

About thirty-five minutes from Ploesti, the bombers descended to treetop level for the run-up to the target. When the Sky Scorpions arrived at the refinery, the Battle of Ploesti had already begun. Gigantic storage tanks, their roofs blown off by 1,000-pound bombs, shot up tongues of flame, setting many of the Liberators on fire. The air was thick with flak bursts and tracer fire as the lumbering bombers, swaying in the propeller turbulence of the Liberators directly in front of them, virtually flew straight down the gun muzzles of Ploesti's defenders.

Col. Alfred Gerstenberg, a Luftwaffe commander who had flown with Göring in the Great War, had turned Ploesti—the refinery as well as the town of 100,000 inhabitants—into "the first air fortress in the world." The refinery was ringed with more flak guns than Berlin, and there were machine guns and fast-firing cannons on factory rooftops and water towers, and inside haystacks and church steeples. The protector of Ploesti also had over 250 fighter planes at fields in the vicinity of the oil complex and had set up 2,000 smoke generators to conceal the refineries. Around the main oil plants he had positioned hundreds of barrage balloons with thick steel cables designed to tear off the light aluminum wings of bombers. Planned as a Yankee surprise, Ploesti turned into a Nazi ambush.

"We flew through sheets of flame, and airplanes were everywhere, some of them on fire and others exploding," recalled Col. Leon W. Johnson, leader of the Flying Eight Balls. The groups led by Johnson and John "Killer" Kane, the son of a Baptist minister, had to fly through explosions ignited by delayed-action bombs dropped by the Liberators that had arrived before them. After ascending briefly to release their bombs, the Liberators continued to fly "on the deck" and in V-shaped formations of three that were so tightly grouped that Capt. William Cameron could see the rivets in the two bombers he was sandwiched between. The dense, greasy smoke created by the oil fires concealed refinery stacks over 200 feet tall. Airman Joseph Tate saw a man come tumbling out of the nose hatch of a flaming Liberator, his parachute tailing behind him. "He drifted over the top of us so close we could see his burned legs."

Ardery's squadron was the last to enter this storm of fire. As he went in he looked to his right and saw that the plane flown by his squadron mate, Lt. Lloyd Hughes, was leaking fuel in great volume. Hughes had to have known it but seemed determined to get to the target, which was behind a solid wall of fire. Within seconds, his plane was turned into an aerial blowtorch and went down.

The battle over the refineries lasted only twenty-seven minutes. After it was over the flame-scorched bombers were set upon by swarms of fighters that hung to them "like snails on a log." It was bedlam, with the bombers soon stretched over a hundred-mile-wide area of the Danube plain, each Liberator fighting its own lonely battle for survival. Over half of the B-24s were shot up and half had run out of ammunition. Some of the planes were so badly damaged that they looked like steel skeletons, their tough framing the only thing holding them together. Bleeding men lay on the flight decks, crewmembers tending to them, hoping they could hold out for another six to seven hours. Ardery's plane "skipped over the tops of trees and tension lines, keeping at almost zero altitude to reduce the effect of ground defenses." As it zoomed over an immense grain field, the top of a haystack slid back and two cleverly hidden Nazi gunners opened fire on them. Ardery lowered the nose of his plane to aim the specially equipped automatic guns he controlled from the cockpit and raked them with lead. "Maybe they were dead; I hoped so."

It was nightfall when Ardery's Liberator touched down at Benghazi, thirteen and a half hours after taking off. The Zero Raiders destroyed over 60 percent of Ploesti's production capacity, but the mammoth oil facility had been running at only half-capacity. Ten thousand slave laborers were brought in, and in a matter of weeks the refinery was producing more oil per day than before the great strike. The lack of a follow-up raid allowed the Nazis to rebuild. The Americans would not hit Ploesti again until April 1944, when they could reach the refineries on high-altitude missions from airfields in captured southern Italy.

Three hundred and ten Americans fliers were killed on the Ploesti Raid, roughly one in five of the men sent out from Benghazi. Another 130 airmen were wounded, and over a hundred became prisoners of war in Romania and Bulgaria. Only thirty-three of the 178 Liberators that had been dispatched to Ploesti survived or were fit to fly the next day. Had Bomber Harris done the job, the losses might have been less, but the civilians of Ploesti would have paid dearly. As it was, only 116 Romanian soldiers and civilians died that black Sunday, making Ploesti one of the only air strikes of the war in which more airmen were killed than civilians. It was also the only American air action of the war in which five Congressional Medals of Honor were awarded. Kane and Johnson were among the recipients; Lloyd Hughes was awarded his medal posthumously. Philip Ardery recommended him for the award, wrote the citation, and had a large poster made with Hughes's picture on it. He hung it on the wall of the squadron room when he and his crewmates returned to England, weakened from dysentery and weight loss, a few weeks later.

The Double Strike

While elements of the Eighth were away in the African desert, plans went forward for the Regensburg-Schweinfurt mission, despite Ira Eaker's continuing opposition. This was Washington's mission. "We were pushed into it before we were ready," Eaker told an interviewer late in his life. "I protested it bitterly." As one of his commanders explained, "It was like lining up the cavalry, shooting your way in and then shooting your way out again." Eaker was not afraid of that kind of fight, but he lacked the horsemen to do the job.

Like Ploesti, everything depended on secrecy and timing, but Regensburg-Schweinfurt was a maximum effort, utilizing nearly every available Fortress in England. In late July, a lead crew—pilot, co-pilot, bombardier, and navigator—from each of the bomb groups in the Eighth's 1st and 4th

Bombardment Wings was called to the headquarters of their respective wing commanders, Brig. Gen. Robert Williams and Col. Curtis LeMay. After being briefed on the mission behind locked and guarded doors, the lead crews were pulled from combat duty and sworn to secrecy.

The lead navigator of the Hundredth was Harry Crosby, now flying with Capt. Everett Blakely, one of his closest friends, in the Hundredth's lead ship. The group's commander for this mission was Maj. Jack Kidd, an operations officer who had wanted to be a pilot since the time he saw Jimmy Doolittle win an air race over a grass field near his boyhood home of Winnetka, Illinois. He was smart, steady, and cool under pressure. He would be flying with Blakely. That August, he was twenty-four years old.

The morning of the mission, August 17, 1943, the aircrews were shaken from their bunks at 1:30 A.M. The men knew immediately "something big was up." They were ordered to pack blankets, extra canteens of water, and toilet articles. Breakfast that morning featured fresh, not powdered, eggs and extra rations of bacon, the special meal the men called the Last Supper. Col. Harding opened the briefing by going to an easel, which had a chart outlining the formation. Everyone listened intently; to miss a word could literally be fatal.

The Hundredth would put up three squadrons, a total of twenty-one Forts. Crosby noticed that Brady was flying on his left wing and that Charles "Crankshaft" Cruikshank was leading the second element, with Frank Murphy navigating and John Egan, their squadron commander, in the co-pilot's seat. The Hundredth was in the last and lowest position—Purple Heart Corner—in the 4th Wing's cavalcade of bombers. Down in the lowest of the three squadrons was Gale Cleven, their finest flier, seated next to co-pilot Norman Scott. Cleven would be the Hundredth's shield in the event the Germans hit the group first and hardest.

Then came the surprise. "Your primary is Regensburg. Your aiming point is the center of the Messerschmitt One Hundred and Nine G aircraft-and-engine-assembly shops. This is the most vital target we've ever gone after. If you destroy it, you destroy thirty percent of the Luftwaffe's single-engine-fighter production."

Another task force, they were told, was going to Schweinfurt. "Their target," the intelligence officer continued, "produces most of the ball bearings in Germany. Three months after they get their target, there won't be an engine operating in the whole country." Not a flier in the room believed him.

All eyes were now on the enormous wall map, which 240 men leaned forward and studied, their silence broken by a few low whistles. "You could have heard an oxygen mask drop." A red string extended from Thorpe

Abbotts to a German city on the Danube River, south and west of Nurem-berg. But instead of "hooking around" toward home it continued into the Austrian Alps, down the rocky spine of Italy, and across the Mediterranean to a desert location in North Africa. No one in the group had yet flown far into Germany, but their new bombers were specially equipped with extra fuel tanks in the wingtips. These Tokyo tanks, which increased range by nearly a thousand miles, would get them to another continent. Some faces turned ashen when the intelligence officer mentioned, in a quick aside, that they would be flying without escorts through the heart of Hitler's most for-midable fighter defense zone.

At 5:30 A.M. the crews taxied their bombers to the head of the landing strip and waited. The weather was excellent over the target, but a heavy summer mist hung over the Thorpe Abbotts aerodrome and every other air station in eastern England. At Kimbolton, home of the 379th Bomb Group, part of that morning's Schweinfurt force, navigator Elmer Bendiner and his crewmates stood under the wing of *Tondelayo* and "tried to see through the mists to the end of the runway. . . . We knew that many of us would die, and still we wanted the battle to begin." Better to get it over with and not have to go through the agony of preparation again the next day.

As messages came from the tower postponing takeoff time once, and then a second time, the men grew anxious and irritable. "Frequent 'piss calls' were needed behind the planes," said a flier from another group. "Some could not get their cigarettes to their mouths because of nerves."

At Bassingbourn, Tex McCrary, the Air Force's ace publicity man, was scheduled to fly in a Fortress called *Our Gang*. "I wanted to be at ringside. And I wanted to find out if I could 'cure' fear," the fear that had overcome him on the only mission he had flown in this war.

"The Jerries know what we are cooking up by now—bet they'll be wait-ing," said one crew member. Then the pilot came on the interphone: the zero hour was pushed back two hours. That was the signal for the crew to tumble out of the plane and wait on the runway. At this point, a friend of McCrary's learned that he was on *Our Gang* and drove out in a car to rescue him. It didn't take him long to talk McCrary out of what he desperately did not want to do.

At Thorpe Abbotts, Lt. Col. Beirne Lay, Jr., waited for the signal from the tower in the co-pilot's seat of *Piccadilly Lily,* one of crew chief Ken Lemmons's planes. Seated next to him was a nervy Irishman named Thomas Murphy. Lay was one of the biggest headquarters chieftains, part of Eaker's Original Seven that came to England to establish the Eighth Air Force. Tired of watching the war from behind a desk, Lay had begged

Eaker for a combat assignment and for the past ten days had been flying missions with the Hundredth to prepare himself to lead a heavy bombardment group, an assignment Eaker had finally promised him. He had originally been scheduled to fly as an observer on a plane called *Alice from Dallas* in Cleven's low squadron, but just before the pilots left for their planes, Cleven persuaded Kidd to move Lay to Murphy's plane, in the more protected squadron.

Sitting in *Piccadilly Lily,* nervously adjusting his watchband, Lay thought about the August morning that he had watched Paul Tibbets's puny force of B-17s take off for Rouen. That had been a maximum effort. On this day, exactly one year later, the Eighth was putting up thirty times the number of Fortresses it had sent to Rouen.

The plan was for LeMay's Regensburg force of 146 bombers to go in first, with the preponderance of the escorts. Williams's far larger Schweinfurt force of 230 bombers was to take off minutes later. The two forces were to fly a similar course, as if they were heading for the same target, and then split apart inside Germany, confusing and dividing the enemy's air defenses. LeMay's force was expected to take the brunt of the German counteroffensive, allowing the Schweinfurt armada to proceed to the target with only light resistance. With LeMay escaping over the Alps, the Schweinfurt force would be left to face the full fury of the Luftwaffe on its return to England. The plan was brutally simple: LeMay would fight his way in and Williams would fight his way out.

They were the two best combat leaders in the Eighth. No one was more responsible than Curtis LeMay for turning the Eighth into an efficient fighting force, and Williams was an experienced and audacious air commander, a dashing, one-eyed pilot who walked with a swagger stick and had test-flown the first Fortresses to come off Boeing's production line. Eaker counted on them, but now weather was threatening to disrupt everything.

At Bomber Command headquarters in High Wycombe, thirty-eight-year-old Frederick Anderson, the Eighth's new bombardment commander, had to make the most difficult decision of his life. He had three choices:

1. Cancel the mission and risk losing, for perhaps as long as two weeks, the ideal weather conditions that prevailed from the coast of Holland all the way to Africa.
2. Damn the English weather and send out both forces at the same time, with the risk of losing a great number of bombers in midair collisions.

3. Send the Regensburg force, which had to leave within the hour in order to make it to Africa by nightfall, and hold the Schweinfurt force until the weather cleared over its bases.

Anderson chose the third and, in hindsight, worst option. The elements held up the Schweinfurt force for another three and a half-hours. This would allow the Luftwaffe to hit the Regensburg force full-on and then regroup and attack the Schweinfurt bombers twice—entering Germany and leaving it. To give Williams's force more protection, most of the Thunderbolts scheduled to fly with LeMay were held back to convoy the Schweinfurt armada to the limit of the fighters' range, which, with improved belly tanks, extended almost to the place where the bombers would enter Germany.

Why did Anderson choose to release the bombers, knowing that the entire mission plan was unraveling in front of him? The Eighth Air Force command was under intense pressure from the airpower advocates in Washington to make this mission work, to prove, in the face of a year-long succession of failures and half-victories, that daylight bombing without escorts could work. Nothing less than the future of American strategic bombing seemed to be at stake on this mission. And if Anderson's bombers hit their targets, and the air planners in Washington were right in their prognostications about the importance of ball bearings, the Eighth might deliver a blow from which Germany could never recover. Such was the hubris of the bomber barons, still operating under flawed assumptions about combat effectiveness.

The mission began surprisingly well. LeMay had been training his crews all summer in instrument takeoffs, and his 4th Bombardment Wing did not lose a single bomber forming up in overcast so thick that the aircraft had to be led out to the runways with flashlights and lanterns. It was 7:30 A.M. when the Regensburg bombers broke through the cloud tops, with Curtis LeMay in the lead plane of the leading 96th Bomb Group. At four miles up, the sun was rising and the sky was a magnificent translucent blue. "We knew we were going to have our hands full, because it was such a beautiful day," a tail gunner from Nebraska recalled, "a swell day" for the Nazis to do some bomber hunting. And there was plenty of prey in the air, the bomber stream extending for fifteen miles across the sky.

When the lead planes reported enemy fighters ahead, Beirne Lay's mouth dried up and he felt his buttocks constrict. It was only a tentative attack, but both sides took damage. Down below, Lay saw a Fortress explode and disappear in an orange ball of flame. It was *Alice from Dallas*. Gale Cleven's last-minute intervention had saved Lay's life.

Near the town of Eupen, Belgium, ten miles from the German border and 300 miles from Regensburg, the last of the escorting Thunderbolts from Zemke's 56th Fighter Group turned back for England. Just then, a hurricane of enemy fighters tore into the bombers, diving, spinning, and firing their wing cannons "from all around the clock." The Germans went after the rear groups—the 95th and 100th Bomb Groups—blowing six Forts out of the sky. "The sight was fantastic and surpassed fiction," Lay wrote in his mission report. "I fought an impulse to close my eyes, and overcame it."

This was the first of a "hailstorm" of fighter assaults that continued almost all the way to the target. "I knew that I was going to die, and so were a lot of others," Lay wrote later. The German pilots were as frightened as he was. "We climbed and made perfect contact with the Boeings," recalled Lt. Alfred Grislawski. "There were so many of them that we were all shaken to the marrow." But their "hunting instinct" was awakened by the realization that the Americans were headed for the heart of their homeland. "These Jerries must have had families in Hamburg to want us this bad," Gale Cleven said later. Many did, and were out for revenge.

The Luftwaffe was up in greater numbers than ever before. Its front-line day defense in the west had recently increased from 250 fighters in March 1943 to over 400, mostly the result of emergency redeployments from the Mediterranean and Russian fronts. And fighting over their own fields, pilots could attack until they were almost out of fuel and ammunition and then land, refuel, and rearm.

For most of the fight, Cleven's sidekick John Egan stayed in the cramped nose of Captain Cruikshank's plane firing a .50 caliber machine gun, while navigator Frank Murphy fired the left nose gun and Lt. Augie Gaspar, the bombardier, handled the gun positioned in the center of the Plexiglas nose. Soon all of them were kneeling in ankle-deep piles of shells, praying that their gun barrels wouldn't melt from the extreme heat of repeated fire. Emergency hatches, unopened parachute packs, exploding engines, and body parts flew by them in the slipstream. Lay saw a German pilot step out of his burning plane, fold himself into a ball as he fell, and do a triple somersault through the Hundredth's formation. "He was evidently making a delayed jump, for I didn't see his parachute open."

The rear portions of LeMay's force had been under unremitting attack for nearly thirty minutes and had lost fourteen bombers, and the task force was still more than a hundred miles from Regensburg. At this point, on what seemed to be a ride into extinction, Lay looked down at Gale Cleven's plane, leader of the low squadron, and saw that its nose had been shot out and that one engine was on fire. As Lay learned later, it had been hit six times by 20mm cannon shells, its bombardier was wounded, and the radio operator, who had just heard that his wife was pregnant, was bleeding to death in a pool of frozen vomit, his legs severed above the knees. "His crew, some of them comparatively inexperienced youngsters, were preparing to bail out," Lay wrote in his report recommending Cleven for the Medal of Honor. "The . . . pilot pleaded repeatedly with Major Cleven to abandon ship. Major Cleven's reply . . . was as follows: 'You son of a bitch. You sit there and take it.' " Cleven's words were heard over the interphone and had a calming effect on the crew.

An hour and a half after the first fighter attack, LeMay's bomber column arrived at the target. "I knew that our bombardiers were grim as death while they synchronized their sights on the great Me-109 shops laying below us in the curve of the winding blue Danube, close to the outskirts of Regensburg," Lay wrote. Moments later, a red light flashed on the instrument panel of *Piccadilly Lily.* "Our bombs were away. We turned from the target toward the snow-capped Alps."

From Regensburg, it was seventy miles to the Alps and from there nearly five hours to North Africa. The German fighters did not have the range to follow them into the mountains, but some determined pilots pursued them part of the way. "You could tell how important getting to the Alps was by listening to all the praying that was going on over the interphone," a gunner would tell a reporter from *Yank.* "It sounded like a flying church."

After eleven hours in the air, Tom Murphy's plane landed in the Algerian desert with its fuel gauges on empty—ten of the survivors from a mission that had seen total crew losses of 240. Beirne Lay slept that night close to the wing of his plane, under a star-filled sky. "My radio headset was back in the ship. And yet I could hear the deep chords of great music."

Men talked themselves to sleep that night in the African desert not knowing how the Schweinfurt force had fared. Around midday, while the Regensburg raiders were fighting their way to the target, the sun finally burned the heavy mist off airfields in England and the Schweinfurt force took to the sky. When it reached Eupen at 2:10 in the afternoon, it arrived, unknowingly, at a historic moment in the Eighth Air Force's battle with the Luftwaffe. "I think that very moment when the P-47s left and we went on to suffer all those casualties was the major turning point [in the air war]," William H. Wheeler, a pilot with the 91st Bomb Group remarked forty years later. "The Air Force had it proved to them that their idea of sending B-17s unescorted on a deep penetration just wasn't valid."

Within minutes General Williams saw on the horizon the yellow noses of the lead planes of the largest Luftwaffe force ever to attack an American bomber formation, an estimated 300 fighters, more than double the number LeMay had had to contend with. It was the beginning of an air fight unprecedented in size and ferocity. So many men bailed out of planes that it looked "like a parachute invasion," said one airman. Elmer Bendiner remembered looking down and "counting the fitful yellow-orange flares" on the ground. They were not houses or towns, he quickly realized; they were Fortresses on fire. "We followed the burning Fortresses all the way to the target," recalled Lt. Col. Lewis E. Lyle of the 303rd Bomb Group. "I flew sixty-nine missions in the war, and none of them was this bad."

Flying over the Rhine, William Wheeler's Fortress was turned into a flaming torch by German fighters. Wheeler was trapped, upside down, in the burning plane as it went spining to earth but somehow made it to the forward escape hatch and out into the slipstream, just as the plane's left wing was torn from the fuselage by an explosion.

His last thought as he cleared the aircraft was of his girlfriend back in England. An hour later, he was sitting on an iron cot in the "dungeon like" jail of a small German town, eating a sandwich of black bread and sausage. It had been sixteen hours since his last meal.

For many survivors, the battle to and from Schweinfurt was a continuous nightmare, no one part clearly distinguishable from the other, except for the rescue—"the blessed sight of soaring Thunderbolts above the Channel coast." Flying their second mission of the day, Zemke's Thunderbolts risked annihilation by the enemy by holding on to their highly combustible drop tanks, made of pressed paper, until they were near the border between Belgium and Germany. The extra fuel allowed them to fly fifteen miles east of Eupen, where they surprised one of the Luftwaffe's elite attack groups just as it was prepared to make a final run at the retreating bombers. The Luftwaffe got the worst of it. Zemke's P-47s shot down at least eleven German fighters and lost only three of their own.

The American bombers began landing around six o'clock, many of them at the first British field they could find. Thirty-six failed to make it back, ten from the 91st Bomb Group. One of them was *Our Gang*. Seeing Tex McCrary walk into the Operations Room that evening, a friend looked up from his work and commented dryly, "Hello luck."

The crew of *Tondelayo* had been in the air for eight hours and forty minutes and under fire for close to six hours. After debriefing, the men staggered to their bunks. As Elmer Bendiner put his head on the pillow, he wondered: "Did we win? Did we lose?"

The next morning the airmen learned in the English papers that they had destroyed the target and won a hard-fought victory. The *London Daily Herald* reported the loss of only two Fortresses, both of which had landed safely in neutral Switzerland. Regensburg was "literally wiped off the map," said a euphoric Lt. General Harold George, one of the original Bomber Mafia, who was in England on an inspection tour; and the Luftwaffe had taken a terrific beating, supposedly losing 288 fighters. "The Hun now has no place to hide," Anderson cabled congratulations to LeMay in North Africa.

At Regensburg, a beautifully preserved medieval city of 80,000 inhabitants, the bombing had been accurate. The target was saturated by high explosives and incendiaries and only a handful of civilians were killed. "I am impressed by the precision with which those bastards bomb," German fighter pilot Heinz Knoke noted in his diary. "It is fantastic."

"We really thought that we had turned the trick, and that perhaps no Messerschmitts would ever be manufactured down there . . . again," LeMay wrote later. "That . . . plant was completely out of action–briefly." LeMay correctly emphasized the last word. The factory was rebuilt in record time and Albert Speer intensified efforts to disperse other fighter assembly plants, hiding them in remote woodland and mountain sites.

At Schweinfurt, the bombing was inaccurate. Three widely separated plants had to be hit and Williams's navigators had trouble locating them, hindered by formation disorganization and swirling smoke from artificial fog generators that rimmed the city. Disoriented bombardiers dropped about a third of their explosives in residential areas of the city, killing 200 civilians, and the bombs that did hit the plants were not powerful enough to smash the important machine tools on the factory floor. The Americans dropped 1,000-pound bombs on Schweinfurt at a time when the British were regularly dropping 4,000- and, in some cases, 8,000-pound bombs. Factory roofs at Schweinfurt that collapsed as a result of bomb damage actually protected the ball bearing machines from major damage. While production dropped immediately by 38 percent, Speer had enough reserve stocks to see Germany through what turned out to be a temporary production setback. Without realizing it, however, the Americans destroyed the shop that was turning out parts to manufacture one of Hitler's secret wonder weapons, the Messerschmitt 262, delaying production of the jet plane that could have prolonged the air war.

In his memoirs Albert Speer wrote of escaping a "catastrophic blow." If the Americans had returned to Schweinfurt and hit it "repeatedly" and with maximum force instead of wasting their time on other less important targets, they could have brought armaments production "to a standstill . . . after four months." Historians have seized on Speer's remarks to attack Allied bombing priorities, but Speer was merely repeating the recommendation of Hap Arnold's Committee of Operations Analysts, which had recommended the concentrated strikes Speer feared. "The enemy economy was far too large . . . to blast it all," Elihu Root, Jr., explained the committee's thinking. "We had to choose vital points where small physical damage would cause great industrial disruption." And the committee agreed that the bombing "should be . . . pressed forward with inexorable energy, because there was bound to be a race between destruction on the one hand and repair and evasion on the other." But how does one press forward without delay after taking such losses?

In August 1943, Speer had no idea how badly the Eighth had been hurt on its double strike. In a press conference in London, General Harold George, one of the original Bomber Mafia at Maxwell Field, claimed that the loss of sixty bombers was worth the damage inflicted on the enemy. But he failed to mention that this was almost a fifth of the attacking force, and that another hundred bombers were permanently lost as a result of battle damage, a total loss of approximately 40 percent of the force sent out from England. In one afternoon, the Eighth had lost almost as many bombers as it had in its first six months of operations. Attacking Schweinfurt "repeatedly" with this depleted fleet in the weeks following the first raid would have been an act of insanity.

Originally, Eighth Air Force planners had expected to deliver a double blow to Schweinfurt, with the RAF blasting the city on the night of August 17. Had such an attack been made, it "might have had an early and severe effect on many vital elements of German front-line strength," according to the postwar testimony of factory managers at Schweinfurt. But weather conditions that night were ideal for attacking a secret Nazi research installation at Peenemünde on the Baltic coast that Allied intelligence had recently discovered. And after bombing Peenemünde, Sir Arthur Harris went right after Berlin. "We can wreck Berlin from end to end if the USAAF will come in on it. It will cost between 400–500 aircraft. It will cost Germany the war." The RAF did not bomb Schweinfurt until the following February, the night after the third American raid, and then only under the insistent pressure of the chief of air staff, Sir Charles Portal. Harris himself defiantly insisted that the target experts that recommended ball bearings were "completely mad."

At the tactical level, the double strike of August 17 was a decisive victory for the German defenses. The fantastically inflated American claim of 288 fighters destroyed was nearly in excess of the entire German force that attacked the Eighth that day. Actual German losses were forty-seven fighters. But Hitler was not celebrating. Germany had been hurt more than the Americans realized. Infuriated by the summer attacks on Hamburg, Regensburg, Schweinfurt, and Peenemünde, Hitler put the blame on Hans Jeschonnek, the Luftwaffe Chief of Staff. On August 18, a despairing Jeschonnek put a bullet in his brain.

Nineteen forty-three was the turning point in the war against Germany. Defeated at Stalingrad, in North Africa, in Sicily, and in the waters of the North Atlantic, Hitler's ground and naval forces were under pressure on all fronts. A week before the Ploesti mission, Italian dictator Benito Mussolini was ousted by a palace rebellion and the already overextended German army was forced to rush crack divisions into southern Italy to meet the expected Allied invasion, which would occur in early September. By then, Germany would be fighting a two-front war—actually a three-front war, in Speer's estimation. The war in the air, in his opinion, was the one Germany could least afford to lose. In the summer of '43, the air front was still holding, but the Allies were increasing the pressure. As Roosevelt told reporters, "Hitler built walls around his 'Fortress Europe' but he forgot to put a roof on it."

With the exception of the Battle of Britain, Western Europe had been a secondary theater for the Luftwaffe until late summer of 1943. Now, with the fatherland under a double assault from the air, what had been the peripheral became the central air theater. All other theaters were bled to feed it, with the result that Wehrmacht soldiers were rarely again to have sufficient air support for military operations, a disabling liability.

Still, Speer was frustrated by Hitler's refusal to take the rising American threat seriously enough. The leader he slavishly worshipped failed to make a distinction between Harris's city-smashing campaign and the less spectacular, but potentially more lethal strategic bombing of the Americans, seeing them wrongheadedly as closely linked efforts to destroy German civilian morale. To Hitler, the American raids of 1943 were minor nuisances compared to Harris's devastating strikes on Germany's densely settled cities, raids he feared would undermine popular support for his regime. Instead of ordering the overwhelming numbers of fighter aircraft for defense that fighter chief Adolf Galland and Field Marshal Erhard

Milch, head of the Luftwaffe's armaments program, were demanding, Hitler concentrated instead on building up antiaircraft batteries around large cities—which shot down less than half as many bombers as fighters did, but produced spectacular morale-boosting fireworks displays—and on producing hugely expensive vengeance weapons. Chief among these reprisal weapons was the V-2 rocket, a short-range ballistic missile being developed by Dr. Wernher von Braun and his team of scientists. "This will be retribution against England," Hitler told his generals after von Braun showed him a color film demonstrating the rocket's supersonic speed and destructive potential. Even an initially skeptical Speer bowed to Hitler's demands and gave both the V-2 program and the Army's program for a V-1 flying bomb—a more primitive weapon than von Braun's unstoppable rocket—top priority. After the Hamburg raids, Hitler became fixated on the idea that "terror can only be broken with terror. . . . The German people," he thundered to his aides, "demand reprisals." By bringing down destruction on English cities he would force the RAF to stop its punishing night raids. "I can only win this war if I destroy more of the enemy's [cities] than he destroys of ours," he told one his generals. But without a strategic force of four-engine bombers to conduct sustained, deeply effective air raids against British cities, he would have to wait for the appearance of his reprisal rockets. (Germany had wanted to mount such a force in the late 1930s, to complement its potent medium bombers, but its designers were never able to correct engine problems with the He 177, the Luftwaffe's hoped-for long-range strategic bomber.)

Meanwhile, more rational minds concentrated on building up the Reich's defenses. Only by secretly countermanding and evading Hitler's wishes was Milch able to produce fighter planes in sufficient numbers to defend the homeland in 1943, and to have Galland deploy those fighters in force against the "daylight raiders," whose precision raids were, in Galland's view, "of greater consequence to the war industry" than the RAF's area attacks. Due in large part to Milch's efforts, fighter production increased by 125 percent in 1943 and rose again the following year. But he and Speer were fighting a losing battle with the combined industrial power of the Anglo-American Allies. When shown fantastic Allied production figures for 1943—151,000 aircraft to the Reich's 43,000—Hitler refused to believe them. And the führer's views mattered even more in 1943, the year he, an army man, assumed almost complete control of air operations, stripping the indolent and technologically ignorant Göring of all but ceremonial power over the Luftwaffe. Only Hitler's deep personal commitment to Göring, whom he spoke of as a "second Wagner" in terms of his breadth of vision and imagination, kept the morphine-addicted *Reichsmarschall* in power.

Equally ominous for the Luftwaffe, massive attrition battles in the air on all fronts were badly eroding aircraft strength, despite increases in production. In the month of August 1943, the Luftwaffe had lost 334 fighters over Western Europe. "Losses at the front," Luftwaffe historian Williamson Murray wrote, "swallowed what industry produced."

The Regensburg-Schweinfurt mission had an equally discouraging effect on the Allied high command; it was as if both sides had lost the battle. That August, at a conference in Quebec to discuss the Normandy invasion, Churchill, with General Marshall's support, dismissed the extravagant claims of the bomber barons and again questioned whether the daylight offensive should continue. Hap Arnold publicly defended Eaker's command, but privately he shared his growing concern with Robert Lovett. "Hap was having a hell of a time hanging on," Lovett recalled. "I can't document it but I think he was beginning to worry about [the future of daylight bombing] because the attrition rate was too high." A month later, after a quick trip to England, the great champion of the idea of the self-defending bomber was writing to Marshall: "Operations over Germany conducted here during the past several weeks indicate definitely that we must provide long-range fighters to accompany daylight bombardment missions."

Asked years later what he considered the major lesson of the European air war, Ted Timberlake, former commander of Ted's Traveling Circus, was quick to reply: the Eighth Air Force's "overestimate" of its major weapon, the B-17. "Prior to World War II, if you told the average officer of the Air Corps that it was going to take [repeated] raids of 1,000 to 1,500 heavy bombers to put out a particular target . . . they would have laughed at you." And back then no one would have believed that the "bomber could not live in an atmosphere that had a good air defense." It took the Ploesti and Regensburg-Schweinfurt missions to fully convert General Arnold. But with the long-range fighter and the thousand-bomber fleet still in the future, he and Eaker had to continue to apply pressure with what they had. So Arnold urged Eaker to go back to Schweinfurt to finish the job as soon as possible.

"[After August 17] life will never be the same," Chaplain James Good Brown wrote in his diary from his tiny room beside the chapel at Ridgewell airbase. His 381st had suffered the highest losses of all bomb groups on the Schweinfurt mission, and the atmosphere on the base was like a "morgue." Brown had been with the 381st Bomb Group since basic training in Pyote,

Texas, when hope ran so high that the group felt it would never lose a man. He had left his wife and his church in Lee, Massachusetts, to be with these men he felt closer to than his own brothers. The 381st was his "parish and congregation." He thought he knew the men, but Schweinfurt had changed them. He was aware of this because airmen unable to sleep came to him in the middle of the night with their fears. Some said they had dreams in which they could actually feel the cold clasp of their dead companions. "Men eat in silence. They arise and leave the table in silence. If they ask for anything at the table, it is a low murmur. Or they may go without butter in order not to talk. On the roads men pass by without acknowledging each other. If they smile, it is forced."

It was the same at Thorpe Abbotts. Nine of the group's bombers—ninety men—were missing, the beginning of the Hundredth's reputation as a "hard-luck outfit." Several days after returning from Africa, navigator Frank Murphy wrote his mother in Atlanta to tell her that the war had become a "nightmare" for him. "I'm still okay and healthy, but can't say how long it'll be this way. . . . Just keep up the letters and pray for me once in a while—I'll certainly need it."

Many ground soldiers worried more about being disfigured and dismembered than dying. Not airmen. If luck ran against them, they expected to be killed, not wounded. In ground combat, for every soldier killed, three or four were wounded. In the Army Air Forces in World War II, over three times as many men were killed as wounded.

What saved these men from despair was the life instinct, always strongest in the young, with their powerful sense of indestructibility. Covering another theater of the war that same month, John Steinbeck wrote that every young and green soldier, scanning the frightened faces of his comrades, "sees death there." But in his heart, he believes that he will be exempt. It was this fantastic delusion that held him together. Writing about Regensburg a half-century later, Frank Murphy recalled the haunting British verse from World War I:

> *The Bells of Hell go ting-a ling-a-ling*
> *For you, but not for me*

CHAPTER EIGHT

Men at War

Men at war were different from men at home. Whatever
they were stateside, they were more of in England.
Whatever was good in them became very good; what was
bad became very bad.

HARRY CROSBY, *A WING AND A PRAYER*

East Anglia, September 6, 1943

At the end of Ira Eaker's summer offensive, it appeared that the enemy was winning the war in the skies over the Reich. For three weeks after the Regensburg-Schweinfurt mission the battered and depleted Eighth Air Force did not venture beyond the protective umbrella of its fighter cover. When it finally did, on September 6, the raid was one of the worst fiascoes in its history.

A blanket of clouds hid the target, a ball bearing plant at Stuttgart, and the bombers began circling the city aimlessly, wasting precious fuel, looking for breaks in the overcast while fighting off the Luftwaffe. Over 230 of the 338 Fortresses dispatched to the target left Stuttgart with their bomb bays filled. Their discouraged bombardiers dropped their excess weight randomly on "targets of opportunity" on their way back to England. Near Paris, the red lights on the fuel gauges of some B-17s began to flicker and minutes later, bombers started to go down into the English Channel. One of them was *Tondelayo*.

"To hit a wave broadside is very much like flying into a stone wall," Elmer Bendiner recalled. Seconds later, torrents of green-gray water came rushing into the plane and it began to sink, but the men kept their composure and all managed to climb into the bomber's two rubber dinghies. Nine hours later, a British rescue boat picked up the ten waxen-faced crewmen.

Eleven other Forts had gone into the water, and by nightfall the British had rescued the crews of all of them. On his return to Kimbolton, Bendiner learned that forty-five Forts were lost in an attack that should have been called back as soon as the bombers hit impossibly heavy weather over the Continent, by which time seventy-six of the Fortresses had aborted. There were costlier missions, but none aroused greater resentment among the crews. Some airmen felt that lives had been sacrificed to put on a good show for Gen. Hap Arnold, who was in England that week pressuring Ira Eaker to once again "carry the flag deep into Germany."

Our Father Who Art in Heaven

After Stuttgart, Ira Eaker began experimenting with night bombing. Churchill was still pressuring Arnold to fold the Eighth into Bomber Command; if forced to bomb at night, Eaker wanted to be ready. That September, a squadron of the 305th Bomb Group flew eight night missions with the RAF, one of them as far as Munich. Losses were minimal and some of the crewmen were convinced that the Americans could bomb successfully at night. In early October, Ralph Nutter, a lead navigator on the Munich mission, was prepared to recommend to his division commander that the Eighth continue night operations until it received long-range escorts. But to Eaker's relief, Arnold remained committed to daylight operations. (In September, the Eighth Air Force was reorganized. The 1st, 2nd, and 4th Bombardment Wings became, respectively, the 1st, 2nd, and 3rd Air Divisions. The 2nd Air Division was an all-Liberator unit. The term "combat wing" continued to refer to an informal battle formation made up of three bomb groups.)

When the weather cleared over Germany on October 8, Eaker launched a succession of maximum-effort missions, a second Blitz Week. After it was over the men would have a more appropriate name for it: Black Week.

The first raid was against heavily defended targets in the Bremen-Vegesack area. The following day, the bombers hit aircraft plants at Anklam, north of Berlin, and at Marienburg, on the Vistula, south of the port of Danzig, the longest mission of the war up to this point. And on the tenth, it was Münster. The Eighth took appalling losses on these strikes—eighty-eight heavy bombers—and the Hundredth was decimated, losing almost 200 men, nearly half its airmen. On the day after Rosie Rosenthal's crew returned alone from Münster—where in twelve minutes the Hundredth lost twelve of thirteen planes—five of the group's original leaders, John Egan, Gale Cleven, Frank Murphy, Howard "Hambone" Hamilton, and John Brady, were in German stockades. Three others, Harry Crosby, John Kidd, and Everett Blakely, were recovering from a harrowing crash near Norwich, England, on October 8.

The Hundredth had arrived in England four months before Münster with 140 flying officers; after Münster, only three of them remained on flying status. A week later, one of these men told a friend that he used to think that "the most mournful sound in the world" was the whistle of a freight train in the middle of the night. That was wrong, he said. It was the "the hum of engines on the flight line" in the darkness before dawn.

The men from Ridgewell were also hit hard that week. At Anklam, along the North Sea, the group lost all of the original fliers that were still left in the outfit, the "old men" the replacements had looked to for inspiration. "We are an entirely new outfit" Chaplain Brown wrote in his diary, "[and] no longer . . . a family." Five days later, on October 14, in the gray hours of first light, the Ridgewell boys were shocked into silence when the briefing officer pulled back the curtain from the wall map and pointed to Schweinfurt. After the briefing, some men walked to the back of the room and knelt in front of the Catholic chaplain for his blessing; others huddled with Chaplain Brown before going to their huts to write a final letter.

The pilot of the lead group of Eighth Air Force Mission Number 115 was J. Kemp McLaughlin of Charleston, West Virginia. This was the same J. Kemp McLaughlin who, a year earlier, had flown his maiden mission to Lille, a mission on which his commanding officer had turned coward in the plane. This time McLaughlin was flying with a rock-steady veteran, Col. Budd Peaslee, air commander of the entire Schweinfurt mission. Together they would lead over 300 heavies to the Franconian city where so many of their friends had died.

That morning, there were more enemy fighters in the air than on the first Schweinfurt mission, and dozens of them were rocket ships: converted twin-engine night fighters, most of them Junkers 88s, capable of launching 250-pound missiles from tubes suspended beneath their wings—called stovepipes by the Germans. These were the rockets that had helped decimate the Hundredth at Münster—fused missiles that streaked toward the bombers and detonated at a predetermined range, creating bursts four times the size of ordinary flak explosions. Unlike machine gun and cannon fire, which killed the bombers slowly, the rockets—when they hit mid-ship— destroyed them instantly. The Junkers launched the missiles out of range of the bombers' guns. The explosions forced the American pilots to take evasive action, breaking up the combat boxes. Then the single-engine fighters swooped in, concentrating on one formation at a time, paying deadly attention to stragglers.

These were tactics designed to produce terror and despair in the American crews. Only halfway to the target, the ordinarily unflappable Peaslee said to McLaughlin, "Captain, I think we've had it," but somehow they got through to the target. At the Initial Point, McLaughlin handed over control of the plane to the bombardier, who flew it through the automatic flight control equipment built into his Norden bombsight. "The run was I guess what you'd call a bombardier's dream," bombardier Edward O'Grady said later. "Colonel Peaslee kept calling me saying, 'Get that target! Get it.' "

He did. The B-17s did fearsome damage but lost sixty bombers to the Germans and another seventeen to crash landings in England. Almost thirty percent of the bombers that had made it into Germany failed to return. Bad weather had prevented the Thunderbolts from rendezvousing with the returning heavies, so the fighter attacks persisted deep into northern France. "It seemed like an endless run through a terrible maze," wrote Elmer Bendiner, who was flying with his old crew in a new B-17G model equipped with a twin-barreled, remote-controlled chin turret. Located directly under the nose, it was designed to discourage frontal attacks. It was no use to them on their way back from Schweinfurt, when most of the attacks came from the rear.

In the tail gun compartment of a Fortress named *Tiger Girl*, nineteen-year-old Eugene T. Carson, "Wing Ding" to his crewmates, was sitting in a heap of empty shell casings firing his twin .50s with the desperation of a doomed man. He knew that if his plane was hit he was a goner; he had forgotten to pack his parachute. "We were being mauled. . . . I could not see how we were going to make it home." When the fighters suddenly broke off their attack, Carson—a former dough man in a bakery in Annville, Pennsylvania—bent forward, rested his head on the window of his gun compartment, and "began to shake and cry uncontrollably."

With the skies clear of Germans, it became ghostly quiet in Captain McLaughlin's ship. When the wheels of the Fortress touched down on English soil, O'Grady raised an American flag from the hatch above his position in the nose. His aunt had given it to him before he went overseas, and his parish priest had blessed it. When the flag went up, Colonel Peaslee "let out a cheer." As they taxied around the perimeter of the airfield, the ground crews snapped to attention and saluted O'Grady's flag. The salutes, McLaughlin knew, were not for the national flag, but for the men "who had made the supreme sacrifice that day."

Black Thursday was the greatest air engagement up to that time—not just a raid but a titanic struggle between two large and murderous air armies, one with 229 bombers and the other with over 300 fighters. The battle line extended for over 800 miles and the action was continuous for three hours and fourteen minutes. Only thirty-three American bombers landed without battle damage, and there were 642 casualties among the 2,900 crewmen, over 18 percent of the force.

The German losses were also deep: over a hundred aircraft destroyed or damaged. After the raid Luftwaffe commanders pleaded for more fighters, but Göring and Hitler replied, as they had before, by pouring more money into revenge weapons. This time, however, they questioned the courage of their pilots. At one stormy meeting with Göring, Adolf Galland became so incensed that he removed his Knight's Cross, the military's most highly regarded award, and slammed it on the table. "The atmosphere was tense and still," Galland wrote later. "The *Reichsmarschall* had literally lost the power of speech, and I looked him firmly in the eye, ready for anything. Nothing happened, and Goering quietly finished what he had had to say. For six months after that I did not wear my war decorations."

When Erhard Milch, director of air-armaments, told Göring that he was concerned about the ability of German fighters to defend the cities of the homeland against ever larger American and British raids, Göring replied that "the nation had lived before there were cities." German fighter production did increase in late 1943, but with the stupendous American industrial machine behind it, the Eighth was better able to absorb large losses than the Luftwaffe.

Even to win a war of attrition is a terrible thing for the victorious side. After Black Thursday, morale in the Eighth plummeted to a new low and commanders worried about a crew revolt. "I will never fly another mission, regardless of the cost," a gunner told his friends in the privacy of their Nissen hut, where twelve of the twenty cots were empty that night.

After Black Thursday, a story spread through the ranks of the Eighth Air Force that, although not true in its particulars, expressed the new mood. It was about a solitary, shot-up B-17 limping home to England. Someone on the plane radioed the tower: "Hello Lazy Fox. This is G for

George, calling Lazy Fox. Will you give me landing instructions, please? Pilot and co-pilot dead, two engines feathered, fire in the radio room, vertical stabilizer gone, no flaps, no brakes, crew bailed out, bombardier flying the ship. Give me landing instructions."

The reply came a few seconds later:

"I hear you G for George. Here are your landing instructions, Repeat slowly, please, repeat slowly. Our Father, who art in heaven . . ."

Myths

When Albert Speer got through by telephone to a plant manager at Schweinfurt, he learned that the damage was far greater than the August raid. The Germans lost 67 percent of their ball bearing production. Even before learning the full extent of the destruction, Hap Arnold was euphoric. "Now we have got Schweinfurt," he told reporters. "It was possible," he added incredulously, that bombing itself could ultimately knock Germany out of the war, with ground troops sent into the scorched and defeated land merely "for police purposes." (He somehow forgot about the Russians, who in the extremely unlikely event of a victory achieved through airpower alone would have swept into Germany, pushed aside Arnold's policing battalions, and taken over the entire country.) Even tight-lipped Curtis LeMay was enthusiastic. "Winter holds no hope for Germany," he told an Associated Press correspondent.

The bomber barons could not possibly have believed their own sunny rhetoric. Intelligence intercepts and reports from secret agents inside the Reich gave them a sobering assessment of Germany's recuperative powers. Albert Speer, it was learned, had appointed his most trusted associate, Paul Kessler, as the new czar of ball bearing production, and Kessler was inaugurating a crash program to disperse production to smaller plants and to purchase additional ball bearings from neutral Sweden and Switzerland. Even after this dispersal program failed when local Nazi leaders successfully fought the introduction of new war industries—bomb targets—into their towns, the ingenious Albert Speer substituted "slide" bearings for ball bearings.

When asked by reporters about additional raids on Schweinfurt, General Frederick Anderson warned the American public not to expect immediate and "sensational" developments in the bombing campaign. "Staging a major air operation every day," he said, "was like expecting land and sea forces to take the island of Sicily every day." But "there is nothing else at this time [except airpower] that can hit at the heart of Germany." He had a point. With Allied ground forces bogged down in a campaign of mud and misery in the mountains of central Italy, and with the Russians bearing the burden of the war against the Wehrmacht on their home soil, the only way the Anglo-American allies could directly hurt Germany was from the skies.

Perhaps the greatest myth of the European air war is the idea that after Black Thursday the American Air Force called a halt to unescorted missions deep inside Germany until long-range fighters became available, because, according to official Air Force historians, the Eighth had temporarily lost air mastery over Germany. In the fall of 1943, neither the Germans nor the Allies had gained air mastery over Northern Europe, so there was no air mastery to lose. The battle was in the balance. The Luftwaffe had shot down ruinous numbers of bombers in October—an average of twenty-eight bombers per mission—but not a single Eighth Air Force raid had been turned back, and the home-front fighter command was paying a hellish price for tactical victories, 248 fighters lost in October alone. This amounted to 17 percent of Germany's total fighter force in the West. Luftwaffe commanders were also concerned about the enhanced range of America's fighter escorts. By October, Thunderbolts equipped with larger drop tanks were seen over German border towns, sightings an obdurate Göring refused to believe. Meeting with his war-weary pilots in early November, Adolf Galland told them that they had yet to achieve "decisive success" against the Boeings.

In an equally fought battle of attrition both sides sometimes believe they are losing. With Overlord planned for the spring of 1944, Allied leaders became increasingly worried that their air forces would not have sufficient time and strength to achieve, not just air superiority, but the air supremacy Eisenhower deemed essential for the success of the largest amphibious invasion in history. For this reason alone the bomber offensive could not have been officially suspended after Black Thursday; the entire invasion depended upon its success. In the grim calculus of total war, it was considered far better to lose a few hundred unprotected bombers than to have entire divisions slaughtered on the beaches of northern France.

Contrary to myth, no directive was issued to call off unescorted deep-penetration raids into the Reich. "There's a lot of muddled thinking by writers on this subject," Curtis LeMay told James Parton after the war. "I don't think there was ever definite waiting for fighters. . . . We had to depend only on what fighters were available." Eaker was undeniably more cautious with his thinned-out bomber fleet in the immediate aftermath of

Black Thursday, but even before he was reinforced in November, he had his staff begin drawing up plans for "a maximum effort" against the enemy aircraft industry, an operation code-named Argument. "This is the complete answer," he told Arnold on October 22, "to [Germany's] propaganda that we cannot take the losses they are able to inflict."

Black Thursday *should* have killed the idea of the self-defending bomber, but it did not. Eaker clung stubbornly to it. "We must continue the battle with unrelenting fury," he cabled Arnold the day after the Schweinfurt raid. "This we shall do." According to Parton, in later years Eaker said that he and Anderson "would have gone right back into the heart of Germany, even without the long-range fighters, if weather had permitted." But the weather refused to cooperate. Beginning in mid-October, heavy clouds masked vital targets inside Germany until early January, making pinpoint bombing impossible. As Parton aptly put it, "Control of the air in the two and half months after Schweinfurt II belonged to the clouds."

But an impatient Arnold would not take weather as an excuse. He continued to press Eaker to take longer risks with the additional planes and crews he was sending him. Arnold was unrelenting because he himself was under continuous pressure to justify a budget of billions and the deployment, worldwide, of almost a third of the Army's manpower. Behind this was his career-long determination to make the United States Air Force completely autonomous. That would happen only if the Eighth proved— and very soon—that daylight strategic bombing could work, with or without long-range fighters. Speaking for the men who paid the price to try to make that experiment work, Elmer Bendiner has written that it is "a pity" that prewar theories of American airpower could not have been tested in a laboratory with "flying guinea pigs."

Flak Farm

The week after Black Thursday, J. Kemp McLaughlin and the officers in his crew were dispatched to a rest home for a week of relaxation and recuperation. Beginning in 1942, the Air Force had begun to establish retreats— "flak farms," airmen called them—for war-weary fliers. Airmen sent there by their squadron flight surgeons were suffering from a mild form of combat exhaustion, were at the midpoint of their tours of duty, or had recently had a mind-shaking experience in the sky. Most of the flak farms were manor houses donated by their owners to the RAF, who, in turn, leased them to the Eighth Air Force. By the end of the war there were fifteen of them. Air Force medical officers visited the rest houses regularly, but responsibility for running them was gradually turned over to the women of the American Red Cross. The aim was to make them "as un-military as possible." At first, separate facilities were established for officers and sergeants; later, entire crews were sometimes sent to the same place, and recognition of rank was discouraged. Lounging around the grounds in baggy sweaters, slacks, and sneakers, off-duty airmen could easily have been mistaken for sportsmen on holiday.

McLaughlin and his fellow flying officers spent their respite from the war at Stanbridge Earles, a Southampton estate that was the site of the home of King Ethelwulf, father of Alfred the Great. The gray-faced estate house, with its cut glass windows and crenellated towers, contained eighteen superbly appointed bedrooms. The punctilious butler woke the men every morning at nine-thirty with trays of orange juice, and apple-cheeked Red Cross hostesses met them at breakfast to help plan their day, a schedule that might include a hunt with hounds or a round of skeet shooting on the baronial back lawn.

When tail gunner Eugene "Wing Ding" Carson was flown to a rest home in southern England after the Schweinfurt mission, he showed little interest in badminton or bicycling. Noticing that the comely young maid assigned to his room was "more than a little friendly," he spent a good part of his week with her, finding this a most "remarkable tonic" for his combat exhaustion.

The mission of the flak farms, according to a Red Cross manual, was to remind men "of the things which made them choose to fly and fight. The stronger their desire to live *for* something, the greater their ability to face their jobs." Put differently, their purpose was to keep men flying by keeping them from going crazy. This backfired on occasion. In a scene that Joseph Heller might have written into *Catch-22,* a crew that had been through a shattering experience in the air returned from a flak farm, where they had had time to dwell on their recent horror and unpromising future, and announced their unanimous decision never again to climb into a four-engine bomber. They were transferred to another base, reduced in rank, and placed on ground duty.

When *Stars and Stripes* reporter Andy Rooney visited the first ever sanctuary for sergeant gunners, he found it a "soldier heaven." At Gremlin Gables-on-the-Thames there were sun-lit lounges, turf tennis courts, and a dock on the river with punts and canoes. In the evenings, men stretched out in overstuffed chairs and flicked cigarette ashes on the carpet, if they felt like it. But the thing they talked about most in this restful setting was the organized murder that had brought them there. In a corner of the lounge, Rooney found three sergeant gunners stretched out on a carpet in front of a record player, reliving a sky fight. ". . . an' this guy is comin' in when I start beatin' at him about a thousand yards." Later that day, a group of gunners chose sides, piled into two river skiffs, and fought a mock air battle as they poled upstream toward the landing dock of a welcoming pub. "Enemy fighters comin' in at three o'clock," the gunner in one skiff shouted out the approach of a rival water boat. "Fighter at nine o'clock. Smear him!" And in seconds, the battle was on, the playful gunners splashing water on one another.

Standing on the lawn at the river's edge, three Air Force psychiatrists looked on like doting parents. "When those kids came here, they were [on] edge, nervous, tight all the way through," one of them commented. "They've been here, that bunch, four days. Look at them now. They're living again, not just existing." But part of living, the doctors should have known, was *not* forgetting about the war. Barbara Graves, director of the Red Cross's rest home division, understood this. In the unreal world airmen were thrown into "a man came to think of his plane, his flying mates and his own skill or endurance as the only familiar elements he has to hold on to," she wrote in a report to Eighth Air Force command. "He attaches a tremendous importance to them and suffers when anything happens to them." To forget the war completely was to forget who you had become and who you could count on when it mattered most. Not the understanding staff of a regal estate on the Thames, but nine other scared men in a Fortress under fire.

That evening at Gremlin Gables-on-the-Thames, after a dinner served with starched napery and centuries-old silver, Rooney accompanied a group of gunners to the garden of a local pub. The men talked, over mild and bitter, about baseball and babes until a British bomber rumbled across the night sky, angling for a nearby landing field. There was a long silence as the airmen followed the plane with their glowing eyes until it disappeared beyond a screen of poplars. One of the men, hands cupped in his chin, elbows on his knees, seemed transfixed by the Lancaster. "That's good," he said, "They're all right coming down like that. It's the other way that bothers me sometimes. When one of those big ships gets it, and goes down, and starts spinning around and around . . . that's no good . . ."

"Yeah, I know what you mean," a gunner standing in the doorway finished the thought. "Sort of like a giant getting killed, kind of."

That's how it was with men who never forgot they would soon be back at work.

Piccadilly

In the weeks after Black Thursday, with a foul weather system lingering over Europe and commanders worried sick about morale, great numbers of three- and seven-day leaves were granted to battle-drained crews. Most of the boys headed for London, which was a different place than Capt. Robert Morgan and his *Memphis Belle* crew visited in the winter of 1943. Back then, there were only 47,000 U.S. airmen in England and, with no replacements in sight, leaves had been given sparingly, making Yankee flyboys a rare sight in the war-bloated city. By the end of the year the number of Air Force personnel on the island had ballooned to over 286,000. These airmen comprised only a quarter of the strength of an immense and ever-increasing American troop buildup in preparation for the cross-Channel invasion. In the last three months of 1943, over 413,000 American troops disembarked at English ports, bringing the number of U.S. service personnel in Great Britain to over 773,000. On D-Day there would be a million and a half American soldiers in the U.K., 28 percent of them—nearly 427,000 men and women—members of the AAF.

Thousands of service personnel were stationed permanently in London, but the greatest number of people in uniform in the city were on leaves of absence from military bases scattered all over the suddenly crowded island nation, a country smaller than Minnesota. Most of them were from Britain, its empire, and the United States, but there were also French, Norwegian, Polish, Dutch, and Czech soldiers, sailors, nurses, and airmen in the city that had become their new capital in exile. "Battered and dirty, worn and scarred, [London] swarmed with scores of different uniforms and it spoke in a hundred different tongues," wrote Sgt. Robert Arbib, the construction engineer who visited the city regularly from his new posting, a short rail ride away. A small number of bomber boys came to London with a woman on their arm. Wing Ding Carson made his maiden trip to the big city with an Air WAC (Women's Army Corps) from Eighth Air Force headquarters whom he had met at his bomber base just after the Schweinfurt disaster, and Harry Crosby, a married man, toured the city with Dot, the Iowa girl he had been in love with before he met his wife. She was stationed at a Red Cross club in Cambridge. Crosby and Carson were the lucky ones. Most American airmen who stepped down from a passenger car at one of London's barrel-vaulted train sheds were in the city alone or with crewmates. As Andy Rooney wrote, "They had been hauling regularly," and needed to "take care of their physical needs."

London in the middle of the war was one of the most sensational places on the planet. Death and suffering had released inhibitions, and everywhere there were people in search of food, friends, liquor, and sex. The streets were jammed beyond belief. There were beggars sawing on old violins, gangs of drunken sailors, and smartly dressed women on the arms of colonels, their high heels clicking, their lipstick exactly right. And up on the rooftops, men and women, bundled against the cold, stood on fireguard, waiting for the sirens and bombs that would throw them into action.

With the Allies on the advance nearly everywhere and invasion talk in the air, London was a welcoming place for young airmen who were taking the fight to Hitler's doorstep. The first stop for American airmen was usually the nearest Red Cross Club, where helpful volunteers made bookings free of charge at commercial hotels or at one of the Red Cross's own dormitory-like facilities. After checking in and dropping off their kits, most men headed straight for Rainbow Corner. Located on the corner of Shaftesbury Avenue and Piccadilly Circus, it was a place as close to home as a GI could find in all of England.

Administered by the American Red Cross, Rainbow Corner had been designed "to create a strictly American atmosphere." There was an exact replica of a small-town corner drugstore in the club's basement, where ice-cold Cokes were sold for a nickel and grilled hamburgers for a dime. Upstairs, in the grand ballroom, servicemen danced with volunteer hostesses to the driving music of soldier bands—the Flying Forts, the Thunderbolts, the Sky Blazers. There was also a lounge with a jukebox and a small dance floor with tables and chairs around it. Lonely GIs dunking donuts in fresh coffee would loaf there, listening to the latest American hits. Rainbow Corner never closed its doors. The key had been symbolically thrown away the day of the grand opening in November 1942.

At a writing desk just across from the drugstore, women volunteers helped homesick servicemen write letters to wives, sweethearts, and mothers. The men's favorite aide was Lady Dellie, a delicate-looking woman with blazing eyes, the sister and dancing partner of Fred Astaire and the wife of Lord Charles Cavendish. "Adele took me under her wing, and clucked like a mother hen," recalled Eugene Carson, who met her when he returned to London without his American girlfriend. "She warned me about all the places where I could get into trouble," warnings that Wing Ding used as a beacon to forbidden pleasures.

The club was always crowded. In one day in late 1943, over 70,000 American troops passed through its doors. Here a soldier could get a cheap room, a hot shower, a haircut, a shoeshine, and a complimentary Bromo-Seltzer. He could have his money changed and his check cashed, play bil-

liards and Ping-Pong, watch a prizefight or a wrestling match, read an
American newspaper, and get useful information about the city and its
sights. And at a time when there were no sightseeing buses in London,
there was a booking service that commissioned a dozen bonafide Cockney
taxi drivers to take GIs—for a price—on tours of historic places. An American boy told a staff member, "You do everything here except blow a
soldier's nose."

Fliers on bigger budgets stayed at the Berkeley, the Savoy, Grosvenor
House, or another of London's regal hotels, dropping in at popular afternoon tea dances. Wing Ding Carson saved his money and spent three
nights with his Air Force lover, Genevieve, at the Berkeley. In bed, locked in
his arms, she told him that she had never been with a man before. Stricken
by an unforeseen attack of conscience, Wing Ding refused to push himself
on her and they both left London disappointed. With Genevieve unable to
obtain a pass, Carson spent his next two leaves in the city at the apartment
of a former ballerina that Lady Dellie had introduced him to at Rainbow
Corner. Their first night together "she danced for me," he fondly recalls.

An American airman's tour of the town usually began at night. The
blacked-out streets were thronged with people, many of them carrying
"torches" (flashlights), and taxies filed past, thin lines of light pointing from
tiny slits in their headlight covers. Although an enemy bomber was a rare
sight in the fall of 1943, searchlight beams crisscrossed the sky and there
were false alarms nearly every night: the wail of sirens followed by short
bursts of antiaircraft fire from sandbag bunkers located all across the city,
even at bus stops. When the sirens went off, no one paid any attention;
pedestrians walking by clubs could hear swing bands playing to the beat of
antiaircraft fire. Adding a macabre touch to the evening, heavy fog rising
off the Thames mixed with swirling clouds of coal smoke from the city's
million and more chimneys.

Preferring to explore London by himself, eighteen-year-old air gunner
Jack Novey wandered into a back-alley pub where there were no Americans in sight. Some RAF boys were gathered around the piano. When they
spotted Novey's silver wings they asked him to join them, the start of a long
evening of song and strong drink.

It was rare for American and British fliers to socialize together. "The
major cause of this," speculated George Orwell, residing in London during
the war, "is the difference in pay. You can't have really close and friendly
relations with someone whose income is five times your own." There was
also the feeling among the British troops that the Americans had a clear

physical advantage over them. They were "generally taller, bulkier, and handsomer then we were. Many were blond giants, with hair cut short in 'combat crops.' . . . Their uniforms and their insignia were showy, beautifully fitting, of excellent material and smart. . . . As far as appearance went, they outclassed us."

English pubs closed early, but for those with stamina the next stop was usually a private club, where liquor could be bought by the bottle. Good gin and scotch continued to be scarce in wartime London, and the hard drink that was readily at hand tasted, said Robert Arbib, "like the bottom of a tanning vat." But the clubs on the West End were hot and noisy, and there were women at the tables, sultry things with thin dresses and thick accents, not a few of them professionals who spoke of love for $8. "Lieutenant, I will take you to zee clouds higher zan you have ever been before. Zen I will bring you down, happier zan you have ever been."

There was "local talent," as well, "good time" girls, Londoners called them. Some were only fifteen and sixteen years old, but most of them were working women in their early twenties, the type of girl who had stayed away from the West End before the war because she didn't have the clothes to wear or the money to spend. Although not professionals, they expected presents—nylon stockings and sweets—for a night in the sack in the crowded flats they shared with two or three other women.

For men so inclined, there were plenty of street whores. The easiest place to find them was in the darkened doorways of the shops around Piccadilly Circus. Even with the police around, the women were brazenly aggressive; Piccadilly Commandos, everyone called them. They went after the willing and unwilling alike. "As we males walked along Piccadilly in [the] darkness," correspondent Walter Cronkite remembered, "we could hear the click of heels announce the arrival of a lady of the night. Wearing cheap perfume, she would run her hand along our pants leg." This, Cronkite noted, was "economic," not sexual, foreplay. "By feeling the pants cloth, the experienced ladies could tell whether the male was in the American or British Army and was an officer or an enlisted man. On that determination hung the price at which she would open the bidding."

In the hard bargaining of Piccadilly Circus, the flick of a cigarette lighter—giving the soldier his first glimpse of the woman's face—could make or break a street deal. If some boys got too rough, the Commandos were capable of handling themselves. The French women walked with growling Dalmatians on leashes, and almost all streetwalkers carried switchblades. Vertical sex, a wall-job, as it was known, could be had for £2, about $8; a "quickie" in a shabby hotel room was prorated according to service rank. Most Commandos preferred wall jobs–Marble Arch style was their term for it. It was cost-efficient, assembly-line sex, and the more naive girls were certain they could not get pregnant that way.

The streetwalkers encouraged, but did not demand, that clients wear protection. For men who had forgotten or already used up their supply of condoms, there were plenty of sleazy vendors around the Circle pretending to sell newspapers. By the end of 1943, there was a venereal disease epidemic in the U.K. A *New York Times* correspondent reported that VD rates among GIs in England were over 25 percent higher than they were at home, and that perhaps half of the cases were contracted in Piccadilly. Soon the American Red Cross was operating prophylactic stations in its clubs, and the Army finally built up a sufficient supply of condoms. The early ones, supplied by the British, were found to be "too small." Not until the spring of 1944 did an effective medical treatment for VD become widely available. Called a PRO-KIT, it combined sulfathiazole and calomel. The VD rate declined at the same time for reasons unconnected to the new cure: the Army began tightening its leave policies in preparation for the cross-Channel landings.

A two-day London stay often ended shabbily for the flyboys. After what he described as a "superbender," Texas-born top turret gunner Jack Corner got up from a table, took a few wobbly steps, and dropped to the floor. A crewmate picked him up, piled him into a cab, took him to Liverpool Street Station, and put him on a train to Ridgewell. His hangover probably lasted longer than his leave.

He's Got It Here

Back at their air stations, after sobering up, husbands and sons mailed off letters to wives and parents describing their recent stay in old London– long, wearying days exploring the city's museums and Thames River landmarks: Big Ben, the Tower of London, and the Houses of Parliament. With such strenuous touring, there had hardly been time to grab a quick beer. Inside a letter to his parents, David McCarthy, a navigator in John Comer's bomb group, slipped a photograph of himself and a friend that they had taken in a cheap street-front studio after consuming too much explosive Algerian wine. When McCarthy's wife visited his parents and was shown the photograph, she commented on how tired the two men looked, adding that they must be suffering from battle fatigue. At which point, McCarthy's father, a man acquainted with drink, looked at her and said, "No, Norma . . . Those two boys are drunk!"

With the Eighth Air Force growing rapidly in the fall of 1943, Ira Eaker was faced with a major community relations problem. This had begun to show itself during the summer buildup in preparation for Blitz Week. That July, Eaker warned his commanders that the relationship between American airmen and British civilians—not counting, of course, attractive English women—"was not as good as it was a few months ago when our force was smaller." Toward the end of the year, the American press picked up on this. "In recent months it has become increasingly obvious that the people of Britain are annoyed by the free-spending, free-loving, free-speaking U.S. troops," *Time* magazine reported that December. *Time* claimed that many Britons thought the American GI was "sloppy, conceited, insensitive, undiscriminating, noisy."

This was borne out by public opinion surveys conducted by Mass-Observation, an independent organization founded in 1937 to record "what the British public believe, think and do." Throughout the war, teams of Mass-Observation investigators conducted polls and sociological surveys all over the U.K. and enlisted 1,500 "correspondents" to keep "diaries of their daily life" that recorded cultural changes in their communities. Asked in 1942 how they felt about Americans, 47 percent of those polled said that they had "favorable" impressions. The following year this fell to 34 percent—at a time when the notoriously arrogant Free French troops received a 52 percent favorable reaction. Asked to specify their main reasons for disliking Americans, "boastfulness," "immaturity," and "materialism" topped the list. "They irritate me beyond words," observed a British housewife. "Loud, bombastic, bragging, self-righteous." Another correspondent complained of their "arrogance, Teutonic massiveness, and lack of courtesy and common decency," along with their brazen assumption that they were winning the war by themselves. "How can one help resenting the full-fed, candy-pampered, gum-chewing swagger of our invaders?" wrote diarist Rosemary Black.

The one opinion that pervaded nearly every survey was a deep-seated British belief that America "was a little child that hasn't grown up." "It is strange to see adult persons with their power over scientific inventions, yet with minds of children of eleven," a chemist told a Mass-Observation interviewer. Even Englishmen favorably disposed toward Americans said that the qualities they found most attractive in them were those ordinarily associated with children: their "childlike desire to talk," their vigor and impulsiveness, their open-handed generosity and friendliness, and their "amusing" lack of inhibitions. "I like them," said a young Mass-Observation correspondent, "but not in the way I like the French—as an equal—but in the way a fond parent likes his children."

This was an issue of growing concern to Eaker and Spaatz, and of course to General Eisenhower, who was preparing that December to return to England to assume supreme command of Overlord. Few things were more important to them than cordial relations between the Americans and their English hosts. In a report sent from North Africa in September 1943, Spaatz had made this point emphatically. There were, he said, "three crimes a member of the Air Force can commit: murder, rape and interference with Anglo-American relations. The first two might conceivably be pardoned, but the third one, never."

More than any other place, London was giving American soldiers a bad reputation, yet no American commander—regular Army or Army Air Force—was willing to reduce the flow of troops into the city. In London, where hundreds of white-helmeted American military police patrolled the streets, the GIs were far easier to control than in the lightly policed country towns, where women and drink were also in shorter supply. A man with a drink and a woman, the generals realized, was far less likely to get into a fight than one who was sober and sex-starved. And following the terrible losses of the summer and early fall, the air command, as John Comer observed, was acutely aware of the psychological necessity of "a big blast" in the big town.

After the first Schweinfurt raid, the combat fliers of Comer's 381st Bomb Group were gathered together in the Operations Room for what everyone expected would be more bad news. There was "gloomy silence" until the men heard an announcement they found hard to believe. "We're giving every combat man a four-day pass, and we'll have personnel trucks ready to leave at 1:30. We'll take you right to the outskirts of London where you can catch a tube into the city. . . . This pass will be mandatory unless excused by the Flight Surgeons."

Eighth Air Force commanders also understood that their men had as many problems with Londoners as Londoners had with them. Unscrupulous taxi drivers and merchants took advantage of the Americans' abysmal ignorance of the local currency to cheat them, and prostitutes did a roaring business as pickpockets, or with their pimps, as outright thieves. One of prostitutes' favorite tricks was to lure Yanks into cheap hotel rooms, put knockout drops in their drinks, and empty their pockets when they hit the floor.

Some Britons were already beginning to publicly blame themselves—or more accurately, women from the bottom of the social heap—for unseemly behavior that was unfairly pinned on the Yanks. For the "comfort" of young American males "there swarmed out of the slums and across the bridges multitudes of drab, ill-favoured adolescent girls and their aunts and mothers, never before seen in the squares of Mayfair and Belgravia," wrote novelist Evelyn Waugh, with unsheathed Tory disdain. "There they passionately and publicly embraced, in blackout and at high noon, and were rewarded with chewing-gum, razor-blades and other rare trade goods."

There was also growing resentment about the large numbers of unescorted women who were frequenting the pubs. Most of them were factory girls and women from the uniformed services out for a good time after putting in ten hours and more for the war effort. Surveys indicate that most innkeepers were tolerant of what many of them saw as an inevitable warborn trend. "Usually when they come in alone they don't go out alone, but who am I to criticize." These hardworking women "need drink occasionally, same as a fellow." There was a general feeling throughout the county, said a Mass-Observation surveyor, that "there's a war on, so why shouldn't people enjoy themselves while they can." Even older women "seem little prejudiced against girls drinking by themselves." As one woman said, "Why should it be supposed that they need an escort? A lot of good men are as escorts! I'd rather have a dog any day."

Seeing an opportunity here, Americans on the make treated their English dates like duchesses. "They opened doors for us, were ever so polite, and gave us their complete attention," remembered a British woman, "whereas our men would leave us alone at a table to shoot darts with their mates."

British males responded with humor. "Heard about the new utility knickers? One Yank and they're off." But resentment lasted until the Yanks were finally gone.

Strangeness both attracts and repels, and so it was with the wartime British and Americans, who knew shockingly little about each other. Until the "friendly" American invasion, most people in the British Isles and the United States had never met a person of the other country. To bridge this knowledge gap, the U.S. Army put together *A Short Guide to Great Britain,* a breezy survey of topics ranging from island geography to "indoor amusements" like darts and beer drinking. The British army printed its own suffocatingly dull guide to transatlantic harmony, *Meet the Americans.* Readers who suffered through these guides learned little of use about their cousins across the pond. With radio broadcasts between the two nations rare, and newsreels presenting only snippets of sensationalized information, untraveled Britons and Americans—and that included most GIs—tended to form their impressions of each other from outlets of mass-produced news and entertainment in their own countries: newspapers and magazines, radio and movies.

Movies were wildly popular in wartime Britain. Even in small country towns, the favorite form of relaxation was an evening at the cinema. Many villagers went to a local theater two or three times a week, which made crowded movie houses excellent places to meet local girls. Courting couples sat in the back, single girls and Yanks on the make in the balcony, and old ladies with sandwiches in the front. Organ recitals—accompanied by vigorous hand clapping and singing—opened the evening, followed by a newsreel and two full-length features. British audiences knew all the Hollywood stars, but for many audiences, America itself was the leading character: large and rich, enterprising and energetic, and irritatingly insular, a can-do nation that valued nothing that was not new. Mass-Observation investigators downplayed the role of Hollywood films in shaping British opinion of Americans. "People feel that there is a great deal of [the] fantastic and [the] unreal in these pictures. They do not regard them as representing America, but as representing a sort of dream stereotype from America." But this seems wrong. The national traits that Britons saw portrayed in Hollywood films were the same personal traits that they found alternately odious and attractive about Americans they met during wartime. Mass-Observation's own findings indicate this. So when an Englishman spotted an American he knew exactly what to expect. And he was usually wrong.

The American troop movement to England was an unprecedented planned migration, but neither the Americans who were sent to Britain, nor the British who were there when they arrived, were a representative national group. The American migration was made up overwhelmingly of young men between the ages of eighteen and twenty-eight, separated from families and the community institutions that have a softening impact on human beings, billeted in rigidly controlled military camps, and sent out in air machines to slaughter and smash. On the other hand, Britain, at war, was not entirely itself. London had never been, nor would it ever be again, the city that American soldiers visited. Neither would the rest of the country, a nation missing nearly its entire supply of young, able-bodied men, with all the disruptions of normal family life that proceed from this: wives without husbands, children without fathers, fathers without sons to help on farms and in shops.

It would take time and familiarity to break down preconceived impressions held by both the British and the Americans. The places where this occured most frequently were the villages and towns that ringed the American airbases, where there were tens of thousands of "ground pounders" who—unlike the fliers or the infantry—were in England for the duration of the war. In these little towns "we found that there were other groups in Britain besides an arrogant aristocracy, an ignorant comical class known as 'cockneys,' and the ubiquitous English butler," wrote Robert Arbib. It was in the small towns of middle and eastern England that Britons learned that not every American male swaggered like the Duke or talked like Bogie.

Animosity against the Americans never disappeared, even in the most accommodating towns of East Anglia. Visiting old friends in Norwich, Mass-Observation diarist Sarah Williams complained that the "whole place looks scruffy. It's the Americans. I went into a restaurant which before the war was all right and it was nauseating. . . . There were several Americans with girls and they were all drunk to the point of vomit. . . . Many girls just fling themselves into the Americans' arms, because they have so much money." Townspeople disgusted with the way their young women threw themselves at the Americans failed to figure that it was often a matter of supply and demand. "What's he got that I haven't got?" a British soldier on leave from an overseas assignment asked some local girls who seemed smitten by a Yank. "He hasn't got anything more than you've got," one of them straightened him out, "but he's got it here."

Sudbury

Eighth Air Force commanders worked with the American Red Cross to try to keep men on base in the intervals between overnight leaves. By late 1943, there were Red Cross Aeroclubs on almost every bomber station. There were game rooms, lounges, libraries, and Saturday night dances. "There was wonderful attendance at our dances," recalled Kay Brainard Hutchins, who signed up for overseas work with the Red Cross after two of her brothers were reported missing in action in bombing operations over Europe. "We'd send out big trucks to pick up English girls and bring them to the club. . . . These factory girls loved the American GIs and they loved the jitter-bugging." The dances were closely chaperoned and no girl was permitted to leave the dance hall. On the morning after a dance, a Red

Cross Clubmobile—a converted single-decker London bus—would arrive to serve donuts and coffee. The "sinkers" were made from equipment in the truck's combination kitchen-lounge, and they would be devoured by hungry boys living in a donut-deprived country.

The men most appreciated the work of the Red Cross girls who lived on the bases, and tried to be, in Andy Rooney's words, "a sort of remote combination of Rita Hayworth-and-your-best-friend's-big-sister." They were the first to notify airmen of illnesses and deaths in their families, and they would surprise them with homemade cakes on their birthday. The Red Cross women were outside the door of the briefing room on every mission day, dressed in their stylish blue-gray uniforms and caps, serving coffee and donuts. They would be the last American women seen by many bomber boys.

For the fliers who returned, there was a neatly stacked pile of sandwiches and a big coffee urn on a table in the debriefing room. But in the hours and days between missions, Kay Hutchins and her co-workers couldn't do as much as they wanted to for the boys. Liquor was freely available on the base, and the dance halls of Sudbury were too much competition for bingo games and the difficult-to-date hostesses at the alcohol-free Aeroclub socials.

Robert Arbib had made friends with an Englishman in Sudbury when his battalion was building the airfield at Debach. At that time an American soldier was a rare sight in town, but when Arbib returned for a visit in early 1944 he found the market town by the River Stour completely transformed by the four airbases that had been built within easy reach. Army trucks and jeeps crowded the crooked medieval streets and every public house was packed to capacity. Expecting to find the townspeople longing for their departure, Arbib instead found a town enlivened by the invaders' presence. Villagers had established an Anglo-American club, where airmen were invited to dances and parties, and Americans were marrying Sudbury girls in the town's venerable stone churches. Few Sudbury houses were without American guests on Sundays. The airmen would arrive loaded with goods they had requisitioned from the mess hall kitchen—canned peaches and pineapples, fresh eggs and bread, corned beef and sweet potatoes. If a visiting Yank happened to stop by the PX, there might be a carton of Camels for father and boxes of chocolates for mother and the kids.

Here and elsewhere, the Yanks were wonderful with children. "Tough, gum-chewing, girl-chasing, hard-drinking GIs—let one small child cross his path and he is lost," remarked one woman. "Your Yank is always a sucker for kids." Airmen hosted parties for local children on Thanksgiving,

Christmas, and the Fourth of July. The boys were given rides in jeeps, and there were Tootsie Rolls, fizzy drinks, and cake for everyone. The airmen were at the age where they were soon going to be fathers, or had just become fathers, and they felt sorry for the English kids. Even the most fortunate of them had few toys or games, and many of them were war orphans, or had not seen their soldier-fathers for years. At Thurleigh, the 306th Bomb Group "adopted" a war orphan, a chubby-cheeked three-year-old named Maureen. The men nicknamed her Sweet Pea and had her baptize a bomber named after her by dipping her hand in paint and placing a palm print on the nose.

Jim Crow in England

Airmen looking for bawdier entertainment crowded the two major cities of East Anglia, Ipswich and Norwich, spending their liberty evenings in dance halls smelling of tobacco and cheap perfume. There were always fights in these places, and some customers came prepared. Robert Arbib remembered "dancing with a lithe, strong Land Army girl at Ipswich, who had come to the dance fully armed with a long and evil-looking dagger at her hip." Men looking for sexual pleasure found that it was dangerous to be choosy; one could be left in the lurch after the liquor stopped flowing in the town at ten o'clock. Then it would be a solitary walk back to the Army trucks gathered in a dark parking lot. At the trucks, drunken soldiers and their "dates" said good night, and men called out for missing friends, some of whom were in the town lockup.

North of Ipswich, in a village called Bamber Bridge, a night of hard drinking and a combustible racial situation led to a violent riot by African-American troops. As the pubs began closing on the unusually warm evening of June 24, 1943, two American MPs, patrolling the town in a jeep, heard that there was trouble at the Old Hob Inn. The popular thatched-roof tavern was located not far from the barracks of the 1511th Quartermaster Truck Regiment, an almost entirely African-American unit (except for the officers) that delivered bombs to Eighth Air Force bases south and east of Lancashire. A dozen or so black soldiers had been drinking at the pub and refused to leave at closing time. When the MPs arrived and tried to arrest one of the men for being out of uniform and not having a pass, an argument erupted and a soldier brandishing a bottle lunged at one of the MPs. The policeman drew his pistol, but was persuaded to holster it by a cool-headed black staff sergeant. As the MPs pulled away, someone threw a bottle. It smashed into the jeep's windshield, spraying the two men with beer. They drove off, vowing to return.

After picking up two other MPs on foot patrol, they spotted the black soldiers from the pub heading back to the base, shouting, singing, and drinking from bottles. When they tried to arrest two of them, an ugly brawl broke out with nightsticks, stones, bottles, and knives. One MP was hit between the eyes by a flying bottle, and another was knocked unconscious by a landscaping stone. Then gunshots rang out and the GIs scattered, carrying off their two wounded buddies, one shot in the back, the other in the stomach. The shaken MPs loaded their own two banged-up men into the jeep and sped off.

When the soldiers arrived back at the post, wild rumors flew through the camp that black men had been gunned down by MPs who were still on the prowl. Roused from their bunks, men raced to the front gate, some of them carrying rifles. A few men managed to get past the guards and slip into town; then a small truck filled with half a dozen armed soldiers smashed through the gate. At that point, the unit's only black officer persuaded most of the remaining men at the gate to return to their barracks. "The guilty ones will suffer," he promised.

A half-hour later, at midnight, the fragile peace was shattered when a group of MPs roared into the camp in two jeeps and an improvised armored car equipped with a mounted machine gun. Men raced for the gun rooms, shot out the locks, and seized rifles. Enraged black men, harboring festering grudges for being called "jigaboos" and "niggers" by white officers and MPs, roamed the streets of Bamber Bridge, firing at MPs and at two of their own white officers. "Get inside," one of the mutineers shouted to a villager who ran a fish-and-chips business, "there's going to be a war." One soldier was heard shouting that he would rather die fighting for his race than against the Germans.

The shooting did not stop until 3:00 A.M. Darkness and poor marksmanship kept down the casualties. Two white soldiers—an MP and an officer—and three black GIs were shot, one of them fatally. At two separate military trials, thirty-two men were found guilty of charges ranging from assault to mutiny. There was no murder charge, for there were no witnesses to the killing. Most, perhaps all, of the men on trial had not fired shots the night of the incident; with wildly conflicting testimony, identifying the shooters proved impossible. Sentences from three months to fifteen years of hard labor were meted out to men who were believed to have been carrying rifles the night of the riot, but all the sentences were reduced on appeal.

Within a year, most of the men were restored to duty. This was due to the swift intervention of Gen. Ira Eaker, a Southerner who told his staff that "90% of the trouble with Negro troops was the fault of the whites."

Later that summer, Eaker combined the dispersed trucking units in England into a special command, which he named the Combat Support Wing. This, he thought, would help foster among black troops "a definite feeling that they are contributing to the combat effort." The aggressive commander of the new Combat Support Wing, Col. George S. Grubb, weeded out seventy-five incompetent and racist white officers, upgraded base recreational facilities, and began using racially mixed MP patrols. Morale and performance improved markedly and both court-martial and VD rates dropped dramatically. Like Eaker, Grubb, who was white, believed that most racial incidents were "provoked by white troops," and that "in general, negro troops are more courteous and well mannered than the white troops."

It was an opinion shared by many British people. When the war began, Britian was a racially homogeneous country with not more than 8,000 black residents, most of them concentrated in London and several other port cities. The vast majority of towns and villages did not contain a single black resident, and many English people had never encountered a person of color. England was overwhelmingly white by design and the government wanted to keep it that way. It forbade "coloured British subjects" of the empire from settling in—for them—the inaptly named mother country. Nor had the government wanted black American GIs. When America entered the war, the British Chiefs of Staff, fearing racial friction, had requested that African-American GIs not be sent to England to build airbases. It would be better, they said, if white engineer units were assigned the task. Foreign Secretary Anthony Eden had the temerity to cast this policy in humanitarian terms, telling American ambassador Winant that the English climate "was badly suited to negroes."

The U.S. War Department would have none of this. It was already under relentless pressure from Congress and African-American leaders to integrate the armed forces. The Air Force, moreover, had made it known that it needed engineering units, and there were not enough whites to fill them. Politics and practicality combined to produce an official policy that blacks be sent to England in rough proportion to the number of blacks in the United States, about one in ten. To the surprise of both the American and the British governments, the African-American troops were warmly welcomed and well treated. They, in turn, found it liberating to move about in a country without legal segregation. British men and women mixed freely with black American soldiers in pubs and restaurants and nearly everyone loved the music they brought with them. Their swing bands excited crowds, and one of their magnificent choral groups, made up of 200 aviation engineers, was invited to perform at the Royal Albert Hall in London.

English people drew a line between the races on only one sensitive issue—interracial dating—but opposition to it was not universal. "The white American airman on the base couldn't understand why a British girl would go out with a black American. To us, it really didn't mean anything," recalled a resident of Thorpe Abbotts.

Fearing racial trouble, U.S. Army policy sanctioned segregation while professing to oppose discrimination. In July 1942, Eisenhower issued an important statement on racial relations. "It is the desire of Headquarters," he stated firmly, "that discrimination against the Negro troops be sedulously avoided." In the same circular, however, he encouraged local commanders to institute a separate-but-equal policy for black and white troops, with the aim of minimizing racial friction. One of his suggestions was a policy of rotating leaves, with rotation based on skin color. This would ensure that blacks and whites were not in the same town on the same evening. In this way, racial segregation became the Army's way of minimizing racial discrimination.

Eisenhower's strictures against racial prejudice were widely ignored. After hauling heavy explosives from dawn to dark, through rain and fog, and over dangerously narrow country roads, the five thousand men of the Air Force's African-American trucking units were often denied billets and meals at bomb bases. Most drivers ate K rations and slept in their trucks.

The Air Force had a long-standing policy of institutional racism. At the beginning of the war, Eleanor Roosevelt joined black leaders to pressure her husband to integrate the historically all-white Army Air Corps and to put black pilots into combat. Hap Arnold grudgingly established an all-black fighter unit, the famous Tuskegee Airmen, named for the Alabama base where they trained. These pursuit pilots served with distinction in the Mediterranean Theater, but the Air Force drew the line on integrating bomber crews, insisting that blacks and whites—especially Southern whites—could never operate efficiently as combat teams. Nor would the Eighth integrate its Fighter Command. Arnold feared that a policy of integration would result in "negro officers serving over white enlisted men." This, he said, would create "an impossible social problem."

In 1942, when the War Department forced the AAF to accept blacks at a rate of 10 percent of its total force, Arnold assigned African-Americans solely to ground support units, where they served in tightly segregated ordnance, quartermaster, engineering, and transportation companies. Eaker eagerly accepted these men but had been unable to persuade Air Force headquarters to train blacks to fill shortages in the ranks of mechanics, air controllers, and weathermen, positions with responsibilities that Arnold believed were beyond the mental capacity of most black recruits. With Arnold's backing, even the American Red Cross in England, though it would officially deny it, had separate clubs for black GIs, staffed by African-American Red Cross workers from the United States. By the end of the war, there were only 12,196 African-American AAF personnel in Britain, all of them in service units. Only eighty-two were officers in a branch of the Air Force in which one in six of the white force was commissioned.

With many English women willing to date black soldiers, there were bound to be racial conflicts, especially when black and white troops were in the same town on leave. "I, alone, have seen five instances of niggers with white women," a white Air Force corporal expressed his outrage in a letter to his family. On a number of occasions, black soldiers were assaulted by white troops from Southern states for walking down village streets holding hands with English girls. "When British soldiers and civilians defended the right of the women to choose their own escorts, military police of both colors and nations had to haul off their battling charges," *Time* reported. In Leicester, white paratroopers from the 82nd Airborne Division got into a brawl with an AAF quartermaster battalion when members of the battalion were seen with white women. The black GIs seized weapons and a truck and a full-scale riot broke out, resulting in the death of an MP.

In Launceston, a picturesque Cornish town, black soldiers who had been refused service in the whites-only section of a pub left quietly but returned later, armed with rifles, machine guns, and bayonets. When MPs ordered them to disperse, they opened fire, seriously wounding two military policemen. There was so much trouble between blacks and whites on leave that Air Force commanders in smaller towns took up Eisenhower's suggestion to rotate passes, establishing separate "Black" and "White" nights. In larger towns, the Army issued passes restricting the use of certain pubs and dance halls to one race only, and used MPs to enforce the segregation. By late 1943, this de facto Jim Crow policy was in place wherever large numbers of black and white troops were stationed in close proximity.

The most rigid form of Jim Crow was practiced in East Anglia, where blacks were needed to perform essential work on bomber bases as truck drivers and ordnance workers. Blacks were stationed at segregated facilities near the bomber stations, but for both races the main nightlife was in larger towns like Ipswich, with its 150 public houses. With their smaller numbers, blacks were restricted to only eight Ipswich pubs, one dance hall, and a segregated Red Cross club. In East Anglia, the inappropriately named River Dove was the designated color line. All villages and towns east of the river were out of bounds for black troops. Blacks found in "white towns" were arrested by military police.

Truman K. Gibson, a black aide to Secretary of War Stimson, wrote an indignant letter to Assistant Secretary of War John J. McCloy condemning the exportation of Dixie-style segregation to England. Gibson's protest was ignored and segregation continued to be used as a way to keep peace between the races.

White airmen who had no desire to compete with blacks for the attention of English women supported the system of alternate-day leaves, even though it restricted their own freedom. The policy of segregated evenings did raise a concern, however. These men wondered what their English girlfriends were doing when they were restricted to base on "colored night."

CHAPTER NINE

The Turning

Out of our zeal for freedom, we shall defend ourselves in
any way that we are able.

HERODOTUS

England, Late October 1943

After his wild spree in London, David McCarthy returned to
Ridgewell to discover that the 381st had already received new
bombers and crews, replacements for heavy losses on the Schweinfurt raid earlier in the month. "The sight of the fresh, new faces of the replacements raised our spirits, [but] we were [still] tired, depressed about the
heavy losses, emotionally exhausted, and frightened beyond description."

October's losses had a far rippling effect. McCarthy's wife, Norma, back
in Lake George, New York, had begun corresponding with the families of
men in the 381st since the squadrons left for England. By the middle of October, she had received a flood of letters, telegrams, and telephone calls
from concerned loved ones who were reading about the Eighth's recent
raids and wanted to know if she had heard any news. The names of the de-
ceased had not yet been published in the newspapers. "The avalanche of
requests for information from the distraught and anxious families had a
frightful effect on Norma," McCarthy learned later. "My father-in-law had
to shield her from the phone and from answering the door."

For the crewmen of the Eighth, November 1 was an important day. Black October, what McCarthy called "the killing month," was behind them; perhaps November would bring better days.

Blind Bombing

The maiden mission of November was to Wilhelmshaven on the 3rd, the Eighth's first big strike since Black Thursday. It was a familiar target, within range of fighter escort, and the bombers met only light opposition. Yet it was a milestone mission, undertaken with unfamiliar "little friends" and in cloud cover that would have grounded a fleet this size a month earlier. From this day forward, American strategic bombing was radically transformed.

At the morning briefings, the flying officers learned that part of their escort would be Lockheed P-38 Lightnings. A number of them had been assigned to the Eighth a year earlier, but had been moved to the Mediterranean before they had a chance to prove themselves. They were known to be unreliable at extreme altitudes, where the paralyzing cold hampered engine performance, but they were fast and fearsome war machines, with slightly greater range than the Thunderbolts, a matter of life and death to the bomber crews. When John Comer's pilot arrived on the flight line that morning and informed his gunners that they would be picked up at the coast by fifty Lightnings, "there were whoops of joy!" The men were counting on them to go after the big rocket-carrying German fighters that had decimated the bomber fleets on Black Thursday. None of the Junkers 88s showed up over Wilhelmshaven, but in later engagements the twin-engine Lightnings would annihilate them.

The Germans were far less worried about the Lightnings than they were about the size of the bomber stream sent out on November 3: 566 heavies and 378 fighters, awesome affirmation of the American Air Force's recuperative powers. Equally alarming to Luftwaffe commanders, Thunderbolts equipped with large drop tanks crossed into Holland and penetrated German airspace in cloud cover that grounded or disabled most of Adolf Galland's defensive force. The Luftwaffe command was shocked that the Eighth had any planes over Germany on this day. In the past, similar weather conditions had pinned American war planes to their bases.

The lead planes of the formations had large domelike devices hanging just aft of their chin turrets, and this new technology spelled long-term trouble for the Luftwaffe. These retractable domes housed the scanners for a new form of air-to-ground radar, H2X, code-named Mickey Mouse (later abbreviated to Mickey), an improved American version of a system, H2S, the British had developed in 1940 to locate targets through thick overcast.

The new American "Pathfinder" force—the 482nd Bomb Group—had been activated that August at Alconbury, in Huntingdonshire, and had flown its first mission the following month, leading elements of the Eighth to the German port city of Emden. On that mission of September 27, the four lead bombers had been equipped with H2S. Wilhelmshaven was the first experiment with H2X.

The system was not terribly sophisticated. A high frequency electrical impulse was transmitted downward through a revolving antenna underneath the bomber, and this beam of energy scanned the earth's surface. The reflected signals picked up by the antenna produced a crude maplike image on a cathode ray tube, or oscilloscope, in the bomber: dark areas for water, light areas for ground, bright areas for cities. (Airborne radar was incapable of distinguishing smaller targets like factories and marshaling yards.) When the target was sighted, the Pathfinder planes dropped sky marker flares for the rest of the bomber stream. "All eyes are on the Mickey ship when we're over the target," a navigator described the procedure. "When Mickey drops his bombs, we drop ours."

The bombing on November 3 was hardly pinpoint-precise; most of the explosives missed the port area and fell inside the city. But it was promising enough to have the Air Force invest more heavily in radar equipment, especially after the heavy bombers of a new American strategic air force in Southern Europe, the Fifteenth, began having as much trouble with the weather as the Eighth.

Northern European weather was the principal reason behind Hap Arnold's decision to establish another heavy bomber outfit in Tunisia in October, commanded by Gen. Jimmy Doolittle. From bases on the recently captured Foggia plain in southern Italy, where the Fifteenth was moved in force the following month, its bombers were capable of reaching targets in the southern and easternmost reaches of the Reich that were beyond the range of the Eighth Air Force. But virulent weather patterns over the Alps and in the rugged mountains surrounding the Fifteenth's bases would result in more total nonoperational days for that far smaller force than for the Eighth.

Radar bombing was a means of keeping pressure on the enemy during the long European winters. Germany depended on perpetual cloud cover even more than it did the Luftwaffe to keep its skies clear of American bombers. In an average winter month, there were only two or three days when visual bombing was possible. In the winter of 1943–44, Pathfinder bombers led forty-eight raids, among them the only missions the Eighth conducted over Germany in November and December. Begun as an experiment, radar bombing soon became routine procedure. Throughout the war, only about half of the Eighth's heavies bombed visually. In the winter of 1943–44, it was 10 percent.

Radar bombing had two other advantages. Flying above a protective blanket of clouds, Eighth Air Force bombers suffered far fewer losses to either flak or fighters. And occasionally, formations sent out in horrible weather to conduct radar raids arrived at their targets several hours later to find that the skies over Germany had unexpectedly cleared, allowing more accurate bombing.

Radar bombing was actually a form of area bombing. Precision was impossible. This was a clear break with Air Force creed, but the alternative—not bombing at all in bad weather—was unacceptable to air commanders committed to crushing the enemy. Throughout the war, there were only two factors that greatly accelerated the rate of American strategic bombing operations: tremendously increased production of bombers and crews, and widespread employment of H2X.

The bomber crews called it what it was—blind bombing—but Hap Arnold, sensitive to public perceptions at home, instructed Eaker and his staff to use less graphic and more technically correct terms, such as "bombing through overcast" or "bombing with navigational devices." By whatever name, radar bombing was an unacknowledged admission by the Eighth that the air war could not be won by precision attacks alone. Another pillar of prewar bombing doctrine had collapsed.

Since targets along a line between water and land were more easily identified by radar, the Eighth largely restricted its missions to Germany in late 1943 to the coastal cities of Emden, Kiel, and Bremen, none of them high-priority Pointblank targets. Other missions were flown to occupied France and Norway. This dismal bombing record has caused some historians to portray the Eighth Air Force as a wounded and nearly defeated force in the months immediately following Schweinfurt II. Wounded yes; nearly defeated, no.

That winter German air commanders had a better idea than postwar historians of what they were up against. It was the ever-growing strength of the American raids, several of them twice the size of the force sent to Schweinfurt, that most worried fighter chief Adolf Galland. American fighter escorts were also starting to show their superiority to their Luftwaffe opponents in fiercely contested dogfights. Galland's fighter force was having trouble with the weather and was experiencing a dangerous leakage of skilled pilots, among them twelve aces who had claimed a total of over 1,000 Allied aircraft. Despite increased German production, the Luftwaffe's single-engine fighter force actually declined by 105 planes in the final three months of 1943, as both pilots and planes were lost in accidents and air fights. As historian Williamson Murray has suggested, the eventual defeat of the German fighter force in the late spring of 1944 "can only be understood in the context of earlier attrition rates."

In early November, Hubert Zemke's 56th Fighter Group, the Wolf Pack, recorded its 100th enemy aircraft destroyed, and Thunderbolts of all groups in the Eighth had by then a three-to-one kill advantage in battles with Messerschmitt 109s and Focke-Wulf 190s. In late 1943, Galland was forced to move units from northern France and the Low Countries back to the Rhine, where they would wait for the American escorts to leave the bombers and then hit the exposed formations in concentrated force. In adopting this defense in depth, Galland played into the hands of Allied military planners in England, who wanted areas near the Channel cleared of enemy fighters that might disrupt the D-Day landings.

Their Pyrrhic victory in Black October left Germany with too few skilled pilots to expertly operate the fighter planes that it had finally begun to produce in greater numbers. Defeat for the Americans brought them more pilots and planes, enough eventually to swamp the Luftwaffe. The astonishing American recovery from Black October, like the Ancient Roman army's recovery from the humiliating defeat administered by Hannibal, showed the enemy what a technologically powerful, ferociously focused people they had warred on.

Germany had begun the war with the world's finest combat air force and its second strongest industrial economy. In 1939, the German aircraft industry was second to none. Aeronautic engineers of staggering creativity headed its design studios, and its factory workforce was superbly trained. But even before massive Allied raids on its plants, the industry was prevented from reaching its full potential by three principal factors: gross mismanagement by incompetent Nazi administrators, chief among them Col. Gen. Ernst Udet, Göring's World War I squadron mate whom Göring had put in charge of the Luftwaffe's technical office in 1936; shortsighted military planning at the highest level; and a deep national commitment to craft, not mass, production.

"The German aircraft and engine industry," wrote historian James S. Corum, "was poorly structured to fight a long, total war. Before the war, even the newest German aircraft factories were small compared with the

British and American ones. Although a large number of small factories made the industry less vulnerable to grand strategic bombing, it also prevented the Luftwaffe from employing the most efficient methods of mass production."

The industry was also hobbled by shortsighted strategic decisions by the führer and his inner circle, military management that arose from the Nazis' arrogant optimism. After the lightning defeat of Poland, the Low Countries, and France in the first year of the war, and the fantastic early success of the Wehrmacht in Russia in the summer of 1941, Hitler failed to mobilize the economy fast enough for total war. He believed that Russia would fall by the end of the year, and that he would then have time to marshal the vast resources of his newly acquired continental empire, should Britain somehow stave off defeat and America enter the fight. Neither Hitler nor Göring fully appreciated the massive material potential of Germany's most powerful enemies, Britain, the Soviet Union, and eventually the United States. Not until the defeat at Stalingrad in January 1943 did Hitler order full mobilization, but by then it was too late. Although German aircraft production would eventually increase by almost 300 percent under Udet's capable successor at the technical office, Erhard Milch (Udet committed suicide in 1941), this was never enough to keep pace with mounting attrition and with far greater production leaps by the Allies. In 1944, Germany aviation factories would put out an impressive 40,000 planes, but that same year, the United States alone would produce 96,000 aircraft, and Allied total aircraft production would outpace German production by 400 percent.

Radar bombing was another sign of accumulating American resolve. A form of warfare unhampered by ethical concerns, founded on sheer military necessity, it was an early warning to Germany of America's determination to fight a war of annihilation. Radar bombing may have been inaccurate but it put continuous pressure on German fighter defenses. "By being able to go across no matter what the weather was and bomb with a radar sight, the H2X . . . forced the German fighter up in the air," Carl Spaatz noted after the war. "And I am certain under those conditions that they had as many operational losses, crashes on landing after going up, as they did in the air fighting itself." He was right.

In late 1943, Galland reported to the German high command that his fighter aircraft "had no instruments for blind flying, no de-icing of the cockpit, no safety arrangements for navigation or automatic pilots." And most of his pilots "had no knowledge of instrument flying or bad-weather methods of landing." Fighter leaders that did manage to break through the weather had to attempt to assemble their scattered formations above the clouds, a nearly impossible stratagem. The result: dispersed, less-effective, attacks. "Numerous German pilots were sitting in their completely iced-up cockpits, half blinded, to become an easy prey for the Thunderbolts. The appalling losses of this period were plainly due to the weather," Galland wrote years later.

Winter weather was brutally difficult for fliers on both sides. After completing high-altitude missions in poorly heated cockpits, American fighter pilots were sometimes so frozen and weak that they had to be pulled from their planes by medical teams. Ice two inches thick built up on the windscreens of fighters and bombers, causing accidents. Fliers also had difficulty relieving themselves. There were only two toilet facilities on a four-engine bomber, a tin can and a "relief tube." Between the waist compartment and the tail there was a can with a lid on it, but as Jack Novey noted, "when you put your butt down on the toilet, the frozen metal would take part of your skin with it. So we just threw the damn thing out of the airplane."

The relief tube, a funnel with a rubber hose that dropped out though the bottom of the plane, was located in the bomb bay. Novey explained, "You were supposed to make your way across this narrow catwalk with bombs hanging on both sides, unzip yourself in this extreme cold, aim into the funnel, and urinate." If someone had already used the tube, it was almost certain that his urine had frozen and that "your pee [would] splash . . . right back up in your face." So crew members simply urinated on the floor. When under fire, they had no choice but to relieve themselves in their pants.

Above the clouds at 60 degrees below zero, under a sun that gave no warmth, navigator Elmer Bendiner, flying his final mission on November 29, was so cold he was barely able to lift his arms to chip frost from the inside of his Plexiglas nose cone. The enemy was all around him, but he found it hard to tell the German fighters from his own escorts. When a Focke Wulf 190 came at them head-on, there was no answering fire. Every forward-facing gun in the entire Fortress formation was frozen. Just then, Bendiner's crew noticed that the oncoming German's guns were mute as well. Passing them without firing a shot, the pilot turned to them and waved. "A meteorological happenstance imposed a truce" and Elmer Bendiner—husband, father, and Hitler-hater—got to go home to his wife and brand-new baby.

Few airmen were trained to cope with the insidious dangers of icing. A treacherous combination of high humidity and freezing temperatures would cause "clear ice" to build up on the bomber's surface "so rapidly," one pilot described the phenomenon, "that the craft became too heavy to fly. When this happened there was no recovery." Under the intolerable weight of gas, bombs, and ice, planes would begin spinning wildly until they fell apart. The only consolation of bombing through clouds full of ice was that it was nearly impossible for enemy fighters to get up to the bombers in lethal numbers. "We fly as a matter of course in weather that back home would ground every aircraft in the country," a bomber pilot wrote his mother.

Electrical suits continued to malfunction with such frequency that many fliers stopped using them, preferring to wear extra layers of clothing. The cold penetrated "with an intensity that was the same as pain," causing some fliers to take strange precautions. Navigator and novelist Sam Halpert described how he used to tie a string around his penis so he could "find the goddamn thing" when he felt the urge.

Silk gloves, worn under heavier gloves, had cut down the incidence of frostbite among waist gunners, but frostbite on men's faces from wind-blast remained a major problem until bombers equipped with Plexiglas waist windows began arriving in England in early 1944. Until then, more men continued to be hospitalized for frostbite than for battle wounds. Casualties from flak and cannon fire had been reduced by the introduction of body armor or "flak suits," as the men called them. The combat body vest was made of overlapping manganese steel plates sewed into a canvas covering. An apron of the same material hooked onto the vest, protecting the groin and upper thighs. The complete suit weighed twenty-two and a half pounds and, though cumbersome, could be shed quickly in an emergency by the pull of a cord.

The new armor was the invention of Col. Malcolm Grow, chief surgeon of the Eighth Air Force. In research conducted at the Central Medical Establishment, he had discovered that 80 percent of combat wounds were caused by low-velocity missiles—flak splinters or fragments of cannon and machine gun shells. Dr. Grow worked with London's Wilkinson Sword Company to develop the flak suit, which was worn with a steel helmet with flaps to accommodate earphones, the design idea of the Metropolitan Museum of Art, specialists in historic body armor. "A London firm, specializing since 1772 in the manufacture of swords, is now beating its product into something much more useful at the moment," the *New York Times* commented. "It is making suits of mail for American airmen. . . . Thus the cycle rolls around again, and American fighters, like the Yankee in King Arthur's Court, find themselves back in medieval armor." By December 1943, over 13,000 flak suits had been delivered to bomber bases in England. They were effective against machine gun fire, flak fragments, and shell splinters. Crews with body armor suffered 58 percent fewer casualties than those without it, but men in mail still died instantaneously when hit straight-on by cannon fire or exploding flak, and men died or were badly mangled when hit in areas of the body that their armor failed to shield.

Forrest Vosler

On a return trip from Bremen on December 13, 1943, radio operator Forrest "Woody" Vosler, a former drill press operator from Livonia, New York, was hit where no man was protected. His plane, *Jersey Bounce Jr.* of the 303rd Bomb Group, "Hell's Angels," had two engines shot out and was still being assailed by a storm of German fighters that had scored a direct hit on tail gunner George Buske. Vosler sat on the edge of the table in his radio compartment and blazed away with his flexible machine gun through the open hatch overhead until an exploding shell ripped his gun apart as he bent over it. Reaching up to where his eyes should have been, he felt a moist mass of loose flesh. Vosler saw blood streaming down the retina inside his eye. Thinking it was on the outside, he was certain he had lost a good part of his face. "I knew I was going to die," he said later. "The fear was intense; it's indescribable, the terror you feel when you realize you're going to die and there's nothing you can do about it. So I started to lose control and . . . go completely berserk." Yet as quickly as he had lost his senses, he became serenely calm. Reaching out his hand, he muttered, "Take me, God, I'm ready."

Near the North Sea, the German fighters melted away. With gas running low, the Fortress's pilot ordered the men to throw everything expendable overboard. Vosler's radio had been disabled, but working by touch, with blood dripping from his face, he managed to repair it and instruct the other gunners where to set the dials for the emergency channel. Then he tapped out a distress signal informing Air/Sea Rescue that *Jersey Bounce Jr.* was about to fall into the North Sea. After that he passed out.

When he regained consciousness, he made a decision. With the plane dropping fast and nothing else left to toss out, he asked the other gunners to lower him through an escape hatch without a parachute. Convinced he was disfigured for life—half a man—he felt "it didn't make any difference whether they threw me out or not." They refused.

Vosler went into the freezing sea with the shell-battered ship. "When we came to a stop we all jumped out the hatch and got on the wings," recalled flight engineer William Simkins. "I got onto the right wing with Vosler. I helped lift Buske out. He was still unconscious. We put him on the wing and went to get the life raft. . . . While we were doing this, Buske started to slide down the wing into the water."

Perched on top of the fuselage, with both eyes filled with blood, Vosler was still able to distinguish blurred shapes. "I knew Buske would be in the water in a fraction of a second. I would have to take action. So I jumped and held out my hand at the same time. I grabbed the antenna wire that runs from the top of the tail to just forward of the starboard radio compartment window. I prayed that it would hold, and I was able to grab Buske around his waist just as he was going into the water . . . If the wire had broken, both of us would have gone into the drink."

Minutes later, the crew of a Norwegian trawler pulled the fliers from the sea. That night, Woody Vosler suffered terribly at Great Yarmouth hospital, but as Andy Rooney wrote sometime later, "The doctors think that Forrest Vosler may be able to see enough out of one eye, the right eye, to distinguish the Congressional Medal of Honor" he was to receive for his day's work in *Jersey Bounce Jr.*

The following August, President Franklin Roosevelt pinned the medal on Woody Vosler's chest at a White House ceremony. He had just regained partial vision in one eye after surgeons removed his other eye. Vosler was the second member of the Hell's Angels to receive the nation's highest award for military valor. The other was Jack Mathis, the Texan who died at his bombsight over Vegesack in March 1943.

Two weeks after Vosler's crew was pulled from the sea, the 303rd celebrated the group's second Christmas in England. It was a mournful occasion. Most of the men were "lost in memories of happier times." They had been asked to stay off the trains so that British soldiers and war workers would have an easier time getting home. "It was a reasonable request," said one airman, "because we had nowhere special to go." The men at Molesworth and other air stations in England had one thing to be thankful for that dismal Christmas: they were still alive. "I'm not listed in 'Who's Who,' " Jack Comer wrote in his diary, "but I am listed in 'Who's Still Around.' "

Doolittle

On January 5, 1944, Hell's Angels flew to Kiel, a port city on the Baltic Sea. It was a typical mission: lots of action, lots of losses. What made it special was that it was the final raid mounted by the man who had built the Eighth Air Force in England. Effective the following day, Gen. Ira C. Eaker was transferred to the Mediterranean to command Allied air operations in that theater. He was being moved to make room in England for his old pal Carl Spaatz.

Spaatz was returning to England with Sir Arthur Tedder to work with General Eisenhower in planning the Normandy invasion. Tedder would be Ike's chief deputy at SHAEF (Supreme Headquarters Allied Expeditionary Force) and Spaatz was given command of a new umbrella organization, United States Strategic Air Forces in Europe (USSTAF). Spaatz would oversee and coordinate the efforts of both the Eighth and Fifteenth Air Forces. In some ways, the Strategic Air Forces was the old Eighth Air Force in new dress. Spaatz settled into his former headquarters at Bushy Park, and appointed Eaker's former bomber commander, Gen. Frederick Anderson, as his chief of operations. But Eighth Air Force Bomber Command was officially disbanded and authority over bombing operations from England was concentrated in the hands of the new overall commander of the Eighth, Lt. Gen. James H. Doolittle, who had been Eisenhower's air officer during Operation Torch before taking over the new Fifteenth Air Force. Doolittle's headquarters were at High Wycombe (Pinetree), where Eaker had established the Eighth's Bomber Command on his arrival in England in February 1942. To complete the reshuffling, Maj. Gen. Nathan F. Twining was brought in from the South Pacific to assume command of the Fifteenth Air Force.

The decision to move Eaker was made the previous month. Eaker had conducted a furious campaign to retain his position, appealing all the way up to Eisenhower and Marshall. He was told his new assignment was a promotion, but in his mind, he had been sacked, and by Hap Arnold, his longtime friend, mentor, and co-author. Swallowing his pride, he begged Arnold to reconsider. "Having started with the Eighth and seen it organized for a major task in this theater, it would be heart-breaking to leave it just before climax." Arnold replied by indirection, congratulating Eaker on his new appointment.

Although Arnold had applied the pressure, the final decision had been made by Eisenhower. He wanted Spaatz in London to help him plan air operations for the invasion. The two had worked together in the

Mediterranean on air support for infantry, a practice "that is not . . . widely understood and takes men of some vision and broad understanding to do . . . right," Eisenhower wrote Marshall explaining his decision. Eisenhower also felt at ease around Spaatz; he liked his even disposition and wry sense of humor. Once, when asked to divulge his secret for getting things done, Spaatz replied, "I drink good whiskey, and I get others to do my work." But Eisenhower knew that Spaatz drove himself as hard as he did his aides.

Eisenhower knew that Spaatz still believed that Germany could be defeated by airpower alone. In a November 1943 meeting with Roosevelt's closest advisor, Harry Hopkins, a meeting witnessed and recorded by Eisenhower's aide, Capt. Harry C. Butcher, Spaatz had insisted that a massive bombing campaign against Nazi oil targets by the Eighth and the Fifteenth Air Forces, a campaign he hoped to launch when the weather cleared in the early spring of 1944, would paralyze the German war machine, making Overlord neither "necessary" nor "desirable." But Spaatz, unlike Bomber Harris, was a team player, and Eisenhower was confident that he would give full support to any invasion plan the Allied leadership fashioned. Finally, it made no sense to Eisenhower to have two men of Spaatz's and Eaker's abilities in the same theater. That would be a wasteful concentration of talent.

Eaker showed no resentment against Spaatz, but his close friendship with Arnold did not survive the controversy. Eaker knew that Arnold had lobbied hard to have him removed. Arnold wanted a more aggressive commander, one who would put up more and larger missions, even in pernicious weather, and one who had a greater sense of urgency about the need for long-range fighter escorts. Arnold was particularly angered by Eaker's decision to launch only two very large missions, with over 500 bombers, against Germany in the entire month of November. At a meeting of the Combined Chiefs of Staff in Cairo on December 4, Arnold made known to Charles Portal and others his deep dissatisfaction with Eaker's performance. "The failure to destroy targets," he told the chiefs, "was due directly to the failure to employ planes in sufficient numbers. A sufficient weight of bombs was not being dropped on the targets to destroy them, nor was the proper priority of targets being followed."

Portal, a close friend, gave Eaker advance warning of Arnold's dissatisfaction with his performance and tried to prevent Eaker's removal, but Arnold wrote Eaker that he could "not see any way clear to make any change in the decisions already reached."

In a for-your-eyes-only letter of late February 1944, Arnold divulged another reason he wanted Spaatz in London as head of the new United States Strategic Air Forces in Europe. It was his "desire" Arnold told Spaatz, "to build an American Air Commander to a high position prior to the defeat of Germany. . . . If you do not remain in a position parallel with [Arthur] Harris, the air war will certainly be won by the RAF, if anybody. Already the spectacular effectiveness of their devastation of cities has placed their contribution in the popular mind at so high a plane that I am having the greatest difficulty in keeping your achievements (far less spectacular to the public) in its proper role not only in publications, but unfortunately in military and naval circles, and, in fact, with the President himself. Therefore, considering only the aspect of proper American share in credit for success in the air war, I feel we must have a high commander" directly involved, as Harris would be, in planning Overlord. Arnold did not have to remind Spaatz that the postwar argument for an independent Air Force would depend on whether or not American bombing was seen as decisive in the defeat of Germany.

Eaker never got over the humiliation of being replaced, and of the way he had been initially notified, not by a personal letter from Arnold, but by a coldly worded cable that reached him, embarrassingly, though channels. "I feel like a pitcher who has been sent to the showers during a World Series game," he confided to a friend. Assistant Secretary of War Robert Lovett wrote Eaker to congratulate him on his new promotion but also "to commiserate with you privately at leaving the Eighth after you have seen the baby through rickets, croup, and measles, and just at the time when it grows into a strong young warrior."

Doolittle took over a force that now had twenty-six heavy bombardment groups and sixteen fighter groups. On a maximum effort he was capable of sending out a fleet of 600 planes—6,000 men—more than an infantry regiment. In addition to the Fifteenth, he also had the direct support of the Ninth Air Force, under Louis Brereton, the commander of the Ploesti mission. A tactical air arm of fighters and medium bombers, the Ninth was being moved from the Mediterranean and reconstituted in England to provide support for American ground forces in the invasion of Fortress Europe, and, for a time, to provide additional escorts for Doolittle's heavies. In all, Doolittle had approximately 1,300 battle-ready bombers and 1,200 fighters.

Doolittle inherited what was fast becoming one of the greatest machines of war ever assembled, but one that continued to be plagued with problems. Strangled by the weather, the Eighth had been unable to mount a deep-penetration raid since Schweinfurt, and combat casualties were running perilously high. In the previous six months, the Eighth had lost sixty-four out of every 100 crews. Air Force statisticians reported to Spaatz that only 26 percent of crews beginning operations in England could expect to complete twenty-five missions. With replacement fliers still not up to planned strength, this was a crisis, one that Spaatz and Doolittle hoped to surmount not by taking fewer casualties, but by building up their force fantastically so that the *percentage* of losses would drop. Such is the brutal logic of wars of attrition.

Doolittle and Spaatz were also under crushing time constraints. With the invasion scheduled for late May, they had until May 1, only three months, to gain air supremacy over Northern Europe. On or around that date, the Eighth Air Force was scheduled to come under the direct authority of Eisenhower and concentrate its efforts on supporting the land invasion and the breakout from the beaches. It was a daunting challenge, but Jimmy Doolittle was up to it. A former racing pilot, the King of the Sky, he was renowned for his daredevil stunts but also for his deep knowledge of the science of aviation. In the interwar years, he had helped develop two of the weapons that would help turn the tide in the air war: high-octane fuel and instrument, or "blind," flying.

Doolittle grew up with the fledgling Army Air Service, setting a succession of speed and distance records to advance Billy Mitchell's campaign for an independent air arm. On temporary leave from his duties, he attended MIT and was awarded one of the first American doctorates in aeronautical engineering. He then went on to test his revolutionary ideas in the sky, stretching the frontiers of aviation. In 1929, he became the first pilot in the world to execute a blind landing, using new performance instruments he had helped to develop. With a hood covering his cockpit, making it blacker than the night around him, he took off, flew a planned course, and landed without incident.

In the 1930s, he left active military service to enter private industry as manager of the Aviation Department of the Shell Oil Company. All the while, as a major in the Army Reserves and a demonstrator of Shell's new aircraft products, he continued to be the country's most celebrated stunt pilot, the most famous airman in America next to Charles Lindbergh, and a hero to thousands of boys who would later serve under him in the Eighth.

In 1940, Doolittle returned to active duty at age forty-three. Two years later, after persuading a number of automobile executives to convert their plants to the production of warplanes, he received the call from Hap Arnold that led to the raid on Tokyo, which made him forever famous. Only five foot four and 140 pounds, forty-seven-year-old Jimmy Doolittle was a driven man who credited boxing with helping him to discipline an unruly temper. At age fifteen, weighing 105 pounds, he won the flyweight amateur boxing championship of the Pacific Coast. Later, he taught his two sons to box, telling them that if they ever beat him he would buy them a car. "The last time I boxed with him he broke my nose and I broke two of his teeth," his son John recalled. "He considered it a moral victory for me because he had to pay to get us both fixed."

But in dealing with people, Doolittle relied on persuasion rather than pugnacity. "It didn't take but two minutes, and you were under his spell," said one of his Tokyo raiders. "Doolittle was a great commander," added another Tokyo pilot, "because he had just the right mix: he was both a forceful leader, and approachable as a man." In North Africa he had flown with his men to gain their respect, and he would have flown with the crews of the Eighth had he not been briefed on ULTRA and D-Day, two of the deepest secrets of the war. Everything in his makeup and personal history—his courage, his flying experience, his managerial background, his compassion for his crews, his technical knowledge of aircraft and foul weather flying, and a sobering prewar trip to Germany to study the Luftwaffe, equipped him for his new responsibilities.

Jimmy Doolittle's first decision as commander of the Eighth would reverse the course of the air war. Under Eaker, the mission of the fighter escorts was to stay within close range of the bombers until enemy fighters attacked. "This policy concerned me," Doolittle explained later, "because fighter aircraft are designed to go after enemy fighters. Fighter pilots are usually pugnacious individuals by nature and are trained to be aggressive in the air. Their machines are specially designed for offensive action." Doolittle wanted his escorts to intercept the enemy's fighters before they reached the bombers, and to strafe enemy fighter fields and transportation targets on their return home, as well as on separate operations. "If it moved, could fly or supported the German war effort, I told my pilots to kill it in place." Spaatz agreed completely, seeing the destruction of the Luftwaffe in the air, on its airfields, and at its fighter factories as the Eighth's paramount responsibility. Eaker's policy of forcing the Luftwaffe up to fight by hitting vital economic targets made no sense, Doolittle argued, if the fighters remained tethered to the bombers.

The decision to change things was made in the office of the Eighth's fighter chief, Gen. William Kepner. Walking into Kepner's office, Doolittle saw a sign on the wall: "The first duty of the Eighth Air Force Fighters is to bring the bombers back alive."

"Bill, who dreamed that up?" Doolittle asked.

"The sign was here when we arrived," Kepner replied.

"Take that damn thing down," Doolittle ordered, "and put up another one saying: 'The first duty of the Eighth Air Force is to destroy German fighters.' "

"You mean you're authorizing me to take the offensive?" Kepner asked.

"I'm directing you to," Doolittle replied sharply.

Kepner was elated. He had been urging Eaker to allow him to unleash his fighters, and he especially liked Doolittle's idea of seeking out and destroying enemy fighters on their airfields. As Doolittle left Kepner's office, he heard his fighter commander tearing down the sign.

Later, Adolf Galland would say that the day the Eighth Air Force's fighters went on the offensive was the day Germany lost the air war. At this time, Hermann Göring was ordering his fighters to avoid the American fighter escorts altogether and concentrate on the bombers. This, Galland said later, was Germany's "greatest tactical error" of the air war. It caused his pilots to lose their élan and develop a deep fear of the American fighters, avoiding them whenever possible.

When Kepner told a group of his fighter pilots that they were going over to the offensive they cheered. "[But] as soon as my decision was announced to the bomb groups," Doolittle recalled, "their commanders descended on me individually and in bunches to tell me, in polite terms of course, that I was a 'killer' and 'murderer.' I had taken away their 'little friends' and they were sure their bomber formations would now be picked off wholesale." It was a "difficult decision to make," Doolittle admitted, "[but] from the time we made it, we began to take ascendancy in the air."

That would not happen right away. In early January, after taking over command of air operations in England, both Spaatz and Doolittle, like Eaker before them, were hamstrung by the weather, which prevented the kind of long-range, strategic bombing the Eighth had been created to carry out. With missions continuing to be canceled with despairing frequency and the wreckage of bombers lost to the weather scattered all over England, it was difficult for the crews as well. At Ridgewell, a Fortress experienced trouble taking off into the gloom and crash-landed. The explosion could be heard for miles. Chaplain Brown helped remove the grotesquely charred bodies from the wreckage and two days later led graveside services for the ten fliers at Madingley Military Cemetery, the Air Force's new burial ground, located on a high, wooded hill overlooking the colleges of Cambridge. Standing over the plain wooden caskets, Brown scanned the faces of the dead fliers' friends. They had lost other comrades over Germany, but like shadows, they had disappeared without a trace. These men were about to go into the cold ground. "The look in their faces read: 'This is my end. I will lie here, too,' " Brown wrote later. "And when I saw this on their faces, a cold chill ran up my back."

Even imperturbable Carl Spaatz began to react to the pressure. On two occasions in early January, fast-changing island weather forced Doolittle to recall bomber formations on their way to targets. Doolittle feared that the planes would be unable to land at socked-in English bases when they returned. When Spaatz learned that the weather had unexpectedly cleared over England after the second mission had been aborted, he had it out with his bomber commander. "I wonder if you've got the guts to lead a big air force," he reprimanded Doolittle. "If you haven't, I'll get someone else who has." When Doolittle tried to explain that he would never gamble with the lives of his men on an "uncalculated risk," Spaatz waved him out of the room.

Within days after the second recall, the two commanders were flying together on an inspection tour of bases in *Boots,* Spaatz's personal B-17. As they approached the last of the fields they planned to visit, the weather turned on them and the pilot was unable to locate the field through the leaden mist. Spotting a small hole in the clouds, he dropped through and began hedgehopping over farms and villages until he found an open pasture to land in. They hit hard and came to a skidding stop a few feet short of a stone fence. As the two generals climbed out of the plane, an ashen-faced Spaatz turned to Doolittle and said, "Jim, I see what you mean about uncalculated risks."

The Mustang

One of the two combat missions that Doolittle had recalled occurred on January 11. It was only a partial recall and the bombers that proceeded to their targets were slaughtered. But what looked like a great German victory was actually a promising turning point for the Eighth in its fight for sky supremacy.

At five-thirty on the morning of the mission, the lights came on in John Comer's hut. Aroused from a deep sleep, Comer listened to the roster of the gunners who were flying that day: "Counce flying 888 with Cline—Balmore flying 912 with Crozier." Jim Counce and George Balmore were Comer's longtime crewmates and best friends, but this time he would not be flying with them. He had completed his twenty-fifth mission a few days before and he was heading home to Corpus Christi, Texas, that morning. Comer went down to the flight line with Counce and Balmore to see them off. A quick handshake and they were gone.

Standing at the local train station an hour or so later, Comer watched the bombers pass overhead. As the fleet of Fortresses and Liberators began assembling in the low, menacing overcast, Comer wondered if the boys should be up there on a day like this.

Air Force meteorologists knew it would be a risky mission. They had predicted a few hours of clear weather over central Germany, allowing only a small window of opportunity for the Eighth to fly its first deep-penetration mission with fighter protection against Pointblank targets. Flying in the formation with the 91st Bomb Group, Robert Morgan's old Bassingbourn-based outfit, was Lester Rentmeester, a pilot raised on a dairy farm near Green Bay, Wisconsin. He had quit the University of Wisconsin's engineering program to join the Air Force and his plane was named after his new bride, *Jeannie Marie*. This was his first mission.

The general target was a fighter production belt whose central cities were Brunswick, Halberstadt, and Oschersleben. The target for his group, part of the 1st Division, was a factory complex in Oschersleben that was turning out more Focke-Wulfs than any other plant in the Reich. At the mission briefing, the crews had been told they would have a large escort of fighters, for the Luftwaffe was certain to be out in impressive numbers, protecting targets only ninety miles west of Berlin. Thunderbolts and Lightnings would take the bombers to within fifty miles of their targets and a single group of P-51 Mustangs, the only group then available in England, would cover the lead formation over the target.

The Mustang was the long-range fighter that everyone in the Eighth had been waiting for. In limited numbers, it had begun escorting bombers the previous month. Most of the bomber crews knew almost nothing about the new plane except that it was a fast and impressive silhouette in the sky. There were rumors, however, that it was having mechanical problems and might not yet be a match for the dreaded Focke-Wulf 190.

As *Jeannie Marie* completed its climb through the clouds and broke into the blue, there were bombers scattered all over the sunlit sky, some of them heading in the opposite direction. The plane's radio operator sent a Morse code message, using secret passwords, asking if the mission had been called off. The reply came within seconds. "Press on."

Back at Eighth Air Force headquarters at High Wycombe, an unsettled Jimmy Doolittle watched the weather map as high, heavy rain clouds swept eastward, across the North Sea, toward Berlin. When the fighter escorts began returning, unable to locate the bombers, Doolittle sent out a message recalling the 2nd and 3rd Divisions. The leading 1st Division, less than a hundred miles from the target, was not told that it would have to go it alone, with only a little help from a single combat wing of the 2nd Division, whose commander had disregarded the recall.

The Luftwaffe was ready that winter morning. In a fantastic underground compound outside Berlin, "The Battle Opera House," the movement of the American bomber stream was being plotted on a wall-size map of frosted glass. With the bombers headed on a direct path for Berlin, Galland sent out every plane he had available. Minutes later, his controllers noticed a flight of enemy fighters hovering over Oschersleben, waiting for the approaching bombers. The Germans were shocked that enemy fighters could fly that far and apparently have enough fuel left for a fight. Galland wanted no part of them; he sent his hunters after the Boeings.

Coming in across Holland, Lester Rentmeester's crew was singing and joking to calm their nerves when a shout was heard on the intercom: "Bandits at ten o'clock high." At least three dozen Focke-Wulfs were directly above their stacked formations and had already begun their dive. It was the start of a six-hour-long battle.

After the first assault, there was a short break in the action. Everyone got quiet in the plane as the forward-facing crewmembers nervously watched a swarm of enemy fighters forming up a mile ahead of them, for what looked like the start of a suicide charge. At precisely that moment, a P-51 Mustang flashed through the enemy formation from behind and sent two German fighters into a flaming descent. "It was a complete surprise," Rentmeester recalled. Never had American fighters taken on the Luftwaffe this far inside the fatherland. But today there were not enough Mustangs. Forty-nine of them had become separated in the clouds, leaving only one to confront at least thirty single-engine German fighters.

The pilot was Maj. James H. Howard, the son of medical missionaries in China. After three years as a Navy carrier pilot in the late 1930s, he had returned to China—where he was born—to join Claire Chennault's American volunteer group, the "Flying Tigers." In eighteen months of flying, mostly over Burma, he had destroyed six Japanese planes and was shot down once. When the Flying Tigers were absorbed by the United States Army Air Forces in 1942, Howard accepted a commission as a major. He had arrived in England in the first week of November with the 354th Fighter Group, the first AAF unit in the European Theater equipped with Mustangs.

For over half an hour, Howard climbed and dove continuously, scattering German planes as they bore in on the bombers. In the course of his one-man blitz, three of his four machine guns jammed, but Howard continued to press home his attack with one gun, making diving, rolling passes through the Luftwaffe formations until he ran low on fuel. The 401st Bomb Group, the focus of the German attack, did not lose a single ship. When Howard landed back in England, there was only one bullet hole in his Mustang. It was one of the greatest feats of combat flying in the war and it earned him the Medal of Honor, the only one awarded to a fighter pilot in the European Theater.

American escort pilots had been ordered not to attack the enemy without the rear support of their wingmen. But "it was up to me to do it," Howard said in an interview. "There were 10-man crews in those bombers and no one else to protect them." A slim, self-effacing man, Howard claimed only two enemy kills and two probables, but the bomber crews who witnessed his one-man fight swore he downed six. "There were an awful lot of them around," Howard told reporter Andy Rooney. "It was just a matter of shooting at them."

What was a small victory for Howard was a large loss for the Eighth Air Force. Using auxiliary belly tanks, the Luftwaffe fighters had been able to stay in contact with the bombers longer than they had for any time up to now. The fighting was as tough as it gets in the sky. The 1st Division reported over 400 individual attacks in three and a half hours. The Germans savaged the American fleet, leaving the burnt carcasses of sixty bombers strewn over the snow-covered landscape of the Reich, exactly the number of losses of Black Thursday. Entombed in two of them were the bodies of Jim Counce and George Balmore.

John Comer got word three days later, just as he was packing his bags at a transfer center to head for the ship that would take him home. Both of their planes had gone down and no chutes were observed. "That night was bitterly cold and it was raining," Comer wrote. "I walked blindly in the rain without cap or raincoat for a long time because a man does not cry in front of other men." Years later, after volunteering for the Fifteenth Air Force and flying fifty additional bombing missions, John Comer named his first-born son James Balmore Comer.

Back in Washington, Hap Arnold fumed. Why had so few bombers hit the targets? Why couldn't the Eighth deliver "some good smashing blows?" It had been a gloomy beginning for Spaatz and Doolittle, but they were encouraged by the performance of the Mustangs, which so far had suffered no losses and claimed fifteen kills. "That plane," said American fighter ace Don Salvatore Gentile, "put the Huns right up against the wall."

The Mustang's belated development was one of the most egregious errors in the history of American airpower. It was the plane the Bomber Mafia had claimed was impossible to build, a fighter that could go as fast and as far as the bombers without losing its fighting characteristics.

The best American fighter plane of the war was built for the British and designed by a German who had worked for Willie Messerschmitt, whose Me 109s shot down more Allied planes than any other aircraft. The North American Aviation Company assigned German-born Edgar Schmued to build it and the company delivered the plane to the Royal Air Force in 1941. At the time, the American Air Force showed little interest in it, buying only two planes for test purposes. Its underpowered Allison engine made it unsuitable for high-altitude flying; the British used it as a low-level tactical fighter. Impressed by its performance and streamlined airframe, Lt. Col. Thomas Hitchcock, an American air attaché in London, wrote a memo to Washington in October 1942 to pass on the idea of Lt. Col. Campbell-Orde of the Air Fighting Development Unit that the Mustang be made into a high-altitude fighter "by crossbreeding it with the Merlin 61 engine" produced by Rolls-Royce, which had been working on the problem since June. The modification transformed the plane into a sensational high-altitude aircraft: a small, streamlined beauty that was faster, lighter, and more nimble than anything in the Nazi arsenal. Suddenly the American Air Force became interested, ordering 2,200 of the British-American hybrids from North American Aviation in late 1942—not nearly enough, but a start.

Schmued and his engineers turned the Mustang into a long-legged performer by placing an 85-gallon fuselage tank to the rear of the armor plate behind the pilot. Not until after the Regensburg-Schweinfurt raid, however, did a suddenly concerned Hap Arnold order the plane rushed to England. When Mustangs began arriving, Ira Eaker, who was dubious about their capabilities as escorts, assigned them to the Ninth Air Force for tactical fighting. Arnold quickly changed that, making an arrangement for the Ninth's Mustangs to fly as bomber escorts under the control of Eighth Air Force Fighter Command. Thereafter, the Eighth got all the Mustangs it wanted from North American Aviation. Beginning with their first long-range escort duty in December, P-51s carried 75-gallon drop tanks, one tank under each wing. Thus equipped, they could fly all the way to Berlin and back.

Six months later, improved models with 108-gallon drop tanks were fly-ing to Poland, a round-trip of 1,700 miles, at speeds approaching 440 miles per hour and at altitudes of up to 40,000 feet—and with six 0.5 caliber ma-chine guns. For low-level work, it could carry a 2,000-pound arsenal of rock-ets or bombs. By then, the positions of the bombers and the fighters had been reversed. The new challenge became to increase the size of the bombers' fuel tanks to give the "big friends" the range of their "little friends."

The Mustang was the outstanding piston-powered fighter of the war. In their first three months of operations, the Mustangs scored three times more kills per sortie than the P-47 Thunderbolts, and twice as many as the P-38 Lightnings. By the end of 1944, every fighter group in the Eighth ex-cept Zemke's 56th, had transitioned to Mustangs. The rest of the Thunder-bolts and the Lightnings were transferred to tactical units that would soon begin bombing bridges, airfields, and supply trains in northern France in preparation for the invasion. After the invasion, they would provide battle-field support for Allied infantry. Modified Lightnings, without arms, contin-ued to be used for high-altitude photo-reconnaissance. In less than a year, the Eighth's Fighter Command had become virtually an all-Mustang force.

After the war, Hap Arnold admitted that it had been "the Air Force's own fault" that this splendid performer had not been made available earlier.

"Mass Against Mass"

The Eighth Air Force was unable to send out a single mission for ten days after the Oschersleben raid. As the discouraging weather stretched into mid-February, Air Force planners waited impatiently to deliver the mas-sive blow against the German aircraft industry they had originally sched-uled for early November 1943. This was Eaker's Operation Argument, which called for continuous, coordinated strikes by the Eighth and Fif-teenth Air Forces and Arthur Harris's Bomber Command. Arnold and Eaker were so desperate to destroy these vital targets that the missions would have gone forward in 1943 without long-range escorts. As it was, the bad weather turned out to be an unexpected blessing, allowing the Eighth to build up the strength of its escort force to nearly 1,300 fighters, over 300 of them Mustangs.

The aim of Operation Argument was nothing less than the annihilation of the Luftwaffe. The strategy: bait them and kill them. Send in the bombers—the bait—to destroy the aircraft factories and then massacre the planes and pilots that came up to defend them. Ira Eaker had tried this earlier. But without sufficient bombers to accomplish the task, and without Mustangs, he had never been able to apply what military strategists call the principle of "mass," the application of overwhelming force. This had been the American strategy of winning wars since Ulysses S. Grant wore down Robert E. Lee.

"My lot was much easier than Eaker's because I began to get more bombers and . . . long-range fighters," Doolittle said in a postwar interview. "It was the Mustang that made me look good." But Doolittle would face stronger enemy opposition. With Galland's enhanced defense forces—nearly a thousand daylight fighters—drawn back into Germany, they would be in a position to savage the bomber streams with tightly massed strikes. It would be, Galland predicted, a battle of "Mass against Mass." As he geared up for the coming fight, Adolf Galland stood on a hinge of history, not knowing which way it would swing.

The battle began on the unpromising morning of February 20, 1944. Clouds, ice, and swirling snow greeted the fliers as they headed for their briefings. Out on the airfields, gassed and ready, was the largest strike force yet assembled by the American Air Force, over a thousand bombers and almost 900 fighters. But few airmen expected to fly that morning. Even the ordinarily aggressive Spaatz was vacillating. The previous day he had received word from Eaker that the Fifteenth Air Force would be unable to participate in the opening of what was called Big Week, the most savage succession of air battles of World War II. Eaker's force would be providing emergency support for Allied troops bottled up on the beaches of Anzio, Italy. This was a caution flag for Spaatz, but his deputy for operations, Gen. Frederick Anderson, pressed him to send out the bombers.

Operation Argument was largely Anderson's plan, hammered out in close cooperation with his assistant, Col. C. Glenn Williamson, an old classmate from West Point. The two air strategists were physical opposites who thought alike. "Anderson is tall, rawboned and supple, temperamentally a well-anchored man, a good talker and an easy mixer," a *Life* reporter described him. "Only seldom will a stranger catch the gleam of purpose beneath the affability. Williamson is short and stumpy and given to long spells of moodiness. Logical, erudite in the detail of his profession, uncompromising, he is one of the foremost theoretical thinkers of the Army Air Forces." The two men were united by deep devotion to the ideas of the ancient Chinese philosopher-general Sun Tzu. One of Sun Tzu's maxims—"The opportunity of defeating the enemy is provided by the enemy himself"—sheds light on the strategy of the updated version of Argument. Having built a magnificent industrial infrastructure for the production of fighter aircraft, Germany would have to defend it strongly. This would pull the Luftwaffe into a closely fought battle of attrition that the beefed-up Eighth Air Force was now confident of winning. As Sun Tzu had prophesized, one of the enemy's greatest strengths would prove its undoing.

When Anderson first drew up his plan in October 1943, he proposed to cut German fighter production by 75 percent in four successive hammer blows. That was a preposterous projection. But the four-month-long weather delay had given him, unexpectedly, a long-range fighter force that would allow him to gravely damage the Luftwaffe by attacking it both on the ground and in the air, employing the new twin-pronged offensive machine—an aggressive phalanx of bombers and fighters—that Doolittle had created by unleashing the escorts.

Originally, Anderson was prepared to lose as many as two-thirds of his crews, 7,000 men, a third of the total number of marines that would die retaking the Pacific. With the escorts, he expected his losses to be less heavy, yet still great: up to 200 bombers on the first day of operations. But the risk had to be taken, he believed; the success of the land invasion, and with it the war itself, depended on knocking out the Luftwaffe.

There was something else at stake. Since arriving in England, the Eighth Air Force had taken on three major target systems: submarine repair facilities, ball bearings, and aircraft production, and had failed to knock out any of them. "On the record," an American reporter wrote, "the American daylight attack was in doubt."

To hit Germany this hard, Anderson needed fantastic luck, weather conditions of a kind which rarely occur in Europe in winter." German fighter production was economically concentrated and geographically dispersed. The main assembly plants were organized into industrial complexes, each one with a principal assembly plant surrounded by smaller factories that manufactured component parts. "The peculiar thing about these complexes," as Williamson later explained, "was that the production flow could be shifted from plant to plant inside the complex or to plants in other complexes. If you knocked out the assembly plant in one complex the tools and workers were quickly shifted to another and the satellite component factories fed right into it. A complex was a big octopus. You had to kill all of it to make it die."

But the American attacks of the previous summer and fall had set in motion a dispersal program. Some of the newer complexes were located in central and southern Germany and others in Austria, Hungary, and Poland. With his targets scattered all over the Reich, and visual bombing an imperative, Anderson would need at least three to four days of clear weather. Since many of the missions would be to the extreme limit of the bombers' range, they would be long flights, requiring good visibility both over the targets at midday and back in England at the end of the day, when the bombers flew back into capricious British weather.

To advise him, Anderson had located an eccentric professor and had him flown to England and made an instant major. His name was Irving P. Krick and he was head of CalTech's meteorological department. As a sideline job, Krick operated a long-range weather forecasting service whose patrons included fruit growers and Hollywood movie studios. Krick's theories were based on the idea that "weather situations" repeat themselves. "A sequence of phenomena which produced a certain kind of weather in the past will, if repeated, produce the same weather again." In England, Krick researched European weather records going back half a century. On February 18 he told Anderson that "a good looking sequence" was in the making. Beginning on the 20th, a high-pressure system would settle in over central and southern Germany and would probably last for three to four days. This was it! Anderson, with Spaatz's approval, scheduled a maximum strike for the morning of February 20.

Anderson was banking everything on Krick's forecast, which was one of three he had received, and the only one that promised clearing skies over Central Europe for a succession of days, beginning the following morning. The night before the mission the skies were "solid" over England and weather reconnaissance planes returned with unanimously bleak reports: there was no foreseeable break in the cloud cover. Anderson knew that takeoffs would have to begin before dawn because of the short European winter days, and that icing conditions would pose extraordinary difficulties for both fighters and bombers. It was "not exactly a no-risk situation," recalled Jimmy Doolittle, whose inclination was to postpone. William Kepner, the fighter commander, agreed, but Anderson remained adamant, even if it meant losing 200 bombers. That night at Park House, poker-faced Carl Spaatz camped by the phone, listening to the conflicting advice of his subordinates. After a sleepless night, he sent out the signal to his base commanders: "Let 'em go."

CHAPTER TEN

Liberated Skies

War is a series of catastrophes that results in a victory.

GEORGES CLEMENCEAU

Dawn, June 6, 1944

In the gray mist before first light, as the Allied invasion armada drew near the French coast, the crews of American bombers spotted a lone Flying Fortress circling just below them. In the co-pilot's seat was Gen. Laurence Kuter, on temporary assignment as Gen. Hap Arnold's personal observer of D-Day operations. Lean, turbulent Larry Kuter was one of the framers of AWPD-1, the master plan for the daylight strategic bombing of Germany. In the late summer of 1942, he had been sent to England to execute that plan as commander of the 1st Bombardment Wing of the Eighth Air Force.

That fall and winter Kuter had launched strike after futile strike against impregnable U-boat pens on France's Brittany coast before being reassigned to the Mediterranean, to Operation Torch, and then to Washington to become Arnold's chief planner of combat operations. When he left for Washington in early 1943, the Luftwaffe ruled the skies over the Continent and the future of daylight bombing was in grave doubt. Now Kuter waited for the sun to confirm his hunch that Germany's fighter force would pose no threat to the tremendous amphibious operation that was about to begin.

On the eve of the invasion, General Eisenhower had assured his troops: "If you see fighting aircraft over you, they will be ours." Neither he nor any other Allied commanders gave voice to his deepest concern—that Hitler had been husbanding hundreds of fighters inside the Reich for a furious effort to hurl the invaders back into the sea. Even Carl Spaatz, who was confident his forces had grievously damaged the Luftwaffe, expected—as Eisenhower did—"lively air opposition."

"I was thinking," Kuter recalled, "that if I were the German operations officer and Providence had promised to allow me to select the weather in which to make my defense, these were the conditions I would have chosen. A solid bank of overcast covered the Normandy coast and extended to mid-Channel. . . . Here was perfect concealment for German airmen. They could dive out of the dense cloud upon the packed Channel below, bomb or strafe any ship and climb back into the protecting clouds in a matter of seconds. They could come and go before a gun was brought to bear or our thousands of fighters were able to intercept. I was apprehensive—more than I would care to admit. The cloudbank could be swarming with Germans. Where was there ever such a target—4,000 ships on a front 18 miles broad?"

As the landing boats carrying the troops headed toward the beaches in the heavy chop, General Kuter's concern disappeared. The air was full of Allied fighters and "columns of Flying Fortresses stretched back to England as far as the eye could follow." There were no signs of German fighters. The "Hun never showed up," Kuter wrote later. "He couldn't because he had nothing left."

On this world-turning day, the Luftwaffe flew fewer than 250 sorties against the most powerful invasion force ever assembled to that time. The infantry battle—the breakout from the beaches and the fight to clear the enemy from Normandy—would not be won for another seven weeks, but command of the sky had already been secured in six weeks of withering aerial combat.

Billy Mitchell and Giulio Douhet had seen bomber warfare's instantaneous, morale-shattering power as a humane alternative to the slow slaughter of trench warfare. But the aerial battles in the months leading up to D-Day were unimaginably costly in men and planes. Unlike the grinding killing of the previous war, however, these air fights were swiftly decisive, clearing the skies over Northern Europe for the Kuter-style strategic bombing that would smash Germany's industrial machine in the final year of the war.

Big Week

The first of these great battles began the ugly February morning Carl Spaatz gave the command to begin Big Week, a six-day-long campaign that was fought all over Western Europe, from the North Sea to the Danube, from Paris to Poland. The target on the first day was the stronghold of Hitler's fighter production: the massive assembly and component plants in the Brunswick-Leipzig area of central Germany, some eighty miles south of Berlin. The weather began to clear beautifully as the bomber stream crossed into German airspace, just as Anderson's eccentric weatherman had predicted. Leading the convoy of 800 silver-winged fighters were the Thunderbolts of Hub Zemke's Wolf Pack, fitted out for the first time with 150-gallon belly tanks that would allow his fighters to penetrate nearly to Hanover, almost 400 miles from their base at Halesworth. "We caught up with the bombers and took up station on the left side of their formation at 22,000 feet," recalled Francis "Gabby" Gabreski, the son of Polish immigrants from Oil City, Pennsylvania. "All was quiet until we were ready to break off escort, about thirty miles west of Hanover." At that point, a formation of twin-engine night fighters, Messerschmitt Bf 110s, came into sight just below them and Gabreski's squadron "bounced them." Only a single German fighter escaped undamaged before Gabreski re-formed his squadron for the long haul home. His Thunderbolts had scored eighteen of the sixty-one victories credited to the American fighters that day.

Tactics had as much to do with it as technology. Prior to Doolittle's order to release the escorts, Luftwaffe pursuit planes would usually assemble at lower altitudes, knowing they would be safe there with the American fighters hovering above them, glued to the bombers. On February 20, the enemy pilots were surprised and slaughtered, and Zemke's 56th Fighter Group did not lose a single plane in the region of the Reich his pilots would soon be calling the Happy Hunting Ground.

That night at Park House, Spaatz, Anderson, and Williamson waited for the mission reports to arrive via Teletype, bracing themselves for heavy losses. "The reports came in all evening" Williamson recalled. "Group after group reported no losses or only one or two. We couldn't believe it." When the Teletype machine stopped ticking, the commanders calculated the cost: twenty-one bombers and four fighters—214 of the nearly 11,000 men who flew the mission. The Germans lost 153 fighters. Spaatz was euphoric, "on the crest of the highest wave he had ever ridden," Williamson recalled.

But men who fight battles see them differently than generals back at headquarters. "To the General sitting before the maps . . . the reports on casualties are encouraging," wrote the novelist and World War II veteran Irwin Shaw. "To the man on the scene the casualties are never encouraging. When he is hit or when the man next to him is hit . . . it is inconceivable at that moment to believe that there is a man [who] . . . can report . . . that everything is going according to plan."

For the three American airmen who won Medals of Honor on February 20, nothing went according to plan. Theirs are the greatest individual stories to come out of Big Week, tales of epic heroism and sacrificial solidarity. On a day when young men had to grow up or fold up, they stood strong.

As an unnamed Fortress of the 305th Bomb Group left the skies over Leipzig, it was jumped by over a dozen enemy fighters. Eight crewmen were hit by cannon fire and one of the bomber's engines was on fire. A shell smashed through the right windshield and exploded in the face of the co-pilot, killing him instantly. When he fell forward, all his weight came down on the control column, sending the bomber into a sudden dive. The pilot, Lt. William R. Lawley, who was severely wounded around the face and neck, struggled to force his dead friend off the controls with his right hand while trying to bring the bomber out of its deep descent with his left. He had to pilot the ship blindly; the windscreen and controls were covered with blood and debris. When he finally brought the bomber out of its near vertical drop of 10,000 feet, he noticed that the damaged engine was still on fire. After leveling off he ordered the crew to bail out, fearing the plane was about to explode, but bombardier Lt. Harry Mason, who had gone to the rear to check on the damage, reported that two of the gunners were badly wounded and could not be moved. One of the crew did bail out, but Lawley went on the interphone and announced that he was going to try to bring the bomber home. England was almost five flying hours away, but he saw no other way to save his two stricken gunners. The other crewmen were given a second opportunity to bail out, but decided to stick with Lawley and their semiconscious comrades.

Suffering from shock and exposure, with freezing air blasting through the shattered windscreen, Lawley was ashen-faced and delirious, and several times he slipped into unconsciousness. Harry Mason tied the co-pilot's body to his seat back with a parka and stood between the seats in the cockpit, reviving Lawley and helping him with the controls. When they reached England, they were flying at barely 1,500 feet on only one engine. After missing the first field they sighted through the drizzle and gloom, Lawley spotted a Canadian fighter strip and tried to lower the wheels. They were stuck. The Fortress hit the concrete runway with wheels up, its exposed belly sending up a shower of sparks that looked like a firestorm. The entire crew was pulled from the wreckage alive, but the two badly wounded gunners were permanently crippled.

After the war, William Lawley kept in touch with his crew. One of his gunners, Ralph Braswell, visited Lawley at his home outside Montgomery, Alabama, before his death in 1999. "He had arthritis," said Braswell, "but after I shook his hands, I said, 'They're beautiful. They saved my life.' "

Five other fliers on the Leipzig mission were saved that afternoon by two of their comrades, S. Sgt. Archibald Mathies and Lt. Walter E. Truemper. Near the target, Carl Moore, the top turret gunner of the Fortress *Ten Horsepower,* flying out of Polebrook with the 351st Bomb Group, spotted two Me 109s coming straight at them. Seconds later, a cannon shell exploded in the cockpit, decapitating co-pilot Ronald Bartley and knocking out pilot C. Richard Nelson. The limp bodies of both pilots slumped forward on the steering columns and, in an eerie parallel, *Ten Horsepower* went into the same kind of dive that nearly finished off William Lawley's Fortress. The centrifugal force created by the spiraling dive immobilized every surviving crewman. "For the next few minutes it was like being inside of a spinning top. We were thrown against the fuselage and held there. We couldn't move," said waist gunner Russell Robinson. Carl Moore managed to crawl forward from the floor below his turret and into the narrow opening between the pilots' seats. The wind that was tearing through the fractured window drove him backward. Summoning all his strength, he leaned forward and cringed in horror at the carnage in the cockpit. Bartley's head was on the floor and the right side of Nelson's face had been sheared off. Convinced that Nelson was dead, Moore grabbed hold of both yokes, one in each hand, and used his elbows to fight off the weight and pressure of the pilots' limp bodies. After a descent of nearly 15,000 feet, with enemy fighters pounding them even as they picked up speed, he pulled the plane out of its dive so suddenly, said wounded radio operator Thomas Sowell, "I felt my eyeballs were going to pop out through my cheek bones."

At this point, navigator Walter Truemper, a former accounting clerk from Aurora, Illinois, made his way up to the cockpit and Moore handed over control of the ship to him. A few minutes later, Scottish-born Archie Mathies, a Pennsylvania coal miner's son who had a few hours' flying experience, climbed out of his ball turret and joined Truemper in the cockpit. The two men crouched in the narrow opening between the seats as they tried to decide what to do. Using their hands to manipulate the elevator and aileron controls, which were on the floor of the cockpit, they managed to keep the bomber airborne. Other crewmen pulled Bartley's body out of the right seat and placed it in the crawlway below the cockpit. Truemper then handed the controls to Mathies and, when the Luftwaffe fighters disappeared, went down into the nose to chart a course back to England. The bombardier had bailed out, after releasing the bombs, but with all four engines running well, the rest of the crew decided to stay with the plane.

The freezing blasts in the cockpit made it impossible for either Mathies or Truemper to take the wheel for more than a few minutes at a time. They set up a rotation, with Mathies doing most of the flying and the two men communicating by hand signals because of the noise of the wind. The crew tried to move Nelson so that Mathies could take the left seat, away from the shot-out window, but they stopped suddenly when they realized he was still alive, hanging by a thread.

When they reached Polebrook, Truemper radioed the control tower. "The copilot is dead. The pilot we think is dead. The bombardier has jumped. I am the navigator, the only commissioned officer on board. What should we do?" Truemper said Mathies believed he could land the plane, and Col. Eugene Romig, the base commander, gave the OK. After Mathies made a high, erratic approach on this first attempt—fatigue and exposure having dulled his reactions—Romig ordered him to circle back and have the crew bail out over the field. The last man to jump was Carl Moore. After shaking hands with Mathies and Truemper, he gave his friends the thumbs-up and disappeared through the rear crew door.

While the crew was bailing out, Romig and Maj. Elzia Ledoux, a squadron commander, boarded a B-17 and took off in an effort to fly alongside *Ten Horsepower* and talk it to the ground by radioing instructions to Mathies. With Mathies flying wildly, alternately climbing and diving, they were unable to get close enough to provide much assistance. After Mathies made a second unsuccessful pass, Romig told Mathies and Truemper to point the bomber out to sea, set the automatic pilot, and bail out. The two men replied that the pilot was still alive and could not be moved. They would not desert him.

After failing to land at a neighboring field, *Ten Horsepower* veered out of control and crash-landed. Mathies and Truemper were killed instantly and were posthumously awarded the Medal of Honor. The wounded pilot they died trying to save survived for only another hour or so. Carl Moore, the last man to see his three dead crewmates, was awarded the Distinguished Service Cross. After the war, the Pittsburgh Coal Company renamed one of its mines for Archie Mathies, the air gunner from Stonehouse, Scotland, who had worked beside his father in a bituminous seam in Liberty, Pennsylvania, before dying a hero on his second combat mission of the war.

Eighth Air Force losses rose alarmingly in the next five days of Big Week. At least 226 of its heavies went down over the Reich, nearly 20 percent of the Eighth's available force. Losses for the Fifteenth were proportional. Back in 1942 an equivalent loss rate would have disabled Eaker's command. In that year Laurence Kuter and his fellow air planners estimated that the Eighth would lose no more then 300 unescorted bombers in the entire air war! But in 1944, this was a battle-hardened, airplane-rich Air Force, infused with a new spirit and prepared to sustain frightful casualties. And now, for the first time, it was certain it was winning, that it had found and was exploiting a vulnerable weak point in Germany's war economy.

Frederick Anderson, the master planner of Big Week, was convinced that the Eighth and Fifteenth Air Forces, working for the first time in close coordination with each other, and with the British night bombers, had dealt a paralyzing blow to Nazi fighter production, bringing it close to "final extinction." He was wrong. During Big Week 10,000 tons of explosives were dropped on eighteen German airframe and ball bearing manufacturing centers, including, yet again, Regensburg and Schweinfurt. This was roughly equal to the tonnage dropped by the Eighth Air Force in its entire first year of operations. The RAF also weighed in heavy, dropping even more tonnage than the Americans. Yet this full-out effort would cost the Germans only a two-month delay in aircraft production.

By the summer of 1944, German fighter plane production would peak, in part due to Big Week. With Hitler's approval, responsibility for production was shifted from Göring's scandalously incompetent Air Ministry to a special agency within Albert Speer's Ministry of Armaments and Munitions. Speer placed one of his expert managers, Karl Otto Saur, in charge of an accelerated program of industrial dispersal. In late 1944, Germany's smaller, ingeniously hidden plants were producing more fighter planes per month than Germany had been producing before Big Week. Allied intelligence never discovered these forest plants, which would have been almost impossible to hit from four miles up anyway.

The second part of Anderson's strategy worked wonderfully. The Luftwaffe came up to protect the aircraft plants and lost over a third of its single-engine fighters and, more critically, 18 percent of its fighter pilots. Even the bombing of the assembly plants produced some significant long-term results. German aircraft production figures would have been even more impressive had the plants not been bombed. And in the months ahead dispersal would cost the industry wasting delays. In these smaller plants, aircraft were produced much more slowly than in the more rationalized larger plants. Dispersal would also leave the scattered aircraft plants heavily dependent on rail transport; trains carrying parts and components would soon become fat targets for marauding American fighter planes. In the end, dispersal "defeated itself." When the German transportation system was decimated by Allied bombing and strafing in late 1944, it became impossible to keep the final assembly plants supplied with the parts to produce finished aircraft. Overrated at the time by Eighth Air Force leaders, and underrated ever since by historians, Big Week was neither a victory nor a loss for the Americans. It was merely the opening engagement of what would be the most prolonged and decisive air battle of World War II.

Berlin

Round two was Berlin, the sixth largest city in the world and the greatest economic and commercial powerhouse on the European continent, with nearly all its industries given over to war production. This was another target the Luftwaffe would have to defend.

Arthur Harris had been conducting a campaign of fire and ruin against Berlin all that winter, bombing indiscriminately and taking intolerable losses against the suddenly revived German night-fighting forces. The American effort would be different. The main aiming points would be industrial, chief among them the great ball bearing works at Erkner, in the suburbs of the capital. And the bombers would be used primarily as bait, to bring the Luftwaffe to battle.

There would also be new tactics. In the past, every big bombing mission launched by the Eighth had included elaborate diversionary raids to confuse the defenders. This time there would be no deception, no feints. The American air commanders would send in the bombers on predictable routes. Placing the bombers at extreme risk would be part of the design. With great numbers of long-range Mustangs arriving in England just after Big Week, Anderson, a hard-minded advocate of total warfare, was spoiling for a fight. Prepare yourself for big losses, he warned Hap Arnold in late February. The Eighth would strike "regardless of cost."

Just when casualties began to rise tremendously, the bomber crews received another dose of bad news. Under prodding from Hap Arnold, General Doolittle extended their tours of duty from twenty-five to thirty missions (and later to thirty-five). Why send home crews, the reasoning went, when they had reached the peak of their efficiency? The decision made Doolittle a greatly hated man on the bomber bases. "We fly the first twenty-five for America and the next five for Jimmy," the crews complained.

Big Week put a terrible strain on the men. It was "the pills that got a lot of the guys through," said radio gunner Laurence "Goldy" Goldstein, "pills to put them to sleep, pills to keep them awake, pills to kill the depression." If the flight surgeons refused to dispense them, some men stole them. For the truly desperate, there was morphine, easily available in first aid kits.

The first Berlin mission was scheduled for March 2. When Doolittle scrubbed it because heavy clouds over the target would make the bombing inaccurate, Anderson blew up. "It doesn't matter if Berlin is overcast. The resulting air battle would result in attrition, which makes it more important than any destruction on the ground," he wrote in his diary. "We've got to stick to this god damn thing."

Berlin would be the toughest target the Eighth ever attacked. Doolittle's crews would be meeting a reconstituted Luftwaffe, with over 70 percent of its fighters based within range of Berlin. The German capital was a 1,100-mile round trip from eastern England, which meant the bombers would be exposed over central Germany for five hours and, if the bad weather prevailed, would have to fly over a six-mile-high cloudbank that would make formation flying difficult. When Doolittle's chief aide urged that the Liberators not be sent because, fully loaded, they could not fly as high as the Forts—"God, [the crews] will just get killed in them"—Anderson had a chilling one word reply, "Well?"

On March 3, a few P-38 Lightnings equipped with auxiliary fuel tanks made it to Berlin, but the bombers could not surmount the clouds and had to turn back. Heavy skies and squalls remained a problem the following day, but when Doolittle sent out a mission recall signal to the fleet, two squadrons from the 95th and one from the Hundredth failed to pick it up, or so they said. The twenty-five-ton ships and their shepherding Mustangs pressed on, navigating by dead reckoning. Vapor trails made by whirling propellers compounded the hazards. Flying in the rarefied atmosphere made the airmen "drowsy and listless, but flak bursts prevented any from nodding." Fighter resistance was swift but the formation was saved, after losing five bombers, by the Mustangs of the 4th Fighter Group, led by Lt. Col. Donald Blakeslee, a former member of the Eagle Squadrons, volunteer American pilots who flew Spitfires for the RAF before America entered the war.

When Col. Harry C. Mumford, the leader of the bomber formation, returned to base in the gathering winter dusk, he expected a reprimand. Instead he received the Silver Star and his picture was featured in *Life* magazine.

It was a ragged performance, but the fact that American planes had reached Berlin in daylight was immensely significant to both the Axis and the Allies. In the first year of the war, Hermann Göring had pledged to Berliners that not a single enemy bomb would drop on the sacred soil of the capital. After the war, an interrogator asked Göring at what point he realized that Germany was doomed. "The first time your bombers came over Hanover, escorted by fighters, I began to be worried. When they came with fighter escorts over Berlin—I knew the jig was up."

Chuck Yeager

On March 5 the weather kept the bombers closer to home. Losses were light, but it was a rough day for the escorts. After getting his first victory over Berlin the previous day, Charles "Chuck" Yeager, a twenty-one-year-old rowdy from Myra, West Virginia, was shot down fifty miles east of Bordeaux, in southwestern France, by three Focke-Wulf 190s. Flying only his eighth combat mission, Yeager—who had enlisted as a mechanic—would survive the war to become the first man to break the sound barrier and the world's most famous test pilot, the featured character in the book and film *The Right Stuff.* "I knew I was going down; I was barely able to unfasten my safety belt and crawl over the seat before my burning P-51 began to snap and roll, heading for the ground. I just fell out of the cockpit when the plane turned upside down—my canopy was shot away." Yeager went into a free fall, not daring to pull his ripcord until he had dropped far enough to avoid getting strafed by one of the pursuing fighters.

"Cold and scared," bleeding from wounds on his feet, and hands, and with a hole in his right calf, Yeager realized the odds of escaping the Nazi security forces were long; none of the men in his squadron who had been shot down had made it back to England. But sitting in the deep brush treating his wounds with sulfa powder and bandages and studying a silk map that was sewn into his flight suit, he was confident. The son of poor but hard-willed hill people, he knew how to hunt and trap and live off the land. He had an Army-issue .45 caliber pistol tucked in his belt and he was a crack shot. "Back home, if we had a job to do, we did it," he recalled. "And my job now [was] to evade capture and escape."

Yeager's objective was Spain, where he knew he would receive help
from British diplomats who had established arrangements for downed
fliers to be sent back to England through Gibraltar. But first he had to evade
German patrols that were searching for him with the aid of low-flying scout
planes. Peeking out of the brush, he saw a woodcutter with a heavy ax, a
weapon he could use. Figuring no French peasant was a match for "a hungry hillbilly," he jumped him, wrestled him to the ground, and stuck his
pistol in his face. The man spoke no English, but grinned nervously and
nodded when Yeager told him he was an American. He would go for help,
he signaled with his hands, but Yeager must stay hidden in the woods. The
Boche were everywhere.

An hour later the woodcutter returned with an old man who spoke
some English. Yeager followed him to a small hotel, where he was taken to
a second-floor bedroom. The regal-looking woman who owned the establishment was sitting on the bed, wrapped in a shawl. Looking directly into
Yeager's eyes, she smiled and said in perfect English, "Why, you're just a
boy. . . . My God, has America run out of men already." After questioning
him to make sure he was not a German agent posing as an American pilot,
she told him her people would help him.

The next morning Yeager was taken to a farmhouse, where he hid in the
hayloft for almost a week. Late one night the local doctor, who had already
treated his wounds, returned with peasant clothing and false identity papers and told Yeager they would be taking "a little journey," one that would
lead, after several weeks of running and hiding, to a clearing on a densely
forested mountain, where Yeager was handed over to a band of heavily
armed men wearing black berets. "I don't have to be told who these guys
are," Yeager remembered his reaction. "These are the Maquis, the French
resistance fighters who live and hide in these mountain pine forests by day
and blow up trains and bridges by night."

Yeager was told to stay with these men until the snow thawed in the
Pyrenees. They would then help him cross into Spain.

The Maquis were a relatively new force in the Resistance. (Maquis is the
Corsican name for the local scrub brush that resistance groups on that island used for cover in their eighteenth-century democratic revolution.)
The first *maquisards* were young men from the isolated, forested regions of
Brittany and southern France who escaped to the hills in late 1942 to evade
the Nazis' labor draft, which would have sentenced them to compulsory
employment in Germany. In the summer of 1943, with invasion talk in the
air, many of these mountain bands had begun to take in other members of

the Resistance and engage in acts of sabotage against the Germans and the collaborationist French militia. At this point, British agents from the SOE (Special Operations Executive), an agency charged with fomenting sabotage and paramilitary operations in Nazi-occupied countries, began to take an interest in them. Agents and arms were dropped to the Maquis by parachute and regular radio communication between the *maquisards* and London was established, with SOE working hand-in-hand with a special branch of America's Office of Strategic Services (OSS)–the predecessor of the CIA–headquartered in London. Looking ahead to the Normandy landings, Prime Minister Churchill requested that additional aircraft from the RAF be made available for arming the most formidable Maquis groups, which were in southwestern France. It was then, in January 1944, that the Eighth Air Force was pulled into the operation, flying the first of its so-called Carpetbagger Missions, under the direction of Lt. Col. Clifford J. Heflin. By the following June, the Allies had increased the number of their supply drops to the Maquis to over 850 a month.

Using the crews from recently disbanded Air Force antisubmarine squadrons, the Carpetbaggers, as the new 801st Bomb Group (redesignated the 492nd BG in August 1944) was called, were originally based north of London and close to Tempsford, the home station for RAF squadrons engaged in parallel operations. Both airbases were marked "Closed to the Public," and fliers who drank in local pubs understood that they would be court-martialed if they talked about their jobs.

The 801st's B-24 Liberators, which were moved in March to Harrington, in the depths of rural Northamptonshire, were especially equipped for the night drops. Blackout curtains covered the waist windows, all armaments were removed except the upper turret and tail turret, and the bombers were painted midnight black. Where the ball turrets had been, a hole was cut into the floor of the fuselage and covered with a removable metal shroud. This was the "Joe-hole," through which undercover agents, or "Joes," were dropped with their parachutes. (Female agents were called "Josephines.") Waist gunners, now called dispatchers, sent down large canisters of supplies from the bomb bays. Closer to D-Day, three-man commando units, called Jedburghs, were dropped to conduct covert operations, often in collaboration with the Maquis.

By the time Flight Officer Yeager hooked up with them, the Maquis were heavily engaged in railroad sabotage to prevent local Wehrmacht units from reinforcing divisions stationed on the Channel coast in preparation for the invasion. "The Maquis hide by day and hit by night," Yeager later described their operations, "blowing up bridges, sabotaging rail lines, hitting trains carrying munitions of military equipment." The Maquis group that Yeager joined was armed with British Sten guns and Spanish .38 Llama automatics, but they were in dire need of explosives. For these, they depended upon Allied airdrops.

One evening, Chuck Yeager was sitting in a lantern-lit barn with his band of forest rebels as they unloaded the contents of the steel canister dropped by parachute from an Allied plane. Eyeing the boxes of explosives, fuses, and timing devices he said to the leader, "I can help you with that stuff." As a boy, he had helped his father "shoot" gas wells with plastic explosives. That night he was put in charge of explosive fuse devices. For as long as he stayed with them, he was the Maquis's "fuse man," a "terrorist bomb-maker" no longer protected by the protocols of the Geneva Conventions. If captured, he would be treated as a saboteur and turned over to the Gestapo for torture questioning and execution. But as he said later, he needed "these guys" if he was going to get to the Pyrenees. Besides, the work was "fun, interesting."

It did not last long. On a night in late March, Yeager was put in the back of a truck with a group of other American airmen the driver had picked up earlier. When the truck screeched to a stop, each of the men was given a hand-drawn map and a knapsack filled with bread, cheese, and chocolate. The driver pointed to a narrow mountain path, and the airmen, on their own, began climbing into sheets of rain and gale-force winds. When the others lagged behind, Yeager teamed up with a powerfully built B-24 navigator named "Pat" Patterson. The two men ascended to 7,000 feet in wet, heavy snow up to their knees, crawling across ridges covered with sheets of ice. When they entered the thinning air they had to stop every ten or fifteen minutes, wondering, as they rested, if they would soon become feed for the huge crows that cawed overhead.

By the third day they were lost, by the fourth they were "almost ready to give up"—exhausted, disoriented, and unable to feel their frozen feet. Walking half-asleep, "staggering like two drunks," they stumbled upon an empty logger's cabin, pushed open the door, and collapsed on the floor, where they slept side by side.

Minutes later, they were jolted awake by a hail of gunfire. It was a German patrol and the soldiers were firing blindly through the front door, suspecting escapees might be in the cabin. Yeager jumped out the rear window and Patterson followed right behind him. Hearing his friend scream, Yeager knew he was hit. In an instant, he grabbed hold of him and jumped on a snow-covered log slide. The two men slid down the flume and landed in a swollen mountain stream. Holding the unconscious airman by the neck, Yeager swam to the other bank and pulled him out of the water. Patterson looked in desperate shape; he was shot in the knee and was "bleeding like a stuck hog," his lower leg barely attached to its upper part by a thick, throbbing tendon. Pulling out his penknife, Yeager cut the tendon and tied the bloody stump with a spare shirt the Maquis had made out of his parachute.

When night descended, he slung his still unconscious friend over his shoulder and began climbing a steep slope, stopping now and then to see if Patterson was alive and fighting off a strong urge to give up and die. At sunrise, Yeager reached the top of the mountain, and in the distance, through the morning haze, he could see "the thin line of a road that must," he thought, "be in Spain."

Too weak to negotiate the steep draw that led down to the road, he dragged Patterson to the edge and pushed him over. Yeager followed behind him, riding on a long stick he held between his bent legs just as he did when he used to slide down a steep hill behind his West Virginia house "using a broomstick as a brake." When the two airmen reached the road, Patterson was so pale and limp that Yeager thought he was dead. Feeling there was nothing more he could do for Patterson, Yeager left him by the road, in clear view, to be picked up by a passing motorist. Then he began walking south.

Reaching a village, Yeager turned himself in to the local police and slept for two days. He was awakened by an American consul and taken to a hospital "where there was nothing to do but sunbathe, eat, and flirt with the chambermaids ... while the American consul tried to free six of us downed airmen from our hellish existence." While still in Spain, he learned that Patterson had been picked up by the Guardia Civil an hour after he had left him and had been taken to a hospital. Within six weeks, Patterson was back in the States. Chuck Yeager had other ideas.

Bloody Monday

The day after Chuck Yeager was shot down over France, the Eighth Air Force returned to Berlin and fought the greatest air battle ever. "A 15-mile-long parade of American bombers thundered across the heart of Berlin for 30 minutes today and set great fires in the stricken Nazi capital after smashing through a huge German fighter screen," the United Press reported. The *New York Times* estimated that a strike of this scale engaged nearly 600,000 men and women on both sides. This figure included 12,000 Allied airmen, almost 1,000 German pilots, 50,000 Allied and 25,000 German ground crewmen, and up to half a million Germans at antiaircraft emplacements that reached all the way from the continental coast to the capital.

"Berlin from the air was a huge, dark city," recalled B-17 gunner Tommy LaMore, the descendant of a Cherokee family that had survived the Trail of Tears. "This was Hitler's town. The big bad boys lived in this neighborhood.... Go ahead, send the Luftwaffe up, go ahead, shoot at us with everything you've got, but here we are, blowing up your houses in front of your master-race eyeballs. I cheered when the bombs left the racks. 'Hold on to your sauerkraut, Adolf!' I yelled."

An Eighth Air Force record of sixty-nine bombers, 10 percent of those that made it to Berlin, was lost to fighters and flak. Nazi radio stations claimed the Forts and Liberators were driven from their targets as they came over the city, but a day later, dispatches by Swedish reporters said that large sections of the capital's industrial suburbs were "still burning" and were "without light, power, gas or telephone service."

The Germans made them pay for this assault on their capital. Fighters lined up fifty abreast and flew into the bomber formations head-on. The defenders closed with the bombers at 200 yards per second and each fighter pilot was able to fire only a half-second burst at 500 yards before having to pull up violently to avoid smashing into the bombers. This was not much time, but "one accurate half second burst from head-on and a kill was guaranteed. Guaranteed!" recalled a German fighter pilot.

The Bloody Hundredth got the worst of it. Discovering a gap in the escort coverage, "[bandits] hit us head on and in pairs," turning fifteen bombers to flame and ruin in less than three minutes, recalled C. B "Red" Harper, the pilot of *Buffalo Gal*. With *Buffalo Gal* burning and full of holes, and with its oxygen system knocked out, Harper jettisoned the bombs and dove to 5,000 feet, where there was breathable air.

By the time Hub Zemke's Thunderbolts arrived in force, the 13th Combat Wing, of which the Hundredth was a part, had lost twenty bombers in twenty-five minutes. Ahead of them, an even stronger formation of German fighters was assembling in front of the most powerful flak defenses in the world, an angry cordon of 750 light and heavy guns. But the American juggernaut muscled its way to the target, presenting a fearsome sight to Berliners on the ground. Taking cover in a slit trench near one of the gun batteries was seventeen-year-old Alexander Witzigmann, on his first day of duty at the flak site. "I was so frightened by the display of strength by the enemy I began to shake."

A mission begins before dawn with the loading of bombs into the bellies of the "heavies."

An intelligence officer conducts a dawn mission briefing.

Flying officers are rushed to their bomber.

Chaplain Father Michael Ragan gives airmen a blessing.

Fortresses line up for takeoff. On the ascent, in the crowded and blackened sky, aerial collisions were common.

In 1943, P-47 Thunderbolts did most of the escort duty for the bombers. Hubert "Hub" Zemke (left), commander of the 56th Fighter Group, "Zemke's Wolf Pack," meets Glenn Miller, whose Army Air Forces Band toured Eighth Air Force bases in 1944.

A navigator sits in the nose of the bomber and charts its course to the target.

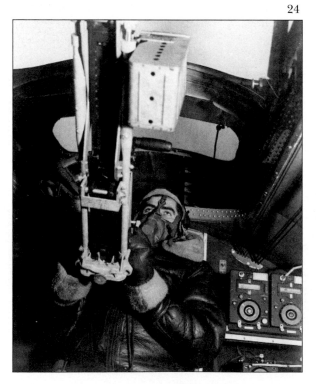

Over the North Sea, this radio gunner fires a few bursts to check his guns. Men went on oxygen at 10,000 feet.

This Fortress waist gunner is protected against subzero temperatures with electrically heated boots and gloves. He wears a "flak apron" into which is sewn overlapping manganese steel squares.

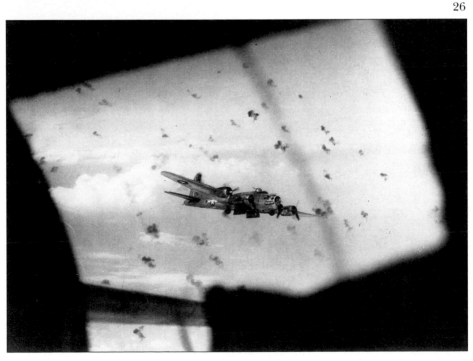

Near the target, the bombers enter the "flak field." Pilots cannot take evasive action, for the bombardiers need a steady platform for greater accuracy.

Fast-changing English weather made the return to base perilous. These two Fortresses collided and disintegrated as they roared through a blanket of clouds that covered their base.

When word arrives that the bombers are returning, men gather at the control tower to "sweat 'em in," counting and trying to identify each bomber.

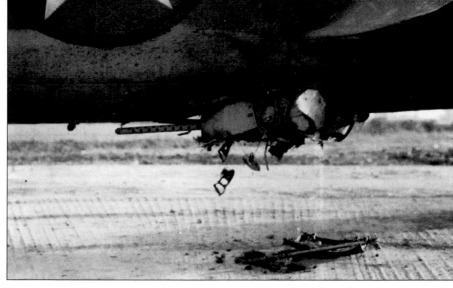

The ball turret gunner was crushed to death when a mechanical malfunction trapped him inside his plastic cage and a damaged electrical system made it impossible to lower the plane's wheels.

The crew of *Carol Dawn* walks down the runway looking for a ride to the debriefing room.

Returning crewmen are served coffee and sandwiches by a Red Cross worker.

The Americans ran into patchy cloud cover over the city and had to bomb through intermittently visible holes in the high thin clouds that raced across the sky. The ball bearing plant at Erkner went untouched and most of the 3,000 tons of explosives fell inside the city, killing and maiming over 700 civilians. But the bombing was not the main reason the Americans were there. They were there for a fighter fight. "They looked each other over as they raced at each other's noses," the historian of the 4th Fighter Group described the opening round. "Each dropped wing tanks, like two boxers shedding robes at the sound of the gong." Of the approximately 400 German defenders that entered the fight at least sixty-six—179 according to Air Force claims—went down, most of them victims of the swift-hitting Mustangs. The "Indians," as the German pilots called them, chalked up an astounding eight-to-one kill ratio in the cutting cold above Berlin, where the pilots' feet went numb and their hands turned purple under fur-lined gloves. "Relief tubes were frozen; some used their pants as diapers and the pants froze." Fighter jockeys kicked the floors of their cockpits and beat their hands to bring up the blood, yet some "were bathed in fright-sweat" as they went straight at the Fw 190s at closing speeds of 600 miles per hour. It was like hand-to-hand combat, opposing pilots getting in so close on their passes they could see each other's eyes.

When they returned to their home base at Debden, Blakeslee's pilots were jubilant, joking, back-slapping, and boasting that it was the "best hunting" they had ever had: fifteen victories for their group alone. In the debriefing hut, the pilots made their reports, devouring chocolate to sustain them until they could reach the mess hall. Then it was to the clubroom, where "The Birdman," as Blakeslee's men called their adored leader, ordered the "Free Beer" sign put on the bar mirror.

It was different at the bomber bases. Over half the Forts that managed to return came in with battle damage, and many of them were "heavily laden with petrified men and stiffs who are laid on the floor." Some of the fliers were furious, angrier at the high command than they were at the enemy. At Thorpe Abbotts, where the group had lost fifteen bombers, men cursed Spaatz and Doolittle for sending them to Berlin when the Germans knew they were coming. The men did not know it yet, but this raid was the turning point in the air war. That day, some Berliners had been given a presentiment of their own awful end. Climbing out of a shelter in the center of the city, Gert Mueller, a technical school student, remembered thinking: "If they can do that once they can do it again!"

New York Times reporter James B. Reston caught the significance of what Berliners would call Bloody Monday. "The time of what was once called air raids has passed," he wrote. "The Allied army of the air has started a campaign of attrition against the Luftwaffe which must be recognized as one of the decisive military campaigns of the war. . . . From now on the Allied leaders of this campaign will send their aerial artillery anywhere in Germany where the German fighters are made and to any point where German fighters will give battle."

With the weather "a mess" on the following day, the fliers of the Bloody Hundredth were allowed to sleep till noon, write letters in the afternoon, and crack a few bottles in the evening. Unexpectedly, around ten o'clock word came in that the group was on mission alert. Red Harper and his friends walked slowly back to their huts and hit the sack. Hardly anyone spoke.

Awakened at 4:00 A.M., Harper's heart took a jump when he looked at the briefing map. No one breathed a word. It was Berlin again and they were going back over the same route they had taken two days before. The group's new commander, Maj. John M. Bennett, had "pitched a fit" when he learned the night before that the Hundredth was being dispatched to Berlin on Wednesday after losing 50 percent of its force that Monday. Bennett had been on the job for barely twenty-four hours, having replaced Chick Harding, who was rushed to the hospital and almost died from gallstone problems he had been ignoring. The men, said Harper, were in a mood for mutiny, and Bennett knew it. Bennett had called wing headquarters the night before the mission and received permission to lead the wing. His boys would need encouragement.

As Bennett led his fifteen bombers out over the North Sea, he wondered how many of them would stay with him. "I was petrified. I had mental pictures of all kinds of personnel failures and abortions." At Dummer Lake, in northern Germany, the place where the Hundredth had been massacred two days before, the Thunderbolts broke for home and the Mustangs that were to take over were late showing up. The Luftwaffe feasted on the opportunity. This time the enemy attacked another wing, the 45th, just ahead of them. Lost and psychologically disoriented, the leader of the shot-up 45th failed to make the turn toward Berlin at the initial point, and Bennett, without hesitation, moved his wing to the front and led the Eighth Air Force to the target.

Galland held his hugely outnumbered fighter force back until the heavies began their bomb run. Then he sent up "whole battle fleets" of defenders. The American machines blasted through this wall of fire, and once through it, fighter opposition over the target was "surprisingly light." The flak, however, was murderous. Men could smell it through their oxygen masks and the concussions shook their bodies. Fragments of the hot shrapnel came up through the bottoms of the bombers, emasculating men. Anticipating this, the gunners of the Hundredth had foraged armor plates from the salvage yard at Thorpe Abbotts and used them, along with their flak vests, for what they called "eunuch protection." The determined city defenders also employed ground-to-air rockets. As Red Harper watched one of them coming up, it seemed like half an hour before it passed in front of him, looking "like a white telephone pole with fire spewing out the tail end."

Only one of the Hundredth's bombers failed to make it back to East Anglia. In all, the Americans lost thirty-seven bombers and eighteen fighters but, once again, they chewed up the enemy's fighters. At Thorpe Abbotts, returning combat crews were given an extra shot of scotch, a new "medical" policy. "Morale," said Red Harper, "went up like a skyrocket."

After the debriefing, Bennett gave the crew of *Buffalo Gal* a forty-eight-hour pass and the men headed straight to London. "We had seen over 200 men in our Bomb Group shot out of the sky during our first five missions . . . and we were all getting a little 'flaked up,' " Red Harper remembered. As they walked down the steps of a cellar restaurant the next evening they unknowingly entered another war zone. Just before their orders of gin and grapefruit juice arrived, an explosion shook the room. The Germans had been bombing London and other British cities for some time in retaliation for the RAF raids on their capital. The thick-crusted Brits were getting used to it and had begun calling it the Baby Blitz. Within minutes, "candles were lighted and the party continued." When a helmeted air raid warden came down the stairs and asked if anyone was hurt, there was no reply. He then asked if any of the women in the room might be pregnant. A husky female voice came from the back of the room, "Blimey Matey, give us a little time, we just got here!"

While Harper's crew was in London, nine planes from the Hundredth went to Berlin and all returned that afternoon. Only six American Fortresses and a single fighter plane were lost on the great raid of March 9, and the pilots and crews did not report a single enemy plane destroyed. "Nazis Shun Battle," the next day's *New York Times* announced. The Germans claimed that a mountain of clouds four miles high had pinned their fighter forces to their airfields, but the mauling they had taken on the two previous raids was the real reason the Luftwaffe did not rise to fight that afternoon. This was something big. It had been less than five months since Schweinfurt II. In that short span of time the Americans had regained the initiative in the skies over the Reich. Aerial supremacy had yet to be won but "we were taking 40 to 50 [enemy fighters] every day we went out," Gen. William Kepner said later.

In a cable to Hap Arnold, Spaatz gave a tersely accurate assessment of Berlin Week. "During the past week . . . three attacks were made without any attempt at deception. Route followed on each attack being exactly the same. . . . [While] it is too early to gauge full effect of destruction of fighter production plus their heavy air wastage, we of course are all confident that the air battle is in our hands." In three days, the Eighth had lost 153 bombers, losses that "were replaced in a matter of hours," an Air Force spokesman told reporters.

This is where the Americans had the advantage, in men even more than machines. Albert Speer's hidden plants continued to pour out planes, but a despairing Adolf Galland did not have enough qualified men to fly them. In March alone, he lost 20 percent of his experienced pilots. In that month the Eighth destroyed more than twice as many enemy planes as it had in 1942 and 1943 combined. In the words of a German historian, "the war of attrition had reached the mortal phase when neither courage nor skill availed further." The effects of these losses on morale are recorded in the diary of a Luftwaffe pilot. "Every time I close the canopy before taking off, I feel that I am closing the lid of my own coffin."

The Cost

For the remainder of March and into April, Spaatz and Doolittle continued to force the fight, sending out heavies on immense radar raids—baiting missions, actually—in blinding weather that made accurate bombing impossible. In April alone, the Eighth Air Force lost 409 heavy bombers, the most it would lose in any single month in the air war, and the Fifteenth's losses shot up from ninety-nine in March to 214.

Some Luftwaffe pilots were fighting with patriotic ferocity. In a spirit of self-sacrifice, a group of such airmen approached Galland with the idea of forming an elite "storm" group to ram the "death-dealing bombers." Galland rejected the idea, but did approve the formation of a volunteer Storm Group squadron, Sturmstaffel I, that employed tactics that any other air force in the world except Japan's would have considered senselessly suicidal. With lighter, faster fighters covering their approach, Fw 190's equipped with heavier armor and armament would form up in "flying wedges," get in as close as possible, and try to shoot down the invaders "at any price," Galland explained. "If during such a storm attack their own air-craft was heavily hit, they could always ram and bail out."

The pilot-depleted Luftwaffe was able to use these tactics with effect only against bombers unprotected by great numbers of escorts. So it simply waited for its opportunities. The relay system that the American fighters employed to protect the bombers gave the enemy plenty of chances to do harm. Each formation of fighters made contact with the bomber stream at a designated point, providing high or parallel coverage until its fuel was exhausted, and then giving way to longer-range fighters. Spitfires gave shallow cover to the bombers on departure and arrival, Thunderbolts and Lightnings took them across the Rhine, and Mustangs ferried them to and from distant targets like Berlin and Munich. In such a system, up to a thousand fighters might be needed to keep forty to a hundred covering the bombers at any one time. When an American bomber formation suffered heavy losses in the spring of 1944, it was almost always because the escorts and bombers failed to make a rendezvous or because a small number of escorts was overwhelmed by a massed German attack. Using these wolf pack tactics, German fighters often outnumbered the escorts by as much as ten to one, giving even the most inexperienced pilots an edge.

On a mission to Berlin on April 29, twenty-year-old co-pilot Truman Smith's group accidentally strayed out of the bomber stream and paid the price, losing ten of the sixty-six ships the Eighth Air Force lost that day. The next morning, Smith was on a road by the base trying to hitch a ride to visit a friend at a nearby bomber station. When an ambulance pulled over, he ran toward the rear of it and reached out to pull open the back door. "No lieutenant!" the driver shouted. "Up front!" It was too late. Smith's mouth dropped when he saw nine bone-white cadavers on stretchers. These were men who had been told that the Luftwaffe was finished.

After the first Berlin raids, morale plummeted at the bomber stations. Again, fatigue and rising losses were precipitants, but crewmen began questioning the military value of the targets they were recently attacking—cloud-covered cities, particularly Berlin, where the bombing seemed to be without clear plan or purpose. In a confidential survey of combat crews that the Eighth Air Force conducted in the spring of 1944, Berlin easily topped the list of targets the men found to be unimportant. Typical comments were:

"Berlin is not a military target."
"Berlin, just propaganda value."

"I don't believe in spite bombing."

"Berlin. Devastation of one city will not break morale."

Some airmen found it hard to be in "the murder business." Lt. Bert Stiles of Denver, Colorado, was one of them. A brooding, darkly handsome co-pilot in the 91st Bomb Group, flying out of Bassingbourn, the former base of the crew of the *Memphis Belle,* Stiles was already a published author. He had dropped out of Colorado College to become a writer, and a number of his short stories had appeared in the *Saturday Evening Post* before his group arrived in England in March 1944. He had brought his Corona typewriter with him, against regulations, and took a notepad on missions to record his impressions. Between missions he wrote short stories and a luminous autobiography, *Serenade to the Big Bird.* Although Bert Stiles felt he was "made for the blue sky, he should have been a war correspondent," said his former fraternity brother and command pilot, Sam Newton. "He would have been another Ernie Pyle."

Sitting at a small writing desk in his room after his first mission, Stiles wondered whether he had the stomach to kill. He had run into some Polish Spitfire pilots in Iceland on his flight to England and they had a blood lust, wanting "to kill every Nazi in the world." It was different with him, a boy from "a land where bombs never fell." To deal out death over Berlin he had to remind himself that there were "sons of bitches" down there that had to be conquered, and that the eight men who had slept in his bed in the four months before he arrived in England were all dead or missing in action.

While Army surveys indicated that the morale of American combat fliers remained higher than that of ground soldiers throughout the war, all these missions packed together, one on top of the other, filthy weather or fair, with the bombers as bait, worked on the men's minds. And some of them broke. "Altogether, we started out for Berlin seven times," recalled John A. Miller of the Hundredth. "Twice our co-pilot went nuts and tried to crash us into the sea. These times the crew fought him off the wheel and we aborted. After the second time he didn't return to our crew. He wasn't a coward; he just couldn't go back to Berlin."

Beginning in March, the number of psychiatric casualties reported by the Central Medical Establishment rose noticeably. The pace was just as punishing for fighter pilots, some of whom flew twenty and more missions a month between March and May. The rate of operations was so rapid that large numbers of fighter pilots and bomber crews were completing their tours of duty in less than two months. With the invasion on the near horizon, no excuses were accepted for not flying. "One morning the flight surgeon was checking every pilot trying to get enough to make up a flight," said fighter pilot Max J. Woolley. "He looked at everyone and most were in bad shape. He asked me, 'How do you feel' I spent about a minute telling him of my severe case of diarrhea. He responded, 'Stick a cork up your ass and enjoy the flight.' "

Binge drinking increased and combat commanders continued to do little about it while officers at headquarters who did not fly in combat had almost no way of controlling those that did. After putting away a dozen drinks too many, a lieutenant from the Hundredth began to make a scene in a swanky London hotel bar. When a staff officer from Pinetree ordered him to his room, the tipsy flier replied. "Colonel, yesterday, at noon, I was over Berlin. Where in the hell were you?"

A few men flew drunk, still high from the night before. "One night I got home from the liberty run to Northampton and found out I was alerted to fly the next morning," recalled Ben Smith, a twenty-year-old Georgia boy who was a radio gunner with *Hell's Angels*. "I was in bad shape. I got the others to pick up my stuff at briefing and went on out to the airplane and stuck the oxygen hose to my nose. I immediately felt better, but it didn't last. When we got over enemy territory . . . I began vomiting. My goggles and oxygen mask frosted over solid and I could not see." Pulling off his mask to shake out the vomit, he swore that he would abstain forever. But on landing he headed straight for the Dirty Duck Pub, just off the base, convinced that his destiny, in the words of the Air Corps anthem, was to live in fame and go down in flames. "Alcohol was the only thing that made our existence bearable," he wrote later.

That was an exaggeration. The Air Force's own surveys of flier morale indicated that "the single factor" that "permitted" most crewmen to continue flying without a mental breakdown" was not alcohol but the "hope for relief" after thirty missions. Strong leadership also helped to hold men together.

One of the Eighth's finest squadron commanders was Maj. James Maitland Stewart, a Princeton honors graduate known to all as Jimmy Stewart, the Hollywood movie idol. After being drafted in 1940 at age thirty-two, the rail-thin, six-foot-four son of an Indiana, Pennsylvania, hardware store merchant had tried to get into the Army Air Force but failed to meet the weight requirement for his height, 148 pounds, by five pounds. Desperately wanting to serve (he later called the draft "the only lottery I ever won"), he appealed the decision, over the heated protests of Louis B. Mayer, his dictatorial boss at MGM. After convincing an Air Force enlistment officer to give him a new test and "this time forget to weigh me," he entered military service as a private, signing his enlistment papers just days after winning an Oscar for his role as a reporter in *The Philadelphia Story.* "It may sound corny," he later explained his decision, "but what's wrong with wanting to fight for your country. Why are people so reluctant to use the word patriotism?"

The slow-talking Stewart, the man movie critics called "tall drawl," was already an accomplished flier with a commercial pilot's license and his own sporty two-seater plane, experience that landed him an assignment with the Army Air Corps as a flight cadet with a monthly salary of $21, exactly $11,979 less per month than he received from MGM. After earning his pilot's wings one month after Pearl Harbor, he pressed for overseas combat duty, but was assigned instead to flight instructor duty in the States. Nobody wanted to take responsibility for putting one of America's most popular movie stars in harm's way. Stewart coaxed and complained until the brass finally relented. In November 1943 he arrived in England as a squadron commander with the 445th Bomb Group, a Liberator outfit stationed in Tibenham, just outside Norwich, in what was known to airmen as B-24 Country. Three months later, he was awarded the Distinguished Flying Cross for holding his formation together under intense enemy pressure on the first day of Big Week. It was one of the twenty combat missions he would fly, not losing a single man to enemy fire or mental breakdown.

Watching him around base, the men of his 703rd Squadron could not believe how closely his real behavior matched his screen persona—getting things accomplished without dramatics and, in his small-town manner, calling the men "fellas," urging them to write their "folks," and peppering his speech, as he did in the movies, with "doggone's" and "gee whizze's." Stewart played the piano at dances in the officers club and helped make chocolate for the squadron. But he was "basically a loner," said his fellow squadron commander Capt. Howard "Doc" Kreidler, of Tilden, Nebraska. On their free days, Stewart and Kreidler would rent a small wooden boat in the village and paddle off by themselves, stretching out and listening to American swing music on a tiny portable radio. Around the men he was "about as unemotional as you can get" Kreidler recalled, but the fliers respected his cool, measured leadership and quiet authenticity. Without any fanfare, "he skipped all the milk runs," said Sgt. John Harold "Robbie" Robinson, one of his squadron gunners, and later the author of a powerful book about his wartime experiences. "High command didn't like that."

"He had tremendous rapport with the men—that languid, humorous way he had of settling them down in some pretty stressful situations," recalled Col. Ramsay D. Potts, Jr., the charismatic group commander of the 453rd Bomb Group, at Old Buckenham, ten miles from Tibenham, where Stewart was transferred in March 1944. At "Old Buc," Stewart was group operations officer, charged with directing bombing operations and briefing the crews. He and Potts, a veteran of the low-level Ploesti raid, were both new appointments. They took over a group that had arrived in England just after Stewart's 445th and suffered staggering casualties during Big Week and over Berlin, including the loss of both its first commander and its group operations officer, the men Stewart and Potts replaced. Morale was sagging, and Potts and Stewart, who shared quarters, began reviving it with a tight discipline and inspiring hands-on leadership.

"They were on the job around the clock, often in Stewart's jeep," wrote Starr Smith, a combat intelligence officer with the group, "on the flight line, checking every detail, laying on practice missions—seldom leaving the base." Spirits improved and so did formation discipline and target proficiency. And there were fewer losses.

Rosie Rosenthal was made of the same stuff as Jimmy Stewart. In May 1944, two months after completing twenty-five missions with the crew of *Rosie's Riveters,* he took over the 350th Bomb Squadron of the Hundredth, whose morale and efficiency had slipped badly, and began to restore the unit to peak performance. "After the first Berlin raids, we had men who were banged up mentally, and a few of them didn't want to fly anymore. I told them they had a moral obligation to fly, and that I would fly with them. We were here to beat Hitler. I also told them that if they didn't fly they would be letting down friends who had helped to keep them alive up to now. The appeal to their pride and respect worked better than the one to their patriotism." Rosenthal knew that without group loyalty—the responsibility that fighting men feel to the men next to them—wars would be impossible. Gale Cleven and John Egan "gave the 100th its personality," wrote Harry Crosby. "Bob Rosenthal helped us want to win the war."

In the end, however, Eighth Air Force morale improved markedly only when casualty rates declined. That began to happen in May 1944, after American fighter pilots had reduced the Luftwaffe's effectiveness. "We did the bombing—the dirty work," said Rosenthal, "We were the decoys, and they took care of the bad boys that had been beating us up. They were guys who made D-Day possible."

Fighter Boys

Rosie Rosenthal, like Bert Stiles and thousands of others, had joined the
Air Force hoping to fly fighter planes. "The fighter boys, with their style
and dash, had it all over us," Rosenthal recalled. "They were up there
alone, in complete control of their planes, free spirits who could take more
chances, be more aggressive than we could."

That spring, two great contests were waged by the fighter boys: one to
break the record of twenty-six aerial victories set by America's "ace of
aces" in World War I, Capt. Eddie Rickenbacker, the other between Don
Blakeslee's 4th Fighter Group, a Mustang outfit, and Zemke's Wolf Pack,
still flying Thunderbolts.

The hero of the Hun-killing tournament, as the pilots called the race to
best Rickenbacker, was Capt. Don Salvatore Gentile, a high school football
hero from Piqua, Ohio, with movie-star looks. Eisenhower called this son
of Italian immigrants a "one-man air force," and this became the title of an
instant biography of him by the famous war correspondent Ira Wolfert. For
a month, Wolfert lived in Gentile's room at Debden and had his publisher
advance the Mustang ace $2,000 for a series of exclusive interviews.

Gentile and his rivals were featured in newsreels in theaters back home
and were front-page copy in papers on both sides of the Atlantic. Reporters
mobbed them after every mission and kept track of their running scores.
The pilots were obliging, drinking their admirers' bourbon and flying low
and menacingly into their camera lenses when they weren't off blasting
"Jerries." Gentile and his wingman, John T. Godfrey, the team Winston
Churchill called the "Damon and Pythias" of the modern age, became national heroes when Gentile destroyed five enemy planes on the ground in
a single day, bringing his score to thirty. When they were sent home to lead
a war bond drive, factory whistles were blown in their honor and New York
taxi drivers begged them for their autographs.

Hub Zemke was equally famous, although he was not drawn to the
limelight. The son of German immigrants from Missoula, Montana,
Zemke had worked in his teens as a gold miner, picking up extra cash as a
saloon brawler. Turning his attention to boxing, he won the middleweight
Golden Gloves title in five western states before he entered the University
of Montana, where he boxed and played football. "He still looks like a half-
back," wrote Tex McCrary, "hard and lean and young at thirty." Once
a month, he would slip into London and enter one of the Rainbow Club's
boxing matches as Corporal Zemke. He carried that pugnacity into
combat.

Zemke's 56th Fighter Group had five of the top aces in the European Theater, including himself, but along with Blakeslee, Zemke excelled as a group leader, not as a deadly shot like Oil City's Gabby Gabreski, the Eighth Air Force's number one ace when the war ended. It was more important to both of them that the group perform well than they be the highest-scoring pilots. "We love fighting," said chiseled, hard-drinking Don Blakeslee, "fighting is a grand sport." His commander, William Kepner, put it more strongly. "A blooded horse will run until he drops, and a fighter pilot will fly until he kills himself or gets killed."

Don Blakeslee was a battle leader for three and half years, flying more than 400 sorties. He fought the Luftwaffe longer than any other American pilot, stopping only when he was sent home under extreme protest. His far-ranging Mustangs, the "Blakesleewaffe," scored big in the spring of 1944. But it was Zemke's outfit, flying a slower, more powerful plane that would end the war with the most aerial victories—665—of any fighter unit in the European Theater. The Thunderbolt, with a more rugged frame than the Mustang and a dive like its name, scored heavily in air-to-ground operations, shredding parked enemy aircraft on strafing missions. Strafing took more nerve than skill and, statistically, was five times as dangerous as escort duty.

Flying as low as ten feet above the ground, at speeds up to 450 miles an hour, pilots flying "beat up" missions, as they were called, had to contend with trees, houses, barns, and high-tension wires before running through a fusillade of fire from antiaircraft batteries and flak towers. On one mission, the Eighth lost two of its top aces, Capt. Walker M. "Bud" Mahurin and Maj. Gerald W. Johnson.

Strafen is a German word meaning to punish, and these terrifying attacks did exactly that. Hitting targets of opportunity on the way back from escort duty soon evolved into independent fighter sweeps, a tactic that Jimmy Doolittle called "organized air guerrilla warfare." Tremendous fighter raids were mounted on days when weather kept the bombers grounded. Up to 700 Mustangs, Lightnings, and Thunderbolts would sweep across the Reich at treetop level, shooting up anything of interest that came into their gun sights, including grazing cattle and hay wagons. In April, low-level fighter attacks accounted for over half of the enemy fighters destroyed in combat operations.

"You need good eyes and a good neck to survive. If you don't have those—you're a goner," said Robert Johnson, one of Zemke's aces. Teamwork, however, was the key to success in fighter warfare. Classic dogfighting, mano a mano battles decided by aerial acrobatics, was rare in the

European air war. Fighters fought in twos: a leader and wingman, one the attacker, the other his protector. Everything depended on finding the enemy first and surprising him—"bouncing" him—preferably from above. "The enemy fighter that you see never shoots you down," Kepner would tell his pilots. "The corollary is you must see every enemy fighter to be safe." A man's machine mattered—its speed, maneuverability, and fire-power—but so did he. A fighter pilot did not become truly effective in the European Theater, William Kepner believed, until he had flown 100 combat hours. By the first day of Big Week, Kepner had a stable of such pilots and that made all the difference, especially when facing inferior pilots.

In 1939, the Luftwaffe had the best trained airmen in the world, fero-ciously dedicated young men who were not assigned to battle units until they had completed 250 hours of flight training. But by mid-1943, the bone-grinding battle of attrition had begun to force the high command to strip its training schools of cadets with only 100 to 150 hours of flying time to fill the cockpits of its front-line fighters. And as a result of shortsighted lo-gistical planning, these German training programs were producing far fewer graduates than the mass production training programs of Britain and the United States, which now required combat pilots to have between 325 to 400 hours of flight training. By the spring of 1944, the Luftwaffe was run-ning out of experienced fighter pilots, and their replacements, unable to handle engine and weather problems, or even land properly on rugged fields, were destroying more of their planes in accidents than the enemy was able to shoot down. In combat, these eighteen- and nineteen-year-old neophytes were hopelessly overmatched. "New German pilots who flew against the highly trained American and British pilots in 1944," writes Luft-waffe historian James S. Corum, "were unlikely to last more than a few weeks in combat before being killed or wounded."

Experience was a greatly prized quality because "the first time you get into combat, you don't see as well as you do later," fighter ace Gerald John-son explained. "You don't really know exactly what you're looking for. . . . Your eyes, if you just look into infinity, sometimes don't focus on anything. After a while, you begin to realize that you're looking for a little speck in the sky, which in just a little bit is going to be an airplane. A lot of [pilots] scan the sky and don't see it. They never develop the ability to really see enemy airplanes." This is why "situational awareness"—good eyes and a good neck—was often the difference between living and dying. That and light-ning-quick reflexes. "The whole thing goes in a series of whooshes. There is no time to think," Gentile told Ira Wolfert. "If you take time to think you will not have time to act. While the fight is on, your mind feels empty."

If fighter pilots lived in a world of split seconds, bomber boys lived in one of agonizing hours, with too much time to think about their own end, which depended inordinately on Lady Fortune. In its testing and training programs the Air Force looked for different qualities in fighter and bomber pilots: physical strength, judgment, emotional stamina, dependability, team play, discipline, and leadership in bomber pilots; rapid hand-eye co-ordination, aggressiveness, boldness, individuality, and a zest for battle in fighter pilots. In a profile of the ideal bomber pilot, the Air Force noted: "The attitude of crew members . . . was that they would gladly let some other crew have the hottest pilot in the group . . . if they could have the man who, when in a tough spot, where a decision which might mean life or death to them had to be made, would quickly . . . make the best possible decision." For bomber pilots, "intellectual traits" were more highly prized than sensory-motor skills. "Love of blood sports, cockiness . . . and lack of high intellectual stature would prove to be good qualifying factors for fighter pilots," said this Air Force study.

While a bomber crew's greatest thrill was surviving a mission, fighter pilots returned from "good hunting" exhilarated, chopping the air with their hands to signify the Germans they had flamed. "The frank pleasure that a fighter group shows following a heavy killing is shocking to outsiders," observed Eighth Air Force psychiatrist Douglas Bond.

But bomber pilots suffered much higher casualties than fighter pilots, and with greater responsibilities as crew commanders, they were more susceptible to mental breakdowns or combat fatigue. "The task of the fighter pilot is ideal for high motivation," Air Force psychologists concluded. Fighter pilots had shorter, more informal briefings—five minutes to the bomber crew's one hour. They took off and formed up much more quickly and less dangerously than bomber pilots, and, unless they were strafing, were rarely the targets of Nazi flak gunners. Alone in the clean medium of the air, the fighter pilot, with certain limitations, could fly as he chose, making his own decisions. This often encouraged explosive reck-lessness and dangerous exhibitionism, yet more often than not it saved pilot's lives, as they could scoot off, climb or dive, anytime it got too hot. A Fortress crew on a bomb run had to sit and take it, like the crew of a sub-marine trapped and under assault on the floor of the ocean. As a staff offi-cer with Blakeslee's Debden outfit wrote: "You have to give the bomber boys this: they were the ones who fought the toughest part of the air war." Their sacrifices made it possible for the fighter boys to finish off the Luft-waffe.

•   •   •

Out-produced and out-fought, the Luftwaffe had lost air superiority over continental Europe by May 1945. The Americans and the British had twenty times more planes than the Germans, and the fuel and skilled pilots to fly them. Under interrogation after the war, Lt. Gen. Karl Koller, chief of the Luftwaffe's operations staff, claimed that if Germany had enjoyed air supremacy in the spring of 1944, "there would have been no invasion, or it would have been turned back with the loss of much blood." But with air ascendancy lost in the great battles between March and May 1944, the Luftwaffe's "task," said Koller, "was to make sacrifices."

Asked why Germany failed to develop a nimble fighter capable of staying in the air as long as the Mustang, Koller replied that German industrialists and engineers insisted that such a plane "could not be built." But the idea might have been revived when the war began to go badly for Germany had Hitler shown interest in it. This is the difference between pliant democracy and rigid despotism. Before the war, the American bomber barons and the airplane industry, had echoed the opinion of German aircraft experts. Yet when the crisis arose, they responded, although almost too late. An invasion whose success seems inevitable only from hindsight was made possible by the introduction into the war of an air machine few believed could be built.

The Great Showdown

Driving the Luftwaffe back into Germany made the invasion possible, but did not guarantee its success. The heavily reinforced Wehrmacht was strongly lodged in northern France, under orders from Hitler to fight to the last man. How could airpower be used to weaken it? The leaders of the Great Alliance had been heatedly debating this question since January 1944, and it was not until early May that an uneasy agreement was reached. It was one of the stormiest policy disputes of the war.

Upon his appointment as supreme commander of Overlord, Eisenhower demanded operational command of the tactical and strategic air forces of Britain and the United States. He had to have this, he insisted, in order to insure that the entire Anglo-American air effort was directed to the immediate support of the invasion. Hap Arnold, Eisenhower's old friend, agreed to this immediately, but the British protested. To get Churchill and his War Cabinet to surrender control of Bomber Command was a Herculean undertaking, and Eisenhower had to threaten to resign to get his way. Unless Arthur Harris's bombers came under his direction, he told

Churchill, he would "simply have to go home." That settled it. Air Vice Marshal Sir Trafford Leigh-Mallory, whose competence Spaatz questioned, was given direction of the invasion's tactical air arm, which included the American Ninth Air Force. And commencing on April 14 and continuing until the Battle of Normandy was won, Arthur Tedder, Eisenhower's chief deputy, would have overall supervision of Bomber Command as well the Eighth and Fifteenth Air Forces.

Having secured control of the bombers, Eisenhower had to decide how to use them in the weeks leading up to the invasion. Everyone agreed that the biggest fight would be the Battle of the Buildup. The Allies were counting on surprise and overwhelming shock power to get a small part of their force onto the beaches on D-Day. After that, victory would go to the side that was able to accrue a preponderance of power. The Germans seemed to have the advantage. Using the excellent road and railway network of Belgium and France, they would be able to resupply their armies more easily than the Allies, who would have to depend upon a vulnerable sea highway running from Normandy's Cotentin Peninsula to capacious supply depots in the south of England. The Allied objective was to isolate the beachhead and cut off the German army in Normandy from its chief sources of supply in the Rhineland and the Ruhr.

A plan put forward by Tedder's scientific advisor, Professor Solly Zuckerman, struck Eisenhower as having the best chance of accomplishing this. Zuckerman proposed a strategic bombing campaign directed at railroad marshaling yards and repair shops in northern France and Belgium. By hitting these inland transportation focal points, the Allies would create a state of chaos and ruin that would stop or radically impair the movement of German reinforcements to the assault area. This, Zuckerman believed, would be more effective than a bridge-busting campaign proposed by an American Air Force target advisory staff of young economists headed up by Walter W. Rostow and Carl Keyson, both of whom would later hold high economic policy positions in the White House during the 1960s. Marshaling yards, in Zuckerman's opinion, were easier targets for heavy bombers than bridges, and their destruction would cause greater disruption of traffic. Zuckerman's proposal became known as the Transportation Plan and it came under scorching criticism from three formidable adversaries: Arthur Harris, Carl Spaatz, and Winston Churchill.

Harris and Spaatz agreed on one thing. The Zuckerman plan would divert them from their shared objective: to bomb Germany out of the war, making an invasion unnecessary. "There could be no greater relief afforded Germany than the cessation or any ponderable reduction of the bombing of Germany proper," Harris wrote in a strident memorandum enunciating his opposition to Zuckerman's plan. "The entire country would go wild with a sense of relief and reborn hope." Harris's position and prestige, however, were undercut by the unsustainable losses his forces had recently taken over Berlin; since the previous November he had lost almost 1,200 bombers. When Harris persisted, claiming that his night bombers were incapable of hitting precision targets like marshaling yards, RAF Chief of Staff Charles Portal called his bluff, instructing Bomber Command to hit six marshaling yards in France. The targets were pulverized. In the words of Max Hastings, "Harris stood confounded by the virtuosity of his own men." As he well knew, his crews had developed the capability to bomb almost as accurately at night as the Eighth did in daylight. After these twin defeats, Harris had no choice but to grudgingly back the Transportation Plan.

While Harris worried about not killing enough Germans, Churchill worried about killing too many Frenchmen. The seventy or so rail centers targeted by Zuckerman were in or near urban areas and intelligence reports indicated that the bombing could kill or cripple as many as 160,000 French and Belgian civilians, suffering that might create "a legacy of hate" that would poison postwar relations with France. As D-Day approached, Churchill softened his opposition. His concern about the "cold blooded butchery" of civilians was somewhat alleviated when the commander of the Free French Forces in the U.K., Maj. Gen. Pierre Koenig, was consulted and replied, "This is war and it is to be expected that people will be killed. . . . We would take twice the anticipated loss to be rid of the Germans." But only a letter from Roosevelt in early May insisting that military considerations must dominate succeeded in persuading the prime minister to throw his full support to a bombing initiative that had already begun over his intermittent protests.

The most seriously considered counterproposal to Zuckerman's Transportation Plan was Carl Spaatz's Oil Plan. Having achieved air superiority with its fighter planes, the American Air Force proposed to exploit that breakthrough by sending its heavies against the industry that kept the diminished Luftwaffe flying and the Wehrmacht in the field. Spaatz's target analysts estimated that American strategic bombers could bring about a 50 percent reduction in Germany's gasoline production with only twenty-five raids—fifteen by the Eighth Air Force and ten by the Fifteenth. The resulting fuel emergency would reduce the mobility of the Wehmacht's motorized divisions and disrupt the delivery of supplies and reinforcements to the Normandy beachhead, a far greater dividend, Spaatz argued, than would accrue from the destruction of easily repaired marshaling yards.

Spaatz tried to make his proposal more appealing to Eisenhower by pointing out that an oil offensive would occupy only half of the American Air Force's operational strength. The other half could still be used to destroy transportation infrastructure in France. But instead of saturating marshaling yards, Spaatz proposed concentrating tactical operations on the bridges that spanned the Seine and Loire rivers, the targets that Lieutenant Rostow's committee recommended.

Hap Arnold urged Marshall to support Spaatz's plan, but Marshall left the final decision to Eisenhower, who leaned heavily on Tedder for advice on air matters. In the end, the American bomber barons' reputation for amplification and their previous record of failure helped kill their case for oil bombing. A year earlier, the Eighth Air Force had argued with equal vehemence that Germany's ball bearing industry was a potentially war-ending target system. Tedder also had some history with this issue. Early in the war, Bomber Command had gone after German oil plants and failed disastrously, missing the targets and losing dozens of crews. "We have been led up the garden path before," Tedder wrote a similarly skeptical Portal.

On March 25, at a tense meeting with all the Anglo-American air chiefs, Eisenhower ruled for Zuckerman, even though Churchill—who was not at the meeting—favored the Oil Plan. Eisenhower did this after Gen. Frederick Anderson, conceded—under close questioning—that the Air Force "could not guarantee that the attacks of oil targets would have an appreciable effect during the initial stages of Overlord." The Oil Plan, he said, "would have a decisive effect within a period of about six months." That was not good enough for Ike. He was most concerned with the first six weeks of the invasion—getting armies ashore and keeping them ashore.

Portal ended the meeting by saying that the Allied air staffs should consider adopting the Oil Plan, but only after the first crisis of Overlord had passed and Allied armies were firmly planted in Normandy. When Eisenhower agreed, "the great showdown," as an American officer called it, ended.

Spaatz bowed to Eisenhower's wishes without a public fight because he had the highest respect for the supreme commander. "If Eisenhower had asked him, in writing, to drop his bombs in the Arctic Ocean on D-Day he would have complied," said Col. Richard D'Oyly, Spaatz's senior target officer. There may have been more to his compliance than that. Although he surely wanted the invasion to succeed, he believed it might fail, and if it did, he did not want his Air Force blamed for obstructionism. "This ___ invasion can't succeed," he had told his staff before the March 25 meeting, "and I don't want any part of the blame. After it fails, we can show them how we can win by bombing."

Nor did Spaatz think he had been completely beaten at the March 25 meeting. Encouraged by the committee's concession that his Oil Plan had "great attractions," Spaatz persuaded Tedder to release a contingent of Liberators from the Fifteenth Air Force to attack Ploesti, a raid that inflicted enough damage to persuade Tedder to permit further raids from Italy. But Spaatz wanted more. He wanted to bomb Germany's synthetic fuel plants, the chief source of its oil supply. Eisenhower told him to wait until late summer, but Spaatz persisted. After a flaming argument with Ike, during which Spaatz may have threatened to resign, Eisenhower gave in—but only a little. He gave Spaatz verbal permission to have his bombers strike synthetic plants on two days in May when the weather was clear over Germany but impossible over France.

On May 12, Jimmy Doolittle sent 886 bombers against a tightly massed complex of synthetic oil plants in central Germany, provoking a tremendous air battle in which the Americans lost forty-six bombers and the Germans over sixty fighters. The ferocity of the fight convinced Spaatz that his target planners had found the enemy's fatal flaw. "On that day the technological war was decided," Albert Speer wrote in his memoirs. A week after the raid, Speer reported to Hitler that "the enemy has struck us at one of our weakest points. If they persist at it this time, we will soon no longer have any fuel production worth mentioning. Our one hope is that the other side has an air force General Staff as scatter-brained as ours!"

After sixteen days of round-the-clock repairs at the plants, the Eighth struck again on May 28 and 29, while the Fifteenth hit Ploesti. The twin blows halved German oil production. ULTRA intercepts confirmed that the Germans were deeply alarmed. "I guess we'll have to give the customer what he wants," Tedder is reported to have said. But with the invasion only a week or so way, the oil offensive would have to wait.

Bombing to Invade

Spaatz's pre-invasion oil raids produced unexpected dividends. The threat of follow-up raids kept the preponderance of German fighter power inside the homeland, even after the Allied ground forces stormed the beaches on June 6, 1944. The Transportation Plan was even more successful. Allied heavy and medium bombers almost completely dismembered the rail network of northern Belgium and France, choking off the main supply channel that fed the German army. And fighter planes pounced on anything that moved on France's roads and railways. On a single day in May, the Ninth Air Force's Fighter Command, headed by Maj. Gen. Elwood "Pete" Quesada, one of America's most innovative air leaders, destroyed so many trains that the fliers dubbed the occasion Chattanooga Day, after the Glenn Miller recording "Chattanooga Choo Choo." A German commander described the roads leading to the Normandy beaches as *Jabo Rennstrecki,* fighter-bomber racecourses.

In a last-minute change in the original Transportation Plan, Allied fighter-bombers smashed the bridges over the Loire and the Seine, cutting off most of Normandy and Brittany from the rest of France. (This was the tactical plan proposed back in March by Spaatz's target planners.) By the last week of May, all routes over the Seine north of Paris were closed to rail traffic. Bridges in the Pas de Calais area were hit even more heavily in a successful effort to convince the enemy that the invasion would come in that area, which was much closer to both southern England, the launch point for the invasion, and northern Germany, its ultimate objective.

Allied planes dropped a total of 71,000 tons of bombs on the French railway system, the equivalent of seven times the explosive power of the uranium bomb that would turn Hiroshima into nothing.

Postwar studies of pre-invasion bombing suggest that the bridge-busting campaign by the low-flying fighter-bombers was more successful in impeding German troop movements than the destruction of French rail centers by the heavies. Using tens of thousands of slave laborers, the Germans repaired marshaling yards and tracks as fast as Allied strategic bombers destroyed them. And these high-altitude attacks on yards located in heavily populated urban areas killed an estimated 12,000 French and Belgian civilians. Tactical raids on bridges and moving locomotives, on the other hand, caused minimal collateral damage and had a more serious impact on the enemy's ability to move its armies. The Wehrmacht would fight a brilliant defensive battle in Normandy, but its fate was almost preordained when Allied airpower won the Battle of the Buildup before the invasion began.

A number of German generals, including Field Marshall Gerd von Rundstedt, overall ground commander in Normandy, and Field Marshal Wilhelm Keitel, head of the German armed forces high command (OKW in its German acronym), told Allied interrogators after the war that the invasion had succeeded only due to "our inability to bring up our reserves at the proper time . . . Nobody can ever prove to me," said Keitel, "that we could not have repelled the invasion had not the superiority of the enemy air force in bombers and fighters made it impossible to throw these divisions in the fight."

Sharing the War

"We waited so long it turned into a joke," Bert Stiles wrote in his journal. "Each time they woke us up in the night somebody would say, 'It's D-day.' But it never was. And then on the sixth of June it was."

That night there was no sleep for anyone in East Anglia. Beginning just after midnight, the skies roared and shivered as thousands of planes—troop carriers, reconnaissance craft, bombers, and fighters—began assembling in the low-hanging clouds. Great groups of them threatened to collide as they flew down a corridor barely ten miles wide. The bombers, in six-ship squadrons, kept out of each other's way only by following searchlight beacons to a point south of London. There the broken overcast pulled itself together and became a solid blanket of gray over which a great parade of over 1,300 heavies thundered toward their targets, led by blinking Pathfinder planes.

Stiles and his crew were part of the "big show." Looking down from four miles up, Stiles could see the tremendous flashes of naval guns, crimson and orange against the dull gray sea. As Gen. Laurence Kuter watched this bomber armada pass over his low-flying B-17 observation plane, a friend he had given up for dead was in a farmhouse in Nazi-controlled France, waiting for word of the invasion.

Not long after surrendering his headquarters job for command of a new Liberator outfit, the 487th, Lt. Col. Beirne Lay, Jr., was shot out of the sky while leading the group on a pre-invasion strike against a marshaling yard at Chaumont, France, south and west of Paris. He and the ship's co-pilot, Lt. Walter Duer, made contact with the Underground, but with all escape routes to Spain closed down by the Gestapo and the destruction of the French rail system, they were taken to a safe house run by the local Maquis. They arrived the night before D-Day.

At daybreak they were shaken awake by the owner, M. Paugoy, a small excitable man with a high-pitched voice. "Le débarquement! Les Américains! Normandie! Normandie!" Leaping from their beds the two fliers could hear the cracking kitchen radio breaking the news. After eating a celebratory breakfast of eggs and toast, they were led to a place in the fields that would be their hideout. "We were examining the vineyard," Lay recalled, "when a sudden roar of engines filled the air. Out of the mists of dawn a 36-ship formation of Messerschmitt-109 fighters, with a large bomb slung beneath each glistening green and gray belly, swept low over the farm as they assembled from a near-by airdrome, staggering slowly under the great load."

Looking up, Walt Duer muttered: "With the fighter cover we'll have over the Channel, I'll bet not one of those bastards gets back to base." As the formation melted into the sky, Beirne Lay felt a "thrill of pride" that American air mastery "had already doomed this remnant of the Luftwaffe to a suicide mission."

The Messerschmitts that the two downed fliers saw that morning were part of a German reserve force of 300 fighters dispatched to the invasion area to reinforce the puny contingent of 150 fighters already there. Most of these fighters became "badly scattered," according to Allied reports, and "reduced in number because of their pilots' incompetence." When the pilots found that most of their forward fields in France had been turned into moonscapes by pre-invasion air assaults, they had to operate from improvised fields well in the rear of the invasion beaches, where they were preyed upon by swarms of Anglo-American fighters and unable to render effective assistance to Wehrmacht units in the invasion zone. Most of the ninety or so planes that attacked the invasion fleet on the evening of D-Day did little damage and were either chased away or slaughtered by Allied fighter planes.

There was no glory that day for the bomber boys. That morning, they had appeared suddenly and spectacularly over the enemy's coastal defenses just before the first landing boats came ashore. Hampered by thick cloud cover and concerned about hitting their own troops, the lead bombardiers, using radar bombsights, delayed their releases. Five thousand tons of explosives fell harmlessly behind German coastal positions. The heavies flew other missions that day against enemy fortifications and key transportation junctures just off the beaches, in the hope of disrupting German efforts to bring up reinforcements, but their air support was not as effective as that provided by Thunderbolts, Mustangs, and low-flying B-26 Marauders. The twin-engine Marauders decimated German defenses on Utah Beach, guaranteeing the American assault forces in the sector an unexpectedly easy landing.

But the Eighth Air Force had already done its indispensable duty. In the five-month battle for the air supremacy that made the invasion possible, the American Air Forces in Europe lost over 2,600 heavy bombers and 980 fighter planes and suffered 18,400 casualties, including 10,000 combat deaths, over half as many men as the Eighth lost in all of 1942 and 1943. These airmen deserve an equal place in the national memory with the approximately 6,000 American soldiers killed, wounded, or missing in action in the amphibious and airborne assault on D-Day.

For nearly every Allied airman who flew that day, it was the greatest experience of the war. "I briefed the crews of the 100th," recalls Rosie Rosenthal, "and I had never seen such a reaction from them. They stood and cheered and roared. This is the day they had been looking toward. I led the group on the third bombing mission of D-Day, toward dusk. We had a rule. No one could talk on the intercom unless it was absolutely necessary—radio discipline. But as we passed over that vast armada and headed over the beaches, a member of our crew started to say a prayer for the people down below and we all joined in. It was one of the most emotional moments of my life."

Flying back to England, Bert Stiles wondered how the "poor bastards down on the beach" were doing. The planes were over them, the warships behind them, but this would be their fight. And then it struck him. "Our war was over, the exclusive war of the 8th and 9th Air Forces by day and the RAF by night. . . . We'd be trucking the bombs over, more of them, more often, but it wasn't our own private show any more. The boys who take it the slow way had the bright lights on them now."

Sharing the war did not bother Lt. Bert Stiles. "Blood is the same whether it spills on aluminum or Normandy mud. It takes guts whether you fly a million-dollar airplane or wade in slow with a fifty-dollar rifle . . . Maybe some of the airpower fanatics will scream that the big brains didn't give us a chance to win it our way." But "the only thing that matters," Stiles wrote on the evening of D-Day, "is to win, win in any way so there is never another one."

CHAPTER ELEVEN

The Fatal Trap

The Kingdom of Heaven runs on righteousness, but the
Kingdom of Earth runs on oil.

ERNEST BEVIN, CHURCHILL'S MINISTER
OF LABOUR AND NATIONAL SERVICE

London, June 1944

Three days after the Allies landed in Normandy, Gen. Hap Arnold arrived in London with Gen. George Marshall for a series of meetings with other leaders of the Great Alliance. With Allied troops planted on French soil, the drive to the German border was about to begin. High on the agenda of the Combined Chiefs of Staff—the supreme Anglo-American military authority, made up of the U.S. Joint Chiefs of Staff and the British Chiefs of Staff—was the role the American Air Force would play in the battle to liberate Western Europe.

Before the main meetings convened, Arnold wanted to assess the air situation in northern France. On the morning of June 12, he and Marshall, accompanied by Eisenhower, boarded the destroyer USS *Thompson* for a tour of the Normandy battlefront. Cutting through the heavy gray seas at thirty knots, the *Thompson* passed a pageant of power that stretched from horizon to horizon: cruisers, battleships, destroyers, and minesweepers, along with Liberty Ships and landing craft that were ferrying over 15,000 assault troops and 3,000 tons of supplies a day to the invasion beaches, where 45,000 Royal Engineers and laborers were building a colossal system of artificial piers and breakwaters, code-named Mulberries, that had been towed across the Channel. Assembled offshore from this instant harbor was "the greatest armada man has ever seen," wrote war correspondent Ernie Pyle. It was "a wonderful but terrifying sight," Arnold wrote in his diary. "If there was ever a bomber's paradise . . . it was the harbor of Portsmouth . . . and this unprecedented mass of ships. . . . What a field day it would [be] for the German Air Force."

On landing, Arnold met with Gen. Pete Quesada, who had built an improvised headquarters for his Ninth Air Force Fighter Command on the Normandy beaches. Quesada assured Arnold that his own intelligence indicated that the Luftwaffe had only sixty planes in combat readiness out of the hundreds sent to oppose the Allied landings, a force capable of only nuisance raids. The Luftwaffe "does not have numbers, does not have crews, lacks training, does not have [the] will to fight, [and] has lost its morale," Quesada told Arnold.

This was the moment the American bomber commanders had been building toward: now they could penetrate German airspace without heavy fighter opposition, knocking out the oil refineries and munitions mills that supported the enemy war effort. And what a force they had available to carry out these industry-killing raids: over 2,100 heavies in Britain and 1,200 in Italy. But strategic bombing was not a priority for Eisenhower and the Joint Chiefs. In the coming months the Eighth Air Force would be called upon to do what it lacked the equipment and experience to do well—provide direct air support for Allied armies operating in Normandy. There was no moving Eisenhower on this. Nor would strategic bombing be even the second priority of the Eighth that summer. In the very week that Arnold was in England a new threat arose, one that further diverted the American bomber barons from what they saw as their ordained, war-ending mission.

During their stay in England, Arnold and the other members of the American Joint Chiefs of Staff were guests at the Sussex estate of J. W. Gibson and his wife, only a short drive from London. Gibson, the world-famous engineer who had designed the Mulberry harbors in Normandy, had converted a former hunting lodge of Henry VIII into a regal country retreat ringed by 200 thickly wooded acres. On the evening of June 15, Arnold retired early to his room to pack for his return journey. Near daybreak, there was "a long series of explosions following one another in quick succession," most of them from the direction of London but a few dangerously close by. Arnold went out onto the grounds and spotted a strange-looking machine circling directly over the Gibson estate, its motor making an unnerving buzzing sound. Then the machine went silent and came tearing out of the clouds in a steep dive, crashing and exploding a mile or so away. Arnold knew at once that it was one of the new pilotless planes the Germans had fired on London the evening of June 12–13. It was a V-1, "Vengeance Weapon 1," as Joseph Goebbels, Nazi Minister for Propaganda and Enlightenment dubbed it, Hitler's personal payback for the bombing of his cities. Within minutes, six more of these V-1's landed a few miles from the Gibson house, leading Arnold to suspect that the Germans had deliberately targeted the American chiefs of staff.

After breakfast, Arnold, who had a passionate interest in new weaponry, was driven to the local village where one of the "Drones" had landed in an orchard, creating a crater six feet across and five feet deep. Around the hole were spread the remains of the "gadget," which looked to him like a small airplane: a cylindrical steel fuselage with short stubby wings, jet-propelled, controlled by an automatic "gyro-pilot," and carrying a one-ton payload. While the V-1s were not precision weapons, Arnold feared that they would, in Eisenhower's words, "dislocate the war effort" if they were aimed in great numbers at the concentration of troops and supplies in the Channel ports and off the beaches at Normandy.

"Our answer," Arnold suggested to Eisenhower the next day, "must be to hit the factories where critical parts are made." Aerial attacks on the launching sites would be futile, Arnold believed; the smaller sites were ingeniously hidden while the larger storage and research sites were virtually bombproof. Some other way had to be found to take them out. In the meantime, Arnold salvaged parts of several V-1s that had struck London and sent them back to Wright Field, near Dayton, Ohio, to see if Air Force scientists could develop a copy of the rocket, a project that would spur the postwar development of an American cruise missile.

The Allies had known about the new German pilotless jet since the previous November, when British intelligence discovered launching sites along the northern coast of France, the "Rocket Gun Coast," the *New York Times* called it. Fearing these projectiles might be armed in the near future with biological, or even atomic weapons, the planners of Overlord ordered bombing raids on the sites. Under the code name Operation Crossbow, the Allied air forces hammered German launching sites—called "ski sites" because of their elevated launching ramps—in the Pas de Calais and on the tip of the Cherbourg peninsula, delaying the scheduled launches until after D-Day. They had also bombed, without much success, immensely larger, mysterious-looking rocket storage and research centers. Now Eisenhower, responding to urgent pleas from the British War Cabinet, ordered the Anglo-American air forces to destroy all German launching sites and storage facilities in northwestern Europe.

Carl Spaatz and Arthur Harris were furious. Their aerial photo intelligence indicated that most of the Luftwaffe's flying bombs were being fired from mobile, heavily camouflaged sites, which were almost impossible to locate. But Eisenhower had Churchill on his neck, and both leaders were concerned about intelligence reports that Hitler was developing—at the larger "hardened" sites—supersonic guided missiles, V-2s, with vastly greater range and destructive power than the V-1s. The Germans were also believed to have in development a supersonic rocket, the V-3, capable of reaching New York City. If the big brains of the Reich, led by boy genius Wernher von Braun, could put a nuclear payload on the New York rocket, they might win the war. German scientists, it turned out, were not close to completing such a rocket and had already given up hope of developing an atomic bomb, but in June 1944, Allied intelligence did not know this.

The V-1s were causing havoc in London. Almost a hundred of them a day landed in the city, creating an unexpected second Blitz that led to the evacuation of a million women and children. Churchill saw the V-1 as a cowardly weapon, armed and aimed by men who would not risk their own lives, as bomber crews did, to destroy others. In a rage, he ordered the RAF to prepare for poison gas attacks on German cities. He was talked out of this, however, by his air chiefs, who warned him that the Germans would respond with bombs loaded with deadly nerve gas, weapons they already had in their arsenal.

Hitler never aimed his flying bombs at invasion embarkation ports, perhaps because of their known inaccuracy, but just as importantly, because of his deep obsession with retaliation bombing. Londoners—pensioners and housewives—were the targets; they would pay for the suffering of Berliners. It was in London that over 90 percent of the V-1 fatalities would occur.

Traveling at a speed of 400 miles per hour and arriving in droves, often in cloudy weather, the pilotless bombs were, at first, difficult to shoot down, flying too low for the high guns stationed around London and too high for the low guns. But swiftly improved British defenses were able to destroy over half of the 7,488 buzz bombs, as they become known in Britain, that reached southern England in the eighty days of the Nazi rocket assault. Some of the flying bombs slammed into the steel cables of the balloon barrage that was set up on the Kent and Sussex approaches to the capital, but most of those destroyed were shot out of the sky by British fighter planes or by newly redesigned antiaircraft guns firing proximity fuse shells that exploded in clusters around their targets. Some audacious British pilots knocked them out of the air without releasing a shot. They would fly alongside a rocket, slip one of their wingtips beneath it, and tip its wing slightly. With the airflow over its wings distorted, the V-1 would roll over and dive straight into the ground. Still, in the first weeks of the second battle of London, large numbers of them—on some days 60 percent—got through. Sent against "a target," in Churchill's words, "18 miles wide by over 20 miles deep," their inaccuracy was almost immaterial.

Over the course of the summer, over 18,000 people were injured and 6,184 killed. The bombs fell so randomly that many Londoners refused to enter air raid shelters, reacting to the "robot bombs" with a nonchalance that bordered on "idiocy," in the words of a local diarist. Even the stands at the racetracks were packed to capacity. Racing "enthusiasts," this Londoner wrote, "have apparently decided that since death can find them anywhere in southern England these days, they'd just as soon be found laying a bet on a promising horse."

The earlier Crossbow missions had not been popular with bomber crews, who had not been told what they were bombing, only that they were hitting military targets ringed by antiaircraft guns. In the summer of '44, some airmen of the Eighth changed their minds about Crossbow after spending time in the city that once again was on the front line of the war.

Flying over the Reich a few days after helping to pull bomb victims out of a smoking London building, Sergeant gunner Harry A. Clark felt no compassion for the people his crew was about to destroy. "Goddamn the Nazi bastards!" he remembered saying to himself as the bombs were released. Watching the dirty clouds rise from the city, he recalled a dead man he had seen in the London wreckage, the inert, mangled body of his son in his arms, the boy's battered head connected to his torso by a few threads of flesh and muscle. "I silently dedicated the destruction our bombs made to them."

Aphrodite

That June, Eighth Air Force pilot Fain Pool had just flown his fourteenth combat mission. A broad-shouldered Oklahoman with thick black hair and a winning smile, his enthusiasm for combat had recently been aroused by what he had seen on a weekend in London: women and children lying in pools of their own blood, their modest homes smashed to dust by "push-button bombs that came without warning in the night."

A few days later, Lieutenant Pool was relaxing in the officers club of the 385th Bomb Group at Great Ashfield when he was summoned to the office of the base commander. Four other pilots were in the room when he arrived. The men were asked to volunteer for a hazardous, highly secret mission, one that involved flying a heavy bomber and bailing out over friendly territory. That was all the commanding officer was able tell them. No crews would be needed; the Air Force wanted only pilots and radio technicians. Their reward for this one job: credit for five bombing missions.

When one pilot asked how long they had to think about volunteering, the colonel told them he wanted their answer immediately. After four of them declined, Pool volunteered. Ten hours later he was unloaded from a plane at a Royal Air Force repair depot called Honington, in Suffolk, where he was taken by jeep to a small American compound at a remote corner of the base. As he entered the green-brown Nissen hut that would be his new quarters, one of the other pilot volunteers stuck out his hand and said, "Hey, fellows, another nut's arrived!"

At their first briefing, the pilots and radio technicians were given a rough outline of the operational plan. The Air Force was going to take ten worn-out Flying Fortresses, tear their insides out, and fill the planes with 20,000 pounds of nitrostarch, a highly explosive orange powder used for demolition. Part of the load would also be napalm, a new invention of warfare. The "Weary Willies," as they were called, would be equipped with remote control radio equipment that would allow them to be directed in flight by "mother ships," B-24 Liberators hovering above and behind them. A few of the drones would be equipped with television cameras mounted in their Plexiglas noses. They would send pictures of the ground to receivers in the control ships so that the robots could be directed precisely to their targets.

A crew of two, a jump pilot and an autopilot engineer, would get the drone into the air at an altitude of 1,800 feet, put it into a gentle dive, set the controls, arm the explosives for an on-impact detonation, and bail out over England. Every door and hatch except one would be bolted shut. The only way out of the plane was through a precariously tight escape hatch in the nose, just behind the inside engine on the pilot's side. The mother ship's remote control system, which fed into the drone's autopilot, would steer the low-flying, unmanned plane to what was described as a maximum-priority target. The largest explosive missile ever made by man would then dive on the target from a height of 600 to 700 feet, well below the enemy's radar horizon.

The project was code-named Aphrodite and it was a spectacular failure.

None of the two-man crews knew the objective of their mission: to destroy four large rocket sites across the Channel. It was thought that these facilities would be ready to launch long-range rockets more lethal than the V-1s within the month. "Aside from the grave threat to London, this weapon directly threatens our war effort," Spaatz wrote Arnold in late July, "since it may be used to destroy communications and port facilities on both sides of the Channel." Only one of these rocket centers was underground, but all were protected by massive ferroconcrete domes thirty to forty feet thick. The men were told that the orders for the operation had come directly from Spaatz and Doolittle, and that the project was the "pride and joy and consuming interest" of the Old Man, Gen. Hap Arnold.

After some preliminary training, the men and planes were moved to a small RAF base at Fersfield, a fog-enshrouded place in the empty Norfolk countryside, not far from the North Sea, where they were confined to the base under the penalty of court-martial. A few days later, they were joined by a detachment of U.S. Navy pilots and radio-control specialists. The Navy had established its own experimental drone program, code-named Anvil, for its Pacific-based aircraft carriers. It had more sophisticated radio and television technology than the Air Force, but Spaatz and Doolittle made sure Aphrodite had priority over Anvil.

The first Air Force mission was scheduled for August 4. Four drones would go, two at a time. The lead plane would be piloted by Lt. Fain Pool. His autopilot engineer would be S. Sgt. Philip Enterline of Kittanning, Pennsylvania. The main target was a German underground site at Mimoyecques, France. Its immense steel doors were opened only once a day, for just thirty minutes. When that happened, the Aphrodite team planned to "stuff a planeload of explosives down its gullet."

When Pool and Enterline climbed into their plane they looked at each other and whistled. It was loaded to the roof line with boxes of nitrostarch, giving it a dangerously high center of gravity. Enterline was worried, but Pool shrugged off his partner's concern; some of the best scientists in the world were involved in the project, he assured Enterline. If the explosives were stacked this high and tight, it was for a damn good reason. Pool's greatest concern was not that he was flying the most powerful single bomb ever assembled up to that time, but that he would be bailing out, at high speed and ridiculously low altitude, through a hole barely two feet wide.

Pool got the plane into the air without trouble. Five minutes later, the second drone cleared the runway. After that, nothing went right. Pool and Enterline had difficulty setting the autopilot and arming the firing system, and the plane spun out of control and began flying dangerously low. Pool, the last one out, jumped from only 500 feet. Landing in a plowed field, he was so glad to be alive he danced a jig. Then he heard an ear-splitting explosion. It was not his plane, he learned later, but the second drone, which stalled out and went into a fatal dive. The radio man parachuted to safety but the pilot, Lt. John Fisher, was incinerated in the wreckage. Pool's robot made it to the target but the guidance system experienced a malfunction and the drone was unable to dive. Flying aimlessly, it became an easy kill for a German flak crew.

The jump crews of the two other drones that were sent out that day survived with injuries. One robot crash-landed far from its target, a large rocket site at Wizernes believed to be a center for V-3 research and development; the other blew up just short of its destination. The day was a debacle.

The Air Force tried again on August 6, again without success, although with no loss of life. Undaunted, the Navy flew its one drone from Fersfield on August 12. It was a PB4Y, a modified B-24 Liberator, the type of plane used for submarine patrol. Its jump pilot was twenty-nine-year-old Joseph Kennedy, Jr., son of the former ambassador to England and brother of John F. Kennedy, a Navy lieutenant who had been badly wounded in the Solomon Islands the year before when his PT boat was cut in half by a Japanese destroyer. Joe Kennedy had plenty of experience with the plane, having flown over fifty missions on submarine patrol in the Bay of Biscay. In a letter of August 10, he assured his brother Jack that he had no intention of risking his "fine neck . . . in any crazy venture." Yet he must have known he could be flying a suicide mission.

His plane, *Zootsuit Black,* carried 24,240 pounds of Torpex, a new explosive that was lighter yet more powerful than nitrostarch. Kennedy and his co-pilot, thirty-five-year-old Wilford J. Willy, the father of three, took off and put the Liberator on a dead-on course for Dover, where they were to bail out and be picked up by a B-17, hopefully before anyone asked them why they had abandoned a perfectly flying bomber in the densely settled London suburbs. Flying directly above them was the head of the Eighth Air Force's photo reconnaisance group, Col. Elliott Roosevelt, a son of FDR. Minutes into the flight, Roosevelt heard two explosions, one second apart. Where *Zootsuit Black* had been there was a flaming orange and yellow ball. The remains of the plane fell to earth near the village of Newdelight Woods; the bodies of Kennedy and Willy were never recovered.

The Navy could not find a clear cause for the crash but it was probably a faulty remote-controlled arming device, which Kennedy had been warned about by an American electronics officer at Fersfield.

By the time the Navy completed work on a new modified drone, the British army had overrun the four mystery targets of the Aphrodite mission in the area west of the Pas de Calais. Intelligence agents found them filled with nothing but rats and rubble. They had been abandoned for months and were being used as decoys by the Germans to divert attention from the mobile sites from which most V-1s were launched, and from research facilities where scientists were working on more advanced rocket technology. They had been abandoned, it was learned, because 12,000-pound British Tallboys, the most powerful unmanned bombs in existence, had done more damage to them than Allied photo intelligence suspected. The entire Aphrodite effort had been wasted on dead targets.

On September 3, the Navy flew its modified drone against U-boat pens on the North Sea island of Heligoland and hit a coal pile instead. This ended its brief flirtation with radio-directed bombers. Arnold stubbornly kept Aphrodite going, even after a succession of equal catastrophes occurred with drones equipped with television cameras. If the war lasted much longer, he wanted to be ready to send waves of war-weary planes into German and Japanese cities and industrial sites. Later in the year he would try to convince Roosevelt to back his plan as a way of finishing off Germany.

The Crossbow campaign was another failure. All through the summer, the brunt of this misguided initiative was born by Harris's Bomber Command, assisted by an equally unenthusiastic Eighth Air Force. Acting on faulty intelligence, the British Air Ministry, which directed the effort, insisted on concentrating on two targets of scant consequence: small rocket sites, which were constantly moved and easily repaired, and large concrete storage sites that the Germans had secretly abandoned in favor of caves and tunnels in the Oise Valley, north of Paris. These caves were eventually found and hit, but too late to effectively blunt the damage that V-1s were inflicting on London.

The Allies paid a price unconscionably disproportionate to the results: almost 2,000 aircrew and 400 four-engine bombers. General Spaatz had been right all along. As Adolf Galland pointed out after the war, "The best way to fight the German V-weapon system, would [have been] to paralyze the German war industry." In the end, infantry accomplished what airpower could not. The V-1 raids stopped in early September when Field Marshal Sir Bernard Law Montgomery's Commonwealth forces broke out of their post-invasion stalemate near the Norman city of Caen and destroyed every launching site in France. Their destruction had no real effect on the war effort but was a blessing for Londoners. "For the first time in ten nightmarish weeks, lots of Londoners," said a local diarist, "climbed into their own beds and slept the sleep of the just and dog-tired."

Cobra

In mid-July, while London was under the heaviest rocket assault of the summer, the Allied invasion armies were still bottled up in Normandy. Their forward units had advanced only twenty-five to thirty miles from the landing beaches, along a narrow front of barely eighty miles. The British Second Army had failed to smash through the enemy's massed panzer strength at Caen, gateway to the flat ground that led to Falaise, forty miles south of the British beaches, where the Allies hoped to build forward airbases to provide cover for the eventual breakout to the German frontier. All the while, the Americans, after taking the port city of Cherbourg, on the northern tip of the Cotentin Peninsula, were fighting a draining war of attrition in the *bocage,* the ancient hedgerows of rural Normandy. Waist-high earthen banks, thick with deep-rooted vegetation and trees up to twenty feet high, bordered each pasture and meadow, and narrow, sunken roads traversed the entire marshy area.

Rooting out the Wehrmacht in this claustrophobic landscape was a slow, deadly business. Snipers were everywhere and the tangled terrain was murder on tanks. Ordered by Hitler to hold every inch of ground, the defenders fought furiously, less for the führer than for self-preservation. With Allied casualties running to well over 100,000, and the Germans threatening to build an iron cordon around the invasion lodgment area, "we faced a real danger of a World War I–type stalemate," Lt. General Omar N. Bradley, commander of the American ground forces, wrote later.

The agony and frustration of static warfare led Allied commanders to resort to a weapon not available in World War I, "a truly massive aerial bombardment that could exceed by many orders of magnitude any artillery preparation possible on the old Western front," in the words of historian Russell F. Weigley. On July 18, Montgomery's British and Canadian forces—assailed by a number of coalition leaders for fighting with excessive caution—attempted a massive breakthrough at Caen, to be preceded by one of the most awesome carpet bombings of the war. The RAF and the

Eighth blasted an enormous gap in the enemy front, allowing Montgomery to take most of the city. But the men of Panzer Group West crawled out of their holes and held their positions on the high ground south of Caen, preventing a breakthrough into the Falaise plain. Their efforts were aided by thousands of bomb craters that stalled Monty's mechanized columns.

Bradley came up with another plan, which unexpectedly turned into one of the supreme military achievements of the European campaign. Operation Cobra would begin with a cataclysmic bombing by the Eighth Air Force. In one hour, over 1,000 heavies would drop 50,000 iron bombs into a tight rectangle just south of a long, straight road that separated the American and German armies in Normandy, near the crossroads town of St. Lô. Bradley's First Army had just taken St. Lô after a bitter fight, placing the Americans on the thin wedge of terrain that separated the *bocage* from the open country to the south. This unprecedented saturation bombing was expected to create a paralyzing effect on surviving enemy troops, setting them up for a breakneck assault by the VII Corps of First Army, led by Maj. Gen. J. Lawton "Lightning Joe" Collins. With seven panzer divisions occupied near Caen and only two facing the American First Army at St. Lô, Bradley had high hopes for the operation.

Carl Spaatz fumed about using his bombers in close support of ground operations, seeing Cobra as yet another wasteful diversion from his oil campaign. But great numbers of his airmen were eager to aid Ernie Pyle's mud, sleet, and rain boys. "A lot of us felt that, but for the grace of God, we could be down there, slugging it out in the hedgerows," recalled Rosie Rosenthal. "At the same time, we knew that pinpoint bombing was more fiction than fact, and that created concern."

Just before the operation, Bradley flew to England to win the assurance of the senior air commanders that their bombers would approach the target from the safest direction, east to west, just south of the St. Lô–Periers road. A north-to-south approach would put them directly over his troops, with the risk of accidentally hitting them. In his memoirs Bradley claims to have gotten his way at the "great conference of [air] marshals." He did on the size of the bomb loads, but not on the approach path to the target. There was heated debate on this, and apparently Bradley mistook the assurances of a few air leaders for the assent of all. Air Chief Marshal Trafford Leigh-Mallory, who was responsible for coordinating Allied strategic bombing in Normandy, took Bradley's side, but representatives from the Eighth Air Force were emphatic that a route parallel to the road was impossible, given the constricted size of the target—a piece of French real estate only a mile and a half wide—and the immense number of bombers that would have to pass over it in a mere sixty minutes. No firm decision was reached, and Bradley must have returned to Normandy with the feeling that Leigh-Mallory, who promised him a force of over 2,200 planes—heavy, medium, and fighter-bombers—would prevail.

There had also been a discussion at the meeting about the size of the safety zone. Not trusting the accuracy of its own bombers, the Eighth Air Force wanted Bradley's troops to withdraw to positions 3,000 yards from the strike zone, giving them a safety margin of two miles. Bradley proposed a fallback of only 800 yards; he wanted his men in close, where they could pounce on the dazed Germans as quickly as possible. A compromise of 1,250 yards was reached, but even that was no guarantee that men would not be felled by friendly fire, Bradley was pointedly warned.

The entire Eighth and part of the Ninth were set to go on July 24, but when the weather worsened, Leigh-Mallory postponed the operation—too late, however, to stop hundreds of heavies and mediums from proceeding to the target, ducking under the clouds, and unloading 700 tons of ordnance. Human error caused "spillage" outside the target zone. Twenty-seven soldiers were killed and another 131 were wounded, all from the 30th Infantry Division.

The next morning Rosie Rosenthal led the 3rd Air Division, part of a force of 1,507 four-motored heavies, back to St. Lô. Again, airmen had orders to approach the target from north to south. As Rosenthal's vanguard neared St. Lô, it ran into scattered clouds and the entire formation had to drop down from the planned bombing altitude, forcing lead bombardiers to scramble to reset their bombsights. Thunderbolts of the Ninth Air Force had already torn into the forward German positions in a four-minute blitz that inadvertently made the work of the heavies more difficult. Billowing clouds of smoke and dust floated up from the battlefield and mingled with enemy flak bursts to obscure the readjusted sight lines of the bombardiers. The bombardier in Rosenthal's ship froze when he spotted the pillars of smoke and dropped late, in the rear of the German lines. But a number of other planes began dropping short, near American troops positioned a mere half-mile from the road, their front lines marked for the airmen by red smoke.

Ernie Pyle was with the American army at St. Lô. "The flight across the sky was slow, studied. I've never known a storm, or a machine, or any resolve of man that had about it the aura of such a ghastly relentlessness. . . . God, how we admired those men up there." Their thundering machines filled the sky with a "doomlike sound," creating a "spectacle of war" that made Pyle and the men he was with forget for a moment the danger they were in. They watched, frozen to their positions, as the exploding bombs crept back toward them, following the smoke line the bombardiers were aiming for, which a light breeze was blowing back over them. Then the "earth trembled and shook." Men hit the dirt, scrambled behind low stone walls, raced for dugouts and slit trenches. Frightened GIs could feel the bomb concussions in their chests and even in their eyes. Within seconds, however, the American bombs stopped crashing down on them, and began landing, as planned, a mile or so ahead. The leading company of Pyle's battalion had taken a terrible pounding, but it attacked "on time, to the minute," advancing 800 yards through the four-mile gap in the German lines. There the entire Army offensive ran into a wall of resistance and stalled.

Watching the battle from a farmhouse, Bradley was despondent. When the casualty reports came in, he was heard saying: "Christ, not again!" One hundred and eleven Americans were killed by Eighth Air Force bombs and at least another 500 were wounded. Among the dead was Lt. Gen. Lesley McNair, who had come from England as an observer. General Eisenhower, who had observed the operation from Bradley's headquarters, swore never again to use heavy bombers in support of ground forces, and Bradley fumed about the overpaid, overdecorated, overrated bomber boys. But part of the reason for the heavy casualties was Bradley's own interest in a quick, slashing assault, one that precluded putting his men in covered positions.

In London, General Doolittle was summoned to the office of Ike's chief of staff, Lt. Gen. Walter Bedell Smith, and blamed for the tragedy. Doolittle accepted responsibility but explained that serving as flying artillery for the infantry was unfair duty for crews trained to hit industrial targets. No bombardment force in existence, he told Smith, could place over 3,300 tons of explosives accurately into an area saturated with swirling smoke.

Doolittle was certain that Smith would call for his removal, but the St. Lô bombing had done far more damage to the enemy than Eisenhower and Bradley had suspected. The American bombers came on "like a conveyor belt," said Lt. Gen. Fritz Bayerlein, commander of Panzer Lehr Division, which took the brunt of the air attack. Bomb blasts burned men and equipment, overturned tanks, destroyed communications, and transformed the front of Panzer Lehr's lines—where over a thousand men lay dazed or dead—into what Bayerlein called a *Mondlandschaft,* a lunar landscape.

Sensing that the enemy's command and communications system had

taken a lethal hit, Lightning Joe Collins decided to gamble. The next morning he called up his reserve armor, smashed through the thin crust of German resistance, and kept moving southward toward the excellent road net
near Avranches. Fighter-bombers of the 9th Tactical Air Command
worked ahead of the tank columns in search and kill missions. Reporters
would call it the St. Lô Breakout, and it was the decisive turning point in
Eisenhower's European Crusade.

This became Lt. Gen. George Patton's show. The apostle of armored
warfare was flown in from England, where he had acted as D-Day decoy,
building up a phony force of cardboard tanks and planes that had convinced the Germans, into late June, that the main Allied landing would be
in the Pas de Calais. Patton took charge of the newly activated Third Army
and began an all-out drive across France at a rate of fifty miles a day, moving with furious resolve from the seaside bluffs of Avranches, into the Brittany peninsula, and then eastward to help destroy the German Seventh
Army. It was one of the most astonishing achievements in the history of
mobile warfare, and it was made possible by close coordination among
tanks, troops, artillery, and the fighter-bombers of the Allied air forces,
which acted as fast-moving aerial artillery for the army.

Eisenhower would change his mind after St. Lô and use heavies again in
direct support of ground troops, but it was always with less decisive results
and more deaths due to friendly fire. The troops loved to have the intimidating four-engine bombers overhead, but the heavies were of far greater
use to the infantry as instruments of interdiction, cutting the enemy lines of
communication. Without the heavies, the St. Lô breakout could have been
achieved only with staggering casualties. But it was Gen. Pete Quesada's
fighter-bombers that did most of the aerial damage after the breakout; operating as armor column cover, they cleared the way for the American
Army's road march to the Rhine.

Quesada, one of the youngest generals in the Air Force, introduced in-
novations in warfare that broke down the rigid division between tactical
and strategic bombing. He took his pilots, who were operating from forward bases in France, to the front lines "so that they could see how much
better off they were than those poor devils who were fighting the Germans
on the ground. I also took them to a collecting station where the wounded
were treated. We eventually imbued these young kids with the idea that
their prime task was support of the land campaign."

The fighter bombers could be called upon on short notice and take out
battlefield targets with far greater lethality than the lumbering Forts and
Liberators. And in the battle for France, Pete Quesada gave them better ar-

mament—deadly 5-inch rockets—as well as new eyes and ears. He put high-frequency radio sets in tanks so tank men and airmen could talk to one another, and he placed his own airmen in radio-equipped tanks as forward air controllers, to better direct fire on German battlefield targets.

By late summer, close air support of infantry—a German innovation—became one of the salient causes of Germany's defeat. With the Luftwaffe almost absent from the skies, the fighter-bombers inflicted lethal damage on German divisions that were pushed back in panic to the western borders of their homeland by swift-moving American infantry, artillery, and armor, reinforced by Canadian, British, and Polish units that finally broke through at Caen. Passing through a corridor of horror known to history as the Falaise Pocket, the Germans were massacred by Allied air-tank battle teams. "It was complete chaos," a German soldier recalled. "That's when I thought, 'This is the end of the world.' "

Two avid observers of the German retreat were Eighth Air Force evaders Beirne Lay, Jr., and Walter Duer. Early that August, they were still hiding out in the farmhouse that turned out to be a secret Maquis storehouse for arms and ammunition dropped by bombers from England. After learning of the St. Lô breakout, they had been following the American advance, village by village, on the silk maps they had in their escape kits. Working from first light to dark in their patron's wheat fields, Lay and Duer waited for their liberation. One evening as they were un-harnessing the horses in the stable, two bright-faced French girls burst through the door, threw their arms around them, and presented them a wreath of red, white, and blue flowers. The Germans had left, the girls said breathlessly. The Americans were only thirty kilometers away.

At breakfast the next morning a band of "fierce looking Maquis, armed to the teeth with Bren guns, pistols, hand grenades and knives," came storming into the kitchen holding out packages of American cigarettes. The two American airmen were handed tommy guns and ordered into the backseat of a battered sedan. With the French guerrillas riding the running boards, gangster-style, their machine guns at the ready, they were driven to one of Patton's armored columns. The next morning they were sent by jeep back through the American lines to Ninth Air Force headquarters in France. "On every side was the wreckage of the Wehrmacht," Lay wrote later. And in the near distance Lay could hear the sounds of battle. It was the Germans "being pounded to death by our fighter-bombers . . . in the slowly closing Falaise gap."

The Germans left behind most of their equipment, along with about

50,000 prisoners and 10,000 dead comrades. Yet at least 50,000 German soldiers managed to escape the Falaise Pocket before it was closed in late August. The Allies would meet them again in front of the Rhine.

The slaughter at Falaise ended the eighty-day-long Battle of Normandy, the most decisive battle on the Western Front. The Germans lost over 400,000 combatants—killed, wounded, or captured—and the Allies suffered over 225,000 casualties, two-thirds of them Americans, among them 8,536 airmen killed and missing. The battle was a prelude to the liberation of Paris and the triumphant Allied drive across France to Germany's western border, a campaign joined by Allied forces that landed on the coast of southern France on August 15. Further north, the Allied armies swept forward almost unopposed from the Seine to the Somme, the Marne, and the Belgian border, through territory famous from the First World War. Just 100 days after the Normandy landings, Allied armies were massed on a 250-mile-long front facing the West Wall, or Siegfried Line, as the Americans called it, the recently strengthened prewar defenses Hitler had built in front of the Rhine. The battle for France was over; the battle for Germany was about to begin.

It would be a murderous fight. Even in its reduced state, the German army remained one of the outstanding fighting forces in the history of arms. To lessen the cost of crushing this still imposing military machine, Carl Spaatz had already begun a major campaign against oil, the Wehmacht's chief source of sustenance.

The Oil War

Although America's strategic bombers remained under the direct control of the Allied supreme commander until September, with a priority obligation to support the ground offensive, Eisenhower had given Spaatz some wiggle room. After D-Day, Spaatz received written permission to go after oil targets when his bombers had favorable weather over Germany and were not needed for Crossbow or infantry support operations. Beginning in late June, the Eighth Air Force made a series of gigantic raids against oil installations north of Munich, while the Fifteenth Air Force continued to pound Ploesti, along with oil facilities in southern Germany, Austria, and Hungary. At the same time, the British Air Ministry directed a protesting Arthur Harris to attack synthetic oil plants in the Ruhr when he was not reducing the cities of that region to cinder and ash. Harris continued to see attacks on German oil installations as a "diversion" from the main task of crushing German resistance. Although he would later admit that the offensive against oil turned out to be "a complete success," he added: "I still do not think that it was reasonable, at that time, to expect that the campaign would succeed; what the Allied strategists did was to bet on an outsider, and it happened to win the race."

This was rubbish. Spaatz had hardly bet on a long shot. ULTRA intercepts and other intelligence reports fully available to Harris provided unambiguous evidence that Allied bombers had finally found a target whose destruction could help turn the course of the European war.

In April 1944, a month before Spaatz began his oil campaign, Germany's synthetic oil industry had been virtually untouched by Allied bombs. This is astounding, given the industry's importance and extreme vulnerability to aerial attack. These were immense plants operating at full blast in cleared land outside German cities, seemingly ideal targets for daylight bombers equipped with the most accurate bombsights ever invented. In over a year and a half of costly bombing operations, American target planners had failed to see that oil plants were much more important than ball bearing factories, which were almost impossible to disable, or aircraft plants that had been moved to remote, cleverly camouflaged sites. Nor, amazingly, did Allied target planners recognize the intimate connection between Germany's synthetic oil industry and its chemical industry, which produced all the essential ingredients for explosives.

In 1943, Hap Arnold's Committee of Operations Analysts, headed by Elihu Root, Jr., had placed oil as the strategic bombing campaign's third most important target, after the aircraft and ball bearing industries. The COA did not give oil the priority it deserved because it erroneously believed that Germany had enough standby refining capacity to cushion the initial shock of bombing. An oil offensive, committee members believed, would not have an immediate impact on enemy "front-line strength," in the air or on the ground. But General Spaatz, backed by his own Air Force target planners, continued to press the issue. Had the American Strategic Air Forces been headed by a less resolute leader, or one committed to other bombing priorities, an already tardy oil campaign might have been dangerously delayed and the war prolonged.

The Americans bore the burden of the oil campaign, the first true test of Air Force doctrine that daylight strategic bombing could disable the German economy. That summer was the beginning of true strategic bombing. During the entire war the Anglo-American air forces dropped more than 1.4 million tons of explosives on Nazi Germany. Over 70 percent of this tonnage was delivered after July 1, 1944, a comparatively small but critical part of it (about 200,000 tons of bombs) on oil targets. The attack on oil plants, beginning in May 1944 was, in Albert Speer's words, the "first heavy blow" delivered against German industry. The effect on production was immediate and far-reaching. If the government did not take emergency action to strengthen the air defenses of the synthetic oil plants, "an impossible situation in the fuel supply for the Wehrmacht and the country will arise . . . by September . . . which must lead to tragic results," Speer warned Hitler.

Oil is the blood of machine-age warfare. No modern state can wage war successfully without a sufficient and secure supply of petroleum products, both fuel and lubricants. Germany began the European war with a precarious fuel situation and within two years it was fighting an energy colossus. America had begun the transition from coal to oil early in the twentieth century and by 1939, oil accounted for half its total energy. In that year, the United States produced twenty times more oil than Germany would at the peak of its wartime production. California alone produced more oil than the Soviet Union, the largest petroleum producer in Europe. Germany, by comparison, relied on coal for 90 percent of its energy. But its army and air force, and much of its navy, ran on oil. That was a serious problem; indigenous oilfields supplied only 7 percent of the country's fuel requirements.

In September 1939, the German army invaded Poland with only a two-to-three-month reserve of aviation and motor gasoline. At that time Germany was importing nearly 70 percent of its liquid fuel, an alarming vulnerability for a nation with imperial ambitions. Hitler was able to enhance German petroleum supplies and avoid a wartime fuel emergency by seizing oilfields in the subdued countries of Hungary and Austria, and in Romania, his client state and Axis ally. Until mid-August 1944, when the Romanian fields were finally put out of operation by the Red Army and the Fifteenth Air Force, Ploesti remained the chief source of German crude oil, providing almost 60 percent of the country's oil imports. But before then, Hitler needed at least three times the output of the fields in the Danube basin to continue to wage total war.

Germany alleviated its energy problem by a feat of chemical alchemy—turning coal, a fuel it possessed in abundance, into oil, one it sorely lacked. By the eve of the American oil offensive, Germany's petroleum industry had made a complete turnabout. It was then producing almost three-quarters of the country's liquid fuel needs, and stocks of both aviation fuel and diesel oil had improved greatly. This was almost entirely due to a tremendous war-generated expansion of the synthetic oil industry—a state-supported combine of petroleum-producing giants run by businessmen in sympathy with the führer's program of foreign conquest and racial cleansing. Chemical companies like I. G. Farben had purged all Jewish executives and were relying increasingly on slave workers from conquered countries and concentration camp inmates procured for them by the SS. (I. G. Farben built one of its synthetic fuel and rubber plants in Poland, next to the mass murder mill at Auschwitz.) By September 1944, a third of the workers in the fuel industry were slave laborers. And well before then, the once independent synthetic oil industry had been forged into an instrument of the führer state, a war-directed conglomerate controlled by Reich Minister of Armaments and Production Albert Speer.

Most of Germany's synthetic oil was produced by hydrogenation plants that used the Bergius process, named after its inventor, Friedrich Bergius, a Nobel Prize–winning chemist. Chemical engineers used hydrogen under high pressure and extreme heat, and in the presence of a catalyst, to convert brown coal into the high-grade gasoline and aviation fuel used in tanks and warplanes. In the first quarter of 1944, synthetic fuel plants located near rich coal deposits in the Ruhr, Silesia, and central Germany, around Leipzig, produced over half of Germany's total supplies of oil, 85 percent of its high-grade motor fuel, and nearly all its aviation gasoline. Even today, no country's synthetic oil industry comes close to Germany's peak wartime production.

The rapid expansion of the German oil industry could have had grievous consequences for the Allies. Just months after German domestic oil production peaked, Albert Speer announced that fighter production had reached an all-time high. If oil targets had not been bombed exactly when they were—in the narrow time frame between May 1944, when German fuel production peaked, and September 1944, when tremendous numbers of enemy fighters were delivered from the factory to the front—these new planes, including jet aircraft, would have been in the air every day. Without the experienced pilots the Luftwaffe had lost earlier in the war, Germany could never have regained air supremacy. But fleets of fighters flown by hastily trained pilots would have made the destruction of the German war economy more time consuming and costly for Allied bombers.

Wartime Germany was a chemical empire built on coal, air, and water. These three basic raw materials formed the foundation of a chemical process—often concentrated in one plant—that used gases derived from coal to produce not only liquid fuels, but 99 percent of Germany's synthetic rubber and nearly all its synthetic methanol, synthetic ammonia, and nitric acid—raw materials used to make military explosives. This was the unseen bonus of the oil campaign: whenever American bombers knocked out two hydrogenation plants—the immense Leuna works, near Merseburg, and a much smaller plant at Ludwigshafen—Germany instantly lost 63 percent of its synthetic nitrogen, 40 percent of its synthetic methanol, and 65 percent of its synthetic rubber. The British and the Americans did not come to a full realization of the organic relationship between Germany's synthetic oil and chemical plants until after the war, when their agents interrogated German ministers and businessmen. This is one of the most dismaying intelligence failures of the war, a failure that is all the more surprising because American oil companies helped build Germany's embryonic synthetic oil industry in the late 1920s, when I. G. Farben opened its Leuna works, the first plant to test the Bergius process. Faulty intelligence resulted in the loss of planes and crews over crude oil refineries that were greatly less important than synthetic oil plants, with their facilities for producing chemical byproducts.

Although Germany's synthetic energy plants were scattered all over the Reich, a high percentage of petroleum production was concentrated in a small number of Bergius hydrogenation plants that were the sole source of Germany's high-grade aviation gasoline and most of its motor fuel. Nearly one-third of Bergius production was concentrated in just two plants: Leuna and Politz, in Polish Silesia, and over a third more in five other plants. Earlier in the war, Speer had lived in mortal fear that the Allied air staffs would target Germany's perilously grouped synthetic plants, which were too large and complex to be dispersed. When the plants were finally bombed, Hitler publicly rebuked I. B. Farben's Karl Krauch, his chief minister of chemical planning, for organizing the industry as if to invite its own destruction from the sky. Yet it was Hitler who had encouraged the economic integration that made German synthetic production overwhelmingly efficient; and he had done nothing to discourage Hermann Göring's misplaced confidence in the Luftwaffe's ability to shield these plants from aerial annihilation.

When the American attacks began, Speer feared that they were the opening salvos of a "long expected and long feared" single-industry offensive. Fortunately for Germany, they were not. On Sir Arthur Tedder's orders, American bombers continued to drop most of their tonnage on targets other than oil. After the war, Speer told American interrogators that a full-out offensive against the synthetic plants by the combined air armadas of England and America—closely spaced raids, night and day, without cease—could [alone] have brought about Germany's surrender . . . in eight weeks."

That is unlikely. This war, like almost all others, had to be won on the ground, but earlier and more sustained attacks on oil would surely have shortened the war on the Western Front by several months.

The American Strategic Air Forces would make 347 separate oil strikes and Britain's Bomber Command would carry out an additional 158. The Eighth Air Force's primary targets were the Leuna works, located three miles from the center of Merseburg and ninety miles southwest of Berlin, and the even larger complex at Politz, in the Silesian coalfields, seventy miles northeast of the capital. Together, these operations produced more than a third of Germany's total Bergius output of liquid fuel.

Leuna was a military-industrial powerhouse. A monument to German chemical wizardry, it produced gasoline for the Luftwaffe, lubricants for Tiger tanks, rubber for Hitler's motorized divisions, and explosives for nearly every German armored and artillery unit. A virtual city, covering three square miles of land and employing 35,000 workers—10,000 of them prisoners or slave laborers—it was the Reich's second largest synthetic oil plant and its second biggest chemical operation. Millions of tons of brown coal, strip-mined from local pits, were fed into it, and billions of gallons of water were pumped into its two-mile-long maze of machines from the plant's own waterworks. Hundreds of miles of underground cables, railroad tracks, and overhead pipes strung together its 250 buildings. The destruction of any part of this interconnected transportation and utilities infrastructure could shut down the entire operation, a fact that made Leuna, like other synthetic plants, highly vulnerable to aerial attack—in fact, almost inherently indefensible.

Over a period of ten months, between May 14, 1944, and April 5, 1945, a total of 6,630 American bombers tried to put Leuna out of business. It was, said one writer, "the grimmest fight to the death ever attempted by an air force." With its enormous size and distinctive features, Leuna should have been easy to spot from 20,000 feet up on a clear day. The first American crews sent against it were told that it could be identified by the sprawling railroad yards just west of its gates and by thirteen fire-belching chimneys, each of them a hundred feet high. But on the bomb run it was difficult for the pilots to see their own wingtips in a midday sky turned to night by greasy black camouflage smoke sent up from hundreds of small ovens.

As the raids got worse for the Germans, their deception and defenses got better. Decoy plant buildings were constructed outside the main plant and, as often as not, were bombed as intensively as the real things. The main problem for the air crews, however, was the circle of antiaircraft guns deployed around the plant, which put up the densest flak field in the world. In three separate attacks by the Eighth, 119 planes were lost and not one bomb fell on the Leuna works.

More than 19,000 of Leuna's workers were members of a highly trained air raid protection organization, equipped with over 600 radar-directed guns. With enough Luftwaffe fighters stationed nearby to put up determined, if only sporadic, resistance, Leuna became the most heavily defended industrial target in Europe.

Earlier that year, Hitler had increased the size of Germany's antiaircraft defense force to nearly a million by moving troops from the Eastern Front and bringing into the force secondary school students, women, and Soviet prisoners of war. By then Germany had over 13,200 heavy antiaircraft guns. Most flak gunners were deployed in batteries of six to twelve guns. Around Leuna and several other oil targets, Speer set up *Grossbatterie,* each of them equipped with up to thirty-six guns capable of firing a barrage or "box" of shells into a prearranged spot. Beginning with the summer oil raids, the Eighth Air Force would lose over twice as many bombers to flak than to fighters. While flak was responsible for 40 percent of the wounds suffered by Eighth Air Force fliers during the first year of the air war, it accounted for 71 percent of the wounds over the entire period of the war.

Flak was a grossly inefficient defensive measure. On average, it took 8,500 rounds from the newest version of the 88mm gun to down a single bomber. Yet it was a devastatingly effective psychological weapon, designed to unnerve the aircrews and impair bombing accuracy. In the summer and early fall of 1944, Germany still had enough ammunition to saturate the sky over its oil plants, maiming and killing great numbers of Allied fliers. By the end of the war, German flak gunners would take down some 5,400 American planes, as opposed to 4,300 shot down by fighters. Merseburg, or "Mercilessburg," as some airmen began calling it, became the most forbidding destination in "the land of doom."

"I can still remember the angry black cloud of exploding flak filling the sky as we approached our target that day," recalled B-17 co-pilot Tom Landry, later the head coach of the Dallas Cowboys. "And I remember the helpless, sinking feeling I felt as we followed our squadron leader into the heart of that cloud." Flying into a wall of flak, Brig. Gen. Gordon P. Saville remembered Laurence Kuter's famous remark back at the Air Corps Tactical School before the war. "While antiaircraft fire may be annoying, it should be ignored."

"Over the [oil plant] the sky looked like some surrealistic painting by Hieronymus Bosch," said Hell's Angels radio gunner Ben Smith. "There was a pall of smoke as thick as a forest fire. . . . Trailing long plumes of smoke, planes were falling, bombers and fighters alike. Parachutes dotted the weird landscape like random wildflowers." While other men turned to prayer to help get them through the flak fields, Ben Smith found that swearing—"a steady stream of blue language"—did the trick. Smith found it impossible to find solace in a God that sent good men to their deaths in flaming planes.

Planes hit by flak had a better chance of making it back to base than ones roughed up by fighters, but that brought the carnage closer to home, increasing crew anxiety. Some bombers landed with 200 to 300 holes in them and with crewmembers in worse shape than their planes: arms and kneecaps sheared off, eyes blown out of their sockets, torsos torn open so widely that flight surgeons could see the dead men's lungs. With the decline of the Luftwaffe, the percentage of bombers lost on raids dropped, but men still died in big bunches. "Every time we came back from a rough mission," Bert Stiles wrote, "we had to shake up the line-up of [our softball team], and twice we had to find a whole new infield."

Flak was insidious; it reduced men to a state of complete helplessness—passive stress, Air Force physicians called it. In frustration, gunners would fire at the flak bursts. No one thought they were crazy.

Crew loyalty was the single most important reason for the low incidence of breakdowns in air combat. But it was harder for some crews to bond when they faced flak rather than fighters. The crisis of combat failed to bring Bert Stiles's crew together, as he had hoped it would. "In the old days before fighter cover . . . [crews] had to know each other, and rely on each other, and bring each other through," Stiles wrote. All the men had to work together, spotting the fighters, calling out their positions for the gunners. "Now it was mostly a matter of luck."

Some men were still flying that summer who had known what it was like back in '43. One of them was S. Sgt. Eugene "Wing Ding" Carson, who had been a tail gunner in the 388th Bomb Group when the fighter war was at its hottest. Carson had flown what he thought was his final mission in the late winter of 1944, but after he returned to Mt. Pocono, Pennsylvania, and was reassigned as a gunnery instructor, he talked his way into a second combat tour with a new outfit, the 92nd Bomb Group. He was back in the war because he had learned that his twin brother, John, serving with the Fifteenth

Air Force, had been shot down over Athens and was reported dead. Wing Ding refused to believe this; he wanted to go back to Europe and find out what had happened to John.

Even with the Luftwaffe derailed, Carson watched the spirits of the crews sink again in the summer of 1944, after reaching a high point around D-Day. The flak had a lot to do with it, but so did fatigue. Although the weather over Germany was unusually pernicious that summer, the Eighth flew almost every day—twenty-eight days in June, twenty-seven in July, twenty-three in August—a pitiless pace. In those three months the Eighth lost 1,022 heavy bombers, approximately half its operational strength, along with 665 fighter planes of the 900 it had constantly on hand. Even at the reduced loss rate of 1.5 percent per sortie for thirty heavy bombing missions, compared to the 3.6 percent rate in April, an airman still stood more than a one-in-three chance of being killed or captured before his tour ended. The only consolation was that more frequent missions put more men closer to going home. The men did, however, receive some relief in late August, when training schools in the States were finally able to provide two crews for each bomber.

This was no consolation for airmen like Ben Smith, who felt, on most days, more dead than alive. The light-spirited Georgia boy had become, in a matter of months, "cynical, irreligious and hard as nails." No longer could he think of home and family; he even stopped writing to his folks, ignoring their pleading letters for news from him. "I had thoroughly desensitized myself," he recalled. "I had taught myself not to feel anything at all. . . . I had grown a crust, and getting rid of it was not easy."

Visitors to the bases noticed that there was something wrong with these boys. Most of them were "quiet, edgy, morose." And many of them drank tremendously and lived only for the day; they lacked the sweeping horizons and large dreams of most boys their age. The replacements arrived excited and eager to perform, but that usually lasted less than a week. Soon they, too, had that "look."

One evening, Ben Smith joined a volleyball game in progress. It was the strangest thing he had ever experienced. No one laughed, no one shouted, no one made a sound. "The entire game was played in silence."

On the oil runs to Merseburg, the bombing seemed as random as the game of life and death in the exploding shrapnel. How could you destroy a target you could not see? The sky over Leuna was so dark from flak, German smoke pots, and exploding oil tanks that "we had no idea how close our bombs came to the target," Tom Landry recalled. Postwar Air Force studies would show that the two most difficult industrial targets to hit in the European Theater of Operations were the two largest: synthetic oil plants and oil refineries. Only 29 percent of the bombs aimed at Leuna on clear days landed inside the plant gates; on radar raids the number dropped to 5.1 percent. One in seven of the bombs failed to explode, mostly because of bad fuses, and one in ten fell on decoy installations or on open ground. Accuracy was compromised by bad weather, human and mechanical error, and stiff enemy defenses—more heavy guns than were used to protect cities like Munich and Frankfurt. On many missions, a skyful of bombers failed to kill or injure a single worker in a mammoth oil plant. After the first raid on Leuna killed 126 workers, plant managers built more and stronger air raid shelters. In twenty-one subsequent raids, only 175 additional workers were killed.

Plant equipment was even better protected than plant workers. Storage tanks were lined with reinforced concrete, and compressors and other vital moving machinery were protected by ingeniously constructed blast walls that were impervious to the 250-to-300-pound bombs favored by the Americans. On even the most successful missions, only 1 to 2 percent of American bombs fell on essential plant machinery. These lucky hits did almost no damage.

The RAF visited Leuna less frequently than the Eighth but caused more destruction to storage tanks and major structures with 2,000- and 4,000-pound bombs capable of penetrating blast walls. American bomb experts continued to insist that it was more effective to use lighter bombs in greater numbers than to drop the big "cookies" favored by Bomber Harris. This miscalculation cost lives. American aircrews had to repeatedly return to the same target in order to destroy it, a practice that would have horrified Curtis LeMay, who was now in the Far East commanding crews flying the new B-29 Superfortresses.

Dropping lighter bombs also made the work of German firefighting crews easier. The fires were less intense and didn't last as long, and Leuna's fire-fighting force of 5,000 men and women had little trouble putting them out. Repairs were more difficult, but at the beginning of the bombing, manageable. After the first American raids on the oil plants, Speer appointed Edmund Geilenberg, his trusted deputy, to a newly created post, commissioner general for emergency measures. His instructions could not have been more explicit. The "successful prosecution of the war," he was told, depended upon the "the reconstruction of these plants." Geilenberg used his dictatorial powers over labor requisition to rush repair crews to stricken plants. In Berlin, the word was "everything for oil." But in pulling workers from the aircraft and munitions industry, along with 7,000 engineers from the armed forces, he weakened other parts of the German war machine. By the late fall of 1944, Geilenberg had assembled a labor army of 350,000 just for oil repairs. In all, Germany had almost 1.5 million persons assigned to air raid defense and repairs, a diversion of manpower that had a grievous impact on war production.

For most of the summer, a combination of foul weather and other bombing priorities prevented the Eighth Air Force from conducting frequent follow-up raids on oil facilities. This gave Geilenberg time to get the plants back into production, if only at a fraction of their former capacity. Working at a furious pace and under extreme discipline, Geilenberg's crews were able to restore smaller hydrogenation plants to almost full production in four to six weeks. This usually gave the plant a two-week period of production before the next air strike and the next cycle of repairs.

Later in the summer, air attacks were timed to coincide with the resumption of production, which was learned by more frequent air reconnaissance. Air Force operations officers made another correction. To adjust for bombing inaccuracy, the Eighth began saturating the plants with explosives, hoping for a few fortunate hits.

This was the big breakthrough. This was how the German oil industry was eventually disabled for good: by relentless carpet bombing that caused simultaneous damage to a number of plants. One plant after another would be mortally wounded. But a plant would be wounded not by a single blow to one of its vital organs—its gas compressors or gas purification plants—but by successive attacks on its electrical grid—its nervous system—and on its gas and water mains—its veins and arteries—parts of the interconnected plant organism without which it could not function.

It was a race, as Speer put it, between "concrete" and "bombs." By the end of the summer, the steadily accumulating effects of bomb damage began to overwhelm the repair forces, keeping down the average monthly output to 9 percent of plant capacity. And the effect on chemical products "was just as bad," Speer said after the war. Bombing raids were taking "such a toll [on] the piping systems in the chemical plants," Speer reported, "that direct hits were no longer required to do extensive damage. Merely the shock of bombs exploding in the vicinity caused leaks everywhere. Repairs were almost impossible." The result was a slow-paced slaughter of the plants. An Air Force created for precision bombing won its greatest victory by carpet bombing.

Victory in the Battle of Leuna would cost the Eighth Air Force 1,280 airmen. Although Leuna would experience a brief revival in the early autumn, the summer attacks damaged the plant irretrievably. A strangulating Allied naval blockade had helped bring down Germany in World War I. A quarter of a century later, Allied bombers imposed an aerial oil blockage on Germany, one that eventually finished off the already diminished Luftwaffe, and seriously curtailed the mobility of the army. After June 1944, German production of aviation fuel for the remainder of the war was 197,000 tons, little more than a month's supply in the period before the raids. And by September, oil imports from Romania had been stopped.

In raids that cost it 230 heavy bombers, the Fifteenth Air Force, aided by the RAF, had reduced the output of the main Ploesti fields by 90 percent by the time the Red Army occupied the smoking ruins of the oil monolith on August 30, 1944. In these raids from primitive bases in southern Italy, the Fifteenth suffered a far higher loss rate than the Eighth throughout the summer of 1944.

The heroism of the crews of the Fifteenth Air Force received only back-page coverage in the American press. The Eighth, the darling of news reporters from the big papers stationed in London, captured the headlines. This lead the airmen of the Fifteenth to compose a ditty, sung to the tune of "As Time Goes By":

> *It's still the same old story,*
> *The Eighth gets all the glory,*
> *While we go out to die.*
> *The fundamental things apply,*
> *As flak goes by.*

Auschwitz

That summer, the Fifteenth Air Force was also pounding oil targets in southern Poland. On July 7, it attacked Blechhammer, a petroleum facility 40 miles northwest of Auschwitz, and on August 20, it made the first of three raids on the I. G. Farben synthetic oil and rubber plant near Monowitz, a prison camp that supplied the Farben works with slave labor. Monowitz-Buna, as it was called, was part of the enormous Auschwitz concentration camp complex and was located less than five miles from the camp's main murder mill, Auschwitz II, or Birkenau, site of the gas chambers and crematoria. "It was the practice to brief bomber groups to steer clear of prisoner-of-war and concentration camps," recalled Milt Groban, a radar navigator-bombardier on the August 20th mission. Air Force target selection officers did not want their crews to kill or injure innocent soldiers and citizens held captive by the Nazis.

Neither Groban nor anyone else on that August mission knew that Auschwitz was Hitler's most notorious extermination camp. Nor did the crews know that Jewish leaders and resistance groups in Europe were at that time pressuring the governments of Great Britain and the United States to bomb the murder machinery at Birkenau. Had this been done, and had thousands of prisoners been killed, it would have been one of the great moral controversies of the war. As it was, the eventual decision not to bomb Birkenau sparked a heated public debate that shows no signs of abating.

In May 1944, Nazi leaders in Hungary, led by Adolf Eichmann, head of the "Jewish section" of the SS, began to round up and ship to Auschwitz the entire Jewish population of the country. The Nazis had already murdered over five million European Jews, and Auschwitz was one of only two killing camps that remained in operation in Poland. Information about the Hungarian deportations, along with the summary of a detailed report of conditions inside Auschwitz compiled by two recent escapees, reached London and Washington in June and early July. This led Jewish and resistance groups with offices in London to implore the British government to bomb the rail connections between Hungary and Auschwitz, along with the crematoria and gas chambers at Birkenau.

By the first week of July, 434,000 Hungarian Jews had been sent to Auschwitz and nearly 90% of them had been murdered. An aroused Churchill, who considered Hitler's Final Solution "the greatest and most horrible crime ever committed in the whole history of the world," instructed his Air Staff to look into the feasibility of bombing the gas chambers. Bombing the railway lines from Budapest to Auschwitz would have little effect, for they could be quickly repaired, but bombing the camp itself, an extreme measure, might persuade the puppet government in Hungary to end the mass deportations. On July 15, after a less than systematic study, the secretary of state for air, Archibald Sinclair, reported that the distance was "too great for the attack to be carried out at night." But Sinclair proposed "to have the proposition put to the Americans . . . to see if they are prepared to try." He added, however, that he was "very doubtful indeed whether, when they have examined it, the Americans will think it possible."

He was right. Appeals from European underground groups to bomb the camp and the rail lines leading to it had already been conveyed to the American War Department by representatives in Switzerland of the War

Refugee Board, established by Roosevelt to aid Jewish victims of the Nazis. Assistant Secretary of War John J. McCloy, in charge of relations between the civilian community and the American military, maintained that bombing the camp would involve a "diversion of considerable air support essential to the success of our forces now engaged in decisive operations." McCloy's response was in line with official War Department policy "that the most effective relief which can be given victims of enemy persecution is to insure the speedy defeat of the Axis." Over 200,000 British and American soldiers and airmen were in German prison camps, yet no plans had been made to liberate them. The official American policy was that all rescue operations should be "the direct result of military operations conducted with the objective of defeating the armed forces of the enemy."

McCloy claimed then and later that summer that a mission to Auschwitz would be an Eighth Air Force operation, a highly risky "round trip flight unescorted of approximately 2,000 miles over enemy territory." He was wrong about this. The actual distance was 1,540 miles and fighter planes would have escorted the bombers to the target. McCloy failed to mention that the Fifteenth Air Force had begun conducting systematic bombing operations in Upper Silesia, in the near vicinity of Auschwitz. Nor did he note, or perhaps he did not know, that on August 2, the day that Carl Spaatz first heard about the request to bomb the camp from Britain's deputy chief of air staff, Norman H. Bottomley, he had been "most sympathetic."

The Eighth Air Force could conceivably have carried out the mission from newly operational bases within easy range of Auschwitz. That June it had begun to fly "shuttle missions" to the Soviet Union, under the code name Frantic. Leaving from England, bombers hit targets deep inside the Reich and, instead of returning home, proceeded to airfields provided by Stalin near Kiev, in the Ukraine. From there they were able to strike targets in Eastern Europe and fly south to Italy and then, after rest and refueling, back to England, conducting bombing operations on every leg of the journey. But Stalin had tight control over what the Fortresses on Operation Frantic bombed, and he made sure that they concentrated on targets that directly aided the Red Army's summer offensive. These bases were also vulnerable to Luftwaffe attacks, for Soviet air defenses in the area were not vigilant. On the night of June 21, Luftwaffe bombers illuminated the airfield at Poltava, Russia, with flares and dropped 110 tons of bombs, destroying or damaging 69 of the 114 Fortresses and igniting the enormous stocks of aviation fuel the Americans had previously brought into Russia. The Luftwaffe returned on the following night and hit the other two Frantic bases. So if a mission had been approved to Auschwitz, Spaatz would have called on the heavies of the Fifteenth Air Force, flying from the risk-free fields in Foggia Italy, 640 miles from the camp.

A formation of heavies from the Fifteenth would have had no trouble reaching Auschwitz, but could it have accomplished its objective without a prohibitive loss of aircrew or prisoners? New research by airpower historians familiar with bombing operations in Europe indicates that the camp's killing machinery could have been put out of operation, although perhaps not with one decisive blow. It may have taken up to four separate missions to destroy the four heavily constructed crematoria and gas chambers. And the bombers would have needed clear skies to have had any hope of hitting their targets without inadvertently bombing the prisoners' barracks, which were located dangerously close to the gas chambers. Like almost all other raids on industrial targets—and this was an industrial target, a murder mill for creating and then disposing of corpses—these strikes, as Air Force historian Richard G. Davis points out, would have had to be spread out over a number of weeks in order to confuse enemy defenses, assess bomb damage by photoreconnaissance, and adjust mission planning to take into consideration changes in enemy defenses. If the raids had begun in July 1944—the earliest feasible time they could have begun because of Allied airpower's complete commitment to the Normandy invasion and the time it would have taken for the American government to reach a decision and have its airmen develop a plan of attack—the Fifteenth would not have been able to complete the job until sometime in September. By then, all the Hungarian Jews at Auschwitz had been murdered. Camp officials, however, continued to import and slaughter Jews from all over Europe until Himmler ordered Auschwitz's gassing machinery dismantled in November, to prevent it from being discovered by the Red Army. So the bombing still might have saved lives.

American fliers would have been lost in these operations, for the I. G. Farben plant had antiaircraft guns capable of reaching planes flying over Auschwitz. But the greatest risk would have been to the prisoners. That summer the Fifteenth Air Force had a commendable accuracy record by the standards of the time. Nonetheless, high-altitude bombing, as we know, was imprecise. Even a slight error by a lead bombardier could have been catastrophic. And after the first raid, the SS would likely have moved prisoners closer to, or even inside the crematoria and gas chambers, to discourage further bombing. And who can claim with certainty that if the gas chambers had been destroyed the SS would not have been able to rebuild them, using slave labor right there in the camp, or perhaps that the Nazis might have resorted to killing the prisoners by other means. Up to 1.5 million Jews had been murdered by rifle squads before the widespread use of gas chambers. Would the Nazis have stopped the killing because of a few bombing raids?

These are unanswerable questions. All that can be said with certainty is that bombing Auschwitz would have been a difficult and dangerous operation, with lives of airmen and inmates at risk. Nonetheless, it could have been done.

But should it have been done? Was such a raid advisable, in the larger context of the war? The Hungarian Jews were sent to their deaths at a pivotal moment in the war for the Western Allies: during the planning and execution of operation Overlord, the battle to liberate France, the attacks on V-weapon sites, and the beginning of the hugely important oil offensive. At the time, it was believed that these operations held the promise of ending the war by the opening of winter. Was it prudent at that time to divert American heavy bombers from their main military objectives? McCloy thought not, nor did Spaatz's second in command, Frederick Anderson. But by historian Richard Davis's calculations, four missions flown against Auschwitz would have diverted only about 7 percent of the Fifteenth's bombers from the oil offensive. And when air commanders were ordered that September to make a similar "diversion" from strategic bombing, a mission of mercy they considered both "costly and hopeless," they saluted and obeyed.

On August 1, 1944, partisan forces in Warsaw, encouraged by Russian radio to believe the Red Army's furious summer offensive would carry across the Vistula to their city, rose against their Nazi occupiers. But meeting stiff resistance, the Russians halted their offensive in the suburbs of Warsaw, on the east bank of the Vistula, and Stalin did not renew it for another six months. Meanwhile, for sixty days the Poles waged an unequal conflict, fighting house to house, mostly with grenades and Molotov cocktails, against heavily reinforced SS troops. Churchill, overriding the strenuous objections of his air commanders, ordered an airdrop of food and guns. The missions were flown by volunteers, many of them Poles, from British bases in Italy, not far from Foggia, and the crews suffered heavy losses. The prime minister pressured a wavering Roosevelt to support the supply drop, and then persuaded Stalin to allow American bombers that had been designated to drop supplies into Warsaw to land at Frantic bases in the Ukraine. On the morning of September 18, a formation of 107 Fortresses left England and dropped over 1,200 containers of food, weapons, and medical supplies into the stricken city. But with the Nazis in control of most of Warsaw, over three-quarters of the containers fell into their hands. The mission was tremendously important for Polish morale, however, and a strong sign of moral concern for their impossible plight.

Roosevelt ordered another Frantic airlift, but on October 2, Stalin withdrew permission for Americans to use Frantic bases to support a rebellion he considered dangerous to his own interests, an uprising led by anticommunist forces tied to the Polish government-in-exile in London. A few days later the Polish rebellion was crushed. There was little left of Warsaw when the Russians entered it in January 1945.

Stalin could also have used his tactical air force to bomb Auschwitz, which was only 100 miles from Soviet front lines in early August 1944, a fact largely ignored in the debate over the bombing of Auschwitz. But the Great Patriotic War was fought to save Russia, not the Jews.

When the Red Army entered Warsaw in January it was a dead city; and when it arrived at Auschwitz that same month its soldiers found only 8,000 or so starving, frostbitten survivors.

Why were the Warsaw Poles supported, and not the Jews at Auschwitz? At the time, the Poles had what the Jews did not, a government in London, one with influence on Churchill. While anti-Semitism in the government bureaucracies of Britain and the United States surely figured in the decision not to push the issue of the bombing with the urgency it deserved, the reason the Poles got their airlift was because they had more political clout than the Jews. As a survivor of Auschwitz recalled, "It was not that the Jews didn't matter; they didn't matter enough." If the Dutch had been marked for slaughter, or if it had been learned that thousands of Allied airmen were being exterminated at Auschwitz, would Britain and America have failed to act with resolve?

In the summer of 1944 bombing had saved lives. On July 2, Spaatz had ordered a massive raid on military targets in the greater Budapest area, raids totally unconnected with the deportations. Many of the bombs fell into the city at the very moment that the Allies, neutral Sweden, and the Vatican were bringing heavy diplomatic pressure on the Hungarian government to end the massacres then taking place. Roosevelt himself issued strongly worded threats to the Hungarian government and appealed to the Hungarian people to help Jews escape and "record the evidence" of racial crimes for later retribution. The puppet government, which was already deeply divided about cooperating with the SS, saw the bombing, erroneously, as the first of a possible series of reprisal raids on Budapest. On July 7, Adm. Miklós Horthy, the Hungarian regent, stood up to Eichmann and ordered an end to the deportations, saving the lives of some 300,000 Jews still in country.

With Auschwitz, however, there was the sensitive issue of killing innocents. The writer and Auschwitz survivor Elie Wiesel wrote that when the camp was hit by stray American bombs on September 13, 1944 "we were not afraid. . . . Every bomb that fell filled us with joy." But other survivors said they owe their lives to the Allied decision not to bomb.

What about the bomber boys? It would be hard to find many veterans of the Eighth and Fifteenth Air Forces who believe that Auschwitz should have been bombed. "We would only have been helping Hitler," said Eighth Air Force navigator Louis Loevsky. Rosie Rosenthal agreed. After participating in Cobra, when American soldiers died under American bombs, he knew that a raid on Auschwitz could have been an even greater calamity. Milt Groban, an observant Jew, said he would have considered himself a traitor to his people had he dropped bombs on Birkenau, "killing some now to save some later."

The most unfortunate thing for America's moral reputation is not that Auschwitz was not bombed—people of conscience are on both sides of the issue—but that the War Department never asked the Air Force to study the feasibility of the operation. The question of whether it was possible for the Americans to bomb Auschwitz successfully was left, instead, to historians to ponder and debate years later, when lives were no longer at stake.

When on October 3, the head of the War Refugee Board, John W. Pehle, passed along another recommendation that Auschwitz be bombed, this one from the Polish government-in-exile, General Spaatz was informed by cable, but not instructed to take action. This was the only time the War Department sent a proposal to bomb Auschwitz to an Air Force official in the European Theater. Gen. Frederick Anderson cautioned Spaatz to "give no encouragement" to the project. The bombing, he said, would not improve the condition of the prisoners and "there is also the possibility of some of the bombs landing on the prisoners. . . . In that event the Germans would be provided with a fine alibi for any wholesale massacre that they might perpetrate." There is no record of Spaatz's reply, but he was not the one to make the decision. "The President could do it. No one else could," McCloy said in an interview with the *Washington Post* in 1983. And there is no reliable record that anyone close to Roosevelt, including McCloy, ever brought the bombing issue to his attention. If someone had reached the president with the idea, he surely would have opposed it. His overriding objective in Europe was to defeat Hitler and bring the boys home. "It was like the Civil War," said Eighth Air Force navigator Paul Slawter. "Winning was more important to Lincoln than anything else. When slaves were freed, it was almost always in the course of strategically important military operations in enemy territory. And that's how the Nazi killing camps were found and the survivors freed."

Roosevelt may have been right, but bombing Auschwitz could conceivably have saved thousands of lives and would have sent a resounding message from America that the destruction of the Jews would not go ignored or unpunished.

The Fatal Trap

Carl Spaatz left no record of how he felt about the bombing of Auschwitz. His overwhelming concern that summer was his oil offensive, which ULTRA intercepts indicated was achieving immense results. That August, Albert Speer admitted to the Japanese ambassador to Berlin that "for the first time, *wehrwirtshaftlich* [war economy] raids, which might deal a really fatal blow to Germany, had begun." Shortages began cropping up everywhere in the Reich, disrupting military operations against the two gigantic land forces converging on Germany from east and west. That August, the German army had abandoned fuel-starved tanks and motor vehicles all over France in its retreat from the Falaise Pocket, and the Luftwaffe was forced to close down most of its training schools. Air cadets were sent to the infantry and instructors went on active duty at fields close to the oil plants. The new pilots would be unequal opponents for American fighter jockeys flying Mustangs powered by 100-octane gasoline, fuel that gave their already superior planes additional range and acceleration. Ten years earlier, Jimmy Doolittle had persuaded his employer, Shell Oil, to begin manufacturing the new, experimental 100-octane gasoline and had pressured the military to procure airplane engines that used it.

"This summer is . . . like a nightmare from which there is no awakening," Luftwaffe pilot Heinz Knoke wrote in his diary. On nearly every mission his brave squadron lost five pilots. For his air commanders to order "battered old crates" to meet thundering formations of American fighters was, he grimly concluded, "nothing less than murder!"

Knoke and his comrades were fighting not just the Allied air forces, but the world's only industrial and oil superpower, the United States of America, a nation that produced more oil than all the other countries on earth combined. From Pearl Harbor until the end of the war, the Allied nations consumed almost seven billion barrels of oil. More than six billion of that came from America, along with 90 percent of the world's 100-octane gasoline. "This is a war of engines and octanes," Josef Stalin offered a toast at a banquet in Churchill's honor. "I drink to the American auto industry and the American oil industry."

With the fuel shortage "unbearable," in Adolf Galland's words, the German air force was caught in a fatal trap. Forced to defend the oil plants that supplied its fuel, it lacked the fuel to defend them adequately.

The countries at war with Germany and Japan controlled 90 percent of the world's natural oil output; the Axis states controlled 3 percent of the output. It was these disparities that had driven Germany and Japan to wars of conquest in Russia and Southeast Asia: to take from others what they lacked. When they both ran desperately low on oil—Japan as a result of an Allied naval blockade and Germany as a result of an Allied aerial blockade—they could not win the world war they had begun.

For Germany, this became apparent when the fuel shortages produced by the summer bombing began to directly affect the army. From July 1944 to the end of the war, the Wehrmacht was denied a sufficient flow of both fuel and ammunition. By early September 1944, supplies of methanol—the main constituent of hexogen, an extremely powerful explosive—had dropped drastically, and so had nitric acid and synthetic rubber production. In order to stretch dwindling supplies of explosives, finished shell cases containing 20 percent rock salt were being shipped to the front. The accelerated Allied bombing program was hurting the German economy in other ways as well. By this point in the war, up to one-third of German artillery production, one-third of the output of the optical industry, and two-thirds of the production of radar and signals equipment was devoted to antiaircraft defenses, and these defenses consumed one-fifth of all ammunition produced. In addition, approximately two million workers were involved in antiaircraft defense, either at the guns or in work crews that repaired bomb damage to factories and cities. "The combined effects of direct destruction and the diversion of resources denied German forces approximately half their battle-front weapons and equipment in 1944," concluded historian Richard Overy.

In trying to protect the industries that produced the oil and explosives the Wehrmacht depended upon to survive and fight, Speer was forced to deprive it of manpower and equipment it badly needed. Here was another fatal trap.

In the summer of 1944, the Luftwaffe lost an average of 300 aircraft per week, most of them on the Eastern and Western fronts. But unknown to the Allies, new units were being formed, and Speer and Galland had reason to believe they would be used not at the fronts, but over the oil plants. Speer had pushed hard for this new policy in his August report to the führer on the state of the oil industry. "If the attacks on the chemical industry continue in the same strength and with the same precision in September as in August the output of the chemical industry will drop still further and the last stocks will be consumed.

"This means that those materials which are necessary for the continuation of a modern war will be lacking in the most important fields. . . .

"There remains only one possibility, and this only with a large amount of luck," he told Hitler. Two things would have to occur almost simultaneously: bad weather would have to set in over Europe for at least three weeks, and the Luftwaffe would have to use that "breathing space" to strengthen itself to the point where it was able "to inflict heavier losses on the enemy and to hinder the compact carpet bombardments by splitting up the bomber formations.

"The Luftwaffe must be ready for this last great strike by the middle of September at the latest. It must throw into this undertaking all its best personnel, its flying instructors and its most successful fighter pilots. . . .

"If this course is taken it will, if successful, mean the beginning of a new air force, or it will mean the end of the German air force."

That fall, Speer got the bad weather he needed to repair some vital oil plants and increase the production of aviation gas for the new Luftwaffe fighter fleet—over 3,000 aircraft—he had been building at his hidden production plants, many of them underground. And Speer and Galland believed they had persuaded Hitler to commit this fighter arm to the defense of the homeland.

But before the Eighth Air Force met the rearmed Luftwaffe in the skies over Germany, it was forced to address what appeared to be a severe morale problem within its own ranks. That summer, Hap Arnold had begun receiving reports that a disturbing number of his bomber crews were landing in the neutral countries of Switzerland and Sweden, not because their planes were in trouble and could not make it home, but because the airmen wanted release from the war.

CHAPTER TWELVE

Prisoners of the Swiss

The Swiss government's holding of American flyers as
hostages and their reason for doing so was one of the best
kept secrets of World War II.

DONALD ARTHUR WATERS,
PILOT, THE BLOODY HUNDREDTH

Switzerland, March 18, 1944

It was a hazy day with broken cloud cover as *Hell's Kitchen,* a B-24 Liberator of the 44th Bomb Group, headed east toward Lake Constance, part of the border between Germany and neutral Switzerland. *Hell's Kitchen* was in trouble. Hit by exploding flak over Friedrichshafen, on the enemy side of the lake, it was down to two engines, with gas gushing from the left wing tanks. The plane was a thousand miles from East Anglia and had no chance of making it there. Dropping out of formation, Lt. George D. Telford told his crew he was going to try to land the plane somewhere in Switzerland.

That morning at the squadron briefing, Telford had been told that if his plane was fatally damaged over the target he could fly toward Swiss airspace and request permission to land. The only thing he knew about Switzerland was that other crews from his bomb division had landed there and never returned.

As *Hell's Kitchen* approached the Swiss border, nineteen-year-old flight engineer Daniel Culler, flying his twenty-fifth and final mission, spotted four Me 109s closing in on them. Sergeant Culler was scared. His gun turret was not functioning properly and he hated aerial combat. A small-town Indiana boy, he was raised as a pacifist by his widowed mother, a devout Quaker. But after Pearl Harbor he had decided that his duty to his country preceded his vow of nonviolence and persuaded his anguished mother to sign his enlistment papers. He had needed her signature because he was not yet eighteen. Up to then, the only creature he had killed was a rabbit he shot to put food on his "meat-starved family's table." Culler was so sensitive about taking lives that he sometimes cried when *Hell's Kitchen*'s bombs were released. "At those times I never saw an enemy, but a fellow human being." Yet he had flown and fought courageously, feeling morally obligated "to fight oppression."

As he and his fellow gunners prepared to open up on the fighters, Lieutenant Telford called out over the intercom that they had Swiss markings—two white crosses—on their sides. They were apparently German-built planes flown by Swiss pilots. Everyone was to hold fire, but stay at the ready. An English-speaking pilot made radio contact with *Hell's Kitchen* and ordered Telford to lower the landing gear or else his plane would be shot down. At that point, the bombardier destroyed the top secret Norden bombsight and the radio operator disabled the radio and tore up the codebook. Dan Culler threw the pieces out the waist window and began devising a plan to set the plane on fire as soon as it landed. Knowing next to nothing about the Swiss, but having heard a rumor that they traded damaged Allied planes to the Germans for fighter aircraft, he wanted to make sure that *Hell's Kitchen* would not end up in enemy hands.

The moment *Hell's Kitchen* touched down at Dubendorf, just outside Geneva, Culler went to the rear of the plane and hid above the wing section near the spot where the large fuel lines converged and were exposed. He planned to cut the lines with a rusty pocketknife, switch on the fuel pump, and set the bomber on fire with a flare gun as soon as the rest of the crew was out of harm's way. As he began cutting the largest hose, and the gas started to spray all over him, he noticed that the tanks on the damaged wing had been completely ruptured by the plane's jarring landing. The entire wing was saturated with gasoline. All he had to do was fire a flare into the vapors. After the rest of the crew had left the plane from the open doors of the bomb bay, Culler walked out onto the catwalk in the bomb bay and prepared to jump from the plane and fire the pistol. Just then a strong hand grabbed hold of one of his feet and pulled him to the ground. Culler had an iron grip on the flare gun and was ready to fire when someone else dropped his full body weight on the arm holding the gun and tore it from his hand.

Culler saw that the men holding him down were Swiss soldiers, and that they had probably saved his life. "I was covered with gasoline. If the gun had gone off, not only would the plane have been blown to bits, but I would have turned into a human torch. With a Swiss rifle pointed to my head and three soldiers holding me down, I looked around and saw Swiss guards with rifles pointed at all of us. It didn't look like a friendly place to me."

Fifteen other American bombers landed safely or crash-landed in Switzerland that day. Culler saw several of the bombers that came into Dubendorf after *Hell's Kitchen,* and all of them, he later recalled, "were in bad shape." Although he did not know it, some of them had been fired on by Swiss pilots and flak gunners. This was not unusual. Over the course of the war, the Swiss would kill at least twenty RAF and sixteen American airmen and injure a large number of others. In all, the Swiss attacked at least twenty-one of the 168 American bombers that intentionally landed in the country, even though most of them showed unmistakable signs of combat damage or distress. By the end of the summer of 1944, over a thousand American fliers would be in Swiss hands, held under military guard and forbidden from leaving the country for the duration of the war. Nearly a thousand more would be interned in neutral Sweden. The story of these fliers is one of the darker secrets of World War II.

The Nazi radio propagandist William Joyce—known to British listeners as "Lord Haw-Haw," due to his accent—claimed that American bomber boys were landing in Sweden and Switzerland with their golf clubs and skis. "We had heard tales of swanky resort hotels, drinking fine wines, eating good food, and dating bad girls," American airman Leroy Newby recalled his wartime impressions of Switzerland. The Swiss government confirmed that the downed airmen were being held in resort hotels, and rumors flew that many planes were landing with nary a scratch on their paintwork. In August 1944, *Collier's* magazine ran a lavish photo spread showing beaming American flyboys skiing, biking, and drinking champagne at Stockholm nightspots with ravishing Swedish blondes.

Alarm bells began going off at Air Force headquarters in Washington when reports came in that in July alone forty-five American bombers and one Mustang had found refuge in Switzerland. Gen. Hap Arnold had been fuming about American landings in neutral countries since the previous March and April, at the height of the Eighth Air Force's climactic battle with the Luftwaffe. Now he sent a steaming message to Tooey Spaatz claiming he had substantial evidence that large numbers of American bombers had landed in neutral countries "without indication of serious battle damage or mechanical failure, or shortage of fuel." There was also, he charged, confirmation from American diplomatic personnel in Sweden who had interviewed interned crews that "the landings were intentional evasions of further combat service."

It took a lot to unhinge the even-tempered Carl Spaatz, but this letter did it. In language that bordered on insubordination, he told Arnold that both he and Ira Eaker, head of Allied air operations in the Mediterranean Theater, "resent the implication that these crews are cowards, are low in morale or lack the will to fight. Such is a base slander against the most courageous group of fighting men in this war."

Arnold—not known for his equanimity—was overreacting. In his memo to Spaatz, he had inflated the amount of evidence he had in front of him from diplomatic personnel in Sweden. His suspicions were based on a single letter from the American consul in Göteborg, William W. Corcoran, a notoriously erratic man. Corcoran accused American airmen interned in that country of "a complete lack of patriotism" and an eagerness to avoid additional military service "by any means possible." These reckless charges had fueled Arnold's concern that the recent landings in neutral countries were a symptom of a greater problem: a dangerous deterioration in crew morale brought on by fatigue and heavy losses. Even before he had written Spaatz, Arnold had set in motion three independent investigations: two of them to interview interned crews and examine American aircraft being held by the Swedes and the Swiss; the other, conducted by a member of headquarters staff, to study combat crew morale in the entire European Theater of Operations.

While these investigations were going forward that August, Arnold received a communiqué from Brig. Gen. Barnwell Rhett Legge, the military attaché at the U.S. legation in Bern, that should have tipped him off about the real situation in Switzerland. Legge claimed that he was having problems trying to dissuade the airmen that Arnold accused of trying to sit out the war in Switzerland from escaping in droves from their "benevolent hosts" and returning, at great personal risk, to England with the help of the French Underground. Why were these airmen fleeing their supposedly comfortable confinement in Alpine resorts? And why was General Legge trying to stop them? These should have been the questions Arnold was asking.

Had Air Force investigators looked more closely into internment conditions in Switzerland, they *would* have found a festering morale crisis, although hardly the kind Arnold suspected. Of the 1,740 American airmen kept in Switzerland during the war, a number that includes both "internees" (1,516 of them) and evaders who landed in enemy territory and found their way into Switzerland, 947 tried to escape, some of them two and three times. By comparison, approximately 1,400 American bomber boys were interned in Sweden and although there are no official numbers, very few tried to escape. Getting back to England from Sweden would have been difficult, and they were well treated in the four camps set aside for them, all of them run by friendly English-speaking Swedish officers who provided the men with plenty of recreational facilities and periodic passes to Stockholm and other large cities. The Swedish government was under heavy diplomatic pressure from the United States for selling iron to Germany and hence hastened the repatriation of American fliers, which eliminated any need for the men to risk escape. And when a few impatient fliers did try to flee the country, Swedish officials, fearing American economic sanctions, were reluctant to stop them.

This was not the situation in Switzerland. Despite vigorous protests from Secretary of State Cordell Hull, the Swiss refused to begin repatriating American internees until the last few months of the war. The country's military police actively hunted down American fliers making for the border, shooting and wounding a number of them. Most of those who were apprehended were sentenced to indeterminate prison terms, with the compliance of General Legge, who was unofficially in charge of American military internees. Using the threat of court-martial, Legge warned American airmen not to escape. Escape attempts would alienate their hosts, Legge told Spaatz's headquarters in England, and slow down the negotiations he was secretly conducting for the airmen's release. But Legge was more concerned with appeasing the Swiss than with freeing the American internees, and when fellow Americans were caught escaping and imprisoned by the Swiss, he monitored their deplorable prison conditions with inexcusable indifference. In the last two years of the war, the "benevolent hosts" of the American airmen threw 187 of them into one of the most abhorrent prison compounds in Europe, a punishment camp run by a sadistic Nazi. One of these unfortunates was Daniel Culler.

Alpine Internment

Within an hour after touching down in Switzerland, Culler's crew and other American crews that landed at Dubendorf that afternoon were taken by armed guards to a large auditorium, where they were briefed by Swiss officials on the conditions of their confinement. They would be taken by train later that day, they were told, to a special camp in an isolated area in the center of the country where they would be quarantined for two weeks and then kept under guard for the remainder of the war. They would be granted liberties, but anyone leaving the confined area without permission would be hunted down and sent to a penitentiary camp. Swiss soldiers were under orders to fire at internees attempting to escape if they failed to heed a "Halt!" order. Since Switzerland was a nonbelligerent, the airmen were not considered either prisoners of war or evaders; having entered the country armed and willingly, they were classified as internees. Yet in almost every respect they were treated like prisoners of war, although they were denied many of the rights granted to POWs under the terms of the Geneva Accords.

Seeing an American general sitting on the stage next to Swiss officials conducting the briefing in the auditorium at Dubendorf must have encouraged the captured airmen. Surely this was a charade; they were expensively trained American warriors and their country had people here who would make sure they got back to their squadrons and into the fight again. But General Legge, a corpulent World War I cavalry officer who dressed in jodhpurs and knee-high leather riding boots, concluded the briefing with a stern warning. Men imprisoned for attempting to escape would have no appeal to either the American consulate or the American military attaché; they would be under Swiss law. The internees would be treated well and should exercise patience, said Legge. The war would be over soon and they would be repatriated. Listening intently, Daniel Culler was confused. The general's warning conflicted with instructions he had received back in England that captured airmen had a duty to try to escape and return to their units. "To my mind, even though they called us internees in a neutral country, the fact that they held us here at gunpoint made us prisoners," Culler wrote years later.

Sergeant Culler's crew was taken to the main American internment camp at Adelboden, a vacant summer resort thirty miles northeast of Lake Geneva. A single winding road led from the railroad depot at Frutigen to Adelboden. The camp commandant, a blond, blue-eyed officer who reminded Culler of every SS man he had seen in the movies, separated the officers from the enlisted men and assigned each group its quarters. The men were put up in stripped-down resort hotels, where they were kept under constant surveillance. They were treated well, although conditions were far from ideal. The entire country was under strict rationing. Hot water, a luxury in wartime Switzerland, was turned on once every ten days, and then for only a few hours. Without coal to heat their quarters in cold weather, the men ate their skimpy meals of black bread, potatoes, and watery soup dressed in their flight suits and gloves. Meat was served only once a week and was awful—usually blood sausage made from mountain goat. With their meager diets, over half the men developed ailments of the mouth and stomach, and medical and dental care was unavailable, except in extreme emergencies. Some men who had been wounded on their last combat mission had to wait months to be admitted to a hospital. Dan Culler landed in Switzerland with a severe case of frostbite and within days the skin on his feet began to turn black. He was told he would be treated the next time a Swiss army doctor came to Adelboden, but one never showed up. The Swiss, all the while, sent medical teams to assist the Wehrmacht on the Eastern Front.

The prevailing problem at Adelboden was boredom and the prevailing sport was drinking, often to excess. The men could purchase their own alcohol with the small stipends they received in lieu of flight pay from the American legation in Bern, and some of them stayed drunk for days at a time. Books and mail arrived from home and airmen were allowed to ski on the local slopes and walk into town unescorted, provided they were back in their quarters by dusk. Girls were scarce in tiny Frutigen but when word spread that young American aviators were filling the cafés, smartly dressed women from Bern and Zurich began frequenting the resort on weekends. "Many were married to officers," recalled a wartime resident, "but they would come to Adelboden alone and have an 'adventure.' They would meet these young pilots who seemed like they were from another world."

Although travel was far more restricted than it was for internees in Sweden, an airman on good behavior might receive a special pass to visit another town if he had a formal invitation from a Swiss family—perhaps the parents of an attractive girl he had met on the local ski slopes. But these high-spirited warriors were out for sex and companionship, not lasting ties. During the entire war, only two American internees married Swiss women. And after a while, boredom, spartan conditions, the growing proximity of Allied armies in France, and what General Legge described as "the call to return to battle," fed the urge to flee. The obstacles, however, were daunting.

Some of the men took hikes deep into the mountains, escorted by armed guards who acted as guides. It was a storybook landscape: church bells chiming every hour, glacial lakes sparkling like giant jewels in the midday sun, but some men came back so depressed that they had to retire to their rooms. Only a crack mountain climber stood a chance of escaping through the massive Alpine peaks that rose, like so many imprisoning walls, around the deep, pine-scented valley. And beyond the impassable ranges, in every direction, lay the Reich. "Ever since that experience in Switzerland, I've been of two minds about mountains," recalled airman Martin Andrews. "I find them beautiful, but also a little bit oppressive."

The guards told Culler that these mountains he loathed prevented their country from being overrun by the German army. They also told him that over 60 percent of the Swiss population was of German descent, and that many Swiss belonged to local Nazi groups and were not likely to assist an American on the run. These were only half-truths.

Swiss Neutrality

With its formidable Alpine front and an army of 435,000 troops, organized into spirited local militias, Switzerland would have been difficult to conquer. But Hitler had no need to subdue this Alpine redoubt; he got most of what he wanted from the Swiss by a combination of intimidation and ideological symmetry.

Most Swiss citizens supported the Allied cause and opposed a Nazi takeover of their country, yet there were at least forty fascist and superpatriotic societies in the country, some with cells and chapters in more than 150 communities, most in the predominantly German-speaking cantons. With the active support of SS head Heinrich Himmler and Propaganda Minister Joseph Goebbels, Berlin funneled money and ideas to many of these pro-Nazi organizations, all of which were aggressively anti-Semitic. The German legation in Bern openly supported a branch of the National Socialist German Workers Party, which boasted tens of thousands of committed followers. "Probably no other country in the whole of Europe," wrote historian Alan Morris Schom, "was so thoroughly infested with similar groups in proportion to its population and geographic area." Most of these organizations drew their membership from the working and lower-middle classes, but the semisecret Swiss Fatherland Association (Schweizerischer Vaterländischer Verband) was dominated by the powerful troika of political, business, and military leaders who ruled wartime Switzerland. (Today, copies of the organization's pro-Nazi, anti-Semitic publications have inexplicably disappeared from every library and scholarly repository in Switzerland.)

The leading members of the Fatherland Association were chiefly responsible for Switzerland's strong economic ties with Nazi Germany and fascist Italy. This relationship was sedulously cultivated by the collaborationist president of the Federal Council—the country's seven-person executive branch—Marcel Edouard Pilet-Golaz, but was rooted in Switzerland's extreme economic vulnerability: its dependence on imports for almost all its fuel and much of its food. Switzerland purchased coal and farm goods from Germany in return for steel. As a neutral, it had a legal right to trade with Germany and Italy, but international law forbade a neutral from supplying war goods almost exclusively to one belligerent nation. The Swiss contravened this decree. Walther Stampfli, a member of the Fatherland Association, organized Swiss industrial production to meet the needs of Hitler's Germany. The leading Swiss banks—Nazi Germany's bankers of choice—helped fund the Third Reich's weapons production, and Swiss industries churned out essential products for the German war machine, including machine tools, aircraft cannons, radio parts, military trucks, freight cars, chemicals, dyes, industrial diamonds, and ball bearings. The gigantic Oerlikon works, headed by Hitler-sympathizer Emil Buhrle, produced 120mm antiaircraft cannons for the Luftwaffe, and other Oerlikon armaments were in the arsenal of nearly every Wehrmacht unit. The Swiss also built armaments factories inside Germany, some of which employed slave labor, under SS direction. Dr. Max Huber, president of the International Red Cross, owned several of these plants in southern Germany. In 1942, over 97 percent of Swiss exports went to the Axis Powers or their collaborators.

Romanian oil was sent by sea to Italy and transshipped by rail across Switzerland to Germany, as were nickel, copper, and chrome from Turkey and the Balkans. There was also an active trade across Swiss territory between Italy and Germany. "Switzerland's rail system, and thus Switzerland itself, effectively belonged to the German Reich," wrote historian Cathryn J. Prince. And Nazi thugs deposited in Swiss bank vaults gold ripped from the teeth of concentration camp victims and artwork confiscated from the homes of prominent German Jews who had been shipped to death factories.

Switzerland did take in some 200,000 refugees during the war, approximately 28,000 of them Jews, but the Jewish Swiss community and other organizations were charged a head tax to support them. And the Swiss turned down tens of thousands of Jews seeking refuge in their country; some were arrested and turned over to authorities in Germany and Vichy France. In 1938, Minister of Justice and Police Dr. Heinrich Rothmund suggested to German officials that German Jews have their passports stamped with a red letter "J" to aid Swiss border guards in identifying them.

In its defense, the wartime Swiss government explained to the Allied powers that it was the unwilling prisoner of geography. After the occupation of Vichy France in November 1942, the country was surrounded by the Axis Powers, the closest free nation was over a thousand miles away. Only extraordinary Allied diplomatic pressure and the realization that the Allies would win the war persuaded the government of this 700-year-old democracy to reverse its economic policy in February 1945 and stop the exportation of war-related products to the Third Reich. But in defiance of the Allied demands, the Swiss National Bank continued to receive convoys of looted gold from the Reichsbank. Not until a week before the end of the European war did the Swiss Federal Council outlaw all Nazi Party cells. "Finally in April 1945, the Swiss surrendered—only a week before General [Alfred] Jodl did," wrote diplomat Dean Acheson, later the U.S. Secretary of State under President Harry Truman.

Fearing reprisals or violations of its territorial integrity, the Swiss government permitted the Luftwaffe to set up a rest facility for its pilots at a fashionable hotel in Davos, a sylvan mountain resort. Distressed German fighter planes were also permitted to land on Swiss airbases that regularly fired on incoming Allied aircraft. "How neutral can you be? You just wanted to land there and kiss Mother Earth and they're shooting at you," complained one American airman. But this bomber boy failed to realize that Swiss gunners had a reason to be vigilant, if often excessively so. Flying frequent and spectacularly large bombing missions close to the Swiss border, the American Air Force routinely violated Swiss airspace, hundreds of intrusions—mostly accidental—that angered Hermann Göring, from whom the Swiss had purchased much of their air force. On several occasions during the war American bombers mistakenly attacked Swiss cities, among them, Bern, Basel, and Zurich. The worst accident occurred on April 1, 1944, when the city of Schaffhausen was devastated by twenty B-24 Liberators that had gotten lost in heavy cloud cover. Thinking they were over an enemy city, they unloaded their bombs on the market center, killing forty civilians and injuring over a hundred more. The Swiss government demanded and received a formal apology and reparations, but this did little to assuage the anger of Swiss in the border communities. It is perhaps not an accident of history that the month that Schaffhausen was bombed, Swiss fighters and flak gunners finished off a badly disabled B-17, *Little Chub,* with two engines smoking and its left wheel shot off, as it attempted to crash-land near Zurich. Six members of the crew were killed, one of them after he was forced to parachute from 600 feet. The U.S. legation filed a protest, claiming that "Swiss fighter aircraft attacked the American plane after the latter had answered the green rocket signal of the Swiss planes by a like signal." The response was curt, mentioning only that the instructions to Swiss air corps personnel "have in fact already been changed, in part due to this happening."

Airmen at Adelboden suffered from the host country's appeasement of Hitler and its rising impatience with Allied air incursions. If Switzerland had been truly neutral, these men and the men in the two additional camps set up for American fliers would have been accorded as many liberties as Allied internees were in Sweden, where many of them worked in the Swedish aircraft industry and were quartered in comfortable guesthouses. As it was, those airmen who stayed in their camps and waited for the end of the war were rarely mistreated by the Swiss army. But those daring to escape entered a heavily armed country where loyalties were mixed and where soldiers, police, and court officials were ordered to be tough on captured American airmen.

The Black Hole of Wauwilermoos

Daniel Culler feared the unknown. Growing up in insular Syracuse, Indiana, he had never wandered more than thirty miles from home. Yet now all he could think about was escaping into the unknown to "rejoin the fight against . . . oppression." His patriotism was so ardent it seems, in retrospect, contrived. But in shedding his Quaker beliefs to kill for his country, he believed that he had given up any chance of entering heaven. His only hope for the hereafter was that God had created a special place, short of heaven but far from hell, for those who committed licensed murder for a clean cause.

The first time Culler escaped, in May 1944, he and two companions got lost and nearly died of exposure in the mountain forests along the Italian border. In excruciating pain from the bleeding scabs on his feet, and so sick from accidentally eating poisoned berries that he could barely walk, Culler returned, by himself, to Adelboden on the same train that he and his companions had taken south to Bellinzona, the largest city on the Italian border. "The most amazing part of my escape was that I had traveled more than five hundred miles on the Swiss public transportation system, and not one time was I ever questioned or asked for any identification." One of the reasons was that he had been passing through the Italian, not the German section of the country, where the police were more vigilant. A report from the Swiss Commission of Internees and Hospitalization, issued after the war, offered an additional explanation. "We did everything we could to prevent the escape of internees. Unfortunately, our efforts were hampered by the fact that a large part of the population felt honor bound to help internees escape in any possible manner."

After reporting to the commandant of Adelboden, Dan Culler was sentenced to ten days' solitary confinement in the Frutigen jail. His companions, he learned later, were caught by Swiss border guards and imprisoned. After serving his sentence, Culler was taken to a high-security punishment prison called Straflager Wauwilermoos or, in English, "punishment camp at the swamp of Wauwil," a village near Lucerne. Culler was never told why he was sent there, or for how long. As he passed through the gates of the prison, his military guard whispered to him. "I'm sorry to bring you to this hellhole. Watch your every step. There are some awful men in here, and you are so young."

Wauwilermoos was a closely packed compound of mud-splattered barracks surrounded by a high barbed wire fence and patrolled by guards with machine guns and attack dogs. Built in 1941, it was a disciplinary camp for lawbreakers and escapees among Switzerland's ballooning population of military internees from nearly a dozen countries. To run it, Swiss authorities could not have chosen a more odious character. Capt. André-Henri Beguin, a former officer in the French Foreign Legion, was as corrupt as he was cruel. At the time, he was under investigation by Swiss authorities for adultery, bribery, embezzlement of prison funds, spying for the Germans, and unlawfully wearing a Nazi uniform (while living in Germany before the war he signed his correspondence, "Heil Hitler"). Grossly overweight, he rarely entered the prison grounds, preferring to run things from behind his desk, where he was occasionally entertained by one of his four mistresses, and where he could conveniently confiscate aid packages mailed to inmates. The officers he appointed were as coarse and corrupt as he was. They treated us "like scum," said Eighth Air Force bombardier James Misuraca. "The Swiss called this a punishment camp but it was more like a concentration camp."

When guards shoved Dan Culler through the door of Barrack Nine he nearly passed out from the stench. Every Indiana barn he had ever been in smelled better than this place. The wooden floor was covered with filthy straw, which the prisoners slept on and used for toilet paper after they vacated in the miasmic slit trench just outside the front door. "What happened to me that night, and many more to follow, was the worst hell any person ever had to endure," Culler wrote in his searing prison memoir. A group of Russian prisoners held him down, stuffed straw in his mouth, and sodomized him repeatedly. "Coming from a small farming community, I never heard of men doing to me what they did. I . . . hadn't even been with a girl, except to hold her hand and give her a light kiss on her cheek or mouth. I was bleeding from all the openings of my body, and I prayed to God to take my life from me."

He was raped again the next morning and forced to have oral sex with several of his assailants, who stuck sticks in his mouth to pry it open. After being knocked unconscious, he awoke to find blood running down his throat. Too weak to move, and with his hands tied behind his back, he was thrown into the waste ditch outside the barracks. "When I finally came to my senses, I crawled from the ditch and tried to wipe myself with straw. I noticed something was hanging from my rectum, and realizing it was skin from the inside, I tried to push it back in."

A few hours later, Culler staggered into Beguin's office, screaming uncontrollably. "They all stared at me as though I [was] some kind of freak, and a sort of nasty grin came across their faces." For the first time in his life, this son of a Quaker minister found himself cursing at another human being. But no one understood him, no one spoke English. Tiring of Culler, André Beguin stood up and pointed toward the door with the riding crop he always carried. His guards promptly tossed Culler out the door. Lying facedown on the dirt path, Culler prayed that the free-roaming guard dogs would finish him off.

Within days Culler's entire body was covered with boils from the lice and rats in the feces-contaminated straw. The rapes continued and became more violent. He began to vomit blood and an unknown yellow substance, and he developed chronic, bloody diarrhea. When a British sergeant major visited the camp to check on the English prisoners, Culler asked him why the Red Cross had not come to inspect this place, why he was being held without trial, and why had the American military attaché in Bern, General Legge, not been informed of his imprisonment? On a later visit the sergeant major told Culler that he had intervened on the American's behalf to the British authorities in Bern but had been told that General Legge refused to believe that the Swiss had a place like Wauwilermoos, and that his official position was that if an American airman tried to escape, he should be subject to Swiss punishment. In Culler's mind, the country he fought for was abandoning him, and Switzerland, the nation that was sending Red Cross representatives to monitor conditions in German prisoner of war camps, was not interested in visiting a medieval-like holding pen less than a hundred miles from the Red Cross's international headquarters in Geneva. "There isn't any abuse [at Wauwilermoos]," an International Red

Cross inspection report noted, "but on the contrary strict control on the part of the commandant of the Camp." There was "iron discipline," said a Swiss major who looked into conditions at Wauwilermoos, but this was "necessary." And Beguin, he added, was the "dream man . . . to direct a camp of this type." The officious Swiss officer concluded his report with the highest praise he thought he could offer. The camp documents, he said, were "kept in perfect order."

Later that year, when General Legge finally learned about Wauwilermoos, he was at first unmoved. Instead of intervening to help the increasing numbers of American fliers who were being held there, he used the punishment prison's very existence to discourage further escapes. Under his signature, he issued a bulletin for the attention of all American Air Force internees in the country warning them that anyone attempting to escape "will receive no support from me against punitive action by the Swiss Internment authorities, which will be 5–6 months' detention at Camp Wauwilermoos." Unknown to the airmen, Legge, under pressure from the State Department, had begun negotiating for the mass repatriation of all American internees, and constant escapes were hindering his efforts. Late in the war, he also made several formal protests to the Swiss government about the deplorable conditions at Wauwilermoos, where dozens of American airmen were being held incommunicado without trial for indefinite periods. This in no way excuses his refusal to personally visit Wauwilermoos or his failure, earlier in the war, to make closer inquiries about its existence.

When Culler was finally taken from Wauwilermoos and given his day in court, he discovered that Swiss justice was a mockery. The military court proceeding was conducted entirely in German, and when it was over, Culler was handed an English translation of the transcript. He would be sent back to Wauwilermoos without medical treatment and for an unstated period of time. The transcript did not contain a single word of his oral testimony describing his rape and the conditions inside the prison. The final indignity was a bill Culler received for 18 francs—compensation for the court's time and trouble.

Back in prison, Culler was tormented by a loud ringing in his ears—the result of beatings suffered at the hands of the Russians. They had been transferred, but sitting alone in a corner of the barracks, wrapped in a thin blanket, Dan Culler felt he was losing his mind. "The last I remember at Wauwilermoos, I was acting like a madman, trying to stuff straw down my throat so I could not breathe." As he began to lose consciousness, he heard the British sergeant major shouting orders at two Swiss guards who were trying to revive him. "After that everything went black."

Later, the sergeant major told him that the British government in Bern, at his insistence, had gotten a Swiss diplomatic official to sign a paper demanding that Culler receive immediate medical treatment. Dan Culler woke up in a Swiss military hospital, and after a few days he was transferred to a tuberculosis sanitarium in Davos, near the Austrian border. From there he escaped to France on September 26, 1944, the way paved for him by his pilot. With the help of Air Force personnel stationed at the Swiss consulate, Lieutenant Telford paid some Swiss operatives to orchestrate his entire crew's escape and hand them over to the Maquis. As they crossed the border on foot, Swiss guards opened fire on them, wounding Telford in the ankle. The Telford crew was flown back to London in an Eighth Air Force C-47 cargo plane with a group of other internees—English and American—who had recently passed over the border. Carl Spaatz had arranged for the airlift.

In August 1944 Spaatz had begun urging Washington to pressure the Swiss to release interned Air Force personnel. He also sent word into Switzerland that airmen would be held to their oath to escape captivity. At this point, American Air Force officers serving in diplomatic positions in Switzerland, as well as members of the U.S. consulate in Zurich, began defying General Legge's orders and actively helping airmen escape. At the instigation of Secretary of State Hull, an underground network was also established by the OSS; fliers were hidden in the American legation in Bern and then sent to the border in boxcars or ferried across Lake Geneva.

Sam Woods, a former Marine pilot who was the American consul general in Zurich, set up an escape network on his own that helped over 200 internees reach France. Clandestinely meeting dozens of them in churches and cemeteries, he provided them with false passports and drove many of them to the frontier in his black sedan. At the border, Woods would enter a Swiss tavern that was connected to a French pub by an underground sewer line, equipped with a telephone hookup. Woods used the phone to alert his French compatriots that a group of Americans was ready to come over. Running this freedom line took money, a lot of it for bribes, but Sam Woods had a steady supply of funds, courtesy of Thomas J. Watson, the founder and president of IBM, who channeled cash to Woods through his company's European office.

As the ground war came closer to Switzerland, General Sam—so anointed by the fliers he spirited to freedom—was sought out by increasing numbers of airmen. Their chances of successful escape had greatly improved now that the German army had been driven from France and the

American Seventh Army, which landed in southern France on August 18, 1944, reached the Swiss border near Geneva.

Around this time, Gen. Hap Arnold received final reports from the investigations he had mounted earlier that summer to determine if American fliers were deliberately evading service by flying into neutral Switzerland and Sweden. Lt. Col. James Wilson, Arnold's appointed representative, had talked with fliers on bomber bases in England and Italy for well over a month but could find no evidence of a morale crisis. Even earlier, word had come back to Arnold from Air Force intelligence investigators that "no crew, with the possible exception of . . . one has purposely landed in Sweden." Despite their generous treatment by the Swedes, most internees were eager to return to England, although some who had been seriously wounded had no burning desire to return to combat. It was also discovered that William Corcoran's sweeping charges against American airmen in Switzerland had been based on interviews with only two crews, and that Corcoran had probably been "misled by the nonchalance and contempt for heroics displayed by most American airmen." What seems to have finally satisfied Arnold was a report from Allen Dulles, head of the OSS in Central Europe, with headquarters in Bern. Dulles, who used Switzerland as the base for his extensive spying operations, indicated that neither he nor American military officials in Switzerland who examined the condition of every American plane that landed there, had found any evidence of airmen trying to evade combat. "I believe this is nothing but ill-willed propaganda inspired by Nazis," Dulles concluded.

After the war, Spaatz, still in a slow burn over Arnold's accusations, would order American repair teams to conduct a close inspection of bombers that landed in Switzerland and were being prepared for return to the U.S. Air Force. The report would conclude that, with the exception of only one or two planes, every American bomber that came down in Switzerland had been either heavily damaged in combat or was dangerously low on fuel.

When France was liberated, the Axis encirclement of Switzerland was broken. With friendly airbases everywhere in France, the attractiveness of landing in Switzerland and Sweden diminished. During the last three months of 1944, only five American heavy bombers landed in Switzerland. All were from the Fifteenth Air Force—battle-ravaged planes that had no chance of returning, over the intimidating Alps, to southern Italy.

In London, Army intelligence and OSS agents put Dan Culler through an exhaustive round of interrogations. No one believed his grisly story about

Wauwilermoos. "Sergeant, you are a God damn liar!" he was told at one point. "There is no such place as Wauwilermoos . . . and if there was, the Swiss would not put any American soldier in there for nothing more than an attempted escape." In desperation, Culler stripped off his shirt and shoes and showed his interrogators the boils all over his body. These men, Culler soon realized, did not want to believe his story. At the time, American diplomats were negotiating a reparations payment to the Swiss government for the accidental bombing of Swiss cities and General Legge was still trying to close a deal with the Swiss for the repatriation of the 600 or so remaining American internees. The American government wanted no negative publicity about the Swiss while these negotiations were in process. If Culler persisted in his story and went public with it, the Army, he was told, would declare him mentally incompetent and put him in a mental detention hospital for years.[*]

After swearing to remain silent about his captivity, standard procedure for both internees and evaders, Daniel Culler was shipped home in November 1944. When he walked into his mother's kitchen and she saw his condition, the first words out of her mouth were, "I warned you about those awful wars!"

---

[*]On February 17, 1945, 473 American airmen were repatriated under an agreement that released two Germans for every American, but the last airmen were not freed until the end of the war. In September 1945, André-Henri Beguin, commander of Wauwilermoos, was arrested by Swiss authorities and charged with adultery, embezzlement, and dishonoring his country. He was convicted, sentenced to a three-year prison term (he served only two years), and stripped of his Swiss citizenship.

CHAPTER THIRTEEN

My Bellyful of War

I wanted wings until I got the
God damned things.
Now, I don't want them anymore.
They taught me how to fly and
sent me here to die.
I've had my bellyful of war.

ARMY AIR CORPS SONG

East Suffolk, September 1944

Before he was interrogated in London, Sgt. Daniel Culler had returned to his air station at Shipdham to collect his personal things: clothing, money, photographs, letters, and a greatly prized bicycle he had locked in a secure place before his last mission. Everything he valued had disappeared without a trace; gone, too, were his old squadron mates—missing in action or shipped back to the States. Culler did not see a single face he recognized.

Even the machines on the hardstands were new. "The old beat-up, mean-looking, camouflaged B-24s were missing, and shiny, new, polished aluminum planes had replaced them," he recalled. With two crews for every ship and the men racing through their tours in a matter of months, many of the fliers did not even bother to baptize their bombers with nose art. Some planes had no names, just numbers, and their crews no longer feared the Luftwaffe. Culler talked to gunners who had flown twenty missions over the course of the summer without seeing a German fighter. The Luftwaffe was dead, and with Allied armies closing in on the Rhine and the Oder that September, the war would be over by Christmas, he was told.

Capt. Ellis "Woody" Woodward of New Orleans was one of the new Eighth Air Force fliers. His group, the 493rd, was stationed at Debach, the airfield Robert Arbib's engineers had helped build, and was the last of the forty heavy bombardment groups to join the Mighty Eighth. The group flew Liberators, but three months later it was converted to Fortresses. It had entered the war on D-Day, and that summer Woodward's crew had seen plenty of carnage in the flak fields over the oil mills, but none of its gunners had fired a shot in anger.

On the morning of September 12, 1944, Woodward, a lead pilot, took his low squadron out over the North Sea and headed toward Magdeburg with a force of over 300 bombers to destroy an ordnance depot. With dark patches of steel floating over the target, it was a dangerous but typical mission, until the bombers began turning for home. At that moment, one of Woodward's gunners shouted "Fighters!" and seconds later their plane was hit by a fusillade of exploding cannon shells. Woodward was leading a flight of a dozen tightly grouped B-17s. Ninety seconds later, he scanned the skies and saw only one other Fortress.

Then everything became quiet. At exactly the moment when his bomber was most vulnerable, the enemy fighters had disappeared. Four hours later, Woodward set down his ruined bomber on an emergency airstrip in England. Seven Fortresses of the 493rd, he learned later, had been lost to enemy fighters, and a number of others had been too badly damaged to stay with the formation. Standing on the runway, watching *Ramp Happy Pappy* being hauled to the salvage yard, Woodward wondered: where did those fighters come from and why did they leave before completing the slaughter?

Unknown to Woodward, Air Force photoreconnaissance planes had recently been reporting alarming evidence of a resurgence of German fighter strength. But not until the day before Woodward's mission had the Luftwaffe struck with force, its first mass attack since before D-Day. Nearly a hundred enemy planes evaded the Mustangs and swooped down, twenty abreast, on a trailing low group of the bomber stream, the Fortresses of the luckless Bloody Hundredth. In five minutes, twelve of the group's bombers disappeared, then eight more from the 92nd went down. The Eighth Air Force toll, after Woodward's squadron was hit the following afternoon, was seventy-five bombers lost in two days. Although Allied intelligence knew that Albert Speer had pulled off a production miracle, not until these attacks did Adolf Galland reveal how the new fighters would be deployed. It was an old strategy with a new twist.

Storm Groups

Employing the element of surprise, Galland's all-volunteer storm squadron, Sturmstaffel I, had enjoyed some success the previous winter, but its ponderous, heavily armored twin-engine fighters, Zerstörers, began to be chewed up by the Mustangs. Galland's solution was to build an even more strongly armed and armored fighter, a modified Fw 190 with enhanced armor plating, a bullet-resistant canopy, two auxiliary fuel tanks, and five fearsome guns. It was called the Sturmbock, or Battering Ram. Flying in Sturmgruppen, waves of up to forty planes, this eight-ton "flying tank" became for a short time the most lethal bomber destroyer of the war.

Galland teamed Storm Group squadrons with groups of faster single-engine fighters. While the angular Me 109s provided top cover, the Storm Groups went straight for the heavies. Concentrating on one part of the bomber stream to achieve maximum shock effect, they usually attacked from the rear, wingtip to wingtip. Pilots held their fire until they were within a hundred yards of the enemy, at the point when the bombers first appeared in the target circle of their gun sights. "From such range we could hardly miss," recalled one Sturmgruppe pilot, "and as the [30mm] explosive rounds struck home we could see the enemy bombers literally falling apart in front of us." After scoring a hit, a Storm Group pilot would dive straight down and head for home to avoid being caught and killed by the faster Mustangs. This is the reason enemy fighters had not stayed to finish off Woody Woodward's squadron.

If a Sturmbock pilot failed to score a direct hit on an enemy bomber he was bound by a solemn oath to ram it. But with pilots desperately scarce in the Reich, Storm Group volunteers were instructed by their local commanders to bail out immediately before or after impact. "The chance of surviving a ramming and jumping out with a parachute, sounds very much like heroic suicide," recalled Werner Vorberg, a squadron captain. Yet, incredibly, more than half of the pilots who rammed American bombers, probably glancingly, reached the ground in their parachutes without serious injury.

Such tactics placed a premium on blazing courage and unquestioning patriotism; few pilots defending the homeland were deficient in either of these qualities. "One must keep in mind," wrote Vorberg, "that the German airmen knew about the escalation of the brutal, unrelenting bombing . . . of residential districts of the central cities, [and] the militarily nonsensical shooting by . . . escort fighters at everything that showed itself below, at farmers behind the plow, at bicycle riders, pedestrians and Red Cross ambulances." They knew, as well, "that if a peace treaty [was] sought, not the slightest mercy was to be expected. . . . This knowledge motivated the storm fighter for his tasks."

The new Storm Groups delivered—and took—frightful casualties. In just two days, September 11 and 12, they lost thirty-eight pilots. Barely reinforced, Vorberg's unit flew on September 27 against over 300 Liberators of the 2nd Bomb Division. The combatants—an air force that had never been turned back and one sworn to protect its home soil—collided in the skies over central Germany. For Jimmy Stewart's old Liberator group, the 445th at Tibenham, it was the blackest day of the war. It suffered more losses than any single combat unit sustained in the history of American aerial warfare.

The 2nd Air Division had expected no trouble from fighters that day. The Luftwaffe had not been seen for over two weeks. So confident were the division's commanders that they had ordered the ball turret guns removed from the bellies of the Liberators so that the planes could carry more bombs. When the Liberators approached the Initial Point and prepared to make their bomb run against industrial targets in Kassel, all thirty-five planes from the 445th suddenly pulled away from the formation. Navigators and pilots in the main force radioed frantic warnings to the group's lead plane, but all they received back was an order to "tighten it up and follow me."

When the errant planes reached Göttingen, about twenty miles from Kassel, and released their bombs, they were hit, low and from the rear, by three Storm Groups. After making their first fire passes, the Sturmbocks hung from the Liberators' propellers and savaged the exposed undersides of the bombers, where the ball turret gunners would have been. As one Liberator after another was turned to smoke and splinters, crews from other bombers, flying further ahead, began "bailing out in rows before they were even attacked," reported Captain Vorberg. Seconds later, a German fighter rammed a Liberator. "As I approached my target I armed the cannon and pulled the trigger," recalled Storm Group pilot Heinz Papenberg. "Nothing happened . . . I thought then about the *Sturm* commitment to ram and decided to do it. I can still see the horrified expression on the face of the tail gunner. . . . My left wing sawed through the bomber's rudder. . . . My wing was so damaged it couldn't hold the plane in the air and I spun away. For a few moments I decided I was going to die. . . . My crate was out of control. I jettisoned the hood and was sucked out of the cockpit."

Papenberg smashed into the tail of his own plane, broke his leg, and lost consciousness. When he came around, he was still free-falling. Moments later—he doesn't remember how—his chute opened. He was only a few hundred feet from the ground.

Back in the skies above the Werra River Valley, where Papenberg had safely landed, American pilots were putting in panicky calls for escorts. The 361st Mustang group arrived just in time to prevent the total destruction of the 445th.

Twenty-five four-engine bombers had been destroyed in six minutes of focused fury. Only four Liberators made it back to Tibenham. Lt. Col. Jimmy Stewart, who had been promoted that July to 2nd Combat Wing headquarters at Hethel, was sent to run the debriefing and settle down the stunned and mostly speechless survivors. Stewart split the men into small groups and tried to get them talking. Survivors suffering from paralyzing shock were unable to utter a word.

Some of the group's Liberators had landed on special "lame duck" fields on the English coast, but most of the missing survivors were in German hands. In the village of Nentershauen, one crewman was shot by a German soldier on leave, and four others were sent to a local labor camp, where they were executed by the guards in the middle of the night. After being roughed up, George Collar and a small group of survivors were sent out to collect the mutilated remains of their buddies. It was ghastly duty. "We traveled up and down the hills and forests all day, picking up approximately a dozen bodies," recalled Collar, whose nose had been broken and both eyes blackened by an irate German farmer. "That night when we returned to the village, we left the wagons containing the bodies at the cemetery . . . and we were taken back to the jail and brought a loaf of bread. . . . It was the last white bread we were to eat until we were liberated in May 1945."

The Eighth Air Force introduced new tactics to combat the Storm Groups. Fighter formations were sent ahead of the bombers to break up the Sturmgruppen before they formed up into their menacing phalanxes. Or else the fighters got behind them and gunned them down one after the other, the courageous German pilots refusing to engage, yet refusing to flee. Some Storm fliers were still able to get through to the bombers, but the escorts almost always caught up with them and made them pay. The faster Me 109s, tethered to the slow-flying Sturmbocks, were massacred by the Mustangs.

On October 12, Chuck Yeager, flying escort for a formation of Liberators, destroyed five Me 109s over Bremen, making him the Eighth Air Force's first "ace-in-a-day." But if Air Force regulations had been adhered to, he would not have been flying that day.

After returning to England from Spain the previous May, Yeager had begun a fight with his base commanders over the War Department regulation that prohibited airmen shot down over occupied Europe from returning to combat duty. "German intelligence kept dossiers on most of us, and knew who had been shot down before; they'd go right to work on your fingernails if you were shot down again," trying to extract information on the French Underground. "[But] I was raised to finish what I started, not slink off after flying only eight missions. Screw the regulations." The brassy West Virginian had taken his protest up the chain of command to Eisenhower himself, who finally relented after the Allies landed in France and the Maquis began operating in the open.

Yeager was a born aerial killer, with matchless vision and reflexes, and, in his flight leader's words, "more balls than brains." But his five victories in one afternoon owed a lot to the dismal performance of the airmen he went up against, two of whom he took down without firing a shot. As he came up on their tails and was about to "wax" them, one pilot panicked and broke sharply left, smashing into his wingman.

Jets

Adolf Galland did not have enough pilots and fuel to send out his suddenly reduced Storm Groups with any regularity. But he had another bullet in his chamber: a plane without propellers, the world's first combat-tested jet fighter. Since July, General Doolittle had been receiving reports about small numbers of jet fighters and rocket-powered planes that were shadowing his bomber formations; they would fly at a safe distance from the bombers and taunt them with their performance capabilities, but rarely engage. The weapon Air Force intelligence was most worried about was the twin-turbo Messerschmitt Me 262, the fastest aircraft in existence. It flew at 540 mph, about 100 mph faster than the Mustang, and it ran on diesel fuel, which Germany possessed in far greater quantity than standard aviation fuel. Eighth Air Force intelligence had badly underestimated the number of conventional fighter planes German industry produced over the previous summer and Spaatz did not want to make the same mistake with the Me 262. If this stunningly fast, powerfully armed plane began to be mass-produced, the Luftwaffe could regain command of the skies over Germany.

Spaatz and Doolittle pressed Hap Arnold to accelerate the production of an effective counterweapon, but America's first jet, the Bell P-59, proved to be no faster than the Mustang, and Spaatz was told that a true high-performance jet aircraft, the P-80A, would not be ready until far into the following year. Britain had a promising jet fighter, the Meteor, but its production schedule was deplorably slow, and it never got into combat. With piston-powered planes his only answer to German jets, Doolittle had begun making systematic attacks on jet fighter production plants that July. They continued into early fall, but were ineffective. The jet aircraft plants were even more cleverly hidden than plants producing conventional aircraft.

"We flyers had one ray of hope in [the fall of 1944] and that was the new jet fighter," recalled a Luftwaffe squadron commander. Historians have long insisted that the Allied air forces were saved from that fate only by the bungling interference of Adolf Hitler. Hermann Göring was one of the sources of this idea. Asked by interrogators after the war, "What was the reason for the delay of the use of the Me 262 as a fighter?" he replied instantly, "Adolf Hitler's madness." This is one of the most persistent myths in airpower history. Hitler did interfere with the development of the plane, but this delayed its appearance by only a few months at most.

In late 1943, when the Me 262 was about to go into serial production, the führer had shocked his technical advisors by ordering its conversion from a fighter to a fighter-bomber, a "Blitz bomber," he called it. Without checking with the engineers and administrators directing the project, Göring had promised the führer that the plane would be ready in large numbers by May 1944, at which point Hitler had hoped to use them in reprisal raids against English cities–"Terror is only broken by terror"–and to repel the Allied invasion of northern France.

Led by Galland, most of the führer's air advisors had wanted him to increase fighter production–propeller planes as well as jets–and to use these aircraft for the protection of war industries. They had unexpectedly gotten what they wanted when production genius Erhard Milch, director of air armament, secretly disregarded Hitler's order and pushed ahead with the development of the Me 262 as a fighter. Hitler had not gotten wind of this until May 1944, when the first Me 262s rolled off the production line and Göring presented it to him as the fighter that would "sweep Allied air power from the skies." The führer had flown into a rage, demanding that the armament be removed and that the Me 262 be fitted out as a bomber. This is when he dismissed Milch and turned over aircraft production to Speer. (Speer later made Milch deputy armament minister.) "You had a great ally in your aerial warfare, the Führer," Göring told American interrogators.

In the next few months, Speer and Galland implored Hitler to alter his plans for the Me 262 and employ every available plane in the Reich in the defense of the synthetic oil plants. That August, in a stormy meeting with Galland and Speer, Hitler had flown out of control and, in a spitting rage, roared: "I want no more planes produced at all. The fighter arm is to be dissolved. Stop aircraft production . . . at once, understand?" He wanted all skilled workers and matériel in the aircraft industry moved immediately into the production of flak guns, he told an incredulous Speer, "a program five times what we have now. We'll shift hundreds of thousands of workers into flak production. Every day I read in the foreign press reports how dangerous flak is. They still have some respect for that, but not for our fighters." And with that, Galland and Speer were ordered from the room.

After being advised about the technical difficulties involved in such a massive transfer of munitions resources, Hitler ordered a more modest increase in flak defenses, but repeated his command to Speer and Karl Saur, Speer's deputy in charge of fighter production, to increase flak defenses at the expense of air defenses. "That was the first command from Hitler that neither Saur nor I obeyed," Speer wrote later. On the following day Speer assembled his armaments staff and told them straight-out: "We must . . . maintain the production of fighter planes at a maximum." By then, Hitler had calmed down somewhat and agreed to Speer's proposal for a new fighter production program. Hitler also came around, although only part of the way, on the Me 262, allowing it to be tested as both a bomber and a fighter, but mass production continued to be delayed by persistent problems with its turbojet engine—the first in the world—and Eighth Air Force attacks in the winter and spring of 1944, beginning with Big Week. These factors, along with the difficulty of training pilots to handle the temperamental and highly combustible aircraft, did more than Hitler's ill-advised intervention to delay its appearance.

As Allied armies pressed closer to the borders of Germany in the late summer of 1944, Hitler finally gave Galland permission to form a jet fighter unit for the defense of the Reich. On October 3, it became operational at two fields close to the Dutch border, directly in the path of the main American bomber route into Germany. The unit was headed by Maj.

Walter Nowotny, one of the Luftwaffe's top aces, with 258 kills. That October, Doolittle and Spaatz thought they would have to fight the battle for air superiority all over again, but Nowotny's pilots destroyed only twenty-two Allied aircraft, at a cost of twenty-six of his unit's thirty planes. Almost all of the losses were the result of technical difficulties and pilot inexperience. "For many pilots the only previous experience of flying such a revolutionary aircraft had consisted of a few circuits of the airfield," wrote Luftwaffe historian Cajus Becker. But Allied pilots did their part. Nowotny's turbojets were dangerously slow in taking off and landing and were able to stay airborne for only an hour or so. Every time one of them was spotted in the sky by a vigilant Allied patrol plane, British and American fighters would rally to its home field and hover there, waiting for its return. "I saw a large airdrome with a six-thousand-foot runway and a lone jet approaching the field from the south at 500 feet," Chuck Yeager described his only victory over a Me 262. "I dove at him. His landing gear was down and he was lining up the runway, coming in at no more than 200 mph, when I dropped on his ass at 500 mph." Yeager poured flaming steel into the jet's wings and the plane crashed short of the runway and disappeared in a cloud of smoke and debris.

On November 8, Walter Nowotny was killed in a crash landing at his home base. Galland, who witnessed his fiery death and learned that same day of three other crashes, withdrew the unit from combat for additional training. While a jet squadron three times larger was being readied, Galland fell back on a strategy that drew on the Luftwaffe's only available source of strength—the 2,500 single-engine fighters Speer had recently delivered, more than double the number of fighters the Luftwaffe possessed in 1943. Galland called his plan for the final defense of the homeland *Der Grosse Schlag,* "The Great Blow."

Since August 1944, Galland had been training a great part of this fighter force for a tremendous attack on a single American bomber formation. He expected to take down as many as 500 bombers and to lose an equal number of his own fighters. "This was going to be the largest and most decisive air battle of the war," he wrote later, an aerial Armageddon. The shock of these unprecedented losses might convince the Eighth Air Force to suspend its raids on the Reich's oil plants and go after its harder-to-hit aircraft industry. Galland hoped that the Wehrmacht could then delay the Russian advance until either "the Western Allies conquered Germany" or a compromise peace was negotiated by the secret enemies of the führer.

In mid-November, the assault armada was ready. At the first sign of clear weather, it would be launched, and Galland expected the battle to decide the fate of the Reich. In the following weeks, the weather remained miserable and Galland was forced to use up to two-thirds, but never all, of this husbanded force in four concentrated attacks on Spaatz's radar-directed bombing operations. "It was a difficult decision to hold back [all of] the defensive fighters," Galland wrote later, "but the leaders kept calm and did not insist on vain and costly forced action."

Even so, these were tremendous air battles in which the Luftwaffe lost a staggering 348 pilots. "The flying in November 1944 was the toughest I encountered during the entire war," reported a German fighter commander. "The odds against us were 20 to 1 and sometimes even 30 to 1." Every time the enemy rose to fight, Mustangs destroyed as much as a quarter of his attacking force, Spaatz reported to Robert Lovett, assistant secretary of war for air. "His pilots are not well trained, although very aggressive," which for them was a catastrophic combination.

One of the American casualties in these terrible November battles was a Mustang pilot of the 339th Fighter Group, the promising writer Bert Stiles. After flying thirty-five bomber missions, Stiles had requested a transfer to a fighter outfit. "I want to fly a real plane," he told an English friend. "I want to feel the wind blowing across my face—to climb, dive, soar, be free." He died in a sky fight over Hanover as part of an American formation that destroyed 132 enemy aircraft.

On November 20, while Galland was still waiting for exactly the right weather, he received crushing news. The air units he had prepared for the Great Blow were to be moved to the Western Front in early December in preparation for "a great land battle." Only two fighter wings would remain in the Reich. Galland had no time to retrain his pilots for the low-altitude air fighting they were about to experience in support of the ground forces. They would leave for their new duties "unprepared and disheartened at the failure of the scheme which had given all of them hope."

The transfer of his pilots was Adolf Galland's last official duty as commander of the Fighter Arm. Having fallen out of favor with both Göring and the führer, he would take no part in the coming operation. That December, his phones were tapped, SS spies were placed on his staff as clerical help, and his political past was investigated, for he had never joined the Nazi Party. At the end of the month, Göring called him to his headquarters and in a two-hour monologue accused him of devising ill-advised tactics, of failing to obey orders, and of setting up "a private dynasty in the Fighter Arm." He then stripped him of his command. Galland asked to be sent to the front as an ordinary pilot, but Göring ordered that he take a leave until his successor was found.

So Germany would fight one of the largest infantry battles of history without its finest air commander.

That November, the führer was completing plans to launch an all-out counteroffensive the following month in the Ardennes Forest, extending north to south, from Belgium to Luxemburg. It would be his last great effort to reverse the course of a war that was going disastrously against Germany, a counterstrike as spectacular in scope and intent as the Great Blow Galland had intended to deliver.

The Battle of the Ruhr

While Hitler plotted his surprise counterstrike, the Allied air barons began the decisive bombing initiative of the European war, one that delivered unrecoverable blows to the entire German war economy, not just one essential part of it. But that campaign began in earnest only when Allied bombers were prevented by cloud cover from accurately hitting their main targets, Germany's oil installations. Ironically, the foul weather that Albert Speer considered the only possible salvation for the German economy opened the way for its utter destruction.

In September 1944, as the Allied armies approached the Siegfried Line, their lightning-like advance across northwestern Europe came to a sudden halt. Eisenhower's forces were the victims of their own success. They had advanced so rapidly that they outran their supply line, which reached all the way back to the invasion beaches, where 90 percent of their fresh supplies still came across from England. The advancing Allied armies were now perilously short of ammunition, medicine, food, and gasoline. Getting these necessities to the front was difficult. The French rail system had not recovered from the Allied air assault in preparation for D-Day, and the Germans were still holding on to a number of major Channel ports, among them Le Havre, Brest, Calais, and Dunkirk. Cargo planes and heavy bombers were enlisted to fly gasoline to the Allied armies stalled along the German frontier, and an emergency around-the-clock truck service was rushed into place. Over 6,000 trucks and trailers and 23,000 men were mobilized to carry fuel, ammunition, and rations from the original landing beaches and the only functioning port in Normandy, at Cherbourg, to the armies advancing on the Rhine. This improvised supply system line could not nearly keep up with the demand for supplies, and there were not enough airfields in the vicinity of the troops for the air lift that was organized to be of much use.

This logistical nightmare focused attention on Antwerp. The British had just captured the Belgian city, one of Europe's largest ports, but had failed to take the Scheldt River estuary, the long narrow approach to the port. If Antwerp were opened, the Allied fuel problems would end; but instead of applying full force to clear the Germans from the banks of the Scheldt, Eisenhower made a risky attempt to win the war by the end of the year. Prodded by Field Marshal Bernard Montgomery, he approved a mission to land paratroopers in Holland, behind the Siegfried Line, and have them drive hard through the industrialized Ruhr in the direction of Berlin.

Code-named Market-Garden, the operation was launched on September 17, 1944, and was a catastrophic failure, with heavy losses, most of them British Airborne troops. Eisenhower then decided to break the Siegfried Line by a series of crushing frontal assaults along the German border. The first attack of that bloody fall and winter was in early October at Aachen, an ancient cultural center just west of the Rhine. After a vicious fight, Aachen became the first major German city to fall, but the Allies were unable to break through to the Rhine. At the southern end of the Allied line, Patton, without sufficient fuel for his tanks, found it equally difficult to reduce the citadel city of Metz. Montgomery did clear the Scheldt estuary and open the port of Antwerp, but in late 1944, the war along the Siegfried Line settled into a stalemate, with Allied infantry moving slowly and at terrible cost against fixed German positions.

That fall, Allied air commanders, released now from Eisenhower's direct control, wrestled with the question of how air power could help finish off Germany.

A new advisory organization—the Combined Strategic Targets Committee—was established but Harris and Spaatz had authority to hit targets of their choosing, subject to the overall control of the Combined Chiefs of Staff and the heads of their respective air forces. A coordinated strategy was called for, but the commanders could not come up with one. In some ways, this was a reprise of the dispute that occurred in the run-up to D-Day, with Spaatz favoring attacks on oil, Harris on industrial cities, and Tedder on transportation targets.

This time Spaatz prevailed, and for the same reason that had put Tedder on top earlier in the year. Back then, the pressing objective was to prepare the way as quickly as possible for the Normandy invasion; now, it was to finish off Germany by Christmas. The Combined Chiefs decided that greatly intensified oil strikes, in conjunction with an autumn offensive by Eisenhower's ground forces, offered the best chance of doing that.

A cagey bureaucratic infighter, Tedder continued to lobby for his own plan, using his considerable leverage with the Chiefs of Staff and the Royal Air Force commander, Sir Charles Portal. Tedder and his chief policy aide, Professor Solly Zuckerman, proposed that the campaign against railways begun in France in the spring of 1944 "should be carried into Germany, since its economic and industrial life, as well as the freedom of military movement, depended on the untrammeled use of a railway system." That September, Allied fighter-bombers, with occasional help from the heavies, had begun attacking rail and water transportation targets in northwestern Germany, but Tedder wanted something far more ambitious: a full-out assault by the Allied air forces, both strategic and tactical, on Germany's transportation infrastructure—its rail, river, and canal traffic. Deprived of these economic arteries, neither the industrial cities that Bomber Harris was pulverizing, nor the synthetic plants that Spaatz was destroying, could continue to function; and factories everywhere in the Reich would be cut off from the raw materials, component parts, and markets they needed to survive. Coordinated assaults against the transportation network would also play havoc with Albert Speer's ingenious but vulnerable system of industrial decentralization. "The more [industries] have been dispersed the more they depend on good communications," Tedder reminded Portal. And the German army's "dependence on communication needs no comment. . . ." Conceding the success of Spaatz's oil offensive, Tedder proposed that transportation and oil be treated as complementary, not competing, target systems.

Zuckerman's intelligence sources indicated that the pre-invasion devastation of the rail system of northern France and Belgium had also fatally weakened the Reichsbahn, the German National Railway, as it was forced to supply cars, locomotives, and rail service lost to Allied bombing in those countries. The system needed only "a slight push," he argued, to topple it. Why, he wondered, did the American "warlords" fail to see what was directly in front of their eyes: the enemy's transportation system on the precipice?

It was not that clear-cut. Eighth Air Force intelligence experts insisted that the attacks on the French railway system had not been as effective as Zuckerman claimed; they had inconvenienced but not incapacitated German troop movements. Why divert the heavies to new targets when oil raids had already put Germany on the ropes? As in Operation Overlord, timing was everything for the Allied leadership. Knocking out the best-run rail system in the world by the end of the year seemed beyond possibility, whereas ULTRA intercepts offered unassailable evidence that the Reich oil industry was about to be sent to the mat.

Zuckerman, an eminent zoologist, insisted that his strategic bombing plan was based on scientific principles and objective analysis. This was preposterous. Strategic bombing was the furthest thing from a science. It was founded more on faith than fact—on incomplete or erratic data, most of it gathered from photoreconnaissance conducted over a part of the world that lay under perpetual cloud cover for great parts of the year. Everything about the strategic bombing was new and untried. The only thing it shared with science was its experimental impulse. Unlike the other military services, the bomber commanders and their advisors had neither precedent nor experience to fall back on.

Flexible Allied air leaders like Tedder and Spaatz had learned how to bomb by the very act of bombing, by experimenting with new tactics and strategy until they found their way to what worked most effectively. Their only correctives were the black-and-white infrared photographs of their reconnaissance pilots and information gleaned from ULTRA intercepts. And the latter were of distressingly limited value because almost all German business communication was by landlines, not encoding machines.

Zuckerman and Tedder forged an excellent war plan, but they were hardly the strategic visionaries they have made themselves out to be in their otherwise excellent autobiographies. They advocated oil attacks focused on the Ruhr, for example, whereas the vastly more important targets of Leuna and Politz lay further east. If Spaatz erred in not giving sufficient attention to transportation bombing, Tedder and Zuckerman made the equal error of not giving oil the emphasis it deserved.

At a crucial meeting of the air chiefs in late October, oil was given top priority, with transportation a distant second. But a proviso unintentionally swung the initiative to Tedder's plan. When weather grounded Spaatz's oil raiders—who needed clear skies to hit synthetic plants with even a measure of accuracy—they were instructed to go after transportation targets, "with blind bombing techniques as necessary." As it turned out, the weather remained atrocious into the following year, throwing the advantage to proponents of railroad bombing. In the last part of the war, the Eighth Air Force would drop nearly half its tonnage on transportation targets. One of the reasons Spaatz did not want to make German railroads his priority—the system's immense size—made it an ideal target of last resort. It was a target that was almost always available.

Bomber Harris was given virtually the same bombing directive as

Spaatz, but with Portal still unable to control him because of Harris's strong ties to Churchill and his immense popularity on the home front, the headstrong air commander did almost as he pleased. In the last three months of 1944, his force dropped 53 percent of its bombs on cities, 15 percent on transportation targets, and only 14 percent on oil facilities. Because of the tremendous lifting capacity of his Lancasters, Harris made a stronger contribution to both the transportation and oil offensives than he is generally credited with. It is a stain on his reputation that he did not do more.

After a saturation attack on Darmstadt on September 11, a raid that ignited a firestorm that consumed over 10,000 people, nearly a tenth of the town's population, Harris zeroed in on the Ruhr and the regions just to the west of it. That autumn and early winter, he unleashed attacks on over thirty industrial cities, some of the same towns his crews had torched the previous year. Much of the wreckage was industrial property and transportation infrastructure—gas plants, electric grids, and water mains, but too much of it was human blood and bones. If the preponderance of the 60,000 tons of explosives Harris's heavy bombers dropped on the cities of Ruhr had been used against oil and rail targets, he would have better served the Allied war effort and his own troubled legacy.

The Allied air forces' communications bombing also centered on the Ruhr, the country's largest producer of coal, iron, and steel. A knockout blow delivered there, Tedder argued, would have a rippling effect on the entire German economy. He turned out to be right but for the wrong reasons. In attacking transportation, the Allies blundered into a war-winning bombing offensive, one that deprived German factories and power plants of the one raw material without which they could not function.

Almost all freight in Germany was shipped by either rail or canal, and the most important commodity that these systems transported was coal, the source of 90 percent of Germany's energy. Just as the Allies failed to see the close connection between Germany's synthetic oil and munitions industries, so they failed to appreciate the full significance of the coal-Reichsbahn relationship. When the Eighth Air Force arrived in England in 1942, its only guide to bombing policy was a hastily prepared plan based on the American—not the German—economy. But the United States was an oil and automobile society, whereas Germany was heavily dependent on coal and railroads. Not even Tedder, who came from a coal-driven economy, had emphasized the close connection between coal and railroads in his passionate pleas for transportation bombing. Depriving some key industries like steel of their coal supplies was one part, not the main thrust of his transportation plan. Here Tedder was the victim of his own intelligence sources. No Allied intelligence agency envisioned what would be the most effective bombing outcome of the European war—the destruction of the Reich's coal-railway nexus.

While oil was essential to the Nazi war machine, coal was even more important. Deprived of it, the entire German economy would collapse. Bad weather and good fortune thus conjoined to produce a devastating assault on Germany's most essential commodity.

Most of Germany's coal reserves were located in three regions: the Ruhr, Upper Silesia, and to a far lesser extent, the Saar—in southwest Germany, on the French-German border. The Ruhr basin was the source of 63 percent of Germany's coking coal, the key ingredient for smelting iron, and 80 percent of its most valuable coal, bituminous, as opposed to lignite, or brown coal, which contains decidedly less energy. Coal from the Ruhr powered the region's own industries, as well as those of central and southern Germany. Upper Silesia's coal met the energy needs of the Berlin metropolitan region. The Allied bombing campaign in the Ruhr was not aimed at the pitheads or production centers, but at transportation arteries that led in and out of them, all of which passed through the enormous marshaling yards of the Reichsbahn. The dispatching centers of all railway freight, these yards were, in Tedder's words, "the heart of the rail system," and yet they had been "relatively untouched." When Allied bombers began systematically destroying them they created a nationwide coal famine that would build in intensity until it brought the entire economy to a standstill in early 1945. "It is ironical," wrote historian Alan S. Milward, "that of all Germany's raw materials the one in which she was best supplied should have been so responsible for the final collapse."

By November, relentless raids by the Allied air forces had severed the Ruhr's waterway connections to the rest of Germany. This created economic havoc, for over a third of the region's coal exports were shipped by water. From this point on, the full burden of keeping the economy running fell on the Reichsbahn. A railway that ordinarily carried three-quarters of the country's freight was now asked to carry nearly all of it. Stated simply, the new bombing philosophy was this: instead of concentrating on the industries that produce the freight, attack the carriers that move it, a rail system being easier to knock out than an entire industrial economy. And when that rail system was destroyed, the economy would crack and collapse. As with oil, it was a battle between the bombers and the repair crews. By November, Speer had almost 200,000 workers engaged in industrial repairs in the Ruhr alone. Fifty thousand of these were "expendable" slave laborers from Holland, but 30,000 had been released from the armaments industry, creating an unavoidable drain on the war economy.

Through a gigantic effort, parts of the system were kept open, but the battle between destruction and reconstruction—always an uneven one—turned disastrously against Germany in the winter of 1944. It was then that attrition became fatal, for it was only after the fifth or sixth bombing attack that a marshaling yard was disabled. As with the oil campaign, it was the frequency and weight of the attacks, not their accuracy, that was most telling. American Air Force publicists lauded the surgical precision of the raids, boasted about killing the enemy's industry with a thousand clean cuts, but the German economy was bludgeoned to death by the blunt instrument of saturation bombing.

Indispensable supply and troop trains could often get through the wreckage on a single track, but only with the greatest difficulty. And fighter-bomber attacks on moving trains made it necessary to move troops to the front almost exclusively at night. It was the near perfect marriage between the strategic and tactical forces that Tedder envisioned. The heavies hit the big, easy-to-spot marshaling yards, and the fighters and medium bombers went after moving trains, viaducts, and bridges.

"The disruption of our communications," Speer warned Hitler that November, "may well lead to a production crisis which will gravely jeopardize our capacity to continue the war." The outcome of "the battle of the Ruhr . . . will determine the fate of our Reich."

Blind Bombing

From September 1944 to the end of the European war, the American forces dropped twice as much tonnage on marshaling yards as any other target, with radar attacks predominating. Attacks on marshaling yards raised troubling moral issues. Unlike oil plants, the big rail yards were located in the central districts of industrial cities, adjacent to workers' housing. These cities—although not their marshaling yards—were easily detected through the clouds with H2X radar. In destroying large marshaling yards the Eighth Air Force destroyed densely settled residential neighborhoods, killing and maiming thousands of civilians. How could this not happen when, by the Air Force's own calculations, only 2 percent of the bombs dropped in a typical radar attack hit within 1,000 feet of the aiming point?

Human error was compounded by Curtis LeMay's militarily effective policy of bombing on the leader. "My squadron was on the tail end of a bombing strike against a railroad yard in a small industrial town," Eighth Air Force pilot Craig Harris described a typical raid against an urban rail center. "There were about 400 bombers in front of us as we approached the target. Our shadow, if we had had one, would have covered almost the entire town. The clouds were so thick we couldn't see a thing on the ground. The lead plane carried the radar equipment. When it passed over the target it dropped its bombs, along with a smoke marker, the signal for the rest of the formation to drop. The planes at the head of the formation wasted the marshaling yard, but the rest of us wasted the town."

Even when bombing was done visually, on clear days, the collateral damage could be enormous. "We bombed the marshalling yards of . . . Mayen," wrote Sgt. John J. Briol of the 457th Bomb Group. "The railroads went right through the center of the town. 'Bombs Away,' and Ozzie [the bombardier] hit the toggle switch." Minutes later the bombs landed, and from his ball turret, Briol had a perfect view of the carnage. "This was a little city of about 2,000 people. We blasted the yards all right and the entire city with it. I saw the whole city disappearing and I suddenly realized again what a rotten business this was."

"The specter of . . . the extermination of innocents would forever lie in the back of my mind as I matured," recalled Eighth Air Force pilot Bernard Thomas Nolan. While some airmen killed without remorse, studies conducted by Eighth Air Force psychiatrists found that most men on heavy-bomber crews could not "tolerate well the guilt of killing," despite the fact that the victims were "remote, almost abstract." For the most part, personal hatred was directed at German leaders, not the pilots the Eighth fought or the people it bombed. "We live with fear but not with a consuming hatred for another human, who given his wish, would not be involved in this madness any more than we," radio operator J. J. Lynch wrote in his combat diary. But the more typical reaction after an ugly raid was to bury the experience.

The Eighth had done blind bombing before but never this remorselessly. Approximately 80 percent of the Eighth's and 70 percent of the Fifteenth's missions during the last three months of 1944 were conducted in dense to moderate cloud cover. Now it was open season on any community that had a major railway facility, and that was almost every city and town of economic consequence in western Germany. In December the arc of destruction widened to include the entire Reich.

If the main target could not be found, Air Force crews were given clearance, beginning in November, to bomb "targets of last resort"–towns or industrial sites "large enough to produce an identifiable return on the H2X scope." This was a policy pressed on Doolittle by Gen. George Marshall, in his haste to conclude the war. The presumption was that such towns had to contain a "military objective" of some kind, even if it was only a single railroad bridge or oil storage tank.

The new bombing directive, dated October 29, 1944, was a clear departure from the Eighth Air Force's standing policy against indiscriminate bombing. Up to this point, the Eighth had rarely aimed its bombs directly at civilians, and it would never employ the fire-raising tactics used by Bomber Harris. But pressure to finish off the enemy created a new situation in which the German people could now expect the neighborhood-destroying raids in daylight they had previously experienced only at night.

The Eighth had a unit called the Air Scouts: former bomber pilots who flew ahead of the attack fleets in Mustangs to alert them by radio about late-breaking weather conditions they might want to avoid. But, for the most part, the weather over Germany during this winter, as during the winter before, ceased to matter in determining whether to send out the force. Bombers were dispatched unless conditions over their home bases were absolutely impossible.

By the winter of 1944, the differences between the bombing practices of the Eighth Air Force and Britain's Bomber Command had narrowed, although they were still significant. The Eighth killed unaccountable numbers of civilians when it began intensively bombing vital urban targets that it could not possibly hit accurately. Bomber Harris continued to launch city-consuming attacks after his night force developed, in 1944, guidance technology that allowed it to hit targets within and around urban areas with considerable accuracy. One air force deliberately targeted civilians; the other, with only a few exceptions, did not. The declared intention of the attacker may be insignificant to the people of a neighborhood shattered by a string of bombs aimed elsewhere. But it is a matter of surpassing significance to the residents of entire cities coldly mapped out for slaughter.

Blind bombing put American airmen, as well as German civilians, in greater jeopardy. "If we fall into most German hands now, they will kill us," John Briol wrote in his diary. But most crewmen on blind bombing missions feared the weather more than the Germans. Lost in heavy clouds, a lead navigator took Lewis Welles's 95th Bomb Group down the bomb run backward. "Lew pulled the nose up until the ship stalled out to avoid hitting another plane," Welles's tail gunner, Rulon Paramore, described the incident in his war journal. "We lost our wing man in the ordeal. The plane that missed us hit him. They both blew up."

That winter, Lt. Kenneth "Deacon" Jones, a twenty-year-old pilot from

Janesville, Wisconsin, took a train to Cambridge for the funeral of a friend from his 389th Bomb Group who was killed in a crash landing in England. It was a mass burial service, "so many names with no one to grieve for them." Bundled up in his trench coat, Jones began to shake with emotion when taps was played. After the service, he and another airman walked to a local pub and ordered a glass for their departed friend. "We took off sometime later, and one full drink was left standing on the bar."

Some men who sought relief from the war in the towns of East Anglia returned to the base more depressed than when they arrived. On a three-day visit to Cambridge, Georgia-born Ben Smith fell in love with the old timbered buildings, the ancient inns, and the lawns and gardens that ran from the backs of the colleges down to the slow-flowing River Cam, from which the town took its name. Twenty miles removed from "death and terror," Smith found "peace and sanctuary" and he did not want to leave. The bus trip back to Molesworth felt as long and depressing as any mission he had ever flown.

Hangar Music

While Ben Smith was at Molesworth, his Hell's Angels group celebrated its 200th mission with a wild three-day party. Military trucks hauled in enormous quantities of scotch and lager and were then dispatched to pick up girls from the local towns. "So it began—non-stop drinking for days on end. The casualty lists mounted. The dispersal tents were booked solid. Bars were filled with wall-to-wall humanity, sodden and riotous." Some of the women stood on the bars and stripped for the boys, and the MPs could not keep drunken couples from sneaking into the Nissen huts to enjoy each other. "Finally it was over," Smith recalled, "and what the Germans had not been able to do, alcohol had! The 303rd Bomb Group was completely out of business."

For its 200th mission party, the Bloody Hundredth chartered a train to pick up hundreds of women in London, most of them of questionable virtue. After being tested for venereal disease, they were billeted in special barracks guarded by MPs, although "most of them didn't sleep there," recalled pilot Keith Lamb. There was clean fun as well. Families from the surrounding villages were invited and there was a traveling English carnival, with rides, concessions, and a fortune-teller. While village children devoured real American hot dogs and rode the gorgeous carousel brought in for the occasion, Fortresses took off for the Reich. When the boys returned that afternoon without a single loss, they joined the merrymakers, drinking bitter and eating thick steaks cooked on open pits near the airfields.

When the sun went down, the action shifted to the big hangar. Fliers and their dates jitterbugged to the driving music of the Hundredth's Century Bombers Orchestra. "Once you'd learned to jitterbug you never wanted to do any other dance," recalled a local woman. "The American boys would swing you around and throw you over their shoulders, and between their legs. Everyone got lost in the music. It was bloody wonderful."

About a week after the party, the commanding officer learned that several London women were still on the base as guests of a group of fliers who were kind enough to share their beds with them. The MPs were sent to roust them, but they refused to leave. The guards were ordered back and the women disappeared from the Nissen hut. "I never saw men look so sad," Rosie Rosenthal recalled the expressions on the faces of the disappointed fliers. Two days later, the same girls were found in the beds of the MPs.

When Lewis Welles's 95th Bomb Group celebrated its 200th mission party the guests of honor were Bing Crosby, Dinah Shore, and Capt. Glenn Miller and his Army Air Force Band. "For an hour the walls of the [hangar] pulsated and vibrated," Welles described Miller's concert in a letter home. "When it seemed as if the roof would fly off the [band] piled into their trucks and took off."

Miller arrived in England with his forty-piece orchestra just after D-Day, causing a sensation in a country where his soft swing music had been copied by nearly every British dance band. During the previous year, the band, with its handsome lead crooner Sgt. Johnny Desmond, "the boy Sinatra," had raised millions for the war effort with a Saturday radio program, *I Sustain the Wings,* and concerts at war bond rallies all across America. But Miller wanted to go to Europe, into the heart of the war, to entertain the airmen with the tunes they listened to on German radio while flying back from the Reich: "In the Mood," "A String of Pearls," "Tuxedo Junction," "Chattanooga Choo Choo," "Pennsylvania 6-5000," and the band's sentimental theme song, "Moonlight Serenade."

At age thirty-eight, with a wife and two toddlers, the lean, scholarly-looking trombonist was three years past the upper age limit for the draft, but "I sincerely feel that I owe a debt of gratitude to my country," he told his disappointed American fans. Miller broke up the band he had formed just four years before and was commissioned a captain in the Army Air Forces. With a boost from Gen. Hap Arnold, he was given permission to organize a new band, filling it with an unlikely combination of jazz musicians and classically trained string players, all of them Air Force volunteers. Some of the band's older players had no desire to go overseas, but Miller lobbied hard for the reassignment and General Eisenhower finally requested that the band be posted in England to broadcast shows for a new radio service of the Allied Expeditionary Force. Some of the musicians had been declared unfit for overseas duty, but Miller had the requirements waived. "You're all going no matter what they said on your service records," he told them. Miller was flown to London to make advance arrangements, the rest of the orchestra followed by sea.

The Miller band arrived in the city at the height of the buzz bomb scare. The musicians found Captain Miller spending most of his time in a bomb shelter underneath the BBC building at 25 Sloane Court, where they were scheduled to do their broadcasts. When a pilotless bomb landed three blocks away, Miller received permission to take the band to Bedford, fifty miles north of London. Here the band was billeted for the next six months, close to the American airbases it visited on a busy summer tour. The day after the band left London, a V-1 rocket slammed into the street directly in front of 25 Sloane Court, shattering buildings and killing over seventy people.

Miller's band played most of its concerts in giant steel hangars and flew from base to base in war-weary bombers marked with bright white paint: *Condemned for Combat*. Music-hungry airmen crowded the stage, stood on the wings of planes, and perched on the beams high overhead, swaying to the sounds of home. "That sound was something in that hangar," a bomber pilot recalled Miller's concert at Attlebridge. "I mean, people went nuts."

In late November, Miller told his orchestra that they would be going to liberated Paris for a Christmas concert, giving the American fighting forces on the continent "a hunk o' home." He would fly ahead to set things up. On December 15, as he and his friend Col. Norman F. Baessell prepared to take off from an RAF field near Bedford, Miller was noticeably nervous. The weather was vile: freezing drizzle and dense fog, and they were in a light, single-engine plane without ditching equipment or parachutes—a Norseman D-64 piloted by RAF flight officer Johnny "Nipper" Morgan. Before they boarded, Morgan had assured them the weather was improving. This was scant consolation to Miller, who had an aversion to flying. The Norseman took off into the gloom and vanished forever.

For forty years, Glenn Miller's death remained an unsolved mystery. In 1984, two members of an RAF bomber crew—the navigator and pilot—came forward with an explanation. On the afternoon of December 15, their four-engine Lancaster was returning from an aborted daylight mission to a marshaling yard in Germany. After their bomb-aimer jettisoned the bombs over the English Channel, the navigator, Fred Shaw, said that he and a gunner—who died in 1983—saw a Norseman aircraft fall from the sky, the victim, apparently, of the concussion created by their discarded bombs, one of them a 4,000-pound "cookie" that exploded near the surface of the sea. "The rear gunner, who was looking around all the time, saw it tip up and go into the sea," Victor Gregory, the pilot, told a *New York Times* reporter. When Gregory was asked why he had not disclosed this information sooner, he said he had forgotten about the incident until Shaw contacted him, and had failed to connect it with Miller's disappearance, which had not been reported for nine days after he left England. Fred Shaw said his curiosity was first aroused in 1954 after seeing the Hollywood film of Glenn Miller's life, starring Jimmy Stewart. Shaw checked his wartime logbook and realized the downed Norseman might have been Miller's plane. For years, his story was discounted by reporters, historians, and Glenn Miller enthusiasts, until it was corroborated by aviation historian Roy Nesbit, who conducted an exhaustive study of meteorological charts and declassified operational documents.

The Battle of the Bulge

On the evening Glenn Miller was scheduled to meet friends in Paris, Field Marshal Gerd von Rundstedt issued the order of the day to the armies he had secretly amassed in the Eifel Mountains, opposite the Ardennes Forest. "Soldiers of the West Front, your great hour has struck. Everything is at stake." At five-thirty the next morning, a thunderous artillery bombardment announced the opening of the assault that would stun the world. This was Hitler's final attempt to turn the tide of the war, a colossal gamble made against the advice of his senior military commanders, including von Rundstedt.

The führer's plan was to raise a new army, the Volksgrenadier, a people's infantry made up of transferred airmen and sailors, retired infantrymen, conscripts from Nazi-occupied countries, and German boys as young as fifteen. It would link up with veteran army units, including the Waffen SS, in a lightning counterattack along an eighty-mile front that ran from southern Belgium to the middle of Luxembourg. The attack would be spearheaded by the hundreds of tanks that Albert Speer's accelerated armaments program had produced that summer, and would be supported by the new Luftwaffe units Galland had assembled for the Great Blow. After breaking through the twisted terrain of the Ardennes, two armies, with another protecting their southern flank, would swing north, across the Meuse River, and capture the port of Antwerp, some 125 miles away. This would cut the flow of supplies to the Allies and split the British and Canadian forces from the American armies to the south. At this point, the Western Allies might agree to a separate peace, allowing Hitler to throw everything he had against the oncoming Bolsheviks.

For his plan to succeed, Hitler needed at least three things: the element of surprise, bad weather, and additional gasoline, which he expected to capture in the fight. "Fog, night, and snow," he predicted, would ground the Allied air arm and give him his victory. In the opening hours of von Rundstedt's offensive, almost a quarter of a million German troops and 900 tanks swept through the thinly defended American lines—a "ghost front" manned by untested units and veterans exhausted by a savage November fight in Germany's Huertgen Forest. Fighting in heavy snow and fog, and caught completely by surprise in dense, untracked forests, defense lines broke down and the Germans made enormous initial advances, creating the great bulge in the American lines that would give the battle its name. All the while, heavy cloud cover extending all the way back to England grounded the Allied air forces, giving the attackers the advantage Hitler had banked on.

How had Hitler pulled off the surprise, amassing a tremendous army directly in front of American lines at a time when the Allies enjoyed air superiority over this entire region? It was a case of the Army's having the intelligence, but not believing it. Aerial and ground reconnaissance had detected a German buildup west of the Rhine, but American ground commanders were convinced it was nothing more than an effort to reinforce existing defensive positions along the Siegfried Line in expectation of a coming Anglo-American offensive to the north and south of the Ardennes, where most of the Allied troops were massed. As historian Charles MacDonald, a veteran of the battle, wrote: The American commanders "looked in a mirror and [saw] there only the reflection of their own intentions."

For a worrisome succession of days, the weather held and the impetus of the surprise assault carried Hitler's panzer armies, the sharp point of the advance, deep into the Ardennes. The heroes who turned the battle were the losers of the first few days. Soldiers in small rifle companies, engineering groups, and antitank teams fought in zero-degree temperatures, slowing the German penetration and giving Eisenhower time to bring up massive reinforcements. Blunting the initial German advance was crucial for another reason. Unknown to the Allies, the Germans had only enough fuel for a five- or six-day attack. Before their gasoline ran out, the armored columns, headed by Col. Joachim Peiper's 1st SS Panzer Division, counted on capturing fuel depots behind enemy lines. The defiant resistance of American GIs defeated these plans, as small units attacked Tiger tanks with bazookas and rifle grenades and raked infantry outfits with small-arms fire, grenades, and mortar. "Our orders were to hold or die," recalled one soldier. "Somehow we held." They and airborne units rushed to the front in trucks held on precariously at crossroads towns like St. Vith and Bastogne; and by the end of the first week of the enemy offensive, Patton's Third Army was racing toward imperiled Bastogne, in one of the most thrilling rescue efforts of the war. All the while, Eisenhower moved a quarter of a million men into the thick of the fight. No army has ever been reinforced in such numbers and at such speed.

Two days before Christmas, the skies cleared and Allied fighters and medium bombers chewed up panzer columns already hobbled by fuel shortages. "We'd look up at the sky and say, 'Thank goodness they're flying again,' " recalled Sgt. Roger Rutland. That day, the Eighth put up every heavy bomber available, an air armada of nearly 20,000 men. It saturated airfields and marshaling yards east of the Rhine, dropping more tonnage than on any other single day of the war.

The following day, the Eighth Air Force lost one of its founders, one of the "original six" that Ira Eaker had brought to England to set up American bombing operations. After spending a year at Eaker's headquarters, Brig. Gen. Frederick Castle had volunteered to take over the newly committed 94th Bomb Group, and after restoring discipline to that unruly outfit, had been given command, in April 1944, of the 4th Combat Wing, the largest in the Eighth Air Force. On Christmas Eve 1944, he led the greatest force in the history of aviation against communications centers and Luftwaffe fighter fields. Flying over Belgium, Castle's plane was forced out of the lead by engine problems. With friendly troops beneath him, he refused to jettison the bombs to gain speed, and his trailing bomber became an easy target for seven Messerschmitts that had been tracking the bomber stream, a formation that stretched for 300 miles, all the way back to the Channel. General Castle's Medal of Honor citation describes what happened next: "Repeated attacks started fires in two engines. . . . Realizing the hopelessness of the situation the bail-out order was given. Without regard for his personal safety he gallantly [took] the controls to afford other crew members an opportunity to escape. Still another attack exploded gasoline tanks . . . and the bomber plunged earthward," with Castle guiding it toward an open field. The explosion spread metal fragments and human remains for over 600 feet.

Attacking pitilessly that day and right through Christmas, the strategic and tactical forces knocked out bridges and rail lines and cratered highways, creating a "supply crisis" that helped doom the German offensive. The Luftwaffe rose to defend the Wehrmacht's lifelines, but lost nearly 250 fighters in five days. Running low on both fuel and ammunition, harassed by American engineering units that blew up bridges and by attack planes that blanketed the skies, Colonel Peiper's SS unit abandoned its tanks and began walking back to Germany. On Christmas Day, Gen. Hasso von Manteuffel's 2nd Panzer Division, having passed St. Vith, ran out of gas only three miles from the Meuse, where it was pilloried by a column led by Gen. Lawton Collins, the hero of the St. Lô breakthrough. The next day advanced columns of Patton's army broke the siege of Bastogne. With these twin defeats, all chances of the Germans reaching Antwerp evaporated, although Hitler insanely ordered his armies to continue to press the fight, refusing to believe that its objectives were beyond reach.

Allied heavy and medium bombers continued to smash rail junctions, bridges, and marshaling yards behind enemy lines, preventing German units from reaching the fighting front. Even soldiers on bicycles could not get through some railway towns wrecked by Allied bombs. The German offensive "would have succeeded," von Rundstedt told Allied interrogators after the war, "if supplies and reserves could have been brought up as quickly as General Patton could move up from the south." That is doubtful, but the destruction of rail transportation west of the Rhine helped seal the fate of the German army in the Ardennes before the onset of the new year.

On New Year's Day, the Luftwaffe, under direct orders from Hitler, undertook a daring offensive to reverse the course of the battle. Before the sun came up, over 800 German fighter pilots made final preparations for an early morning strike against Allied fighter fields in Holland, Belgium, and northern France. The objective was to catch the fighters while they were still on the ground, paralyzing a good part of the enemy's air force "in one stroke." Some of the German squadrons took to the air barely an hour after celebrating the New Year. "We danced, laughed, and drank until quite suddenly—on a gesture from the Kommandeur—the orchestra stopped playing," recalled Lt. Gunther Bloemetz. " 'Meine Herren,' the Kommandeur's voice rang out across the silent room, 'we will check our watches. Take-off in fifty minutes!' "

With the winter sun beginning to rise on the horizon, the pilots were in their planes, two of them dressed in their mess uniforms—white shirts, patent leather shoes, and white gloves. If captured, they wanted the enemy to know "they have to deal with superior people." Moments later, "sixty aircraft thundered across the airfield, blowing the virgin snow of New Year's Eve into the whirling clouds with their take-off." Approaching their targets at treetop level, the attack forces caught the British and American tactical commands with their pants down, destroying or damaging over 450 planes, most of them on the ground. But in Operation Baseplate the Luftwaffe fighter arm lost over 400 piston-engine aircraft and 237 pilots, including fifty-nine of the force's commanders. It was the greatest single catastrophe the Luftwaffe would suffer. "In this forced action we sacrificed our last substance," said Galland, who had prepared most of these pilots for the Great Blow.

In the previous year, the Luftwaffe had lost over 13,000 aircraft, destroyed or damaged beyond repair, in combat operations on all fronts. After Baseplate the single-engine fighters would be able to mount only occasional, harassing attacks on the Allied bombers. That December, the Luftwaffe had accepted shipments of over 2,900 new combat aircraft, but without sufficient fuel and pilots, most of these spanking-new planes would spend the rest of the war in air parks with blocks on their wheels.

By the first week of January, the Allies were on the advance in the Ardennes, slowly pushing the Germans out of the seventy-mile-deep bulge, a monthlong operation. In January 1945, the U.S. Army suffered more battle casualties—over 39,000—than in any other month in the fight for northwest Europe. The best friends the GIs had in the final weeks of the battle were the Allied air forces. Clouds of Thunderbolts and British Typhoons flew in over the treetops, following the tracks of German tanks in the snow. All the while, the Eighth Air Force continued to savage marshaling yards on both sides of the Rhine, creating transportation delays and deep shortages of weapons and ammunition. Essential supplies continued to get through to the Wehrmacht, but with immense difficulty, as two entire transportation systems, one in the Cologne area, the other around Frankfurt, were turned into railway "deserts." And as von Rundstedt's armies retreated from the frigid forests of Belgium, they were fatally delayed by gasoline shortages caused by Spaatz's oil offensive. By the end of January, the enemy's brilliant fighting retreat turned into a rout, a race back to the Siegfried Line, where the battle had begun six weeks earlier.

The Battle of the Bulge was almost entirely an American fight, the biggest and costliest in lives ever fought by the U.S. Army. Over one million German and Allied soldiers were engaged, 600,000 of them Americans. Nineteen thousand Americans were killed, 47,000 wounded, and 15,000 captured. The Germans suffered over 100,000 casualties. It was preeminently a riflemen's battle, but airpower had been indispensable.

January was the climax of the Allied air campaign against Hitler's war economy. The Reichsbahn was damaged beyond hope of recovery; with this, the coal famine turned into an irreversible energy catastrophe. The Ruhr—the beating heart of the German economy and the chief source of its coal and iron ore—was almost completely cut off from the rest of the country. Deprived of the raw materials essential to production, gasworks, power plants, and munitions, mills either closed down or were forced to drastically curtail output. And with Germany's rail system under daily assault, component parts, including ball bearings, could not reach the final points of production. Unable to ship the products it was still able to manufacture efficiently, the entire ball bearing industry collapsed.

Allied oil raids compounded the chaos caused by the coal crisis. Heavy cloud cover in the late autumn had helped the oil industry recover a small part of its productive capacity. But Allied bombers got through to their targets with enough regularity that fall and winter to demolish any hopes that Speer might have had to salvage the sinking industry. By late January, it was impossible for either the Luftwaffe or the motorized units of the Wehrmacht to organize effective resistance in the West. By then, the general economic situation had become irremediable. The final curtain had fallen on the German war economy.

From January 1945 on, German armies on both the Eastern and Western fronts would experience severe shortages of both fuel and weapons, the direct result of the bomber war. "When the Allied breakthroughs [occurred] west of the Rhine in February, across the Rhine in March, and throughout Germany in April, lack of gasoline in countless local situations was the direct factor behind the destruction or surrender of vast quantities of tanks, guns, trucks, and of thousands upon thousands of enemy troops," said Gen. Omar Bradley. And by Joseph Stalin's own admission, Russian victories in Silesia in February and March 1945, and the Red Army's final drive on Berlin, were aided by the enemy's fuel crisis, the massive impairment of his rail system, and the transfer of German fighters from the Eastern Front to the defense of homeland industries.

Interrogated after the war, the German high command was almost equally divided on the question of which air attacks had hurt the Reich the most: those on transportation or oil. Field Marshal Keitel thought transport raids because of their direct importance to military operations and war production; Göring said oil raids—"Without fuel, nobody can conduct a war." But German field commanders on the Western Front—men actively conducting operations—realized that it was the *simultaneous* blows against oil and transportation that had made it impossible to conduct effective ground operations. "Three factors defeated us in the West," said von Rundstedt. "First, the unheard of superiority of your air force, which made all movement in daytime impossible; second, the lack of motor fuel—oil and gas—so that the Panzers and even the remaining Luftwaffe were unable to move; third, the systematic destruction of all railway communications so that it was impossible to bring [a] single railway train across the Rhine. This made impossible the reshuffling of troops and robbed us of all mobility."

Gen. Georg Thomas, former head of one of Germany's major war production boards, put it most succinctly: "Victory is production, and you destroyed German production. Victory is movement—you paralyzed us." Conducted simultaneously and unsparingly in the fall and winter of 1944–45, the oil and transportation offensives hastened the end of a war that could have dragged on into late 1945.

The January Crisis

In January 1945, the air commanders who had destroyed the German economy failed to realize it. Persistent cloud cover prevented photoreconnaissance planes from gaining a complete picture of the destruction that Allied bombing had wrought. Not until February, when the weather improved and Sir Norman Bottomley, the RAF's deputy chief of air staff, ordered a thorough review of ULTRA intercepts of German commercial message traffic, would a complete picture emerge of the extent of the damage done to the German transportation system. Bottomley's investigators would discover thousands of enemy reports describing the parlous state of the national economy. In its enthusiasm for oil over transportation bombing, the Combined Strategic Targets Committee had either failed to scrutinize carefully or deliberately ignored these reports.

Lacking this invaluable information in early January, the Anglo-American air chiefs were despondent. "The fighting quality of the German ground armies is still very high," Assistant Secretary of War Robert Lovett described the prevailing pessimism of American air leaders. "Their offensive possibilities are still large. . . . The recuperative power of German industry has exceeded our expectations . . . [and] the morale of the civilian population has shown no signs as yet of breaking."

In a remarkable letter to Carl Spaatz, Hap Arnold conceded for the first time in the war that "we may not be able to force capitulation of the Germans by air attacks." At a January 11 conference of Allied air leaders, Gen. Frederick Anderson reported that "from the strategic point of view, the picture is very sad," a verdict that Jimmy Doolittle backed "100%." Anderson had just seen a disturbing report prepared by Brig. Gen. George C. M. McDonald, the Eighth Air Force's intelligence chief. It warned that "a staggering proportion of German aircraft production" was going into the "jet program," and that if the war continued beyond June, jet-powered fighters, in numbers approaching 700, could be capable of completely upsetting "the present balance of aerial power in Europe."

ULTRA intercepts also indicated that Germany had begun a production program to assemble fast, silent-running submarines with supplemental electric motors that would allow them to remain submerged for up to seventy-two hours. By January, almost a hundred new boats were under construction and three dozen were already in training exercises in the Baltic Sea. The new U-boats, said A. V. Alexander, the first lord of the admiralty, were capable of inflicting "losses of a level we suffered in spring 1943."

"Our estimate of the situation does not lead up to the conclusion that German strength will crack in the near future," Spaatz wrote Arnold in early January. "Unless our ground armies succeed in obtaining a significant victory over German ground armies west of the Rhine in the reasonably near future, it will be necessary to reorient ourselves and prepare for a long, drawn out war." The Combined Chiefs of Staff agreed. The European war they had confidently expected to win by Christmas 1944 looked to them like it might last far into 1945, with the defeat of Japan coming eighteen months after that.

At the conclusion of a February 2 meeting of the Allied air commanders, Gen. Frederick Anderson delivered an impassioned plea for "replanning the strategic air offensive on the assumption of a longer duration of the war." The oil and transportation offenses would have to be prosecuted with renewed vigor, and heavy attacks would have to be made on jet aircraft plants and submarine assembly yards at Hamburg and Bremen.

Draconian measures against German population centers might also be required to extinguish the last embers of Nazi resistance. This threatened to put Berlin back on top of the Eighth Air Force's bombing agenda. And from Robert Lovett's office came a dramatic plan to form a new fighter-bomber raiding force, named after the legendary Confederate cavalry leader Jeb Stuart, an idea that had originated with Gen. Pete Quesada. Its purported aim was "the systematic destruction of enemy communications, small factories, power plants etc. deep inside Germany." But it was really a thinly disguised proposal for terror raids designed to break the morale of German citizens in the hundreds of towns that had not yet felt the fury of Allied air attacks. "If the power of the German people to resist is to be further reduced," Lovett ominously suggested to Arnold, "it seems likely that we must spread the destruction of industry into the smaller cities and towns now being used for production under the German system of dispersal."

Arnold's headquarters staff dismissed Lovett's plan. His proposal for the "early provision" of 500 additional aircraft to carry it out was not within "current AAF capabilities." But Arnold urged Spaatz to consider equally "visionary" plans that "would result in greater destruction than we are getting now. . . . Air power must not let the war in the west become a stalemate."

In early January, Hap Arnold and other discouraged leaders of the Anglo-American coalition were banking heavily on the success of a massive Soviet offensive that was about to begin. Hopefully this would force Hitler to heavily reinforce the Eastern Front and prevent his depleted forces at the West Wall from mounting a strong defense along the Rhine.

The fate of thousands of Allied prisoners of war also rode on the fortunes of the Red Army. Among the POWs being held by the Germans in camps along the eastern reaches of the Reich, directly in the path of the impending Soviet advance, were 95,000 Americans, including over 30,000 airmen. One of these camps was Stalag Luft III in Sagan, part of German-occupied Polish Silesia, one of a half-dozen Luftwaffe-run stockades for Anglo-American airmen.

On the morning of January 12, Stalin unleashed the Red Army's final winter offensive. Eight days later, elements of the Soviet army smashed into Silesia, depriving Germany of one of its great coal-producing regions. On January 27, with the Russians closing in on Posen and Breslau, cities to the north and south of Sagan, Hitler ordered the Luftwaffe to evacuate the prison camps that were about to be liberated. He wanted to keep the Anglo-American terror-fliers as hostages, possible bargaining chips for a separate peace agreement with the Western Allies.

Listening to the thunderous discharges of Soviet artillery, airmen at Stalag Luft III grew concerned about their approaching fate. As prisoners, they had felt a strange sense of security. Despite the hardships, their lives had not been endangered unless they had tried to escape; they were actually safer in a German stalag than in an American bomber over the Reich. "Now real fear set in," said navigator Lou Loevsky, "the kind of fear we had felt when we jumped from our burning bombers into the land of the people we were bombing."

CHAPTER FOURTEEN

The Wire

It was always with us—that fence—And we were on the wrong side of it.

EUGENE E. HALMOS, PRISONER OF WAR,
EIGHTH AIR FORCE

Berlin, March 22, 1944

As Lt. Louis Loevsky was falling to earth over bombed-out Berlin, he had two concerns: what he was wearing around his neck and what he had left behind in England. "Even before I pulled the ripcord, it occurred to me that I risked being shot by the Gestapo or the SS if I kept on my dog tags, which were marked with an 'H,' Hebrew, to ensure that I received a proper burial. I also knew that if I ripped them off and threw them away I risked being shot as a spy. Since our military briefings had not covered these minor details, I decided to risk being shot as a Jew."

Loevsky's second problem was this. In a matter of minutes he was either going to be killed or captured. In either case, he would be listed as missing in action and his personal belongings, including some horribly embarrassing items, would be shipped home to his parents in Lyndhurst, New Jersey. A week before his 466th Bomb Group had been shipped out to England some of the men went to the base PX and bought big boxes of Hershey chocolate bars. The English girls were said to love them. Loevsky had taken a bolder approach, buying a gross of condoms and stuffing them into the pockets of every uniform he possessed, including the one he had on. "Here I was free-falling over Berlin and I was thinking to myself, 'Holy shit! When my parents open that Air Force footlocker they'll think: 'What kind of a sex fiend did we raise?' " Asked years later if he was sexually hyperactive at the time, Loevsky replied: "No, just an optimist."

Loevsky was the twenty-four-year-old navigator of the Liberator *Terry and the Pirates*. Hit by flak over the target, the bomber careened out of control and collided with another B-24, the *Brand,* shearing off its tail and sending it into a fatal spin. Before the *Brand* exploded, one of its propellers smashed into the underside of *Terry and the Pirates,* trapping the bombardier, Leonard Smith, in the forward gun turret, directly underneath the Plexiglas nose. Smith was in pain and shock, and in his delirium he pulled off his gloves and oxygen mask. "He was rapidly turning blue, at 23,000 feet, and with the temperature nearly 40 degrees below zero, I knew he'd have severe frostbite in no time," Loevsky remembered. "I had to get him out of there quick.

"I'm a little guy [five foot four] and he was a big guy, so it was a hell of a struggle, but I managed to hook an arm around his chest and pull him out; then I let the bombs go. I had no idea where they landed, but I knew we had lost some of our guys in that collision and I didn't want our mission to have been in vain.

"After that, I booted Len out of the plane and jumped right behind him; Bill Terry, our pilot, followed right behind me. I landed in a tree on a downtown Berlin street."

Two Wehrmacht soldiers apprehended him and marched him at gunpoint through the bomb-blasted city to their headquarters. "As we went along, civilians began gathering around us, and soon we had an infuriated mob to contend with. People began to spit on me, make throat-cutting motions with their hands, and chant in perfect English, 'Hang him! string him up!' The German soldiers were forced to lower their rifles to contain the crowd. If it hadn't been for them I'm sure there would have been a necktie party."

When they arrived at headquarters, Loevsky met up with Len Smith, who had somehow managed to pull the ripcord with his severely frostbitten hands and land on the roof of a small hotel. Later, Loevsky learned that his pilot was dead. The Germans informed the Eighth Air Force that Bill Terry's body had been found near the wreckage of the plane he had gone down in. Loevsky knew this was not right; he had seen his pilot jump from *Terry and the Pirates*. "I have no evidence for it," he said years afterward, "but I'm convinced that he was either shot in his chute or killed by irate civilians. We were really pasting Berlin and other German cities and we were warned to avoid German civilians if we were shot down. Reports had come back to us that they were beating and even lynching American fliers, '*kinder* killers [child killers],' they called us."

Terrorfliegers

Unlike most infantrymen who were captured by the Germans, airmen were apprehended alone because they came out of the sky alone, which made it impossible to determine how many of them were beaten or killed. There are, however, dozens of documented cases of the murder and brutal mistreatment of the reviled *Terrorfliegers* (terror fliers), bomber boys as well as fighter pilots. At the time Lou Loevsky was captured, American bombs were falling regularly into residential areas of Berlin and other cities, and long-range fighter escorts were under orders to dive low and strafe targets of opportunity on their return to England. These were usually enemy airfields and marshaling yards, but the German government reported attacks on passenger trains, schoolyards, cyclists, pedestrians, and peasants at the plow—and called for reprisals. "It would be demanding too much of us . . . to expect that we should silently accomodate ourselves as victims to this unlimited barbarity," declared Minister of Propaganda Joseph Goebbels.

An unknown number of German civilians were killed in fighter sweeps over small towns and villages, killings verified by film taken from the gun cameras of downed American Thunderbolts and Mustangs. But many of the German reports of civilian casualties were the rank fabrications of Nazi propagandists intent on inflaming public opinion. Sensational reports also appeared in German papers describing killer squads of American bomber boys recruited from gangland Chicago to fly "murder raids" against cities like Berlin and Hamburg. In late 1943, the photograph of a B-17 bombardier wearing a flight jacket with the words "Murder, Inc." emblazoned on the back had appeared on the front page of a Berlin newspaper; soon a story on the bombardier's life was featured in a popular German magazine. The writer claimed that Lt. Kenneth Williams of the 351st Bomb Group was one of Al Capone's stone-cold killers who had been freed from Alcatraz at the insistence of President Roosevelt in order to organize an Air Force outfit called Murder, Inc., whose supposed objective was to massacre German women and children. Each air assassin was reputedly paid $50,000 a mission. "Gangster Williams is now in our hands," a Nazi radio broadcaster gloated. "He is living proof of America's murder lust. He belongs to America's secret weapon—a mass murder league—which has been set loose against us."

The truth was more prosaic. When Kenneth Williams and his crewmates had arrived in England they were assigned a war-weary Fortress, *Murder, Inc.;* and in a burst of bravado Williams had an enlisted man paint the bomber's nickname on the back of his leather flight jacket. He was never to fly in *Murder, Inc.,* however. With the old bomber under repair in a hangar, Williams's crew had flown its first two missions in standby planes. After the crew was shot down on their second mission, a German sergeant took pictures of Williams in his flight jacket, and in one photo he was posing with his back to the camera. This was the photograph Nazi propagandists feasted on.

Investigators from the Luftwaffe did not take the story seriously, but thousands of Germans did. Captured near Bremen, Eighth Air Force airman Roger Burwell was loaded onto a truck and driven through the streets of the still burning city, where he saw the body of a fellow American flier hanging from a lamppost. "I was glad that I was in the hands of the military rather than a mob of civilians," Burwell said later.

Göring had issued instructions early in the war that captured enemy airmen were to be protected by Luftwaffe police from the inflamed wrath of the German citizenry. A famous World War I flying ace, Göring believed in the universal kinship of fliers, Knights of the Sky. He also wanted to ensure that his own captured airmen were treated humanely by their Allied "comrades." By early 1944, however, official German policy had begun to shift ominously, at the insistence of the führer. In late May of that year, Goebbels published an editorial in a Nazi Party paper condemning Anglo-American air attacks against "defenseless" women and children as "naked murder," not warfare. In the future, Germans should not be expected to protect "enemy man-hunters" from the righteous wrath of the people. It will be, Dr. Goebbels declared, "an eye for an eye, a tooth for a tooth."

Less than a week later, Martin Bormann, Hitler's private secretary, and one of the most sinister figures in the Reich, issued a secret circular to local Nazi Party officials detailing alleged incidents of Anglo-American fighter pilots deliberately targeting civilians. A number of captured airmen "were," he admitted, "lynched on the spot immediately after capture by the populace, which was incensed to the highest degree." These mob attacks had gone unpunished, a policy of noninterference that must be continued, he insisted. As Hitler's generals testified after the war, the führer wanted downed terror aviators "to be surrendered to public fury." Hitler's Security Police chief, Ernst Kaltenbrunner, obliged, informing his entire security force that "pogroms of the populace against the English and American terror-fliers are not to be interfered with. On the contrary, this hostile mood is to be encouraged."

Shortly after Bormann's circular was issued, the German high command, under pressure from the führer, issued a highly secret and patently criminal order. Oral briefings—not traceable written orders—were to be given to all military officers concerned to prevent intervention by soldiers against citizens who attacked *Luftgangsters* (air gangsters). And from the deepest reaches of the Nazi bureaucracy, direct orders occasionally went out to execute downed airmen. At a postwar investigation into the murder of four Anglo-American fliers, a party functionary named Hugo Gruner testified that he had received orders from the local Nazi leader, Robert Wagner, to "execute any Allied airman taken prisoner." Gruner carried out this command with ruthless resolve, discharging a machine gun burst into the back of each airman. The limp bodies were then "dragged by the feet and cast into the Rhine."

Finally, on March 15, 1945, a month after the firebombing of Dresden, Hitler issued a blanket command that all downed terror fliers were to be shot or lynched on capture. This was, in his demented mind, not just an act of retribution. He was also angered by mass surrenders of German troops to Eisenhower's forces. "The soldiers on the Eastern front fight far better," he told General Heinz Guderian. "The reason they give in so easily in the West is simply the fault of that stupid Geneva convention [which Germany and the Western Allies, but not Russia, had signed] which promises them good treatment as prisoners. We must scrap the idiotic thing."

Even Heinrich Himmler's SS was unwilling to carry out Hitler's bestial command, for fear of postwar Allied retribution. At the Nuremberg war crimes trials, Alfred Jodl, chief of the operations staff of the German high command, testified that he and other Wehrmacht leaders had used "delaying tactics, a kind of passive resistance," to block Hitler's measures to turn over "low-level fliers" to "lynch justice." These stratagems, he admitted, were only "occasionally successful."

The motivation of the German high staff was hardly humanitarian. Their paramount concern was the protection of German airmen in enemy hands, and the impact such egregious violations of the Geneva Conventions would have on the morale of remaining Luftwaffe fliers. Expediency, not moral concern, saved the lives of thousands of downed Allied airmen in the last months of the war. But with the Nazi Party's encouragement, and with the more than occasional surrender by the Wehrmacht to Hitler's madness, vigilante violence continued. When a B-24 Liberator was shot down over Mecklenburg on June 21, 1944, all nine crewmembers were executed on the pretext of "attempting to escape." In another documented incident, the Gestapo was marching six American fliers through the town of Rüsselsheim, which they had bombed the previous day, when workers from a local factory came pouring into the street, demanding that the Americans be lynched. According to witnesses, two women began screaming, "There are the terrorizers of last night, kill the dogs! We can't have pity!" One of the women threw a brick and the mob soon joined in, pelting the airmen with stones and beating them with farm tools until they collapsed and died—one airman pleading before he took a fatal blow, "Don't kill me. I've got a wife and two children." The bodies of the airmen were left unburied for a day before they were thrown into a communal grave. After the war, a military court at Darmstadt sentenced five German civilians to death for the murders. The two women who incited the crowd also received death sentences, but General Eisenhower reduced their punishment to thirty years' imprisonment.

Two years after the war, at an American military court at Dachau, a Wehrmacht doctor, Max Schmidt, admitted that he had cut off the head of an American flier, boiled it and bleached it, plucked out the eyes, and sent it to his wife "as a souvenir." The court sentenced Schmidt to ten years' imprisonment for abusing the dead body of a combatant. Official records of the Nuremberg trials contain at least sixty-six legally documented incidents of killings or beatings of unarmed American airmen in the custody of the Reich, over 70 percent of the offenses being murder.

Downed Allied airmen felt safer in the hands of the German military than they did with the local citizenry they had bombed. Luftwaffe police and interrogators were in official charge of captured airmen, and their tactics for extracting information were rough but rarely barbaric. After being captured, Lou Loevsky was shipped with other downed American airmen to Dulag Luft, the Luftwaffe interrogation center for Allied airmen at

Oberursel, a suburb of Frankfurt am Main.* After being strip-searched, he was placed in solitary confinement in an unheated cell that was "colder than a Nazi's heart." The windowless room was only a few inches wider than his cot and was unlit; without his watch he had no idea whether it was day or night. After a meal of stale black bread and evil-tasting ersatz coffee made from oak leaves and coal, Loevsky was removed from his cell for interrogation. "They knew I was a greenhorn, had been shot down on my first mission, and had nothing to give them, so they released me after a few days of questioning. The airmen who blabbed or were high-ranking officers usually stayed longer."

The Luftwaffe interrogators at Dulag Luft were deeply skilled specialists who preferred methods more subtle than the rubber hose. All of them spoke fluent English and some had spent time in England or America; one of them was a former piano salesman from Yonkers, New York, who had returned to the fatherland after Hitler took power. The Luftwaffe resisted Gestapo and SS pressure to be harder on the captured airmen. After the war, Hanns Scharff, the famous master interrogator at Oberursel, claimed that he and his colleagues "were horrified when our German radio stations broadcast a statement issued by [Goebbels] . . . that all Allied airmen falling into German hands in the future were to be declared to be 'fair game' in the eyes of the populace. . . . [We] stood fast. Our orders remained the same as before . . . we were to fully protect the prisoners." If a prisoner was an officer, the smoothly proficient Scharff—a man said to be able to "extract a confession of infidelity from a nun"—would begin by offering him chocolate and cigarettes and then draw him into some light banter about American baseball or movies. The conversation became so congenial that many airmen were unaware that the interrogation had begun. Luftwaffe interrogators tried to impress airmen with the thick files they already had on them and their bomb group. "You will not be telling us anything we do not

---

* The term "Dulag Luft" originally referred to both the interrogation center and a transit camp across the road from it for prisoners awaiting shipment to permanent prison compounds. Later, the transit camp was moved, first to a park in central Frankfurt, near the main railroad station (to discourage Allied bombing of the city), and later, after that camp was destroyed by Allied bombers in late March 1944, to the town of Wetzlar, about thirty miles north of Frankfurt. The Germans called both these transit camps Dulag Luft and the main interrogation center in Oberursel Auswertestelle West (Evaluation Center, West), to distinguish it from a similar interrogation center for Soviet airmen on the Eastern Front. But the American Air Force and most of the prisoners held at Oberursel continued to call the interrogation center Dulag Luft, short for Durchgangslager der Luftwaffe—or Air Force Transit Camp. In this account, I have followed the Army Air Forces' precedent.

already know." At one point in his interrogation a smiling Luftwaffe major asked Roger Burwell why the men in his 381st Bomb Group at Ridgewell had not yet fixed the broken clock in their officers club.

Airmen who refused to provide military or personal information were usually threatened verbally. Some were told that their families would not be informed they were alive and "safe" until they began to cooperate; men captured without identification tags were warned that they could be turned over to the Gestapo to be executed as spies. One stubbornly tight-lipped officer—married and with children—was told that if he persisted in his obstinacy, a report would go out the next day from the German radio station in Calais that the night before he was shot down he had been at the Grosvenor House in London, in room 413, with an attractive blond woman. Knowing that the information was exactly correct, the major is reported to have fainted on the spot.

Such threats were rarely carried out. "Under mental pressure because of his civilian-looking flying clothes, the [prisoner] told all," a captured interrogation report reads. Prisoners were also softened up by the appalling conditions at Dulag Luft: the tomblike isolation, the starvation rations, and the mice that ran free in the dank cells, and crawled in prisoners' pockets searching for food. Sometimes the promise of a shower, a shave, and a hot meal was sufficient to loosen a man's tongue. The guards also fiendishly manipulated the temperatures in the cells, shutting off the electric wall heaters in the winter and turning them up to intolerable levels, to 130 degrees, in warmer weather. Hundreds of airmen arrived at Dulag Luft wounded and were denied medical treatment, a flagrant violation of the Geneva Conventions regarding prisoners of war. "[My interrogator] said he could see that I was injured and needed treatment and that my being stubborn would only delay my being sent to a hospital," Roger Burwell recalled. On the other hand, high-ranking Allied fliers believed to possess specialized military information were taken on hunting trips or invited to raucous drinking parties with German officers.

It was the interrogators' immense amount of information about American Air Force operations that was their most effective tool in extracting information. In intelligence briefings back in England, airmen had been warned about what to expect, but the "apparent omniscience" of their captors unnerved more than a few of them. "[My interrogator] actually inquired about my mother's health in Terre Haute and asked how my kid sister was doing in high school," recalled one flier.

Many POWs assumed that the Germans had spies on every American airbase in England. There is no evidence, however, that their agents had penetrated a single air station. They didn't have to. Most of the information was gathered from Allied sources by Dulag Luft's efficient staff, who scrutinized American magazines and newspapers brought in from neutral Portugal, including *Stars and Stripes,* a rich source of hometown information about airmen. Additional information, including logbooks, briefing notes, and airmen's personal diaries, was gathered from clothing and other personal belongings found in the charred wreckage of bombers. These documents often contained highly secret data about flight patterns, the effectiveness of German defenses, and targets marked for future bombing. An officer in the American Air Force's Counter Intelligence Corps noted at the time that "it was not uncommon for large German manufacturers to ask the Luftwaffe if their factories were on the list, and if so, when they could expect to be bombed." German linguists also monitored Allied airmen's wireless communications. According to Hanns Scharff, the interrogators at Dulag Luft had at their disposal a copious file in which "nearly every single word spoken in the air from plane to plane or from base to plane or vice-versa was carefully noted." As Air Force counter intelligence experts noted in their own secret files, "nothing in the way of documents, written or printed, was too insignificant to merit close scrutiny" by the intelligence staff at Dulag Luft.

A case in point is the airmen's ration cards. Every American flier in the European Theater received exactly the same kind of card, and there was nothing on the card to indicate where he was stationed. But investigators at Dulag Luft were able to identify an airman's bomb group by the way his card was canceled. At Thorpe Abbotts, for example, the clerks on duty in the PX marked the cards with a heavy black pencil. The PX counter was made of rough board. All the cards canceled there carried the impression of its distinctive pattern in the black pencil markings. The Air Force's Counter Intelligence Corps estimated that 80 percent of the information obtained by Dulag Luft was supplied by captured documents and monitored radio traffic, with the remainder coming from POW interrogations. After the war, when he was hired as an interpreter by the American military, Hanns Scharff estimated that all but twenty of the more than 500 airmen he questioned disclosed operational and tactical information that proved useful to the Luftwaffe. Few of these airmen, he emphasized, did it knowingly, or through intimidation or a conscious desire to improve the conditions of their confinement. "I suppose he got something out of me," said one flier, "but to this day I haven't the least idea what it could have been."

After being released from Dulag Luft, Loevsky and several dozen other

airmen were taken by tram to Frankfurt, where they were herded onto cattle cars and sent deep into German-occupied territory to Stalag Luft III
(Air Camp number three), near the town of Sagan, a hundred miles southeast of Berlin, one of the half-dozen main POW camps operated by the
Luftwaffe—hence the term "Luft," or air—for Allied airmen. (The Wehrmacht and the Kriegsmarine ran their own stalag systems.)* Two of the camps,
Stalag Luft III and Stalag Luft I, near the town of Barth on the desolate
shores of the Baltic, were officers camps; the others were entirely for sergeants or for sergeants and a sprinkling of officers. By the end of the war
there would be approximately 33,000 Army Air Forces personnel in German prison camps, a little less than one-third of the total number (93,941)
of Americans captured and interned by the Germans in the European Theater.

At Sagan, two of the most powerful men in the prisoner hierarchy were
Gale Cleven and John Egan from the Bloody Hundredth. Egan was a
member of the prisoners' secret intelligence committee in charge of escape
activities, and Cleven was a valued education officer. Both worked closely
with the Hundredth's first commander, Col. Darr Alkire, the senior American officer in charge of one of the prison's five compounds, to establish a
military-style command structure, with the men organized to do everything imaginable to make life difficult for the "goons," as the prisoners
called their guards. "We were thrown together, the Germans and us, in this
bleak pine forest in Upper Silesia, one big unhappy family," Cleven recalled. And it was "a rapidly growing family. The more we punished the
Germans the more airmen poured through the gates of our stalag." All of
them were victims of a terrifying air experience that had dropped them
suddenly and unexpectedly into the hands of the enemy; all had been put
into solitary confinement and closely interrogated by the Luftwaffe. At
least half of them were still suffering from wounds and a number of them
were permanently maimed or disfigured. They arrived exhausted, hungry,
and distraught, many of them wrapped in bandages or hobbling on
crutches, with lost, faraway looks in their eyes, surprised and angry, even
ashamed, that they had been captured. "It's a strange thing when you go to
war. You somehow never expect to be taken prisoner," recalled Eugene E.
Halmos, a B-24 navigator who had been a magazine writer in New York
City before the war. Every combat flier arriving in England knew he might
be killed or wounded. "But taken prisoner? That's a role few men picture

---

* *Stalag* is short for *Stammlager,* or base camp, and is the term Germans used in World
War II for prisoner of war camps for officers and enlisted men.

for themselves." As American bomber pilot Hank Plume said long after the war, "If I had known I was going to be a POW I'd have done a better job preparing for it."

The Great Escape

They were "kriegies," slang for *Kriegsgefangenen,* "prisoners of war" in German. Most of them had been told when captured, "For you the war is over." That was "a lie," said Lou Loevsky. "Capture was the beginning of our longest mission."

Arriving at the camp's main building for delousing and processing, a new "purge" of prisoners would see groups of fellow American fliers crowding close to the gates of their compounds, shouting and waving. "Practically everyone recognized someone and almost immediately a great outcry arose," recalled one prisoner. " 'Hey, Joe, how in the hell did you get here? Come on in, the water's fine!' . . . 'Henry! Have you seen Bill? I've been expecting him.' . . . 'You've had it chums. . . . For you the vor iss ofer.' "

After being photographed, fingerprinted, and assigned a POW number, Lou Loevsky received his bedding and eating utensils: two thin army blankets, one sheet, a burlap mattress cover filled with wood shavings, a small linen towel, a mixing bowl and cup, and a knife, fork, and spoon engraved with swastikas.

Loevsky entered a place alive with excitement. Seventy-six RAF prisoners had escaped from North Compound several days before he arrived, crawling through a thirty-foot-deep tunnel that a thousand men had been digging for over a year. The breakout, later called the Great Escape, had taken place on the night of March 24–25, and the escape parties, each led by a German-speaking prisoner, had scattered in a dozen different directions. The SS and the Gestapo were called in and the government issued a *Grossfahndung,* the highest search order in the Reich: almost five million Germans took some part in the roundup. When Loevsky arrived at Sagan, the escapees were still believed to be on the loose and there was "a feeling of euphoria in the camp."

Unknown to the men, all but three of the escapees had been quickly apprehended, and on Hitler's orders, fifty of them were executed by the Gestapo and cremated to destroy the physical evidence of cold-blooded murder. The führer had wanted all seventy-six prisoners shot, but his generals persuaded him to reduce the number to fifty.

It was the duty of captured Anglo-American officers to do everything in their power to escape. Escapes—although not successful ones—were common, and prisoners who were caught were sent to the "cooler," a grim solitary confinement lockup, for a period of roughly ten days. Since the punishment for escape was not extreme, many of the kriegies considered it a kind of game. So on April 6 when the senior British officer, Herbert M. Massy, was informed that forty-one (the number was later changed to fifty) of his escaping officers had been shot "while resisting arrest or attempting further escape from arrest," he was stunned. How many were wounded? he demanded to know. No one was wounded, he was told. When word reached the prisoners, they were "plunged into anger, shock, and despair," said Loevsky. "I'll never forget the words of our compound commander, Col. Delmar T. Spivey, when he called us together: 'Gentlemen, we're helpless and hopeless.' This was my introduction to Stalag Luft III."

Camp Kommandant Col. Friedrich-Wilhelm von Lindeiner-Wildau was arrested and a chain reaction was set in motion that led to a September 30 order from Martin Bormann to transfer control of all POW camps from the armed services to the SS. Fortunately for the kriegies, Himmler delegated prisoner of war matters to SS-Obergruppenführer Gottlob Berger, a man with a sharply developed sense of survival. Knowing that Germany could not win the war, he hoped that his humane treatment of Anglo-American POWs in the last stage of the conflict would save him from the hangman. Berger allowed the Luftwaffe to retain operational control of their camps. The prisoners were warned, however, that future escapes would bring their lives under the direct authority of Himmler, who, rumor had it, wanted to dispose of all prisoners of war. Posters were placed in conspicuous places in all stalags: "The escape from prison camps is no longer a sport."

Some Jewish prisoners began to fear they might be sent to concentration camps. In December 1944, the kriegies at Sagan learned of the camps from other prisoners who had recently spent time in one of the worst of them. In the summer of 1944, 168 Allied fliers—eighty-two of them Americans—were evading capture in civilian clothes in Nazi-occupied France when they were betrayed by a Gestapo spy that infiltrated their escape line. Charged with being saboteurs and terrorists, they were shipped off in cattle cars to Buchenwald, near Weimar, Germany, where they spent nine horrifying weeks before a sympathetic Luftwaffe officer intervened and had them transferred to Sagan. They arrived in a pitiful state. "They were like . . . skeletons, with sunken chests, hollow eyes, and stick-like limbs," recalled one POW. Questioning them, "we realized how bad it would be if [any of us] went into a concentration camp."

If Himmler, and not Berger, had been in active control of the POW camps, it is likely that thousands of Jewish war prisoners would have been sent to one of the special SS slave labor camps like Berga, sixty miles from Buchenwald. There, 350 American infantrymen captured in the Battle of the Bulge, men known or thought to be Jewish, worked alongside concentration camp inmates excavating tremendous tunnels for an underground synthetic oil plant.

After the Great Escape, relations between prisoners and Luftwaffe guards deteriorated badly at all the camps, particularly Sagan. Colonel Spivey, who had been in charge of a school for Air Force gunners in the States before being shot down in August 1943 while on an inspection mission in the European Theater, instructed his men to leave the room if a German entered it, unless ordered to remain. Nazi propaganda about *Luftgangsters,* along with intensified RAF raids on Berlin, "made our guards increasingly surly," wrote David Westheimer, later the author of *Von Ryan's Express,* a best-selling prisoner of war novel. "Shooting into the camp [from the watchtowers], very rare in the past, increased. . . . When nerves on both sides of the wire were stretched tautest, Brigadier General Arthur W. Vanaman turned up at Stalag Luft III. The rumor spread quickly that he bailed out of a B-17 over Germany, which later got back to England with all its regular crew unharmed, and that he spoke fluent German, was a prewar acquaintance of Hermann Goering, and had been sent to defuse the situation."

Vanaman did know Göring from his four years as assistant air attaché in Berlin before Pearl Harbor, but he had not been sent to Stalag Luft III to calm the waters. He was there because he had made the stupidest mistake of his life. As the Eighth Air Force's new chief of intelligence, he had been briefed on ULTRA shortly after arriving in England. Then he decided, after gaining Doolittle's reluctant permission, to fly in combat so that his intelligence staff would have greater respect for him. On his third mission, his Fortress was struck by flak and one of the engines caught fire. The pilot hit the bailout button and Vanaman was the first man out of the plane. Moments later, the pilot got the fire under control cancelled the bail-out order, and headed back to England with the four remaining crewmen. Word of Vanaman's capture sent shock waves through the top Allied command structure. Eisenhower was furious at Doolittle for giving Vanaman permission to fly over the Reich with knowledge of the Allies' most closely kept military secret. "When Van went down, we thought we lost everything," said Gen. Laurence Kuter in a postwar interview. "He had all of the highly classified stuff. He should have never, ever been there." Fortunately, the rank-conscious Germans did not interrogate him. The highest-ranking Air Force officer captured during the war, Vanaman was brought to Berlin, treated with deference, and told he would be sent to a comfortable castle in Dresden for special prisoners. Pounding the table for effect, he insisted that he be sent to the largest Air Force POW camp. When he arrived at Stalag Luft III he replaced Col. Charles Goodrich as senior American officer. He was assigned to Center Compound and made his predecessor, Spivey, his chief of staff.

Vanaman had injured his back on his fall into Germany, and at night he would tear off small pieces of his bandages and tape them over his mouth to prevent himself from talking in his sleep and revealing his sensational secret. Using mind control, he succeeded in driving the very word ULTRA out of his head. "When I came out of Germany I did not know and remember the code word ULTRA," he recalled in a postwar interview. "It's funny what a man can do with his mind."

That October the prisoners received word from Washington, through secret channels, that devising escape plans was no longer their duty as American soldiers. The risks were too great, and with Anglo-American armies within striking distance of the Rhine, the prisoners' liberation seemed imminent. Some men continued to hatch escape plans and dig tunnels, if only as antidote to depression. Both they and the kriegies who decided to stay put lived in hope that fall and winter of 1944, but it was not an easy time for them. "Just keeping up your hopes, which was all part of keeping your sanity, was tremendously difficult," said Loevsky, the son of a struggling immigrant brass maker. "I wouldn't take crap from the Germans or anyone else, but some nights I wanted to cry I was so damn lonely and scared." Loevsky had a recurring dream. "I have never been a practicing Jew, but in my dream I was asked by some fellow Jewish prisoners to join them in private prayer services in the barracks. The dream was always the same. The guards would crash through the door, herd us into the pine forest, and shoot us. I couldn't shake that dream, nor could I share it with anyone else. I was a tough guy. I had a reputation."

Life in the Bag

Stalag Luft III had been opened in April 1942 as a small, high-security camp for RAF airmen. But by late 1944 its prison population had swelled to more than 10,000, with over half of the new prisoners American fliers. For purposes of control, the kriegies were kept in five separate compounds—North, South, East, Central, and West—with the German guard force and command staff quartered in their own compound. In one corner of the camp was the *Vorlager.* It contained special facilities for the kriegies, including an infirmary, a bathhouse, a storage building, and the cooler. RAF airmen were segregated in the North and South Compounds; the other three compounds were reserved for American prisoners. Each compound contained a dozen or so weather-beaten barracks called blocks, a cookhouse, a shower building, a laundry, and a combination theater and chapel. Scattered around the drab gray barracks buildings were playing fields for baseball, football, and soccer that had been built by the kriegies.

A barracks building housed up to 150 men in double- and triple-decker bunks. There were from twelve to fifteen sleeping rooms of varying sizes, each furnished with a few benches, some shabby wooden lockers, and a table with a 20-watt bulb hanging straight down from the ceiling over it, exactly as it is pictured in the popular postwar film *Stalag 17.* This was the only electric light in the combine. Men made their own primitive lamps with tin containers filled with the grease that floated on the top of their rank-smelling soup. High-ranking officers were given two- and four-man rooms; the other officers slept twelve to fifteen to a room, and the orderlies—sergeant gunners who had been sent to the camp in the summer of 1944 at the request of the compound leaders—were housed in a large, crowded room in the center of the barracks. They did much of the cleaning, washing, and cooking for the officers, the only labor they were required to perform. By the terms of the Geneva Conventions, flying officers were not permitted to do work for the detaining power.

At each end of the narrow central hallway that separated the living areas was a washroom, with cold-water faucets; a cramped communal kitchen containing two coal-burning stoves; and a small latrine that was used only after nightly lockups. Large daytime pit latrines, or "aborts," were located between the barracks. The blocks had been shabbily constructed by Russian slave laborers; heavy rains overwhelmed their thin beaverboard roofing, turning some rooms into "miniature lakes." And in the ferocious Silesian winters, freezing blasts of wind penetrated the cracks in the walls, forcing the men to sleep in their clothing. Some airmen retained remnants of their flying uniforms, but most wore military clothing supplied by the U.S. Army and delivered by the International Red Cross. Additional clothing arrived in personal packages from home. "Everything you owned, you wore to keep warm," recalled Elmer Lian, an airman from Fairdale, North Dakota.

In summer, swirling clouds of sand would blow into the rooms and the dirt would embed itself in the men's clothing, under their nails, and in their skin. Lice and bedbugs lurked in the mattresses, and the aborts overflowed regularly, filling the air around the living areas with a deplorable smell.

Staying alive was the prisoners' paramount concern; security the Germans'. A stalag was enclosed by two high metal fences, running parallel to each other; between them was a dense thicket of rolled concertina wire with long, sharp barbs. Three-story wooden sentry towers—"Goon Boxes"—were placed around the perimeters of the compounds. They were equipped with powerful searchlights and manned by guards with expressionless faces. About thirty feet from the perimeter fence—and inside the camp—was a low-hanging wire (in some camps it was a rail). Prisoners were warned that if they crossed this "warning wire" for any reason, even to retrieve a baseball, they would be shot on the spot.

The barracks were built two feet off the ground to discourage tunneling. "Ferrets," English-speaking security guards dressed in blue overalls and equipped with metal probes, would sneak under the barracks to check for tunnel-building activity. The ferrets used the small crawl spaces in the attics of the barracks to eavesdrop on kriegie conversations, and they placed hidden listening devices all over the compound. They also conducted unannounced searches, often in the middle of the night. Mattresses were torn open, beds overturned, wooden floors ripped up, and the prisoners' meager possessions tossed about, chewed up by guard dogs, and sometimes stolen.

At ten o'clock at night, the German guards shuttered the windows and barricaded the barracks doors with heavy wooden bars. Sentries with Schmeisser machine pistols slung around their necks patrolled the camp the entire night, their snarling Alsatians pulling at their leashes. These attack dogs were trained on Allied uniforms in the woods outside the camp and were so unpredictably vicious that they occasionally turned on their masters. "If the shutters were open after dark, it was risky to put your hand out the window lest it be snapped off at the wrist," recalled John Vietor, a pilot with the Fifteenth Air Force who was a "guest of the Führer" in Stalag Luft I at Barth.

Similar incidents occurred at other camps. In Stalag Luft VI, a sergeant's camp in East Prussia, Eighth Air Force radio gunner Glen A. Jostad, a shy Wisconsin farm boy, counted sixteen holes in the walls of his compound after the guards opened fire for no apparent reason.

Guards were tougher on prisoners in sergeant's camps. At Stalag Luft IV in the Reich province of Pomerania (now Poland), the most notorious of the guards was Sgt. Hans Schmidt. Known to the kriegies as "Big Stoop," he was a slow-moving giant of a man, six foot seven inches tall and nearly three hundred pounds; and he was a twisted sadist. Sneaking up behind prisoners, he would slap their ears with his unnaturally large hands, bringing men to their knees with pain and rupturing the eardrums of several of them. Big Stoop patrolled the compounds with his eyes cast down, swinging a thick leather belt. Air Force gunner George Guderley watched helplessly as Schmidt beat a prisoner senseless with that belt, using the buckle to inflict scalp wounds so deep that the bone of the man's skull was exposed. "He wasn't even human," says Guderley, a street-tough Chicagoan. "He was a beast. I would have killed him if I had had the chance."

In all matters save security, the Luftwaffe kept a loose leash on the prisoners, allowing them to run the day-to-day affairs of the compounds. At 7:00 A.M. there was roll call—*Appell*. The prisoners stood at attention in a hollow square on the parade ground as the camp officials performed a count. When the tally was complete, sometimes after as many as ten recounts, the Germans would salute the Allied Senior Officers, and they, in turn, would dismiss their men. For the rest of the day, until lockup, the kriegies were under the unofficial authority of their own military superiors. A senior Allied officer was in charge of each compound (in the enlisted men's stalags the prisoners elected a Man of Confidence). Answering to him were block commanders, each responsible for a barracks or block. Camp leaders acted as go-betweens in negotiations with the Germans and communicated with delegates of the Swiss government, which acted as the Protecting Power in Germany. The Geneva Conventions of 1929 called on belligerents to accept the aid of Protecting Powers to help resolve disputes over prisoners of war and to conduct regular camp inspections to ensure that living conditions were in line with the standards set down in the Geneva codes. The International Committee of the Red Cross, an independent humanitarian agency headquartered in Geneva, also conducted inspections, under the auspices of the Geneva Conventions on prisoners of war. When inspections were scheduled, the Germans would invariably make hurried improvements in camp conditions, improvements that rarely lasted longer than the visits of the inspectors.

Every stalag had its central security committee. At Stalag Luft III it was called the Big X and was run by a charismatic Eighth Air Force fighter pilot, Lt. Col. Albert P. "Bub" Clark, one of the first Americans to be shot down in the war and the officer who had been in charge of security in North Compound for the Great Escape. All escape plans were to be cleared with X. If a plan was given a reasonable chance of succeeding and did not interfere with another escape plan, it could expect to receive X's approval and active assistance. Each compound also had its own security committee to guard against infiltration by Gestapo plants. Before being assigned to their barracks, new kriegies were interrogated by the members of the committee. "We also interviewed them to find out what their skills and backgrounds were as far as things that might help us [to plan escapes]," Bub Clark recalled. Men with special skills were assigned to small, secret "factories" located all over the compound. Peacetime photographers became expert forgers, making passports, German ration cards, and travel passes; the documents were made to look official with rubber stamps fashioned from the heels of men's flying boots. Miniature compasses were assembled with needles, razor blades, and small pieces of glass—the metal magnetized by stolen German magnets. Camp tailors made German uniforms out of old blankets, burlap bags, towels, and clothing from home; the uniforms were dyed gray in a solution made by boiling book bindings. Amateur sculptors used blocks of wood to make fake German pistols that looked exactly like those the guards carried. "We never failed to find someone who could do the things that needed to be done," said Clark.

While these men were at work, or while a tunnel gang was burrowing under a blockhouse, men called "stooges" were placed on guard at each of the barracks's entrances. If a German approached, a stooge would shout, "Goon Up!" and clandestine work would cease.

Tunneling was difficult and dangerous work, especially at Sagan, where the sandy soil seemed to be perpetually shifting. The two-man tunneling crews—"moles"—worked on their stomachs, using their elbows for locomotion. Bed slates from the combines were used to shore up tunnels, digging tools were fashioned by kriegie metalworkers, and fresh air from handcrafted bellows was fed into the tunnels through ducts made of empty Klim ("milk" spelled backward) cans. Entrances were hidden under burning stoves and bathhouse drains. The work lasted months and some tunnels reached as far as several hundred feet. Excavated soil was disposed of by flushing it down the barracks' toilets and by filling mattresses and lockers. There were also "penguins," men assigned to carry freshly dug dirt in sausage-shaped cloth bags hidden inside their loose-fitting trousers. The

bags hung from a long sling around their necks. The penguins would wad-
dle around the camp perimeter, slowly releasing the sandy soil by pulling
on a string attached to openings in the bags. Other men walked behind
them, kicking dark-colored dirty sand over the freshly excavated yellow
sand, which even smelled different from the surface sand.

All this was for naught. As a kriegie leader reported after the war,
"Every time a group of prisoners . . . crawled underground to a point outside the camp there was the saddening anticlimax of finding German
guards pointing rifles into their exit hole and ordering them to solitary confinement."

The writer Damon Runyon has one of his characters intone: "Life is six
to five against." Chances of escaping a German stalag were slimmer than
that. The men knew it, and realized, as well, that to have any chance of
making it through German lines they had be wearing either civilian clothes
or an enemy uniform, a virtual guarantee that they would be shot on the
spot if apprehended by the Gestapo. There are no reliable records, but in
the entire war probably less than 2 percent of American prisoners attempted to escape German camps and an unknown number made it to
freedom. British intelligence sources claim that 28,349 British Commonwealth and Allied (Greek, Polish, French, Czech, and Russian) soldiers and
7,498 Americans escaped from camps or evaded capture in World War II,
with evaders vastly outnumbering escapees.*

After the Great Escape no prisoner who set out for freedom from a Luftwaffe camp reached an Allied or neutral country. In an effort to keep the
men orderly and in strong spirits, military discipline was enforced by Allied officers. "If you left them alone, they would have gone to seed, grown
beards, gotten slovenly," Bub Clark recalled. "They would have just un-
raveled. But we had hut inspections on Saturday mornings; we marched
them. . . . We took every opportunity to keep them from forgetting that
they were military men and their country would need them when they got
home."

POW life was resolutely communal. Men formed themselves into
"combines," groups of from four to a dozen kriegies who lived together in

---

* There is no agreed-upon figure about how many of either group, escapees or evaders,
made it to freedom. Nor is there a reliable breakdown between the number of escapees
and the number of prisoners. The American escape agency, MIS-X, claimed that there
were over 12,000 Americans who escaped or evaded. A high official at MI-9, the British
escape organization, argues that the true number probably lies somewhere between the
British and American figures.

a cramped room and shared virtually everything. "In this group we live, find our friends," Eugene Halmos wrote in his secret prison diary, which he kept on scraps of paper. The combines prepared most of their own meals in the barracks. The camp cookhouse supplied only one cooked ration a day, usually barley soup that had the consistency of glue and was served with tiny white bugs floating on the surface. The bugs were prized; they provided protein. The Germans also dispensed uncooked rations for the kriegies to prepare in their makeshift kitchens: worm-infested potatoes, margarine that looked like axle grease, and blutwurst, a sausage made from onions and congealed animal blood. All meals were eaten with "goon bread," a hard black concoction whose ingredients included sawdust. The Luftwaffe food was so bad that some new prisoners refused to eat it. A freshly arrived kriegie, a cocky captain wearing his officer's hat at a "jaunty angle," was assigned to Lou Loevsky's combine. On his first evening in camp he stared at a foul-looking piece of meat and growled, "What the fuck is that." Told it was sausage made from the blood of slaughtered animals, he pushed his portion aside and announced, "I'd sooner eat shit." The following day he returned to the table, his stomach growling, pointed at the blutwurst, and said, "Please pass the shit."

German rations were supplemented by more nutritious food that arrived in Red Cross parcels. Each kriegie usually received one parcel a week. The Allied armed forces paid for and packaged these parcels, which were shipped into Germany by the Swiss Red Cross. In addition to cigarettes and Army-issue chocolate bars, each cardboard "suitcase" contained about ten pounds of canned food: raisins, tuna, liver pâté, corned beef, sugar, jam, Spam, prunes, crackers, powdered coffee, and a one-pound can of condensed milk. Red Cross parcels saved thousands of kriegies from debilitating dietary disorders. The combines split up the contents of the parcels equally, except for cigarettes, chocolate bars, and jam. Theft occurred but it was not common. "You could lay a piece of bread on your pillow, and no one would ever touch it," said Elmer Lian.

One of the most ingenious of the prisoners' self-created institutions was "Foodaco." At this "Stalag Swap Shop," located in the camp cookhouse, Red Cross food was exchanged in a highly regulated barter system, with cigarettes serving as the principal medium of exchange. Each item had its own price, or point value, one cigarette equaling one point. Foodaco (an abbreviation for "food account") also stocked toilet articles and spare clothing. There was a surcharge on each item. The "money" was used to bribe nicotine-starved guards for escape and survival equipment: cameras, clothing, radio parts, and small tools.

Combines were allocated "stove-time" in the barracks kitchen to cook hot meals from the rations they received from the Germans and the Red Cross. "Cooks surrounded the stove, poking, prodding, stirring, testing," and recipes were exchanged with avidity. Men who had never touched a skillet proved to be surprisingly inventive. Having no flour, they made biscuits from crackers and tasty soups from Spam and German onions. And thirsty kriegies found ways of making home brew from the raisins, prunes, and sugar. Three drinks produced a pleasant glow, four caused a stomach eruption.

The Germans rarely provided fresh vegetables, so the men dug "victory gardens" behind the barracks, planting radishes, carrots, kale, lettuce, and onions. But this kriegie ingenuity produced a daily diet that barely sustained life. "You could tell an old-timer in camp by the fact that he didn't bother to pick out the maggots when eating his barley," said Roger Burwell, who was quartered in Loevsky's compound.

Historians have made much of the Germans' general adherence to the Geneva codes and the low death rate in the stalags, approximately 5 deaths per 1,000 prisoners, but the Germans provided neither food nor clothing that met the standards of the Geneva agreements. A normal-sized man at that time required 3,000 calories a day to lead a reasonably active life; the Germans provided from 1,500 to 1,900. And airmen at the officers camps were fed far better than sergeants imprisoned in separate stalags or infantrymen held in camps in other parts of the Reich.

Medical services in all the stalags were scandalous; the equipment was medieval and the number of trained personnel inadequate. Captured airmen who were seriously wounded were sent first to a German hospital, where they received good care. But few patients received essential followups after they were shipped to stalags. "We had men in camp with arms and legs missing . . . ," recalled Sgt. Richard H. Hoffman, a prisoner in Stalag XVIIB, in Krems, Austria. "The [American] medics . . . set up a therapy room to help [them] . . . The wounded exercised their stumps using homemade weights and pulleys in an attempt to make their limbs stronger. . . . The Germans would not supply artificial limbs."

At Stalag Luft IV, in Pomerania, where Big Stoop patrolled the compounds, Capt. Leslie Caplan, an American flight surgeon, handled a staggering sick load brought on by overcrowding, pervasive filth (the camp had no communal showers), parasitic sand fleas, and starvation rations. This was the worst of the Luft camps, presided over by Lt. Col. Aribert Bombach, a strident Nazi who had lost his family in an Allied bombing raid. Here, in the summer of 1944, a group of nearly 2,000 Anglo-

American fliers were victims of one of the most fiendish acts of cruelty committed by the Germans in their prison camps.

These sergeant gunners were being transferred from Stalag Luft VI at Hydekrug, a desolate town in East Prussia on the border with Lithuania, and in the direct path of a furious Russian summer offensive. On the sweltering afternoon of July 14, the Hydekrug sergeants were taken in closed cattle cars to the port of Memel on the Baltic Sea, where they were herded into the stinking holds of two rusty coal freighters, "packed in," said one POW, "worse than slaves in the old slave ships." The stench was so horrible that one prisoner, upon first entering the hold, would only go halfway down. He clung to a ship's ladder for the entire time at sea. He was Sgt. John W. Carson, the missing twin brother of Eighth Air Force tail gunner Eugene "Wing Ding" Carson. A radio gunner with the Fifteenth Air Force, he had been shot down over Athens, Greece, in late December 1943, and the Air Force had been unable to locate him.

After two days at sea, the ship that carried John Carson's group laid anchor at the German port city of Swinemunde, at the mouth of the Oder River. There the airmen were placed in boxcars and handcuffed in pairs. The next morning they reached a remote railroad juncture called Kiefheide. When the guards pulled back the doors of the cars, the men crawled and fell to the ground "in sickening slow motion, yelling and crying," recalls B-17 pilot Tommy LaMore, a prisoner at Luft IV who had been enlisted to help move the new POWs to the camp.

The Hydekrug prisoners were covered with scrapes and sores, vomit and excrement, and they were cursing at the Germans.

"Go ahead and kill us now, you Kraut shitbags!"

"The men," LaMore would write, "were beyond reason, ready to charge the guards."

Capt. Walther Pickhardt, a camp guard renowned for his brutality, was there to make sure that did not happen. Waving a pistol and raising himself to his full five feet three inches, he was inciting a group of prison guards and young naval cadets who happened to be in the area. The Kriegsmarine cadets were standing around him, dressed in their freshly pressed uniforms, their shining bayonets unsheathed. "These are the people who bombed your women and children. Now is the time for revenge," Pickhardt shrieked. When the suffering men were unloaded from the cars, Pickhardt ordered his guards to march them up a narrow road through a dense pine forest. "As soon as we started up the road, orders were given for us to increase our pace, and the Kreigsmarines began to hit some of the prisoners with the butts of their rifles and to prick us with bayonets," recalled William

D. Henderson, an Eighth Air Force tail gunner from Mississippi. "They continued to yell at us to run faster. They then turned dogs loose on the column."

Hidden machine gun nests had been placed on both sides of the forest road. Pickhardt wanted to provoke his prisoners to try to escape into the inviting woods, but none of them took the bait.

There had not been enough chains for all of the prisoners, and those not shackled were able to run at a dead heat. Many of the men who were handcuffed together fell. When they did, the marines and the dogs were on them, the marines shouting out the names of bomb-damaged German cities as they pricked and stabbed them, *"Eine für Hamburg, Eine für Köln!"* Some of the prisoners were still suffering from war wounds; others were broken down and deathly sick from the Baltic nightmare. Sgt. Edwin W. Hayes was handcuffed to his best friend, Robert Richards, who had an open wound in his leg and had lost an eye when he was shot down. When Richards stumbled, Hayes pulled him up and carried him the rest of the way. Other men did the same for weaker comrades shackled to them. "It was a time of heroism unsung," said prison poet Robert Doherty. "Brother carried brother."

After a two-mile run, the prisoners emerged from the forest into a broad clearing, with the pine-board camp in front of them. The men threw themselves on the ground, and Pickhardt called off the dogs. None of the estimated 150 men who were bitten and stabbed on the Hydekrug Run died, but some were permanently disabled.

"Like everyone else," recalls John Carson, "I settled into the routine of obedience and slow starvation." It would have been easier to die than to live. But after learning from some POWs from the 92nd Bomb Group that his twin brother was back in England on a second tour of duty, he knew that Wing Ding had come back looking for him. "I was determined to survive."

Bomber crewmen were trained to cooperate, and this training served them well in the camps, as it had on the Hydekrug Run. The strain of living together in close quarters with twelve to sixteen men for months, even years, led to friction, flare-ups, and occasional fistfights. But the barracks of the Luft camps, like the compartments of the bombers, were surprisingly harmonious places. Men of vastly different backgrounds buried their differences as well as their prejudices, "bending to the will of better judgment," as one airman put it.

Some men found it more difficult to live with themselves than with their mates. Time was the enemy of every kriegie. "Each day was born to be killed, a slow, agonizing process," wrote a POW. In a diary he kept throughout his two-year confinement at Barth, Fortress pilot Francis "Budd" Gerald endowed "the wire" that penned him in with human characteristics, "a silent, stern tyrant. [It] is barbed—there are exactly 8,369 barbs in his stark perimeter in front of our barracks. I have counted them. We all count them, often. There used to be 8,370 barbs, but recently one has rusted and fallen off. This was quite an event.

"You can cheat 'the wire'—but not for long. . . . You can turn your back to him and escape him by building a picture frame out of a tin can, or doing your weekly wash, or scribbling out a poem. . . . But when you look up again, he is there . . . blocking every dream, every plan, every vain soaring of enthusiasm . . ."

A persistent reminder of the prisoners' helplessness, "the wire" drove a number of men over the brink—"barbed wire disease," as the kriegies called it. Its most conspicuous symptom was a "demoralizing melancholia," a feeling of being hopelessly trapped. In its more pernicious form it devolved into a "captivity psychosis" that left a victim unable to concentrate or even remember his name. Afflicted men became apathetic and inattentive and would spend entire days in their bunks vacantly staring at the walls. Others fell from listlessness into a paralyzing depression, unable to talk or even communicate with their hands. The inherent uncertainty of POW confinement aggravated the condition. Unlike most criminals in a civilian prison, kriegies never knew when they would be freed, if at all. This led some grievously sick men to prefer death to continued confinement.

On a rare summer night when the prisoners' windows were left open, John Vietor and a friend saw a bombardier crawl out of his barracks and make a suicidal rush for the wire. "A few seconds later we heard a shot and the subdued snarling of a dog. . . . In a minute a blinding glare of searchlight swept the area. . . . Ten feet away was the prostrate body of a wounded prisoner. Standing over him was a growling Alsatian and a stocky guard still holding his pistol."

At night, in the fetid combines, it was impossible to distinguish the anguished cries of men with barbed wire disease from those of men haunted by night dreams: visions of exploding planes, flaming parachutes, and baked bodies. "One night I heard a man call out, 'Waist gunner to pilot . . . Joe's been hit hard. Dear God, he's been shot in half!' " wrote Richard Hoffman in his searing prison memoir. "There was silence, then muffled sobs."

During the war, thousands of American infantrymen feigned insanity in order to be removed from the line and sent to a field hospital and then back home. No one feigned insanity in a stalag. Conditions in the camp hospitals were as appalling as they were in the barracks, and the Germans refused to repatriate prisoners suffering from mental disorders. Prisoners counted on friends to help them keep their moorings. "I feel I'm on the verge," a crewmate of Glen Jostad confided to him one evening. "Keep an eye on me. If you see me acting crazy, get hold of me." This helped. Still, a number of prisoners overcome with despair tried to take their lives. B-24 bombardier Lt. Philip B. Miller tells of a quiet, withdrawn man in his combine at Barth who cut his throat and wrists with a razor blade "and lost enough blood to paint a house. There was an excellent British doctor who stitched him up and he was returned to the compound."

There are no reliable records on suicides in the stalags, but by all accounts the number was low. Most kriegies bore up under the pressure and more than a few actually profited from the experience. "The most wonderful friends I've ever had came out of these camps," Lt. Col. Bub Clark said later. "None of us felt it was a total dead loss as an experience. A lot of us learned a lot about ourselves. And we certainly learned how to get along with people under difficult circumstances, which is a very important lesson." The deprivations kriegies endured led many of them to a keener appreciation of things they had previously taken for granted. In his prison memoir, John Vietor quoted the ancient Arab proverb:

> *I murmured because I had no shoes*
> *Until I met a man who had no feet.*

In his first weeks at Sagan in July 1944, Eugene Halmos fell into a soul-deadening depression. "Always the wire around you. . . . Always the towers with the guards. . . . Always no place to go." But he quickly learned that "the trick was to keep busy." The camp had a couple of foils, so he took up fencing and began pushing himself to get involved in organized activities. By early August, he found himself writing in his diary: "Amazingly, in such a place, you broaden your horizons." With David Westheimer, he found books "the best escape." Generous donations from the American Red Cross, the YMCA, and folks back home allowed the Luft camps to amass substantial libraries. The library in South Compound of Stalag Luft III occupied two adjoining barracks rooms, one of them furnished with armchairs and settees the prisoners had made from packing cases. Immediately after roll call, there would be "a mad rush for the best seats and the best books." Almost every day, a group of regulars could be found in the reference section, some of them preparing for their return to college after the war. Nicholas Katzenbach, the navigator of a medium bomber flying out of Italy and, years later, a United States attorney general, read with such disciplined purpose that when he returned from the war he was able to skip his final undergraduate years at Princeton. He persuaded the university to give him two years' worth of classroom examinations in six weeks so that he could graduate with his class. "What my father did . . . took on a sort of mythic value in our household," wrote his son John, author of the prisoner of war novel *Hart's War.* "The lesson was simple: An opportunity could be created out of any situation, no matter how harsh."

Katzenbach's friend David Westheimer began reading almost entirely to kill time, but soon found himself transported to unexpected worlds. "In the bag, books often conveyed vivid images undreamed of by their authors, a richness beyond anything experienced by a casual reader in an easy chair in a comfortable room. . . . 'As Millicent ran along the path, twigs brushed her legs.' Legs. I saw legs, all right. Bare legs. And everything above them, also bare."

The most popular items in the kriegie libraries were Swiss movie magazines featuring photographs of impossibly gorgeous Hollywood queens. Cherry-lipped Betty Grable was a huge hit, but in a poll taken at Stalag Luft III, sultry Ingrid Bergman easily beat her out as "The Girl Kriegies in West Camp Would Most Like to Have Open Their Klim Cans."

The kriegies also established their own "colleges." The one at Sagan offered almost forty courses, all taught by the prisoners. There were courses on chemistry, mathematics, physics, philosophy, Latin, literature, history, auto mechanics, marketing, accounting, printing, and bodybuilding. Textbooks were scarce but the YMCA supplied blackboards and plenty of notebooks. One POW wrote home that he was studying French and English literature at "Sagan U" and was reading *War and Peace* for pleasure. By the end of the war, a number of American colleges and universities were offering credit for rigorous courses taught by qualified prison instructors.

All of the Luft camps had exuberant theater groups. Some men had stage experience, but enthusiasm was more plentiful than talent. With materials supplied by the YMCA, the kriegies made costumes and stage scenery, and they built surprisingly comfortable theater seats from Red Cross food crates. Chandeliers were fashioned from tin cans, and with YMCA instruments the men formed their own symphony orchestras with names like the Luftbandsters and the Sagan Serenaders. Professionally trained musicians wrote their own music from memory on scraps of toilet paper and taught the uninitiated how to read music. The YMCA supplied playbooks but the prisoners wrote and produced dozens of their own plays.

The theater was an all-purpose facility. "After we got our loudspeaker system and hundreds of symphonic recordings from the YMCA, we would darken the theater in the early afternoon," Colonel Spivey remembered, "and [our orchestra leader] would play Mozart, Beethoven, or some other famous composer, explaining the music as it was played. The theater would almost always be filled on such occasions." The men couldn't get enough music. South Compound at Sagan received a portable phonograph from the Red Cross that was passed around from combine to combine, along with stacks of mildewed records. "When it was our turn the phonograph was never off," recalled Westheimer. "Overnight was best. We played it long after lights out. One man would volunteer to stay up to wind it and change records while the others lay in their sacks listening, blissful and yearning, to the same records over and over again. 'Rosalita,' 'You Are Always in My Heart,' 'That Old Black Magic,' and a dozen or so others."

Kriegie dreams were filled with women, and the men's letters to wives and girlfriends were sexually charged. One POW told his wife to have the bedroom ceiling repainted in her favorite color; she would be seeing a lot of it when he returned. Occasionally, some village women would walk teasingly outside the perimeter of the camp, swaying their bottoms and driving the men mad. The sight of untouchable women drove some prisoners to despair. Two British fliers were walking around the camp perimeter at Sagan on a brilliant Sunday morning reminiscing about what they would be doing if they were back home on a day like this. Unexpectedly, two attractive women emerged from a path in the woods and began walking along the line of the camp fence. As they passed by, one of them said in a soft voice, "Good morning gentlemen, what a beautiful morning."

"Those few words . . . hit us like a laser beam right between the eyes," said John Cordwell. "And we didn't have to say anything to each other. We staggered back, went back to our beds, and went into complete depression. We lay there for weeks until we shook it off."

Glee clubs and jazz bands also held forth in the camp theaters, and on Sundays, church services were offered by courageous chaplains who had volunteered to parachute into Germany to be with the prisoners. Religion provided solace, but mail was more important. Prisoners were permitted to send three letters and four postcards a month. After passing the censor, each communiqué took three to four months to reach its addressee–the delay caused by its having to pass through both the prisoners' own and the German censors. (The job of the kriegie censors was to make sure that no prisoner inadvertently disclosed escape plans or clandestine operations within the compounds.) The amount of incoming mail was not restricted, but the German delivery system was wildly erratic, leading some men to suspect, incorrectly, that the enemy was torturing them by withholding letters from home. Incoming mail contained some choice passages, which men sometimes shared with their fellow prisoners. One captain received a sweater from a woman through the Red Cross. After he wrote to thank her, she replied, "I am sorry that a prisoner received the sweater I knitted. I made it for a fighting man." Another flier received unexpected news from his wife: "Dear Harry, I hope you are broadminded. I just had a baby. . . . He is such a nice fellow . . . he is sending you some cigarettes."

On a wall next to his bunk, an enterprising kriegie created a gallery of "impatient maidens," row upon row of snapshots of women, including one in her bridal dress, who had sent "Dear John" letters to husbands and boyfriends at Sagan. The photographs were donated by the jilted kriegies. "There was a lot of laughter in the camp," said Lou Loevsky. "Even the cuckolds laughed at themselves. Life was so grim you needed humor to keep your sanity."

Nothing did more to raise or lower prisoner morale than mail call, with the possible exception of war news. Kriegies got their war information from three sources: new prisoners, Allied and German radio broadcasts, and clandestinely published camp news sheets. Unlike the gossipy kriegie newspapers, these newsletters contained breaking information from the world's war fronts. "The only truthful newspaper in Germany" is how editor Lowell Bennett, a former international correspondent, described *Pow Wow* (Prisoners of War Waiting on Winning), the daily underground newspaper he helped establish at Stalag Luft I. The war news it reported was obtained from a radio set hidden in a barracks wall of one of the British compounds. The nails that held the receiver in place acted as terminals, to which an antenna and earphone cables were attached. The parts to make the radio had been smuggled into the camp by German guards in exchange for American cigarettes. A typist printed the news on toilet paper that was delivered to Bennett's compound by a British liaison officer who had prior permission from the Germans to carry important open messages between the Allied leaders of the various compounds. The British officer carried the news in a hollow wristwatch. To avoid detection, he would adjust the hands to the proper time of day in case he was stopped and searched by the guards. The scraps of toilet paper were then passed on to Bennett and his staff, who went to work preparing a hand-typed, single-sheet paper. Only four copies of each issue were produced on carbon paper, which was made by smoking sheets of plain paper over tin-can lamps, one copy for each of the American compounds; the resourceful British produced their own news sheet. Couriers delivered the sheets to barracks security officers, who read them aloud to the men, usually in the washroom, with stooges placed at both ends of the barracks and in front of the washroom window. The paper was then tossed in the barracks's wood-stove.

The Germans ultimately found out about both *Pow Wow* and the secret radio. The barracks where the paper was produced was searched more than any other at Barth, but the 2,000-word sheet never missed a deadline. Nor did the Germans ever discover the location of the radio.

Each Luft camp had its own newspaper, and when war news arrived the progress of the Allied armies was pinpointed on large handmade maps that were posted on the walls of the blocks. The news was encouraging in fall of 1944. Both the Western Allies and the Red Army were on Germany's frontiers and the skies were filled almost every day with silver bombers from England. Every time a formation of them flew overhead, the kriegies would gather outdoors and let loose roars of approval.

But as winter approached and the Western Allies became stalled along the Siegfried Line, the mood in the stalags turned somber. That December word reached the camps of the furious German counteroffensive in the Ardennes. "Our guards, most of them old and fat Wehrmacht soldiers, were jubilant," Gale Cleven remembered. A mood of despair crept through the ranks, and older prisoners especially began to speak in "hushed tones" about the possibility "of lifelong imprisonment." The temperature plummeted and men stayed in bed all day to keep warm. Both food and mail became depressingly scarce as Allied planes savaged German rails and roads. Only a small backlog of Red Cross food parcels from Geneva kept the men from starving on their diets of thin soup, worm-ridden vegetables, and goon bread. Even bright-spirited Eugene Halmos began to despair. "The day of deliverance from here is receding further and further into the future," he confided to his diary. The only consolation Lou Loevsky had that dreary winter was news from England that his footlocker had been purged. A friend had confiscated the condoms before his belongings were shipped home.

The war news dampened but did not kill the Christmas spirit. At Stalag Luft I, the airmen decorated their combines with scraps of paper they painted with watercolors donated by the Red Cross. And they built a camp Christmas tree with a broom handle and strips of wire cut from Klim cans and decorated it with toilet paper cut and colored to simulate needled foliage. "Slivers of cellophane from cigarette packages were strung out like tinsel. The varicolored paper of soap wrappers, tin-can labels, and note-book covers were meticulously cut to make decorations. [And] razor-shredded paper produced snow." A chaplain—a rugged Briton who had been captured at Dunkirk in 1940—celebrated midnight services in the mess hall and a choir of nearly 2,000 men, most of them standing outdoors, was accompanied by a small YMCA organ.

The weather on Christmas morning was cold but splendidly clear, and the airmen at Stalag Luft III were issued special Red Cross parcels filled with canned turkey, cookies, and plum pudding. The Germans even pitched in, handing out cheap party hats and noisemakers. The prisoners tried to make the best of it, but for most of them it was an "empty show." Like other men, Eugene Halmos's thoughts were entirely of home. Wait-ing for him, and for the honeymoon the couple never had, was a girl named Ann.

The families of the German guards were visiting Sagan that day, and the kriegies could see them through the fence. For men with young children, this was pure torture. When the mail unexpectedly arrived at Barth that Christmas Day, John Vietor tore open two letters from his father, filled with happy news from home. Then he opened a third letter. It was from a boyhood friend offering condolences for the death of Vietor's father.

On New Year's Day, with the Americans still fighting in the Arctic land-scape of the Ardennes, the BBC announced that the Red Army, camped on the banks of the Vistula, was preparing to move out. Nearly four million men and 10,000 tanks formed a front that stretched from the Baltic to the Balkans. Part of this overpowering invasion force was poised to advance across western Poland to the Oder, the border between Poland and Ger-many, and then "Forward, into the fascist lair!" That put them on a collision course with Sagan, strategically situated between the Vistula and the Oder.

The Russian advance produced mixed feelings among the kriegies: hope that liberation was near, conjoined with fear that the Germans would dispose of them before the avenging Soviets arrived.

News of the Russian offensive had a mixed impact, as well, at Eighth Air Force headquarters near London. Here was an opportunity to use bomb-ing to hasten the Soviet advance and bring the war to a speedy end. But Gen. Frederick Anderson and other advocates of hard war insisted that the bombing would have to be cataclysmic, for the enemy had shown he had plenty of powder left in his arsenal. War industries would have to be smashed, but so would civilian morale. The Eighth Air Force had reached a moral divide—and was about to cross it.

CHAPTER FIFTEEN

Terror Without End

We have not yet killed enough. We must make this War so fatal and horrible that a Century will pass before new demagogues and traitors will dare to resort to violence and war to achieve their ends.

GEN. WILLIAM TECUMSEH SHERMAN,
AUGUST 20, 1863

England, January 30, 1945

That evening, Jimmy Doolittle received an urgent directive from Carl Spaatz. The aiming point of the Eighth Air Force's next mission was the center of Berlin. As on its previous strikes against the German capital, the Eighth would target government buildings that were nerve centers of genocidal warfare, but this time the principal targets were not military installations. They were railway passenger stations overflowing with refugees, mostly women, children, and the elderly. These panic-stricken families were fleeing their homes in the easternmost regions of the Reich, blood-drenched lands being overrun by the Red Army on a revenge march of rape, pillage, and mass murder. To General Doolittle, this was terror bombing and he urged Spaatz to reconsider his order.

What kind of behavior is morally justifiable to bring down a repugnant regime that refuses to surrender, even in the face of certain defeat? Hitler's insane orders to fight to the finish would subject Germany to a veritable rain of ruin in the last months of the war. The Japanese government's decision to continue the war after the fall of the Philippines in early 1945 would make the end of the war even more terrible for the people in that country's combustible cities of paper and wood. On the evening of March 9, Gen. Curtis LeMay would send his Saipan-based fleet of B-29 Superfortresses on a low-level incendiary raid against Tokyo that would kill at least 100,000 people and burn sixteen square miles of the city, an area equivalent to two-thirds of Manhattan Island. The great Tokyo raid was merely the first of sixty-four firebombings that incinerated hundreds of thousands of Japanese civilians. In Tokyo, Osaka, and Nagoya alone, the areas leveled (almost 100 square miles) would exceed the areas destroyed in all German cities during the entire war by the Anglo-American air forces (approximately seventy-nine square miles).

It has been argued that the March 1945 Tokyo raid was a historic turning point in American military policy, the abandonment of long-standing restraint against the indiscriminate killing of noncombatants. But that moral threshold had been crossed on the morning of February 3, 1945, when the entire Eighth Air Force appeared in the freezing skies over Berlin.

Thunderclap

The Berlin raid had its genesis in a plan Carl Spaatz had originally opposed. In July 1944, the British Chiefs of Staff suggested to the prime minister "that the time might well come in the not-too-distant future when an all-out attack by every means at our disposal on German civilian morale might be decisive. . . . The method by which such an attack should be carried out should be examined and all possible preparations made." Thunderclap, the plan's code name, was to be an apocalyptic Anglo-American air assault on Berlin—a continuous four-day blitz designed to deliver a *"coup de grâce* to German morale" by killing and maiming over a quarter-million people and demolishing the administrative center of the Nazi government. "Such an attack resulting in so many deaths, the great majority of which will be key personnel, cannot help but have shattering effect on political and civilian morale all over Germany," declared Chief of Air Staff Charles Portal.

Thunderclap was not to be unleashed until Germany was on the brink of defeat, when a crippling blow to civilian morale stood a reasonable chance of forcing an organized surrender, or igniting a popular uprising against the Nazi regime. But that "psychological" moment might be fast approaching, the British Chiefs of Staff believed that July, as two determined armies converged on Germany from the east and the west. British planners, however, were unable to obtain American cooperation. Spaatz, with strong support from Air Force headquarters in Washington, led the opposition, arguing against joining the RAF in what would be obliteration bombing—the purposeful targeting of civilians. It was one thing to kill noncombatants in raids on military installations inside urban centers, a "revolting necessity," in the opinion of most American air commanders. It was quite another to aim bombs at residential neighborhoods. It "[is] contrary to our national ideals to wage war against civilians," declared Maj. Gen. Laurence Kuter, now Hap Arnold's assistant chief for plans and combat operations. Brig. Gen. Charles P. Cabell, a key tactical planner, went further, denouncing Thunderclap as a "baby killing" scheme.

These air commanders were not soft-shelled humanitarians; their policy was founded squarely on military considerations. "It wasn't for religious or moral reasons that I didn't go along with [Thunderclap]," Carl Spaatz would later tell Air Force historians. He was waging all-out warfare against a perversely evil enemy, and morale bombing was not, in his estimation, a war-winning policy. "Our entire target policy has been founded on the fact that it was uneconomic to bomb any except military objectives and the German productive capacity," Kuter said, speaking for Spaatz, Doolittle, and other air leaders who remained committed to economic bombing. The German people had been hammered from the air for four years by the British without any sign of a general breakdown in resolve or an upsurge of organized opposition to the regime. Now the British were asking the Americans to join them in yet another, and even greater, effort to break morale. This led Spaatz to question their motives for advancing Thunderclap at this late moment in the war. "There is no doubt in my mind that the RAF wants very much to have the U.S. Air Forces tarred with the morale bombing aftermath which we feel will be terrific," he wrote Arnold.

Winston Churchill also opposed Thunderclap and that ended the discussion. "At the present moment, none of the German leaders has any interest but fighting to the last man, hoping he will be that last man," he noted shrewdly. Instead of delivering a leveling blow on the government center of Berlin, the prime minister suggested making a list of war criminals that would be executed if they fell into Allied hands. This, he thought, might place some distance between the Nazi leadership and the German people, who feared sweeping reprisals against all Germans if the war was lost.

The idea behind Thunderclap never died, however. In late August,

Eisenhower told Spaatz to be "prepared to take part in anything that gives real promise to ending the war quickly." Spaatz should continue to hit economic and tactical targets, Ike instructed, "unless in my opinion an opportunity arises where a sudden and devastating blow may have an incalculable result." That fall and early winter, with the German army showing unexpectedly strong resistance on the Western Front, Thunderclap was premature. But in January, when Marshal Georgi Zhukov executed a lightning advance to the Oder River, within forty miles of Berlin, the time had arrived, some top planners argued, for Eisenhower's "sudden and devastating blow."

The plan settled upon was not the original Thunderclap. Berlin remained a target, but sobered British intelligence experts now considered it "very doubtful" that an attack on the Thunderclap scale in the near future . . . would be decisive." The aim was to continue to progressively weaken Germany rather than trying to deliver a single aerial deathblow. This could be accomplished most effectively, the British believed, by aggressively supporting the Russian ground offensive. With the western Allies still recovering from the heavy German assault in the Ardennes in December 1944 and not yet ready to resume their march to the Rhine, bombing German positions along the Eastern Front would assist the only military initiative that stood a reasonable chance of breaking the enemy by the conclusion of winter. A secret report by the British Joint Intelligence Committee suggested that a massive bombing of Berlin, the main transportation nexus of eastern Germany and a city inundated with millions of refugees, "would be bound to create great confusion, interfere with the orderly movement of troops to the front and hamper the German military and administrative machine." Adding urgency to the bombing was the belief that the Sixth SS Panzer Army had just left Belgium and would be passing through Berlin on its way to the collapsing Eastern Front. Blasting these cities might also have "a political value in demonstrating to the Russians . . . a desire on the part of the British and Americans to assist them in the present battle," thereby improving Churchill and Roosevelt's bargaining position with Stalin at the upcoming meeting of the Big Three at Yalta, scheduled for the first week of February.

Although not Thunderclap, this was a bombing design of chilling resolve; rail stations bursting with homeless people would be targeted, not to break morale, but to create transportation and urban "confusion." When Bomber Harris was shown the plan, he recommended additional strikes on the Saxon cities of Chemnitz, Leipzig, and Dresden, all major railroad centers close to the Eastern Front and swollen with refugees.

At this point, Winston Churchill jumped into the discussions, asking his secretary of state for air, Sir Archibald Sinclair, "whether Berlin, and no doubt other large cities in East Germany, should not now be considered especially attractive targets. . . . Pray report to me to-morrow what is going to be done." The prime minister's impatience was fueled by a recent intelligence report indicating that German resistance might collapse by mid-April if the Soviets broke through into Germany. Otherwise, the war could drag on into November.

Churchill's intervention sped up the timetable. Sinclair informed the prime minister that the attacks would commence as soon as weather and moon conditions were favorable. At this point the Russians were given advance notice; and later, at the Yalta Conference, Stalin himself asked that Dresden be bombed, along with Leipzig and Berlin. (The official records of the conference indicate that the only targets the Soviet representatives specified were Berlin and Leipzig. But recently, the official interpreter for the British Chiefs of Staff, who attended every session of the Yalta meetings, has come forward with the revelation that Stalin himself requested verbally, and quite strongly, that Dresden be added to the list of the eastern German cities the Anglo-Americans planned to bomb.)

When Spaatz was briefed on the British plan, he revealed that his staff was already planning a major raid on Berlin, although not one that targeted refugees. Spaatz had equal faith in the Soviet offensive. "The power of the Russian advance is the greatest strategic factor at the present time in this war," he wrote Hap Arnold, "and . . . I believe it should be strongly supported" by bombing Berlin, the "focal point in the control and supply of the defense against Zhukov's spearhead." Up to this point, the revised Thunderclap had been entirely a British plan. Presently, a new joint bombing directive was issued by Spaatz and Air Vice Marshal Norman Bottomley: the Eighth would hit the center of Berlin while the RAF, with American assistance, would bomb the other three rail junctions. At Spaatz's insistence, there was a proviso: these city targets were to be bombed only when weather ruled against attacks on oil installations.

Why did Carl Spaatz agree to a plan that was in direct violation of his long-stated policy against targeting civilians? Heavy pressure from Hap Arnold to end the war quickly was a major factor. That January, Arnold was snapping at Spaatz's heels, his anger and anxiety bringing on a fourth heart attack in mid-January, one that nearly killed Arnold at his desk. Arnold's frustration with the inability of American airpower to finish off Germany spilled over in a succession of intemperate communiqués to his

European commander. "With [our] tremendous striking power, it would seem to me that we should get much better and much more decisive results than we are getting now," he wrote Spaatz. "I am not criticizing, because frankly I don't know the answer and what I am now doing is letting my thoughts run wild with the hope that out of this you get a glimmer, a light, a new thought, or something which will help us to bring this war to a close sooner." With his "thoughts running wild," Arnold had recently tried to revive his disastrous pet project, Aphrodite. The previous fall, he had approved the use of war-weary bombers as unmanned robots against German industrial targets, some of them located in major urban centers. Although all eleven robots that were launched failed to make contact with their targets, Arnold continued to press the Combined Chiefs of Staff for an ambitious expansion of the experiment, one that called for the employment of over 500 "Weary Willies" against large industrial targets, "as an irritant and possibly a means of breaking down the morale of the people of interior Germany."

Arnold was a "terrorizing and intimidating" figure to high-ranking Air Force officers. (In a fiery argument with a former assistant secretary of war, he picked up the crippled man's cane and threw it at him.) And he had considerable influence with Gen. George Marshall, who, on his behalf, waived the regulation that forced officers with heart disease to retire (Marshall himself had a serious heart murmur). Arnold may have gotten his way on Aphrodite had the British not strenuously objected. Churchill and Portal feared retaliation attacks on London by hundreds of unmanned German planes that had been rendered nonoperational because of shortages of fuel and pilots. (The Germans had already tried to hit London with combat-damaged Junkers 88 bombers guided by automatic pilot.) While Spaatz was unenthusiastic about the Weary Willies project, Arnold continued to push it until Roosevelt's successor, President Harry Truman, at Churchill's urging, buried it in the last month of the war.

Writing to a convalescing Arnold in early 1945, Spaatz tried to rein in his boss's raging impetuosity. The war would not be won by new and untried measures, he told him emphatically. Victory would be achieved by grinding warfare, on the ground and in the air, with unrelenting attacks on oil and transportation. But not knowing yet how badly his air offensive had hurt the enemy's economy, Spaatz was also frustrated by Germany's steely resiliency, and was willing, at this point, to condone at least one unprecedented measure—a terror raid on Berlin. This was a raid he could square with his beliefs: it was not morale bombing and it accorded with his desire

to assist the Russian ground offensive. (Unknown to Spaatz or any other
Allied commander, Albert Speer had decided in late January that the war
was lost, although the self-protecting minister of armaments did not have
the courage to inform his führer of this until March 15.)

The final push came from George Marshall. Anxious to move all American war resources to the Pacific as soon as possible, Marshall was willing to
give "morale" bombing a try. Gen. Frederick Anderson met with Marshall
just before the Yalta summit and Marshall told him he wanted Munich
bombed, along with the cities along the Berlin–Leipzig–Dresden rail
nexus. Intelligence reports that had come across Marshall's desk indicated
that government offices were being evacuated from Berlin to Munich in expectation of even heavier bombing raids on the capital. "Attacks on Munich would probably be of great benefit because it would show the people
that are being evacuated to Munich that there is no hope," Marshall told
Anderson.

Generals Eisenhower and Bradley agreed. President Roosevelt did not
have to be consulted. The American military command was thoroughly
apprised of his insistence on hard war against Germany. The Germans had
started the First World War, yet not a single ground battle had been fought
on their home soil. "It is of the utmost importance that every person in Germany should realize that this time [unlike World War I] Germany is a defeated nation," Roosevelt told Secretary of War Stimson. "The fact that
they are a defeated nation, collectively and individually, must be so impressed upon them that they will hesitate to start any new war. . . .

"Too many people here and in England hold to the view that the German people as a whole are not responsible for what has taken place—that
only a few Nazi leaders are responsible. That unfortunately is not based on
fact. The German people as a whole must have it driven home to them that
the whole nation has been engaged in a lawless conspiracy against the de-
cencies of modern civilization."

In September 1939, when Germany began World War II, Roosevelt
had sent appeals to all belligerents to refrain from "the inhumane barbarism" of bombing civilians. Three years later, the president was telling
Congress that the Allies intended to hit Germany "from the air heavily and
relentlessly." The people who "bombed Warsaw, Rotterdam, London, and
Coventry are going to get it."

In February 1945, the Americans planned to hit Germany harder than
they ever had before, with the clear intent of sowing terror and chaos. It
would begin with Berlin in the first week of February, and Munich soon afterward. (Weather and other target priorities prevented the Fifteenth Air

Force from hitting Munich until March 24, and with a different objective than Marshall had originally suggested.) No one in the Allied high command believed that Germany could still win the war, but no one doubted that it had the will and capability to battle on with suicidal resolve. And with England once again under round-the-clock assault from Nazi rocket bombs, there were few voices urging restraint.

Nazi Rockets

On September 7, 1944, a British official went before the press and announced: "Except possibly for a few last shots the Battle of London is over." The flying bomb barrage had ended. The following day there were two tremendous back-to-back explosions in the city. To calm fears, the government encouraged rumors that several gas mains had exploded. After more explosions rocked the city in the next weeks, a Londoner saw an American soldier building a fence around an enormous crater. Had a Nazi rocket landed there, he asked? "No, man," said the GI, "that's no rocket; it's one of those flying gas mains."

Until the following March, when the launch sites of the new V-2 rockets were overrun by Allied troops, the people of the southern cities of England would have to live through the uncertainty and daily terror of yet another Blitz. Not as many would die as in the first Blitz, but with this new vengeance weapon, German scientists "had raised the art of killing to the highest peak of science and efficiency ever attained," wrote one reporter. Like the V-1, the new weapon was wildly inaccurate, killing indiscriminately. In all, 2,700 Britons died and another 6,500 were badly mangled; almost equal numbers were killed and maimed in Antwerp, Brussels, and Paris. But unlike the V-1, neither early warning nor interception was possible. From small, difficult-to-detect launching pads in occupied Holland, these twelve-ton supersonic rockets climbed seventy miles into the stratosphere and hurtled silently to earth at speeds of up to 4,000 miles per hour—too fast to be seen. This made them greatly more frightening than the noisier, slower-moving V-1 flying bombs. "If I'm going to be killed," a London woman commented sardonically, "I would like to have the excitement of knowing it's going to happen."

The British government was so concerned about public panic that it was not until November 10 that Churchill revealed that many of the missiles aimed at England—the Germans had also resumed firing V-1s—were supersonic rockets carrying one-ton warheads. They were the most feared weapons the world had yet seen. Designed on a wilderness Baltic island by scientists working under the odious opportunist Dr. Wernher von Braun, they were produced at a supersecret facility called Mittelwerk, a system of deep storage tunnels in an isolated valley of the Harz Mountains. Albert Speer had personally selected the site, near the small city of Nordhausen, after the British bombed the original production facility at Peenemünde. And he approved the use of concentration camp laborers who were shipped in from Buchenwald and worked in the medieval-like tunnels under SS supervision. Until the 3rd Armored Division liberated the facility in early April 1945, 60,000 prisoners passed through the Mittelwerk slave system and over one-third of them died of starvation, disease, and murder. Another 1,500 were killed in two successive RAF raids on the facility.

The A-4, as the Germans called their new liquid-fuel weapon, was the world's first short-range ballistic missile, "the grandfather of all modern guided missile and space boosters." At the same time that it was being aimed at English cities, von Braun and his team of physicists and engineers were also trying to rush into production an ICBM—intercontinental ballistic missile—the A-10, or New York rocket, named for the city it was intended to hit. Allied intelligence knew about this project and suspected the Germans were also developing an atomic bomb. The future of the world could have been horrifyingly altered had the Nazis built the bomb and perfected a long-range delivery system. But Hitler's persecution of Jewish scientists, along with his interest in more conventional vengeance weapons, robbed both programs of industrial resources and indispensable talent. In May 1945, an American intelligence team found that German scientists were "about as far as we were in 1940, before we had begun any large work on the [atomic] bomb at all." Even the transatlantic rocket would not have been operational until 1947, at the earliest.

But no one on the Allied side knew this in January 1945, when Thunderclap-style bombing operations were being discussed by Anglo-American air barons. What London-based war leaders *did* know was what they witnessed in their midst. At the height of that Christmas season, 164 shoppers and two infants in prams were obliterated when a V-2 smashed into a London Woolworth's. This was after 115 British women were killed with terrifying suddenness while waiting in line at a food market for their weekly meat ration.

The launch sites for the new rockets were small and heavily camouflaged and their underground manufacturing facility was virtually bombproof. The only way the RAF could hit back at the enemy was to target his cities. Although there is no mention of retaliation in the planning documents for the February bombing campaign against the cities of eastern Germany, it had to be in the thoughts of those who directed air operations from London.

As the Eighth Air Force's Berlin raid was in the final hours of its planning stage an extraordinary thing happened. Gen. Jimmy Doolittle asked Spaatz to reconsider his directive. "There are no . . . important strictly military targets in the designated area," he wired him; and to bomb the city accurately the Eighth would have to bomb visually, exposing the crews to murderous antiaircraft fire.

Doolittle was that rare Eighth Air Force commander who opposed terror bombing on both military and moral grounds. And unlike Spaatz, he saw the Berlin raid as an effort to "lower German morale"; to terrorize people but also to destroy their will to endure. "The chances of terrorizing into submission, by merely an increased concentration of bombing, a people who have been subjected to intense bombing for four years is extremely remote," he told Spaatz, who had made exactly the same argument against Thunderclap the previous summer. Doolittle's final appeal was to Spaatz's conscience and, more directly, to his widely known concern for the Air Force's postwar legacy. "We will, in what may be one of our last and best remembered operations regardless of its effectiveness, violate the basic American principle of precision bombing of targets of strictly military significance for which our tactics were designed and our crews trained and indoctrinated." Leave area bombing to the British, he pleaded, and continue to concentrate on strictly military targets. Even if inadequate technology and hostile weather conspired to prevent these targets from being hit accurately, the American effort would still be seen by history as well intentioned.

Spaatz's clipped reply came in the form of an order, with no appending explanation: "Hit Berlin whenever [weather] conditions do not indicate possibility of visual bombing of oil targets but do permit operations to Berlin." He further informed Doolittle that his own weather forecasters had assured him that this would be a radar operation, and hence safer for the crews. What went without saying was that bad weather meant badly inaccurate bombing, "women and children day treatment," Doolittle's bomber boys called their radar missions.

On the morning of February 2, Doolittle massed every available bomber in his command, but heavy cloud cover nixed the mission. When Spaatz ordered a massive raid for the following day, Doolittle cabled him for a clarification, hoping that Spaatz would reconsider. "Is Berlin still open to air attack? Do you want priority oil targets hit in preference to Berlin if they definitely become visual? Do you want center city hit or definitely military targets . . . on the Western outskirts?"

Spaatz replied within the hour by telephone, later documenting the gist of his message in a bluntly worded note: "Hit oil if visually assured; otherwise, Berlin—center of city."

To cloak what was unquestionably an area raid, Spaatz instructed Doolittle to "stress" in his news releases "effort to disrupt reinforcement of the Eastern Front and increase administrative confusion." Doolittle did that, but he also added some military targets to the bomb list, including marshaling yards and munitions factories.

Six years before his death in 1974, Spaatz came as close as he ever would to admitting that the Berlin raid of February 3 was terror bombing in all but name. "We never had as our target, in [Nazi-occupied] Europe, anything except a military target—except Berlin."

February 3, 1945

At 3:30 A.M., a sharp voice broke the silence in the cavelike hut. "Gentlemen, you're operational! Now!" Aiming his flashlight at the sleeping men's faces, the first sergeant shouted even louder, "Out of the sack." Then he was gone, the most hated man on the base.

This would be the thirteenth mission for Capt. Charles Alling and his crew, part of the 34th Bomb Group flying out of Mendlesham, in Norfolk. Lean and athletic, with sharply cut features, Chuck Alling was a natural leader—bright, well trained, and rock-steady under pressure. That morning, as he slid out of his cot and walked through the chill air to the washroom, his thoughts were of home. If war had not intervened, he would have returned that week to Wesleyan University for the spring semester; but here he was, an ocean away, preparing his mind to lead nine other college-age boys into the most treacherous airspace in the world.

Outside Alling's Nissen hut an Army truck waited, its brown tarpaulin billowing in the wind. Alling and his fellow officers jumped aboard and huddled together in silence with other crews on the frost-covered wooden benches. As the truck sped toward the officers' mess hall, the men stared blankly at the flapping canvas. The only sign of life in the darkened truck was the glow of a dozen or so cigarettes.

At breakfast no one uttered a word. When someone wanted the salt or the pepper he pointed to it. "There was no conversation," Alling recalled.

"Guys were tense and anxious and some may have wondered if their time was up." They had been briefed for a Berlin raid the morning before, so no one was surprised an hour later when the intelligence officer drew back the curtain over the wall-size map of Western Europe and a line of red tape formed an aerial assault avenue to "Big-Ass Berlin." The men knew that the Eighth had been there before, delivering its heaviest punishment the previous winter, before most of them had arrived in England. But at many bases the fliers were told that this time it would be different: the aiming point was the thickly populated city center. Gestapo, SS, and other odious Nazis would die in great numbers in their office buildings, but so would noncombatants. "We were told today that if we had any scruples about bombing civilians, it was hard luck for us because from now on we'll be bombing and strafing women, children, everybody," ball turret gunner John Briol, of the 457th Bombardment Group, wrote in his diary.

At the air station of the 95th Bomb Group, the sergeant gunners were advised to carry their Army-issue sidearms. "If you go down over the target area you are going to need [them] . . . because the [target] is the center of town—arms, legs, and assholes." The briefing officer "put it just like that," recalled James Henrietta, radio operator on pilot Lewis Welles's plane. "In other words, there was no military target there, it was just get whoever you can get. . . . It was just to demoralize."

After being brought up to date on the weather and the state of the enemy defenses, Alling and his fellow officers were driven out to *Miss Prudy,* the silver Fortress they had named for Alling's sister, who was struck down at age twenty-one by spinal meningitis just days before her brother was shipped overseas. By 4:43 *Miss Prudy* was aloft, cutting through black skies and menacing fog, the lead ship in the group's high squadron. As the sun rose, the fog lifted, and the outward-bound bombers began forming up, wingtip to wingtip. "Sometimes they look white and as graceful as gulls against the blue; at others they look black and sinister as they come and go between the clouds," an East Anglian described these majestic air fleets. "But the impressive thing—the thing that makes land-girls pause in their stringing of the hop fields and makes conductors of country buses lean out and look up from their platforms—the impressive thing is the numbers. Never in the Battle of Britain, in the days when the Luftwaffe was beaten over these fields and woods, did the Germans send over such vast fleets. Never were their bombers four-engined monsters, such as these of the Americans [that] go out in their scores and hundreds. . . .

"They have an appointment abroad, and they're keeping it."

More than 900 Fortresses and over half as many escort fighters were dispatched to the target, the largest force ever sent against a single city. (That same morning, the Eighth's 2nd Air Division dispatched over 400 Liberators to the Magdeburg synthetic oil plant, where better weather was predicted.) The Berlin-bound air train was 300 miles long; by the time the forward elements nosed into Germany there were still bombers over the North Sea.

In *The Warriors,* his classic account of ground combat in Europe, American intelligence officer J. Glenn Gray called attention to the "aesthetic appeal of war," the "powerful fascination" and emotional attractions of warfare. Waist gunner John Morris felt the pull of what Gray called "war as spectacle" as he gazed in wonder from his gun portal at the tightly disciplined bomber formations cutting through the north German skies, contrails flaring white and fluffy behind every battle-bound squadron.

The first bombers over the target flew into unexpectedly beautiful skies, high blue and crystal clear, wonderful weather for bombing but also for flak gunners. And Berlin had more of them than any city in existence. Just as his pilot announced over the interphone—"She's clear as a bell over Berlin, guys . . . not a goddamn cloud in the area," Lt. Robert Hand, flying his thirty-fifth and final mission, began to experience the familiar symptoms of combat panic: sweat began to pour out of his flak helmet, his vision blurred, and his entire upper body began to shake. His was the third group over the target, and ahead he saw "a veritable mountain of black puffs." Two shells burst below them, tossing his Fortress around "like a rowboat in the rapids." The lead ship dropped its load and Hand released his ship's string of bombs seconds later. Then his squadron banked and headed into protective cloud cover just outside the target area. As they did, Hand saw a ship just behind them take a direct hit—one of the twenty-five bombers lost that day. A black ball of smoke was all that was left of ten men and three tons of metal. "It just doesn't seem possible that anything that large could disappear so fast," Hand said later.

Bob Hand and Chuck Alling made it back to England that day. Robert "Rosie" Rosenthal, flying his fifty-second mission, did not.

Almost every American in the air this day was seeing Berlin for the first time, but Rosie had been there several times before with his original crew, Rosie's Riveters, most memorably on March 8, 1944, during the week the Mighty Eighth broke the back of the Luftwaffe. That was to have been his twenty-fifth and final mission, but at a celebration that night Rosie had decided he would continue flying. "Go home to the ice cream, the girls, the ball games, and all in one piece. You deserve a break," his friend Saul

Levitt pleaded with him. It was no use. "I had to do what I could for as long as I was able," Rosie said later.

Two months into his second tour of duty, flying as a command pilot, Rosenthal made a hair-raising landing on an emergency field in England on his return from Berlin, bringing down the bomber with three engines out and half the tail sheared off by a runaway propeller. The following September, his lead Fortress was hit by flak over Nuremberg and crash-landed in northern France, an area controlled by American forces. Rosie was pulled from the cockpit with a broken arm and nose and was flown, unconscious, to a military hospital in Oxford. When he returned to Thorpe Abbotts five weeks later, he was assigned to wing headquarters, a desk job he loathed. He wanted to be back in the fight and he made such a pest of himself he was returned to the Hundredth, promoted to major, and given command of his original squadron, the 418th.

Approaching Berlin on February 3, 1945, Major Rosenthal was flying in the co-pilot's chair in the lead plane, a place reserved for the officer appointed that day to lead the entire 3rd Division. Nearing the Initial Point, Rosie's division encountered thick columns of smoke sent aloft by raging fires set by the 1st Division. "The smoke came up over 7,000 feet," said one airman, causing most of the 3rd Division to miss their main targets and hit residential districts east of the main target. "Before we left Germany I tuned in a propaganda broadcast from Berlin," said radio operator Clifford Whipple. "The announcer said, 'Every man, woman and child is out fighting the flames.' "

Turning into the bomb run, Rosie's plane was hit by exploding flak. Two crewmen were killed instantly and flames began shooting from one of the engines. When dense white smoke began filling the cockpit, Capt. John Ernst looked over at Rosie for guidance. Without saying a word, Rosie pointed straight ahead with his left hand.

After Ernst completed the bomb run, Rosie radioed the deputy lead to take over command of the division; and when his shattered plane reached the Oder River, where he knew the Red Army would be, he pushed the alarm bell, the signal to abandon ship. At that moment, the Fortress was hit a second time and a raging oil fire began consuming the central section of the bomber. Other crews looked on in horror, watching for chutes, as the blazing Fortress began to go into a slow, sickening spiral. Six chutes were spotted; then there was an explosion and, seconds later, aircraft number 44 8379 disappeared from sight. "Rosie, the Indomitable, [is] gone," Harry Crosby wrote in disbelief that night from his hut at Thorpe Abbotts.

Unknown to Crosby, that day his friend had fought a solitary fight for survival—and had won. No one watching the dying bomber that morning could have known what happened inside it. Taking the controls from Ernst just after the plane was hit a second time, Rosenthal ordered the pilot to bail out; then, alone with two dead crewmen, he struggled to get to the forward escape hatch in the nose of the plane. With the autopilot disabled, the plane was dropping fast, in a dizzying spin, and Rosenthal was pinned down by centrifugal stress. "I could barely move. It felt like I was in quicksand, but somehow I managed to reach the open hatch and squeeze through it just before the plane blew up." Rosenthal bailed out when his bomber was barely 2,000 feet from the ground and landed with body-breaking force, fracturing the same arm he had broken on the September 10 mission to Nuremburg. Hiding in a bomb crater, his .45 pistol in his left hand, he saw three soldiers with red stars on their hats approaching. Thinking he was a German, one of the Russian soldiers came at him with the butt of his gun. At that point, Rosie threw his arms in the air and shouted, "Americanski! Coca-Cola! Lucky Strike! Roosevelt, Churchill, Stalin!" Seconds later, the Russian was holding Rosenthal in a bear hug and kissing his cheeks.

Rosenthal was passed back through the lines to Moscow, where he became the guest of American ambassador Averell Harriman. From there he sent a telegram to Thorpe Abbotts, asking his buddies to reserve a plane for him; his war, he said, was not over. And so "the Rosenthal legend was kept intact," Saul Levitt recalled. "It was a real legend, made up of the following ingredients: that he could have stopped flying and that he couldn't get killed."

Robert Rosenthal would forever remember the sight he saw only minutes after he landed behind Russian lines. As two Red Army soldiers led him to a jeep, he looked back instinctively in the direction of Berlin: out on the horizon was a solid curtain of lurid crimson and black. It looked like the end of the world.

Flying over Berlin, Lt. John Welch, John Briol's co-pilot, thought about the people down below, under the bombs. His squadron's target was the Friedrichstrasse railroad station, which he had been told would be bursting at the seams with refugees. "God, help them," he whispered as his bombardier released a load of 500-pound explosives.

A week or so after the Berlin raid, a report was smuggled out of Germany by Herie Granberg, a Swedish newspaper correspondent who had taken refuge during the bombing in an underground railway tunnel. "The ground heaved, lights flickered. It seemed the concrete walls bulged. People scrambled about like frightened animals." As more bombs rained down, the lights went out and great clouds of dust filled the tunnel. The chalky dust penetrated people's eyes, blinding them as they knelt on the railroad tracks and prayed. When the bombing ended, Granberg found dead and dying victims scattered all over the square in front of the station.

At the same time, in another neighborhood in the city center, Ursula von Kardorff, a young Berlin newspaper reporter, was racing through the streets in search of friends and family, "carried along by the stream of people who had been bombed out, their faces gray and their backs bent, heavily laden with their belongings." Von Kardorff loathed Hitler, blaming him for a barbaric racial war and the death of her two brothers on the fighting fronts. Part of her accepted the bombing as Germany's due, but she thought it cruelly ironic that the working-class neighborhood she was passing through, where she had friends who shared her political sentiments, had gotten "the worst of it. . . . Not a patch of sky to be seen, only clouds of poisonous yellow smoke," she wrote that night in her secret diary, an incendiary document that would have placed her life in jeopardy had it been discovered by the police. "When evening fell over the burning city one hardly noticed it, because it had been so dark all day."

For several days after the raid, earth-shaking explosions from delayed-action time bombs could be heard throughout the city. Water, gas, telephone service, and electricity were knocked out. Unexploded bombs and vast puddles of filthy water from burst mains made the streets impassable; and clouds of smoke hung for days over the stricken city. Propaganda Minister Joseph Goebbels announced that looters would be shot on the spot, but gangs of drunken soldiers fleeing from the collapsing Eastern Front roamed the ruined city, smashing store windows, pillaging linen and silver, glassware and porcelain, stealing cars from garages, and killing chickens and pigs. Amid the smoking rubble, Herie Granberg found three discarded Nazi Party badges. "If I had taken the trouble, I probably could have found more."

After deliberation, Hitler decided the government must remain in Berlin "and there await either a miracle or annihilation," in the words of Hans-Georg von Studnitz, a despairing official in the German Foreign Ministry. To leave would set a cowardly example for the Berliners the führer had called upon to resist to the end. Nor would there be an evacuation, even of the refugees. "After suffering terrible casualties in yesterday's great air attacks, the homeless masses are trapped in the still burning capital and must share whatever new disaster may befall it," Goebbels declared. "Should a similar great crisis arise in Germany, say in 150 years' time," Goebbels told the führer, "our grandchildren may look back on us as a heroic example of steadfastness."

To this day, there are no reliable figures on the number of Berliners killed on February 3. The dead from previous raids were still trapped in the ruins with the victims of the most recent attack. Adding to the confusion, there were perhaps three million refugees from the eastern Reich crammed into the heart of the city, part of one of the greatest human migrations in history. Thousands of them were cremated where they fell, making either identification or reporting of their death impossible. Early estimates by the Eighth Air Force and Swedish reporters put the number of dead at around 25,000, while a respected German historian has recently arrived at a much lower figure, approximately 3,000. If correct, even this suspiciously low figure represents the most Berliners killed in a single raid in the entire war, during which the city was bombed 363 times, with a total loss of 50,000 citizens. What is known for certain is that an astounding 120,000 people were made homeless by the February 3 bombing.

The RAF had previously dropped bigger bomb loads on the city, but, as the *New York Times* reported, "Never was a target area so saturated." The main targets in the civil and military government area—the Reichschancellery (built over Hitler's hideaway, the bombproof Führerbunker), the Ministry of Propaganda, the Air Ministry, the Foreign Office, Gestapo headquarters, and the despised People's Court, which dealt out retributive justice to Germans who wavered in their support of the regime—"were smothered under eighteen concentrations of high explosives," the Air Force reported. Two central railway stations and the enormous Tempelhof marshaling yard took equally heavy hits. Also destroyed or heavily damaged were major electronics, leather, printing, and clothing plants, along with hotels, newspaper offices, department stores, and residential neighborhoods adjacent to the main targets. Yet it could have been worse, perhaps, like Hamburg, a complete urban holocaust, had the Eighth returned as planned three days later; but weather caused the mission to be canceled.

After-action reports verify the oral testimony of airmen that this was a terror raid. "Berlin, Saturday. Barrage flak, weakening as each group went over," wrote a toggler (bomb releaser) on the Fortress *Supermouse*. "No damage to ship. Visual! 5 x 1000 pounders. Shacked women and children!" Some airmen were untroubled by remorse or guilt. The coldly anonymous nature of bomber warfare made it possible for some human beings to deal out death without the slightest sense of personal responsibility. "I never *saw* any of those people," pilot Lewis Welles said years later. "I never *knew* any of those people. I came home, had a good meal, crawled in between clean sheets and went to sleep." Others saw the bombing as justifiable retribution. "The German people supported Hitler in his rampage over Europe. He did not do it by himself," chaplain James Good Brown spoke for the fliers of the 381st Bomb Group he talked to after the raid. For Brown's men, there was little difference between soldiers in uniform and civilians who made the planes, guns, and gas, and supplied the emotional and financial capital that allowed Hitler to continue his orgy of murder and aggression. These were the extreme reactions of airmen: moral indifference and righteous revenge. The dominant response was perhaps that of pilot Harry S. Mitchell, Jr. "It was a terrible thing to see those bombs going right into the heart of the city but only terrible until I saw the lead ship, about fifty feet away, get a direct burst and break in two," he wrote in his battle diary. "One of the boys that went with that ship . . . had 55 missions. His wife is going to have a baby this month too."

This was a mission that lived for years in the minds of many of the crewmen. "This one . . . bothered me for a long time," said Lewis Welles's radio operator, James Henrietta. "In fact it still does. . . . I'm thinking we're bombing out a lot of people who maybe were helpless victims."

On February 17, German radio reported that the Wehrmacht was conferring a "special decoration" upon General Spaatz—the Order of the White Feather. He was receiving it for "exceptional cowardice" in laying a "carpet of bombs" across a city "crowded with hundreds of thousands of refugees, principally women and children, who had fled before the organized savagery and terrorism of the Bolshevik Communist Red Army." No mention was made of Guernica, Coventry, the rocket assault on London, or the Luftwaffe's bombing of Stalingrad in late August 1942, aerial hammer blows that killed 40,000 Russians, many of them refugees, to the triumphant cheers of German troops positioned on the opposite bank of the River Don. Speaking on BBC radio earlier in the war from his California home-in-exile, the Nobel Prize–winning novelist Thomas Mann had sent a dark warning to his countrymen, "Did Germany believe that she would never have to pay for the atrocities that her leap into barbarism seemed to allow?"

Dresden

It was planned as a one-two punch, a combined RAF–Eighth Air Force assault on a city whose prewar population of 600,000 had recently ballooned to nearly a million as a result of an influx of refugees from the east. The

Eighth Air Force was to hit Dresden first, mounting a "precision" raid on its rail facilities, but inclement weather caused a postponement. That gave Bomber Harris the first shot at the city.

On the unseasonably pleasant evening of February 13, two waves of Lancasters, over 800 bombers, approached the beautiful river town known for its chinaware, its spacious parks, and its fanciful architecture. Dresdeners called their city Florence on the Elbe. That was before it was turned into a desert of stone and ash.

As at Hamburg in the summer of 1943, a catastrophic combination of explosive and incendiary bombs set off a firestorm, this one incinerating or suffocating at least 35,000 people, about 11,000 fewer than did the Hamburg conflagration. The Eighth Air Force flew in that morning and the next, hitting a centrally located marshaling yard and spilling errant explosives into surrounding residential neighborhoods, where thousands of people had gone to escape the fire.

Kurt Vonnegut, an American infantryman captured in the Battle of the Bulge, had been moved to Dresden several days before the bombing to be part of a forced work detail. "The boxcar doors were opened, and the doorways framed the loveliest city that most of the Americans had ever seen." It looked to Vonnegut like Oz.

The prisoners were marched to a slaughterhouse and housed in one of the buildings, a concrete shelter for pigs that were being readied for the butcher's knife. The number over the building was five. Vonnegut was in the meat locker when the bombs fell. It was a safe place.

The prisoners were not permitted to come out of the shelter until noon the next day. "Dresden was like the moon now, nothing but minerals. The stones were hot. Everybody else in the neighborhood was dead," Vonnegut later wrote in his novel *Slaughterhouse-Five*.

Vonnegut was lucky to have been herded into a secure shelter. In all of Dresden there was not a single public air raid bunker of the kind found in other sizable German cities—multistory buildings or underground compartments constructed of heavy concrete, with gas filters, ventilation, emergency exits, fire prevention, and first aid facilities. Dresdeners were forced to rely on the storage basements of train stations and other large public buildings, and the coal cellars of private houses and apartment buildings. The scandalously corrupt governor of Saxony, Martin Mutschmann, had ignored the pleas of city officials for substantial shelters, although he had the SS build reinforced concrete bunkers beneath his office and in the garden behind his home.

Not only was Dresden unprotected, it was defenseless. The local Luft-waffe airfield was lined with newly built fighter planes, but the pilots were under orders not to fly lest they deplete the fatherland's meager fuel supply, which was being hoarded for a final defense. And the city's flak guns had been moved that winter to the Ruhr and to the Oder front. Dresden was what Bomber Harris called an intact city; in five years of war, it had been bombed only twice, both times by the Americans: on October 7, 1944, as a secondary target, and on January 16, 1945. The Eighth had hit industrial targets in and around the main marshaling yard near the city center, killing hundreds of workers but doing no damage to Dresden's jewel-like historic core.

"We felt safe," remembered Liselotte Klemich, a housewife with three children. Before the inferno, false rumors were circulating that Churchill had an aging aunt in Dresden and that this was the reason the city had been spared the fate of Hamburg and Berlin. "Gradually we also began thinking that Dresden would remain intact because of the wonderful art treasures and because the city itself was so beautiful. We had become very careless. Most of the time I didn't even wake my children when there was an alarm. But on this particular evening, when I turned on the radio . . . [around nine-thirty] I was horrified to hear that large bomber formations were on their way and that we were to take shelter immediately. I woke and dressed my three small daughters and helped them into their little rucksacks that contained extra underwear. I took along a briefcase, which held a fireproof box with family documents, all of my jewelry, and a large sum of money. We dashed down into the [basement] shelter. Most of the others were already there. They had looks of horror on their faces."

As people sobbed and prayed, Frau Klemich clung to her children, thinking, "They will be taken now." She worried as well for the unborn child she was carrying in her womb.

From eight feet underground, the incoming British machines could be heard overhead. "It was as if a huge noisy conveyor belt was rolling over us, a noise punctuated with detonations and tremors," recalled Götz Bergander, the eighteen-year-old son of the manager of a local distillery. Harris's crews were trained to raise city-consuming fires, but up to now they had been able to start only three full-scale urban holocausts: Hamburg, Kassel, and Darmstadt. To create a hurricane-like firestorm everything had to go horrifyingly right. It did at Dresden.

The unopposed Lancasters, flying into a cloudless sky, dropped a lethal mixture of explosives and incendiaries into a city of highly flammable, tightly massed buildings that contained vast stores of winter heating fuel.

The high explosives—many of them 4,000-pound air bombs, or "cookies"—were designed to collapse buildings, sever water mains, and create gaping craters in the streets in order to hinder or trap firefighters and emergency teams. They were also expected to blow out windows and doors to create drafts that would allow smaller fires started by hundreds of thousands of "stick" incendiaries to spread and merge, producing, in Vonnegut's words, "one big flame," a flame that would eat "everything organic, everything that would burn." The rain of high explosives had another objective: to intimidate city dwellers, keeping them in their shelters so they could not extinguish with sand, or remove with tongs, the small, sparking incendiaries that landed on the roofs of their houses and apartment buildings.

When the first attack ended, there was tomblike silence in Bergander's shelter, a state-of-the-art facility that had been built beneath the Bramsch distillery by his father, a noted engineer. "Coming out of the shelter was unforgettable. The night sky was illuminated with pink and red. The houses were silhouettes and a red cloud of smoke hovered over everything." Bergander was so thunderstruck he forgot his fear and climbed onto the roof of the distillery to take a photograph of the flaming sky. "People ran toward us totally distraught, smeared with ash, and with wet blankets wrapped around their heads." These Dresdeners were running from the Altstadt, the oldest, most beautifully preserved part of the city, the center of civic life, and the target of the first wave of Lancasters.

The firestorm did not reach a crescendo until after the second RAF attack, just after 1:00 A.M. By then, the thousands of small fires set by the incendiaries had burned their way through roofs and attics and created raging house fires that grew ferociously and merged with fires created by the second torrent of bombs. These bombs fell into areas south of the Altstadt, chiefly the Grosser Garten, Dresden's magnificent greensward, where tens of thousands of fear-driven victims had taken refuge.

The crews of the second flight of Lancasters had orders to hit the Altmarkt, the historic marketplace in the city center, but seeing that it was already a roiling sea of flames, they made an on-the-spot decision; flying on, they dropped their tonnage where they saw no fires, burning what had not yet been burned.

Every Dresdener heard the thunderous explosions of the "air bombs," but people in the shelters failed to pick up a more insidious sound—the slap, slap, slap of four-pound magnesium canisters dropping on tiled roofs. These thermite-filled incendiaries, which the Germans wrongly called phosphorous bombs, were the great killers of the night, causing over five times more damage and death than conventional iron bombs. In no time at all, Dresden was engulfed by a firestorm of biblical proportions and the city's firefighters were overwhelmed, confined to attacking the smaller fires around the perimeter of the gale and creating avenues of escape for people caught in the maelstrom.

Most center-city dwellers who tried to ride out the storm in their coal cellars were doomed. Even well-constructed air raid bunkers offered little protection from firestorms. Seventy percent of Dresden's fire victims succumbed to carbon monoxide poisoning released by combustion; many of them died swiftly and painlessly without a burn on their bodies.

Frau Klemich's shelter was not in the direct path of the firestorm and she and her children survived both bombing attacks. Anne Wahle, living in another part of town, nearly did not. An American-born woman who had married a German officer before the war, she was fighting her way to safety with her three small children and their live-in nurse. "The heat was almost unbearable, and the sudden gusts of wind made us grab at each other for fear of being blown away. It was almost impossible to see through the sparks that kept whirling around us like a red blizzard, and we kept peering through them for a sign of some kind of shelter."

People's shoes melted into the hot asphalt of the streets, and the fire moved so swiftly that many were reduced to atoms before they had time to remove their shoes. The fire melted iron and steel, turned stone into powder, and caused trees to explode from the heat of their own resin. People running from the fire could feel its heat through their backs, burning their lungs.

But it was the gale-force wind—not the staggering heat—that made the most frightful impression on the survivors. What appeared to be hurricane-like winds were actually convection whirls, or fire devils—superheated columns of extremely hot air rising from the fire and sent in a rotating, tornado-like motion by cooler, descending air. In this way—by drawing cooler, heavier air into the vacuum left by its escaping hotter, lighter air—a great fire produces its own wind, a whirling wind that throws burning debris far in advance of the main fire, setting new fires. These smaller fires burned together, trapping life between the main fire coming from behind and the new fire racing back toward it. Caught in this pincerlike fire action, many Dresdeners became disoriented and panicked.

Anne Wahle saw a woman approaching from the opposite direction pushing a large pram with her two children "sitting bolt upright like dolls. . . . Wildly she raced past us, straight into the fire. . . . She and her children instantly disappeared in the flames." Some trapped and despairing souls simply knelt down in the street and awaited their awful end.

A little later, Wahle and her family spotted a house that was still standing and found shelter in its basement. The next morning they tried to escape the city. The streets were eerily empty and almost every house they passed was a scorched ruin. "Where had everyone gone? Were they all dead or still crouching in cellars?" They soon discovered when they neared the Grosser Garten, where blackened body parts were hanging from the trees. Walking on, they passed row upon row of corpses set on the clipped lawn like charred logs. These pitiful victims, their facial features melted into a molten mass, their bodies grotesquely shrunk, had rushed from their burning houses in the old city to what they thought was a refuge. "The water in the fountain basin still rippled peacefully in the pale sunlight," Anne Wahle recalled after the war, when she returned to America. "I thought of the children that only yesterday were sailing their boats there."

Wahle and her family made it out of the city that night and eventually found their way to the home of their nurse's family in the Austrian Alps. But Liselotte Klemich and her children were in Dresden the next day, Ash Wednesday, when the Eighth Air Force appeared overhead, flying into pillars of smoke that rose to 15,000 feet above the city. Three hundred eleven Fortresses dropped 771 tons of explosives and incendiaries into the suffering city, hitting the Friedrichstadt marshaling yard and passenger station and an industrial neighborhood adjacent to the yard. Also hit were a smaller marshaling yard and at least three compact residential areas outside the city center. With the targets obscured by clouds and drifting black haze, most of the squadrons were forced to aim their bombs by radar, and a few made "accidental" releases. Photo intelligence and after-action reports by radar operators note that the "majority of bombs" fell into the marshaling yards or "heavily built areas of the city," some of them near the yards, others as far as "8–10 miles beyond target."

The damage would have been greater if all the American bomb groups sent to Dresden had reached their destination. Three of them became disoriented in a cloudbank over central Germany and, thinking they had hit Dresden, bombed Prague.

Götz Bergander's neighborhood was near the Friedrichstadt marshaling yards. Bombs fell all around his residence, but neither he nor anyone else in his shelter was harmed. The family's apartment block was ruined, however, and Götz's mother, only forty-four years old, suffered a heart attack. The Berganders and their neighbors moved their beds into the shelter, which became their nighttime abode for the remainder of the war.

There were thousands of homeless souls in Bergander's neighborhood when the American bombers had first appeared overhead, people who had escaped from the old city. They "really felt as if they were coming in for special persecution on the 14 February noon raid," Bergander said later. The raid had not been planned this insidiously, but to the victims it surely looked like it had. As historian Richard Taylor noted: first the British bombed the Altstadt, then the Grosser Garten, where thousands of victims from the Altstadt had fled. Finally, the Americans bombed the untouched areas in the western suburbs. "It was as if the enemy had anticipated the Dresdeners' every move, and then killed them like cattle cunningly driven into holding pens."

Dresdeners, along with a number of historians of the bombing, most prominently the Englishman David Irving, would later claim that P-51 Mustangs of the 20th Fighter Group machine-gunned surviving fire victims on the Elbe meadows and in the area of the Grosser Garten, piling one massacre upon another. This could not have happened. The 20th Fighter Group was in Prague that day with the bombers that had flown off course; and neither German nor American records make mention of strafing activities anywhere near the Dresden area on the days of the American bombing raids. Joseph Goebbels, who would have pounced on such information, had nothing to say about low-level fighter attacks on the people of Dresden.

On February 15, over 200 Fortresses of the Eighth Air Force returned to Dresden, diverted there by foul weather over their primary target, an oil plant near Leipzig. Some damage was done to the industrial suburbs, but not a single bomb fell on the aiming point, the city's marshaling yards.

As the Americans flew back to their bases, a Nazi official went on the radio. "Not a single detached building remains intact or capable of reconstruction. The town area is devoid of human life. A great city has been wiped from the map of Europe." Wartime German reports listed up to 400,000 dead. New research by Götz Bergander, who has written a scrupulous account of the bombing, puts the number killed between 35,000 and 40,000. But with the city crammed with several hundred thousand refugees, who can know how many died?

For weeks after the fire raid, Berlin reporter Ursula von Kardorff, who had recently decided to leave her job and home for a safe haven in the countryside, heard "dreadful stories" of people digging bodies out of Dresden's ruins. "The British prided themselves particularly on having killed so many refugees. This barbarity is not much different from our own. It is inhuman for anyone to pour high explosives and phosphorous on refugees, old people, mothers and children."

"The fire kept burning for weeks," recalled Liselotte Klemich. "I wasn't there for the cleaning up of the bodies. We read about that in the newspapers. They swept the bodies together and burned them in the market place." Allied POWs worked on the cleanup, pulling shriveled bodies from the ruins–"corpse mining," Kurt Vonnegut called this gruesome duty. POWs used pitchforks to toss the shrunken bodies onto farmers' wagons and carts. They were then piled on iron grates in the city's central market, soaked with benzene, and immolated by SS extermination experts brought in from a local concentration camp. The ashes were later buried in mass graves. The vast cremation lasted into March, and for weeks afterward Allied prisoners who worked in the cleanup were unable to get the smell of burning flesh off their clothing.

"The idea was to hasten the end of the war," Vonnegut wrote in his novel. "Only one person ever got any benefit from the bombing of Dresden, and he is me," Vonnegut said later. "I wrote an antiwar novel that made lots of money."

Eighth Air Force waist gunner John Morris disagreed. "I'm not ashamed of having gone to Dresden . . . on February 15; it was legitimate military strategy and I'm convinced that it hastened the arrival of VE-Day. . . . The Wehrmacht was falling back before the Russian army all along the eastern front. . . . But once they reached the sacred soil of the Fatherland, they could be expected to regroup and become lethal again for a last-ditch fight. . . . So it was sound strategy to prevent the Wehrmacht from reaching the relative safety of home base. And we did so: we bombed the hell out of the railroad marshaling yards and road hubs along its lines of retreat–all up and down Germany's eastern border–Stettin, Berlin, Frankfort-am-Oder, Leipzig–as well as Dresden. . . .

"I don't rejoice in the 35,000 Germans killed there. Incidentally, I doubt that there were many Jews in that number; the good burghers of Dresden had just recently shipped the last of them off to Auschwitz."

That is almost right. Victor Klemperer, a professor at the city's Technical University, was one of only 198 registered Jews in Dresden when the first Lancasters came plowing through the cloudless February sky. The rest had either escaped, committed suicide, or been sent to Auschwitz and other murder mills. A decorated World War I veteran and a devoted German patriot, Klemperer had lost his job, his home, and his life's savings in the racial hysteria that swept the city after Hitler came to power. He had not been deported, however, because he was married to an "Aryan," a racially pure German. This changed on February 13, when all Jews capable of physical labor were ordered to report three days later for transportation to an unknown "work" camp, an order they regarded as a death sentence.

Henni Brenner's father was one of these remaining Dresden Jews. "The morning he received the order to report for the transport . . . he became very depressed," his daughter recalled, "and said, 'Henni, only a miracle, a bolt from the blue can save us now.' " As soon as the bombs began falling, Brenner and his family ripped the degrading yellow stars from their clothing and started to make their way out of the stricken city. Among the other escapees were Victor Klemperer and his wife, Eva. They spent three months on the run before finding safety in a Bavarian village occupied by American troops.

Before the elder Brenner left, he insisted on seeing the Gestapo building. "We couldn't get that far," says his daughter, "because everything was burning, but from a distance we saw that it was ablaze. Well, then we felt some satisfaction."

Was Dresden a legitimate military target? General Doolittle thought so. Although disturbed by the immensity of the damage caused by the British, he considered Dresden a key transportation center—the junction of three important trunk lines of the Reichsbahn. Twenty-eight army trains, carrying a total of almost 20,000 soldiers, were passing through the city every day in early February. The Friedrichstadt marshaling yard, the principal target of Doolittle's Fortresses, was one of the most important in eastern Germany. The night before the RAF raid, American POWs were being moved through this switching yard. "For nearly twelve hours German troops and equipment rolled into and out of Dresden," recalled one of the prisoners, Col. Harold E. Cook. "I saw with my own eyes that Dresden was an armed camp: thousands of German troops, tanks and artillery and miles of freight cars loaded with supplies supporting and transporting German logistics towards the east to meet the Russians."

Germany's seventh largest city, Dresden was a thriving center for the manufacture of gun sights, radar equipment, bomb fuses, electronic components, and poison gas for both the Luftwaffe and the Wehrmacht. In 1945, approximately 50,000 of the city's industrial workers were engaged in war work.

Not far from Dresden there was a work camp called Schlieben, where Jewish inmates produced Panzerfausts, the deadly antitank rockets that would become the favorite weapons of the fanatical Hitler Youth in their final suicidal battles against Allied troops. In the early hours of February

14, the slave laborers of Schlieben watched Dresden burn. "It was like heaven for us," recalled Ben Halfgott, "for we knew that the end of the war must be near and our salvation was at hand."

Half a century later, John Morris was asked why Dresden was bombed so late in the war. How could we have known then, he replied, that the war would be over by early May? On Ash Wednesday the American Army was still burying its dead from the Battle of the Bulge.

Sir Arthur Harris argues unassailably in his memoirs that "the attack on Dresden was at the time considered a military necessity by more important people than myself." But the critical question is not why or when Dresden was bombed, but how it was bombed. Why conduct a city-destroying raid when a selective strike on rail facilities would have more closely fit the purposes of the revised Thunderclap plan? This was entirely Harris's decision. In the absence of vigilant government supervision of Harris's bombing policies (both British and American civilian leaders left operational matters in the hands of their air commanders), Harris had near complete control over the mission. Not surprisingly, Dresden was treated no differently than other German cities he had either eradicated or attempted to eradicate.

It was a question of proportion. As Götz Bergander has said, "Even in war, the ends must relate to the means. Here, the means seemed wildly out of proportion to the end. I will not say that Dresden should not have been bombed—it was a rail center, and thus an important target. I will not say Dresden was an exceptional case as compared to other German cities. But I do not understand why it had to be done on such a huge scale."

Dresden had not been specially marked for immolation. There was nothing exceptional about the raid except the unexpected magnitude of the devastation. Harris planned this mission exactly as he had planned the thirty-eight other city-busting raids his force carried out in the first three months of 1945. Dresden was a routine incendiary mission that happened to go exactly right. "From our point of view it was only a fluke," recalled the eminent physicist Freeman Dyson, who was a civilian scientist working at Bomber Command headquarters. "We had attacked Berlin sixteen times [previously] and with the same kind of force that attacked Dresden once. There was nothing special about Dresden except that for once everything worked as we intended. . . . Dresden was like a hole in one in a game of golf." Casualties were appallingly high, but not disproportionate to RAF fire raids on at least five other German cities: Pforzheim, Darmstadt, Kassel, Hamburg, and Wuppertal.

It was also a routine raid for the Eighth Air Force, "business as usual." Indeed, no combined air operation better illustrates the differences between the fast-converging, though still distinct, late-war bombing policies of the RAF and the Eighth Air Force. Two powerful air forces were sent to the same city within hours of each other and with the same strategic objective: the interdiction of the Berlin–Leipzig–Dresden rail corridor. But the two commanders, Doolittle and Harris, employed different bombing techniques. One air force tried to kill an urban rail system, the other tried to erase an entire city.

Both failed to achieve their objective. After the raid, Harris boasted: "Dresden was a mass of munitions works, an intact government center, and a key transportation point to the East. It is now none of those things." That is inaccurate. While the fire raid dealt the city's industries and rail network a staggering blow, the economic disruption would have been far greater had Bomber Command targeted the suburban areas where most of Dresden's manufacturing might was concentrated.

The American raid and its follow-up were equally disappointing to Air Force strategic planners. Rail service was partially restored in Dresden within two weeks, and military trains soon began passing through the city's marshaling yards. Dresden was finally eliminated as a rail nexus in the same way that German transportation centers in the Ruhr had been eliminated: by repeated attacks, in this case, two well-executed missions on March 2 and April 17. The last blow was decisive. Nearly 600 Eighth Air Force bombers pulverized the city's marshaling yards, severing the last surviving north–south link in the Reich. At least 500 civilians were killed, but it was as accurate a raid as the Americans were capable of executing against an urban military target.

The Eighth Air Force was never capable of precisely hitting a marshaling yard obscured by clouds or smoke. Young men died trying, but headquarters was apparently not satisfied with heroic failure. After the war, it cleansed its bombing records. During the war, Eighth Air Force's group commanders made no attempt to disguise what they were doing. While the targets might be designated as "marshalling yards," the after-action summaries are perfectly clear about what was destroyed. "The low squadron pattern hit in the central city area and compact residential district fully built up," reads a typical mission summary, this one from the October 7, 1944, Dresden raid. Yet after the war, when anonymous Air Force historians compiled two massive statistical compendiums of American strategic bombing missions—reports still widely used by independent historians—neither volume listed "city area" as a target category. As Richard Davis, a senior historian with the Air Force History Support Office, wrote: "The unknown hand or hands" that put together the reports "changed all raids striking city areas to 'marshalling yards' or 'port' or 'industrial areas.' " And all raids on central Berlin were changed to a special category expressly reserved for that city, "Military & Civil Government Area." It is as if the American Air Force in Europe never sent a single sortie against an enemy city.

This calculated policy of obfuscation began during the war with the press releases of the Air Force's formidable public relations machine, second to no other in the services, not even that of the Marines. After the Dresden raid, Gen. Frederick Anderson cabled a worried Hap Arnold with this reassuring news: "Public relations officers have been advised to take exceptional care that the military nature of targets attacked in the future be specified and emphasized in all cases. As in the past the statement that an attack was made on such and such a city will be avoided; specific targets will be described."

The bomb loads carried on urban missions—the ratio of blast bombs to incendiaries—tell the real story. Incendiary bombs have no blast effect and were, therefore, not generally used against hardened targets—industrial plants, marshaling yards, and heavy military machinery. Their sole purpose was to destroy "soft" targets, such as houses, barracks, commercial buildings, and government offices. Yet in the Eighth Air Force's Dresden mission of February 14—a marshaling yard raid—the ratio of explosives to incendiaries was 60 percent to 40 percent, a lethal cocktail for an area, not a precision, raid.

This was not unusual. On radar raids, American strategic bombers regularly used a high percentage of incendiaries on rail targets in other cities: Cologne (27 percent), Nuremberg (30 percent), Berlin (37 percent), and Munich (41 percent), although very few fire bombs were used in attacks on the French rail system in the run-up to D-Day, for fear of killing French civilians. In a follow-up raid on Berlin on February 26, 1945, over a thousand American bombers, using radar guidance and carrying a bomb load that was 44 percent incendiaries, knocked out the city's three central rail stations and started raging fires that swept through unintended target areas, including residential neighborhoods. Three weeks later, on March 18, the Eighth mounted its heaviest Berlin mission of the war, dropping over half a million incendiaries. Berlin's size, its modern construction, its excellent firefighting force, its formidable flak defenses, and its broad imperial avenues, which acted as firebreaks, made it harder to burn than

Dresden. Otherwise, any one of these late-war "transportation" raids could have ignited a firestorm.

The Eighth Air Force was not trying to burn Berlin or any other German city. Knowing that it could not hit its central city targets accurately, especially with radar, it had its bombers carry large loads of incendiaries in order to widen the circle of destruction, which increased the chances that the intended target would suffer damage. It also, of course, increased the likelihood that large numbers of noncombatants would die, especially with most American bombing being done by radar in the winter of 1944–45. To compensate for inaccuracy caused by imprecise radar equipment, weather, German resistance, equipment malfunction, and human error by men who were asked to do a precise, high-pressure task while under enemy fire, American bomber crews frequently carpet bombed, said Fifteenth Air Force radar navigator-bombardier Milt Groban. "A common intervalometer setting, with 500-pound bombs, was 400 feet. This meant," Groban explained, "that bombs would be released sequentially so as to make a string 4,800 feet long. A typical four-squadron group of fifty bombers would drop fifty of these approximately mile-long strings through a target. We usually hit something—frequently a bomb or two hit or damaged the target." To distinguish themselves from the British, the Americans asked to be judged by what they aimed at, not by what they hit. But the alternative to inaccurate bombing was not to bomb at all and risk contributing to the prolongation of Nazi tyranny against, among others, slave laborers, POWs, and concentration camp inmates.

The difference between Eighth Air Force transportation bombing and RAF area bombing was more clear-cut in cities in which most or all of the major industries were located in the suburbs. On the evening of September 11–12, 1944, Bomber Command set off a firestorm that in less than an hour obliterated the entire urban core of Darmstadt, a residential city with no major rail yards or war industries. Yet the raid was ineffective. With 90 percent of the city's industries located in the unburned suburbs, Darmstadt's war production was almost fully restored within a month. That December, the Eighth Air Force bombed Darmstadt's suburban industries, a large target, easily spotted, even by radar. This strategic strike delivered an "industrial *coup de grâce*" without major loss of life or civilian property in the sections of the city that were spared in the RAF's September holocaust.

• • •

The multiple raids on Berlin and Dresden in February and March of 1945 were part of an immense acceleration of the air war. By the end of 1944, almost four-fifths of German towns with over 100,000 inhabitants had already been destroyed; and that was before Allied bombing operations peaked. In the first four months of 1945, the Anglo-American air forces dropped over twice the tonnage of bombs on Germany that the RAF had dropped in all of 1943. "It is soul destroying to wait, day and night, for the inevitable disaster," sixty-eight-year-old Mathilde Wolff-Mönckeberg wrote to her grown children, who were living outside the Reich. This German matron had refused to leave her "poor burning destroyed" Hamburg when a mass evacuation occurred in the late summer of 1943, one of dozens of wartime evacuations that displaced ten million people, mostly mothers and their children (working women without children and most women with older children were forbidden from evacuating).

As long as the German government did not seek peace, there was no reason to stop the bombing. It is what was bombed and how it was bombed that is questionable, both morally and militarily. The world's focus on Dresden has obscured equal excesses. Pforzheim was a medium-size city in southwestern Germany that produced precision instruments and had marginal value to the Wehrmacht as a juncture for military trains. Ten days after the Dresden raid, Harris's crews destroyed over 80 percent of the town's developed area and wiped out over a quarter of its wartime population (compared to roughly 5 percent in Dresden). "The whole place has been burned out," Harris reported to his fellow air commanders on March 1. "This attack," he added with evident satisfaction, "[is] what [is] popularly known as a deliberate terror attack." Bomber Command had now destroyed sixty-three German towns "in this fashion," he declared.

He was not finished. On the night of March 16–17, his fleets destroyed Würzburg, a historic cathedral and university center in northern Bavaria. Nearly 90 percent of the city's built-up area was burned out, and 5,000 of its 100,000 inhabitants were killed. This inexcusable, out-of-control bombing of early 1945 should stand as a warning to nations that launch wars of naked aggression. When the people who are the targets of their malice are forced to fight for their very survival, they will, if they are strong enough, fight with unhinged fury, with the aim of completely crushing the enemy (unlike World War I, this war would end with a surrender, not a peace treaty). In such a fight "the wonder is that moral scruples entered as much into the calculus as they did," wrote historian Richard Kohn.

The German people became victims of the "hatred their leaders had systematically sown," wrote Gen. Hans Rumpf, former head of the Reich's firefighting service. "It was the ordinary men and women and their children who had to pay the bill." But millions of these "ordinary" Germans— and General Rumpf himself—had backed Hitler's sinister purposes, and in doing so they put themselves, their cities, and their children at terrible risk. Writing half a century after the war, the German novelist W. G. Sebald concluded his controversial book on the air war, *On the Natural History of Destruction,* with this thought. "The majority of Germans today know, or so at least it is to be hoped, that we actually provoked the annihilation of the cities in which we once lived."

Clarion

No German town was safe from attack in early 1945. One of the most controversial air operations of the war, code-named Clarion, was aimed at undefended or lightly defended targets all over the Reich. First suggested by Arnold and then refined by Spaatz, it called for "widespread simultaneous attacks" by waves of warplanes—American and British—striking from low altitudes against previously un-bombed transportation targets in small towns and villages. Light and heavy bombers, accompanied by fighter planes, would be sent out against these towns with the aim of overwhelming Reichsbahn repair crews and precipitating "a crisis" among railway workers. "As a result of our continued pressure against transportation objectives, morale of railway employees is known to be infirm at best," an Air Force planning document observed, "and it may well be that repeated attacks using all forces available will result in mass desertion from work."

Another mission objective was to create shock among millions of Germans who had thus far escaped the heavy bombing. With little or no Luftwaffe opposition expected, American air leaders wanted to impress upon these people, as William Tecumseh Sherman's virtually unopposed March to the Sea had impressed upon Southerners, "the hopelessness of their situation."

Clarion created a rift within the American air leadership. Jimmy Doolittle opposed it and so did Ira Eaker, still head of the Mediterranean Allied air forces. Both feared that it would divert attention from the oil campaign. Clarion, moreover, would "absolutely convince the Germans that we are the barbarians they say we are," Eaker wrote Spaatz, in a straight-from-the-heart personal letter, "for it would be perfectly obvious to them that this is primarily a large scale attack on civilians. . . . Of all the people killed in this attack over 95% of them can be expected to be civilians." Gen. Charles Cabell added, "This is the same old baby killing plan of the . . . psychological boys, dressed up in a new Kimono. It is a poor psychological plan and a worse rail plan."

Eaker had no moral objections to the incidental killing of German civilians in attacks on strategic objectives, but Clarion, in his view, did not target objectives of major economic or military value. Eaker also worried about the effect the raid would have on the Air Force's wartime legacy. "We should never allow the history of this war to convict us of throwing the strategic bomber at the man in the street," he wrote Spaatz. This had to have made an impression on Spaatz, who had used a similar argument against Thunderclap when it was first proposed by the British the previous summer. But feeling pressure from Arnold to end the war quickly, and knowing that both Marshall and Roosevelt wanted Germans everywhere to feel the weight of the war, passing on that terrible experience, in Roosevelt's words, "from father to son, hence to grandson," Spaatz ordered the operation to go forward. Bombardment commanders were warned to take special care in their press releases to dispel the idea "that this operation is aimed at civilian populations or intended to terrorize them." But Spaatz had to know that terror bombing was built into the structure of a low-level raid by thousands of planes.

Clarion was launched on February 22. For two days, over 3,500 bombers and nearly 5,000 fighters roamed over a quarter-million square miles of the Reich, bombing and strafing rail yards, passenger stations, bridges, grade crossings, motor vehicles, and canal barges. Among the targets were Heidelberg, a university town, and Baden-Baden, a health resort. There are no records of civilian casualties and Allied losses were light.

The Air Force leaders pronounced Clarion a "spectacular success" and a repeat performance was scheduled for March 3. But follow-up intelligence indicated mission failure: repair crews were not overwhelmed, there was no apparent erosion of German morale, high-priority military traffic continued to get through. And one of the towns heavily hit was in Switzerland—the second time Schaffhausen was accidentally bombed by the Eighth Air Force.

At a press briefing, Air Force officials put a curious spin on the mission, claiming that it was impossible to destroy the morale of a people whose morale had already been destroyed. But Spaatz canceled the March operation and began concentrating almost exclusively on what had been his three salient late-war objectives: destroying Germany's oil industry, dislocating its rail system, and providing support for Eisenhower's armies.* Before he could bring down the curtain on his final air campaigns of the war, however, Spaatz had to deal with the United States Air Force's most embarrassing press-relations gaffe of the war.

Three days after the Dresden raid, an Associated Press correspondent named Howard Cowan issued a dispatch that would cause consternation at SHAEF (Supreme Headquarters Allied Expeditionary Force). "The Allied Air Commanders have made the long awaited decision to adopt deliberate terror bombing of German population centers as a ruthless expedient to hastening Hitler's doom.

"More raids such as the British and American heavy bombers carried out recently on the residential sections of Berlin, Dresden, Chemnitz and Cottbus are in store for the Reich, and the avowed purpose will be creating more confusion in the German traffic and sapping German morale."

Cowan had gotten his information at a press briefing conducted by C. M. Grierson, an RAF intelligence officer on SHAEF's air staff. Dresden had been attacked, Grierson told reporters, to stop the movement of troops and supplies to the Eastern Front, to break up a gathering center for evacuees, and to smash "what morale there is left to have any effect on." Grierson never used the term "terror bombing." But Cowan, with good reason, interpreted his rare public admission that civilians had been targeted as an official concession by the Allied air command that it had begun a policy of slaughter bombing to shorten the war. Cowan must have been convinced of this when a SHAEF censor, improbably and inexplicably, approved his dispatch for public release.

Cowan's story became headline news in American papers, causing the American Air Force immense embarrassment. With Hap Arnold still convalescing from his heart attack in Coral Gables, Florida, crisis management was handed over to his deputy commander, Gen. Barney Giles, and to Robert Lovett, who at George Marshall's insistence effectively became the air chief. Over Arnold's signature, Air Force headquarters demanded an

---

* The Allies' final drive to the Rhine began on the evening Clarion was launched, and might further explain why Spaatz supported an air operation that he realistically expected to paralyze German rail communications for no more than "several days." Perhaps he hoped that Clarion could cause enough damage to enemy supply lines in the Rhineland to allow Gen. Courtney H. Hodges's Ninth Army to execute, with minimal opposition, its river crossing near Cologne.

immediate explanation from Spaatz. Were the Berlin and Dresden raids terror bombing, or were military targets given priority?

Spaatz's reply was reassuring. Grierson had exceeded both his knowledge of bombing policy as well as his authority, Spaatz insisted; his views represented those of Bomber Harris, perhaps, but not American air commanders. As Frederick Anderson explained, it was a case of "absolute stupidity by an incompetent officer." Both the Berlin and Dresden raids were, he and Spaatz assured headquarters, continuations of previous policy. Cologne, Münster, Frankfurt, and other transportation centers in western Germany continued to be hit with furious intent, yet these missions were not labeled, as similar raids in eastern Germany were, "as terror attacks against populations." The recent assaults on eastern German cities signaled a change not in bombing policy, but in bombing "locale." The targets were troop and military supply shipments, not refugees.

These explanations satisfied Arnold, who, from his sickbed, was eager to push the issue under the rug. They were less satisfactory to Secretary of War Stimson, who had wanted Dresden preserved in order to become the postwar "center of a new Germany which will be less Prussianized and be dedicated to freedom." And they did not sit well with Spaatz's director of intelligence, Gen. George McDonald.

In one of the most remarkable internal communications in American Air Force history, McDonald wrote to Gen. Frederick Anderson on February 21 vehemently protesting the Bottomley-Spaatz directive, issued in late January, calling for the bombing of transportation targets in Berlin, Leipzig, Dresden, and other eastern German cities. "This directive puts . . . the American Army Air Forces unequivocally into the business of area bombardment of congested civil populations." It was issued at a time, moreover, when "no intelligence available to this Directorate indicates that destruction of these three cities will decisively effect [sic] the enemy's 'capacity for armed resistance.' " The destruction of these cities as transport centers "might delay but could not critically disrupt essential movement of troops and supplies," McDonald insisted. "Nor can the elusive, if not illusionary target of morale justify the importance accorded these cities. The desideratum of morale attack is revolt. All authorities are agreed that the German people are powerless if not actually disinclined to revolt against present controls."

If the Eighth Air Force's previous bombardment policy and practice were shown to be ineffective, McDonald added caustically, "we should face the issue squarely and . . . abandon all other target priorities . . . and settle wholeheartedly to the extermination of populations and the razing of cities.

"If such a practice is sincerely considered the shortest way to victory it follows as a corollary that our ground forces, similarly, should be directed to kill all civilians and demolish all buildings in the Reich, instead of restricting their energies to the armed enemy." The present bombing directive, McDonald concluded, "repudiates our past purposes and practices and links us inseparably with a dream and design of aerial warfare limited to indiscriminate homicide and destruction. . . . It is therefore recommended that high authority be requested in the strongest possible terms to review our directive so as to permit the Army Air Forces to continue their own demonstrated methods of making the most effective contribution to the conquest of the enemy."

The Cowan affair, the alarming opposition to terror raids in Spaatz's own command, and the diplomatic crisis ignited by the accidental bombing of Swiss territory prompted Spaatz to issue a new bombing directive on March 1. It restated, in the strongest language yet, that only military objectives were to be attacked. It also put in place strict precautions to prevent another bombing of Switzerland, where there were still American fliers that the Air Force was attempting to repatriate.

In March the military bombing reached a wartime peak; a monthly high of almost 170,000 tons of bombs was dropped on Germany, 102,000 of them by the Americans. That month the Eighth Air Force sent out bombers on twenty-six days, dispatching a thousand or more of them on twenty of those missions. Some of the bombing was overkill, but this should be hardly surprising to students of warfare. Wars between powerful nations have a built-in dynamic, a demonic capacity for acceleration and excess, not necessarily by deliberate decision, but by the process of harnessing a people's emotional and material resources to total victory. Then, too, a military enterprise of the vast cost and size of the strategic bombing offensive acquired a momentum of its own when it reached the apex of its destructive capability. Once the planes, bombs, and crews were assembled in overwhelming force, "simply letting the aircraft and their valuable freight stand idle on the airfields of eastern England ran counter to any healthy economic instinct," W. G. Sebald argued cuttingly. So American bomber boys continued to fly and die in excess of the numbers needed to dismantle the enemy's war machine, whereas in the first years of the conflict they had flown and died in numbers insufficient to the task.

Still confined to his sickbed in Florida, Arnold received a message from headquarters alerting him to Secretary Stimson's continuing concern that the Dresden bombing may have been both unnecessary and excessive. Across the top of it Arnold wrote in bold script: "We must not get soft. War must be destructive and to a certain extent inhumane and ruthless."

And what was the lingering mood in Dresden? While Götz Bergander doubts that the bombing shortened the war, he is convinced that the shock of the attack—its suddenness and annihilating fury—"contributed in a fundamental way to a change of heart. This expressed itself at that time in the words: Better an end to terror than terror without end."

This was the "change of heart" Allied air barons had hoped their terror bombing would produce. But as we will see, it came too late in the war to have a direct effect on its outcome, and it exhibited itself in an inward-looking fatalism that made victims of the bombing incapable of openly challenging Nazi rule. "Everyone is so overcome by his own personal worries that he no longer cares about the fate of Germany," one woman expressed the prevailing mood. "It is far more important that one gets something to eat, that shoes will last a little longer, and above all whether there will be an air raid. Will we have a roof over our heads tomorrow, or even be alive?"

In the meantime, all that these victims of the bombing could do was suffer and struggle to survive, wondering, in the words of Mathilde Wolff-Mönckeberg, "when it will be our turn." This was the exact predicament of the Allied bomber crews.

CHAPTER SIXTEEN

The Chimneys
Hardly Ever Fall Down

Everywhere I looked lay the ruins of the city, heaps of stone
and rubbish with only the chimneys sticking out like fingers
up into the twilight sky. The chimneys hardly ever fall
down.

SYBILLA KNAUTH,
AN AMERICAN WOMAN LIVING IN LEIPZIG

Dresden, March 2, 1945

At ten o'clock that morning, as the crew of *Miss Prudy* approached
the ruined city for another attack on its marshaling yards, Chuck
Alling noticed a few tiny specks on the horizon. Seconds later, a
pack of German fighters swooped down on them, rolling as they fired. The
attack caught the bomber crews off guard. A deep fuel famine had "whittled down to the bone" the Luftwaffe's fighter defense, and air-to-air opposition had been feeble in the first two months of 1945.

The Alling crew was not surprised, however, to see a few "sinister looking" Me 262s in the assault force. They had been told to be on the lookout
for the Nazi wonder planes, which had begun to appear again in small
numbers that February, four months after Maj. Walter Nowotny's first jet
fighter unit had been disbanded. Up to now, few of the enemy's jets had

tangled with the tightly massed bomber formations, but this attack by over a hundred German fighters, more than a few of them Me 262s, was part of the Luftwaffe's final stand against the American day raiders.

The next day another formation of Eighth Air Force bombers encountered the largest jet fighter force to date, losing six bombers and three Mustangs to about three dozen determined Me 262s. During the previous month, jet fighters had attacked sporadically in twos and threes, but on this day they flew in unison and with deadly effect. Then, on the morning of March 18, after a two-week-long lull due to bad weather, an equal number of German jets, along with conventional piston-engine fighters, lined up across the sky to face a Berlin-bound fleet of 1,329 bombers and over 700 long-range fighters, the heaviest raid of the war against the German capital. It was a battle unlike any the Americans had yet fought, pitting conventional, piston-engine planes against aircraft and air-to-air missiles of the next age of aerial warfare.

In this, the most tremendous air battle of 1945, up to thirty jets flashed through the escort screen of Mustangs and destroyed two Fortresses within a minute, three more in the next three minutes, and two more right after that—a total of seven kills in eight minutes, three of them bombers from the hard-luck Bloody Hundredth. Then six more jets joined the fight. These were the fastest, most powerfully armed planes to appear in the skies over Germany—Me 262s equipped with the newest weapon of the war, the R4M air-to-air rocket. Each rocket-bearing jet carried twenty-four of these missiles in wooden racks under its wings. A single hit was capable of bringing down a heavy bomber, but the jet pilots compounded the killing power of their rockets by forming up in phalanxes and firing them simultaneously, creating annihilating "lanes of fire" through the Eighth's tightly grouped defensive formations.

The jets launched their high-velocity missiles from close range with pinpoint accuracy. "Shattered fuselages, broken-off wings, ripped-out engines, shards of aluminum, and fragments of every size whirled through the air," recalled a German pilot. "It looked as if someone had emptied out an ashtray." The Eighth lost six Mustangs and thirteen heavies, while the enemy lost only three pilots in an air fight in which they were outnumbered nearly a hundred to one.

For the next several weeks, German jets were on the prowl nearly every day. By the end of March, they had destroyed sixty-three bombers. This was attrition the machine-rich Americans could effortlessly sustain, but General Doolittle feared that the air war had entered a new and ominous phase. Air Force intelligence reports indicated that Albert Speer's bombproof underground plants were producing jets at a rate of over three dozen a week. And unlike most of the Luftwaffe pilots that the Eighth had been encountering that winter, these fliers seemed highly experienced. "[They] never allowed themselves to be caught in a bad position . . . [and] it was impossible to catch or climb with them," an American fighter squadron noted in its combat report.

The crack German aviators were the core of a freshly formed combat wing of approximately sixty aircraft, Jagdgeschwader 7 (JG 7). The unit had become fully operational in late February, when it began to carry the burden of the Luftwaffe's defensive battle. In another surprise, Hitler had recalled Adolf Galland to active duty in January, ordering him to form a second jet unit, Jagdverband 44 (JV 44), an elite cadre of fifty pilots. The legendary fighter commander who had started the war as a squadron leader would end his national service as one, piloting the aircraft he had failed to convince Hitler to produce in overmastering numbers.

Galland recruited the best of Germany's piston-engine aces, comrades he had flown with and caroused with. Some were "coaxed" out of their hospital beds and flew with artificial limbs; others reported for duty "without consent of transfer orders. Most had seen action since the first day of the war," Galland would write later, "and all of them had been wounded." Coarsened by failure, few of them expected to reverse the course of the war, but all thirsted for the honor and glory of being "the first jet boys" of the dying Luftwaffe. "The magic word 'jet,' " said Galland, "had brought us together."

Stationed near Munich, the "Squadron of Experts" ran into trouble even before it first met the enemy in the sky on April 5. After the Berlin battle of March 18, Doolittle ordered pulverizing carpet-bombing raids on all jet airfields. And as in the fall of 1944, American fighter planes began flying standing patrols over the airdromes in the hope of destroying the superior planes when they became easy kills—taking off and landing. Rat catching, the fighter jockeys called it.

Even in close combat, American Mustang pilots learned how to fight the jets. Flying a wonderfully maneuverable plane with a superior turning radius, they were able, in groups—rarely singly, as Chuck Yeager had—to get the jump on Me 262s in dogfights, and after "bouncing" them, killing them. "In a man against man battle . . . our pilots had not the least chance against an Me 262," observed Col. William C. Clark, commander of the American 339th Fighter Group. "The aircraft was simply too fast. We countered its superior speed with our numerical superiority."

Like the bomber war, it became a battle of attrition, one the Germans could not win. Despite Speer's prodigious efforts, a jet produced was not necessarily a jet delivered, for Germany's transportation system was virtually destroyed just as the underground plants began to roll out the jets in sizable numbers. By April, fewer than 200 of the more than 1,200 Me 262s available—about one in six—were operating in combat units, and these tiny outfits, stationed at widely dispersed bases, were under harassing fire from Allied planes.

Then there was the manpower problem. By early April, barely two weeks into the Luftwaffe's final fight with the bombers, Germany had all but run out of skilled pilots. Rank amateurs were asked to attempt the impossible—to skillfully maneuver, in the fury of combat, the fastest, most heavily armed, and most mechanically unreliable aircraft on earth. "They didn't know the aircraft, the enemy, his tactics, our own tactics, or the very refined Reich Defense system—and what was more, they were almost all insufficiently trained," recalled one of the few remaining veteran pilots of JG 7. Unable to fly on instruments in wicked weather, alarming numbers of them failed to form up into well-organized strike forces; attacking singly or in pairs, they suffered unsustainable battle losses. More were lost in air accidents than in combat.

By this time, the Luftwaffe's precariously thin defensive force was squeezed into a narrow ribbon of territory in central Germany, running from Berlin to Munich. From bases in this region the Germans launched a suicidal operation not unlike the kamikaze attacks that were being directed against the American fleet assembled that same month off Okinawa for the final battle of the Pacific war. This all-or-nothing operation was the brainchild of a Luftwaffe bomber ace, Oberst Hajo Hermann. A flaming nationalist, he was convinced that the Me 262 was Germany's only chance to avoid surrender terms more degrading than those of the Treaty of Versailles. "But its introduction into service would take time," he later described his thinking, "and we desperately needed some means of inflicting an unacceptably high loss rate on one . . . American raiding formation . . . so that we would gain a breathing space to get the jet fighters into service in large numbers."

Hermann's plan was loosely based on the ramming tactics of the old Sturmgruppe units. They had been unsuccessful in their semisuicidal attacks of the previous year because their ponderous Fw 190s, overladen with arms and armor, were easy pickings for American fighter escorts. Only when accompanied by a screen of faster-flying fighters had they been able to inflict losses on the enemy. In a plan submitted to Göring in late

1944, Hermann proposed using a different attack plane, a high-altitude version of the Me 109, stripped of armor and carrying only a single machine gun for self-defense. After assembling 5,000 to 6,000 feet above the bombers, each pilot would pick a target and dive straight down on it and slam into the weakest structural part of a heavy bomber, the section of the fuselage just in front of the tail assembly. A well-placed hit was capable of breaking a bomber in two.

The Sturmgruppe pilots had tried to ram the bombers only if they were unable to destroy them at close range with their cannons; Hermann's squads would use ramming as the sole means of attack. But unlike the Japanese kamikazes, German suicide pilots would try to hit the bombers in such a way that they would be able to parachute from their ruined planes and fight another day for the fatherland. Using up to 800 planes flying on fuel husbanded for this climactic mission, Hermann hoped to destroy as many as 400 bombers, with an anticipated loss of 200 heroes of the homeland.

Hitler and Göring approved the plan, but warned Hermann not to squander veteran pilots. Only air cadets would be used. In February, a call went out to fighter training schools for volunteers and Hermann soon had more pilots than he had planes at his makeshift base, a fighter field at Stendal, near the Elbe River. They called themselves the Sonderkommando Elbe and their operation's code name was Wehrwolf.

Training—mostly political indoctrination designed to fuel patriotic fervor—was accelerated with news of the fast collapsing Western Front. "It was in March of 1945 that we broke the back of the German army," recalled Major Chet Hansen, General Bradley's chief of staff. At Cologne, Coblenz, Bonn, and every other point that Allied troops reached the Rhine, the Germans blew the bridges as they retreated eastward. But on March 7, a task force of the 9th Armored Division captured the Ludendorff Bridge in the town of Remagen, south of Bonn, before the Germans could set off the explosives. This allowed the American First Army to penetrate the Rhineland plain. A weak enemy effort to hurry in reinforcements was thwarted by Allied airpower. Twenty of the twenty-five main marshaling yards in the region were disabled, part of what one reporter called "the greatest air blitz of the war."

In the last week of March, four armies, including Patton's Third, crossed the Rhine on barges and on pontoon bridges constructed with breakneck speed by brigades of engineers. German armies in the Ruhr Valley were encircled and captured, leaving the Allies with 325,000 prisoners of the dying Reich. "Germany's most valuable industrial section no longer served her war effort," Air Force historians described the enemy's final plight. "And behind the Ruhr lay a demoralized population, a stricken industry, a beaten army, and a fading government."

On April 2, one month after capturing Cologne, the third largest city in Germany, American troops celebrated Mass in the city's bomb-battered cathedral. Now Göring was forced to act. At the break of dawn on April 7, he ordered the unprepared Elbe unit into action against an approaching force of over a thousand American heavies. As 120 student pilots climbed into the clouds to rendezvous with a supporting force of piston-engine fighters and jets from JG 7, patriotic music was broadcast on their headphones, along with the ringing exhortations of a Nazi matron reminding them of "dead wives and children buried in the ruins of our towns."

Not all of the suicide fighters were brain-numbed Nazi zealots. Many had volunteered because they saw no future for themselves or their country, no alternative but to fight and die in the absence of promises from the Allies of a nonvindictive peace. "There can be no doubt that our propaganda has failed to provide the German soldier with a positive reason for surrender," declared a report prepared by the psychological combat team of the American First Army. "Most of the official statements, on the contrary, have made him feel that he can gain nothing from a future that brings defeat. . . . Propaganda playing up a hard but bearable existence for Germany, backed by some kind of official assurances, would give the average German soldier a positive reason to end the fight." As the boys of the Elbe force gathered in the blue to meet the Americans, they believed, in their clouded despair, that they were fighting to protect Germany from a vindictive peace settlement that would leave it prostrate and forever feeble, with a great part of it under the Bolshevik heel. Draw blood, and lots of it, and the wounded Americans, with a war still to be won in the Pacific, might seek a separate peace.

It was a brutal but one-sided fight. Fifty German fighter planes, including a dozen jets, broke through the Mustangs and reached the bombers. At least eight suicide planes rammed American heavies and brought them down, smashing into their nose sections or tearing into their fuselages and using their whirling propellers as buzz saws. Men died gruesomely in bombers that were cut open like tin cans, their torn bodies swept away by blasting winds. Ten other bombers went down, but some heavies that were rammed miraculously survived, and so did dozens of the pilots of the ramming force.

The Luftwaffe paid dearly for its desperation, losing up to three-quarters of the fighters sent on the mission. "The first use of our suicide fighters has not produced the success hoped for," Göbbels wrote in his diary. "But . . . this is only an initial trial which is to be repeated in the next few days, hopefully with better results." But Sonderkommando Elbe never flew again.

Three days later, the Eighth was sent out to complete the thunderous raids it had launched the previous day on jet fighter bases. Göring put over fifty Me 262s in the air against almost 2,000 Allied aircraft, and the jets had sixteen confirmed kills, all but three of the heavies the Eighth lost that day. It was the jets' most successful single day against the bombers, but the Americans shot down nearly half the assault force. American fighter planes destroyed another 284 German aircraft on the ground, among them at least twenty-five jets. It was a loss of operational jet aircraft that proved fatal to the Luftwaffe. The defense of Berlin and all of central Germany was abandoned, and the decimated fighter units that remained were transferred to primitive grass airfields in southern Bavaria. In the annals of the Eighth Air Force, April 10 is "the day of the great jet massacre."

On April 19, seven days after the death of President Roosevelt, the Eighth Air Force had its final fight with the Luftwaffe. The target was the marshaling yard at Aussig, Czechoslovakia. It was a tactical operation requested by the Army to prevent supplies from being delivered to German forces holding out against the Russians in the Prague area. Chuck Alling's *Miss Prudy* led the 34th Bomb Group, and the Americans hit their target dead-on. Just as they did, two jets streaked past Alling's left window and seconds later four Fortresses disappeared. Then the Mustangs entered the fight and destroyed the two jets that had ended the lives of forty American boys in a blink. Before Alling's disoriented gunners could swing their heavy weapons around fast enough to track it, another jet made a swift pass from eight o'clock and claimed a fifth Fortress. This was *Dead Man's Hand,* piloted by Lt. Robert F. Glazener and flying, as many bombers did at the end of the war, without its usual complement of two waist gunners. The aircraft, on its 111th combat mission for the 447th Bomb Group, was the last Eighth Air Force heavy bomber lost to enemy fighters in the war. Alling and his men saw no parachutes, but learned later that seven of the eight crewmen managed to escape the flaming plane and were later liberated by American troops.

After the war, Allied interrogators asked the Luftwaffe's chief of staff Karl Koller what would have happened if Germany had had jet planes in great numbers earlier in the war. The general answered without hesitation. Had the Luftwaffe been able to put 500 to 600 Me 262s in "continuous operation by autumn 1944 at the latest," the American daylight "bombing terror" would have been "broken."

This is doubtful. Technical setbacks in the development of the turbojet engine and Hitler's initial insistence that the Me 262 be used as a bomber prevented Germany from winning the technological battle against time that might have blunted the daylight offensive. Even if Germany had had those 500 or so jets that Koller mentioned, it would have been able to stop the "bombing terror" for only a short time—the time it would have taken the American Air Force to ship to England part of the fast-growing fleet of the B-29 Superfortresses it had begun sending to the Central Pacific in mid-1944. A gigantic leap forward in aviation technology, the Superfortress was bigger, faster, and more heavily armed than its older brother, the Flying Fortress. Flying at speeds of over 350 miles per hour at altitudes up to 40,000 feet—where the performance of smaller-engine planes, including jets, was wildly erratic—and equipped with revolutionary remote-controlled guns, it would have been a formidable aircraft for the first-generation German jets and their pitifully inexperienced pilots to contend with. With their high rates of fuel consumption, these jets, moreover, could operate only within twenty-five miles of their bases.

Even if the Me 262s had been able somehow to prolong the war into the late summer of 1945, Germany, not Japan, would probably have been the target of the first atomic bombs, weapons initially developed for use against the Nazis by scientific teams dominated by Jews. "If the Germans had not surrendered I would have flown the bomb over there," *Enola Gay* commander and former Eighth Air Force pilot Paul Tibbets said after the war. "I would have taken some satisfaction in that—because they shot me up. . . . My instructions were to create an elite bombing force . . . with the understanding that, when trained, they would be divided into two groups: one to be sent to Europe and the other to the Pacific. There was no Japanese target priority. All our early planning assumed that we would make almost simultaneous bomb drops on Germany and Japan."

Had B-29s been deployed in England, it would have taken only a short time to lengthen runways to accommodate them; and even before the atomic bomb was ready, these long-winged destruction machines, in this emergency situation, would likely have dropped enormous loads of incendiaries on German cities, creating a dozen more Dresden-like conflagrations. Clearly, America was prepared to do this to Germany "when," in Hap Arnold's words, "the occasion warrants."

In 1943, at Dugway Proving Ground, a desolate desert compound in

Utah, Hollywood set designers from RKO's Authenticity Division and engineers from Standard Oil, under contract with the Army's Chemical Warfare Service, built two working-class neighborhoods, one German, the other Japanese. These were exact replicas—right down to the furniture and bed coverings—of workers' housing in Tokyo and Berlin. To ensure the authenticity of the German village, the Army recruited the renowned Modernist architect Eric Mendelsohn, a recent German-Jewish émigré, and he designed six brick tenements, the type of closely packed rent barracks in Berlin's suburbs that the Eighth Air Force bombed repeatedly in early 1945. Both mock villages in the saltbrush desert were firebombed and rebuilt repeatedly, experiments that led to incendiaries capable of penetrating the roofs of German buildings. At Dugway, the Army also performed experiments with M-69 napalm, the insidious new weapon of war developed by Standard Oil. "If we are going to have a total war [against Germany] we might as well make it as horrible as possible," said Assistant Secretary of War Robert Lovett. In late 1944, Lovett had encouraged the Air Force to begin making plans for massive napalm raids on German troop concentrations and cities. For Germany, a war prolonged by jet fighter resistance would have brought not a more lenient peace—a Nazi pipe dream—but Gomorrah-like extermination, napalm hurricanes followed by atomic typhoons.

As it was, the air force that began the war as the most feared on earth, the scourge of Guernica, Warsaw, and Rotterdam, met its end at a tiny landing strip in Salzburg, with American Mustangs circling overhead like vultures covering their prey. But the victors did not dive and attack, recalled Adolf Galland, who was standing on the field with his gathering of aces, the lucky few that had survived a savage six-year air war. "They obviously hoped soon to be flying the German jet fighters that had given them so much trouble." As the first column of American tanks rattled onto the airfield, Galland's pilots poured gasoline over their futuristic turbojets and set them on fire.

The Strategic Bombing Survey

Even before the air war ended, Gen. Frederick Anderson, Spaatz's second in command, was anxious to see the results firsthand. In mid-April, the general requisitioned a light plane and a C-47 transport, loaded two jeeps on the transport, and set out with a small Air Force team on an eight-day air and land tour of cities and industries the Americans had bombed. In his personal retinue were a photographer, an intelligence officer, and a historian, Dr. Bruce C. Hopper.

It was a hair-raising excursion. Anderson, who knew "his targets as a boy knows his marbles," flew the tiny plane at treetop level, "boring right down into the skeletons of ball-bearing plants," Hopper observed in his log. The main roads were choked with refugees, and the retreating Wehrmacht had heavily mined parts of the Autobahn, but Anderson, driving one of the jeeps airlifted by the C-47, stuck to the twisting back roads, speeding through villages that had yet to be liberated. With all the bridges over the River Main blown out, Anderson confiscated an abandoned wooden boat and he and the intelligence officer, both seasoned fishermen, rowed across to Schweinfurt, battling a heavy current that threatened to carry the party of four over a milldam. A few days later, the men almost met their end as Anderson maneuvered his plane, in stormy weather and without an altimeter, through steep valleys in search of a break in a mountain wall. Later, in Nuremberg, they rode into the center of the recently liberated city with an armed escort of "trigger happy G.I.'s," as entire buildings collapsed thunderously into the streets. When their jeep broke down near Schweinfurt, Anderson's entourage rode on the backs of a farmer's cows to a bombed-out ball bearing plant.

Hopper's unpublished field notes read like those of an archaeologist surveying the ruins of a far-distant civilization: "Darmstadt, a shambles seemingly without a roof intact. . . . Frankfurt. Looks like Pompeii magnified . . . Kassel . . . just miles of rust staring to the sky . . . Würzburg, a crumpled mass of peanut shells. Leuna . . . an enormous desert of iron skeletons. . . . Magdeburg . . . another ghost city. . . . Cologne . . . indescribable. One gets a feeling of horror; nothing, nothing is left."

At several of their stops, Anderson's group dined with American journalists, and all agreed that they were witnessing "destruction and chaos in a degree never before known in the world." The cities they had passed through were not living communities; they were wounds in the earth, said correspondent Leonard Mosley. In their entire tour, the only sign of industrial life Anderson's group witnessed was a single moving train.

If Anderson needed moral vindication for the desolation his bombers caused he found it at Buchenwald, where half-burned skeletons still lay on the warm furnace floors and human bones were set in piles taller than any living person. "Here is the antidote for qualms about strategic bombing," Hopper wrote in his log.

*   *   *

As Anderson's group was completing their on-site survey, the American Air Force was already into the second month of gathering data for a systematic study of the economic and psychological effects of strategic bombing on Germany: *The United States Strategic Bombing Survey (European War)*. Spearhead Teams of Army officers had crossed the Rhine in March, on the heels of the Allied armies, and were digging in the ruins of munitions mills and oil refineries in search of documents. Traveling in jeeps and weapons carriers, and carrying satchels of chocolate, cigarettes, and soap to encourage local cooperation, they entered some combat zones ahead of American tank columns and came under withering fire. Four members of the field teams, two of them civilians, were killed and four others suffered serious wounds.

This was one of the most wide-sweeping social research projects ever undertaken, a massive fact-finding effort that yielded over 208 published reports. These volumes make the American air war over the Reich "among the most brilliantly illuminated military campaigns of all time." Some of the early discoveries were the result of a mix of luck and excellent detective work. Canvasing the twisted remains of the I. G. Farben hydrogenation works at Ludwigshafen-Oppau, a field team ran into the plant director, who led them to an air raid bunker containing stacks of statistics on plant damage and casualties. Another team discovered four caches of oil industry documents that had been hidden in a string of villages deep in a pine forest—one pile in an abandoned brewery, another in a cattle barn. Other Spearhead Teams unearthed records in mineshafts, village graveyards, and deep holes dug in forest clearings. Among the finds was sixteen barrels of documents on the workings of the German synthetic oil industry, including highly sensitive information about assistance given by the Germans to the Japanese in their less successful attempts to manufacture synthetic fuel.

In Cologne, a spearhead group located the Reichsbahn offices on the west bank of the Rhine. As members of the team began searching the building, they came under fire from hostile troops garrisoned just across the river. After calling in two American rifle platoons to provide cover, they went on hands and knees and gathered up railroad records that were strewn on the floors of abandoned offices.

Other work began in occupied France and Belgium. Under the leadership of Rensis Likert, a noted expert in the measurement of public opinion, the survey's Morale Division questioned hundreds of former French POWs, Yugoslav refugees, and slave laborers who had escaped from the Nazis. Teams of interrogators then fanned out all over Germany, interviewing almost 4,000 civilians in thirty-four towns. All the while, members of the survey's Economic Divisions hunted down and interrogated plant managers and city officials.

After the German surrender, a team that included Technical Sergeant Paul Baran—the son of affluent Polish Jews, former OSS operative, and later controversial Marxist economist at Stanford University—was secretly airlifted into Soviet-occupied Berlin to obtain economic statistics from Dr. Rolf Wagenfuehr, the chief statistician of the Speer ministry, who was reputed to be a "roast beef" Nazi, brown (Nazi) on the outside, red (communist) on the inside. Locating Wagenfuehr's whereabouts from a Berliner that Baran had met at Harvard before the war, Baran arranged a meeting. Wagenfuehr surrendered to Baran a copy of a manuscript he had just completed, "The Rise and Fall of the German War Economy." When Baran asked Wagenfuehr to accompany the team back to western Germany, he refused, saying he had already "cast his lot with the Russians." That night Paul Baran led a "posse" into the Soviet sector and, said one team member, "quite literally, lifted Wagenfuehr out of bed from beside his wife." The statistician was flown back to western Germany and not returned, despite heavy pressure from the Red Army, until he had given Air Force researchers the information they needed.

Later that summer, Baran interrogated a German steel tycoon. Taking notice of Baran's ill-fitting uniform, wildly disheveled hair, and pronounced Jewish features, the insolent German informed him that he was accustomed to speaking only with "leaders of industry. Who are you?" Baran replied that his position invested him with authority to keep the German mogul in prison for one day for each question he refused to answer. The answers thereafter were fast and full.

Baran had been brought into the survey by his former Harvard colleague John Kenneth Galbraith, later a renowned economist and public intellectual, and, under President John F. Kennedy, ambassador to India. A witty and polished liberal iconoclast, forever challenging the "conventional wisdom," a phrase the notoriously immodest economist claimed to have invented, Galbraith had been recruited by George Ball, a future undersecretary of state and ambassador to the United Nations. The two men had worked together briefly in Washington in the early war years and were equally skeptical of the ability of bombing to win wars. Galbraith's feelings ran deeper; he considered bomber warfare "a hideous thing."

When Ball approached him, the Canadian-born Galbraith was a senior editor at *Fortune* magazine, having recently left a top position with President Roosevelt's Office of Price Administration. Although hesitant to leave

Fortune, he thought his skepticism about bombing would provide a needed corrective to the runaway enthusiasm of the bomber chiefs. He finally signed on when Ball, joined by Paul Nitze, a young government economist and future Pentagon official, convinced him that the survey would be a civilian-run operation, "independent of the Air Force, although advised and supported by it."

Arnold and Carl Spaatz had wanted it that way. The idea for the survey was theirs; it could furnish important data for the bombing of Japan and lay the foundation for future airpower doctrine. To give the survey wide autonomy, Arnold convinced Roosevelt to make it a blue-ribbon presidential commission. Air Force leaders were confident that an unbiased investigation would come to the conclusion that airpower had been instrumental in the defeat of Germany, a position they believed in, Galbraith observed, "as others believed in the Holy Spirit." An endorsement of airpower's indispensability by an independent presidential committee would also aid the Air Force in its upcoming fight for autonomy. For this reason, Arnold resisted offers by the Royal Air Force to conduct a joint Anglo-American survey. The British produced a separate and less-inclusive study, which was not released for general publication until 1998.

Failing to land the prominent, impartial public figure he hoped to head the survey, Arnold had to settle for Franklin D'Olier, the president of the Prudential Life Insurance Company and a former World War I artillery captain. Active direction of the survey, however, soon passed to Henry Alexander, a New York lawyer and J. P. Morgan partner. Other top positions went to fixtures of American business and the bar, men from old New England families and storied banking firms. But the real power lay in the heads of the directorates or working committees. They were called divisions, and a separate division was established for every major target or objective of the bomber war: oil, transportation, morale, and so forth. The divisions were headed and staffed by men of rising reputation and clear competence: engineers, scientists, economists, lawyers, psychologists, statisticians, and managers. George Ball was put in charge of the Transportation Division and Galbraith headed a committee that looked into the "overall economic effects" of bombing on German mobilization.

Galbraith's staff of "economic warriors" were, he wrote later, "a roster of the famous of the next economic generation." Besides Baran, the group included Burton H. Klein, Galbraith's chief assistant and later a leading economics theorist; Nicholas (later Lord) Kaldor, a Cambridge University luminary; E. F. Schumacher, later the author of the groundbreaking environmental book *Small Is Beautiful;* and G. Griffith Johnson, a future assistant secretary of state. They were joined by a handful of "unlikely warriors," among them the British poet W. H. Auden and the composer Nicolas Nabokov, appointments that left Hap Arnold dumbstruck. Only one prominent Air Force general was given a position of influence on the committee and that was entirely advisory. He was Orvil A. Anderson, Jimmy Doolittle's former deputy commander of operations, the only one in the leadership thoroughly versed in Air Force bombing procedures.

The survey's directors were faced with an unprecedented task. As Hanson Baldwin of the *New York Times* observed, "Probably for the first time in history a military campaign is undergoing a minute examination and critique from an official, but predominantly civilian board." Looking on with concern, Army and Navy leaders wondered what had possessed Hap Arnold to create such a dangerous threat to the military's prerogatives. "The idea does not appeal to them," Baldwin wrote; "they fear the committee may set a precedent for similar review and critiques of ground and naval campaigns."

An overseas office was set up in London, in Eisenhower's old headquarters on Grosvenor Square; and after the Army consolidated control of the Rhineland, forward headquarters was established at the Park Hotel in Bad Nauheim, a luxurious health spa near Frankfurt. Galbraith and Ball arrived there in mid-April. When not in the field interrogating Nazis, they assembled their staffs in the hotel's leather and wood wine bar for lively debates about the impact of strategic bombing, which Galbraith was determined to prove was minimal. As he told friends, by the time he joined the Bombing Survey he had mastered "the first principle of warfare: Naturally suspect what air generals tell you." (Galbraith's disdain for the military extended, apparently, to ordinary GIs. On a flight back to the States in the summer of 1945, "a much decorated sergeant shared a seat with me and asked if I would like to hear of his war adventures," Galbraith related in his memoirs. "I told him I would not. He made several attempts at conversation, which I rejected. Finally he asked me who I thought would win the World Series. I asked him what leagues were playing that year.")

Did Strategic Bombing Work?

By early April, there was little left to bomb in Germany. The oil war had been won. Synthetic plants were down to 6 percent of normal output and production of aviation gasoline had stopped altogether. The oil campaign "clipped the wings of the Luftwaffe" and impaired the Wehrmacht's mobility, preventing it from protecting coal resources that powered the synthetic plants. In February 1945, the Wehrmacht had amassed up to 1,500 tanks to stop the Red Army's drive into the Upper Silesian coalfields, but could not properly deploy them because of fuel shortages. By then the German army was operating under a self-imposed speed limit of 17 mph and under a standing order that "anyone using fuel for purposes other than the immediate conduct of operation will be considered a saboteur and court-martialed without mercy."

In the last year of the war, Speer's deputy, Edmund Geilenberg, had been put in charge of an emergency program to build seven underground hydrogenation plants. Unlike the aircraft industry, synthetic oil production was too large and complex an operation to put belowground quickly; and none of the plants was completed.

It could have been different. Early in the war, oil engineers had proposed moving production underground, but were told by Nazi officials that the war would be won before such plants could be completed. Instead of being rewarded for their initiative, the engineers were warned by the Gestapo that if they continued to press for such a program they would be shipped off to a concentration camp for "questioning the Reich's impregnability." If the underground program had been started in 1942, and well-ventilated plants had been built close to coal supplies, with a network of secure pipelines to transport the oil, "the German oil industry might have been relatively safe from bombings," in the opinion of American oil experts recruited by the U.S. Strategic Bombing Survey. But it was a case of too little too late. One year after taking on the herculean task of putting German oil production underground, Edmund Geilenberg was found running a small bicycle repair shop in northern Germany.

By early April 1945, the Allied air forces' transportation campaign had also achieved its major objectives. Germany's river and canal network had been disabled and its rail system was in ruins, and with it, the coal industry that powered the economy. While there is still debate over whether Allied bombers should have focused on cutting rail lines at bridges, underpasses, tunnels, and viaducts instead of smashing marshaling yards, where repair crews were stationed to quickly mend the damage, Allied airpower's slow strangulation of rail and river systems was probably the greatest single cause of Germany's economic collapse.

No nation today can prevail in a total war without an industrial economy, and Germany did not have one in early 1945. It had almost no oil, and although it had plenty of coal, Allied airpower made it impossible for

Germany to move it. "Even a first-class military power—rugged and resilient as Germany was—cannot live long under the full-scale and free exploitation of air weapons over the heart of its territory," the framers of the U.S. Strategic Bombing Survey report would conclude. For the first time in modern history the economy of a world power had been utterly destroyed, and along with it, all of that country's major cities. To regard the hundreds of fuel-starved factories that remained undamaged as "industry," war correspondent Julian Bach observed, "is to mistake the carcass for the beast."

Although the economy did not completely collapse until Allied armies were on German soil, prepared to deliver the deathblow, unrecoverable disruptions had begun much earlier. And Eisenhower's armies would not have been on Germany's doorstep without airpower.

This is not the impression most people have of the outcome of the Allied bombing campaign. Moral outrage over terror bombing (the British historian J. F. C. Fuller has argued that Bomber Harris's "appalling slaughterings . . . would have disgraced Attila the Hun") and the enormous expenses of bomber operations—money, critics charge, that could have been used more productively in other facets of the Allied war effort—have led to assessments of strategic bombing that undervalue its impact on the German war effort. Prominent journalists and historians have insisted that strategic bombing failed to curtail German production and that urban bombing actually strengthened the will of the German people to resist. And these critics cite the findings of the United States Strategic Bombing Survey as support for their conclusions.

It is one thing to challenge the Air Force's claims about strategic bombing and quite another to argue that the Bombing Survey says what it decidedly does not say. How that survey's conclusions came to be widely misrepresented is one of the puzzles of modern military scholarship. John Kenneth Galbraith is a major contributor to the confusion. In his Vietnam-era writings he called the air war against Germany a "disastrous" failure, leaving unsuspecting readers to assume that he had arrived at this conclusion in 1945. In his understandable opposition to President Lyndon Johnson's first large-scale bombing of North Vietnam, Operation Rolling Thunder, Galbraith insisted that strategic bombing had never worked, not in Vietnam, not in Korea, not even in World War II. Galbraith's biographer, Richard Parker, argues the point even more insistently than his subject. The U.S. Strategic Bombing Survey found that strategic bombing "hadn't in fact succeeded in destroying—or even in seriously hindering—the

Germans' war production capacities. . . . Even the special targeting of oil and rail facilities after D-Day did little more than slow the German army and air force, rather than cripple them."

This is a misrepresentation of both Galbraith's conclusions and those of the survey's summary report. The real story is different, complex, and intellectually intriguing.

In the late summer of 1945, the Bomb Survey completed its fieldwork and its division heads returned to London and Washington to write their reports. Galbraith based his division's study of the overall effects of bombing on German war production on information provided mainly by two sources: Rolf Wagenfuehr and Albert Speer. Wagenfuehr provided invaluable statistics on German wartime production, but Speer gave Galbraith much more—inside information about Nazi war planning and policy.

On the day after the German surrender, two members of Galbraith's Spearhead Team, Lt. George Sklarz and Technical Sergeant Harold Fassberg, found Speer quite by accident in an office building in Flensburg, the resort town on the Danish border where Adm. Karl Dönitz, Hitler's anointed successor, had established a rump government. At the time, this was the only part of Germany that had not been occupied by the Allies, and Speer was living in a sixteenth-century castle surrounded by a lake-size moat and guarded by SS troops. When Galbraith flew to Flensburg with George Ball, Paul Nitze, Burton Klein, and a bevy of interpreters, he and his party were driven to Speer's retreat, where they were greeted by the courtly Nazi minister, tall and erect and dressed in a smartly tailored brown uniform.

Speer was the person Galbraith and Ball had most wanted to see, the "miracle man" who possessed unsurpassed information about the inner workings of the military economy he had run with near dictatorial powers in the final years of the war. Meeting him, said George Ball, was "like stumbling on the page of answers after one had worked on a puzzle for months." Realizing the game was up, Speer agreed to what amounted to seven days of exhaustive interviews—our "bombing high school," the Reichsminister called their marathon sessions.

Before his arrest seven days later by British troops, Speer was pleasingly eager to provide information. When the Americans met him on their second day in Flensburg, he was dressed in a plain business suit, which made him look like a youthful college professor; and like most professors, he delighted in being the center of attention. "With charm and apparently spontaneous candor, he evoked in us a sympathy of which we were all secretly ashamed," Ball admitted later. "What had he then known of the Holocaust?" Fearing, perhaps, that it might break the mood of leisurely affability, no one dared ask.

Seated on a small sofa with his hands folded over his knees, rocking slowly back and forth as he spoke, Speer told the astonishing story of how he had turned a wastefully inefficient war economy into a focused production machine. From fragments of these interviews and from Wagenfuehr's statistical tables, Galbraith and his "economic warriors" fashioned an arresting theory about German economic performance, one that found its way into the strategic bombing surveys of both the United States and Britain and shaped the postwar work of leading historians and economists, among them Burton Klein, Galbraith's future thesis student at Harvard and author of the seminal work *Germany's Economic Preparations for War.*

This is the theory of the Blitzkrieg Economy, which purports to dispel one of the most popular conceptions about the Nazis: that from the opening months of the war they had ruthlessly mobilized the resources of the German state for total war. German war management "was for a long time halfhearted and incompetent," Speer told Galbraith's team. Nazi Germany had initially mobilized at a level sufficient only to support a series of "cheap and easy" victories over its European neighbors. These were Blitzkrieg Wars, later proponents of the theory called them, wars won by lightning-quick ground and air assaults. And they were supported by the Blitzkrieg Economy, a production system mobilized only for the short term. It was a guns-and-butter economy that did not compel the civilian population to make deep sacrifices, for Hitler feared that a program of radical home-front austerity might trigger social discontent that would undermine the war effort, just as such measures had done in World War I Germany. After Germany defeated France faster than even Hitler envisioned, weapons production was "intentionally run down," Galbraith would argue after examining Rolf Wagenfuehr's economic figures. Even on the eve of Soviet invasion, "no preparation had been made to obtain a genuinely large-scale increase of armament production." Russian resistance would collapse in a matter of months, Hitler was convinced. So most German factory hands continued to work only one shift, and women were not recruited into the industrial labor force.

Germany's failure to prepare for a prolonged war finally backfired when the Wehrmacht was stopped in front of Moscow in the winter of 1941–42, short of clothing and equipment for the brutal winter campaign. That February, Speer was appointed minister for armaments and munitions and inaugurated a program of all-out mobilization.

Liberators fly at treetop level on the approach to enemy oil refineries at Ploesti, Romania, in August 1943. Fifty-four of the 178 bombers were lost, and five fliers earned the Medal of Honor.

Sgt. Joseph James Walters is escorted to a hiding place by two Belgian men, father and son. Walters landed in an apple tree in his parachute after his Fortress was shot down on the Regensburg-Schweinfurt mission, one of sixty bombers lost that day. A Belgian factory worker took this photograph.

The air war went badly for the Eighth until the arrival in late 1943 of the P-51 Mustang, a long-range fighter that could escort the bombers all the way to Berlin.

In the lead-up to D-Day, Thunderbolts like the one piloted by the Eighth's leading ace Francis S. "Gabby" Gabreski helped the Mustangs gain air supremacy over northern Europe.

In 1944–45, the Eighth hit two targets that disabled the German economy: synthetic oil plants and railway marshaling yards. Leuna, a giant synthetic oil plant near Meresburg, was one of the best-defended places in Germany. The photo recon plane that took this picture of the damaged plant was shot down by antiaircraft fire.

Most marshaling yards were located in or near city centers, making it virtually impossible to bomb them without causing major damage in residential neighborhoods nearby.

Maj. Jimmy Stewart, the Hollywood film star, was one of the Eighth's leading combat commanders.

With a diminished German fighter force, flak became the greatest threat to bomber crews. Pilot Lawrence M. DeLancey landed this Fortress after its nose section was shot away by flak.

A flak helmet was no protection from an exploding 20mm shell from a German fighter plane. This boy survived.

A Liberator is cut in two by cannon fire from a Me-262, a German fighter jet introduced late in the war.

The Eighth established rest homes for men who had gone through traumatic air experiences. The estates were run by Air Force medical personnel and Red Cross hostesses.

Air gunners of the 381st Bomb Group celebrate V-E Day.

Some 28,000 Eighth Air Force airmen were liberated from POW camps at the end of the war. One of them was Lou Loevsky (right), seen here with crewmate Leonard Smith.

Over 45,000 British women married American servicemen during the war.
A shipload of "war brides" and their babies leaves Southampton Harbor in
January 1946 to rejoin their husbands in the States.

At Horsham St. Faith, village folk wave farewell to a Liberator of the 458th
Bomb Group as it heads home.

The American Air Force's failure to appreciate the true character of the Nazi war economy was "one of the greatest, perhaps the greatest miscalculation of the war," Galbraith was convinced after speaking with Speer. It led to two years of appallingly ineffective bombing, culminating in the great 1943 raids against the ball bearing factories of Schweinfurt, operations that Galbraith considered the "most disastrous . . . in the history of aerial warfare." When the Eighth Air Force arrived in England, its bomber commanders assumed they were attacking a fully mobilized economy, an industrial system that was "a tightly stretched drum," one that had no "slack," no reserves of plant, labor, and materials that could be moved from the peacetime to the wartime economy to replace what was lost through bombing. But the Hermann Göring–led economy was as "fat and incompetent" as its leader, Speer informed Galbraith and other American interrogators. Göring and other leading Nazis lived in "astonishing luxury" and practiced "unlimited graft." (That Speer said this in the drawing room of a sumptuous seaside estate he had appropriated for his own pleasure was an irony that Galbraith chose to ignore in his published accounts of the interrogation.)

When Speer and his technocrats were given virtually full direction of the war economy a year after Speer became minister of armaments, they reduced the influence of both the military and the party in decision-making and began the move from craft to mass production in pivotal industries, using the principles of Henry Ford to standardize and simplify factory practices. After the Americans began bombing aircraft and munitions plants, Speer decentralized the control of manufacturing and moved much of the production system underground. For almost two years, this still undermobilized economy was resistant to a knockout blow from the air. With plenty of slack available, Speer was able to move ball bearing operations to other sites and shift workers in the consumer goods sector of the economy that were put out of jobs by Bomber Harris's city-busting raids—clerks, salesmen, and waiters—to better use in war plants. These measures allowed Speer to increase production of tanks and planes into the late summer of 1944. According to Wagenfuehr's statistics, munitions production at that time was more than three times what it had been before heavy bombing began.

This is a compelling theory: the story of how an uncorrupted production genius almost single-handedly frustrated and defeated for over two years the combined efforts of the two greatest bomber forces in existence. Recently, however, the foundations of the Blitzkrieg theory have been shaken. Modern scholars, among them the military historians

Richard Overy and Williamson Murray, and economic historian Werner Abelshauser, see one, not two, wartime Germanys, a nation that had begun preparing in the mid-1930s for a global war of racial conquest and that "followed a path of ever-strengthening mobilization" into the 1940s. Beginning as early as 1939, there were severe cutbacks in consumer production and steadily rising rates of military spending, which rose nearly 400 percent just before Speer's ascendancy. By then, most consumer goods industries were being forced to devote over half their output to the military, and Germany had mobilized a much greater part of its female workforce than Great Britain.

Although it intended to, Germany could not rearm in depth in the late 1930s and early 1940s, Williamson Murray argued, because it suffered from a shortage of almost every strategic raw material essential for war making except coal. In addition to oil, it had to import iron ore, copper, lead, zinc, bauxite, and the nonferrous metals used to make high-grade steel: nickel, manganese, tungsten, vanadium, and molybdenum. Germany had a shortage of skilled and unskilled labor as well.

Another problem for Hitler, Overy points out, was that his economic preparations for war were out of step with diplomatic realities. Germany's invasion of Poland incited the full-scale continental war that Hitler had not planned to launch until the mid-1940s, after he had consolidated Germany's power in Central Europe. When total war came unexpectedly, the economy lacked strong strategic guidance and administration. It was, as Speer correctly told Galbraith, incompetently run. But Speer's production miracle was not achieved by converting a Blitzkrieg Economy into a total war economy. Speer simply used more efficiently, and with less military interference, resources already being committed to all-out war; he and his teams of industrialists and engineers brought to peak performance a war economy that had already begun to be rationalized in 1941 by his predecessor as munitions overlord, Fritz Todt, who was killed in a plane crash in February 1942. And now with Hitler's vast European conquests, Speer had virtually the entire continent to draw upon for his shortages of labor and raw materials: oil from Ploesti; coal from Silesia; copper, lead, zinc, and bauxite from the Balkans; and iron ore from Sweden, a compliant neutral country. Speer's economic empire included aircraft, munitions, and electronics factories in Holland, France, and Czechoslovakia; and these countries and others supplied Germany with slave laborers, prisoners of war, and contract laborers, in all, almost eight million foreign workers, nearly three million of them from Poland and Russia. The tremendous expansion in production that Speer oversaw from 1942 to mid-1944 "did not depend to any great extent on the supposed slack within the prewar economy," Murray pointed out in his important book, *The Change in the European Balance of Power, 1938–39.* "Rather, it occurred because the Germans were able to exploit ruthlessly the resources of the occupied and neutral countries within their sphere of control."

Speer admitted this to Allied interrogators in 1945 in testimony that directly contradicts Dr. Wagenfuehr, a statistician who was not actually privy to military and economic policy-making. As historian Sebastian Cox pointed out, it was only "much later, when he was preparing his memoirs, [that] Speer came to accept much of the Wagenfuehr thesis, probably because it made his own achievements as the Reich Armaments Minister appear even more substantial than they really were, and showed him to be a realist and a pragmatist surrounded by fantasists with little real understanding of the problems."

What significance does this new interpretation of the German war economy have for understanding the bomber war? If mobilization already was in full swing in 1942, then Spaatz and Tedder were at least partially right. Although Germany's entire economic fabric was not stretched tight by 1944, at least two vital areas were: oil and transportation. This made them perfect target systems when they were finally hit, Germany having no reserves of either gasoline or rolling stock to replace what was lost to the bombers.

In Galbraith's report for the Bombing Survey, he writes that prior to the summer of 1944, Allied bombing had "no appreciable effect either on German munitions production or on the national output in general." While this seems to support the idea that strategic bombing failed, Galbraith goes on to argue in his report that the oil and transportation campaigns eventually conjoined to deliver unrecoverable damage to the economy, dramatically reducing steel, oil, and aircraft production. He even concedes that bombing conducted *prior* to the summer of 1944 had placed a ceiling on Germany's production of combat aircraft, that it was "possible that production would have been 15–20% higher in the absence of bombing."

Evidence unavailable to Galbraith's economic team indicates that the ceiling was considerably lower. In January 1945, German officials from Speer's Ministry of Armaments assessed what might have been produced the previous year without Allied bombing. They concluded that German industry had made roughly 36 percent fewer tanks, 31 percent fewer military aircraft, and 42 percent fewer trucks. These unrealized gains helped prevent wartime Germany from becoming an economic superpower.

At Flensburg, Albert Speer argued that World War II was preeminently an "economic war," a war between rival production systems, and that it "was decided through attacks from the air," beginning with Spaatz's oil raids in May 1944. This testimony is absent from Galbraith's published reminiscences about his meeting with Speer. "The losses inflicted by the American and British air fleets," Speer said, "constituted for Germany the greatest lost battle of the war," and it was the Americans, he emphasized, who delivered the most telling blows.

There is good reason to question Speer's testimony to American Air Force interrogators. Knowing he would soon be tried as a war criminal, he was surely tempted to tell them what they wanted to hear–that American economic bombing was more effective than British area bombing. But Speer told British interrogators exactly the same thing. "The American attacks, which followed a definite system of assault on industrial targets, were by far the most dangerous. It was in fact these attacks which caused the breakdown of the German armaments industry." In the words of Field Marshal Erhard Milch, deputy armaments minister under Speer, "The British inflicted grievous and bloody injuries upon us, but the Americans stabbed us to the heart."

Historical debates about the economic impact of bombing tend to ignore one of bombing's signal contributions to victory: its impact on the land war. Both critics and defenders of the Anglo-American bombing campaign tend to fall into the error of segmented thinking, considering the contributions of the ground and air forces in "mutual isolation." This is not how the war in Europe was fought. Like Trident, Poseidon's weapon, the three sharp prongs of Allied war-making power–the air, sea, and ground forces–operated in tandem, as did the Allies' strategic and tactical air forces, when under Eisenhower's control. The armies of democracy that marched to the Elbe could not have landed in northern France without domination of the air and sea lanes to Hitler's Fortress Europe. This oceanic and aerial supremacy was achieved through the defeat of both Göring's fighter forces and Dönitz's U-boats.* While American fighter boys did most of the damage in the aerial victories that made D-Day possible, the Luftwaffe would not have come up to fight had the bombers not been there, attacking targets the Germans had to defend and taking sufficient losses.

And the infantry breakout from Normandy would have been nearly im-

---

* No landing would have been possible in 1944, moreover, without the suffering and sacrifice of the Red Army and the Russian people on Germany's Eastern Front, where more citizens and soldiers died than on all the other fronts of the war combined.

possible without tactical air support and attacks by both fighters and bombers on the French transportation system, continuous and devastating raids that isolated the battlefield and prevented the enemy from bringing up deciding numbers of reinforcements.

Bombing attacks on the German transportation system began too late to prevent the Wehrmacht from conducting a tenacious holding action on the Western Front in late 1944, and a punishing counteroffensive in the Ardennes. But by the early winter of 1945, Allied bombing had destroyed Germany's rail and water transportation systems and caused severe production losses in the coal-starved armaments industry. Even the weapons and ammunition that continued to be produced in greatly reduced quantity could not get through to the troops. This prevented the Wehrmacht from mounting, on Hitler's orders, a final, fanatical defense on Germany's frontiers, a Götterdämmerung that would have lengthened the war at a frightful cost in lives.

Even Galbraith admitted this in a little-noticed section of his report for the Strategic Bombing Survey. If Germany had somehow been able to extend the war into the late spring and early summer 1945, the double-barreled bombing assault on transportation and oil would have brought armaments production "to a complete standstill," he wrote, "[and] German armies, completely bereft of ammunition and motive power, would almost certainly have had to cease fighting."

America's strategic bombing commanders were not enthusiastic proponents of interservice cooperation. It was Adm. Ernest King's unrelenting pressure that led to the effective deployment of B-24 Liberators against German U-boats, and Eisenhower's authority as supreme commander that forced Carl Spaatz to "divert" bombers to tactical operations that helped turn the course of the war in Europe. In the real war, as opposed to the paper war fought in the classrooms at Maxwell Field in the 1930s, the idea that airpower alone could defeat an industrialized and highly militarized nation died as fast as the concept of the self-defending bomber.

The World War II record of the Eighth Air Force is mixed. Early in the war, its target planning was abysmal. It bombed U-boat pens that were indestructible and ball bearing factories whose machine tools it was incapable of destroying with undersize 500-pound bombs. The deep penetration raids against Schweinfurt's ball bearing complex should not have been mounted until a larger bomber force was assembled and protected by long-range fighters. In miscalculating the ability of the unfortunately named Fortress to stand up to the Luftwaffe, American air planners needlessly sacrificed the lives of young men who were unable to fully appreciate the desperate nature of their missions.

Through a policy of trial and error the Eighth Air Force eventually found the right targets, but it ignored one of extreme importance: Germany's electric power network. Dismantling the enemy's highly vulnerable power and switching stations would have undermined its oil industry, which relied heavily on electric power. Prewar American air planners, led by Haywood Hansell, had designated the destruction of the German electric power system as a primary objective of the strategic bombing offensive, but Spaatz failed to attack it for the same reason he had originally hesitated to hit the German rail net: the system seemed too large and spread out to effectively disable. But by early 1944, Germany's electric power system was as overextended as its rail system, "taut and vulnerable" and "open to attack," in General Hansell's postwar assessment. Had the largest electric power plants been hit in that year, "all evidence indicates that the destruction . . . would have had a catastrophic effect on Germany's war production," the U.S. Strategic Bombing Survey concluded.

The Allied bombing effort in World War II has been more closely scrutinized than any other military operation in history, but almost none of its critics points out one of its most dangerous shortcomings: the failure to place air operations—what to bomb, how to bomb, and when to bomb—under closer civilian scrutiny. The Allies had air commanders of surpassing ability, but they were given too loose a leash.

Yet these air commanders and their valiant crews conducted a determined campaign—the war's longest continuous battle—that was as critical to securing victory in Europe as the Battle of the Atlantic. After years of frustration and appalling losses, the Combined Bomber Offensive finally began delivering lethal blows to the German war machine in the winter and spring of 1944. From that point on, it was second in strategic importance only to the Red Army's defeat of the Wehrmacht and the great Western invasion of 1944, an operation that could not have gone forward without Allied air superiority. Along with the authors of the United States Strategic Bombing Survey, Germany's most distinguished historian of the air war, Horst Boog, has argued that the Anglo-American air offensive was "decisive in the war . . . From the early summer of 1944 it brought about a lethal invasion of the German machinery of war, without which the war might have continued as an unending horror for an unforeseeable time, at least until the use of the first atom bomb."

The Inner Front

Once the Anglo-American air forces reached full strength—a total of 28,000 combat aircraft—they were democracy's terrible swift sword.* Gathering in their immensity over the North Sea and the southern Alps, these air armadas released over two million tons of bombs on the Reich. The cost in lives lost was appalling. The Eighth Air Force, the largest aerial striking force in the war, sustained between 26,000 and 28,000 fatalities, roughly one-tenth of the Americans killed in World War II. Taking the lower number, this was 12.3 percent of the 210,000 Eighth Air Force crewmen who flew in combat. Of all branches of the American armed forces, only submarine crews in the Pacific had a higher fatality rate: almost 23 percent. In addition, an estimated 28,000 Eighth Air Force crewmembers were shot out of the sky and became prisoners of war. If they and the estimated 18,000 men who were wounded are added to the casualty list, the number of those lost in operations, not including untold numbers of psychological casualties, is at least 72,000, over 34 percent of those who experienced combat. This is the highest casualty rate in the American armed forces in World War II.

For much of the war both Bomber Command and the Eighth Air Force ran a casualty rate in excess of 50 percent of crew force. In the Eighth Air Force, the pioneers of 1942–43 paid the heaviest cost. Only one in five of these fliers completed their tours of duty. Of the 110,000 aircrew in Bomber Command, 56,000 were killed, a loss rate of 51 percent, the highest casualty rate of any of the Commonwealth's armed forces in the war.

German losses were also staggering. Over the course of the war, roughly 70,000 aircrew were killed in action and another 25,000 wounded. Luftwaffe loss rates were exceeded only by U-boat crews, and, by some estimates, were higher.

The biggest losses were on the ground. Five years of bombing inflicted wholesale damage on over sixty-one German cities with a population exceeding 100,000. In most of these places half or more of their built-up areas were burned and exploded out of existence—128 square miles of thickly settled urban space. Many of these cities had been reduced to "suburban rings surrounding destroyed cores."

---

* At peak strength the Eighth Air Force had approximately 200,000 personnel, 2,800 heavy bombers, and over 1,400 fighter planes. There were 40 bombardment groups and fifteen fighter groups. More than 350,000 Americans served in the Eighth during the war. Seventeen Medals of Honor were awarded to its crewmen, and the Eighth had 261 fighter aces. By comparison, at maximum strength the Fifteenth Air Force had 1,190 bombers.

A total of 25 million Germans, almost a third of the nation's wartime population and nearly half its industrial workforce, was bombed heavily. And somewhere between 500,000 and 600,000 noncombatants residing in the Reich, free and unfree, perished under the bombs. This is roughly twice the number of combat fatalities sustained by American forces in combat in Europe and the Pacific. (Of the 405,399 members of the armed forces who died in the war, 291,557 were killed in combat operations.) At least 800,000 other noncombatants were seriously injured. The overwhelming majority of those killed and maimed were women, the elderly, and children under five years of age; most children over that age had been evacuated to the countryside. Most of these victims were part of the 96 percent of German urban dwellers who could not find space in the limited number of fortresslike government bunkers.

At least three million dwelling units were destroyed–20 percent of the housing in the country–and probably another three million were heavily damaged. By some estimates, twenty million people, 500,000 of them in Hamburg alone, were made homeless. Berlin, the victim of 310 raids, was 70 percent destroyed. Cologne's suffering was proportionally greater. It was 80 percent destroyed.

It is almost implausible to suggest that destruction and death on this scale bolstered morale, which can be loosely defined as a people's support for the war and confidence in victory, attitudes exhibited in such areas as work attendance, compliance with wartime restrictions, and faith in wartime leaders. In interrogations conducted after the war, German military and government leaders insisted that the spirit of the German people remained unbroken throughout the war. "[You] underestimated . . . the powers of resistance of the German people," Albert Speer told RAF interrogators. "Other peoples, as perhaps the Italians, would have certainly collapsed under a similar series of night attacks and would have been unable to undertake further war production"–but not the iron-willed Teutonic people, he insisted.

"Even after the heaviest attack, it was normally possible to get over 90 percent of the workers back to the plant the next day to clean up the debris and to carry on production whenever possible," Robert Ley, chief of the Nazi German Labor Front, told Allied intelligence. "This," he stressed, "was done on the basis of voluntary appeals, not orders to the workers."

More than half a century after the war, the former Bomber Command advisor Freeman Dyson remained convinced that "there is overwhelming evidence that the bombing of cities strengthened rather than weakened the determination of the Germans to fight the war to the bitter end. The notion that bombing would cause a breakdown of civilian morale turned out to be fantasy."

The United States Strategic Bombing Survey, the most comprehensive study of German wartime morale, came to a markedly different conclusion, one that has been buttressed by recent research in German archives. "Bombing seriously depressed the morale of German civilians," the survey's Morale Division stated in its final report. "Its psychological effects were defeatism, fear, hopelessness, fatalism, and apathy. War weariness, willingness to surrender, loss of hope in a German victory, distrust of leaders, feelings of disunity, and demoralizing fear were all more common among bombed than among unbombed people." The assertion that bombing bolstered morale "is an invention of Nazi propaganda which has been absorbed uncritically by subsequent scholars," argued historian Neil Gregor.

But even though German morale did eventually collapse, wartime proponents of morale bombing badly misjudged the nature and political impact of that collapse. This makes their decision to conduct terror bombing highly questionable.

German civilian morale fluctuated wildly in the first years of the war, rising when national armies were triumphantly on the move and the home front was relatively secure, and falling in the wake of shocking setbacks, such as the firebombing of Hamburg and the defeat at Stalingrad. Once massive urban bombing began in 1943 and accelerated after D-Day, morale fell steadily by gradients that roughly coincided with the number of bombs that were dropped. We know this because historians have uncovered "mood" reports prepared by local officials of the Nazi Party security service (Sicherheitsdienst–SD). These intelligence reports on popular opinion give a different picture of morale in bombed cities like Nuremberg and Schweinfurt than the national reports prepared by senior officials in the SD. The latter reports play into one of the staples of Goebbels's propaganda machine: the idea of the *Schicksalsgemeinschaft*, or community of fate. This is a group spirit that reputedly united the people on the home front with the soldiers on the battlefield in a common patriotic cause: to unquestioningly and forever support the regime. SS chief Heinrich Himmler gave expression to this community of fate idea as early as 1937. "In the coming war we shall fight not only on the land, on the sea, and in the air. There will a fourth theater of operations—the inner front. That front will decide on the continued existence or the irrevocable death of the German nation."

Early in the war the party was successful in sustaining local morale after

bombing raids, less with patriotic rhetoric than with generous, personal-
ized assistance to suffering people. "The organizations for bomb-damage
worked wonders," recalled Christina Knauth, a young American interned
with her mother and two sisters in heavily bombed Leipzig. "It was all in
the hands of the Party and the work of these organizations won the party a
lot of prestige. . . . People were taken care of . . . right away, even if it was
only with tents and field kitchens."

In Leipzig and other German cities, the party worked closely with local
support groups to provide bomb victims temporary shelter, meals at communal kitchens, medical attention, and ration cards to purchase clothing
and pay emergency boarding expenses. The party also took care of all hospital bills and burial expenses. Within a month, a typical family that had
lost its home could be expected to be relocated in permanent quarters in
another part of the city. There, family members were visited by local party
officials, who helped them complete claims for damage reimbursement. In
their moment of greatest need, the party was there for them and was continuously supportive. "This disaster, which hits Nazis and anti-Nazis alike,
is welding the people together," Hitler-hater Ursula von Kardorff wrote
of the pre–D-Day bombing. "After every raid special rations are issued—
cigarettes, coffee, meat. As Dostoyevsky's Grand Inquisitor said, 'Give
them bread and they will back you up.' If the British think that they are
going to undermine our morale they are barking up the wrong tree."

Neighbors also helped one another. In Leipzig, the early raids changed
the "moral" character of the city, as one of the Knauth sisters observed.
"The most immediate thing was that everybody became talkative and
friendly and companionable. Leipzigers were never that before, but they
were now. . . . Everyone helped everybody else; they had to, of course, but
somehow they seemed to want to—to draw closer to their neighbors so that
they would have company and not feel alone. That's the way people get
when they come to the edge of the grave and still are alive."

This was in February 1944. Heavier bombing brought great changes, although the Knauth family did not experience them. They were released by
German authorities and made their way back to the United States. Beginning in the summer of 1944, when bombing became the common experience of German people living in cities, the party's relief organizations were
swamped by the scale of the devastation, and party propaganda began to
fall on unreceptive ears. People began to openly resist evacuation, not
wanting to break up their families; and families sent to other regions were
often coolly received by people with clashing religious and cultural backgrounds. "The old dislike between Prussians and Bavarians got worse

when Berliners were evacuated to Munich," reported one of the Knauth sisters. Growing numbers of evacuees decided that the daily danger they faced in their home cities was more bearable than "the 'hell' in the homes of their hosts," reported a government official. Defying orders straight from the führer, thousands of them headed home. With the Luftwaffe conspicuously absent from the skies and Allied armies closing in on them, only the most die-hard Germans held out hope for victory. Signs of demoralization, defeatism, and social disintegration abounded. There was ugly competition for space in public shelters; and shelters themselves, with people "penned more closely together than animals in a stable," became breeding grounds for disaffection and unpatriotic gossip, much of it directed at local party officials who had their own private bunkers.

When the air raid sirens stopped wailing, people emerged from their holes, wrapped wet clothing around their faces to allow themselves to breathe in the swirling hot dust and dirt, and began looking for their homes. Without streets or buildings to guide them, some disoriented families had to rely on the sun to get their bearings. In heavily bombed areas, the rubble was piled higher than some standing buildings and people were without water, heat, electricity, telephone service, and public transportation, often for weeks. Workers whose houses had been bombed left their jobs for long, unexcused periods, and the morale of workers who did show up at the plants was at "low ebb," the Berlin Chamber of Commerce reported in the winter of 1945.

Ursula von Kardorff and her friends noticed that increasing numbers of Berliners who had suffered under the bombs failed to report for work regularly, and that those who showed up every day were in a high state of anxiety. Sickness also cut into job performance. In cities without sufficient power or fuel there were epidemics of respiratory diseases; women suffering from nervous tension stopped menstruating or, in their despair, stopped wanting to have children; and doctors reported increases in the number of patients suffering from coronary disease. Fatal heart attacks acquired a new name: they were called "shelter deaths."

It was the truly innocent, not the soldiers of production, that suffered most terribly. Terrified children screamed uncontrollably in dark cellars and bunkers, and children pulled from the smoking wreckage of their homes went into prolonged periods of shock, assaulted by dreadful nightmares. A Berlin woman watched a young girl standing on a pile of broken bricks, picking up and dusting off each brick before she threw it away. Her entire family was buried under the bricks and she had gone mad.

Bombing inflicted deep psychological wounds on people of all ages.

How could it not have? Sleep-deprived people were pressed together underground day after day wondering when it was their turn to be torn beyond recognition and carried away by the authorities—after they used bolt cutters to remove the victims' jewelry. Medical research teams of the U.S. Strategic Bombing Survey noted that more than one-third of the people who experienced a major air raid suffered "relatively permanent psychological effects, that is, the terror transcends the immediate raid to such an extent that it is reinstated by the next alert."

Today we call this post-traumatic stress disorder, a condition that was also prevalent among the crews who delivered the bombs. After the war, Yale University psychologist Irving Janis led a wide-ranging investigation of the psychological effects of urban bombing and reached the same conclusion as American Air Force doctors who had treated distressed bomber boys at clinics in England: people on the front lines do not "adapt" or become habituated to life-threatening conditions. There is no such thing as "getting used to it." Chronic tension and anxiety only increase with further exposure to anxiety-inducing situations. Both the bomber boys and the people they bombed lived in constant fear of the dreaded direct hit. "I never became accustomed to the raid and bombing," a German respondent told an American bombing-study worker. "I don't think anybody did. I was always afraid and shaking and nervous." Ninety-one percent of Germans interviewed by Bomb Survey investigators said that the bombing was "the greatest hardship" of the war for them.

Bombing confused its victims. After a while, they did not know whom to blame. Earlier in the war the tendency was to excoriate the British and scream for reprisals. But when the bombing accelerated and German bombers and vengeance rockets failed to bring down equal suffering on the English, the Nazi government began to be singled out for censure. By 1945, the party and its supreme leader became the principal targets of public frustration. "We have the Führer to thank for this," a man from bomb-ravaged Dusseldorf had the guts to say in front of an SS soldier. In early 1945, increasing numbers of provincial investigators working for the SD began to report a general refusal in heavily bombed areas to give the Hitler salute, and more than a few vocal housewives saw the raids as divine revenge for the atrocities committed against the Jews. One prophetic woman blurted out in public that this war was "easy" for the führer. "He doesn't have to look after a family. If worst comes to the worst in the war, he'll leave us all in the mess and put a bullet through his head!"

Berliners joked that the explosive effects of American bombs were so great that portraits of the führer "flew out of the windows." And written on posters inscribed with the slogan "The Führer is always right" were pleas to "Put an end to the war." Hitler's failure to visit the ruins, as Churchill so famously had, strained the credulity of Nazi officials who tried to comfort bombed-out people by telling them that the führer had "inquired after their fate by telephone."

The annihilation of Dresden was one of the final blows to national morale. People fleeing the city spread stories of ruin and despair, feeding hyperinflated fears that this was the fate that awaited all German cities. "When this catastrophe became known to the whole of Germany, morale disintegrated everywhere," observed one German officer.

Well before this, many Germans had reached the point where they were almost beyond caring. Traumatized by repeated bombing, they resigned themselves to their fate, not to death, but to defeat and persistent suffering. In Berlin, people's fatalism was expressed in the mordant comment: "Enjoy the war while you can, folks, because the peace will be terrible." This was not behavior that nurtured revolt. Passivity produced a malleable urban citizenry, people who might have lost their patriotic passion yet continued to follow orders. "Many find themselves in a condition of absolute fatalism. One cannot change what's going on therefore there is no point in worrying about it. They leave everything up to the leadership," observed a party official. Untold numbers of people who ceased to believe in the righteousness of the Nazi war continued to support the regime, fearing that "defeat would be calamitous."

Party officials began to complain that the people were so ground down and apathetic that it was almost impossible to carry on organized political activities; not surprisingly, attendance at party meetings declined. People no longer cared about politics; the "essentials—food and housing"—were their consuming concern. But for party leaders there was a salubrious side effect. Citizens overwhelmed by the "elementary problems of existence . . . [do] not have the time or the energy to engage in preparation for revolution," reads a provincial SD report.

Ursula von Kardorff saw her friends—bright, engaged people, most of them committed opponents of the regime—retreating into their private lives. "Everyone is concerned with his own affairs. Is my house still standing? Where can I get a few tiles for the roof or some cardboard for the windows? Where is the safest shelter?" Coping was the ruling concern. "Our life in Berlin," a housewife wrote in her diary, "[has] now sunk to a mere animal fight for existence." People meeting in the streets greeted each other with a new expression: "BU," short for *"Bleib übrig,"* literally meaning: "Be a survivor."

Some people were unable to bear their pain stoically. Worn and haggard, they sat listlessly in their battered homes, sobbing quietly, but occasionally breaking apart completely, hysterically "screaming and weeping, or trembling violently." In Berlin, broken people "staggered like sleepwalkers through the streets . . . clinging to some object, the only thing saved from their goods and chattels—a vase, a pan, or some other useless thing seized at random."

Such public displays of grief or pain were frowned upon, for almost everyone in a heavily bombed city was a victim. Most people understood that they should suffer silently and privately. Passivity and perpetual listlessness were the prevailing psychological symptoms of those broken by the bombing. "Those who lost their families, their homes, their all, were generally too disheartened to respond to consolation. They became indifferent and so utterly apathetic as not even to hate the fliers who had destroyed their homes." Lethargy, pessimism, and the retreat from social activity—clear signs of mental depression—became so prevalent that wartime German doctors described the last stages of the conflict as the "war of the vegetative neurosis."

Stoicism had its limits. When the bombing accelerated tremendously in early 1945 and the Soviet army, "the Red Genghis Khan," began its final drive to Berlin—a threat feared even more than the bombing—some of the strongest-willed people began to crack. Ursula von Kardorff, who had vowed that the bombing would never break her morale and that of her fellow Berliners, wrote that she and her friends were now "in a state of hysterics." Crisis continued to draw people together, but these were spiritless gatherings. "People are herding together like deer in a storm," von Kardorff wrote in her diary.

Government mood reports from the winter of 1944–45 catch the deepening discontent, the product of three converging calamities: bombing, the approach of the Allied armies, and the collapse of the economy. "Newspaper articles, in which the people are told that the days of the air terror are numbered, have exactly the opposite effect of what they had been intended for. If, subsequently, another raid occurs the depression of the people is all the worse. The faith in our leading men, including the Führer, is rapidly disappearing. They are thoroughly fed up with Goebbels' articles and speeches and say that he has lied to the German people and talked too big." According to historian Gerald Kirwin, Allied bombing "did irreparable harm to the prestige of the Nazi media."

"Why does nobody go crazy?" von Kardorff asked herself after the thunderous American raid of February 3. "Why does nobody go out in the street and shout, 'I've had enough?' Why is there not a revolution?" Yet she herself knew the answer. "One can only beat this regime with its own weapons, with brutality, treachery and murder," she quoted a friend in her diary, "and we are not able to use those weapons."

This was the problem with terror bombing. It was a blunt instrument designed to crush the morale of German workers to the point where they either rose up against their government or dropped their tools in order to protect their homes and families, but it did neither. Terror bombing was founded on a flawed understanding of how people react to crushing catastrophes, and on an impossibly optimistic view of the German people's opportunities to revolt. The fantasy of terror bombing was not, as Freeman Dyson claimed, that it depressed morale. The fantasy was that depressed morale would have war-ending consequences.

In assessing the impact of bombing on German morale, a distinction must be made between "attitude," *Stimmung* in German, and "behavior," *Haltung,* with the understanding that attitude does not invariably or predictably affect behavior. Thousands of workers did stay away from their jobs when their homes were bombed or breakdowns in public transportation made it impossible for them to get to work. But even emotionally defeated people continued to report for work right up to the surrender. This was not a manifestation of Aryan toughness or unflagging support for cause and country, as Speer alleged. It was a symptom of a sad state of affairs in which there were few realistic alternatives but to remain on the factory treadmill. With the Nazi relief system depleted, work was the only way to put food on the family table; and in a time of crisis and chaos, the orderly routines of work provided some people with a measure of emotional stability. A German coal miner commented, "As long as I am at work I don't remember, but when I get home I'm afraid."

As the country neared collapse, some discouraged workers became, in their fear and helplessness, more dependent on authority—that of the factory boss as well as the local Nazi hierarchy. This was, after all, a society that prized obedience and discipline, character traits that helped prevent dissatisfaction from escalating into public dissent and absenteeism from rising to levels where it would have had a severe impact on war production. When crisis and character failed to sustain work discipline, the state stepped in. The SS and the Gestapo infiltrated stool pigeons into factories, and Hitler Youth fanatics turned in their own parents for speaking out against the regime. Police hunted down absentee workers, and discipline was so rigid in some munitions mills that if word reached workers on the factory floor that their neighborhood was being bombed, they were not permitted to leave until the end of their shift. If a loved one was killed, survivors were forbidden to wear traditional mourning dress. The Gestapo ensured compliance. French slave laborers who worked side by side with Germans told American interrogators that their co-workers had been more afraid of the police than the bombs. Then there were those—we'll never know how many—who continued to support Hitler and his war in the hope of a last-minute miracle.

Morale bombing failed to achieve both its aims. In a police state that prized industriousness and obedience, discouraged workers remained, on the whole, productive workers, if only out of fear or habit. And dissidence, when it appeared, became little more than powerless rage.

What did the air barons who advocated morale bombing think the German people would do if and when their morale collapsed? Clearly, they had no idea. Germans of conscience, as well as those who came to their senses toward the end and admitted the futility of continuing the war, lived in a society in which complaining people were hanged from lampposts by Nazi vigilantes for the crime of "defeatism." As one worker said, "Rather than let them string me up I'll be glad to believe in victory."

Even Arthur Harris was dubious about morale bombing, a strategic objective he inherited when he took over Bomber Command in 1942. He called it a "counsel of despair" and doubted that any meaningful result would accrue even if demoralization did occur "with the concentration camp round the corner." As we have seen, he bombed German cities to kill German workers not morale. In killing workers he shattered the infrastructure that sustained their lives—urban power stations, water supplies, streetcar lines, and most importantly, housing, the "billets" of the citizen "soldiers of production." As he famously told his crews before sending them to Berlin, "Tonight you go to the Big City. You have an opportunity to light a fire in the belly of the enemy and burn his Black Heart out." While the oceans of fire he created in German cities were far less damaging to Nazi war production than raids on transportation and oil refineries, area bombing at least had a clearer rationale than the terror bombing that the American air leaders, in their despair and frustration, ordered their crews to carry out at the end of the war.

It would be wrong, however, to criminalize the behavior of Carl Spaatz and Frederick Anderson. If these commanders are guilty of anything it is of misjudging the depths of Nazi unreason. In the last months of the war, an already defeated enemy insanely fought on, as historian Richard Bessel argued, because "all Nazism had to offer was war and destruction, war without end or an end through war."

The Eighth Air Force engaged in terror bombing for four weeks. The RAF conducted terror raids for three years. But in fairness to Britain's Bomber Command, all area bombing was not morale bombing, and all British bombing was not area bombing. Even though Arthur Harris had to be pressured, Bomber Command did hit synthetic oil plants and marshaling yards; and Harris was eager to destroy Germany's aircraft and tank industries. His area raids, while not nearly as militarily effective as the Americans' so-called precision raids, did hurt the German war effort. RAF urban raids killed untold numbers of German skilled workers, and the damage these wasting raids caused to infrastructure and utilities curtailed the economic performance of urban-based war industries.

But area bombings' most important contributions were indirect. British urban raids provoked Hitler to demand immediate retaliation against English cities. In late 1943, Göring told his staff that "all they [the German people] wished to hear when a hospital or children's home in Germany is destroyed is that we have destroyed the same thing in England; then they [are] satisfied." The U.S. Strategic Bombing Survey estimated that the resources used on vengeance weapons would have enabled Germany to produce an additional 24,000 fighter planes and perhaps develop an effective ground-to-air missile.

Area bombing, along with American raids, caused other diversions of Germany's war resources. Beginning with Hitler's invasion of the Soviet Union, Stalin had been pressing Churchill and Roosevelt for a "second front" in northwestern Europe. In 1943 Allied bombing became that second front, a continuous air invasion that brought Germany a burden it could not bear. To defend the homeland in 1944, the Luftwaffe was forced to call upon over two-thirds of its fighter force, aircraft that were urgently needed on the Eastern Front. Eight hundred thousand military personnel were mobilized for air defense work, more soldiers than the Wehrmacht had in Italy. Fully one-third of German artillery production was devoted to antiaircraft guns and 50 percent of electrotechnical production to radar and signals equipment for the antiaircraft effort. And up to 1.5 million laborers—free and enslaved—were employed in air raid damage work. In 1944, the German air defense system called on the services of 4.5 million workers and consumed a third of the nation's total war resources. Digging shelters and distributing gas masks, cleaning up bomb debris and pulling the dead from battered buildings, working as fire wardens and firefighters, nurse's aides and social workers, airplane spotters and emergency ambulance drivers, millions of German civilians were enlisted in the bomber war, acting as a "home front army."

Arms and men used in one place cannot be used somewhere else simultaneously. Without Allied bombing, up to a quarter of a million German men and 7,500 heavy guns employed for air defense could have been sent to the Eastern Front in 1943, where they would have been deployed against Red Army tanks. This would not have secured a German victory, but it might have delayed a Soviet counteroffensive.

There is even evidence that urban bombing eroded troop morale. In letters from home, the families of German soldiers described the bombing "in most lurid or poignant terms," American bombing survey teams discovered after examining thousands of pieces of captured mail. Soldiers returning from leave described these scenes of devastation to their comrades; one soldier reported how he saw his native city turned into "a sea of flames and smoke." Others returned home and were unable to find loved ones who had been lost in the ruins or evacuated to other towns. Gen. Alfred Jodl, one of Hitler's closest military advisors, told Allied investigators that the bombing had a profound "psychological effect" on Wehrmacht troops. "While previously the soldier believed that by fighting at the front he was protecting his native land, his wife, and his children, this factor was completely eliminated and replaced by the realization . . . 'What am I fighting for . . . I can be as courageous as possible and still at home everything [is] smashed to bits.' "

This mirrored the mood of Rebel soldiers in the trenches that encircled Richmond in the fading months of the American Civil War. These pinned-down Confederates, tens of thousands of them from the Deep South, were ordered to stay at their posts while William Tecumseh Sherman destroyed their homes and towns and turned their wives and children into refugees. Wehrmacht troops "fought well and the number of deserters was always very small, but they were no longer as enthusiastic as before," and were less willing to resist the enemy, Jodl claimed.

The Combined Bomber Offensive also delivered emotional shocks that helped to change German attitudes that needed to be changed, not to win the war, but to secure the peace. The final months of Ursula von Kardorff's war experience illustrate this point. After her Berlin flat was destroyed by Allied bombs in the late winter of 1944, von Kardorff quit her job and left the city for a secluded village in rural Swabia, where life was "like something in a picture." Then in April the "new masters" arrived, their Sherman tanks rumbling down the main street of the village, their Fortresses roaring overhead in "brilliant precision . . . just as though they were flying over their own country."

"Men in khaki" were "everywhere" and, for Ursula, they brought with them the promise of freedom—freedom from the ever-looming threat of arrest, torture, and death. When she heard reports on British radio of the shattering "discoveries" the Allies had made at German concentration camps, she shared the shocking news with her new rural neighbors, most of them party fellow-travelers. They answered with looks of cold disapproval. "It's all a pack of lies."

Passing through villages in Swabia and other provinces, Allied soldiers and war correspondents encountered a citizenry broken by war and eager to surrender but without remorse or deep feelings of accountability. The photojournalist Lee Miller, the only woman to accompany the American Army from the beaches of Normandy to Hitler's Eagle's Nest at Berchtesgaden, found Germans "repugnant" in their "hypocrisy. . . . No one in Germany has ever heard of a concentration camp, no one had ever been a Nazi," and "no Germans, unless they are underground resistance workers or concentration camp inmates, find that Hitler did anything wrong except lose." To Miller and fellow reporters like Martha Gellhorn, Germany gave no evidence of knowing it was sick even in the hour of its death.

The bombing appeared to have changed few people's minds about the Jews, or even about Germany's right to seize the land and wealth of its European neighbors, conquests that were "provoked by its encirclement by enemies that meant it harm," Germans told *New York Times* reporter Raymond Daniell. But as in Japan, the bombing did discredit the old leadership, weakening its emotional hold on the people, the first and essential step in the long process of eradicating fascism and militarism. It was the shocking experience of becoming "the world's vastest ruin," not a repudiation of the propelling impulses of National Socialism, that initially broke the link between the party and the people, smoothing the way for the slow transition to a society pledged to peace and democracy. The U.S. Bombing Survey concluded that the morale effects of bombing were more important "for the denazification of Germany than for hastening military defeat. . . . Bombing brought home to the German people the full impact of modern war with all its suffering. The imprint on the German nation will be lasting."

Then and Now

The American Air Force entered World War II with the fantastic notion that aerial warfare could be waged at minimal cost to enemy noncombatants, that destruction and death could be contained by new aiming instruments. But bomber warfare brought the battle front to the home front with a wanton destructiveness that would have outraged even General William Tecumseh Sherman. Approximately 1.5 million people, more than one-half of them women, were killed by bombs in World War II, as opposed to roughly 3,000 in World War I, a 500-fold increase in civilian mortality.

Yet American air leaders in Europe never publicly admitted that they were waging what the *New York Times* reporter Percy Knauth called "total air war—the kind of total war that Germany fought . . . although with less effective means." The American air chiefs knew what they were doing, Knauth argued, but were afraid to admit it, for fear that the truth might split public opinion at home.

They need not have worried. The American people solidly supported the Combined Bomber Offensive, as they would the dropping of atomic bombs on Japan. In early 1944, when the British pacifist Vera Brittain published a scorching indictment of RAF terror bombing, "Massacre by Bombing," in *Fellowship,* the organ of the pacifist Fellowship of Reconciliation, the prominent journalist William Shirer accused her of being a dupe for Joseph Goebbels's propaganda machine. That February, the *New York Times* reported that its mailing was running fifty to one against Brittain's essay, which supported the war but urged that it be conducted humanely. The editorial position of the *Times* was not unlike the opinion of George Orwell, who in his own answer to Vera Brittain in the London press wrote that "there is something very distasteful in accepting war as an instrument and at the same time wanting to dodge responsibility for its more obviously barbarous features."

Before Pearl Harbor, Percy Knauth believed with Vera Brittain that the bombing of noncombatants should be made an international war crime. What he saw in the war convinced him that he had been naive. "We did not realize that war knows nothing of humanitarianism. . . . We did not realize that the bombing of military and so-called civilian targets together is the only way in which air warfare can be waged effectively—that it is impossible to separate the two."

But neither Knauth, nor any other reporter who covered the war, believed that bombing killed more civilians than ground warfare. As Orwell wrote in 1944: "Heaven knows how many people our [air] blitz on Germany and the occupied countries has killed and will kill, but you can be quite certain it will never come anywhere near the slaughter that has happened on the Russian front." Orwell, like Knauth, was sensitive to the killing of another group of innocents, besides women, children, and the elderly. " 'Normal' or 'legitimate' warfare picks out and slaughters all the healthiest and bravest of the young male population." The same humanitarians who screamed with horror at the bombing of German towns, Orwell noted, applauded every time a German U-boat went to the bottom with fifty and more brave young men dying horribly by suffocation.

That is just one of the ways in which war is inherently barbarous and therefore to be avoided if the cause is not right. And here is where World War II holds a lesson for humanity. The Nazis did not think of themselves as savages, and that made them irredeemable. But as Orwell wrote: "If we see ourselves as the savages we are, some improvement is possible, or at least thinkable."

The war shattered another of Percy Knauth's notions: the idea that there was a clear distinction between American and British bombing policies. In the spring of 1945, he visited an aircraft plant near Nuremberg that had been "precision" bombed by the Eighth Air Force. Outside the plant there was a housing development for the workers. The Germans could have moved the workers out of these cottages, far from harm's way, but they did not. So when the Americans destroyed the factory they also destroyed the workers' homes. "In some of them a few people were still living, women and children of the workers' families. They were wild-eyed, dirty, and half-starved. By night they barricaded themselves in the cave-like ruins of their homes, fearing rape by passing refugees or soldiers. Their clothes were in rags. In some ways they looked almost as bad as the prisoners of Buchenwald."

After the war, navigator Paul Slawter of the 493rd Bomb Group, an aspiring writer, read Percy Knauth's powerful book, *Germany in Defeat*. "What he said about there being no distinction between our bombing and that of the British got me thinking about an encounter I had with an RAF bomber pilot in a London pub sometime in the fall of 1944, just before I completed my tour of duty," he said in an interview. "He was a big guy, a Scotsman, and a terrific talker. At one point he looked at me said, 'You know, we do the same thing, although you chaps won't admit it. We do area raids on area targets and you Yanks do area raids on pinpoint targets.'

"That got a laugh out of me," Slawter recalled. "I didn't want to argue with the guy. I was tired and homesick, and didn't want to talk about the war. And anyway, he was right. Our bombing was pretty messy.

"Long afterward, I revisited that conversation in my mind and thought I had missed an opportunity. I should have told him, 'We *are* different than you, not better, just different. It has nothing to do with courage or concern for women and children, or anything like that. It's the job we are given, the orders we carry out, that make us different. Our commanders have a better idea how to beat the enemy: by destroying his industries, not his cities, and by trying to do this as accurately as possible. Yes, we miss a lot, can't be helped, but in warfare or anything else, intent surely matters.'

"But remember," Paul Slawter said, "I wasn't there in the closing months of the war when we joined the British in dumping bombs in the middle of cities in the crazy belief that this would stop the Germans from fighting and working."

CHAPTER SEVENTEEN

A Pageant of Misery

Our airmen who were prisoners of the Germans are special. They were there, in the belly of the beast. They saw and experienced the tyranny that other airmen knew only from afar.

ROBERT "ROSIE" ROSENTHAL,
HUNDREDTH BOMB GROUP

London, March 28, 1945

That morning Winston Churchill sent a note to Charles Portal, head of the Royal Air Force. "It seems to me that the moment has come when the question of bombing of German cities simply for the sake of increasing the terror, though under other pretexts, should be reviewed. Otherwise we shall come into control of an utterly ruined land. . . . The destruction of Dresden remains a serious query against the conduct of Allied bombing. . . . I feel the need for more precise concentration upon military objectives, such as oil and communications behind the immediate battle-zone, rather than on mere acts of terror and wanton destruction, however impressive."

Portal was indignant. Although unsuccessful in pressuring Arthur Harris to concentrate on the military targets the prime minister now seemed to favor exclusively, he resented the implication that Bomber Command had become solely a terror force. It had played an instrumental role in both the oil and transportation campaigns, and that January, it was Churchill who had pressed the RAF to begin "basting" the cities of eastern Germany. Was he now trying to bring down the blame for Dresden entirely on Bomber Command? Portal thought so.

Shown a copy of the prime minister's note, Arthur Harris branded it an "insult both to the bombing policy of the Air Ministry and to the manner in which that policy has been executed by Bomber Command." Unlike Portal, however, he believed that area bombing should continue. "I do not personally regard the whole of the remaining cities of Germany as worth the bones of one British Grenadier," he fumed.

When Portal suggested that Churchill withdraw his "minute," the prime minister wisely agreed and drafted a milder one. A week later, the British discontinued their area offensive and began discussions with the Americans to end the entire strategic air campaign. Both air forces had run out of strategic targets to bomb.

On April 16, Carl Spaatz sent a directive to his two European bombardment commanders, Jimmy Doolittle in England and Nathan Twining in Italy. "The advances of the Ground Forces have brought to a close the Strategic Air War waged by the United States Strategic Air Forces and the Royal Air Force Bomber Command. It has been won with a decisiveness becoming increasingly evident as our armies overrun Germany. From now on, our Strategic Air Forces must operate with our Tactical Air Forces in close cooperation with our armies."

Nine days later, the Eighth Air Force flew its final heavy bombing mission of the European war, a series of raids on the sprawling Skoda Works at Pilsen, Czechoslovakia, and smaller targets in Austria. It was a tactical mission requested by the ground forces, not a strategic raid. The Czech munitions mill was believed to be supplying tanks and heavy guns to German forces in that area of the collapsing Reich, and there were railroad centers in and around Salzburg that were still moving enemy troops and supplies.

Part of the Pilsen force, the 384th Bomb Group, took off from Grafton Underwood in the English Midlands, the same airfield from which the Eighth Air Force mounted its first heavy bombing mission of the war on August 17, 1942. On that short run to Rouen there had been no losses. On April 25, 1945 Heavy Bombing Mission Number 968, six bombers succumbed to withering flak fire over the Skoda Works. The forty-two crewmen missing in action were the last combat casualties sustained by the Eighth Air Force. The next day, Soviet and American armies met at the Elbe River and Nazi Germany was cut in half. The wheel of history turned.

One of the fliers who made it back from Pilsen defined the uncrushable spirit of the air force that helped bring Germany to ruin. Twenty-seven-year-old Lt. Col. Immanuel "Manny" Klette, son of a Lutheran minister who had emigrated from Germany, had arrived in England in early 1943, when an American bomber crewman's average life expectancy was fifteen missions. He flew against the toughest targets—St. Nazaire, Vegesack, and Schweinfurt—and was wounded by flak on one mission and sustained five fractures in a crash landing in England. When he regained the use of his legs, he joined the 91st Bomb Group at Bassingbourn and took command of one of its radar-equipped Pathfinder squadrons. Although not required to fly, he led his men on every difficult mission, including the big one to Berlin on February 3, 1945. "I asked him to stay on the ground more," said his commanding officer. "But he still continued to go. I got my dander up and ordered him only to go when his turn to lead came up. He still went. What the hell are you going to do with a man like that?" Manny Klette's trip to Pilsen on April 25 was his ninety-first bombardment raid of the war, a record for the European Theater.

Another Kind of Air Force

The last cargo dropped by the Eighth Air Force was food for starving people. In late April, the Germans still held an iron grip on great parts of the Netherlands. To blunt the Allied advance and punish persistent Dutch resistance, the fanatical Nazi commanders had cut off food supplies to the people and opened the dikes, flooding much of the country's low-lying farmland. By the spring of 1945, over 12,000 Dutch had died of starvation and another four and a half million were suffering from malnutrition, reduced to eating tulip bulbs when stocks of vile-tasting sugar beets ran out. "Unless a gift comes from heaven," a Dutch woman wrote her brother in England, "we will soon die."

In the last week of April, with the die-hard Nazi garrison still refusing to surrender, General Eisenhower pressured German civil authorities in the Netherlands to agree to a cease-fire that would allow British and American bombers to airdrop food supplies. If they did anything to disrupt the food drop, Eisenhower warned them, the Allies would treat "every officer and man responsible for such interference as violators of the laws of war."

The airlift was a lifesaver for the Dutch and a greatly needed psychological lift for American bomber boys, some of whom were having trouble dealing with their jobs as state-sanctioned destroyers. "In long, late-night talks . . . [we wondered] what was happening to us? Were we machines? Were we avengers?" recalled Harry Crosby, the former bombardier with the Bloody Hundredth who was now an operations officer. On May 1, the day the world learned of Adolf Hitler's suicide, the Eighth became, in Crosby's words, "another kind of air force"—not strategic or tactical but humanitarian, part of a mission the British called Operation Manna, the Americans, less reverentially, Operation Chowhound. By agreement with the Germans, only skeleton crews—crews without gunners—were authorized to fly, but that order was almost universally disregarded. "Everyone wanted to fly," Crosby recalled. Even maintenance men and chaplains boarded the heavies after loading the bomb bays with boxes of Army rations and sacks of potatoes donated by British farmers.

The bombers entered Dutch airspace in single file as low as 200 feet, and released their cargo in open areas marked with huge red crosses. It was a "free" drop—no parachutes were attached to the food cartons—but servicemen had made their own small parachutes out of handkerchiefs and scraps of cloth, filled them with candy, cigarettes, and food from home, and dropped them randomly. Resistance fighters who had hidden the parachutes of downed Allied fliers they had saved from the Gestapo retrieved them from haystacks and storage cellars, painted them vivid colors, and fashioned them into "happiness clothes"—hats, scarves, and skirts. They joined tens of thousands of their grateful countrymen who crowded the drop zones, in defiance of Nazi orders, and waved small British and American flags they had saved for the hour of their liberation. On the outskirts of Amsterdam, Chuck Alling's Fortress passed over fields of brilliantly colored tulips. In one of them, the heads of the flowers had been clipped to say, "MANY THANKS, YANKS."

"I felt better about Manna-Chowhound than I did about Operation Clarion," said Harry Crosby.

While Chowhound was in full swing, General Doolittle authorized 30,000 Eighth Air Force ground personnel "to make aerial tours of Germany to see with their own eyes what they had helped to bring about." Mechanics, bomb-loaders, cooks, truck drivers, control tower operators, and typists were taken on low-level aerial sweeps of bomb-blasted German cities— "trolley missions," the men called them. "One city was like another . . . gray, flattened and dead," a member of the Hundredth Bomb Group scribbled in his diary. "There will never be a new Germany," said Danny Roy Moore of Homer, Louisiana. "They can never rebuild, no way."

Even the men who had wrought this destruction could hardly believe the magnitude of it. Eighth Air Force pilot Kenneth "Deacon" Jones flew a trolley mission on May 3, 1945, and recorded his impressions in a pocket-size notebook. Jones had eagerly awaited the day he could fly over Germany without fear, yet looking down at a ruined land he felt only "emptiness." The powerhouse industries of the Rhine Valley had been smashed to splinters, but so, too, had homes and hospitals, schools and social halls, and great parts of the cathedrals of Lübeck, Mainz, Münster, and Cologne. "European mankind must blush with shame," Joseph Goebbels had declared, "to think that a twenty-year-old American, Canadian or Australian terror pilot can, and is allowed to, destroy a painting by Albrecht Dürer or Titian, and commit sacrilege against the most venerable names of mankind." But Deacon Jones never doubted that the bombs he dropped on Germany were punishment to fit the crime.

Jones's trolley tour was different from that of most others. His commanding officer wanted the men to walk the streets of a city that Allied bombs had silenced, to see and smell the wastage of total war. Landing at an airbase on the border between Holland and Germany, the men boarded Army trucks that took them to Cologne, the turbulent river port of nearly a million people that had been turned into a mausoleum by thirty-three months of bombing, most of it by the British. Many of the 40,000 people who remained in Cologne had become cave dwellers, troglodytes sharing candlelit coal cellars with disease-carrying rats and flies. "Insolent and fat," the rats lived on the decaying corpses that had not been removed from the wreckage. As Jones walked through this ghostlike place, its streets lined with gaunt, smokeless chimneys, the rubble stacked up to form hills a hundred feet high, he felt like he was visiting the lowest depths of hell.

The airmen were told that the Nazis had fled Cologne in panic, taking with them virtually every man and woman who might have helped alleviate the suffering of those left behind. There were no city officials, no doctors or nurses, no police or social workers; and Cologne's hearty lovers of Rhine wine and potato dumplings were reduced to an animallike existence, digging for food in rank-smelling piles of broken brick and iron. Yet in this city that had almost ceased to exist, Deacon Jones saw frail German women sweeping and washing what remained of their sidewalks and streets. It did not seem to bother them that the rubble-strewn streets they were cleaning were "fantastically impassable." Jones understood. In this unearthly place it was important to reaffirm "that life must go on." But most of Cologne's survivors, he noticed, remained out of sight, holed up in their subterranean haunts, as if they did not want to take in what had been done to them.*

As the GI trucks rumbled down the streets Jones could see the cold fury in the faces of the "rubble women" they passed. Here were the air gangsters who had brought this great sorrow down on them. Hours before, their incoming B-24s had thundered overhead so low that their bomb bays were clearly visible from the ground, reigniting people's memories of the "rocking explosions" that had shattered their lives, "the hammering of the sky upon the earth."

The trucks stopped in the center of Cologne, and the men piled out for a walk through the city. Stopping for a moment to make an entry in his diary, Jones wondered how anyone could proclaim "we won" after seeing these ruins; yet winning, he knew, had been tremendously necessary. Back at the airstrip, as he fired up the engines of his bomber, he had only one thought: a deep desire never "to come this way again—for any reason." Never had untouched America appealed to him more urgently.

As he crossed the North Sea under a low canopy of clouds he felt a door closing on his youth. "I was twenty years old and felt ancient."

The Blizzard March

The Eighth Air Force had one more mission. Allied prisoners of war had to be brought out of southern Germany and Austria to transit camps in

---

* In Heinrich Böll's autobiographical novel, *The Silent Angel,* a war-weary German soldier returns to recently liberated Cologne and is taken in by a woman who refuses to open the shutters in her apartment, which overlooks the city. One morning, after she leaves the room to get dressed, he pushes the shutters open, looks out at the "charred ruins of the city," and then quickly closes them. "Now within, it was dim and quiet once more. . . . He understood why she hadn't wanted to open the window."

In a recent essay on the air war, the late German novelist W. G. Sebald wrote that after the war, there was "a tacit agreement, equally binding on everyone [in Germany], that the true state of material and moral ruin in which the country found itself was not to be described. The darkest aspects of the final act of destruction, as experienced by the great majority of the German population, remained under a kind of taboo like a shameful family secret."

Sebald hailed Böll's *The Silent Angel* as one of the only works written by the war generation that provide "some idea of the depths of the horror then threatening to overwhelm any who really looked at the ruins around them." This, he speculated, is the reason it was not published until 1992.

northern France, where they would be fed, reclothed, and given medical care before being sent home. "Revival missions," they were called.

Rosie Rosenthal—back at Thorpe Abbotts and fully recovered from wounds suffered on the Berlin raid of February 3—was one of the first to volunteer. "I had rejoined the Hundredth too late to get another crack at the Germans but this was a mission I really wanted to fly." It was a mercy run to Linz, Austria, and the liberated prisoners were French POWs. "After that, I wanted to fly down to southern Germany to pick up our own liberated airmen, but that was not a mission assigned to the Hundredth."

"We were waiting to be picked up at a place called Moosburg, near Munich, an enormous prison camp where General Patton had liberated us," recalled Lt. Lou Loevsky. "It was like a bolt from the blue. One day we were slaves, the next day we were free. On the day we were liberated a lot of the men broke down and cried. I didn't. I willed myself not to cry. I thought I was dreaming and that if I cried I would wake up and still be a prisoner."

None of these airmen had begun his imprisonment at Moosburg. The Allied fliers had arrived there at the very end of the war, after long forced marches from camps along Germany's Eastern Front. For three months they had been lost to the world outside their confinement; even the Red Cross had been unable to track them. They had traveled by foot and rail through the spreading chaos of the dying Reich, witnesses to both the suffering they had caused with their bombs and the barbarism they had risked their lives to eradicate. "What many of us saw and experienced, no one at home would have believed," said the Bloody Hundredth's Gale Cleven.

It is a story that begins on January 27, 1945, and has no end, for no airman on the march outlived the burden of his experience. On that day, with the Russians closing in on Posen and Breslau, approximately eighty miles north and south of Sagan, Hitler ordered the Luftwaffe to move the prisoners of Stalag Luft III to camps west of Berlin. Additional orders went out to evacuate other stalags in the path of the Russian stampede. Among the hundreds of thousands of prisoners held by the Germans were 95,000 Americans, 38,000 of them airmen—bomber crewmen and fighter pilots from outfits all over Europe. Hitler had wanted these fliers kept as hostages for any eventuality. One of his twisted ideas was to billet them in towns heavily bombed by the Anglo-Americans. Another was to execute them if the bombing continued.

On the evening of January 27, the prisoners in South Compound of Stalag Luft III were being treated to a kriegie production of the popular Broadway comedy *You Can't Take It with You*. Midway through the first act, the doors burst open and Col. Charles Goodrich, senior officer of the compound, stormed down the center aisle, leaped onto the stage, and held out his arms to call for silence. "The goons have . . . given us thirty minutes to be at the front gate. Get your stuff together and line up."

Messengers raced through the compounds to spread the word, and men started packing emergency rations they had stowed away: chocolate, sugar, dried fruit, and cheese. Like most other prisoners, David Westheimer thought he was prepared for the cold. He wore two pairs of socks, wool long johns, a wool shirt and pants, a sweater, a battle dress jacket, a stocking cap, a muffler, a greatcoat, and two pairs of gloves. It had been snowing all day, and by nightfall, as the men lined up in threes outside their barracks, the snow was heavy on the ground and the wind was blowing fiercely from the west, the direction in which they would be marching. Waiting in the dark for the order to march, the men of South Compound stomped their feet in the soft snow to try to keep them warm. Some men started to shake, terrified at moving out into an unknown future. "Prison life wasn't a picnic," said Gale Cleven, "but it was relatively safe. Outside the wire, who knows what awaited us."

The 2,000 prisoners of South Compound were the first to leave Stalag Luft III. The men of West Compound followed, led by Col. Darr Alkire, the first commander of the Hundredth Bomb Group. John Egan and Buck Cleven, who had lived together in the stalag, fell in line behind Alkire. Col. Delmar Spivey's Center Compound was the last to leave, at around 3:00 A.M. At the head of that trailing column was Gen. Arthur Vanaman, limping noticeably from wounds suffered when he had parachuted into Germany and become the highest-ranking officer in enemy hands. As the prisoners marched past the camp warehouse, each man was handed a Red Cross box weighing about eleven pounds. These "suitcases" were too heavy to carry, so the men tore them open and stuffed their favorite items into their overcoat pockets and knapsacks: chocolate D-bars, prunes, and cigarettes. Camp guards were waiting for them outside the gate, their snarling sentry dogs pulling menacingly at their leashes, their machine guns mounted on horse-drawn wagons. A few Hitler Youth had joined the guards, as had some big-bellied members of the Volkssturm, Hitler's ragtag home guard. Anyone attempting to escape would be shot, the goons announced. "So off we went," recalled Lou Loevsky, "destination unknown."

As Lt. A. Edwin Stern of the Bloody Hundredth marched into the silent pine forest outside the darkened camp, a terrible thought ran through his mind. The previous spring, when he was captured near Berlin, a woman jumped out of the unruly crowd that surrounded him and spat in his face, and a group of hard-faced Nazi Youth threw stones at him. Now he was going out among these people he had bombed, German settlers who had been transplanted to Silesia, to Lebensraum created by Hitler's quick conquest of Poland. What would the reception be like?

But most of the prisoners were in high spirits when they began the march. "There was lots of joking and friendly banter about Uncle Joe's boys overtaking us and freeing us in a day or so," said Cleven. "Six or seven hours later no one was laughing." Nearly everyone had fallen into a despairing silence, each man folded into his own thoughts, fighting a private battle against the cold.

Marching into the teeth of the worst European blizzard in decades, some prisoners were temporarily blinded by the lacerating snow. Heads bowed, shoulders hunched against the winds, men slept as they walked. When a defeated man staggered to his knees from exhaustion and exposure, his buddies would pull him up and slip cubes of sugar into his mouth.

The cold blurred lines of authority and created a community of misery among the prisoners and their guards. Middle-aged guards who were too exhausted to tote their rifles handed them to prisoners to carry. *"Alles ist kaput,"* they would mutter sourly. At one point, Lieutenant Stern lifted his gaze and through the swirling snow spotted two Americans helping one of the older guards, who could go no further. Two days into the march, two guards and four Americans died. There was talk of escape, even mutiny, but the American commanders ordered their men to stay together and orderly. They were deep inside the Reich and all that was out there beyond the frozen road was the killing cold. Better to face it together than alone.

The Germans gave them no food or water, and at night, the prisoners were billeted in barns, churches, chicken houses, and abandoned concentration camps. One evening Darr Alkire's group slept in a pottery factory worked by Polish and French slave laborers from a local prison camp. Some of the women offered their bodies for American cigarettes, chocolate bars, and soap, but most of the sex-starved men were too exhausted to oblige. Cleven and Egan sprawled out on the concrete floor, blessedly heated by giant kilns in the basement. "It was hard to get any shut-eye," says Cleven. "Men were screaming in their sleep that they couldn't march another step." After a long rest, they reached another village. By this time, their guards barely paid attention to them. The Germans were caught up in their own battles for survival. Only the sentry dogs, released from their leashes, stalked the edges of the column.

The line of prisoners extended for almost thirty miles along the route

Napoleon had taken back from Moscow, and the narrow road was jammed with refugees fleeing the oncoming Russians. Their sorrowful caravan was part of the greatest panic migration in European history. In that week, there were over seven million people, most of them from Silesia, Pomerania, and East Prussia, heading back to the fatherland. By the end of January, nearly 50,000 refugees were pouring into Berlin every day, part of the stream of displaced humanity that would be targeted at train stations by American bombers on February 3. "[We pass] silent, deserted towns where refugees line the roads in horse- and cattle-drawn carts, waiting to move out," the former New York journalist Eugene Halmos wrote in his secret diary. "Little kids peek . . . out, red-faced with the cold, from under huge piles of household goods." Enormous hay wagons, pulled by starving horses, their bones showing through their shanks, rattled past them on the road. Stone-faced patriarchs rode up front and watched impassively as the prisoners offered small pieces of chocolate to the children huddled in the backs of the wagons. Occasionally, a ragged Wehrmacht regiment passed them on the road, heading in the opposite direction, toward the westward-moving Russians. These were not the goose-stepping conquerors that the men had seen in the newsreels back home. They looked impossibly young and tremendously afraid, and some of them asked the prisoners for food.

On February 1, the first waves of prisoners arrived in the garrison town of Spremberg, where the Germans finally issued them food: bowls of diluted barley gruel and black bread. Alkire's group had walked over sixty miles in five days. After devouring their food, they walked the final mile to the railroad station, where they were pushed into closed cattle cars. The cars had no markings identifying them as carriers of POWs and this alarmed the men. They knew American fighter planes would be stalking the rail lines. "Where are we going?" one of the prisoners asked a guard. "Another camp," came the unwelcome reply. "You will not like it."

A few days later, General Vanaman's group stumbled into Spremberg. There Spivey learned from the guards that his men would be shipped by rail to where the prisoners of South Compound had just been sent—a large camp in the town of Moosburg, in eastern Bavaria. He and Vanaman would not be accompanying them. They were to be taken to Berlin on a secret mission, and then repatriated to Switzerland, their reward for getting their men to Spremberg in good order. Spivey protested. He wanted to stay with his men, and he didn't want them to think that he and Vanaman had worked out a private deal for their own release. But the guards were adamant. As

Spivey stood on the sidewalk and watched his 2,000 men march down the street toward the rail station, he shouted to them "to keep their chins up."

"Conditions inside the boxcars were unspeakably hideous," navigator Frank Murphy, of the Hundredth Bomb Group, wrote in his account of the march. "We could not lie down; we either stood or sat on blankets on the hard floor packed together with our knees drawn up tightly under our chins. . . . Many men passed out from the cold and lack of food. Others were so ill they vomited or lost control of their bowels and we had no way to clean ourselves. Some men were so miserable they cried."

Two days later, toward midnight, Frank Murphy's group arrived at a railroad siding in Moosburg. When the train stopped, men started screaming for the doors of the cattle cars to be opened. They wanted fresh air, food, and water, but they were left in the locked cars for the entire night. When the doors were opened just after dawn, most of the prisoners were too weak to move; the guards had to climb into the cars and shove them out. Their clothes soiled by vomit and feces, the men were marched to the gates of Stalag VIIA, a catch basin for every segment of humanity the Nazis had warred on. This vermin-infested pigsty would be their home for the remainder of the war.

Limbo

A week earlier, Darr Alkire's group had arrived at an equally abysmal camp on the outskirts of Nuremberg, about eighty miles north of Moosburg. Eighth Air Force pilot William H. Wheeler, a prisoner for eighteen months after being shot down on the Regensburg-Schweinfurt raid, was with them. When the guards pulled open the door of his boxcar, Wheeler saw that they were in a large marshaling yard and noticed that the Luftwaffe guards were backed by black-uniformed SS troops. The Germans were prepared for trouble. "The anger and rage of the POWs was close to being suicidal," Wheeler recalled. They shouted curses in German and appeared ready to riot. Then word came through the ranks from Alkire to calm down so they could get to the camp, where there was food and water.

Stalag XIIID had no heat or beds and was located only two miles from a freight yard that was a favorite target of Allied bombers. Here the airmen got a taste of their own poison, as the Eighth Air Force and Bomber Command pounded the city day and night. The men took cover in shallow slit trenches they dug outside their barracks, holding blankets and coats over their heads to protect themselves from showers of spent shrapnel from enemy antiaircraft guns. The British dropped bombs the size of small trucks and some of them fell close to the camp, sending shock waves across the ground capable of breaking bones. "I prayed (not just for myself)," recalled an Eighth Air Force flier, "but mainly that no American city would ever see anything like it." Colonel Alkire went to the Kommandant in a rage and demanded that his men be moved to another camp. There were no other places to put them, he was told. Would they rather be placed inside burning Nuremberg?

The men learned to live with the bombs. Hunger was the greater enemy. Within a week after the prisoners arrived at Nuremberg, the Germans ran out of barley soup and potatoes and began serving dehydrated vegetables infested with weevils and worms. Some prisoners sorted out the bugs; others devoured them and discouraged weaker men from eating their food so they could have it.

On the first of April, prisoners heard on their hidden radios that the American Seventh Army was advancing directly toward Nuremberg. Two days later, over 15,000 emaciated POWs were formed into columns and put on the road to Munich. This was a hot zone and they were in daily danger from friendly air fire. Passing a marshaling yard, they saw a squadron of Thunderbolts diving straight at them with guns blazing. Three airmen were killed and three others wounded. The next day the men put a huge replica of an American Air Corps insignia on the road, with an arrow pointing in the direction of the march. "This ended the bombing of the column," said the group's medic, Sgt. Gordon K. Butts.

The march had begun under bright skies, but by the first afternoon a cold rain began to fall and it tracked the airmen for days. To maintain order, Alkire had to have more food. He wanted Red Cross parcels immediately, he told the German captain in charge of the march. If any of his men died, he would hold him personally responsible.

Unknown to Alkire, General Vanaman and Colonel Spivey had already taken care of this. After being brought to Berlin, they met with representatives of SS Lt. Gen. Gottlob Berger, who was still in charge of air force prison camps. Working through the Swiss government, Berger made arrangements for Red Cross supplies to be delivered from Geneva to Allied prisoners of war who were being moved from the Eastern Front. Like his earlier effort to prevent his own SS from taking over control of the Luft camps after the Great Escape, this was a calculated effort by Berger to appease the approaching Western Allies.

The Americans and the British provided a fleet of 200 trucks and two special trains, and the Germans guaranteed their safe passage under an emergency relief agreement engineered by Eisenhower. Prodded by Churchill, who feared that Hitler planned "to murder some or all of the prisoners," Eisenhower also sent a pointed message to the Combined Chiefs of Staff in Washington. "Acts of violence may be perpetrated against prisoners of war and massacres might be instigated by SS troops or the Gestapo under cover of the general disorder." Preparations were then made to send Special Forces units from the advancing Allied armies to liberate camps close to the front lines. And airborne troops began training in England to mount rescue missions to prison camps farther behind German lines, paratrooper raids similar to those carried out by Gen. Douglas MacArthur's forces in the Philippines. The war ended, however, before any rescue efforts were attempted.*

After arranging for Red Cross food relief, Berger summoned Vanaman and Spivey to his heavily guarded headquarters. He wanted Vanaman to take a message to Eisenhower conveying his desire to negotiate—by secret radio codes—a separate peace with the Western Allies. This would allow a reinvigorated Wehrmacht to push the Russians back to the Oder. High-ranking army officers would then murder Hitler and Himmler—who were madmen, Berger said—and arrange an "orderly and correct surrender" of the country to the Western Allies. Berger would do this, he told Spivey and Vanaman, to save his country from the Bolshevik beasts. He also claimed that he wanted to save the lives of Allied POWs, whom Hitler was threatening to kill as payback for Dresden.

Vanaman agreed to work with Berger, but only after Berger promised to stop the forced POW marches and speed up the delivery of food to the men. He and Spivey were then smuggled into neutral Switzerland. From there Vanaman was flown to France to meet with General Spaatz. Spaatz was incredulous when he heard Berger's peace proposal. "Somebody sure pulled your leg," he told Vanaman. He then sent Vanaman to Washington to get rid of him. The general made a full report to the War Department, which was conspicuously ignored. No one in the Allied command structure would have agreed to this craven deal with a man Vanaman and Spivey considered, in their equal abhorrence of the communists, "a Great German." The United States "would be in a much better position today," an unchanged Vanaman said in an interview in 1967, "if we had done just

---

* Similar emergency planning had not been set in motion to rescue the Hungarian Jews at Auschwitz.

what Berger wanted us to do—negotiate a peace with the Western Allies. . . . The Russians had long supply lines, and I think [the Wehrmacht] could have driven them back . . . to the borders of Germany."

After the war, Spivey visited Berger frequently and invited him to POW gatherings in the United States, where he honored him as the man who saved Americans from starvation and mass murder. According to Berger, in the early spring of 1945 Hitler had ordered all Allied airmen held by the Germans to be taken to his mountaintop fortress and retreat at Berchtesgaden, in the Bavarian Alps south of Munich. They were to be held there as hostages while he tried to negotiate a favorable truce with the Western Allies. If Roosevelt and Churchill were uncooperative, the 35,000 airmen would be executed. Eva Braun, Hitler's mistress, reputedly opposed the order on moral grounds, and knowing that Berger did as well, arranged for Hitler to give the signed order to him. Through a clever bureaucratic ruse, Berger made sure it was never executed.

Berger claimed this happened on April 22, although there are no witnesses or documents to support his story. On that day, Hitler had decided to stay—and die—in his Berlin bunker. Having made that decision, why would he have given an order to move POWs to his Alpine redoubt?

If Berger didn't save Allied POWs from a death sentence, he did try unsuccessfully to stop the POW marches and he was able to hasten the delivery of Red Cross parcels to prisoners on the move. Several days after his final meeting with Vanaman and Spivey, a convoy of Red Cross trucks from Switzerland located Darr Alkire's column and delivered 4,000 packages of food. While the kriegies sat in an open field eating chocolate bars and downing cans of condensed milk, they learned from the BBC that other American airmen, mostly sergeants, were on forced marches in other parts of Germany. The Red Cross was trying to monitor these marches, but with Germany in chaos, it was unable to find out how many men there were, where they were, or where they were headed. Red Cross representatives did inform London and Washington that sources inside Germany indicated that these men were in grave danger. Family and friends of the prisoners "must be ready for bad news," a representative of the American Red Cross announced.

The Gunners

The prisoners in danger were from Stalag Luft IV in Pomerania, some of them still recovering from puncture wounds suffered on the Hydekrug

Run. They had been evacuated in late January, as the Russians approached their camp. Some were sent to other camps further west, but 6,000 of them, mostly Americans, were split into two columns and were marching westward along a narrow corridor bordering the Baltic Sea, just north of the main Russian drive on Berlin. The guards told them it would be "a three-day hike" to their next destination, but many of the men would still be on the road, walking aimlessly, when the Germans surrendered in early May. No one will ever know how many men died on this starvation march, but surely hundreds did, in what was for American airmen the European equivalent of the Bataan Death March of April 1942.

Dr. Leslie Caplan, the chief medical officer at Stalag Luft IV, remained in the rear of the column, picking up the sick and the dying as they fell behind in mounting numbers, suffering from diphtheria, pneumonia, tuberculosis, dysentery, and frostbite. Caplan did what he could for them with his small staff of volunteer medics, who performed minor surgery in barnyard filth, lancing infected ulcers on men's feet with scalpels fashioned from safety razors tied to twigs. Sick prisoners seeking shelter for the night were denied access to barns because farmers complained they were too lice-ridden to sleep with their livestock. "It was obvious," Caplan later told investigators, "that the welfare of German cattle was placed above our welfare."

The worst trial occurred on February 14, when the prisoners were forced to march thirty-five kilometers. "Men had rampaging dysentery and they weren't even allowed to stop and relieve themselves," said Sgt. George Guderley. "We'd march through a town, and the men would slow down a bit, drop their drawers, and let fly. . . . With the Russians only fifteen to twenty miles behind us, we weren't even allowed to stop for a drink of water. So men, without looking, would reach down and scoop up handfuls of snow and put them in their mouths. But the khaki-colored snow was full of urine and bloody feces, and these men were ingesting hepatitis and yellow jaundice."

That night the snow gave way to a cold, driving rain, and the spiritless men slept on soggy ground "littered by the feces of dysenteric prisoners" who were marching ahead of them, and they drank from ditches that had been used as latrines. Men who were certain they would not make it to morning said their farewells to friends before nodding off. "It was the worst night of my life," Guderley, the tough Chicagoan, remembered. "It was worse than bailing out of a burning bomber."

Some men survived the march by being selfish—hoarding and hiding food and firewood—but most of them formed combines, groups of two or three prisoners who searched for food and firewood together and shared everything, even their body heat. The buddy system saved lives. "Day 35 was my day of reckoning," Sgt. Joseph O'Donnell recalled. On that day, the scrawny ball turret gunner from Riverside, New Jersey, almost gave up. Collapsing beside the road in his soaking wet clothing, he stared at his reflection in a cold pool of water. It was the first time he had seen his face since he left the camp. "I saw a harried, starved, unshaven . . . skeleton," he wrote days later in his logbook. Convinced he had no chance of surviving, O'Donnell decided he would die right there, sitting like a beggar by the road. "But my top-turret gunner picked me up, carried me to a barn, covered me with straw, and by morning I felt a little better."

On March 28, when they reached a town just west of the Elbe River, the prisoners were loaded into boxcars and taken to Stalag XIB in Falling-bostel, thirty miles away, a collection pen for tens of thousands of prisoners of all nationalities. "We wanted to get back in prison, where there was food and shelter," Guderley recalled. "But we quickly found out that this vile pit was worse than Luft IV."

A week later, O'Donnell's column was gathered together and put on another forced march. This time the guards directed them eastward, to escape the oncoming Anglo-American armies. They doubled back and covered much of the same territory they had traversed the previous month. As they marched in warmer weather, eating the flesh of horses killed by American fighter planes, they heard the rumble of friendly artillery in the distance. This raised hopes, but by the twentieth day, some men wondered if they had sufficient strength to hold on.

Traveling through rural Germany, the sergeant gunners of Stalag Luft IV did not encounter pathetic processions of refugees or pass towns flattened by Allied bombs. And the only barbarity they experienced was inflicted on them. Another group of marching prisoners saw the deepest depths of Nazi depravity. They were from Stalag XVIIB,* a prison containing over 4,200 noncommissioned officers of the American Air Force, as well as 26,000 POWs from France, Russia, Italy, and smaller nations.

---

* The camp was later made famous by *Stalag 17,* a Broadway play that was made into a successful Hollywood film directed by Billy Wilder and starring William Holden, whose performance won him an Academy Award for Best Actor. The play was written in captivity by two Army Air Force gunners, Donald Bevan and Edmund Trzcinski, who played a character in the film.

On April 8th, the American POWs, marching in eight separate groups, evacuated their camp near Krems, Austria, as the Red Army began its encirclement of Vienna, only fifty miles away. No reason was given for moving only the Americans, but the Germans were probably hoping to use them as bargaining chips in any negotiations they might enter into with the U.S. Army.

Several days later, as the prisoners approached the city of Linz, Sgt. Richard H. Hoffman, a B-24 tail gunner, saw German soldiers herding hundreds of people onto the road. As the column of humanity came closer, one of the kriegies cried out: "Who are these people?"

"Untermenschen," replied a guard—subhumans.

They were walking skeletons with sunken chests and mouths without teeth, and they had a scary, faraway look in their eyes. Ignoring orders not to speak to them, a number of POWs called out in several languages, asking them who they were. They were Jews and political prisoners, mostly Hungarians, and they were from a camp called Mauthausen. They were being marched to the front to build gun emplacements for their enslavers.

Then a shot rang out and one of the wretched souls, seated on the ground, fell over on his side, a geyser of blood spurting from his head. An SS officer holstered his pistol and approached another man sitting on the road. He gave him a good kick and ordered him to get up. The man tried, but couldn't. In an instant, the German pulled out his pistol and shot him in the forehead.

As the airmen moved down the road in shocked silence, many of them felt a commingling of revulsion and fear: hatred for the Germans and the terrifying realization that this might happen to them. "I wanted to . . . charge into the Germans and kill them all, but dear God I was afraid," Hoffman recalled.

On the streets of the town of Mauthausen, Sergeant Hoffman's group saw more bullet-marked bodies lying in spreading puddles of their own blood. When Allied prisoners stopped to rest, hardly anyone spoke. Close to Linz, a Nazi stronghold, nearly every town they passed through had been heavily bombed. "Citizens, mostly women, children, and old people, were sitting on piles of bricks and debris, shocked into silence and staring at the ruins," Hoffman recalls. But after what they had just seen, the men found it hard to summon up compassion for the people of these wasted towns.

Crossing the Danube, the airmen marched in the direction of Braunau am Inn, Hitler's birthplace. On April 18, they came to a hastily built camp in a pine forest by the River Inn. There they met up with POWs from Stalag XVIIA who had arrived just before them and built crude huts inside a barbed-wire enclosure. There was only a light guard detachment, but the other prisoners warned the new men not to try to escape. The American Army was on the opposite bank of the river, where white sheets could be seen hanging from the upper windows of nearly every house.

Liberation

Less than a hundred miles to the west, the main body of Darr Alkire's column had just reached Moosburg's Stalag VIIA. Gale Cleven was no longer with them. He had escaped the evening the marchers reached the Danube, after telling Alkire that he was convinced the Germans planned to fall back into the Alps and stage a desperate stand, using American airmen as negotiating pawns. His friend John Egan agreed with him, but had to stay behind; Alkire had put him in charge of security operations on the march.

That night, Cleven and two other men had crawled through an open stockade filled with manure, with Egan providing cover by priming a rusty old pump, the squealing and scraping drawing the attention of the guards. But it was the manure that saved them. "It was Chanel No. 5," Cleven said later. "It took the dogs off our scent. Once out of the stockade, we took off through muddy fields and slept that evening in a grove of willows. We had no map, no compass, but we figured if we kept moving west and traveled by night we'd soon run into our boys."

By now the prison population at Moosburg had ballooned to over 100,000—slave laborers, freshly transferred concentration camp inmates, and POWs like Lou Loevsky who had been there for weeks. On Sunday morning, April 29, bullets began to whistle through the camp and heavy arms fire erupted all around it. Finding cover, John Egan scrawled in his notebook. "Right now a fair-sized war is going on all around us." It was a battle between advance elements of Patton's Third Army and SS troops for control of the town of Moosburg. Looking around, Egan noticed that the camp guards were gone. They had been ordered to reinforce the SS. "1230 April 29. . . . The fighting has moved away (I hope) . . . and you can see 'Old Glory' [flying from the steeple of the village church]. The town has been taken. My first glimpse of the red, white and blue in 19 months," Egan wrote from the now quiet camp.

Thousands of American prisoners, tears streaming down their cheeks, stood at attention, saluting the flag. Then a Sherman tank smashed through the main gate and the men rushed toward it, patting and kissing it, and holding out their hands to touch their emancipators as they popped up out of their hatches. A captain climbed out of the tank and announced that he had come for his brother. Seconds later, a prisoner ran toward the Sherman and the brothers embraced. Another tanker freed his son, a lieutenant in the American Air Force. "FOR US THE WAR IS OVER!" Eugene Halmos wrote in his diary. It was ten months to the day since he had been shot down over Holland.

Someone lowered the Nazi Swastika and ran the Stars and Stripes up the camp flagpole. Then up went the other flags the men had hidden in anticipation of this day: the Union Jack, the Red Star of Russia, the French Tricolors, and the flags of nearly every other Allied nation. The prisoners went wild. "We cheered even louder," said airman Roger Burwell, "when a truckload of bread showed up." It was "real WHITE bread, which tastes like cake to us." That night, Alkire informed his men that they would be flown to France in seven to ten days.

On May 1, George Patton arrived at Moosburg in a long Packard touring car, accompanied by an entourage of reporters and newsreel cameramen. Striding through the camp like a conquering king, his ivory-handled pistols bouncing on his hips, he stopped suddenly to examine the pale shrunken bodies of Frank Murphy and his Sagan buddies. "I'm going to kill these sons-of-bitches for this," he muttered in a low, cold voice.

That night freed prisoners from every nation in Europe paraded in the streets of Moosburg, showing off the booty they had "liberated" from German homes and stores: cases of cognac and wine, pigs and lambs, crossbows and sabers, top hats and hunting rifles. American POWs snaked through the crowds in stolen German bicycles, motorcycles, and command cars, throwing flowers and flashing victory signs. All the while, Sherman tanks pushed through this madcap scene, followed by long lines of stone-eyed soldiers. Patton's men were marching south to stamp out the dying embers of Nazi resistance.

The next morning, at a forest camp near Braunau, Sgt. Richard Hoffman went down to the River Inn for a drink of water. On his way back, he spotted a car climbing the mountain road. It was the camp Kommandant's staff car, and when it came to a stop in the compound, the German got out, walked stiffly around the back of the car, and opened the other door. Out stepped an American Army captain wearing a steel helmet. "I figured the poor bastard had gotten captured," Hoffman recalled. But Hoffman noticed that the American was carrying an automatic pistol. "Prisoners don't carry .45s. I ran toward the car and let out a rebel yell." As he did, POWs rushed toward the American officer, their arms waving wildly. The captain stepped on a tree stump, raised his hands for silence, and announced: "Men, you are back under the control of the United States Army. Your German camp Kommandant came into Braunau several hours ago and surrendered to our forces."

Two days later, Joe O'Donnell, Leslie Caplan, and hundreds of other haggard prisoners stumbled into spearheads of the British Eighth Army near the city of Hanover. It was the twenty-sixth day of their second forced march, and for O'Donnell, his eighty-sixth day on the road since he had left Poland. George Guderley would have been with them but he had not made the second march. With the help of a sympathetic German guard, he had hidden out in the Russian compound at Fallingbostel to avoid going on the road again. Two weeks later the camp was liberated by a British tank column.

A walking skeleton, O'Donnell was flown to an Army hospital in England. John Carson and other airmen who were not gravely ill were flown to Camp Lucky Strike, a tent city near the port of Le Havre that held nearly 50,000 liberated prisoners. There they were fed, deloused, and given toilet kits, new uniforms, and stacks of French currency. On May 6, when word spread through the camp that the Germans were about to surrender, the ex-kriegies began preparing for a celebration.

V-E Day

At 2:41 A.M. on May 7, at Eisenhower's headquarters in the cathedral city of Rheims, Col. Gen. Alfred Jodl signed the documents of the Act of Military Surrender. Under the terms, the unconditional surrender of Germany was to take effect at one minute before midnight on May 8, 1945, V-E Day. But when Stalin protested that the war was not officially over until the Germans ratified the treaty in the presence of Marshal Zhukov, the conqueror of Berlin, Eisenhower was "directed to withhold news of the first signing until the second could be accomplished."

A large delegation of dignitaries and reporters, led by Air Chief Marshal Tedder, flew to Berlin on May 7 to meet Marshal Zhukov and a German delegation headed by Field Marshal Wilhelm Keitel, head of the German Armed Forces High Command (OKW) and, with Jodl, one of Hitler's servile sycophants—nodding donkeys, Albert Speer called them. Gen. Carl Spaatz, who had witnessed the first surrender at SHAEF headquarters in Rheims, accompanied Tedder as the American representative.

The surrender talks were held at a military engineering college in a small suburb called Karlshorst. After twelve hours of wrangling over the exact wording of the instrument of surrender, the Allied representatives, along with a noisy retinue of reporters and photographers, gathered in a large, austere conference room. General Zhukov sat at the head of a plain wooden table, with Tedder on his right and Spaatz on his left. A Russian guard brought in the German delegation, headed by Field Marshal Keitel. Staring straight ahead, Keitel raised his marshal's baton in salute, sat down at the table, and "surveyed the room as he might have looked over the terrain of a battlefield," observed Capt. Harry Butcher, Eisenhower's aide. Here was the "Prussian and Nazi arrogance which I, and all others who saw, will forever carry in our minds."

After the last Nazi put his signature on the document, Zhukov rose and asked the Germans to leave the hall. When the door closed behind them, the Russian officers rose as one man and let out a thunderous cheer, and began bear-hugging one another. It was well past midnight, but servants suddenly appeared and set up a brilliant banquet, with bottles of wine, champagne, vodka, and brandy set beside every plate. The Russians broke into song and "Marshal Zhukov himself danced the *Russkaya* to loud cheers from his generals." The celebration lasted far into the morning and at least three generals had to be carried out of the room. "I was glad to note," said Tedder, "that none of them was British."

The next morning, Tedder and Spaatz asked to be taken through the heart of Berlin on their way to Tempelhof airport, south of the city. "This is a city of the dead," wrote correspondent Harold King, who toured the Nazi capital with them. "I have seen Stalingrad; I have lived through the entire London Blitz . . . but the scene of utter destruction, desolation and death which meets the eye in Berlin as far as the eye can rove in all directions is something that almost baffles description. . . . The town is literally unrecognizable. . . . From the [still standing] Brandenburg Gate, everything within a radius of from 2 to 5 miles is destroyed." What bombs had left intact, Russian artillery had finished off. The wreckage was not unlike that of Cologne. Only in Berlin one had the sense that not just a city but a nation, and with it, an ugly idea, had come to ruin.

The German surrender, said Churchill, was "the signal for the greatest outburst of joy in the history of mankind." London was the epicenter of that celebration, and the prime minister got caught in it on his way to the House of Commons to make the victory announcement. "Instantly, he was surrounded by people—people running, standing on tiptoe, holding up babies so that they could be told later they had seen him, and shouting affection-ately the absurd little nursery maid name, 'Winnie, Winnie!' " wrote London diarist Mollie Panter-Downes.

"London simply went crazy," recalled Lt. Rosie Rosenthal, who was on leave in the city when the news broke at 3:00 P.M. on Tuesday, May 8. "I'd be walking through a throng of people with a pretty girl on my arm and all of a sudden she was gone, replaced by another one. It was a madhouse, a beautiful, beautiful madhouse.

"We had an airman with us who had taken the pledge; had never had a drink. We lost him for an hour or so and then found him dead drunk in the gutter."

Piccadilly Circus attracted the most boisterous crowds. At Rainbow Corner, the Red Cross put on a tremendous party. Swing bands played continuously and soldiers and laughing girls "formed a conga line down the middle of Piccadilly."

That night the twin brothers John and Gene Carson had a long-awaited reunion. After being discharged from Camp Lucky Strike, John Carson had crossed the Channel in an English ship and gone to Rainbow Corner to look for Wing Ding. He ran into Adele Astaire, who still worked at the club as a volunteer, and she told him she knew his brother and would arrange for him to be at the club on the evening of May 8, not knowing that this would be V-E Day. "I can still see my brother coming down the left side of the hall to greet me," John recalled.

It was the night of their young lives. Wing Ding showed his brother around London, taught him how to drink heavy English beer, and took him to the Windmill Theatre, his favorite burlesque club. After the show, John met a member of the cast, a busty blond dancer who was about eigh-teen years old. Fifty years later he could still remember her address.

Out in East Anglia, at the airbases and in the villages, the celebration was less boisterous. The Japanese were fighting on furiously, and thou-sands of men from East Anglia were serving with the British armed forces in the Pacific. Word had already come back to many a country cottage that a husband or a son was in an enemy prison compound. "My main feeling on V-Day was an intense loneliness," said a Norwich woman. "A day like that seems so unreal without one's husband."

American airmen missed their wives and sweethearts, and they also had their minds on the Pacific, as they awaited orders to be moved to that "other war" that they had had little time to think about until now. Still, it was excellent to end this one. That night bonfires burned in village squares and the East Anglian sky was turned into "a fairyland of color" by home-made rockets and fireworks and flares shot from Air Force Very pistols. "Spirits did not flag until midnight," reported a local writer.

The parties lasted longer at the American air stations, where there was free whiskey and beer. Ground crew personnel, who were most familiar with the locals, streamed out of the gates and packed their favorite pubs, their English girlfriends on their arms. But at Mendlesham, home of the 34th Bomb Group, the commanding officer ordered the men confined to the base. "As odd as it may seem, most of us didn't want to go anyway," says Chuck Alling. They wanted to celebrate as a unit and in their own way. Religious services were held in the chapel every hour and all the crews attended at least once, ending each service with the "Battle Hymn of the Republic," the men's voices rising to the line, "Mine eyes have seen the glory of the coming of the Lord . . ."

That night the bar at the Mendlesham officers club was three deep with airmen lifting their glasses in salute to fallen friends.

"It is midnight," Ursula von Kardorff wrote in her diary from the German village she had escaped to. "Unconditional surrender comes into effect from this moment. All over the world they are singing hymns of victory and the bells are ringing out. And what about us? . . . We have lost the war, but if we had won it everything would have been still more horrible than it is."

On May 8, liberated POW Richard Hoffman of Stalag XVIIA was in a transition camp near Nancy, where he was reunited with his crew. That morning the crew had gotten word that they would be shipped home the following day. To celebrate, they walked into the city, taking with them more wine than they could handle. Still physically weak and dehydrated, they were all deliriously drunk after a few swallows. "Suddenly, horns, church bells, and sirens cut loose," Hoffman recalled. Frenchmen came running out of their houses and flooded the streets, embracing one another and shedding tears of joy.

That night Hoffman clung to his mattress as the room spun around and around until he mercifully passed out. The next morning, as his boat nudged out of Le Havre's war-wrecked harbor, music was piped in over the loudspeaker system. The first song was "Don't Fence Me In."

May 8 was Gale Cleven's last night at Thorpe Abbotts. Using the North Star and a homemade compass, he and his companion George Aring had made it back from Moosburg. On their first night as evaders they had gotten separated from Cleven's best friend from college, George Neithammer, who had been a prisoner with him at Sagan. When an American Piper Cub flew overhead, they figured it was safe to walk by daylight, and with the help of friendly German farmers they ran into remnants of the American 45th Division. "I was so skinny," Cleven recalled, "that if I stood just right, I didn't have a shadow."

Within a week, Cleven was reunited with his old outfit, just days before the end of the war. "The fabulous Cleven" was back, and "everyone wanted to meet him," recalled a veteran of the Hundredth. Cleven sat around the officers club talking to the men, his cap tilted back "in the same old careless way, his right leg swung lazily over the arm of a chair, turning the clock back nineteen months." But he soon tired of this. "I begged to fly just one last time, for the Germans had rather upset me, but they wouldn't let me. They told me our war, the bomber war, was over. So I said, the hell with it, send me home, I've got a girl I want to marry."

Home was Hobbs, New Mexico, where his father had been transferred from Wyoming, and where Gale had met his fiancée before going off to war. He left Thorpe Abbotts on V-E Day, shedding tears when the men of his old squadron presented him with an engraved English silver set and a watch. "I'm just a baby," he said, and stumbled out of the barracks and into the soggy night without his raincoat.

Then he was gone for good and without a good-bye. Arriving at the front door of his home in New Mexico, he got the bad news. The next day he was on the road, thumbing a ride to Casper, Wyoming, to serve as a pallbearer for George Neithammer. His friend had been caught somewhere in Germany and shot.

When John Egan arrived in Hobbs to be the best man at his friend's wedding, he was carrying a silk parachute. The bride's mother knew at once what it was for, and in a day and night fashioned it into a wedding dress. As the bride walked down the aisle with her father, Egan leaned in toward Cleven and whispered, "Where's the ripcord?"

The House That Flak Built

The last American airmen to be liberated were the ones the American high command had hoped to get out first. Stalag Luft I was a camp of "air aces," prize hostages, it was feared, for Nazi die-hards. This was "Zemke's Stalag." When Hubert "Hub" Zemke arrived at Barth on the Baltic with a special escort in December 1944, he became, by rank, the senior Allied officer, in charge of almost 7,000 men. For almost two years, German pilots had been hunting him hard, and his luck finally ran out on his final scheduled mission, when his Mustang lost a wing in a thunderstorm and he was forced to parachute into the hands of the enemy.

Five other American aces were with Zemke, among them Lt. Col. Francis "Gabby" Gabreski, holder of the Eighth Air Force record of twenty-eight enemy fighters destroyed in aerial combat, and Maj. Gerald Johnson, with eighteen kills to his credit. Gabreski and Johnson had served under Zemke in his famed "Hun-hating" Thunderbolt outfit, the 56th Fighter Group, before Zemke was transferred to a Mustang squadron in the spring of 1944. Gabreski, too, had gone down on the last mission he was to have flown. On July 20, 1944, he crash-landed on a strafing operation against a German airfield.

Other Air Corps heroes at Stalag Luft I were Lt. Col. Charles "Ross" Greening, a flight leader on Gen. Jimmy Doolittle's Tokyo Raid before he was moved to the European Theater of Operations, and Fortress pilot John "Red" Morgan, awarded the Medal of Honor in 1943, and shot down over Berlin on March 6, 1944. As Lowell Bennett, editor of *Pow Wow,* the camp's underground newspaper, noted—for many of its guests "life had been much more difficult *before* reaching . . . the house that flak built."

Bennett's story was even more fantastic than Morgan's. After Germany invaded Poland in September 1939, he left Montclair State Teachers College in New Jersey and went to Finland to fight the invading Russians. When Finland succumbed, he joined the French Foreign Legion in North Africa and later became an American Volunteer Ambulance Corps driver in France, where he was captured by the Germans. He escaped from a prison camp and wrote a book about the North African campaign. After that, he signed on as a war correspondent on the London staff of the International News Service. In December 1943, he and two other reporters were shot down while covering an RAF night raid on the German capital. Of the four reporters who flew with Bomber Command "to watch Berlin burn," only Edward R. Murrow returned. Parachuting into Berlin from his stricken bomber, Bennett again became a prisoner of the Nazis. His editors first heard from him when he filed a dispatch "from somewhere inside Nazi Germany" saying he had eluded his captors and was writing a book of his experiences in longhand. In May, his editors heard from him. He was "in the klink again," he said—charged with espionage and sentenced to solitary confinement for the duration of the war. Bennett escaped two more times before being sent to Stalag Luft I.

• • •

While Richard Hoffman and other liberated airmen celebrated V-E Day in France, the men of Stalag Luft I were still behind barbed wire, prisoners—not of the Germans—but of their own commanders. The Luftwaffe had left and was replaced by Colonel Zemke's security police, who imposed "a discipline at least equally that under the Germans," Bennett observed. Guards were posted at the gates, and men were warned that they would be court-martialed after the war if they were caught attempting to escape. Zemke had made arrangements to have his men flown out by the Eighth Air Force, but a Red Army commander, who had recently arrived at Barth, insisted that an agreement signed at Yalta by Churchill and Roosevelt prohibited Anglo-Americans from flying over Russian-held territory. "We are technically free, but I am worried," B-17 co-pilot Alan Newcomb wrote in his prison logbook, which he kept on scraps of toilet paper. "I get frequent dizzy spells, my heart seems to pound at an alarming rate, and I am filled with a vague, threatening fear of everything and everybody." Newcomb, who had recently graduated from Ohio Wesleyan University, felt he was about to go "crazy."

The chaos and terrifying uncertainty had begun on the afternoon of April 28, when the prisoners first learned that the Red Army was less than twenty-five miles away and driving furiously toward them. The Kommandant, Oberst von Warnstadt, called in Zemke, the son of German immigrants, and informed him that he had orders to evacuate the camp immediately and march the prisoners to an undisclosed location near Hamburg, 150 miles away. If he tried to do that, Zemke warned him, the prison's secretly trained commando forces would rush the guards and take over the stalag. Zemke persuaded the Kommandant that it would be in his best interest to turn the camp over to him and flee from the Russians with his staff.

The next morning, American Air Force personnel were manning the guard towers and Old Glory was flying from the compound flagpole. Later that day, Zemke sent out reconnaissance patrols to make contact with the Red Army. After locating the Russians, a small party, including Zemke, Bennett, and a translator, drove out to their headquarters. After a breakfast of champagne, vodka, and fried eggs, the Americans returned to the camp. On their way back they passed detachments of the Red Army advancing toward Berlin with terrible purpose. There were hay wagons loaded with crates, bundles, and drunken women, and beside them, marching in disorganized columns, were Siberian, Mongolian, and Ukrainian soldiers—red-faced and wild-looking from a brutal winter campaign. The troops were singing folk songs, drinking vodka straight from the bottle, and spitting curses at the shuttered windows of the German houses they passed. Occasionally a soldier would leave the line to chase a chicken in a farmyard and snap its neck when he caught it. When Zemke's party stopped to speak to a Russian lieutenant, a barking dog interrupted them. "The Russian nonchalantly shot it." Bennett could see trouble ahead.

The next day a drunken Cossack soldier rode into camp on a white farm horse. "Why are these men still behind wire?" he wanted to know. "Tear down the fences. Go home. You're free!" he shouted to the Americans in Zemke's compound, and shot his long-barreled pistol in the air for emphasis. When Zemke tried to quiet him, the sodden Russian put a gun to the colonel's head and cocked the hammer. At that point, "the camp went stark raving mad," said one prisoner. Men that had begun to feel that they were prisoners again under Zemke's iron rule tore down the fences and hundreds of them fled, either to join the Russians and freed slave laborers in looting and burning the town of Barth, or to the west, to hook up with the Allied armies.

The following morning almost two dozen German women were found strangled or shot in the vicinity of the camp. Every morning after that, terrified women and children from Barth came out to the American camp and begged to be let in, some young women offering their bodies in exchange for sanctuary. The supplicants stayed into the night, and slept in fields underneath the high watchtowers for safety. "This is something we never expected to see," said airman Forrest Howell, "the Germans seeking protection with us."

Fearing anarchy, Zemke issued an order that only his men were permitted to enter and leave the camp, but he was unable to keep out armed and inebriated Red Army soldiers, or control their behavior in or outside the camp. "Hundreds of Jerries have been shot or have committed suicide," wrote Newcomb. "Three women shot themselves about a hundred yards from my barracks and we sent out a detail to bury them. The Mayor of Barth killed himself . . . and rape cases from six to sixty are brought to our doctors by the Jerries." Desperate German fathers invited Americans into their homes to sleep with their daughters in order to keep the Russians away. One American airman saw a dozen or more Russian soldiers, in their high black boots, lined up outside a cottage waiting for their turn to violate a German girl.

The next day a Russian colonel drove a herd of confiscated cattle into the American camp and killed them with a machine gun. Prisoners who had been butchers in peacetime cut up the beef, and that night the men of

Zemke's stalag had steak and schnapps for dinner. Later, drunken Americans stole horses and carriages, rigged them like Roman chariots, and raced through the narrow streets of the town, firing revolvers in the air and yelling "Tovarich" to startled Russians. "But most of us obeyed Zemke's orders and stayed in the camp," recalled bombardier Oscar G. Richard III, a sweet-natured kid from Sunshine, Louisiana. "I believe that Colonel Zemke was the main reason we eventually got out of Barth without losing many men."

When the main body of the Russian force arrived, the officers cooperated with Zemke in keeping the men in camp. They clamped a curfew on the town and sent the Americans they found in Barth, some of them in the beds of fräuleins, back to the American stalag, where the barbed wire fence had been repaired.

Zemke's commandos found a small concentration camp near Barth and several of the camp doctors went out to treat the liberated inmates—Jews and political prisoners who had been slave laborers in a local aircraft factory. Lowell Bennett accompanied them. The SS guards had fled weeks before, leaving the already enfeebled prisoners to starve. Nearly 300 had already succumbed. Allied doctors commandeered burial parties from among the people of Barth. "The Germans who dug mass graves for the dead were initially uncertain whether the trenches were for themselves or the prisoners," Bennett wrote later.

Walking away from the camp, Gabby Gabreski noticed something strange. Bodies were hanging from the fences at the far end of the main compound. In a final act of chilling barbarity, the fleeing SS had locked the gates and, unknown to the prisoners, had charged the electric fence. Dead victims—their eyes frozen open in looks of astonishment—were clasping the wire. "This validated the war for me as no propaganda campaign ever could have," said Gabreski.

Nerves were stretched dangerously tight in Zemke's stalag. The swing music that blared over the camp loudspeakers was making the men desperately homesick, and Alan Newcomb wasn't the only one feeling that he was about to go insane. In despair, more than 300 impatient men escaped on German bicycles and horses and in stolen cars and carriages. Lowell Bennett and three of his friends joined the exodus. They confiscated a tiny two-cylinder car from the camp motor pool, loaded it with Red Cross parcels, and glued a paper to the windshield that said, in Russian: "Press—Pass Freely." They were off on a 400-mile journey to the American lines.

"Complete indescribable chaos existed everywhere," Bennett wrote in his published account of the trip. Bennett had seen the remains of an army's defeat in France in 1940, but "this was a thousand times worse"— mile after mile of burned-out tanks, planes, and artillery pieces and road- side ditches piled high with the bloated corpses of Wehrmacht soldiers. Standing forlorn by the road were parentless children with their names pinned to their sweaters. This was liberated, lawless Germany. Could it ever be put back together again, Bennett wondered?

After crossing into the American zone, Bennett's group caught a plane to Paris, where they celebrated V-E Day in a hotel in the center of the city.

The men in Zemke's stalag spent V-E Day listening to confiscated German radios for news about their rescue. On May 12, they finally received word that a fleet of Flying Fortresses would be landing at the local airstrip that af- ternoon. In secret negotiations at the Elbe River, the Russians had agreed to an airlift on the condition that the Americans surrender a Nazi prisoner the Russians wanted very badly. Former Red Army commander Andrei Vlasov had been captured by the Germans and had formed, with their help, an army of Russian prisoners of war to liberate the motherland from Stalinism. Now he would be returned to the country he had betrayed.

Late that afternoon, a roar went up from Zemke's stalag. Overhead was a wing of silver bombers, circling in the sky. The time was 2:30 P.M. At that moment Col. Andrei Vlasov was being handed over to the Russians. This was the prearranged signal for the bombers to land.

By Zemke's orders, the British went first, since they had been in captiv- ity longer. The American airmen left the next morning, marching out of camp in a long column—6,250 freedom-starved men. The Fortresses roared in one minute apart and left their propellers spinning. Twenty to thirty men were packed into each plane. No one had a parachute, and no one cared.

Heading toward Le Havre, the bombers descended to 500 feet to give the airmen a close-up view of some of the cities they had wrecked. "I grabbed a spot near one of the waist windows so I could see Germany once more from the air," recalled Oscar Richard. Passing over the corpse of a German city, Richard remarked to the men sitting next to him, "That could be us. That could be America. Nobody said we had to win this war."

The Forts landed near Rouen, where the men boarded a train for Camp Lucky Strike. From there, Richard "hitchhiked" a ride back to England with an aircrew from his bomb group, the 384th. They had flown to France to search for some of their squadron mates, and were happy to meet up with one of their unit's "pioneer" fliers. When they landed at Grafton Un- derwood, the field from which the Eighth Air Force had begun the Ameri-

can air war, Oscar Richard felt like a stranger. "The only personnel I knew
were a few of the ground officers. . . . And the airmen I saw looked a lot
younger than the men I had flown with." The briefing room still had a huge
map of Western Europe hanging from the wall and the equipment room
was stacked high with combat gear, but the smell of fear and cigarette
smoke was gone.

That night Lieutenant Richard walked to his Nissen hut and slipped into
his bunk. As he lay there his thoughts went back to the day he first arrived
in England, in the winter of 1943, when the Eighth Air Force was taking a
pounding from the Luftwaffe and the arithmetic of survival was running
hard against the bomber crews. Then, through an open window, he
thought he heard the wheezing and coughing of Wright Cyclone engines
and the shouts of crew chiefs preparing the "big-ass birds" for the next
day's run. A familiar fear ran through his body . . . and then he was asleep.

They left in a hurry, sometimes before people who had grown fond of them
had a chance to say good-bye. Nine-year-old Frank Patton lived near an
airfield at Eye, home of the 490th Bomb Group. His mother did the men's
laundry and he ferried it back and forth to them on his bicycle. They rewarded him with candy bars and coffee and soon he was bringing them
baskets of fresh farmer's eggs. The ground crews got to like him and let him
hang out in their tents by the hardstands. They taught him how to smoke
cigars and to swear with proper vehemence.

On a drizzly day in August, after the fighting had stopped, Frank Patton
cycled to the base and found the gates unguarded. The huts were empty
and the planes were gone. "It was the saddest day of my life," he said fifty
years later.

At Horsham St. Faith, there was a proper farewell. A hundred or so
local folk, dressed in their Sunday finest, gathered on the field and waved
farewell to a Liberator of the 458th Bomb Group as it taxied down the runway. Alice Bingham was in her nightgown when she took a photograph of
one of the last of the group's Liberators flying directly over her home on
Pinewood Close. Looking up at it, she remembered how one of these long-
winged beauties had once crashed through her garden and flattened a
neighbor's cottage. "In those days, we had coal fires and the undercarriage
wheels used to cut through the smoke as they flew low over our roofs."

"I still remember the Yanks," recalled a Suffolk woman, "almost more
than I remember the war itself."

Leaving was easy because at the end of the journey was home. But men
could not forget friends who were left behind. Before leaving England, Eu-

gene "Wing Ding" Carson visited the American cemetery at Madingley, on a hill outside Cambridge. He went to say good-bye to his crewmate Mike Chaklos, who was killed on a mission in early 1944. "As I walked among the markers I silently cried my heart out," Carson recalled.

Decades later, when the pull of the past proved too strong to resist, Carson wrote his own story of the war. He closed it with a poem from the hand of an anonymous author.

> *Oh do not let the Dead March play*
> *O'er these at Madingley do stay*
> *For they were young and old-style gay,*
> *Play their music of the day;*
> *Tunes of Dorsey, songs of Bing,*
> *Let them hear Glenn Miller's swing*
> *Then too the crosses well may sway*
> *With those at Madingley do stay.*

Epilogue

The Eighth Air Force began its great movement back to the United States on May 19, 1945. The bomber boys flew their own planes; the ground echelons and fighter pilots went by sea. Those who made the ocean crossing were first taken on Liberty trucks to the local English train station, where many of the men were met by their new brides. "War is very screwy," wrote a reporter from *Stars and Stripes*. "The husbands now go home and sweat out their English wives." For over seven months, there was not enough shipping for the 45,000 or so British women who had married American servicemen. They had to wait until U.S. soldiers and sailors from all over the globe were brought home.

Most of the war brides were either pregnant or with one or two small children when they finally received word in late December that immigration restrictions had been waived for them and ships were available to bring them to their new homes and husbands. "Operation Diaper Run," as the press dubbed it, was launched from Southampton harbor on January 26, 1946. On board the SS *Argentina* were 452 war brides, 173 small children, and one war bridegroom. His wife, a Women's Air Corps volunteer in England, had already been sent back to New York. "As we sailed from Southampton . . . we ran into a British troopship of . . . returning souls who booed us out of sight," recalled one of the departing brides.

At New York City and Newport News, Virginia, the two entry ports, it was not always a joyous reunion. Some wives had known their husbands for only a few weeks and had forgotten what they looked like. One London woman spotted a man dressed like a pimp walking up the gangplank. "Oh God," she thought, "hope mine doesn't look like that." Dozens of husbands had changed their minds and didn't show up; others wished they hadn't. "Some [women] were caught sleeping with the sailors while aboard ship," war bride Ann Holmes related. "When their husbands met them in New York, [they] were given the opportunity to refuse these women. And many of them did. The women were sent back." Countless wives arrived in port to learn that their husbands, who had been sent to the Pacific for "a double dose of war," had not yet returned.

After leaving England, the Eighth Air Force was redeployed to recently conquered Okinawa under Jimmy Doolittle, who had led the first American air raid on Japan in 1942. Carl Spaatz was given command of the U.S. Strategic Air Forces in the Pacific, with headquarters on Guam. On August 6, after receiving authority from Washington, Spaatz ordered his former Eighth Air Force pilot Paul Tibbets to drop a uranium bomb on Hiroshima. Three days later, a more powerful plutonium bomb obliterated over half the city of Nagasaki. Spaatz then told Doolittle that if he wanted to get his Eighth Air Force in combat with the Japanese he had better organize an operation for the next day, for the war would soon be over. Doolittle had been assigned 720 B-29s and many of them were war-ready, but he stood them down. "If the war's over," he told Spaatz, "I will not risk one airplane nor a single bomber crew member just to be able to say the 8th Air Force had operated against the Japanese in the Pacific." After Europe, his boys had nothing to prove.

Three weeks later, Carl Spaatz was on the deck of the battleship *Missouri* for the Japanese surrender, making him the only person to witness all three major Axis capitulations. After the war, he succeeded the gravely ill Hap Arnold as commanding general of the U.S. Army Air Forces. He was at the helm on September 17, 1947, when the Air Force finally won its release from the Army and became an independent branch of the American military. Fittingly, Carl Spaatz became the first chief of staff. From across the grave, Billy Mitchell must have smiled.

Robert "Rosie" Rosenthal was in B-29 training in Florida when the Japanese surrendered. On returning from England, he had gone straight to Washington, right to Arnold's office, and lobbied for a combat command in the Pacific. Gen. Orvil Anderson had tried to change his mind—"you've had enough, let others go"—but Rosenthal had been adamant. With the war over, he was still not through.

Back home in Brooklyn, working for his old Manhattan law firm, he found himself in an unsettled state. "Throughout my war service, I had been tightly disciplined. I put a brake on my emotions and probably held too much inside me. Now I began to unravel. I couldn't concentrate, couldn't focus on my work. We were working on some important law cases but the work seemed humdrum compared to what I had just been through."

Rosenthal had been closely following the news of the Nuremberg war crimes tribunal, which had convened in November 1945, and felt he ought to be there. On trial were the monsters he had gone to war to destroy. "When I heard that the Army was searching for prosecutors for the smaller trials that were to follow the showcase trials I took the train to Washington and got a position on the staff." On the ship that took him back to Europe in July 1946 he met Phillis Heller, a Navy lawyer who would also be joining the American legal staff in Nuremberg. He and the radiant girl with the oddly spelled first name fell in love instantly and were engaged ten days later. "We wanted to get married right away but Phillis told me she had promised to ask her father's permission," Rosenthal recalled. "I thought that was great. I was marrying an old-fashioned girl. I wrote her father a long letter and he wrote back saying, 'Robert, you two young people are making a big mistake. Come home at once.' I told Phillis, 'I guess that's it.' And she said, 'What are you talking about? I said I had to *ask* his permission. We did. Now we can get married.'

"I knew then I was in trouble—I was taking a lawyer for my wife."

On September 14, 1946, the couple exchanged vows in Nuremberg, the city the U.S. Army had pronounced "91 percent dead." They lived in a bomb-damaged, miserably heated flat not far from the Palace of Justice. Although they were too busy to mingle with their neighbors, the German people they did meet were unwilling to talk about the bombing. "People walked silently through the ruins, not even turning to look at them," Rosie observed later. "It was as if these enormous pyramids of rubble didn't exist and they were still living in the lovely prewar city.

"The bombing had ruined the people as well as the city. They were in desperate straits that winter. Women's clothes were unkempt, old men were unshaven, and there were hardly any young people to be seen. Families didn't have enough food and there was no economy, only a thriving black market.

"One evening Phillis and I were walking alone by the river and we sensed that someone was following us. When we stopped, he stopped. Phillis was smoking a cigarette and when she tossed it in the gutter, this man rushed up, picked it up, and disappeared into the shadows. Cigarettes, even butts, were valuable items on the black market and we assumed he planned to trade it. That's what the people of the Thousand Year Reich had been reduced to.

"You had to feel sorry for them, yet I refused to believe that the German people were not responsible for Hitler, especially here in Nuremberg, the city where the Nazis held their Roman-like rallies and where adoring women had thrown flowers on Hitler's motorcade.

"There was no need for a campaign of retribution against these ordinary people who had supported Hitler. They had suffered enough. Let them live with what they had done, and what had been done to them. That would be punishment enough. But the Nazi leaders and their criminal henchmen had to be treated differently."

The leading Nazis—Göring, Speer, Dönitz, and others—were still being tried that September, but the Rosenthals began preparing cases against additional war criminals—Wehrmacht officers, Nazi functionaries, and German industrialists who had worked closely with the party. These cases were to be brought before U.S. military tribunals, also held at Nuremberg, beginning in November 1946. Phillis Rosenthal investigated I. G. Farben, the Nazi-controlled chemical conglomerate that had used concentration camp labor. Her husband's job was to investigate the racial crimes committed by those who served under Göring, Jodl, and Keitel. "I interrogated all three of them. Göring was arrogant and unrepentant but the army generals talked to me in a grandfatherly way, claiming, with quiet indignation, that they had nothing to do with the Nazi atrocities. Keitel was especially insistent that he had adhered to the German military's code of honor. They lied, of course.

"Seeing these strutting conquerors after they were sentenced—powerless, pathetic, and preparing for the hangman—was the closure I needed. Justice had overtaken evil. My war was over."

Acknowledgments

L ooking back, I realize that this book began the moment I discovered my father's World War II Army Air Forces flying jacket in my grandparents' attic. At the time, I was a small boy visiting my grandparents in the row house where my mother and her sister Helen, new brides of boys called to service, spent the war years. A year later, my mother was wearing that jacket, hanging up the family wash in the backyard, when she told me we would be going that evening to the Strand Theater to see *The Glenn Miller Story*, starring Jimmy Stewart, a real-life Eighth Air Force hero, as I learned from my father after the show. The jacket finally became mine after I saw Gregory Peck in *Twelve O'Clock High*, the finest movie ever made on the Eighth Air Force. It is a wonder that it took me so long to write this book about one of the outstanding fighting outfits in the history of arms.

I started work on the story before I met Robert "Rosie" Rosenthal, but from that point forward he was its inspiring force. He was unfailingly generous with his time and put me in touch with other veterans of his Bombardment Group, the Bloody Hundredth. I met Rosie in Savannah, Georgia, at the Mighty Eighth Air Force Heritage Museum, and its passionately committed staff soon made the museum the mother ship of this effort. Most helpful was the Director of Oral History, Dr. Vivian Rogers-Price, who made available her impressive collection of interviews with Eighth

Air Force veterans and located more photographs in the museum's fabulous collection than I could ever hope to use. The museum's former head, C. J. Roberts, and its present director, Dr. Walter E. Brown, went out of their way to make my regular visits to Savannah both productive and enjoyable.

Whenever I ran into problems, Eighth Air Force veterans, among them Gale Cleven, Sherman Small, Lou Loevsky, Hank Plume, Craig Harris, and the late Paul Slawter, made time to answer my questions. And there was always Rosie.

In the five years it took to research and write this story I interviewed over 250 veterans of the Eighth Air Force. They were modest to a man, never calling attention to themselves, insisting that the only heroes were the men who didn't make it back. As they leave us, we can only hope we will see their like again.

The historian's work would be impossible without dedicated research librarians. At every repository I visited I had the good fortune to run into gracious people like Stan Spurgeon, who gave a full week of his time guiding me through the extraordinary oral history collection at the American Airpower Heritage Museum in Midland, Texas. Space prevents me from giving the names of the dozens of research librarians who provided expert assistance, but I have listed their institutions in the bibliography.

I am especially indebted to the children of departed Eighth Air Force veterans for making available to me their fathers' letters and diaries. Special thanks to Pat Caruso and Suzi Tiernan, the daughters of airmen Francis Gerald and Paul Slawter.

Lafayette College could not have been more helpful. Karen Haduck, the director of Skillman Library's interlibrary loan service, kept finding old documents and books I thought were unobtainable. At one time or another, almost the entire research staff of Skillman Library—and especially Terese Heidenwolf—had a part in this effort. By anticipating my every need, the library's director, Neil McElroy, made working at Skillman the equivalent of working at a major research repository.

Lafayette College and the Mellon Foundation provided funding that allowed me to assemble an extraordinary team of student researchers led by Alix Kenney, Marisa Floriani, and Emily Goldberg and assisted by Jessica Cygler, Miriam Habeeb, and Margarita Karasoulas. Alix was particularly helpful at the Library of Congress and the National Archives, and she located many of the photographs in this book. The indispensable Kathy Anckaitis allowed me to keep my eye on the ball by taking on work that would have overwhelmed me.

Two distinguished military historians, Williamson Murray and Conrad Crane, and the deeply knowledgeable historian of the 100th Bomb Group's Photo Archives, Michael P. Faley, read a draft of the manuscript and offered discerning criticism, saving me from embarrassing errors and omissions. Donald Meyerson, a friend of thirty-five years and a decorated combat veteran, read the book as it was being made and helped shape it in conversations that went on continuously, often late into the night. Another close friend, James Tiernan, read parts of the manuscript and helped immensely with research in the United Kingdom at the Imperial War Museum, the Mass-Observation Archive, and museums at old Eighth Air Force bases run by volunteer enthusiasts. Special thanks to Ron Batley of the 100th Bomb Group Memorial Museum at Thorpe Abbotts for hosting me in East Anglia and arranging interviews with villagers who knew the American bomber boys during the war. Travel assistance provided by the National D-Day Museum in New Orleans helped me conduct research in Germany and four other countries in continental Europe. Susan Wedlake of the American Embassy's Cultural Affairs Office in London arranged for me to give the book a test run in lectures at, among other places, Oxford and Cambridge Universities. And I made my first visit to old Eighth Air Force bases while I was in residence at All Souls College, Oxford.

Writing may be the loneliest occupation there is, but two friends, Bob Bender, my editor, and Gina Maccoby, my agent, were always there with support and astute advice. I have published four books with Bob and his superb assistant, Johanna Li, and six with Gina, and they were never more helpful than with this one. Gypsy da Silva and Fred Chase were once again my copyeditors—and keen-eyed critics. Intern Dahlia Adler was their very able assistant. Then there is my mother, Frances Miller, who has been the most inspiring and encouraging person in my life, and who urged me to write this book.

Every book I write should be dedicated to Rose. As more than a few of my friends have said: no Rose, no books. But this one is for our six grandchildren—the gang at the Black Cat Bar—the gathering place in our home named by my granddaughter Alyssa and dedicated to the memory of my father, Donald L. Miller.

Notes

List of Abbreviations

AAF–*The Army Air Forces in World War II*
AHM–Airpower Heritage Museum, Midland, Texas
AFHRA–Air Force Historical Research Agency, Maxwell Air Force Base, Alabama
Arnold MSS–Henry H. Arnold Papers, Library of Congress
EC–Eisenhower Center, New Orleans, Louisiana
Major War Criminals–*Trial of Major War Criminals Before the International Military Tribunal*
ME–Mighty Eighth Air Force Heritage Museum, Savannah, Georgia
M-O–Mass-Observation Archive, University of Sussex, UK
NA–National Archives, College Park, Maryland
Nazi Conspiracy–Office of the United States Chief of Counsel for Prosecution of
  Axis Criminality, Nazi Conspiracy and Aggression
NYT–*New York Times*
NA-UK–The National Archives, Kew, UK, formerly called the Public Records Office
S&S–*Stars and Stripes*
SIA–Archives of the Swiss Internees Association, Jackson, New Jersey
Spaatz MSS–Carl Spaatz Papers, Library of Congress
Target–*Target: Germany: The Army Air Forces' Official Story of the VIII Bomber Command's
  First Year over Europe*
Trials of War Criminals–*Trials of War Criminals Before the Nuremberg Military Tribunals*
USMHI–U.S. Military History Institute, Carlisle Barracks, Pennsylvania
USSBS–United States Strategic Bombing Survey

Prologue: The Bloody Hundredth

3   *"How many"*: Sam Halpert, *A Real Good War* (London: Cassell, 1997), 44.

4   *"No one"*: John Keegan, "We Wanted Beady-Eyed Guys Just Absolutely Holding the Course," *Smithsonian Magazine* 14, no. 5 (1993): 37–38.

4   *"we turned"*: Bernard R. Jacobs, unpublished memoir, Eisenhower Center, New Orleans, LA [hereafter EC].

5   *"Perhaps at no time"*: Starr Smith, *Jimmy Stewart: Bomber Pilot* (St. Paul: Zenith, 2005), 67.

5   *"We have no"*: Quoted in Max Hastings, *Bomber Command* (1979; repr., NY: Simon & Schuster, 1989), 116.

7   *In October 1943—Seventy-seven percent:* James S. Nanney, *Army Air Forces Medical Services in World War II* (Washington, DC: Air Force History and Museums Program, 1998), 20; Malcolm Grow, in Albert E. Cowdrey, *Fighting for Life: American Military Medicine in World War II* (NY: Free Press, 1994), 233; for the medical services of the Army Air Forces, see Wesley Frank Craven and James Lea Cate, eds., *The Army Air Forces in World War II,* vol. 7 (Chicago: University of Chicago Press), chap. 13, [hereafter *AAF*].

7   *"Anyone who flies"– "These were not"*: Saul Levitt, "The Squadron Leader," *Yank,* November 7, 1943, 6–7.

7   *"I can out-drink"*: Author interview with Gale W. Cleven, April 2, 2003.

8   *"House of Lords"*: Levitt, "Squadron," 6.

8   *"I never liked it"*: Cleven interview, April 2, 2003.

8   *"he had a heart"*: Author interview with James P. Thayer, March 22, 2003.

8   *"living through"– "His words"*: Beirne Lay, Jr., "I Saw Regensburg Destroyed," *Saturday Evening Post,* November 6, 1943, 9–11, 85–88.

9   *"I didn't get it"– "So I"*: Author interview with Gale W. Cleven, March 28, 2003.

9   *"electrified the base"*: Harry H. Crosby, *A Wing and a Prayer* (NY: HarperCollins, 1993), 148.

9   *"I carried"*: Quoted in Frank D. Murphy, *Luck of the Draw: Reflections on the Air War in Europe* (Trumbull, CT: FNP Military Division, 2001), 124.

9   *"the man who"*: Cleven interview, April 2, 2003.

9   *"watched the two"– "For some reason"*: Crosby, *Wing,* 148, 46.

9   *"Their fear"*: Cleven interview, April 2, 2003.

10   *"and faster"– "In my pitiful"*: Author interview with Gale W. Cleven, March 8, 2003; Gale Cleven diary, in the possession of its author.

10   *"None of them"– "missing men"*: Jack W. Sheridan, *They Never Had It So Good: A Personal, Unofficial History of the 350th Bombardment Squadron (H) 100th Bombardment Group (H) USAAF, 1942–1945* (San Francisco: Strik-Rath, 1946), 94–95; Crosby, *Wing,* 163.

10   *"How did"– "I want to pitch"*: John Francis Callahan, ed., *Contrails, My War Record: A History of World War Two as Recorded at U.S. Army Air Force Station #139, Thorpe Abbotts, near Diss, county of Norfolk, England* (NY: J. F. Callahan, 1947), 66; Author interview with Gale W. Cleven, March 8, 2003.

10   *"John, I am"*: Crosby, *Wing,* 167.

10   *"The target"– "Built up section"*: "Munster, October 10, 1943," 519.332, Air Force

Historical Research Agency, Maxwell Air Force Base, Alabama [hereafter AFHRA]; author interview with Gen. Thomas Jeffrey, March 27, 2003; Field Order Number 113, 3rd Bomb Group Division, National Archives, College Park, Maryland [hereafter NA]

11 *"we were going"*: Contrails, 66.

11 *"Don't get the notion"*: Cleven interview, April 2, 2003.

11 *"I felt I was there"*: Quoted in Ian L. Hawkins, *The Munster Raid: Before and After* (Trumbull, CT: FNP Military Division, 1999), 79–80.

12 *"It was a Sunday"*: Quoted in ibid., 80.

12 *"I'd been raised"–"this [is] war"–"I made up"*: All quotes in ibid., 74–75.

12 *"We were just too tired"*: Quoted in ibid., 78.

12 *"Did all"–"Egan's gone"*: Crosby, *Wing,* 168.

13 *"When I arrived"–"No one came"*: Author interviews with Robert Rosenthal, March 21, 2002; March 29, 2003.

13 *"I had read"*: Rosenthal interview, March 29, 2003.

14 *"that was a lot"*: Author interview with Robert Rosenthal, March 22, 2003.

14 *"It was near"*: Rosenthal interview, March 29, 2003; "The Bombardment Group," GP-100-HI, May 1945, 14, AFHRA.

14 *"The doors"*: Denton Scott, "A Yank Reporter Takes a Flight to Lorient," *Yank,* March 14, 1943, 14.

15 *"We felt pretty easy"*: Douglas I. Gordon-Forbes, "The Battle That Beat the Luftwaffe," in Carl Spaatz Papers, Library of Congress [hereafter Spaatz MSS].

15 *"heading back"–"Jesus Christ"*: Contrails, 66–67.

15 *"a horrendous"*: Murphy, *Luck,* 167.

15 *"[Our bombardier came up]"–"Go ahead Brady"–"We prattled"–"I [was] very dead"*: Contrails, 67–68.

16 *"the single most vicious"*: Jeffrey interview, March 27, 2003.

16 *"the greatest concentration"–"Red balls"*: Gordon-Forbes, "Battle," Spaatz MSS.

17 *"The German fighters"*: Quoted in Hawkins, *Munster,* 100; author interview with Frank Murphy, January 23, 2002.

17 *"I think this attack"*: Rosenthal interview, March 29, 2003.

17 *"We go four"*: Bert Stiles, *Serenade to the Big Bird* (Atglen, PA: Schiffer, 2001), 104.

17 *"Almost as soon"–"a hundred miles"*: Murphy interview.

18 *"Suddenly, it"*: Murphy, *Luck,* 168–69.

18 *"I was at my gun"*: Gordon-Forbes, "Battle," Spaatz MSS.

18 *"a fantastic panorama"*: Quoted in Hawkins, *Munster,* 134.

18 *"It was like flying"*: Quoted in ibid., 124–25.

18 *"What happens"*: Halpert, *Real Good War,* 91, 105.

18 *"In that split second"*: Gordon-Forbes, "Battle," Spaatz MSS.

19 *"From our position"–"burning fiercely"*: Quoted in Hawkins, *Munster,* 134–35.

19 *"The earth shook"*: Quoted in ibid., 136.

19 *"It was an inferno"*: Quoted in ibid., 138.

19 *"We had a big rocket hole"–"In a situation"*: Author interview with Robert Rosenthal, March 20, 2002.

20 *"Directly ahead"*: Gordon-Forbes, "Battle," Spaatz MSS.

20 *Zemke's 56th:* "Tactical Commanders Report, October 10, 1943, 65th Fighter Wing," 519.332, AFHRA.

20 *"Are they all"–"I didn't feel relieved":* Rosenthal interview, March 29, 2003.

21 *Münster losses:* "Munster Losses," Spaatz MSS; Roger A. Freeman, *The Mighty Eighth: A History of the Units, Men and Machines of the US 8th Air Force* (1970; repr., NY: Cassell, 2000), 77; John R. Nilsson, *The Story of the Century* (Beverly Hills: John R. Nilsson, 1946), 58; Hawkins, *Munster,* 181–82.

22 *"The Bloody Hundredth":* Crosby, *Wing,* 171; Nilsson, *Century,* 27, 58.

22 *"They were fairly":* Author interview with Frank Murphy, November 30, 2005.

23 *"My God":* Murphy, *Luck,* 180.

23 *"about a million fleas":* Author interview with Gale W. Cleven, April 12, 2003.

23 *"What the hell"–"Well, that's":* Ibid., April 3, 2003.

24 *"It was good":* Ibid., April 12, 2003.

24 *"When we got":* Quoted in Gerald Astor, *The Mighty Eighth: The Air War in Europe as Told by the Men Who Fought It* (NY: Dell, 1997), 36.

Chapter 1: The Bomber Mafia

25 *"It would have":* Paul W. Tibbets, *Return of the Enola Gay* (Columbus, OH: Mid Coast Marketing, 1998), 82.

26 *"Where are the American bombers?"–"Now they will":* Author interview with Paul W. Tibbets, January 28, 2002.

27 *"The cameramen":* Spaatz, Command Diary, July 11, 1942, Spaatz MSS.

27 *"[our] theory":* Eaker to Arnold, August 8, 1942, Henry H. Arnold Papers, Library of Congress [hereafter Arnold MSS].

28 *"Laddie, ye'll":* Quoted in William R. Laidlaw, "Yankee Doodle Flies to War," *Air Power History,* Winter 1989, 11.

28 *"evidently had":* Ira C. Eaker, "General Eaker Leads First U.S. Bomber Raid," *Life,* September 14, 1942, 37–38.

28 *"Everyone was yelling"–"By God":* Laidlaw, "Yankee Doodle," 13.

29 *"One swallow":* Quoted in James Parton, *"Air Force Spoken Here": General Ira Eaker and the Command of the Air* (Bethesda, MD: Adler & Adler, 1986), 175.

29 *"exceptionally good":* Eaker, "General Eaker," 380.

29 *"We ruined Rouen":* Typed copy of press clipping, Spaatz MSS.

29 *"like a happy"–"Saturday after":* Laidlaw, "Yankee Doodle," 13.

29 *"It was a cakewalk":* Quoted in Astor, *Eighth,* 37.

30 *"The most perfect":* Laidlaw, "Yankee Doodle," 13.

30 *"In a strategic":* Ibid., 14.

30 *"Of all branches":* John Steinbeck, *Bombs Away: The Story of a Bomber Team* (NY: Paragon House, 1942), 19.

31 *"They had":* Budd J. Peaslee, *Heritage of Valor: The Eighth Air Force in World War II* (Philadelphia: J. B. Lippincott, 1964), 269.

31 *"The attack on Rouen":* Arnold press release, August 18, 2003, Spaatz MSS.

31 *"The first bomb mission":* Peaslee, *Heritage,* 86.

31 *"Strategic bombing":* U.S. Army Air Forces, *Target: Germany: The Army Air Forces'*

Official Story of the VIII Bomber Command's First Year over Europe (NY: Simon & Schuster, 1943), 19 [hereafter *Target*].

32 *"We could cross":* William Mitchell, *Memoir of World War I: From Start to Finish of Our Greatest War* (NY: Random House, 1960), 59.

32 *"the art of war":* Ibid., 10.

32 *"the airplane":* Russell F. Weigley, *The American Way of War: A History of United States Military Strategy and Policy* (NY: Macmillan, 1973), 225.

32 *"The air offensive":* Henry H. Arnold, *Global Mission* (London: Hutchinson, 1951), 69.

33 *Arnold:* Ira C. Eaker, "Hap Arnold: The Anatomy of Leadership," *Air Force Magazine* 60 (September 1977): 83.

33 *"I was sure":* Isaac D. Levine, *Mitchell, Pioneer of Air Power* (NY: Duell, Sloan & Pearce, 1943), 142; quoted in Mark Clodfelter, "Molding," in Phillip S. Meilinger, ed., *The Paths of Heaven: The Evolution of Airpower Theory* (Maxwell Air Force Base, AL: Air University Press, 1997), 87.

34 *"violent to a":* Giulio Douhet, "Probable Aspects of Future War," a 1928 monograph published in USAF Warriors Studies edition of Giulio Douhet, *The Command of the Air,* trans. Dino Farrari (Washington, DC: Office of Air Force History, 1983), 197; This volume of *The Command of the Air* consists of five separate works written by Douhet, including the original 1921 edition of *The Command of the Air* and the 1928 monograph "Probable Aspects of Future War."

34 *"It is not enough":* Douhet, *Command,* 34. For a perceptive critique of Douhet's ideas, see Bernard Brodie, *Strategy in the Missile Air* (Princeton: Princeton University Press, 1959), chap. 3; and Brodie, "The Heritage of Douhet," *Air University Quarterly Review* 6 (1953): 64–69, 120–26. For Mitchell's ideas on hitting vital centers, see Mitchell, *Winged Defense: The Development and Possibilities of Modern Air Power—Economic and Military* (NY: Putnam, 1925), 214; and Mitchell, *Skyways: A Book on Modern Aeronautics* (Philadelphia: J. B. Lippincott, 1930), 253.

34 *"the entire nation":* Quoted in Alfred F. Hurley, *Billy Mitchell: Crusader for Air Power* (NY: Franklin Watts, 1964), 43; Phillip S. Meilinger, "Giulio Douhet and the Origins of Airpower Theory," in Meilinger, *Paths,* 33.

34 *"War is no longer":* Douhet, "Probable Aspects," in *Command,* 195–96.

34 *"The limitations":* Ibid., 181, 196.

34 *"One senses":* Brodie, "Heritage," 125.

35 *civilians were singled out:* Mitchell, *Skyways,* 63; Alan Stephens, "The True Believers: Air Power Between the Wars," in Alan Stephens, ed., *The War in the Air, 1914–1994* (Maxwell Air Force Base, AL: Air University Press, 2001), 40.

35 *"the decisive blows":* Douhet, *Command,* 61.

35 *"a few gas bombs":* Mitchell, *Skyways,* 63, 262–63; Mitchell, *Winged Defense,* 16. For provocative discussions of Mitchell's ideas, see Michael Sherry, *The Rise of American Air Power: The Creation of Armageddon* (New Haven: Yale University Press, 1987), chap. 2; and Robert Frank Futrell, *Ideas, Concepts, Doctrine: Basic Thinking in the United States Air Force, 1907–1960,* vol. 1 (Maxwell Air Force Base, AL: Air University Press, 1989), 21–22.

35 *"the armored knights":* Quoted in Hurley, *Mitchell,* 93; see also "General

Mitchell's Daring Speech," *Aviation* 29 (October 29, 1924): 1160; Mitchell, *Winged Defense,* 16; William Mitchell, "Notes on the Multi-Motored Bombardment Group Day and Night," AFHRA.

35   *"Air power has brought":* Mitchell, *Winged Defense,* vii.

35   *"merciless pounding":* Douhet, *Command,* 58, 22, 61.

36   *"The history":* George F. Eliot, *Bombs Bursting in Air: The Influence of Air Power on International Relations* (NY: Reynal & Hitchcock, 1939), 11–13.

36   *"drop their eggs":* Quoted in Lee Kennett, *A History of Strategic Bombing* (NY: Scribner, 1982), 33.

36   *"Napoleon of the Air":* Quoted in Elihu Rose, "The Court-Martial of Billy Mitchell," *MHQ* 8, no. 3 (Spring 1996): 20.

36   *"can hit a town":* Quoted in Kennett, *Strategic,* 49.

36   *"moral blockade":* Thomas H. Greer, *The Development of Air Doctrine in the Army Air Arm, 1917–1941* (Maxwell Air Force Base, AL: Air University Press, 1955), 15.

36   *"has as its objective":* Quoted in Hurley, *Mitchell,* 37.

37   *"Mitchell's stay":* DeWitt S. Copp, *A Few Great Captains* (Garden City: Doubleday, 1980), 39.

37   *"criminal negligence": New York Times,* September 2, 4, 1925 [hereafter *NYT*].

37   *"He wouldn't rest":* Arnold, *Global,* 117.

37   *"Like all zealots":* James H. "Jimmy" Doolittle, with Carroll V. Glines, *I Could Never Be So Lucky Again* (NY: Bantam, 1992), 104.

38   *"battle of ideas":* Arnold, *Global,* 82.

38   *Bomber Mafia:* Peter R. Faber, "Interwar US Army Aviation and the Air School Tactical School: Incubators of American Airpower," in *Paths,* 216; Clodfelter, "Molding," in *Paths,* 107.

38   *" 'Mitchellism' ": AAF,* vol. 1, 28. For a good biography of Arnold, see Dik Alan Daso, *Hap Arnold and the Evolution of American Airpower* (Washington, DC: Smithsonian Institution Press, 2000).

38   *Air Corps Tactical School:* Claire Lee Chennault, *Way of a Fighter: The Memoirs of Claire Lee Chennault* (NY: Putnam, 1949), 20; see also Raymond R. Flugel, "United States Air Power Doctrine: A Study of the Influence of William Mitchell and Giulio Douhet at the Air Corps Tactical School" (Ph.D. diss., University of Oklahoma, 1965).

38   *"We are not concerned":* Quoted in Robert T. Finney, "History of the Air Corps Tactical School, 1920–1940," imprint 1955 by the Research Studies Institute, USAF Historical Division, Air University, p. 58. For the ideas of the ACTS, see especially Haywood S. Hansell, Jr., *The Strategic Air War Against Germany and Japan: A Memoir* (Washington, DC: Office of Air Force History, 1986).

39   *Norden bombsight–"merchant of death":* Stephen L. McFarland, *America's Pursuit of Precision Bombing, 1910–1945* (Washington, DC: Smithsonian Institution Press, 1995), 209; Robert L. O'Connell, "Arms and Men: The Norden Bombsight," *MHQ* 2, no. 4 (Summer 1990): 66–67.

39   *"The idea of killing":* Hansell, *Strategic,* 13.

40   *"[It] combined":* Keegan, "We Wanted," 34–35.

40 *"choke points":* Haywood S. Hansell, Jr., *The Air Plan That Defeated Hitler* (Atlanta: Higgins-McArthur, 1972), 33–34.

40 *"the true combat plane":* Douhet, *Command,* 132.

41 *"abstract science":* Arnold, *Global,* 115–16.

41 *"A well-planned":* Quoted in Hansell, *Air Plan,* 15.

42 *"seeking attrition":* Hansell, *Strategic,* 13; Hansell, *Air Plan,* 40.

42 *"We just closed":* Interview with Laurence S. Kuter, October 3, 1974, K239.0512-810, AFHRA.

42 *"an excuse":* Quoted in McFarland, *Pursuit,* 92.

42 *"For Mitchell":* Williamson Murray, "The Influence of Pre-War Anglo-American Doctrine on the Air Campaigns of the Second World War," in Horst Boog, ed., *The Conduct of the Air War in the Second World War* (New York: Berg, 1992), 238.

43 *"[I bring you] peace":* Quoted in Keith Feiling, *The Life of Neville Chamberlain* (London: Macmillan, 1946), 381.

43 *"sure . . . that we":* Quoted in Robert E. Sherwood, *Roosevelt and Hopkins, an Intimate History* (NY: Harper, 1950), 99-100.

43 *"ruthless bombing":* Quoted in Eugene M. Emme, "The American Dimension," in Mark K. Wells, ed., *Air Power: Promise and Reality* (Chicago: Imprint, 2000), 66. For Roosevelt's support of air power, see Jeffery S. Underwood, *The Wings of Democracy: The Influence of Air Power on the Roosevelt Administration, 1933–1941* (College Station: Texas A&M University Press, 1991).

43 *"battle of the":* Arnold, *Global,* 177–80; *AAF,* vol. 1, 107.

43 *"in an inspiring sense":* Robert A. Lovett, "The Civilian-Military Teamwork in Warfare," in James Parton, ed., *Impact: The Army Air Forces' Confidential Picture History of World War II, "Bombing Fortress Europe,"* republished by the National Historical Society, Harrisburg, PA, 1989, ix.

43 *"The difficult we do":* Eaker, "Hap Arnold," 91–92.

44 *"ruthlessly":* Richard G. Davis, *Hap: Henry H. Arnold, Military Aviator* (Washington, DC: Air Force History and Museums Program, 1997), 1.

44 *"Most of the":* Laurence S. Kuter, "The General vs. the Establishment: General H. H. Arnold and the Air Staff," *Aerospace Historian* 21 (December 1974): 188.

44 *"slave driver":* Ibid., 188–89.

44 *"Spaatz was a":* Interview with Lt. Gen. Elwood R. Quesada, June 22, 1977, K239.0512-1485, AFHRA.

44 *"I never learned":* Quoted in Ira Eaker, "Memories of Six Air Chiefs: Westover, Arnold, Spaatz: Part II," *Aerospace Historian* 20 (December 1973): 195.

45 *"adored each other":* Quesada interview, June 22, 1977.

45 *"plans but not planes":* Arnold, quoted in *AAF,* vol. 1, 150.

45 *Roosevelt called for: AAF,* vol. 1, 12–13, 107.

45 *"In forty-five minutes":* San Francisco Chronicle, February 18, 1947, 1. For Roosevelt's air construction program, see Irving B. Holley, Jr., *Buying Aircraft: Matériel Procurement for the Army Air Forces* (Washington, DC: Office of the Chief of Military History, Department of the Army, 1964); and Benjamin S. Kelsey, *The Dragon's Teeth: The Creation of United States Air Power for World War II* (Washington, DC: Smithsonian Institution Press, 1982).

45   *mass production: AAF,* vol. 6, xxv.

45   *"fantastically impossible": AAF,* vol. 6, xx–xxi.

45   *"Never before":* Thomas M. Coffey, *Hap: The Story of the U.S. Air Force and the Man Who Built It, General Henry H. "Hap" Arnold* (NY: Viking, 1982), 1.

45   *"provided the leadership":* Lovett, "Civilian Military," in *Impact,* ix.

45   *Army Air Forces established: AAF,* vol. 6, 15.

46   *"read like a":* Greer, *Development,* 124.

46   *"to conduct a sustained":* Hansell, *Strategic,* 62.

46   *The escort they called for:* Ibid., 37. The best summary of AWPD-1 is in Hansell, *Air Plan.*

46   *"Magna Carta":* Arnold, *Mission,* 129.

46   *"could no more":* William Wister Haines, *Command Decision* (Boston: Little, Brown, 1947), 159.

Chapter 2: Eaker's Amateurs

47   *"shook the":* Samuel Eliot Morison, *Two-Ocean War: A Short History of the United States Navy in the Second World War* (Boston: Little, Brown, 1963), 59.

48   *"I want":* Interview with Ira C. Eaker, November 1974, AFHRA.

47   *it "looked":* Arnold, *Global,* 174.

49   *"our shortest route":* Quoted in David Reynolds, *Rich Relations: The American Occupation of Britain, 1942–1945* (1996; repr., London: Phoenix, 2000), 91.

49   *"I do not believe":* Ira C. Eaker, "Some Observations on Air Power," in Wells, *Air Power,* 143.

49   *"Few men":* Parton, *"Air Force,"* 156–57.

49   *"You assemble":* Quoted in ibid., 128–29.

50   *"We had been warned"–"jockeyed slightly"–"Arrived at":* Armstrong quoted in ibid., 133–34; Eaker, "Senior Officers Briefing," U.S. Army Military History Institute, Carlisle Barracks, PA [hereafter USMHI].

51   *Leslie Howard: NYT,* June 4, 1943.

51   *"England would live":* Churchill quoted in Angus Calder, *The People's War: Britain, 1939–1945* (New York: Pantheon, 1969), 264.

51   *almost a garrison state:* Jose Harris, "Great Britain: The People's War?," in David Reynolds, Warren K. Kimball, and A. O. Chubarian, eds., *Allies at War: The Soviet, American, and British Experience, 1939–1945* (NY: St. Martin's, 1994), 238–39.

52   *"This is a war":* Quoted in Calder, *People's War,* 17.

52   *"What a different":* Quoted in Leonard Mosely, *Backs to the Wall: The Heroic Story of the People of London During WWII* (NY: Random House, 1971), 260.

52   *"didn't understand"–"successful bomb warfare":* Harrison E. Salisbury, *A Journey for Our Times: A Memoir* (NY: Carroll & Graf, 1993), 94–95.

53   *RAF raid on the night of May 15–16:* War Cabinet meetings, 14 May 1940 and 15 May 1940, The National Archive, Kew, UK, formerly called the Public Record Office; Horst Boog et al., *Germany and the Second World War,* vol. 6, *The Global War,* ed., Research Institute for Military History, Potsdam, Germany; trans. Ewald Osers et al. (NY: Oxford University Press, 2001), 498–500.

53 *reprisal raid on Berlin:* Francis K. Mason, *Battle over Britain: A History of the German Air Assaults on Great Britain, 1917–18 and July–December 1940, and the Development of Britain's Air Defence Between World Wars* (Oscela, WI: Motorbooks International, 1980) 1st printing 1969), 364–65.

53 *terror raid on Mannheim:* Boog et al., Germany and the Second World War, vol. 6, 507.

53 *"[bombing represented]":* Max Hastings, "The Lonely Passion of Bomber Harris," MHQ 6, no. 2 (1994): 65.

54 *"the morale":* Directive Number 22, quoted in Charles Webster and Noble Frankland, *The Strategic Air Offensive Against Germany,* vol. 4, *Annexes and Appendices* (London: Her Majesty's Stationery Office, 1961), Appendix 8.

54 *"in short supply":* "Eaker Briefing," USMHI, 15.

55 *"I was convinced":* Sir Arthur Harris, *Bomber Offensive* (London: Collins, 1947), 147.

55 *"We should never":* Quoted in Hastings, *Bomber Command,* 107.

56 *"Harris, who had been":* Quoted in Parton, *"Air Force,"* 139–40.

56 *"British officers":* Quoted in ibid., 153.

56 *"We won't do":* Undated press clipping, Spaatz MSS.

57 *"God knows":* Quoted in Parton, *"Air Force,"* 130.

57 *"You might":* Harris, *Bomber Offensive,* 15.

57 *"he relished it":* Parton, *"Air Force,"* 140.

57 *"I don't believe"–If the atomic bomb:* Interview with Ira Eaker, May 22, 1962, by Dr. Goldberg and Dr. Hildreth, AFHRA.

57 *"If you need":* Norman Longmate, *The GI's: The Americans in Britain 1942–1945* (NY: Scribner, 1975), 80.

58 *"distinct American":* AAF, vol. 2, 631.

58 *"Of all the moments":* Arnold, *Global,* 180.

59 *"England is the place":* Quoted in ibid., 182.

59 *"several tricky turns"–"These youthful":* Tibbets, *Enola,* 74–79.

62 *"a Channel full":* Arnold, *Global,* 174.

62 *Arnold was furious:* Ibid., 183.

63 *"rode upon":* Eaker, "Some Observations," AFHRA.

63 *"We didn't know":* Quoted in Joe Gray Taylor, "They Taught Tactics!" *Aerospace Historian* 13 (Summer 1966): 69; see also Arnold, *Global,* 198.

Chapter 3: The Dangerous Sky

64 *"On September 6":* Peaslee, *Heritage,* 92.

64 *"He was"–"backhand shot":* All Tibbets quotes from author interview with Paul W. Tibbets, January 28, 2002, and Tibbets, *Enola,* 92.

66 *"Paul, you did"–"parades and":* Tibbets, *Enola,* 92–96.

67 *"He looked puzzled"–"Though it":* All McLaughlin quotes from J. Kemp McLaughlin, *The Mighty Eighth in WW II: A Memoir* (Lexington: University Press of Kentucky, 2000), 1–7, 81.

67 *"first real brawl":* Target, 35.

67 *"unprecedented":* Ibid.

68 *"field day":* AAF, vol. 2, 221.

68 *"We were living":* Curtis E. LeMay and MacKinlay Kantor, *Mission with LeMay: My Story* (Garden City, NY: Doubleday, 1965), 251.

68 *"Which pickle":* Quoted in Michael J. Nisos, "The Bombardier and His Bombsight," *Air Force Magazine* (September 1981): 106.

68 *With hot slugs:* Lt. Charles H. Franks, "Bombardier–Warrior in a Greenhouse," *Stars and Stripes,* April 27, 1944, 1 [hereafter *S&S*].

68 *excitable pilots:* Col. John C. Flanagan, "Report on Survey of Aircrew Personnel in the Eighth, Twelfth, and Fifteenth Air Forces," April 1944, 23, 141.28B, AFHRA.

69 *"When a new crew":* Ibid., 37.

69 *"expressed as":* Stephens, in Alan Stephens, ed., *The War in the Air, 1914–1994* (Maxwell Air Force Base, AL: Air University Press, 2001), 47.

69 *"so large":* ORS Special Report No. 3, "Preliminary Report on Bombing Accuracy," January 4, 1943, 2, 520.130b 1, AFHRA.

69 *"As we came":* Tibbets, *Enola,* 99.

69 *British Broadcasting Corporation:* AAF, vol. 2, 239.

69 *Civilian casualties (France):* Ibid., 221, 239.

69 *"in strong formation":* Ibid., 222; Eaker, Report, August 31, 1942, 142.052, AFHRA.

69 *"I assured him":* Arnold to Spaatz, August 19, 1942, Spaatz MSS.

70 *"All the raids":* "U.S. High Altitude Bombers Hit Nazis," *Life,* October 19, 1942, 29.

70 *"the most critical":* Horst Boog et al., *Germany and the Second World War,* vol. 6, 597.

70 *Operation Torch:* For a magnificent account of Torch, see Rick Atkinson, *An Army at Dawn: The War in North Africa, 1942–1943* (NY: Henry Holt, 2002).

71 *"Son, I've got":* Quoted in Tibbets, *Enola,* 108.

71 *"You can't have that":* Target, 45.

71 *"I can remember":* Quoted in Richard G. Davis, *Carl A. Spaatz and the Air War in Europe* (Washington, DC: Center for Air Force History, 1993), 105.

71 *"living and working":* Ibid., 105.

71 *"Tooey":* Quoted in ibid., 105.

72 *"What is left":* Quoted in ibid., 109.

73 *"Elaborate entertaining"–"he had to":* Parton, *"Air Force,"* 202–3.

73 *"The Battle of the Atlantic":* Quoted in Nathan Miller, *War at Sea: A Naval History of World War II* (NY: Oxford University Press, 1995), 349.

74 *"The only thing":* Quoted in John Keegan, *The Second World War* (NY: Viking, 1989), 104.

74 *U-boats sank:* Jerome M. O'Connor, "In the Lair of the Wolf Pack," *World War II,* July 2002, 34.

75 *"From four miles up"–"hard, maybe impossible":* AAF, vol. 2, 247–48.

75 *"[is] one of the":* Quoted in ibid., 238.

75 *"first priority":* "Target Priorities for the Eighth Air Force," May 15, 1945, 6, Spaatz MSS.

75 *"like ping-pong balls"*: Edward Jablonski, *America in the Air War* (Alexandria: Time-Life, 1982), 63.

75 *"asked for their fate"*: AFF, vol. 2, 247; French Free Forces, "Information on Bombing of 21 October, 1942, Submarine Bases of Lorient," 18 November, 1942, 520.310B 1, AFHRA.

76 *"You always get"*: Target, 47.

76 *"insufficiently prepared"*: Adolf Galland, *The First and The Last: The Rise and Fall of the German Fighter Forces, 1938–1945* (New York: Ballantine, 1973), 140.

76 *"colossal defensive"*: Quoted in Longmate, *GI's,* 140.

76 *"As a result"*: Oberstleutenant Kogler, "Lecture on G.A.F., March 15, 1945," United States Strategic Air Forces in Europe, Office of the Director of Intelligence, April 6, 1945, AFHRA.

76 *"Not only had"– "these birds"*: Galland, *First,* 140–41.

77 *"cars and refrigerators"*: Asher Lee, *Goering, Air Leader* (London: Duckworth, 1992), 58.

77 *"side show"*: Boog et al., *Germany in the Second World War,* vol. 6, 551.

77 *bomber offensive would fail:* Galland, *First,* 184, 193–95.

77 *"a dangerous gap"*: Boog et al., *Germany in the Second World War,* vol. 6, 551.

78 *weak spot in their defenses:* AAF, vol. 2, 264.

78 *"from all buttonholes"*: Dale VanBlair, "Three Years in the Army Air Forces," unpublished MSS, EC.

78 *"Once you are"*: Kogler, "Lecture," AFHRA.

78 *306th losses:* Russell A. Strong, *First over Germany: A History of the 306th Bombardment Group* (Winston-Salem: Hunter, 1982), 53.

78 *"Who's afraid"*: Longmate, *GI's,* 144.

78 *"If it's going"– "The important thing"– "the solemnity"*: Robert Morgan, with Ron Powers, *The Man Who Flew the Memphis Belle: Memoir of a WW II Bomber Pilot* (New York: Dutton, 2001), 116–17; author interview with Robert Morgan, July 26, 2003.

79 *"You must always"*: Morgan, *Memphis,* 112–13.

79 *"We'd heard"*: Ibid., 114.

79 *"A courtly"*: Bernard R. Jacobs memoir, EC.

80 *"Bombardiers"*: Morgan, *Memphis,* 115–16.

81 *"Don't like my"*: Quoted in John R. (Tex) McCrary and David E. Scherman, *First of the Many: A Journal of Action with the Men of the Eighth Air Force* (NY: Simon & Schuster, 1944), 36.

81 *"The interior of a B-17"*: Jack Novey, *The Cold Blue Sky: A B-17 Gunner in World War Two* (Charlottesville: Howell Press, 1997), 51–54.

83 *"hung like"– "against that terrible"– "that could"– "that monitored"– "[me] to determine"– "like an insect's sting"– "as on the bridge"*: Elmer Bendiner, *The Fall of Fortresses: A Personal Account of the Most Daring, and Deadly, American Air Battles of World War II* (NY: Putnam, 1980), 41.

84 *"embedded in"*: John Hersey, *The War Lover* (NY: Bantam, 1960), 169.

84 *"The coordinated"*: Major General David Grant, "A Day at the Office," quoted in Ian L. Hawkins, ed., *B-17s over Berlin: Personal Stories from the 95th Bomb Group (H)* (Washington, DC: Brassey's, 1990), 63–64.

84 *"it was nip"–"Breaking out":* Jacobs memoir.

85 *"Those frontal assaults":* Morgan interview, July 26, 2003.

85 *Some bombers flew so close:* Paul Tibbets interview, Lou Reda Productions, October 14, 2000.

86 *"Once or twice":* John Morris, testimony, EC.

86 *"God, you gotta":* Quoted in Brendan Gill, "Young Man Behind Plexiglas," *New Yorker,* August 12, 1944, 484.

86 *bombing Brest:* Morgan, *Memphis Belle,* 117.

86 *"a hard and terrible":* Scott, "Yank Reporter," 9.

86 *"devoid of all"–"The swearing":* Ibid., 8–9.

87 *"There you must go":* Anonymous, "24 Hours of a Bomber Pilot," *Harper's Magazine,* August 1944, 290.

87 *"After a couple":* Jacobs memoir.

87 *"When a crewman":* Ralph H. Nutter, *With the Possum and the Eagle: The Memoir of a Navigator's War over Germany and Japan* (Novato, CA: Presidio, 2002), 51.

87 *"ticket home":* Author interview with George Manfred, February 12, 2003.

88 *"Them specks":* Oram C. [Bud] Hutton and Andy Rooney, *Air Gunner* (NY: Farrar & Rinehart, 1944), 69.

88 *"as fast as"–"the steel gray":* Ibid., 70, 72; *Target,* 50.

88 *"The men who"–"Even planes":* Ernie Pyle, "Individual Air Heroes Scarce in This War," news clipping, November 10, 1942, Ernie Pyle Papers, Lilly Library, Indiana University, Bloomington, Indiana.

88 *"[These men]" are not:* Assistant Chief of Air Staff, Intelligence, interview with Col. Malcolm Grow, fall 1943, AFHRA.

89 *"I can't explain":* Novey, *Cold Blue Sky,* 135.

89 *"We never worried":* John M. Redding, *Skyways to Berlin: With the American Flyers in England* (NY: Bobbs-Merrill, 1943), 284.

89 *"Flying men":* Pyle, "Air Heroes."

89 *"By early October":* AAF, vol. 2, 233.

89 *Bad weather:* Oron P. South, *Medical Support in a Combat Air Force: A Study of Medical Leadership in WW II* (Maxwell Air Force Base, AFB: 1956), 4–5.

90 *atmospheric "terrain":* AAF, vol. 7, 311.

90 *weather reduced operations:* The United States Strategic Bombing Survey [hereafter USSBS], *Bombing Accuracy, USAAF Heavy and Medium Bombers in the ETO* (Washington, DC: U.S. Government Printing Office, 1945), 2.

90 *"eight missions":* Beirne Lay, Jr., and Sy Bartlett, *Twelve O'Clock High!* (1948; repr., NY: Dodd, Mead, 1975), 30.

90 *"far worse":* Target, 54.

90 *frostbite:* South, *Medical Support,* 3.

90 *"Men who walked":* William F. Sheeley, "Frostbite in the 8th Air Force," *Air Surgeon's Bulletin* 2, no. 1 (January 1945), 23.

91 *"so badly":* Ibid.

91 *"by the time":* All Moffat quotes in Marshall J. Thixton, George E. Moffat, and John J. O'Neil, *Bombs Away by Pathfinders of the Eighth Air Force* (Trumbull, CT: FNP Military Division, 1998), 97–100.

91 *cold hands:* Interview with Colonel Grow.

92   *"Six weeks later"*: Quoted in South, *Medical Support*, 22–23.

92   *"we put"*: Quoted in Nanney, *Medical Services*, 23.

92   *"That's the thing"*: McCrary and Scherman, *First*, 8–9.

92   *"This is a real"*: Sheeley, "Frostbite," 23.

92   *"wait for everything"*: Ibid.

92   *aerotitis media*: AAF, vol. 7, 399–400.

93   *"aero-medical nightmare"*: Douglas H. Robinson, *The Dangerous Sky: A History of Aviation Medicine* (Henley-on-Thames, UK: G. T. Foulis, 1973), 179.

93   *"It's altogether"*: Halpert, *Real Good War*, 87.

93   *died from anoxia*: South, *Medical Support*, 14.

93   *"We did not contemplate"*: Interview with Colonel Grow.

94   *"I crawled"–"It had been"*: Moffat quoted in Thixton et al., *Bombs Away*, 74–77.

94   *Strange things happened*: Cowdrey, *Fighting for Life*, 227.

94   *Aviation medicine*: South, *Medical Support*, 44–45; Nanney, *Medical Services*, 19.

95   *Grow and Armstrong's work*: Nanney, *Medical Services*, 18–19.

95   *Central Medical Establishment*: Interview with Maj. Gen. Harry G. Armstrong, April 8, 13, 20, 1976, K239.0512-967, AFHRA.

95   *"the care of the flyer"*: South, *Medical Support*, 37, 42.

95   *"They all came"*: Armstrong interview; "306 Bomb Group Surgeon History 1944," 520.7411-4A, AFHRA.

Chapter 4: Airman Down!

97   *"The water looked"–"He'd go down"–"Soon a small"*: Target, 41–42; see also Roger A. Freeman, Alan Crouchman, and Vic Maslen, *Mighty Eighth War Diary* (London: Jane's, 1981), 19–20; and Freeman, *The Mighty Eighth War Manual* (London: Cassell, 2001), 110.

97   *"Unless you"*: Quoted in South, *Medical Support*, 12.

99   *99 percent*: South, *Medical Support*, 11.

99   *44 percent*: Grow interview; Merle Olmsted, "Down in the Drink," *Journal of the American Aviation Historical Society*, Fall 1998, 174.

99   *"We all said"*: S&S, April 10, 1944, 3.

99   *escape risks*: J. M. Langley, *Fight Another Day* (London: Collins, 1974), 251.

99   *Comet Line*: Sherri Greene Ottis, *Silent Heroes: Downed Airmen and the French Underground* (Lexington: University of Kentucky Press, 2001), 124–25.

100   *"parcels"–"No one"*: Yvonne Daley-Brusselmans, *Belgium Rendez-Vous 127 Revisited* (Manhattan, KS: Sunflower University Press, 2001), 68; author interview with Yvonne Daley-Brusselmans, January 20, 2002.

100   *airmen's dog tags*: Daley-Brusselmans, *Belgium*, 55.

100   *To raise the money*: Ottis, *Silent*, 123, 129.

101   *moles–"a long walk"*: Daley-Brusselmans, *Belgium*, 50–51.

101   *The Gestapo infiltrated*: Margaret Rossiter, *Women in the Resistance* (NY: Praeger, 1986), 23; Ottis, *Silent*, 2–3, 22, 120.

101   *"Andrée de Jongh was"*: W. R. Armstrong, "The Lifeline called Comet," *Reader's Digest*, vol. 5 (June 1, 1979), reprinted in *Reader's Digest True Stories of Great Escapes* (Pleasantville, NY: Reader's Digest, 1977), 85.

102 *"[The men] eat up"*: James Good Brown, *The Mighty Men of the 381st, Heroes All: A Chaplain's Inside Story of the Men of the 381st Bomb Group* (Salt Lake City: Publishers Press, 1994), 230–31.

102 *"You can't rely"*: Quoted in Nutter, *Possum,* 18–19.

103 *"Finally, just"*: Nutter, *Possum,* 21–22.

103 *"What took you"–"You are all confined"*: Quotes in ibid., 22–23.

103 *"he was the greatest air leader"*: Author interview with Robert Rosenthal, April 2, 2002; see also Victor Davis Hanson, "The Right Man," *MHQ* 8, no. 3 (Spring 1996): 6.

104 *"The work was hard"*: LeMay, *Mission,* 37.

104 *"We were more afraid"*: Cleven interview, April 2, 2003.

104 *"I can forgive"*: Quoted in Beirne Lay, Jr., "The Background," in *Impact, Destruction From the Air,* vii, copy at Mighty Eighth Air Force Heritage Museum, Savannah, Georgia [hereafter ME]; LeMay, *Mission,* 265–66.

104 *"He doesn't want"–"civilians"–"We needed"*: Nutter, *Possum,* 9.

104 *ill-prepared:* LeMay, *Mission,* 217; see also Thomas M. Coffey, *Iron Eagle: The Turbulent Life of General Curtis LeMay* (NY: Crown, 1986), 28.

105 *"It was LeMay"*: Andy Rooney, *My War* (NY: Times Books, 1995), 123.

105 *"He had* been": LeMay, *Mission,* 229–30.

105 *"The flak is murder"–"Hell's bells"–"we might as well"*: All quotes from Curtis E. LeMay, "Strategic Air Power: Destroying the Enemy's War Resources; 2. The Command Realities," *Aerospace Historian,* Spring 1980, 9–10.

106 *"If we're going"*: LeMay, *Mission,* 241–42.

106 *"Losses go"*: Quoted in Nutter, *Possum,* 33–34.

106 *"howling"*: LeMay, *Mission,* 241–42.

106 *Losses shot up:* Boog, et al. *Germany and the Second World War,* vol. 6, 595.

106 *"When I went"*: Author interview with Robert Morgan, July 26, 2003; Morgan, *Memphis,* 132–33.

106 *"pawns"*: Capt. S. T. Parker quoted in Menno Duerksen, *The Memphis Belle: Now the Real Story of World War II's Most Famous Warplane* (Memphis Castle, 1987), 167.

106 *"Is anyone scared?"*: Col. Maurice Preston, Commander, 367th Bomb Group, quoted in Martin Middlebrook, *Schweinfurt-Regensburg Mission* (NY: Scribner, 1983), 61.

107 *"sleepy and groggy"–"nothing"*: LeMay, *Mission,* 255–56.

107 *"lead crews"–"the common denominator"*: LeMay, "Strategic Air Power," 12.

107 *"Air discipline"*: "U.S. Tactics," Spaatz MSS.

107 *"Possum"*: Parton, *"Air Force,"* 179.

108 *LeMay and Hansell:* LeMay to Gen. Robin Olds, January 12, 1943, Curtis LeMay Papers, Library of Congress.

108 *"on the leader"*: McFarland, *Strategic,* 171–72.

108 *"platform"–"The Automatic"*: Author interview with Craig Harris, October 2, 2002.

109 *"point precision bombing"–"but the fighter"*: Interview with General H. S. Hansell, August 9, 1943, Office of Assistant Chief of Air Staff Intelligence, 142.052, AFHRA.

109 *Douhet and Mitchell:* "U.S. Tactics," Spaatz MSS; "Air Operations: Training and

Organization, December 1, 1942–October 31, 1943," 1–12, Spaatz MSS. When two or more combat wings were directed against a single target, the force was designated an air task force.

109   *"It would be":* Hansell interview, August 9, 1943.

110   *"Can Do":* Nutter, *Possum,* 37. For the difference between air war theory and combat realities, see Williamson Murray, "The Influence of Pre-War Anglo-American Doctrine on the Air Campaigns of the Second World War," in Boog, *Conduct,* chap. 13.

Chapter 5: The Anatomy of Courage

112   *"Ira, I've got"-"stupid":* All quotes from Ira C. Eaker, "Some Observations of Wars and Warriors," AFHRA.

112   *"Only you":* Parton, "Eaker," 33.

112   *"I had been told"-"Young man":* Ira C. Eaker, "Some Memories of Winston Churchill," *Aerospace Historian* 19 (September 1972), 122; Eaker interview, USMHI; Parton, *"Air Force,"* 221.

112   *"Be patient":* Eaker, "The Case for Day Bombing," Spaatz MSS; Davis, *Spaatz,* 162.

113   *"You have not entirely":* Eaker, "Observations," AFHRA.

113   *"He rolled":* Eaker, "Churchill," 123.

113   *"When I see"-"for a time":* Eaker interview, USMHI; Eaker, "Churchill," 124; interview with Gen. Ira Eaker, Imperial War Museum, London, England.

113   *"I decided":* Winston Churchill, *The Second World War,* vol. 4, *The Hinge of Fate* (Boston: Houghton Mifflin, 1950), 679.

113   *"economical method":* Eaker, "Case," Spaatz MSS.

113   *At Casablanca:* Casablanca Directive, January 21, 1943, Spaatz MSS.

114   *"The Eighth Air Force":* Author interview with Andy Rooney, August 20, 2002.

114   *"I was not happy":* Salisbury, *Journey,* 193; Harrison E. Salisbury, *Heroes of My Time* (NY: Walker, 1993), 95.

115   *"God help Hitler":* Denton Scott, "School for Gunners," *Yank,* February 2, 1943, 6–7; See also Andrew A. Rooney, "Rehearsal for a Bombing Raid," *S&S,* January 9, 1943, 2.

115   *"I remember thinking":* Rooney, *My War,* 124.

115   *"Everything was quiet"-"what appeared"-"Lt. Casey":* Andrew A. Rooney, "How It Feels to Bomb Germany," *S&S,* February 27, 1943, 1,4; Rooney, *My War,* 130; Rooney, "Rehearsal," 2; Gladwin Hill, "Reporters Fly on U.S. Raid," *NYT,* February 27, 1943.

116   *Bob Post: NYT,* February 2, 1943; Walter Cronkite, *A Reporter's Life* (NY: Alfred A. Knopf, 1996), 99; Jim Hamilton, *The Writing 69th: Civilian War Correspondents Accompany a U.S. Bombing Raid on Germany During World War II* (Marshfield, MA: Privately printed, 1999), 13. Post was one of only two American reporters killed in the European air war.

116   *"waving his arms":* Morgan, *Memphis,* 173.

117   *"No training":* Quoted in Axel Madsen, *William Wyler: The Authorized Biography* (NY: Thomas Y. Crowell, 1973), 228.

117   *"So we got":* Quoted in Jan Herman, *A Talent for Trouble: The Life of Hollywood's Most Acclaimed Director, William Wyler* (NY: Putnam, 1995), 259.

117   *"It was a way"—"To the German":* Morgan, *Memphis,* 97–98.

118   *"I told him, O.K.":* Morgan interview, July 26, 2003.

118   *"I've got to get"—"his own skin":* Both quotes in Madsen, *Wyler,* 236.

118   *"Hey Pappy":* Quoted in Lyn Tornabene, *Long Live the King: A Biography of Clark Gable* (NY: Putnam, 1976), 267.

119   *"highly important":* Tornabene, *Long Live,* 276; see also Steven Agoratus, "Clark Gable in the Eighth Air Force," *Air Power History* 46, no. 1 (Spring 1999): 6.

119   *"where the going":* *S&S,* April 19, 1943, 2.

119   *"It's murder"—"I hear Gable's"—"like a gorilla"—"How could":* Quoted in Tornabene, *Long Live,* 290.

119   *"will deal":* *S&S,* January 6, 1943, 1.

120   *"Today a new":* "Bomber Command Review of 1943," Spaatz MSS; Redding, *Skyways,* 19.

120   *"No dog":* *AAF,* vol. 2, 316.

120   *"Instead of a bogus":* Nutter, *Possum,* 61.

120   *"The Eighth Air Force":* Salisbury, *Journey,* 195; Parton, *"Air Force,"* 294–95.

121   *"one of the great":* Rooney, *My War,* 141.

121   *"We were all":* Cronkite, *Reporter's Life,* 289.

121   *"the worst kind":* Rooney, *My War,* 99.

121   *"Air Force trade journal":* Hutton and Rooney, *Story of the Stars and Stripes,* 26.

121   *"they rarely":* Rooney interview, August 20, 2002.

121   *"buried under":* Andrew A. Rooney, "This Is the Eighth Air Force," *S&S,* August 17, 1943, 1.

121   *"too sad"—"The gears"—"There were":* Rooney, *My War,* 99–100.

122   *"The boys in the Forts":* McCrary and Scherman, *First,* 8.

122   *Wylie, poll:* Philip Wylie, *Generation of Vipers* (NY: Holt, Rinehart & Winston, 1942), passim; Michael C. C. Adams, *The Best War Ever: America and World War II* (Baltimore: Johns Hopkins University Press, 1994), 8–9.

122   *"the best that ever":* McCrary and Scherman, *First,* 107.

123   *"See you boys"—"A hunk of flak":* All quotes from Jim Duggan, "The Brothers," *Yank,* August 8, 1943, 2–3.

124   *"You don't start hating":* Quoted in McCrary and Scherman, *First,* 86.

124   *"Our morale":* LeMay, *Mission,* 277.

124   *20 percent:* Hansell interview, August 9, 1943, AFHRA.

124   *"a new morbid game":* Hansell, *Strategic,* 83.

124   *"to fly in the":* Salisbury, *Journey,* 196.

125   *"The monthly dances"—"with a burst"—"seduced women":* Donald W. Hastings, David G. Wright, Bernard C. Glueck, *Psychiatric Experiences of the Eighth Air Force, First Year of Combat, July 4, 1942–July 4, 1943* (NY: Josiah Macy, Jr., Foundation, 1944), 138–39.

125   *insanity:* Hastings, "Psychiatric," 72.

125   *CME study:* Maj. Howard B. Burchell and Maj. Douglas B. Bond, "A Study of

100 Successful Airmen with Particular Respect to Their Motivation and Resistance to Combat Stress," December 1944, 520.7411-1, AFHRA.

125 *"flak-happy":* Hastings et al. *Psychiatric Experiences,* 6–7; Roy R. Grinker and John P. Spiegel, *Men Under Stress* (Philadelphia: Blakiston, 1945), 85, 313.

125 *Clint Hammond:* Author interview with Clinton Hammond, April 7, 2002.

125 *Ralph Nutter:* Nutter, *Possum,* 74.

126 *"yellow"–"listening to":* Hastings, *Psychiatric Experiences,* 42, 241–47; South, *Medical Support,* 91; Douglas D. Bond, *The Love and Fear of Flying* (New York: International Universities Press, 1952), 92.

126 *"as contagious":* Hastings, *Psychiatric Experiences,* 203.

126 *"infected":* Interview with Brig. Gen. David Grant, Air Surgeon, Assistant Chief of Air Staff, Intelligence, July 1, 1943, 142.052, AFHRA.

126 *"lacking in moral fiber"–"for the good":* Bond, *Love and Fear,* 156; "Medical Facilities, Administration, and Supply," p. 21, AFHRA.

126 *Enlisted men:* Hastings, *Psychiatric Experiences,* 111; Flanagan, "Report."

127 *"stigmatized"–"head shrinkers":* Douglas D. Bond, "General Neuropsychiatric History," in Lt. Gen. Hal B. Jennings, Jr., ed., *Neuropsychiatry in World War II,* vol. 2, *Overseas Theaters* (Washington, DC: Office of the Surgeon General, Department of the Army, 1973), 853; Nutter, *Possum,* 74.

127 *"Bomber bases":* Rooney interview; Rooney, *My War,* 139; Interview with Crew from 324th Sq. 91st Group, Air Forces Intelligence Section, March 19, 1943, AFHRA.

127 *"war weary":* AAF, vol. 2, 309, 396.

127 *only one in five:* Hansell, *Strategic,* 85.

127 *"flying fatigue"–"operational fatigue"–"chronic fear":* Hastings, *Psychiatric Experiences,* 28, 34; South, *Medical Support,* 85.

128 *225,000 airmen–"lack of moral fiber"–"lacking moral fiber":* Maj. Douglas D. Bond, "Statistical Survey of Emotional Casualties of the Eighth Air Force Aircrews, May 25, 1945," 520.7421, AFHRA. The Central Medical Establishment, which accepted only cases referred to it by flight surgeons and combat commanders, examined 1,716 emotional casualties, of which 1,230 were permanently grounded; Bond, *Courage,* 70–72; Flanagan, "Report"; Eighth Air Force, "Diagnosis and Disposition of Combat Crews Suffering from Emotional Disorders," January 1, 1944, 520.7411-2, AFHRA.

129 *" 'getting used to combat' ":* John W. Appel, "Prevention of Manpower Losses from Psychiatric Disorder," unclassified document, Mental Hygiene Branch, Medical Corps, John E. Sloan Papers, USMHI; John W. Appel and G. W. Beebe, "Preventive Psychiatry," *Journal of the American Medical Association* 131 (1946), 1469–76. One of the classic texts on combat breakdown is Albert J. Glass, "Combat Exhaustion," *United States Armed Forces Medical Journal,* 2, no. 10 (1951), 1471–78.

129 *"emotional disorders"–"has been by far":* Bond, "Statistical Survey"; Hastings, *Psychiatric Experiences,* passim.

129 *"My nervous system":* Quoted in Thomas M. Coffey, *Hap: The Story of the U.S. Air Force and the Man Who Built It, General Henry H. "Hap" Arnold* (NY: Viking, 1982), 63.

129 *"How is courage spent":* Charles M. W. Moran, *The Anatomy of Courage* (Boston: Houghton Mifflin, 1967), xii; Hastings, *Psychiatric Experiences,* 6; Grinker and Spiegel, *Men Under Stress,* 33.

130 *differences between air and ground combat:* Grinker and Spiegel, *Men Under Stress,* 29, 95, 97.

130 *"True psychoses":* Hastings, *Psychiatric Experiences,* 28.

130 *"by keeping alive"–"You leave your imagination":* Moran, *Anatomy,* 101.

130 *"narcissistic defenses":* Jon A. Shaw, "Comments on the Individual Psychology of Combat Exhaustion," *Military Medicine* 148 (March 1983), 223.

130 *"nothing can happen":* Bond, *Love and Fear,* 81; Moran, *Anatomy,* 32.

131 *"the essence":* Sigmund Freud, *Inhibitions, Symptoms, and Anxiety* (London: Hogarth, 1948), 81.

131 *"In the presence":* Moran, *Anatomy,* 38.

131 *"I can still see":* Author interview with Sherman Small, September 27, 2002.

131 *Chance:* Bond, *Love and Fear,* 131; Lt. David G. Wright, *Notes on Men and Groups Under Stress of Combat: For the Use of Flight Surgeons in Operational Units* (NY: Josiah Macy, Jr., Foundation, 1945), 12–15.

131 *"I have a yellow":* Quoted in Bond, *Love and Fear,* 11.

131 *"It is not difficult":* Headquarters, First Central Medical Establishment, "Factual Data," March 8, 1945, Spaatz MSS.

131 *flight surgeon:* Mae Mills Link and Hubert A. Coleman, *Medical Support of the Army Air Forces in WW II* (Washington, DC: Office of the Surgeon General, 1955), 671.

132 *"to get to know":* Andrew A. Rooney, "Fort Takes a Psychiatrist to Lorient," *S&S,* May 19, 1943, 1.

132 *military psychology:* Wright, *Notes on Men and Groups;* the Josiah Macy, Jr., Foundation published four other volumes during the war on combat fatigue, its diagnosis and treatment; see David R. Jones, Jr., "The Macy Reports: Combat Fatigue in World War II Fliers," *Aviation, Space, and Environmental Medicine* 58 (August 1987), 807–11.

132 *"[Airmen] seldom":* David G. Wright, "Report on Observations on Operational Bombing Missions," June 14, 1943, 520.7421, AFHRA.

132 *fifty-three flight surgeons:* South, *Medical Support,* 72.

132 *"positive, preventive":* Wright, "Report on Observations"; Wright, *Notes on Men and Groups,* 18; Douglas D. Bond, "How Can the Flight Surgeon Better Treat Anxiety?" in Wright, *Notes on Men and Groups,* 20.

132 *"He was with us"–"that you'd have"–"the nearest":* Saul Levitt, "Flight Surgeon," *S&S,* January 2, 1944, 22–23.

133 *"Doctor, Chaplain":* "Combat Veterans Evaluate the Flight Surgeons," *Air Surgeon's Bulletin* 2 (September 1945), 276–77; "Informal Report on Flight Surgeon's Activities," May 23, 1944, 520.C58-1, AFHRA; "Combat Veterans," 277.

133 *"It is . . . much easier":* Hastings, *Psychiatric Experiences,* 180–81.

134 *"The therapist can play":* Grinker and Spiegel, *Men Under Stress,* 170–72.

134 *Bond replaced Hastings:* Howard Erb and Douglas Bond, "The Use of Sodium Amytal Narcosis in the Treatment of Emotional Disturbances of Combat

Crews," October 1944, 520.7421 AFHRA; Bond, *Love and Fear,* 116. By May 1944, a total of 311 patients had received sodium amytal narcosis at one of the CME centers. Bond continued to use Pentothal in milder dosages as a diagnostic tool to measure the extent of a patient's suppressed anxiety, while Grinker and Spiegel employed it as a therapeutic device at the Air Force's new Don Cesar hospital in St. Petersburg, Florida, where emotionally distressed airmen were sent, beginning in 1944. See Bond, *Love and Fear,* 113.

134 *sixty-nine men given narcosis treatment:* Hastings, *Psychiatric Experiences,* passim.

135 *"in an atmosphere":* Bond, *Love and Fear,* 109; Mark K. Wells, *Courage and Air Warfare: the Allied Crew Experience in the Second World War* (Portland, Or: F. Cass, 1995), 81.

135 *What possesses:* Grinker and Spiegel, *Men Under Stress,* 28; Jon A. Shaw, "Psychodynamic Considerations in the Adaptation to Combat," in Gregory Belenky, *Contemporary Studies in Combat Psychiatry* (Westport, CT: Greenwood, 1987), 117; Moran, *Anatomy,* i.

135 *"Courage . . . is a moral":* Moran, *Anatomy,* 61.

135 *"It was love":* Herbert Spiegel, "Psychiatry with an Infantry Battalion in North Africa," in Jennings, *Overseas Theaters,* 115; Grinker and Spiegel, *Men Under Stress,* 39, 45.

135 *"War happens":* Eric Sevareid, *Not So Wild a Dream* (NY: Alfred A. Knopf, 1946), 494–95. See also Chris Hedges, *War Is a Force That Gives Us Meaning* (NY: Public Affairs, 2002). This is one of the great books written on warfare, its horror as well as its tragic appeal.

135 *"no matter what":* Grinker and Spiegel, *Men Under Stress,* 113.

135 *"group ego":* Jon P. Spiegel, "Effects of Combat Flying Stress," in David Wright, ed., *Observations on Combat Flying Personnel* (NY: Josiah Macy, Jr., Foundation, 1945), 21; Grinker and Spiegel, *Men Under Stress,* 25.

136 *"clung for support"–"something a man":* Moran, *Anatomy,* 16.

136 *"If another group"–"If one more group":* Flanagan, "Report," 86.

136 *"So I can go home!":* Grinker and Spiegel, *Men Under Stress,* 181–82; Morris Fishbein, ed., *Doctors at War* (NY: Dutton, 1945), 291.

136 *"single factor":* South, *Medical Support,* 76.

136 *"Last winter":* Hansell interview, August 9, 1943, AFHRA.

137 *"The mud":* LeMay, *Mission,* 247.

137 *"A lot of them":* Ibid., 251.

137 *"If it hadn't":* Morgan interview, July 26, 2003; Morgan, *Memphis,* 135.

137 *"This had nothing":* Morgan interview, July 26, 2003.

137 *"Tea dances":* Morgan, *Memphis,* 138.

138 *"One of our officers":* Morgan interview, July 26, 2003.

138 *"The Yanks were":* Quoted in Juliet Gardiner, *Overpaid, Oversexed, and Over Here: The American GI in World War II Britain* (NY: Abbeville, 1992), 108.

138 *"to lie":* Morgan interview, July 26, 2003. For Morgan in London, see also Duerksen, *Memphis Belle,* 68.

138 *"Everywhere we went":* Morgan interview, July 26, 2003.

138 *"but he was a sucker":* Quoted in Tornabene, *Long Live,* 291.

138 *"We didn't want":* Morgan interview, July 26, 2003.

139   *"Don't make friends":* Quoted in Salisbury, *Journey,* 193.

139   *stronger fighter resistance: AAF,* vol. 2, 311, 333–34.

139   *"If you ever":* Quoted in Tornabene, *Long Live,* 292.

139   *"The current position"–"they bomb":* All Eaker quotes in Copp, *Forged,* 372–77.

140   *"eight mouths":* Quoted in Copp, *Forged,* 376–77.

140   *"The crews wanted":* Rooney, *My War,* 136.

141   *"a real fuckup":* Ibid., 108.

141   *"The visibility":* McCrary and Scherman, *First,* 54–55.

141   *"a helluva fire"–"The ammunition":* Redding, *Skyways,* 267.

141   *"Suddenly":* Andrew A. Rooney, "Fortress Gunner," *S&S,* July 16, 1943, 4.

141   *"why Smith stayed":* Redding, *Skyways,* 266.

141   *"Glancing over"–"I jumped"–"That FW":* Rooney, "Fortress Gunner," *S&S,* July 16, 1943, 4.

142   *"We saw Smith":* Redding, *Skyways,* 268.

142   *"It was a miracle":* Ibid., 273.

142   *"a dream-come-true":* Strong, *First,* 109–10.

143   *"He was":* Redding, *Skyways,* 266.

143   *Eighth Air Force losses:* "Combat Casualties, 1943," AFHRA.

144   *"People like me":* Interview with H. S. Hansell, January 1, 1967, K239.0512-629 C.1, AFHRA; Hansell interview, August 9, 1942, AFHRA.

144   *Robert Lovett:* Lovett to Henry Arnold, June 18, 19, 1943, Robert Lovett Papers, NA.

144   *one historian has called:* Copp, *Forged,* 413.

144   *"the absolute necessity":* Arnold to Barney Giles, June 22, 1943, Arnold MSS.

144   *"The spectacle":* Quoted in Taylor, "They Taught Tactics!," 69.

145   *"never before equaled":* Peaslee, *Heritage,* 110.

145   *"Rosky":* Andrew A. Rooney, "25 Times," *S&S,* April 16, 1943, 2.

145   *"just another day"–"went crazy":* Morgan interview, July 26, 2003.

145   *"I gave it":* Morgan, *Memphis,* 210.

145   *"The whole base":* Morgan interview, July 26, 2003.

145   *"No problem"–"I almost didn't":* Quoted in Herman, *Talent,* 259.

146   *"He's scaring":* Quoted in Tornabene, *Long Live,* 293.

146   *"This has to be shown":* Quoted in Herman, *Talent,* 265.

147   *"a story that every":* NYT, April 14, 1944, 1.

147   *"an escape to reality":* Quoted in Madsen, *Wyler,* 258.

147   *"We had lost":* Karl Dönitz, trans. R. H. Stevens and David Woodward, *Memoirs: Ten Years and Twenty Days* (NY: LeBure Books, 1959), 341.

148   *over 63 percent:* USSBS, *German Submarine Industry Report* (Washington, DC: U.S. Government Printing Office, 1945), 31.

148   *"Maybe so":* Morgan interview, July 26, 2003.

148   *"an inexcusable waste"–"not picking"–"It was a heartbreaking job":* Kuter interview, October 13, 1974, AFHRA.

149   *"happy endings":* Rooney, *My War,* 136.

150   *"with his arms":* Quoted in ibid., 116.

151   *"We couldn't bring":* Quoted in ibid., 118–19.

Chapter 6: Teach Them to Kill

153 *"Where are we?"—"Our official welcome"—"Time, please":* All quotes are from Robert S. Arbib, Jr., *Here We Are Together: The Notebook of an American Soldier in Britain* (London: Longmans, Green, 1946), 1–5, 9–13, 21.

156 *"clearing eight miles":* R. Douglas Brown, *East Anglia, 1941* (Lavenham, UK: Terence Dalton, 1986), 85.

156 *"It was as if":* Arbib, *Together,* 18–19.

156 *"They didn't take kindly":* Bill Ong, in Edwin R. W. Hale and John Frayn Turner, *The Yanks Are Coming* (Tunbridge Wells, UK: Midas, 1983), 79.

157 *"English mud": Target,* 78.

157 *"why the Germans":* Ong, in *Yanks,* 79.

157 *"Across the green fields":* Bud Hutton, "American Engineers Rush to Build Bases for Bombers Across England," *S&S,* September 5, 1942, 5.

157 *"light enough to see":* Arbib, *Together,* 50–51.

157 *By D-Day:* Saul Levitt, "The Army's Gypsy-Builders," *Yank,* March 19, 1944, 5.

157 *"gray-green":* Arbib, *Together,* 50.

157 *"Call us mules":* Quoted in Levitt, "Gypsy-Builders," 4.

157 *"We watched him":* Ong, in *Yanks,* 81–82.

158 *"an evening":* Arbib, *Together,* 53; English impressions of the Americans are preserved in diaries housed at the Mass-Observation Archive, University of Sussex, UK [hereafter MO-A].

158 *"There were incidents":* Arbib, *Together,* 26–27.

158 *"We couldn't":* Ibid., 21.

158 *"Jitterbugging was"—"what had happened"—"No dice":* Ong, in *Yanks,* 80.

159 *"The Army engineer":* Levitt, "Gypsy-Builders," 5.

159 *friendly invasion:* Gardiner, *Overpaid,* 67.

159 *"We went":* Quoted in Longmate, *GI's,* 91.

160 *"The motley crew":* Quoted in ibid., 88.

160 *"Nothing in their lives":* Quoted in R. Douglas Brown, *East Anglia, 1939* (Lavenham, UK: Terence Dalton, 1980), 7.

160 *"Even the sky":* Quoted in Longmate, *GI's,* 149.

160 *Pointblank:* "Combined Bomber Offense Plan," Arnold MSS; *AAF,* vol. 2, 665.

162 *"making wild statements":* Quoted in Parton, *"Air Force,"* 279.

162 *"playing safe":* Arnold to Gen. Frank Andrews, April 26, 1943, Arnold MSS.

162 *"it began to look":* Parton, *"Air Force,"* 277.

162 *"I am [not] a horse":* Eaker to Arnold, June 29, 1943, Eaker MSS.

162 *"One of my principal":* Ibid.

163 *"a deep-seated cancer":* Peaslee, *Heritage,* 151.

163 *"I could hear":* All Comer quotes from John Comer, *Combat Crew* (privately printed, 1986, repr., NY: Pocket Books, 1989), ix–xii.

164 *Air Force growth:* United States Army Air Forces, *The Official Guide to the Army Air Forces: A Directory, Almanac, and Chronicle of Achievement* (NY: Simon & Schuster, 1944), 42.

164 *"AAF training":* Ibid., 116.

164 *Medical and physical requirements: AAF,* vol. 7, 516.

164   *"the best physical":* Steinbeck, *Bombs Away,* 32.

164   *Golden Age of Aviation:* Gordon W. Weir, "Navigating Through World War II," unpublished MSS, ME, 7; David McCarthy, *Fear No More: A B-17 Navigator's Journey* (Pittsburgh: Cottage Wordsmiths, 1991), 60–66.

165   *"nothing else":* Tibbets, *Return of the Enola Gay,* 21.

165   *Air Force classification center:* Richard C. Baynes, "Replacement Crew," privately printed MSS, ME, 4.

165   *"every time we turn":* Undated letter, "The Military Career of 1st Lt. Kenneth O. Shrewsbury," MSS, ME.

165   *"learned to be": Official Guide,* 103.

165   *"drama":* Quoted in Stephen E. Ambrose, *The Wild Blue: The Men and Boys Who Flew the B-24s over Germany* (NY: Simon & Schuster, 2001), 60.

165   *"to kill, maim":* Peaslee, *Heritage,* 28, 36.

166   *"acrobatics, lazy eights":* Baynes, "Replacement," 10.

166   *"more relaxed":* Ibid., 18.

166   *"One a day":* Williamson Murray, *Luftwaffe* (Baltimore: Nautical & Aviation Publishing, 1985), 177.

166   *"I was presented":* Bendiner, *Fall,* 38.

167   *"It was around":* Ibid., 56, 59.

167   *Crosby's crew:* Crosby, *Wing,* 33.

168   *"Then he smiled again":* Ibid.

168   *"who approached the monsters":* Contrails, 6.

168   *"We did all":* Interview with Kenneth Lemmons, July 28, 1988, Airpower Heritage Museum, Midland, Texas [hereafter AHM].

168   *"Men of the":* Contrails, 6.

168   *New Year's Day:* Richard Le Strange and James R. Brown, *Century Bombers: The Story of the Bloody Hundredth* (100th Bomb Group Memorial Museum, Thorpe Abbotts, UK, 1989), 3.

169   *"the flight to war":* Peaslee, *Heritage,* 41.

169   *"It was":* Ken Lemmons, Cindy Goodman, and Jan Riddling, *The Forgotten Man: The Mechanic: The Kenneth A. Lemmons Story* (Little Rock: CinJan Productions, 1999), 23.

170   *"There was so much":* Sheridan, *Never,* 39–40; Peaslee, *Heritage,* 39.

170   *"became a part":* Sheridan, *Never,* 42.

170   *"the whole of the ship":* Ibid., 43.

170   *"The wits of the outfit":* Contrails, 14.

171   *"doorstep of the Nazis":* Sheridan, *Never,* 46.

171   *"You've made a mistake":* Lemmons, *Forgotten,* 27.

171   *"The whole family":* Sheridan, *Never,* 50.

171   *"One day":* Author interview with Gordon E. Deben, July 11, 2002, Thorpe Abbotts, England.

171   *"The countryside":* Saul Levitt, "Diary of a Flying Fortress Radio Operator," *Yank,* November 21, 1943, 4.

172   *"a colony":* Saul Levitt, *The Sun Is Silent* (New York: Harper & Brothers, 1951), 86.

172   *Crosby's crew:* Murphy, *Luck,* 54, 83.

172 *"All of us"*: Lemmons interview, AHM; Lemmons, *Forgotten,* 28.

172 *"The hardstands were"*: Lemmons, *Forgotten,* 32.

173 *"the number of American airmen"*: Hutton and Rooney, *Air Gunner,* 23.

173 *"They rode"*: Author interview with Ken Everett, July 10, 2002, Thorpe Abbotts, England.

173 *"They had tons"*: Author interview with John Goldsmith, July 10, 2002, Thorpe Abbotts.

174 *"Fancy going"*: Douglas R. Brown, *East Anglia 1942* (Lavenham, UK: Terence Dalton, 1988), 161.

174 *"What bothered"*: Goldsmith interview.

174 *"I hear the Krauts"—"like so many beasts"*: Levitt, *Sun,* 87, 88, 94.

Chapter 7: The Bells of Hell

176 *"Hearing the explosion"*: Brown, *Mighty Men,* 50–51.

177 *"With a big belching"*: Lemmons, *Forgotten,* 36.

177 *"We couldn't"*: Ibid., 37.

178 *"It's a wonder"*: Ibid., 29–30.

178 *"a nation of mechanics"*: Burt Evans, "Air Force Mechanics," *Yank,* February 27, 1944, 6.

178 *"we loved them"*: Lemmons, *Forgotten,* 42.

179 *"raunchy discipline"*: Crosby, *Wing,* 62.

179 *Neil "Chick" Harding*: On July 1, 1943, Harding replaced Col. Harold Huglin, who, after less than a month, was relieved of command due to stomach ulcers.

179 *"flesh and brain"*: Nilsson, *Story of the Century,* 10.

179 *"All positions"*: Crosby, *Wing,* 100–101.

180 *"the heaviest and most"*: AAF, vol. 2, 674.

180 *"Smoke lies"*: Hector Hawton, *Night Bombing* (London: Thomas Nelson, 1944), passim.

180 *"Suddenly there came"*: Quoted in Martin Middlebrook, *The Battle of Hamburg: Allied Bomber Forces Against a German City in 1943* (London: Allan Lane, 1980), 258.

181 *"It was as though"*: Quoted in Desmond Flower and James Reeves, eds., *The War: 1939–1945: A Documentary History* (NY: Da Capo, 1997), 564–65.

181 *"became insane"*: Quoted in Middlebrook, *Hamburg,* 268.

181 *"yelled like animals"*: All quotes from Else Wendel, *Hausfrau at War: A German Woman's Account of Life in Hitler's Reich* (London: Odhams, 1957), 188.

181 *"lay like fried eels"—"Nothing to remember"*: Quoted in Middlebrook, *Hamburg,* 276.

181 *"We stacked"*: Uwe Koster in Johannes Steinhoff, *Voices from the Third Reich* (NY: Da Capo, 1994), 212.

182 *"rushed into"*: Mathilde Wolff-Mönckeberg, *On the Other Side: To My Children: From Germany, 1940–1945* (London: Mayflower, 1979), 71.

182 *"A wave of terror"*: Quoted in Flower and Reeves, *The War,* 564–65; Max Seydewitz, *Civil Life in Wartime Germany: The Story of the Home Front* (NY: Viking, 1945), 305.

182 *"Well, at any rate"*: Wendel, *Hausfrau,* 189–90. For a similar incident involving the baked corpse of a child, see Friedrich Percyval Reck-Malleczewen, *Diary of a Man in Despair* (NY: Macmillan, 1970, translated by Paul Rubens; first published in Germany in 1947), 189.

182 *thirteen square miles:* USSBS, *Hamburg Field Report,* vol. 1, Text (Washington, DC: U.S. Government Printing Office, 1947), 32; USSBS, *Over-all Report (European War)* (Washington, DC: U.S. Government Printing Office, 1945), 92.

183 *"no possible way"*: Reck-Malleczewen, *Diary,* 189.

183 *"Psychologically"*: Galland, *First,* 159–60.

183 *"Hamburg"–"You'll straighten all that"*: Albert Speer, *Inside the Third Reich: Memoirs* (1970; repr., NY: Simon & Schuster, 1977), 284. See also Ian Kershaw, *Hitler, 1936–1945: Nemesis* (NY: W. W. Norton, 2000), 598.

183 *"took on almost"*: Michael Sherry, *Rise,* 155.

183 *"to strike a target"*: Hastings, *Bomber Command,* 208.

184 *"Even at 17,000 feet"–"I couldn't"*: Novey, *Cold Blue,* 47–48.

184 *"Mad Dictator"*: Comer, *Combat Crew,* 5.

185 *"I tried to apply"*: Quoted in Hutton and Rooney, *Air Gunner,* 217.

185 *"safe"*: Andrew A. Rooney, "Congressional Medal Awarded Texas Flier," *S&S,* December 20, 1943, 1; Rooney, "Flier Dropped with Arm Gone Is Safe in Reich," *S&S,* December 7, 1943, 1.

185 *"Achilles' heel"*: USSBS, "Interview with Officials of the Kugelfisher Company," May 2, 1945, 137.315-4, AFHRA.

186 *"the taproot"*: Quoted in James Dugan and Carroll Stewart, *Ploesti: The Great Ground-Air Battle of 1 August 1943* (1962; rev. ed., Washington, DC: Brassey's, 2002), 3.

186 *"the outgrowth"*: LeMay, *Mission,* 289.

186 *"It is better to cause"–"bottleneck"–"with relentless"*: AAF, vol. 2, 355.

187 *German oil:* USSBS, *Oil Division, Final Report* (Washington, DC: U.S. Government Printing Office, 1947), 1.

187 *Tidal Wave:* AC/AS Intelligence Division, "The Ploesti Mission," 151–56, AFHRA.

189 *"This was the type"*: Philip Ardery, *Bomber Pilot: A Memoir of World War II* (Lexington: University Press of Kentucky, 1978), 97.

189 *"When we walked"*: Quoted in McCrary and Scherman, *First,* 200.

189 *Father Gerald Beck:* Ardery, *Bomber Pilot,* 93–94.

189 *"some idiot"*: Quoted in Frank Way and Robert Sternfels, *Burning Hitler's Black Gold!* (Privately printed, 2000), 23. See also Jay A. Stout, *Fortress Ploesti: The Campaign to Destroy Hitler's Oil Supply* (Havertown, PA: Casemate, 2003), 34.

189 *"You got good connections"–"Make contact"*: Quoted in Dugan and Steward, *Ploesti,* 82.

190 *"Our success"*: William R. Cameron, "Ploesti," *Air Force Magazine* 54 (August 1971), 59.

190 *"the first air fortress"*: Dugan and Stewart, *Ploesti,* 33.

191 *"We flew through"*: Quoted in Jablonski, *America in the Air War,* 73.

191 *"on the deck"*: Cameron, "Ploesti," 61.

191   *"He drifted"*: Quoted in Dugan and Stewart, *Ploesti,* 47; Andrew A. Rooney, "He Won Highest American Award," *S&S,* November 23, 1943, 2.

191   *"like snails"*: Quoted in Ronald H. Bailey, *The Air War in Europe* (Alexandria: Time-Life, 1979), 130.

191   *"skipped over"–"Maybe they were dead"*: Ardery, *Bomber Pilot,* 106.

192   *Ploesti recovers:* Dugan and Stewart, *Ploesti,* 222.

192   *"We were pushed"–"I protested"–"It was like"*: Quoted in Middlebrook, *Schweinfurt-Regensburg,* 28.

193   *"something big"*: Murphy, *Luck,* 114.

193   *Last supper:* Cleven interview, April 2, 2003.

193   *"Your primary"*: Lay, "Regensburg," 10; all noncited quotes in the Regensburg section are from Lay, "Regensburg," 9–11, 85–88.

194   *"hooking around"*: Le Strange, *Century Bombers,* 20.

194   *"tried to see through"*: Bendiner, *Fall,* 14–15.

194   *"Frequent 'piss calls' "*: Brian D. O'Neill, *Half a Wing, Three Engines and a Prayer: B-17s over Germany* (NY: McGraw-Hill, 1999), 40.

194   *"I wanted to be"*: All McCrary and crew quotes from McCrary and Scherman, *First,* 100–10.

196   *Anderson's decision:* Brig. Gen. Frederick L. Anderson, "Report of Operations, 17 August 1943," Eaker MSS.

196   *"We knew we were"*: Quoted in Charles Brand, "The Regensburg Raid," *Yank,* September 12, 1943, 3; Col. Beirne Lay Jr., "Personal Report on the Regensburg Mission," 17 August 1943," GP-100-SU-RE, AFHRA.

197   *"The sight was fantastic"*: Lay, "Personal Report."

197   *"I knew that"–"We climbed"–"hunting instinct"*: Quoted in Middlebrook, *Schweinfurt-Regensburg,* 106.

197   *"These Jerries"*: Cleven interview, April 3, 2003.

197   *Luftwaffe strength:* Murray, *Luftwaffe,* 174–75; Cajus Bekker, *The Luftwaffe War Diaries* (Garden City: Doubleday, 1968), 319; for suspiciously higher figures, see "Report on the CBO," October 12, 1943, 520.310B IV, AFHRA; see also USSBS, interview with Dr. Kurt Tank, April 17, 24, 1945, AFHRA.

197   *"He was evidently"*: Lay, "Regensburg," passim; Lay, "Personal Report."

198   *"His crew"*: Lay, "Regensburg," passim; Lay, "Personal Report." At the mission debriefing, and later in life, Cleven refused to make an issue of the incident. "I was just trying to steady my pilot. He needed some support." The pilot, Norman Scott, who strenuously denied he had panicked on the mission, was sent to another base and assigned ground duty. Cleven interview, April 2, 2003.

198   *"I knew that"*: Lay, "Regensburg," 88; Lay, "Personal Report."

198   *"You could tell"*: Quoted in Brand, "Regensburg," 3.

198   *"My radio"*: Lay, "Regensburg," 88.

198   *"I think that very moment"*: Quoted in Middlebrook, *Schweinfurt-Regensburg,* 192.

199   *"like a parachute invasion"*: Quoted in O'Neill, *Half a Wing,* 43.

199   *"counting the fitful"*: Bendiner, *Fall,* 172.

199   *"We followed"*: Author interview with Lewis E. Lyle, January 27, 2001.

199   *"dungeon like"*: William H. Wheeler, *Shootdown: A World II Bomber Pilot's Experi-*

ence as a Prisoner of War in Germany (Shippensburg, PA: Burd Street Press, 2002), 1–11.

199   *"the blessed sight":* Bendiner, *Fall,* 174.

199   *"Hello luck":* McCrary and Scherman, *First,* 110.

200   *"Did we win?":* Bendiner, *Fall,* 174–75.

200   *"literally wiped off":* S&S, August 26, 1943; *AAF,* vol. 2, 683.

200   *"The Hun":* Anderson to LeMay, August 18, 1943, Curtis LeMay Papers, Library of Congress.

200   *"I am impressed":* Heinz Knoke, *I Flew for the Führer* (1953; repr., Mechanicsburg, PA: Stackpole, 1997), 98.

200   *"We really thought":* LeMay, *Mission,* 295.

200   *While production dropped:* USSBS, interview with Kurt Tank, May 19, 1945, AFHRA.

201   *"catastrophic blow":* Speer, *Inside,* 284–85.

201   *"The enemy economy":* Elihu Root, Jr., to Guido Perera, in Guido R. Perera, *Leaves from My Book of Life* (Boston: Stinehour, 1974), 151.

201   *40 percent of the force:* Freeman, *War Diary,* 89–90.

201   *"might have had":* Perera, *Leaves,* 139.

201   *"We can wreck Berlin":* Quoted in Hastings, *Bomber Command,* 257.

202   *"completely mad":* Perera, *Leaves,* 157.

202   *Actual German losses:* Middlebrook, *Schweinfurt-Regensburg,* 286.

202   *"Hitler built":* Undated transcription of press release, Spaatz MSS.

203   *antiaircraft batteries:* Boog et al., *Germany and the Second World War,* vol. 6, 616.

203   *"This will be":* Albert Speer, *The Slave State: Heinrich Himmler's Masterplan for SS Supremacy* (London: Weidenfeld & Nicolson, 1981), 208.

203   *"terror can only":* Quoted in Murray, *Luftwaffe,* 174.

203   *"I can only win":* Quoted in R. J. Overy, "Hitler and Air Strategy," *Journal of Contemporary History* 15, no. 3 (July 1980): 411.

203   *He 177:* James S. Corum, *The Luftwaffe: Creating the Operational Air War, 1918–1940* (Lawrence: University Press of Kansas, 1997), 267–68. Production of a long-range bomber was also deterred by Col. Gen. Ernst Udet's preference for dive-bombers. Just after the war, the British Air Ministry produced a solid general history of the Luftwaffe, see Air Ministry, *The Rise and Fall of the German Air Force, 1933–1945* (London: 1948; repr., NY: St. Martin's, 1983).

203   *"daylight raiders"–"of greater consequence":* Galland, *First,* 178.

203   *production figures:* R. J. Overy, *Goering: The "Iron Man"* (London: Routledge & Kegan Paul, 1984), 193.

203   *"second Wagner":* Overy, "Hitler and Air Strategy," 417.

204   *"Losses at the front":* Murray, *Luftwaffe,* 180.

204   *"Hap was having":* Quoted in Coffey, *Hap,* 321.

204   *"Operations over Germany":* Arnold to Gen. George Marshall, September 3, 1943, Arnold MSS.

204   *"overestimate"–"bomber could not live":* Interview with Gen. E. J. Timberlake, L239.0512-792, AFHRA.

204   *"life will never be":* Brown, *Mighty,* 112–13, 117–19.

205   *"hard-luck outfit":* Crosby, *Wing,* 122.

205   "nightmare": Murphy, *Luck*, 125.

205   *killed and wounded:* John C. McManus, *Deadly Sky: The American Combat Airman in World War II* (Novato, CA: Presidio, 2000), 190.

205   "sees death there": *New York Herald Tribune*, October 3, 1943, 43.

205   "The Bells of Hell": Quoted in Murphy, *Luck*, 130.

Chapter 8: Men at War

206   *Stuttgart:* Freeman, *War Diary*, 106.

207   "To hit a wave": Bendiner, *Fall*, 198, 200.

207   "carry the flag": Ibid., 188.

207   *night bombing:* Nutter, *Possum*, 131–37.

208   *Crosby crash:* Harry Crosby, "This Is What Happened," *Yank* (December 26, 1943), 8.

208   "the most mournful": Sheridan, *Never*, 98.

208   "old men"–"We are an entirely": Brown, *Mighty Men*, 214–15.

209   "Captain, I think"–"The run was": Quoted in McLaughlin, *Mighty Eighth*, 105; Peaslee, *Heritage*, 221.

209   "It seemed like": Bendiner, *Fall*, 223.

209   "We were being mauled"–"began to shake": Eugene T. Carson, *Wing Ding: Memories of a Tailgunner* (Privately printed, 2000), 83–84.

210   "let out a cheer"–"who had made": McLaughlin, *Mighty Eighth*, 109.

210   *Black Thursday:* William Emerson, "Operation POINTBLANK: A Tale of Bombers and Fighters," in Harry R. Borowski, ed., *The Harmon Memorial Lectures in Military History, 1959–1987: A Collection of the First Thirty Harmon Lectures Given at the United States Air Force Academy* (Washington, DC: Office of Air Force History, 1988), 445.

210   *Air Force casualties: AAF,* vol. 2, 702.

210   *over 18 percent:* Lt. Gen. Ira C. Eaker and Arthur G. B. Metcalf, "Conversation with Albert Speer," *Air Force Magazine* (April 1977), 54.

210   *German losses:* USAF memorandum, June 28, 1949, K110.8-22, AFHRA.

210   "The atmosphere": Quoted in Flower and Reeves, *War*, 571.

210   "the nation had lived": Quoted in Murray, *Luftwaffe*, 218.

210   "I will never fly": George G. Roberts, "Black Thursday," in Kenneth N. Nail, ed., *Mississippians and the Mighty Eighth* (Tupelo: Mississippi Chapter, Eighth Air Force Historical Society, 1999), 20.

210   "Hello Lazy Fox": *Yank," the GI Story of the War,* by the staff of *Yank, the Army Weekly,* edited by Debs Myers, Jonathan Kilbourn, and Richard Harrity (NY: Duell, Sloan & Pearce, 1947), 71.

211   *Speer:* Speer, *Inside*, 286.

211   "Now we have": Quoted in *AAF,* vol. 2, 704.

211   "It was possible": *S&S,* October 21, 1943; *NYT,* October 16, 1943, 1.

211   "Winter holds": *S&S,* October 16, 1943.

211   *ball bearings:* Speer, *Inside*, 286; USSBS, *The German Anti-Friction Bearing Industry* (Washington, DC: U.S. Government Printing Office, 1945), 2, 40–45, 103–20; Martin Fritz, "Swedish Ball-Bearings and the German War Economy,"

Scandinavian Economic Review (1975), 15–35. Fritz estimates that the Swedish contribution to the total German supply of ball bearings was less than 10 percent.

211 *"sensational"–"Staging a": S&S,* October 18, 1943.

212 *lost air mastery: AAF,* vol. 2, 705. I am guilty of the same mistake in my previous book, *The Story of World War II* (NY: Simon & Schuster, 2001), 275.

212 *Luftwaffe losses:* Murray, *Luftwaffe,* 215; Stephen L. McFarland and Wesley Phillips Newton, *To Command the Sky: The Battle for Air Superiority over Germany, 1942–1944* (Washington, DC: Smithsonian Institution Press, 1991), 134–36.

212 *twenty-eight bombers:* Eighth Air Force, "Eighth Air Force Tactical Development, August 1942–May 1945, 92, AFHRA. This informative report was prepared immediately after the war under the direction of Maj. Gen. Orvil A. Anderson, former deputy commander for operations, Eighth Air Force.

212 *"decisive success":* Quoted in Murray, *Luftwaffe,* 216.

212 *"There's a lot":* Excerpt from James Parton interview with LeMay, April 16, 1985, reproduced in Parton, *"Air Force,"* 517.

213 *"a maximum effort":* Eaker to Arnold, October 22, 1943, Arnold MSS.

213 *"We must continue":* Eaker to Arnold, October 15, 1943, Eaker MSS.

213 *"would have gone"–"Control of the air":* Parton, *"Air Force,"* 325, 328; Eaker to Arnold, November 16, 1943, Spaatz MSS. For a different interpretation of the post-Schweinfurt situation, see McFarland and Newton, *Command,* 133–34.

213 *Arnold pressure: AAF,* vol. 2, 735; "Air Plan for the Defeat of Germany," Arnold memo, November 1, 1943, Arnold MSS.

213 *"a pity":* Bendiner, *Fall,* 236.

214 *"as un-military":* Ann Newdeck, "Coombe House Was a Flak Farm," January 27, 1944, reprinted in *8th Air Force News* 4 (February 1978), 1.

214 *"more than a little friendly":* Carson, *Wing Ding,* 105–6.

214 *"of the things":* Quoted in Lande, *Somewhere,* 125.

214 *This backfired:* Bendiner, *Fall,* 206.

214 *"soldier heaven"–"an' this guy"–"When those kids":* Hutton and Rooney, *Air Gunner,* 97–104.

215 *"a man came to think":* Quoted in Lande, *Somewhere,* 125.

215 *"That's good":* Hutton and Rooney, *Air Gunner,* 97–106. See also Headquarters, European Theater of Operations, "Research Findings and Recommendations," July 11, 1944, Spaatz MSS.

216 *American troop buildup:* Reynolds, *Rich Relations,* 102–3. Forty percent of U.S. military personnel in England were ground troops and 30 percent belonged to Services of Supply.

216 *"Battered and dirty":* Arbib, *Together,* 85, 203.

216 *"They had been hauling":* Hutton and Rooney, *Air Gunner,* 133.

217 *"to create a strictly":* Reynolds, *Rich Relations,* 160.

217 *"Adele took me":* Carson, *Wing Ding,* 101.

218 *"You do everything":* Quoted in Verbon F. Gay, *The Story of Rainbow Corner: The American Red Cross Club near Piccadilly Circus, London* (London: Fanfare, 1944), 16, 23–24.

218 *"she danced for me":* Carson, *Wing Ding,* 116.

218   *Jack Novey:* Novey, *Cold Blue,* 82.

218   *"The major cause":* Quoted in Gardiner, *Overpaid,* 56.

219   *"generally taller":* Quoted in ibid., 110–11.

219   *"like the bottom":* Arbib, *Together,* 88.

219   *"Lieutenant, I will":* Quoted in Crosby, *Wing,* 207.

219   *"local talent"–"good time":* "Behavior of Women in Public Houses," 2–5, Mass-Observation Study, MO-A.

219   *"As we males":* Cronkite, *Reporter's Life,* 91.

220   *"quickie":* Longmate, *GI's,* 231.

220   *venereal disease:* Reynolds, *Rich Relations,* 205.

220   New York Times: *NYT,* June 2, 4, 1943.

220   *"too small":* Reynolds, *Rich Relations,* 207.

220   *cure for VD:* Pixie J. Wilson, "The Campaign Against Venereal Disease," MO-A; Reynolds, *Rich Relations,* 208.

220   *"superbender":* Comer, *Combat Crew,* 54.

221   *"No, Norma":* Quoted in McCarthy, *Fear No More,* 78.

221   *"was not as good":* Eaker to Commands, July 14, 1943, Eaker MSS.

221   *"In recent months":* Time, December 6, 1943, 36, 39.

221   *"what the British"–"correspondents"–"favorable" impressions:* "What the British Think of the Americans," November 1942, MO-A.

221   *34 percent–"They irritate me"–"was a little child":* "Anti-Americanism," January, 1947, 1–12, MO-A; Philip Ziegler, *London at War: 1939–45* (New York: Alfred A. Knopf, 1995), 217.

221   *"It is strange":* Mass-Observation Panel on the Americans, 1945, 7, MO-A.

221   *"childlike desire"–"I like them":* Mass-Observation Bulletin, "Portrait of an American," No. 7, April, 1947, 1–2; "Feelings About Americans," 1943, 11–12; Mass-Observation Panel on the Americans, February–March directive, 1945, all in MO-A.

222   *"three crimes":* "Report," September 20, 1943, Spaatz MSS.

222   *"a big blast"–"gloomy silence":* Comer, *Combat Crew,* 51.

223   *"comfort":* Quoted in Ziegler, *London at War,* 220.

223   *"Usually when they come in"–"there's a war on"–"Why should it":* "Women in Pubs," 1943, MO-A.

223   *"They opened doors":* Author interview with Peggy Granham, July 11, 2002.

223   *"Heard about":* Longmate, *GI's,* 271; Mass-Observation Panel on the Americans, 1945, 1.

223   *"indoor amusements":* A Short Guide to Great Britain (Washington, DC: War and Navy Departments, 1942), 5.

223   Meet the Americans: Man in the Street, *Meet the Americans* (London: Martin Secker & Warburg, 1943).

224   *"People feel":* "Opinion on America," February, 1942, 11–13, MO-A.

225   *"we found":* Arbib, *Together,* 91.

225   *"whole place looks":* Sarah Williams diary, MO-A.

225   *"What's he got":* Quoted in Gardiner, *Overpaid,* 130.

225   *"There was wonderful":* Interview with Kay Brainard Hutchins, September 7, 1996, AHM.

226 *"a sort of":* Hutton and Rooney, *Air Gunner,* 21.

226 *"Tough, gum-chewing":* Quoted in Brown, *East Anglia, 1943,* 41; Arbib, *Together,* 75–77, 173.

227 *"dancing with":* Arbib, *Together,* 56.

228 *"The guilty ones":* Quoted in Kenneth P. Werrell, "Mutiny at Army Air Force Station 569: Bamber Bridge, England, June 1943," *Aerospace Historian,* December 1975, 203. See also Alan M. Osur, *Blacks in the Army Air Forces During World War II: The Problem of Race Relations* (Washington, DC: Office of Air Force History, 1977), 99–102.

228 *"jigaboos"–"Get inside":* "Preliminary Report on the Alleged Mutiny at Bamber Bridge, June 26, 1943," 510.0, AFHRA; Werrell, "Mutiny," 204; Osur, *Blacks,* 99.

228 *The shooting:* "Alleged Mutiny at Bamber Bridge," July 13, 1943, 519.771-1, AFHRA; Werrell, "Mutiny," 206–7.

229 *"90% of the trouble":* Staff meeting, July 10, 1943, Eaker MSS.

229 *"a definite feeling":* Eaker to ETOUSA, August 11, 1943, 519.201-25, AFHRA.

229 *"provoked by":* Quoted in Reynolds, *Rich Relations,* 322.

229 *"coloured British subjects":* Reynolds, *Rich Relations,* 217.

229 *"was badly suited":* Quoted in ibid.

229 *warmly welcomed: Time,* October 19, 1942, 32.

230 *"The white American":* Author interview with Ken Everett, July 11, 2002. For British opinion of the Americans, see also Roger A. Freeman, *The Friendly Invasion* (Norwich, UK: East Anglia Tourist Board in conjunction with Terence Dalton, 1992). For race relations, see Graham Smith, *When Jim Crow Met John Bull: Black American Soldiers in World War II Britain* (NY: St. Martin's, 1987).

230 *"It is the desire":* ETO HQ, "Policy on Negroes," July 16, 1942, in Ulysses Lee, *U.S. Army in World War II: The Employment of Negro Troops* (Washington, DC: Office of the Chief of Military History, Department of the Army, 1966), 624.

230 *Eisenhower's strictures: AAF,* vol. 2, 655.

230 *"negro officers serving":* Arnold quoted in Osur, *Blacks,* 22–23.

231 *Red Cross:* George Korson, *At His Side: The Story of the American Red Cross Overseas in World War II* (NY: Coward-McCann, 1945), 260.

231 *12,196 African-American AAF personnel:* Osur, *Blacks,* 96.

231 *"I, alone":* Quoted in ibid., 96.

231 *"When British soldiers": Time,* October 19, 1945, 34.

231 *In Launceston:* Smith, *Jim Crow,* 144–45.

232 *"white towns":* Ibid., 108.

232 *Truman K. Gibson:* Truman K. Gibson to Assistant Secretary of War, December 17, 1943, 250.1, RG 332, NA.

232 *alternate-day leaves:* 8th AF Provost Marshal, report, November 10, 1943, Spaatz MSS.

232 *"colored night":* Smith, *Jim Crow,* 114.

Chapter 9: The Turning

233 *"The sight"–"The avalanche":* McCarthy, *Fear,* 71, 79–81, 88.

234 *"the killing month":* McCarthy, *Fear,* 82.

234 *"there were whoops":* Comer, *Combat Crew,* 179.

234 *size of the bomber stream:* "Lecture on G.A.F., March 15, 1945," Headquarters, United States Strategic Air Forces in Europe, report of April 6, 1945, of a lecture given by Oberstleutnant Kogler on the German air force, 00217374, AFHRA; Murray, *Luftwaffe,* 22.

235 *"All eyes are":* Halpert, *Real Good War,* 251. Of the eleven Pathfinders on this mission, six carried H2X and five H2S; see Thixton, *Bombs Away,* 68. The Eighth was already experimenting with two other British finding aides, Gee and Oboe, both of them navigational devices relying on beams transmitted from ground stations.

235 *Fifteenth Air Force:* USSBS, *Weather Factors,* 20. For the entire war, weather prevented the Eighth from launching missions on 25 percent of all days; the number of nonoperational days for the Fifteenth Air Force was 37 percent.

236 *blind bombing:* Arnold to Spaatz, January 5, 1944; Spaatz to Arnold, January 10, 1944, Spaatz MSS.

237 *Luftwaffe losses in 1943:* Galland, *First,* 187; McFarland and Newton, *Command,* 135.

237 *"can only be":* Murray, *Luftwaffe,* 223; McFarland and Newton, *Command,* 136. In late 1943, the Luftwaffe was losing more planes to accidents and friendly flak fire than to enemy aircraft. See "German Airforce Losses in the West, September 1, 1943–December 31, 1943," 1945, K512.621 VII/148, AFHRA.

237 *defense in depth:* Generalleutnant Joseph Schmid, "Day and Night Aerial Warfare over the Reich," September 15, 1943–December 31, 1943, 1954, vol. 1, "Luftwaffe Operations in the West," 1943–45, K113.107-158-160, AFHRA.

237 *Ancient Roman army's:* See Victor Davis Hanson, *Carnage and Culture: Landmark Battles in the Rise of Western Power* (NY: Doubleday, 2001), 111.

237 *"The German aircraft":* James S. Corum, "Defeat of the Luftwaffe, 1935–1945," in Robin Higham and Stephen J. Harris, eds., *Why Air Forces Fail: The Anatomy of Defeat* (Lexington: University Press of Kentucky, 2006), 213. The best in-depth studies of the German aviation industry in the prewar and early war years are Corum, *Luftwaffe,* Edward Homze, *Arming the Luftwaffe* (Lincoln: University of Nebraska Press, 1976), and Murray, *Luftwaffe.*

238 *400 percent:* Corum, "Defeat," in Higham and Harris, *Why Air Forces Fail,* 214.

238 *war of annihilation:* For the Grant-like American strategy of annihilation, see Weigley, *American Way.*

238 *"By being able":* Interview with General Spaatz, AFHRA.

238 *"had no instruments"–"Numerous German pilots":* Galland, *First,* 190.

239 *"relief tube"–"when you put":* Novey, *Cold Blue,* 128–29.

239 *"A meteorological":* Bendiner, *Fall,* 244.

240 *"clear ice"–"so rapidly":* Dale O. Smith, *Screaming Eagle: Memoirs of a B-17 Group Commander* (Chapel Hill: Algonquin, 1990), 61.

240 *"We fly":* Harry M. Conley, *No Foxholes in the Sky* (Trumbull, CT: FNP Military Division, 2002), 210.

240 *Electrical suits:* Lester F. Rentmeester, "Big Brothers and Little Friends: A Memoir of the Air War Against Germany," *Wisconsin Magazine of History* 77 (Autumn 1990): 39.

240   *"with an intensity":* Novey, *Cold Blue,* 130.

240   *"find the goddamn thing":* Halpert, *Real Good War,* 106.

240   *"flak suits":* Malcolm C. Grow and Robert C. Lyons, "Body Armour: A Brief Study of Its Development," *Air Surgeon's Bulletin* 2 (January 1945): 9.

240   *"A London firm":* Quoted in *Contrails,* 65.

241   *13,000 flak suits:* Brig. Gen. Malcolm Grow, "The Use of Body Armor in Aviation During Wartime," April 1946, 141.282–6 II, AFHRA; Robinson, *Dangerous Sky,* 180; Martin J. Miller, Jr., "The Armored Airmen: World War II U.S. Army Air Force Body Armor Program," *Aerospace Historian* 32 (March 1985): 27–32.

241   *"I knew I was"–"When we came"–"I knew Buske":* All quotes from O'Neill, *Half a Wing,* 262–68, and Judd Katz, "Interview of Medal of Honor Recipients: Forrest L. Vosler, Gunter AFS, AL, March 5, 1986, K239.0512-1703, AFHRA. See also "Mission and Pro Reports, January through December 1943, 303rd Bombardment Group (H)," GP-303-HI, AFHRA. The plane's mission report is reprinted in Harry D. Gobrecht, *Might in Flight: Daily Diary of the Eighth Air Force's Hell's Angels, 303rd Bombardment Group (H)* (San Clemente, CA: 303rd Bomb Group Association, 1997), 298. See also Hutton and Rooney, *Air Gunner,* 226.

242   *"The doctors think":* Hutton and Rooney, *Air Gunner,* 225–28.

242   *"lost in memories"–"It was a reasonable"–"I'm not listed":* Comer, *Combat Crew,* 243, 249.

243   *"Having started":* Eaker to Arnold, December 19, 1943, Eaker MSS.

243   *Arnold replied:* Arnold to Eaker, December 18, 21, 1943, Eaker MSS.

244   *"that is not":* Eisenhower to Marshall, December 25, 1943, in Alfred D. Chandler, ed., *The Papers of Dwight David Eisenhower,* vol. 3, *The War Years* (Baltimore: Johns Hopkins University Press, 1970), 1612.

244   *"I drink":* Quoted in Edgar F. Puryear, *American Generalship: Character Is Everything; the Art of Command* (Novato, CA: Presidio, 2000), 269.

244   *"necessary":* Harry Butcher, *My Three Years with Eisenhower: The Personal Diary of Captain Harry C. Butcher, USNR, Naval Aide to General Eisenhower, 1942 to 1945* (NY: Simon & Schuster, 1946), 447–48.

244   *"The failure":* Quoted in Davis, *Spaatz,* 271. Eaker dispatched over 600 bombers on November 3 and November 26, 1943.

244   *"not see any way":* Arnold to Eaker, December 21, 1943, Eaker MSS.

245   *"desire":* Arnold to Spaatz, n.d. [Spaatz received the letter on March 1, 1943], 168.491 AF/CHO, microfilm reel A 1657, AFHRA.

245   *coldly worded cable:* Arnold to Gen. Jacob Devers for Eaker, December 18, 1943, Eaker MSS. See also interview with General Barney M. Giles, 1974, 98–99, K239.0512-814, AFHRA.

245   *"I feel like a pitcher":* Eaker to James Fechet, December 22, 1943, Eaker MSS.

245   *"to commiserate":* Lovett to Eaker, December 28, 1943, Eaker MSS.

245   *Eighth Air Force strength:* McFarland and Newton, *Command,* 155; Doolittle, *Lucky,* 354.

246   *Eighth Air Force casualties:* Memo for the chief of staff from General Arnold, December 27, 1943, Arnold MSS.

247   *"The last time I boxed":* Interview with John P. Doolittle, Lou Reda Productions,

Easton, PA. For an excellent brief biography of Doolittle, see Dik Alan Daso, *Doolittle: Aerospace Visionary* (Washington, DC: Potomac Books, 2003).

247   *"It didn't take"–"Doolittle was":* Both quotes in Craig Nelson, *The First Heroes: The Extraordinary Story of the Doolittle Raid–America's First World War II Victory* (NY: Penguin, 2003), 33, 41.

247   *Under Eaker . . . fighter escorts:* Eighth Air Force, "Minutes of General and Special Staff Meetings," November 29, 1943, 520.141, AFHRA.

247   *"This policy":* Quoted in Spaatz to CG, Eighth Air Force, January 11, 1944, Spaatz MSS.

247   *"If it moved":* "Jimmy Doolittle and the Emergence of American Air Power," interview by Colin D. Heaton, *World War II,* May 2003, 50.

247   *"The first duty":* Doolittle, *Lucky,* 352–53. For Kepner's reaction, see Davis, *Spaatz,* 302.

248   *Germany lost the air war:* Galland, *First,* 187, 206. Galland credited Spaatz, not Doolittle, with this decision. "I had a chance later to correct Galland," Doolittle said in an interview after Galland's book was published, "Interview with Doolittle," n.d., AFHRA.

248   *"greatest tactical error":* "Interrogation of General Galland," 168.6005-83, AFHRA.

248   *"[But] as soon":* Doolittle, *Lucky,* 353; interview with Gen. James H. Doolittle, August 24, 1979, K239.0512-1206, AFHRA.

248   *"difficult decision to make":* Interview with Gen. James H. Doolittle, April 21, 1969, AFHRA; interview with Doolittle, August 24, 1979.

249   *"The look in their faces":* Brown, *Mighty Men,* 280–81, 288; Ron MacKay, *Ridgewell's Flying Fortresses: The 381st Bombardment Group (H) in World War II* (Atglen, PA: Schiffer, 2000), 74.

249   *"I wonder if"–"uncalculated risk":* Doolittle, *Lucky,* 355.

249   *"Jim, I see":* Doolittle, "Daylight Precision Bombing," in James Parton, ed., *Impact: The Army Air Forces' Confidential Picture History of World War II,* vol. 6, *Pounding the Axis* (Harrisburg, PA: National Historical Society, 1989), xv.

249   *"Counce flying":* Comer, *Combat Crew,* 263; *AAF,* vol. 3, 22.

250   *Lester Rentmeester:* Rentmeester, "Big Brothers," 38.

250   *"Press on":* Ibid., 41.

251   *"The Battle Opera House":* Galland, *First,* 203.

251   *"Bandits at ten o'clock"–"It was a complete surprise":* Rentmeester, "Big Brothers," 43.

252   *"it was up to me":* Press release, March 18, 1995, on the death of General James H. Howard, http://www.Arlingtoncemetery.net/jhoward.htm.

252   *"There were an":* Andrew Rooney, "Bombers Hail One-Man Air Force," *S&S,* January 19, 1944.

252   *"That night was":* Comer, *Combat Crew,* 266–67.

252   *"some good smashing blows?":* Arnold to Spaatz, January 24, 1944, 168.491, AFHRA.

253   *"That plane":* Don Salvatore Gentile and Ira Wolfert, *One-Man Air Force* (NY: L. B. Fischer, 1944), 16.

253   *Edgar Schmued:* Ray Wagner, *Mustang Designer: Edgar Schmued and the P-51* (Washington, DC: Smithsonian Institution Press, 1990), 113.

253 *"by crossbreeding": AAF*, vol. 6, 219.

253 *Schmued . . . turned the Mustang:* Anthony Furse, *Wilfrid Freeman: The Genius Behind Allied Survival and Air Supremacy, 1939 to 1945* (Staplehurst, UK: Spellmount, 2000), 229. The Packard Motor Company made the Merlin engines for the American Mustangs.

253 *Arnold order the plane rushed to England:* Eaker to Arnold, October 15, 1943, Arnold MSS.

253 *drop tanks:* Interview with Gen. B. M. Giles, October 1, 1966, K239.0512-779, AFHRA.

253 *flying to Poland:* Narrative History, Headquarters, 8th AF, February 1944, 17, HD 520.02-5, AFHRA.

254 *Mustang combat record:* "Combat Record P-47s, P-38s, P-51s in U.K., Nov., Dec. 1943 and January 1944," 520.3108B V, AFHRA.

254 *all-Mustang force:* Bernard Lawrence Boylan, "The Development of the American Long-Range Escort Fighter," Ph.D. diss., 1955, University of Missouri, 44, 99, 218–19.

254 *"the Air Force's own fault":* Arnold, *Global,* 376.

254 *Argument:* Murray, *Luftwaffe,* 226.

255 *"My lot was":* Heaton, "Doolittle," 50.

255 *"Mass against Mass":* Galland, *First,* 205.

255 *"Anderson is tall":* Charles J. V. Murphy, "The Unknown Battle," *Life,* October 16, 1944, 104.

255 *"The opportunity":* Quoted in ibid.

256 *October 1943:* Murphy, "Unknown," 104.

256 *prepared to lose:* Walton S. Moody, "Big Week: Gaining Air Superiority over the Luftwaffe," *Air Power History* 41, no. 2 (Summer 1994): passim.

256 *"On the record":* Murphy, "Unknown," 102.

256 *weather conditions–"The peculiar thing"–"weather situations"–"A sequence":* Ibid., 107.

257 *"not exactly":* Doolittle, *Lucky,* 366; *AAF,* vol. 3, 32.

257 *Kepner . . . agreed:* Davis, *Spaatz,* 322.

257 *Park House:* Hansell, *Air Plan,* 181; Davis, *Spaatz,* 322.

257 *"Let 'em go":* AAF*, vol. 3, 33, 31.

Chapter 10: Liberated Skies

259 *"If you see":* Quoted in Emerson, "POINTBLANK," in Borowski, *Harmon Lectures,* 447.

259 *"lively air opposition":* Dwight D. Eisenhower to George C. Marshall, George C. Marshall Papers, George C. Marshall Research Library, Lexington, VA.

259 *"I was thinking"–"columns of"–"Hun never":* Quoted in Murphy, "Unknown Battle," 97.

259 *250 sorties: AAF,* vol. 3, 194–95.

260 *"We caught up":* Francis Gabreski, as told to Carl Molesworth, *Gabby: A Fighter Pilot's Life* (NY: Orion, 1991), 147–48; *S&S,* February 22, 1944, 1, 4.

260 *fighter tactics:* Hubert Zemke and Roger A. Freeman, *Zemke's Wolf Pack: The Story of Hub Zemke and the 56th Fighter Group in the Skies over Europe* (NY: Orion,

1989), 145–46; Walter Boyne, *Aces in Command: Fighter Pilots as Combat Leaders* (Washington, DC: Brassey's, 2001), 97.

260   *"The reports came in":* Quoted in Murphy, "Unknown Battle," 109; *AAF,* vol. 3, 34.

260   *"on the crest":* Quoted in Davis, *Spaatz,* 323; see also *S&S,* February 22, 1944, 1, 4; and Freeman, *War Diary,* 183–84.

261   *"To the General":* Irwin Shaw, *The Young Lions* (NY: Random House, 1948), 463–65.

261   *William R. Lawley:* Interview with Col. William R. Lawley, Air Force Oral History Program, October 5, 1971, K239.0512-487, AFHRA.

262   *"He had arthritis":* Richard Goldstein, "William Lawley, 78, Won Medal of Honor," *NYT,* June 1, 1999, C13.

262   *"For the next few minutes":* All quotes on this incident are from the powerful book by Rick School and Jeff Rogers, *Valor at Polebrook: The Last Flight of Ten Horsepower* (Kimberly, WI: Cross Roads, 2000), 44–45, 49, 63, 66.

263   *They would not desert him:* Medal of Honor citation, Archibald Mathies, General Orders, No. 52, War Department, Washington, D.C., 22 June 1944, NA.

264   *weak point:* Combined Operational Planning Committee, "Third Periodic Report on Enemy Daylight Fighter Defenses and Interception Tactics," 15 February 1944–2 March 1944," March 26, 1944, Spaatz MSS; Emerson, "POINTBLANK," 455.

264   *"final extinction":* Anderson to Arnold, February 27, 1944, Spaatz MSS.

264   *two-month delay in aircraft production: AAF,* vol. 3, 43, 45.

264   *Karl Otto Saur:* Speer, *Inside,* 349; *AAF,* vol. 3, 44.

264   *18 percent of its fighter pilots:* Murray, *Luftwaffe,* 229; *AAF,* vol. 3, 68–69.

265   *Dispersal:* USSBS, *Aircraft Division Industry Report* (Washington, DC: U. S. Government Printing Office, 1945), 5.

265   *"defeated itself":* Ibid., 6–7.

265   *"regardless of cost":* Anderson to Arnold, February 27, 1944, Spaatz MSS.

266   *extended their tours of duty:* Arnold to Doolittle, February 11, 1944, 519.245, Doolittle to Arnold, March 4, 1944, 168.6007, both at AFHRA.

266   *"the pills that got":* Author interview with Larry Goldstein, August 7, 2002.

266   *"It doesn't matter":* Quoted in McFarland and Newton, *Command,* 197; Anderson to Arnold, February 27, 1944, Spaatz MSS; Gen. F. L. Anderson to Gen. O. A. Anderson, transcript of telephone conversation, February 29, 1944, Spaatz MSS.

266   *over 70 percent of its fighters:* Generalleutnant Josef Schmid, "The Struggle for Air Supremacy over the Reich, 1 January 1944–31 March 1944," 1954, K113.107-158-160, AFHRA.

266   *"God"–"Well?":* Quoted in McFarland and Newton, *Command,* 197; See also Ardery, *Bomber Pilot,* 167.

266   *"drowsy and listless":* Grover C. Hall, *1000 Destroyed: The Life and Times of the 4th Fighter Group* (Montgomery, AL: Brown, 1946), 164–65.

267   *Harry C. Mumford:* Interview with William E. Charles, 1983, AHM; Bud Hutton, "First U.S. Bombs Dropped on Berlin," *S&S,* March 6, 1944, 1–2.

267   *"The first time":* Quoted in Hall, *1000,* 160.

267 *"I knew I was going"*–*"Cold and scared"*–*"Back home"*: General Chuck Yeager and Leo Janos, *Yeager: An Autobiography* (NY: Bantam, 1985), 26.

268 *"a hungry hillbilly"*: All quotes from ibid., 26–32; The account in Yeager's auto-biography differs in some details from the story he told to a British debriefing officer on his return to England; see "Escape and Evasion Case File for Flight Officer Charles (Chuck) Yeager," 338-660-YEAGER, NA.

268 *The Maquis:* Gordon A. Harrison, *Cross-Channel Attack* (Washington, DC: Office of the Chief of Military History, Department of the Army, 1951), 203; Julian Jackson, *France: The Dark Years, 1940–1944* (Oxford: Oxford University Press, 2001), 484.

269 *The Carpetbaggers:* "A 'Carpetbagger' with the French Forces of the Interior," in "They Flew at Night," privately printed by the 801st/492nd Bombardment Group Association, in ME. For a comprehensive history, see Ben Parnell, *Carpetbaggers: America's Secret War in Europe* (Austin: Eakin, 1987).

269 *"The Maquis hide"*: Yeager, *Yeager*, 34–35.

270 *"I can help"*–*"these guys"*: Ibid., 33, 35.

270 *"fun, interesting"*: U.S. Air Force Oral History Interview with Brig. Gen. Charles E. Yeager, April 28–May 1, 1980, K239.0512-1204 C.2, AFHRA.

270 *"almost ready"*–*"bleeding like"*: Ibid.

271 *"the thin line"*–*"using a broomstick"*: All quotes in Yeager, *Yeager*, 38–40.

271 *"where there"*: Yeager, *Yeager*, 40–43.

271 *"A 15-mile-long parade"*: Quoted in Hall, *1000*, 174.

271 *The* New York Times: Drew Middleton, "U.S. Bombers Rain Fire on Berlin," *NYT*, March 9, 1944, 1.

272 *"Berlin from the air"*: Tommy LaMore and Dan A. Baker, *One Man's War: The WW II Saga of Tommy LaMore* (NY: Taylor, 2002), 80–81.

272 *"still burning"*: "Reich Capital Aflame," *S&S*, March 8, 1944, 1.

272 *"one accurate"*: Quoted in Jeffrey Ethell and Alfred Price, *Target Berlin: Mission 250: 6 March 1944* (London: Greenhill, 2002), 24.

272 *"[bandits] hit us"*: C. B. (Red) Harper, *Buffalo Gal* (Privately printed, n.d.), 90.

272 *"I was so frightened"*: Quoted in Ethell and Price, *Target*, 87.

273 *3,000 tons of explosives:* Gen. T. T. Milton, "A Participant Remembers," *Air Force Magazine,* January 1980, 80–81.

273 *"They looked"*: All quotes in Hall, *1000*, 139.

273 *Air Force claims:* "Eighth Air Force Claims: VIII Bomber Command Narrative of Operations, 1943–1944," 519.332, AFHRA; "VIII Fighter Command Narrative of Operations, 1943–1944," 168.6005-55, AFHRA; Freeman, *War Diary*, 194–95.

273 *"Relief tubes"*–*"were bathed"*–*"best hunting"*–*"The Birdman"*: Hall, *1000*, 181, 186–87.

273 *"heavily laden"*: Harper, *Buffalo*, 101.

273 *"If they can"*: Quoted in Ethell and Price, *Target*, 100.

273 *"The time of what was"*: James B. Reston, "Berlin Blow," *NYT*, March 7, 1944, 4.

274 *"a mess"*: Harper, *Buffalo*, 94–95.

274 *"pitched a fit"*: Ibid., 101.

274 *"I was petrified"*: John Bennett, Jr., *Letters from England* (San Antonio: Privately

printed, 1945), 43–44; interview with John M. Bennett, November 14, 1984, AHM.

274 *"whole battle fleets":* "Over 850 Forts," *S&S,* March 9, 1944, 1; Frederick Graham, "Bomber Men Awed by Havoc in Berlin," *NYT,* March 7, 5.

274 *"surprisingly light"–"eunuch protection"–"like a white":* Harper, *Buffalo,* 83, 96.

275 *"medical":* Le Strange, *Century Bombers,* 95.

275 *"Morale":* Harper, *Buffalo,* 109.

275 *"We had seen"–"candles were lighted"–"Blimey Matey":* Ibid., 99, 103.

275 *"Nazis Shun Battle":* Drew Middleton, "Nazis Shun Battle," *NYT,* March 10, 1944, 1.

276 *"we were taking":* Interview with Maj. Gen. William E. Kepner, July 15, 1944, Spaatz MSS.

276 *"During the past week":* Spaatz to Arnold, March 11, 1944, Spaatz MSS.

276 *Eighth had lost:* Combined Operations Planning Committee, "Fourth Periodic Report on Enemy Daylight Fighter Defense . . . Period 3 March 1944–31 March 1944," April 6, 1944, Spaatz MSS.

276 *"were replaced":* Time, March 20, 1944, 26.

276 *German losses:* Murray, *Luftwaffe,* 239–40.

276 *"the war of attrition":* Bekker, *Luftwaffe War Diaries,* 352.

276 *"Every time I close":* Quoted in Emerson, "POINTBLANK," 469.

276 *April losses:* Murray, *Luftwaffe,* 262.

276 *"storm" group–"death-dealing"–"at any price":* Galland, *First,* 196.

277 *"No lieutenant!":* Quoted in Truman Smith, *The Wrong Stuff: The Adventures and Misadventures of an 8th Air Force Aviator* (St. Petersburg: Southern Heritage Press, 1996), 85–99.

277 *"Berlin is not":* "Survey of Combat Crews in Heavy Bombardment Groups in ETO, June, 1944," 11, AFHRA.

278 *"the murder business":* Author interview with Paul Slawter, November 24, 1998.

278 *"made for"–"He would":* Bert Stiles, *Serenade to the World from 30,000: And Other Stories and Essays,* edited by Roland Bishop Dickinson and Robert Floyd Cooper (Sacramento: Bishop, 1999), 27, 65.

278 *"to kill every Nazi"–"sons of bitches":* Stiles, "And So to Get Started," in Stiles, *30,000,* 70, 77–84; Stiles, *Serenade to the Big Bird: A New Edition of the Classic B-17 Tribute* (Atglen, PA: Schiffer, 2001), 14–15, 37, 104.

278 *Army surveys:* "Survey of Heavy Bomber Crews," May–June 1944, 520.701, AFHRA.

278 *"Altogether, we started":* Quoted in Bowman, *Castles,* 134.

278 *psychiatric casualties:* "Statistical Survey of Emotional Casualties of the Eighth Air Force Aircrews, 25 May, 1945," 520.7421, AFHRA; Davis, *Spaatz,* 379–80.

278 *fighter pilots:* Kepner interview, July 15, 1944, Spaatz MSS.

278 *"One morning":* Quoted in Astor, *Mighty,* 262.

279 *"Colonel, yesterday":* Quoted in *Contrails,* 75–76.

279 *"One night I got home":* Ben Smith, *Chick's Crew: A Tale of the Eighth Air Force* (Privately printed, 1978), 54–56, 71, in ME; interview with Charles W. Bordner, May 13, 1989, AHM.

279 *"the single factor":* South, *Medical Support,* 76.

279 *"the only lottery"—"this time forget":* Quoted in Cleveland Amory, "The Man Everyone in Hollywood Liked," *Parade,* October 21, 1964, 9.

280 *"It may sound corny":* Quoted in Smith, *Jimmy Stewart,* 29.

280 *Distinguished Flying Cross: S&S,* March 4, 1944, 4.

280 *"basically a loner"—"about as unemotional":* Quoted in Donald Dewey, *James Stewart: A Biography* (Atlanta: Turner, 1996), 246.

280 *"he skipped"—"High command":* John Harold Robinson, *A Reason to Live: Moments of Love, Happiness and Sorrow* (Memphis: Castle, 1988), 333.

280 *"He had tremendous":* Ramsey D. Potts quoted in Dewey, *Stewart,* 251; *Washington Star,* April 1, 1944.

281 *hands-on leadership:* Smith, *Jimmy Stewart,* 126.

281 *"They were on the job":* Ibid.; interview with James Stewart, Imperial War Museum Sound Archive, London, England.

281 *"After the first":* Rosenthal interview, March 21, 2002.

281 *"gave the 100th":* Crosby, *Wing,* 320.

281 *"We did the bombing":* Rosenthal interview, March 21, 2002.

282 *"The fighter boys":* Ibid.

282 *"one-man air force":* Gentile, *One-Man Air Force,* 2–3; Hall, *1000,* 268–89. Rickenbacker's official score of twenty-six included four balloons.

282 *"Damon and Pythias":* Quoted in Jablonski, *Air War,* 64.

282 *"He still looks":* McCrary and Scherman, *First,* 20.

283 *"We love fighting":* Quoted in Hall, *1000,* 71.

283 *"A blooded horse":* Kepner interview, July 15, 1944 Spaatz MSS.

283 *"Blakesleewaffe":* Charles Bright, ed. *Historical Dictionary of the U.S. Air Force* (Westport, CT: Greenwood, 1992), 650.

283 *strafing missions:* Fighter Loss Summary, 24 August 1943–31 May 1944, William E. Kepner Papers, 168, 6005-57, AFHRA.

283 *"organized air guerilla warfare":* Eighth Air Force Fighter Command, Report, 6 April 1944, 520.310D, AFHRA; Stephen L. McFarland, "The Evolution of the American Strategic Fighter in Europe, 1942–44," *Journal of Strategic Studies,* June 1987, 199–200.

283 *"You need good eyes":* Zemke and Freeman, *Zemke's Wolf Pack,* 165.

284 *"bouncing":* Interview with W. R. Dunn, November 2, 1973, K239.0512-922 C. 1, AFHRA.

284 *"The enemy fighter":* Interview with Kepner, July 15, 1944, Spaatz MSS.

284 *"New German pilots":* Corum, "Defeat," in Higham and Harris, *Why Air Forces Fail,* 221.

284 *"The first time":* Interview with Gen. Gerald W. Johnson, February 23–24, 1989, K239.0512-1857, AFHRA.

284 *"situational awareness":* Wells, *Courage,* 38.

284 *"The whole thing":* Gentile, *One-Man,* 8.

285 *"The attitude":* Flanagan, "Report," 13–36.

285 *"good hunting":* Hall, *1000,* 261.

285 *"The frank pleasure":* Bond, *Love and Fear,* 40.

285 *higher casualties:* Samuel A. Stouffer et al. *The American Soldier: Adjustment During Army Life,* vol. 1 (Princeton: Princeton University Press, 1949), 407; "Diag-

nosis and Disposition of Combat Crews Suffering from Emotional Disorders,"
520.7411-2, AFHRA.

285   *"The task":* Flanagan, "Report," 13, 16, 30–36.

285   *recklessness:* Maj. Gerald Krosnick, "Anxiety Reaction in Fighter Pilots," in
Wright, "Observations," 55.

285   *"You have to give":* Hall, *1000,* 161–62, 287.

286   *"there would have been"–"could not be built":* USSBS, interview with Lt. Gen. Karl
Koller, 1945, 519.619-23, AFHRA; Kepner interview, July 15, 1944, Spaatz
MSS; Adolf Galland, "Defeat of the Luftwaffe: Fundamental Cause," *Air Uni-
versity Quarterly Review* 6 (Spring 1953): 35.

286   *Hap Arnold . . . agreed:* Arnold to Eisenhower, January 21, 1944, Eisenhower Library, Abilene, Kansas.

287   *"simply have to go home":* Quoted in Stephen E. Ambrose, *D-Day: June 6, 1944:
The Climactic Battle of World War II* (NY: Simon & Schuster, 1944), 96.

287   *Transportation Plan:* For a succinct, if not unbiased, history of the American
plan and the entire pre-invasion planning debate, see W. W. Rostow, *Pre-
Invasion Bombing Strategy: General Eisenhower's Decision of March 25, 1944*
(Austin: University of Texas Press, 1981).

287   *Harris and Spaatz agreed:* Davis, *Spaatz,* 269, 350.

287   *"There could be"–"The entire country":* Quoted in Murray, *Luftwaffe,* 249.

288   *"Harris stood confounded":* Hastings, *Bomber Command,* 276.

288   *intelligence reports:* Arthur William Tedder, *With Prejudice: The War Memoirs of
Marshal of the Royal Air Force, Lord Tedder* (Boston: Little, Brown, 1966), 521.

288   *"a legacy of hate":* Winston Churchill, *The Second World War,* vol. 5, *Closing the
Ring* (Boston: Houghton Mifflin, 1951), 466–67; Eisenhower to Churchill,
April 5, 1944, Eisenhower Library, Abilene, Kansas.

288   *"cold blooded butchery"–"This is war":* Quotes in Forrest C. Pogue, *The Supreme
Command* (Washington, DC: Office of the Chief of Military History, Department of the Army, 1954), 132.

288   *letter from Roosevelt:* Tedder, *With Prejudice,* 531–32; Churchill, *Closing the Ring,*
466–67.

288   *Oil Plan:* "Plan for the Completion of the Combined Bomber Offensive,"
March 5, 1944, Spaatz MSS; *AAF,* vol. 3, 174–75; memo, Spaatz to Portal, "Use
of Strategic Bombers in Support of OVERLORD," March 31, 1944, Spaatz
MSS.

289   *Arnold urged Marshall:* Arnold to Chief of Staff, March 13, 1944, Arnold MSS.

289   *On March 25:* Tedder, *With Prejudice,* 526.

289   *"could not guarantee":* Anderson quoted in Rostow, *Pre-Invasion,* 34-35; the minutes of this March 25 meeting are in Rostow, *Pre-Invasion.*

289   *"the great showdown":* Quoted in ibid., 45.

289   *"If Eisenhower had asked":* Quoted ibid., 44.

290   *"This–––invasion":* Quoted in ibid., 45.

290   *"great attractions":* Rostow, *Pre-Invasion,* 95.

290   *Spaatz . . . resign:* Davis, *Spaatz,* 392.

290   *He gave Spaatz: AAF,* vol. 3, 175.

290   *"On that day"–"the enemy has struck":* Speer, *Inside,* 346–47.

290 *ULTRA intercepts:* William Wister Haines, *Ultra and the History of the United States Strategic Air Forces in Europe vs. the German Air Force* (Frederick, MD: University Publications of America, 1990, originally published in 1945), 99.

290 *"I guess we'll":* Quoted in Rostow, *Pre-Invasion,* 52.

291 *dismembered the rail network:* ETO, "Effectiveness of Air Attack Against Rail Transportation in the Battle of France," June 1, 1945, 164, 138.4-37, AFHRA.

291 "Jabo Rennstrecki": Quoted in Thomas Alexander Hughes, *Over Lord: General Pete Quesada and the Triumph of Tactical Air Power in World War II* (NY: Free Press, 1995), 12.

291 *pre-invasion bombing:* Alan J. Levine, *The Strategic Bombing of Germany, 1940–1945* (New York: Praeger, 1992), 135; Rostow, *Pre-Invasion,* passim; Chester Wilmont, *The Struggle for Europe* (NY: Harper, 1952), 233–38.

291 *"our inability to bring":* Interrogation of Field Marshal Wilhelm Keitel, 1945, 519.619-23, AFHRA; see also Gerd von Rundstedt interview with Carl Spaatz, May 1945, Spaatz MSS.

292 *"We waited"–"big show":* Stiles, *Serenade,* 90–93.

292 *Beirne Lay:* Beirne Lay, Jr., *Presumed Dead* (NY: Dodd, Mead, 1980; originally published in 1945 as *I've Had It*), 125.

292 *"Le débarquement!"–"We were examining"–"With the fighter cover":* All quotes from ibid., 102–3.

293 *"badly scattered": AAF,* vol. 3, 195. The Germans attempted approximately 250 sorties against the invasion force.

293 *the Eighth on D-Day: AAF,* vol. 3, 143, 192.

293 *Air Force losses:* Office of Air Force History, Washington, DC, "Losses of the Eighth and Fifteenth Air Forces"; Davis, *Spaatz,* Appendix 5, 23, 24; U.S. War Department, Office of Statistical Control, *Army Air Forces Statistical Digest, World War II* (Washington, DC: U.S. Government Printing Office, 1945), tables 118 and 136.

294 *"poor bastards"–"Blood is the same"–"the only thing":* Stiles, *Serenade,* 90–93.

Chapter 11: The Fatal Trap

296 *"the greatest armada":* Ernie Pyle, Scripps Howard wire copy, June 16, 1944, copy in Lilly Library, Indiana University, Bloomington, Indiana.

296 *"a wonderful"–"does not have"–"a long series":* All Arnold quotes in this section are from John W. Huston, ed., *American Airpower Comes of Age: General Henry H. "Hap" Arnold's War Diaries* (Maxwell Air Force Base, AL: Air University Press, 2001), 148–59, and Arnold, *Global,* 238–39. For German raids against the Normandy beachhead, see Spaatz to Arnold, July 17, 1944, Arnold MSS.

297 *"Vengeance Weapon 1":* For the origins of the V-1 project, see Michael J. Neufeld, *The Rocket and the Reich: Peenemünde and the Coming of the Ballistic Missile Era* (Cambridge: Harvard University Press, 1999), 147–48.

297 *"dislocate the war effort":* Dwight D. Eisenhower, *Crusade in Europe* (Garden City: Doubleday, 1948), 260.

297 *cruise missile:* For Arnold's interest in the cruise missile, see Kenneth P. Werrell,

The Evolution of the Cruise Missile (Maxwell Air Force Base, AL: Air University Press, 1985).

297 *"Rocket Gun Coast":* Quoted in *AAF,* vol. 3, 95.

297 *Operation Crossbow:* USSBS, *V-Weapons (Crossbow) Campaign* (Washington, DC: Military Analysis Division, U.S. Government Printing Office, 1945), 1.

298 *poison gas: AAF,* vol. 3, 530; Secretary, British Chiefs of Staff committee to the Prime Minister, July 5, 1944, Arnold MSS.

299 *"a target":* Quoted in Jack Olsen, *Aphrodite: Desperate Mission* (NY: Putnam, 1970), 48; "The Flying Bomb," British Information Services, November 1944, copy in ME.

299 *over 18,000 people:* Statistics on V-1s are from Alfred Price, "V-weapons," in Ian Dear and M. R. D. Foot, eds., *Oxford Companion to World War II* (Oxford: Oxford University Press, 2001), 798. Over 10,000 flying bombs were launched against England; roughly 2,000 of them exploded prematurely. Of the 7,446 that reached Britain, 3,957 were shot down.

299 *"idiocy":* Panter-Downes, *London War Notes,* 333, 335, 339.

299 *"Goddamn the Nazi":* Harry A. Dolph, *The Evader: An American Airman's Eight Months with the Dutch Underground* (Austin: Eaken, 1991), 28–31.

300 *"push-button bombs":* Olsen, *Aphrodite,* 29. All Pool quotes are from Olsen, *Aphrodite,* 27–30.

300 *"Hey, fellows":* Ibid., 30.

301 *rocket sites:* Butcher, *Three Years,* 35.

301 *"Aside from":* Spaatz to Arnold, July 22, 1944, Spaatz MSS.

301 *"pride and joy":* Spaatz to War Department, June 20, 1944, Spaatz MSS.; Olsen, *Aphrodite,* 152.

301 *"stuff a planeload":* Olsen, *Aphrodite,* 95.

302 *debacle:* "Report on Aphrodite Project," January 20, 1945, 527.431A-A, AFHRA; Olsen, *Aphrodite,* 100.

302 *"fine neck":* Quoted in Robert Dallek, *An Unfinished Life: John F. Kennedy, 1917–1963* (Boston: Little, Brown, 2003), 106.

302 *Kennedy's death:* Doolittle to Spaatz, August 12, 1944, Spaatz MSS.

303 *cause for the crash:* Olsen, *Aphrodite,* 228–29. In 2001, a man who had served in the war as a British telecommunications mechanic offered a different explanation. The Americans had failed to warn the British to turn off their radar in the path of the plane and a strong pulse from one of the English ground radar stations set off the delicate radio controls of Kennedy's Liberator, triggering a lethal jet explosion. See Dallek, *Unfinished,* 107. This explanation is impossible to substantiate.

303 *dead targets:* USSBS, *V-Weapons,* passim; Olsen, *Aphrodite,* 254.

303 *Arnold stubbornly kept Aphrodite going:* Spaatz to Doolittle, September 7, 1944, Anderson Diary, Papers of F. L. Anderson, Hoover Institute on War, Revolution and Peace, Stanford University.

303 *almost 2,000 aircrew:* USSBS, *V-Weapons,* 24.

303 *"The best way":* Galland, *First,* 235.

304 *"For the first time":* Panter-Downes, *London War Notes,* 342–43.

304 *"we faced a real":* Omar N. Bradley and Clay Blair, *A General's Life: An Autobiography* (NY: Simon & Schuster, 1983), 272.

304 *"a truly massive":* Russell F. Weigley, *Eisenhower's Lieutenants: The Campaign of France and Germany, 1944–1945* (Bloomington: Indiana University Press, 1981) 137–38.

304 *carpet bombings:* Carlo D'Este, *Decision in Normandy* (NY: Dutton, 1988), 394.

305 *Operation Cobra:* For an excellent analysis of Cobra, see John J. Sullivan, "The Botched Air Support of Operation Cobra," *Parameters: Journal of the US Army War College* 18, no. 1 (March 1988): 106.

305 *Carl Spaatz fumed:* U.S. Air Force Historical Study No. 88, "The Employment of Strategic Bombers in a Tactical Role, 1941–1951" (USAF Historical Division, Research Studies Institute, Air University, 1954), 75–76.

305 *"A lot of us":* Rosenthal interview, March 29, 2003.

305 *Bradley flew to England:* Omar N. Bradley, 25 July 1944, Chester Hansen Papers, USMHI.

305 *"great conference":* Quoted in Weigley, *Eisenhower's Lieutenants,* 138; Omar Bradley, *A Soldier's Story* (NY: Henry Holt, 1951), 341.

306 *A compromise of 1,250 yards:* John H. deRussy memorandum, "Summary of Planning and Execution of Missions 24 and 25 July 1944," 520.453A, AFHRA; Harold Ohlke, "Report of the Investigation of Bombing, July 24–25," Spaatz MSS.

306 *Twenty-seven soldiers:* Sullivan, "Cobra," 103.

306 *Rosenthal's ship:* Rosenthal interview, March 29, 2003.

306 *"The flight across":* Ernie Pyle, *Brave Men* (NY: Henry Holt, 1944), 298–301.

307 *"Christ, not again!":* Quoted in Hughes, *Over Lord,* 216.

307 *killed by Eighth Air Force:* Kenneth Heckler, "VII Corps in Operation COBRA," unpublished report, Modern Military Records Division, NA.

307 *never again:* Bradley, *General's Life,* 280.

307 *Doolittle:* Doolittle, *Lucky,* 375–76; Hoyt Vandenberg War Diary, 27 July 1944, Hoyt Vandenberg Papers, LC.

307 *"like a conveyor belt":* Fritz Bayerlein interview, "Panzer-Lehr Division," 24–25 July 1944, Historical Division Headquarters, U.S. Army Europe, copy in USMHI.

308 *Lightning Joe Collins:* Collins tells his own story in *Lightning Joe: An Autobiography* (Baton Rouge: Louisiana State University Press, 1979).

308 *Eisenhower and heavies:* For more on this theme, see Ian Gooderson, *Air Power at the Battlefront: Allied Close Air Support in Europe, 1943–45* (London: Frank Cass, 1998).

308 *dropping supplies: AAF,* vol. 3, 502–3.

308 *"so that they could see":* Lt. Gen. Elwood R. Quesada, "Tactical Air Power," *Impact* (May 1945; repr., Washington, DC: Office of Assistant Chief of Air Staff, Intelligence, 1992), passim.

309 *"It was complete chaos":* Quoted in Stephen Ambrose, *Citizen Soldiers: The U.S. Army from the Normandy Beaches to the Bulge to the Surrender of Germany, June 7, 1944–May 7, 1945* (NY: Simon & Schuster, 1997), 102.

309 *"fierce looking":* Lay, *Presumed,* 105–19. All other Lay quotes in Lay, *Presumed.*

310 *Battle of Normandy casualties:* D'Este, *Normandy,* 517.

310 *written permission:* Eisenhower to Tedder, June 29, 1944, copy in Spaatz MSS; USSBS, *The Effects of Strategic Bombing on the German War Economy* (Washington, DC: U.S. Government Printing Office, 1945), 4–5.

310 *"diversion"–"a complete success":* Harris, *Bomber Offensive,* 220.

311 *"front-line strength":* AAF, vol. 2, 358.

311 *The Americans bore the burden:* "Air Offensive Against the German Oil Industry," January 29, 1945, AFHRA.

311 *Over 70 percent:* USSBS, *Statistical Appendix* (Washington, DC: U.S. Government Printing Office, 1947), 11, 13; USSBS, *Over-all Report (European War)* (Washington, DC: U.S. Government Printing Office, 1945), 71: USSBS, *Oil Division, Final Report* (Washington, DC: U.S. Government Printing Office, second edition, January 1947), 2.

312 *"first heavy blow":* Interrogations of Albert Speer, 30 May 1945 and 18 July 1945, in Webster and Frankland, *Strategic Air Offensive,* vol. 4, 371–95.

312 *"an impossible situation":* Speer to Hitler, June 30, 1944, 137.1-3, AFHRA; interrogation of Speer, July 18, 1945, in Webster and Frankland, *Strategic Air Offensive,* vol. 4, 379.

312 *half its total energy:* USSBS, *Oil Division, Final Report,* 15.

312 *coal for 90 percent–supplied only 7 percent:* Raymond G. Stokes, "The Oil Industry in Nazi Germany, 1936–1945," *Business History Review* 59 (Summer 1985): 1.

312 *two-to-three-month reserve:* USSBS, *Oil Division, Final Report,* 1.

312 *Romanian fields:* Daniel Yergin, *The Prize: The Epic Quest for Oil, Money and Power* (NY: Simon & Schuster, 1991), 334.

313 *synthetic oil industry:* USSBS, *The German Oil Industry, Ministerial Report, Team 78* (Washington, DC: U.S. Government Printing Office, second edition, 1947), 3–15, 38, 80.

313 *Albert Speer:* Ibid., 75.

313 *85 percent–Even today:* Stokes, "Oil Industry," 276. For Germany's oil industry, see also Arnold Krammer, "Fueling the Third Reich," *Technology and Culture* 19 (June 1978): 394–422.

313 *used the Fischer-Tropsch process:* Allied intelligence estimated that the Fischer-Tropsch plants produced 1.3 million tons per year. The correct figure was .5 million tons. The amount of fuel produced by the crude oil refineries was about one million tons less than Allied intelligence reported. See Charles Webster and Noble Frankland, *The Strategic Air Offensive Against Germany, 1939–1945,* vol. 3, *Victory* (London: Her Majesty's Stationery Office, 1961), 226; and USSBS, *German Oil Industry,* 79–84.

313 *chemical empire:* USSBS, *Oil Division, Final Report,* 1.

314 *Leuna . . . Ludwigshafen:* USSBS, *German Oil Industry,* 4; USSBS, *Ludwigshafen-Oppau Works of I G Farbenindustrie, A G, Ludwigshafen, Germany* (Washington, DC: U.S. Government Printing Office, August 4, 1945), passim.

314 *oil and chemical plants:* The nitrogen produced in the synthetic plants was also used to make fertilizers. Allied intelligence projected that most of the damage to the chemical plants would fall on the agricultural economy. See USSBS, *Powder, Explosives, Special Rockets and Jet Propellants, War Gases and Smoke Acid* (Washington, DC: U.S. Government Printing Office, 1945), passim.

314　*concentrated . . . rebuked . . . Karl Krauch:* USSAF, *Oil Division, Final Report,* 12–14; Speer, *Inside,* 347–49.

314　*"long expected":* Interrogation of Speer, July 18, 1945, in Webster and Frankland, *Strategic Air Offensive,* vol. 4, 379; USSBS, *German Oil Industry,* 53.

315　*"could [alone] have":* USSBS, "Interrogation of Reichsminister Albert Speer," May 15–22, 1945, 371-19, AFHRA.

315　*more than a third of Germany's total Bergius output:* Ronald C. Cooke and Ron Conyers Nesbit, *Target: Hitler's Oil: Allied Attacks on German Oil Supplies, 1939–1945* (London: William Kimber, 1985), 140.

315　*"the grimmest fight"–defenses got better:* William Bayles, "The Story Behind the Nazi Defeat: The Strategic Bombing Attack on Hitler's Oil Supply," *American Mercury* 62 (January 1946): 91; USSBS, *Ammonkiakwerke Merseburg G.m.b.H., Leuna, Germany* (Washington, DC: U.S. Government Printing Office, July 23, 1946), 1–6; Volta Torrey, "The Nine Lives of Leuna," *Popular Science Monthly,* November 1945, 127.

316　*13,200 heavy antiaircraft guns:* Boog et al., *Germany and the Second World War,* vol. 6, 616. For a history of German flak defenses, see Edward B. Westermann, *Flak: German Anti-aircraft Defenses, 1914–1945* (Lawrence: University Press of Kansas, 2001).

316　*71 percent of the wounds: AAF Statistical Digest, World War II,* December 1945, 255, 134. 11-6, AFHRA. Figures on wounds are from Link and Coleman, *Medical Support,* 697. From September 1944 to May 1945 the Eighth lost 551 bombers to fighters and 1,263 to flak. The German triple-purpose 88 had an effective ceiling of 26,000 feet; 105mm guns could reach to 30,000 feet. From the standpoint of crew position, bombardiers received the greatest number of flak wounds, followed by tail gunners and navigators.

316　*Flak was a grossly inefficient:* USSBS, APO 413, "Interviews with Generals von Axthelm and Lt. Col. Sieber, July 12–13, 1945," 137.315-68, AFHRA; A. D. von Renz, "The Development of German Anti-aircraft Weapons and Equipment of All Types up to 1945," 258–80, AFHRA.

316　*5,400 American planes: AAF Statistical Digest: World War II,* 255–56.

316　*"the land of doom":* Gordon W. Weir, "Navigating Through World War II," MSS, ME; see also Stiles, *Serenade,* 75.

316　*"I can still remember":* Tom Landry, with Gregg Lewis, *Tom Landry: An Autobiography* (NY: HarperCollins, 1991), 69. Landry served with the 493rd BG, stationed near Debach.

317　*"While antiaircraft fire":* Quoted in Geoffrey Perret, *Winged Victory: The Army Air Forces in World War II* (NY: Random House, 1993), 331.

317　*"Over the [oil plant]":* Smith, "Chick's Crew," 97–98, 121, 157, 159–60.

317　*"Every time we came back":* Stiles, *Serenade,* 75.

317　*passive stress:* Bond, *Love and Fear,* 88.

317　*"In the old days":* Stiles, *Serenade,* 83, 86.

318　*Eighth lost 1,022 heavy bombers: AAF,* vol. 3, 303, 306.

318　*more than a one-in-three chance:* Davis, *Spaatz,* 446. The actual figure was 36 percent.

318   *"cynical, irreligious"*: All Smith quotes in Smith, "Chick's Crew," 137–39, 147–49, 171–73.

318   *"we had no idea"*: Landry, *Landry,* 69.

318   *Postwar Air Force studies:* USSBS, *Bombing Accuracy, USAAF, Heavy and Medium Bombers in ETO* (Washington, DC: U.S. Government Printing Office, January 1947), 1.

319   *One in seven of the bombs–plant equipment–firefighting:* USSBS, *Leuna,* 20, 51; 8th Air Force, "Memo for Selection of MPI and Bombs and Fuzes for Attack Against Synthetic Plants," November 7, 1944, 520.310n B VIII, AFHRA.

319   *"successful prosecution"*: Speer to Martin Bormann, September 16, 1944, in Webster and Frankland, *Strategic Air Offensive,* vol. 4, 348.

320   *labor army:* Interrogation of Speer, July 18, 1945, in Webster and Frankland, *Strategic Air Offensive,* vol. 4, 381; USSBS, *German Oil Industry,* 57.

320   *oil industry disabled:* Ibid., 382.

320   *"concrete" and "bombs"*: Ibid., 380.

320   *9 percent of plant capacity:* USSBS, *Leuna,* 1–4; USSBS, *German Oil Industry,* 4–5.

320   *"was just as bad"*: USSBS, Interrogation of Speer, May 15–20, 1945.

320   *"such a toll"*: Speer, *Inside,* 350.

321   *aviation fuel: AAF,* vol. 3, 303; USSBS, *German Oil Industry,* 59; Alan S. Milward, *The German Economy at War* (London: Athlone, 1965), passim.

321   *Ploesti:* Fifteenth Air Force, *The Air Battle of Ploesti* (Bari, Italy, 1944), passim.

321   *on August 20:* Headquarters, 97th Bombardment Group (H), Group Intelligence Office, Special Narrative Report; Mission: 20 August 1944, Oswiecim Synthetic 0/R, Poland, 670.322, AFHRA. Oswiecim was the Polish name for Auschwitz.

321   *"It was the practice"*: Milt Groban, "To the Editor," *Commentary* 7 (July 1978), 10.

322   *heated public debate:* The controversy was first raised by historian David Wyman's passionate essay "Why Auschwitz Was Never Bombed," *Commentary* 65 (May 1978): 36–47, and his book *The Abandonment of the Jews: America and the Holocaust, 1941–1945* (NY: Pantheon, 1984). The literature on the issue is voluminous. There is, however, an excellent anthology of essays and documents, Michael J. Neufeld and Michael Berenbaum, eds., *The Bombing of Auschwitz: Should the Allies Have Attempted It?* (NY: St. Martin's, in association with the United States Holocaust Memorial Museum, 2000).

322   *"the greatest"*: Quoted in Miller, *Story,* 520.

322   *"too great"*: Quoted in Martin Gilbert, "The Contemporary Case for the Feasibility of Bombing Auschwitz," in Neufeld and Berenbaum, *The Bombing of Auschwitz,* 71.

322   *Appeals from European underground groups:* Message to War Refugee Board from Roswell McClelland, no. 4291, 6 July, copy in United States Holocaust Memorial Museum, subject file: Camps–Auschwitz; the complete reports and maps of the camp did not reach the Allied governments until November.

323   *"diversion of considerable"*: Memo, Thomas T. Handy, Assistant Chief of Staff, "The Proposed Air Action to Impede Deportation of Hungarian and Slovak Jews," June 23, 1944, NA.

323   *"that the most effective relief"*: Lt. Gen. Joseph T. McNarney, Memorandum for the Assistant Secretary of War, 28 January 1944, NA.

323   *"the direct result"*: Maj. Gen. Thomas T. Handy to the Chief of Staff, February 8, 1944, NA.

323   *"round trip flight"*: Quoted in Morton Mintz, "Why Didn't We Bomb Auschwitz," *Washington Post* (April 17, 1983), D2.

323   *"most sympathetic"*: Gilbert, "The Contemporary Case," in Neufeld and Berenbaum, *The Bombing of Auschwitz,* 2.

323   *"shuttle missions"*: *AAF,* vol. 3, 308–16.

324   *640 miles:* Eaker to Spaatz, April 27, 1944, Spaatz MSS.

324   *airpower historians:* Rondall Rice, "Bombing Auschwitz: US 15th Air Force and the Military Aspects of a Possible Attack," *War in History* 6 (1999): 205–29; Richard G. Davis, "The Bombing of Auschwitz: Comments on a Historical Speculation," in Neufeld and Berenbaum, *Bombing of Auschwitz,* 214–26.

324   *Richard G. Davis:* Davis, "Bombing of Auschwitz," in Neufeld and Berenbaum, *The Bombing of Auschwitz,* passim.

324   *Anti-aircraft guns:* Headquarters Fifth Wing, Annex to Operations Order no. 671 for 20 August 1944, 19 August 1944, 670.332, AFHRA.

324   *accuracy record:* Rice, "Bombing Auschwitz," in Neufeld and Berenbaum, *The Bombing of Auschwitz,* 222.

324   *rebuild gas chambers:* Davis, "Bombing of Auschwitz," in Neufeld and Berenbaum, *The Bombing of Auschwitz,* 223.

325   *Frederick Anderson:* Anderson to Spaatz, Spaatz MSS.

325   *about 7 percent:* Davis, "Bombing of Auschwitz," in Neufeld and Berenbaum, *The Bombing of Auschwitz,* 221.

325   *"costly and hopeless"*: *AAF,* vol. 3, 316.

325   *ordered an airdrop:* Norman Davies, *Rising '44: The Battle for Warsaw* (NY: Viking, 2004), 374–81.

325   *September 18: AAF,* vol. 3, 316–17.

326   *Stalin withdrew permission:* Ibid.

326   *Great Patriotic War:* Jeffrey Herf, "The Nazi Extermination Camps and the Ally to the East: Could the Red Army and Air Force Have Stopped or Slowed the Final Solution?" *Kritika: Explorations in Russian and Eurasian History* 4 (Fall 2003): 929.

326   *arrived at Auschwitz:* Martin Gilbert, *Auschwitz and the Allies* (NY: Holt, Rinehart & Winston, 1981), 331–37.

326   *"It was not"*: Quoted in Gilbert, "The Contemporary Case," in Neufeld and Berenbaum, *Bombing of Auschwitz,* 75.

326   *Spaatz had ordered a massive raid:* Davis, "Bombing of Auschwitz," in Neufeld and Berenbaum, *The Bombing of Auschwitz,* 217.

326   *"record the evidence"*: Quoted in Roger M. Williams, "Why Wasn't Auschwitz Bombed?", *Commonweal* 105 (November 1978): 748.

327   *"we were not afraid"*: Elie Wiesel, *Night,* trans. Stella Rodway (NY: Hill & Wang, 1969), 71; Auschwitz survivor quoted in William J. Vanden Heuvel and Rafael Medoff, "Should the Allies Have Bombed Auschwitz?" http://hnn.us/articles/4268.html.

327 *Lou Loevsky:* Author interview with Louis Loevsky, June 16, 2006.

327 *Rosie Rosenthal:* Author interview with Robert Rosenthal, April 11, 2006.

327 *Milt Groban:* Groban, "Letter," 10.

327 *This was the only time:* Wyman, "Why Auschwitz," 41.

327 *Anderson cautioned Spaatz:* Anderson to Spaatz, October 5, 1944, Spaatz MSS. In November, after finally receiving a copy of the full text of the report by the two recent escapees from Auschwitz, a shocked John Pehle, who up to then had not recommended bombing, changed his mind and urged immediate action. Word had reached him that the killing process had been stepped up; see US, Executive Office of the President, War Refugee Board, German Extermination Camps–Auschwitz and Birkenau, November 1944, copy in United States Holocaust Memorial Museum, subject file: Camps–Auschwitz Bombing to Camps–Auschwitz WRB Report.

327 *"The President could do it":* Quoted in Mintz, "Why Didn't," D1.

327 *no reliable record:* For almost his entire life, McCloy maintained that he never brought the issue to Roosevelt. But in a taped private conversation with Henry Morgenthau III in 1986, when he was eighty-eight years old, McCloy said he did inform Roosevelt and that the president vehemently rejected the idea of bombing Auschwitz, claiming that the Nazis would find other ways to kill the prisoners, and that the Air Force would be accused of killing innocent people. There is no written record of this conversation between McCloy and Roosevelt, yet historian Michael Beschloss took McCloy at his word in his recent book *The Conquerors.* Even David Wyman, the historian who first made the case for the bombing of Auschwitz, said he had been unable to find, in years of archival research, "evidence that the bombing question ever came to Roosevelt." Wyman quoted in Mintz, "Why Didn't We Bomb Auschwitz?", D2; Michael Beschloss, *The Conquerors: Roosevelt, Truman and the Destruction of Hitler's Germany, 1941–1945* (NY: Simon & Schuster, 2002), 66–67.

328 *"for the first time":* Quoted in Davis, *Spaatz,* 442.

328 *Shortages . . . in the Reich:* USSBS, *Defeat of the German Air Force* (Washington, DC: U.S. Government Printing Office, 1945), 11.

328 *100-octane gasoline–Doolittle:* German Oil Industry, 59–60; *AAF,* vol. 3, 303; Doolittle, *Lucky,* 174–77.

328 *"This summer is":* Knoke, *I Flew,* 166–69.

328 *Allied nations consumed:* Yergin, *Prize,* 379. For Hitler and oil, see also Richard Overy, *Why the Allies Won* (New York: W. W. Norton, 1997), chap. 7.

328 *"This is a war":* Quoted in Yergin, *Prize,* 382.

329 *"unbearable":* Galland, *First,* 229; Speer to Hitler, August 30, 1944, in Webster and Frankland, *Strategic Air Offensive,* vol. 4, 331.

329 *90 percent of the world's natural oil output:* Overy, *Why the Allies,* 228.

329 *supplies of methanol–explosives:* Methanol output dropped from an essential production of 34,000 tons a month to 8,750. Nitric acid and synthetic rubber production were more than halved. USSBS, *Oil Division,* 3–4; Speer, *Inside,* 406; Speer to Hitler, August 30, 1944, in Webster and Frankland, *Strategic Air Offensive,* vol. 4, 330.

329 *"The combined effects":* Overy, *Why the Allies,* 131.

330 *"If the attacks":* Speer to Hitler, Report of 30 August 1944, in Webster and Frankland, *Strategic Air Offensive,* vol. 4, 332–33.

330 *Galland believed:* Galland, *First,* 237.

Chapter 12: Prisoners of the Swiss

332 *"meat-starved":* All Culler quotes from Dan Culler, *Black Hole of Wauwilermoos* (Green Valley, AZ: Circle of Thorns, 1995), 104, 156–64.

333 *Fifteen other American bombers:* Archives of the Swiss Internees Association, Jackson, NJ, (hereafter SIA).

333 *"were in bad shape":* Culler, *Black Hole,* 165.

333 *Swiss would kill:* Cathryn J. Prince, *Shot from the Sky: American POWs in Switzerland* (Annapolis: Naval Institute Press, 2003), 23–24.

333 *"We had heard":* Quoted in Stephen Tanner, *Refuge from the Reich: American Airmen and Switzerland During World War II* (Rockville Center, NY: Sarpedon, 2000), 16.

333 Collier's: John Bishop, "Swedish Stopover: Interned American Fliers," *Collier's,* August 26, 1944, 25–26.

334 *"without indication":* Arnold to Spaatz, July 27, 1944, Spaatz MSS.

334 *"resent the implication":* Spaatz to Arnold, July 29, 1945, Spaatz MSS.

334 *"a complete lack":* William W. Corcoran to Hershel V. Johnson, May 23, 1944, Spaatz MSS.

334 *"benevolent hosts":* U.S. Military Attaché, Bern, to Arnold, August 2, 1944, Arnold MSS.

335 *947 tried to escape—Sweden:* Prince, *Shot from the Sky,* 43, 190.

335 *Legge told Spaatz's headquarters:* Maj. Benjamin E. Norman to Brig. Gen. George C. McDonald, October 5, 1944, Spaatz MSS; Prince, *Shot from the Sky,* 122–23.

336 *"To my mind":* Culler, *Black Hole,* 168.

336 *rationing:* Testimony of Lt. Wallace Orville Northfelt, for the War Crimes Office, Judge Advocate General's Department, War Department, USA, September 17, 1945, NA.

337 *alcohol:* Author interview with Robert Long, January 4, 2005.

337 *"Many were married":* Quoted in Prince, *Shot from the Sky,* 87–88.

337 *"the call to return":* Ibid., 123.

338 *"Ever since that experience":* Quoted in Tanner, *Refuge,* 140.

338 *The German legation:* Alan Morris Schom, "A Survey of Nazi and Pro-Nazi Groups in Switzerland: 1930–1945," 1, Simon Wiesenthal Center, http://www.wiesenthal.com/swiss/survey/noframes/conclusions.htm; Jerrold M. Packard, *Neither Friend nor Foe: The European Neutrals in World War II* (NY: Macmillan, 1992), 10.

338 *"Probably no other country":* Schom, "A Survey," http://www.wiesenthal.com/swiss/survey/noframes/conclusions. htm.

338 *economic ties with Nazi Germany:* Ibid., 1–5, Conclusions.

339 *Romanian oil . . . Italy . . . Germany:* Urs Schwarz, *The Eye of the Hurricane: Switzerland in World War Two* (Boulder: Westview, 1980), 22; Packard, *Neither Friend nor Foe,* 71–75.

339 *"Switzerland's rail system":* Prince, *Shot from the Sky,* 174.

339 *Jews seeking refuge:* Schom, "A Survey," 15–16, 18–19; Alfred Häsler, *The Lifeboat Is Full: Switzerland and the Refugees, 1933–1945* (NY: Funk & Wagnalls, 1969), 49; Thomas Sancton, "A Painful Lesson," *Time,* February 24, 1997, 41; Alan Cowell, "Swiss Begin to Question Heroism in War," *NYT,* February 8, 1997; Jonathan Petropoulos, "Co-Opting Nazi Germany: Neutrality in Europe During World War II," *Dimensions: A Journal of Holocaust Studies* 7, no. 1 (1997): 15–21.

340 *"Finally in April 1945":* Quoted in Prince, *Shot from the Sky,* 163; Gerhard Weinberg, *The World at Arms: A Global History of WWII* (Cambridge: Cambridge University Press, 1995) 397–98. Pilet-Golaz served as president from January 1940 until November 1944, when the council finally forced him to step down.

340 *"How neutral":* Quoted in Prince, *Shot from the Sky,* 22.

340 *"Swiss fighter aircraft":* Legation of the United States of America to the Federal Political Department, Bern, June 5, 1944, NA.

341 *"have in fact":* Leland Harrison to Cordell Hull, June 13, 1944, NA.

341 *"rejoin the fight":* Culler, *Black Hole,* 104, 170.

341 *"The most amazing":* Ibid., 196.

342 *"We did everything":* Quoted in Tanner, *Refuge,* 187.

342 *"I'm sorry to bring":* Culler, *Black Hole,* 207.

342 *"like scum":* Testimony of James I. Misuraca, SIA.

342 *"What happened to me":* All Culler quotes from Culler, *Black Hole,* 212–14.

343 *"There isn't any abuse"–"iron discipline":* Quoted in Prince, *Shot from the Sky,* 160–61.

344 *"will receive no support":* Brig. Gen. B. R. Legge, "To All U.S.A.A.F. Internees," September 14, 1944, SIA.

344 *formal protests:* Brig. Gen. B. R. Legge to Col. Divisionnaire Dolfuss, October 19, 1944, NA; Legge to Leland Harrison, American minister, Bern, November 1, 1944, NA.

344 *Culler . . . day in court:* Culler, *Black Hole,* 235; Prince, *Shot from the Sky,* 158.

344 *"The last I remember":* Culler, *Black Hole,* 248.

345 *wounding Telford:* Escape and Evasion Reports, George Telford, September 30, 1944, Daniel Culler, October 1, 1944, NA.

345 *Spaatz . . . pressure the Swiss:* Maj. Benjamin E. Norman to Brig. Gen. George C. McDonald, October 5, 1944, Spaatz MSS.

345 *Sam Woods . . . Thomas J. Watson:* John V. H. Dippel, *Two Against Hitler: Stealing the Nazis' Best-Kept Secrets* (New York: Praeger, 1992), 126–27, 194; Prince, *Shot from the Sky,* 126–28.

346 *Lt. Col. James Wilson:* Memo, Lt. Col. James W. Wilson, "Combat Crew Morale in the Eighth Air Force," September 15, 1944, 168.49, AFHRA.

346 *"no crew":* Office of the Director of Intelligence, Headquarters, United States Strategic Air Forces in Europe, "Interrogation of Lt. Robert A. Hill, 21 June 1944," Spaatz MSS; Col. Charles E. Rayens to Military Attaché, American Embassy, London, June 8, 1944, Spaatz MSS.

346 *"misled by":* USSTAF Surgeon General, "Memorandum Report on Morale of Combat Crew Personnel of the Eighth Air Force, August 31, 1944," 519.701, AFHRA; *AAF,* vol. 3, 307.

346   *"I believe this is":* Quoted in Tanner, *Refuge,* 209.

346   *The report would conclude:* Hans-Heiri Stapfer and Gino Künzle, *Strangers in a Strange Land,* vol. 2, *Escape to Neutrality* (Carrollton, TX: Squadron/Signal Publications, 1992).

346   *Army intelligence and OSS:* Culler, *Black Hole,* 317–18.

347   *"Sergeant, you are":* Quoted in ibid., 316.

347   *"I warned you":* Quoted in ibid., 338.

Chapter 13: My Bellyful of War

348   *"The old beat-up":* Culler, *Black Hole,* 304–5.

349   *Ellis "Woody" Woodward:* Ellis M. Woodward, "Nazi Germany's Luftwaffe Storm Groups: The Untold Story," 104–11, MSS, ME; later published as *Flying School: Combat Hell* (Baltimore: American Literary Press, 1998).

349   *September 12, 1944:* Headquarters, 493rd Bombardment Group, Mission Report, Mission no. 455, September 13, 1944, NA.

350   *Battering Ram:* Adam Lynch, "Kassel: Mission Disaster," *Military Heritage* 1, no. 4 (February, 2000): 56. The plane's official name was Fw 190A 8/R8.

350   *"From such range":* Quoted in Alfred Price, *The Last Year of the Luftwaffe: May 1944 to May 1945* (Osceola, WI: Motorbooks, 1991), 52.

350   *"The chance of surviving"–"One must keep in mind":* Vorberg in Woodward, *Flying School,* 161.

351   *"tighten it up":* Quoted in Lynch, "Kassel," 57.

351   *the Sturmbocks hung:* Aaron Elson interview with Web Uebelhoer, September 30, 1999, www.kasselmission.com.

351   *"bailing out in rows":* Vorberg in Woodward, *Flying School,* 163.

351   *"As I approached":* Testimony of Heinz Papenberg, n.d., www.militariacollecting.com.

352   *"We traveled":* Quoted in Bowman, *Great American Air,* 110; Lynch, "Kassel," 60.

352   *new tactics to combat the Storm Groups:* Galland, "Birth, Life and Death," 58, Spaatz MSS.

353   *"German intelligence"–"more balls than brains":* Yeager, *Yeager,* 44, 58.

354   *Spaatz and Doolittle pressed Hap Arnold:* Arnold to Spaatz, September 21, 1944, Spaatz MSS; Doolittle, *Lucky,* 385.

354   *"We flyers had one":* Kogler, "Lecture on the German Air Force," 12, 14.

354   *"What was the reason":* Army Air Force, Enemy Intelligence Summaries, Interrogation of Hermann Göring, May 29, 1945, 519.619–3, AFHRA.

354   *"Terror is only":* Quoted in Joachim Fest, *Speer: The Final Verdict* (San Diego: Harcourt, 2001), 168. See also Galland, *First,* 259; Kershaw, *Hitler: Nemesis,* 635.

354   *"sweep Allied air power"–"You had a great ally":* Göring interview, June 29, 1945, AFHRA.

355   *"I want no more planes"–"a program five times":* Speer, *Inside,* 408.

355   *"That was the first command"–"We must":* Ibid., 409.

355   *ME 262 tested:* Galland, *First,* 260.

355 *These factors:* Manfred Boehm, *JG 7: The World's First Jet Fighter Unit, 1944–1945,* translated by David Johnson (Atglen, PA: Schiffer, 1992), 189.

356 *Nowotny's pilots destroyed:* Kenn C. Rust and William N. Hess, "The German Jets and the U.S. Army Air Force," *American Aviation Historical Society Journal* 8 (Fall 1963): 168.

356 *"For many pilots":* Bekker, *Luftwaffe War Diaries,* 356.

356 *"I saw a large airdrome":* Yeager, *Yeager,* 61.

356 *"The Great Blow":* Galland, *First,* 232–33.

356 *"This was going"–"the Western Allies":* Galland, "Birth, Life and Death," 59, Spaatz MSS; Galland, *First,* 241.

357 *"It was a difficult":* Galland, *First,* 241. See also *AAF,* vol. 4, 657–58.

357 *"The flying in November 1944":* Quoted in Price, *Last Year,* 111.

357 *"His pilots":* Spaatz to Lovett, December 13, 1944, Spaatz MSS.

357 *"I want to fly":* Cooper, *Serenade to the Blue Lady,* 220. Stiles was killed on November 26, 1944.

357 *"a great land battle":* Galland, *First,* 241.

357 *"unprepared and disheartened":* Galland, "Birth, Life and Death," 59, Spaatz MSS.

357 *"a private dynasty":* Ibid., 61.

358 *outran their supply line:* Alfred D. Chandler, Jr., et al., eds., *The Papers of Dwight David Eisenhower,* vol. 4 (Baltimore: Johns Hopkins University Press, 1970), 2118.

359 *Combined Strategic Targets Committee:* Spaatz to Arnold, October 4, 1944, Spaatz MSS.

359 *The Combined Chiefs decided:* Spaatz was less sanguine than most other Allied war leaders about the chances of defeating Germany by Christmas 1944. See Spaatz to Lovett, October 1, 1944, Spaatz MSS.

360 *"should be carried":* Solly Zuckerman, *From Apes to Warlords* (New York: Harper & Row, 1978), 290.

360 *"The more [industries]"–"dependence on communication":* Tedder, "Notes on Air Policy to Be Adopted with a View to Rapid Defeat of Germany," October 26, 1944, Spaatz MSS.

360 *"a slight push":* Zuckerman, *From Apes,* 305.

361 *German business communication:* For an insightful analysis of the Allied strategic air forces intelligence systems, see Alfred C. Mierzejewski, *The Collapse of the German War Economy, 1944–1945: Allied Air Power and the German National Railway* (Chapel Hill: University of North Carolina Press, 1988), chap. 4.

361 *"with blind bombing techniques":* "Directive No. 2 for the Control of Strategic Bomber Forces in Europe," Spaatz MSS.

361 *half its tonnage:* USSBS, *Effects of Strategic Bombing on German Transportation* (Washington, DC: U.S. Government Printing Office, 1947), 12.

362 *his force dropped 53 percent:* John Terraine, *A Time for Courage: The Royal Air Force in the European War, 1939–1945* (NY: Macmillan, 1985), 675.

363 *Germany's coal reserves:* Mierzejewski, *German War Economy,* 23–24, 33; Milward, *German Economy,* 173.

363 *"the heart of the rail system"–"relatively untouched":* Tedder, "Notes on Air Policy," Spaatz MSS.

363 *"It is ironical":* Milward, *German Economy,* 173.

363 *Speer had almost 200,000 workers:* Speer to Hitler, November 11, 1944, in Webster and Frankland, *Strategic Air Offensive,* vol. 4. 349–51.

364 *battle between destruction and reconstruction:* USSBS, *German Transportation,* 4; USSBS interview with General Peters, June 3, 1945, 137.315–23, AFHRA.

364 *"The disruption":* Quoted in Tedder, *With Prejudice,* 637–38; USSBS, *German Transportation,* 3.

364 *"the battle of the Ruhr":* Speer to Hitler, November 11, 1944, in Webster and Frankland, *Strategic Air Offensive,* vol. 4, 349–56. For the American reaction to the bombing, see Spaatz to Arnold, December 13, 1944, Spaatz MSS.

364 *From September 1944:* USSBS, *Air Force Rate of Operations* (Washington, DC: U.S. Government Printing Office, 1947), Exhibit 24d.

364 *only 2 percent:* Eighth Air Force, Operational Analysis Section, "Report on Bombing Accuracy Eighth Air Force, September 31–December 1944," 5–7, April 20, 22, 1945, Spaatz MSS; USSBS, *Bombing Accuracy: ASAF Heavy and Medium Bombers in the ETO* (Washington, DC: U.S. Government Printing Office, 1947), 4.

364 *"My squadron was on":* Author interview with Craig Harris, September 17, 2003. Doolittle's postwar testimony supports Harris's description; see interview with Gen. James H. Doolittle by Ronald Schaffer, August 24, 1979, K239 .0512–1206, AFHRA.

365 *"We bombed":* John Briol, *Dead Engine Kids: World War II Diary of John J. Briol,* ed. John F. Welch (Rapid City, SD: Silver Wings Aviation, 1993), 166.

365 *"The specter of":* Bernard Thomas Nolan, *Isaiah's Eagles Rising: A Generation of Airmen* (Philadelphia: Xlibris, 2002), 201.

365 *"tolerate well"–"remote, almost abstract":* Hastings et al., *Psychiatric Experiences,* 21–22; Grinker and Spiegel, *Men Under Stress,* 24–25, 35–36.

365 *"We live with fear":* J. J. Lynch, "One Mo' Time," unpublished MSS, 45, ME.

365 *Approximately 80 percent:* USSBS, *Air Force Rate of Operations,* Exhibit 24d.

365 *"targets of last resort"–"large enough"–"military objective":* Headquarters, Eighth Air Force, Office of the Commanding General, "Attack of Secondary and Last Resort Targets," October 29, 1944, 519.5991–1, AFHRA.

366 *Air Scouts:* Samuel W. Taylor, "Phantom Air Force," *Yank* (May 4, 1945), 4–6.

366 *with considerable accuracy:* The British had a more rigorous training program for operators of air-to-ground bombing guidance systems. RAF radar technicians went through a demanding ten-month training course, whereas Eighth Air Force H2X operators received only four weeks of training. For more on this theme, see W. Hays Parks, " 'Precision' and 'Area' Bombing: Who Did Which, and When?" *Journal of Strategic Studies* 18, no. 1 (March 1995): 157.

366 *"If we fall into":* Briol, *Dead Engine Kids,* 166.

366 *"Lew pulled":* Curtis Rice, *Coming In on a Wing and a Prayer: The World War II Life and Experiences of Lewis F. Welles* (Cambridge, MA: Acme Book Binding, 2000), 298.

367 *"so many names":* Kenneth "Deacon" Jones, war diary, ME.

367 *"death and terror":* Smith, "Chick's Crew," 151–55.

367 *"So it began"—"Finally it was over":* Ibid., 133.

367 *"most of them":* Keith Lamb, "Thirty-Five Times: My Experiences as a B-17 Bomber Pilot during World War II," 59–60, unpublished MSS, ME.

368 *"Once you'd learned":* Author interview with Betty Smith, March 6, 2005.

368 *"I never saw men":* Rosenthal interview, March 7, 2002.

368 *Glenn Miller:* After arriving in England the band was renamed the American Band of the Supreme Allied Command, and later that summer, the American Band of the Allied Expeditionary Force.

368 *"For an hour":* Rice, *Wing and a Prayer,* 230.

368 *"I sincerely feel":* Quoted in Geoffrey Butcher, *Next to a Letter from Home: Major Glenn Miller's Wartime Band* (Edinburgh: Mainstream, 1986), 6.

369 *"You're all going":* Quoted in ibid., 39.

369 *"That sound":* Quoted in ibid., 119.

369 *"a hunk":* Chris Way, *Glenn Miller in Britain: Then and Now* (London: Battle of Britain Prints, 1996), 10.

370 *"The rear gunner":* Jo Thomas, "R.A.F. Bombs May Have Downed Glenn Miller Plane," *NYT,* December 31, 1985, C9.

370 *"Soldiers of the":* Quoted in Miller, *Story,* 339.

371 *"Fog, night, and snow":* Ed Cunningham, in *"Yank," the GI Story of the War,* ed. Myers et al., 167.

371 *"looked in a mirror":* Charles B. MacDonald, *The Mighty Endeavor: The American War in Europe* (1986; repr., NY: Da Capo, 1992), 395; *AAF,* vol. 3, xxi.

372 *"Our orders":* Richard F. Proulx, "Twilight of the Gods—Remember Us," unpublished essay, EC.

372 *"We'd look up":* Rodger Rutland, oral testimony, WGBH, *American Experience,* Boston.

372 *"Repeated attacks":* Medal of Honor citation, Brig. Gen. Frederick W. Castle, Air Force History Support Office; Beirne Lay, Jr., "A Comrade's Tribute to Brigadier General Frederick W. Castle," *Washington Post,* January 20, 1945.

373 *"supply crisis":* AAF, vol. 3, xxi, 711, 695.

373 *"would have succeeded":* Interrogation of Field Marshal Rundstedt, by Louis P. Lochner, May 4, 1945, AFHRA; Hughes, *Over Lord,* 289.

373 *destruction of rail transportation:* USSBS, interview no. 55, Field Marshal Wilhelm Keitel, July 5, 1945, 137.315-55, AFHRA; USSBS, interview no. 17, Col. Gen. Jodl, June 7, 1945, 431-1545A, AFHRA.

373 *On New Year's Day:* Göring interview.

373 *"in one stroke":* Galland, *First,* 243; Göring interview.

373 *"We danced"—"they have to deal"—"sixty aircraft":* All quotes in Norman L. R. Franks, *The Battle of the Airfields: 1st January 1945* (London: William Kimber, 1982), 20–21.

374 *Baseplate:* USSTAF, Interrogation of General Koller, September 1945, 19, AFHRA; Davis, *Spaatz,* 535.

374 *"In this forced action":* Galland, *First,* 243.

374 *lost over 13,000 aircraft:* Matthew Cooper, *The German Air Force: 1933–1945, An Anatomy of Failure* (NY: Jane's, 1981), 370.

374 *2,900 new combat aircraft:* Price, *Last Year,* 129.

374 *savage marshaling yards:* USSBS, *The Impact of the Allied Air Effort on German Logistics* (Washington, DC: Military Analysis Division, 1947), 4–5.

374 *railway "deserts":* USSBS, *German Logistics,* 22.

375 *Deprived of the raw materials:* USSBS, *German Transportation,* 53–54; testimony of Major Gallenkamp, German intelligence officer, "Factors in Germany's Defeat," AFHRA.

375 *Allied oil raids:* Milward, *Collapse,* 170.

375 *"When the Allied breakthroughs":* USSBS, *Over-all Report (European War),* 44.

375 *Joseph Stalin's own admission:* Ibid.

376 *"Without fuel":* Göring interview. See also Galland testimony, "Factors in Germany's Defeat."

376 *"Three factors":* Interrogation of von Rundstedt.

376 *"Victory is production":* "Factors in Germany's Defeat," summaries of interrogations of German officers, Gen. George Thomas, June 2, 1945, AFHRA.

376 *failed to realize:* Notes of the Allied Air Commanders' Conference, January 11, 1944, Spaatz MSS.

376 *Norman Bottomley:* Frances H. Hinsley, *British Intelligence in the Second World War,* vol. 3 (London: Her Majesty's Stationery Office, 1988), 526–27, 856–57; Mierzejewski, *German War Economy,* 167.

376 *"The fighting quality":* Lovett, "Personal Memorandum for General Arnold," January 9, 1945, Spaatz MSS.

377 *"we may not be able":* Quoted in *AAF,* vol. 4, 716.

377 *"from the strategic"–"100%":* Notes of the Allied Air Commanders' Conference, January 11, 1945, Spaatz MSS.

377 *"a staggering proportion"–"the present balance":* McDonald to Spaatz, January 3, 1945, Spaatz MSS.

377 *ULTRA intercepts:* Notes of the Allied Air Commanders' Conference, January 25, 1945, Spaatz MSS.

377 *"losses of a level":* Quoted in Miller, *War at Sea,* 502.

377 *"Our estimate":* Spaatz to Arnold, January 7, 1945, Spaatz MSS.

377 *Combined Chiefs of staff agreed:* Frederick L. Anderson to Spaatz, February 2, 1945, Spaatz MSS.

377 *"re-planning the strategic air offensive":* Headquarters, United States Strategic Air Forces in Europe, Staff Meeting, February 2, 1945, Spaatz MSS.

378 *"the systematic destruction"–"If the power":* Lovett, "Personal Memorandum for General Arnold," January 9, 1945, Spaatz MSS.

378 *"early provision"–"visionary":* Arnold to Spaatz, January 14, 1945, Spaatz MSS; *AAF,* vol. 4, 716.

379 *"Now real fear":* Author interview with Louis Loevsky, November 3, 2004.

Chapter 14: The Wire

380 *"Even before":* All quotes from author interview with Louis Loevsky, October 2, 2002, April 24, 2003.

382 *"It would be demanding":* Reich Minister Dr. Goebbels, "A Word on the Enemy Air Terror," reproduced in *Trials of War Criminals Before the Nuremberg Military*

Tribunals [hereafter *Trials of War Criminals*], vol. 11, (Washington, DC: U.S. Government Printing Office, 1950), 168; Office of United States Chief of Counsel for Prosecution of Axis Criminality, Nazi Conspiracy and Aggression [hereafter Nazi Conspiracy], Supplement B (Washington, DC: U.S. Government Printing Office), 75; testimony of Walter Warlimont, *Trials of War Criminals,* vol. 11, 182. See also David A. Foy, *For You the War Is Over: American Prisoners of War in Nazi Germany* (NY: Stein & Day, 1984), 23.

382 *gun cameras:* Raymond F. Toliver with Hanns J. Scharff, *The Interrogator: The Story of Hanns Scharff, Luftwaffe's Master Interrogator* (Fallbrook, CA: Aero, 1978), 229.

383 *"Gangster Williams":* Quoted in Foy, *For You,* 22.

383 *The truth:* Kenneth D. Williams, "The Saga of 'Murder Inc.'," *8th Air Force News* 12, no. 1 (January 1986): 1–3, 6.

383 *"I was glad":* Roger Burwell, "My War," ME, 20.

383 *Göring had issued instructions:* Nazi Conspiracy, 74.

383 *"defenseless" women—"an eye for":* Goebbels, in *Trials of War Criminals,* vol. 11, 166–69. See also S. P. MacKenzie, "The Treatment of Prisoners of War in World War II," *Journal of Modern History* 66 (September 1994): 494; and Arthur A. Durand, *Stalag Luft III: The Secret Story* (Baton Rouge: Louisiana State University Press, 1988), 50. In 1943 Himmler had issued an order stating that it was not the responsibility of German police to interfere in disputes between German civilians and captured Allied airmen; *London Times,* December 18, 1945.

384 *"were lynched on the spot":* Szymon Datner, *Crimes Against POWs: Responsibility of the Wehrmacht* (Warszawa: Zachodnia Agencja Prasowa, 1964), 194; MacKenzie, "Treatment," 494.

384 *"to be surrendered":* Nazi Conspiracy, 76.

384 *"pogroms":* Affidavit of Walter Schellenberg of the Security Service quoted in *London Times,* January 3, 1946. See also affidavit of Bertus Gerdes, deputy gauleiter of Bavaria, quoted in *London Times,* January 3, 1946.

384 *"execute any"—"dragged by the feet":* Datner, *Crimes,* 199–201.

384 *March 15, 1945: London Daily Telegraph,* March 16, 1946.

384 *"The soldiers":* Gen. Heinz Guderian, *Panzer Leader,* trans. Constantine Fitzgibbon (London: Michael Joseph, 1952), 427.

384 *"delaying tactics":* Jodl testimony, *Trial of the Major War Criminals Before the International Military Tribunal* [hereafter *Major War Criminals*], vol. 15 (Nuremberg, Germany, 1948), 297.

385 *"attempting to escape":* Datner, *Crimes,* 200–201.

385 *"There are the terrorizers"—"Don't kill me":* Special Information on Conditions in Germany, Headquarters, United States Tactical Air Force in Europe, Intelligence Report, 4, AFHRA; Foy, *For You,* 42–43; order by General Schmidt, 11 December 1944, in *Trials of War Criminals,* vol. 11, 179; *London Times,* November 10, 1945.

385 *"as a souvenir":* Datner, *Crimes,* 203–4.

385 *Official records:* Testimony of Major R. Sealy, 2 November 1945, in *Trials of War Criminals,* vol. 11, 181–82.

385 *Dulag Luft:* "Auswertestelle West," A.D.I. (K) Report 328, 1945, Troy H. Middleton Library, Louisiana State University, Baton Rouge, Louisiana.

386 *"colder than"–"They knew":* Loevsky interview, October 21, 2004.

386 *Luftwaffe interrogators:* Cleven interview, January 14, 2002.

386 *"were horrified":* Scharff in Toliver, *Interrogator,* 217.

386 *"extract a confession":* Toliver, *Interrogator,* 17.

386 *"You will not be telling":* "German Interrogation of Prisoners of War," Headquarters AAF Intelligence Summary, No. 45, January 1–15, AFHRA; author interview with Hank Plume, August 6, 2004.

387 *broken clock:* Burwell, "My War," 23.

387 *tight-lipped officer:* Delmar T. Spivey, *POW Odyssey: Recollections of Center Compound, Stalag Luft III and the Secret German Peace Mission in WW II* (Attleboro, MA: Colonial Lithograph, 1984), 22.

387 *threats were rarely carried out:* Hanns Joachim Scharff, "Without Torture," *Argosy,* May 1950, 88.

387 *"Under mental pressure":* A.K.I. (K) Report 328, LSU.

387 *"[My interrogator] said":* Burwell, "My War," 21.

387 *"apparent omniscience":* John Vietor, *Time Out: American Airmen at Stalag Luft I* (NY: Richard R. Smith, 1951), 29.

387 *"actually inquired":* Eric Friedheim, "Welcome to Dulag Luft," *Air Force,* 28 (September 1945): 16.

388 *"it was not uncommon":* The staff report on Dulag Luft written by Capt. Gorden DeFosset of the Army Counter Intelligence Corps is described in Friedheim, "Welcome," 16–17, 73.

388 *"nearly every single word":* Scharff in Toliver, *Interrogator,* 133.

388 *"nothing in the way"–ration cards:* Friedheim, "Welcome," 17.

388 *Hanns Scharff estimated:* Toliver, *Interrogator,* 190–91; Edwin A. Bland, Jr., "German Methods for Interrogation of Captured Allied Aircrews" (thesis, Air Command and Staff School of Air University, Maxwell Air Force Base, Alabama, 1948), 13–15.

388 *"I suppose":* Toliver, *Interrogator,* 17; Durand, *Stalag Luft III,* 70. In early 1945, Oberursel was evacuated by the Germans and Scharff was captured and arrested on April 16, 1945.

388 *Loevsky and several dozen:* Loevsky interview, October 2, 2002.

389 *By the end of the war:* "World War II Statistics," Center for Internee Rights, Miami Beach, Florida. For a slightly higher figure see *Study of Former Prisoners of War, Studies and Analysis Service, Office of Planning and Program, Veterans Administration* (Washington, DC: 1980), 31. Sagan is now called Zagan.

389 *"We were thrown":* Cleven interview, April 18, 2003.

389 *wounds:* "Captain Leslie Caplan, Death March Medic," *Air Force Association,* August 25, 1982, in Joseph P. O'Donnell, *The Shoeleather Express* (Privately printed, n.d.), 59; Loevsky interview, October 2, 2002.

389 *"It's a strange thing":* Eugene E. Halmos, Jr., *The Wrong Side of the Fence: A United States Army Air Corps POW in World War II* (Shippensburg, PA: White Mane, 1996), xiv.

390 *"If I had known":* Plume interview, August 6, 2004.

390 *"a lie":* Loevsky interview, October 2, 2002.

390 *"Practically everyone":* Spivey, *Stalag Luft III,* 32; Vietor, *Time Out,* 43.

390 *"a feeling of euphoria":* Loevsky interview, October 2, 2002.

391 *"while resisting arrest":* Paul Brickhill, *The Great Escape* (1950; repr., NY: Ballantine, 1961), 200.

391 *"plunged into anger":* Loevsky interview, October 2, 2002.

391 *Guttlob Berger:* Berger testimony, in *Trials of War Criminals,* vol. 13, 59.

391 *"They were like":* RAF flier John Cordwell interviewed in *Behind the Wire,* a documentary film produced in 1994 by A. Allen Zimmerman for the Eighth Air Force Historical Society. For the Buchenwald airmen, see Thomas Childers's riveting account, *In the Shadows of War: An American Pilot's Odyssey Through Occupied France and the Camps of Nazi Germany* (NY: Henry Holt, 2003); and Mitchell G. Bard, *Forgotten Victims: The Abandonment of the Americans in Hitler's Camps* (Boulder: Westview, 1994).

392 *Berga:* For the Berga POWs, see Roger Cohen's extraordinary work, *Soldiers and Slaves: American POWs Trapped in the Nazis' Final Gamble* (NY: Alfred A. Knopf, 2005).

392 *"made our guards":* David Westheimer, *Sitting It Out: A World War II POW Memoir* (Houston: Rice University Press, 1992), 253.

393 *"When Van went down":* Interview with Laurence Kuter, October 3, 1974, K239.0512-810, AFHRA.

393 *"When I came out":* U.S. Air Force Oral History Interview with Maj. Gen. Arthur W. Vanaman, February 10–12, 1976, K239.0512-855, AFHRA.

393 *"Just keeping up":* Loevsky interviews, October 2, 2002, May 9, 2005.

394 *"miniature lakes":* Bob Neary, *Stalag Luft III* (Privately printed, 1946), 40.

395 *"Everything you owned":* Elmer Lain interview, February 10, 1990, AHM.

395 *"If the shutters":* Vietor, *Time Out,* 96.

396 *Glen A. Jostad:* Author interview with Glen A. Jostad, June 10, 2005.

396 *"He wasn't even human":* Author interview with George Guderly, May 7, 2003.

396 *Red Cross: International Committee of the Red Cross, Report of the ICRC on Its Activities During the Second World War* (Geneva, 1948), 1, 222–28.

397 *"We also interviewed":* All Clark quotes from Clark interview, *Behind the Wire.*

398 *"Every time a group":* Lowell Bennett, *Parachute to Berlin* (New York: Vanguard, 1945), 199.

398 *British intelligence sources:* MI9's August 31, 1945, report, "Statistical Summary: Return of Escapers and Evaders up to 30 June 1945," is reproduced in M. R. Foot and J. M. Langley, *MI9: Escape and Evasion, 1939–1945* (Boston: Little, Brown, 1980), Appendix I.

398 *"If you left them":* USAF Oral History Interview with Gen. Albert P. Clark, June 20–21, 1979, K239.0512-1130, AFHRA.

399 *"In this group":* Halmos, *Wrong Side,* 35.

399 *"jaunty angle"–"What the fuck":* Loevsky interview, October 2, 2002.

399 *"You could lay":* Lain interview, February 10, 1990.

400 *"Cooks surrounded":* Westheimer, *Sitting It Out,* 195.

400 *"victory gardens":* Halmos, *Wrong Side,* 27.

400 *"You could tell":* Burwell, "My War," 26.

400 *calories:* Protecting Power Report No. 1, concerning the December 9, 1942, visit by Dr. Schaeffeler, "Stalag Luft III" folder, Record Group 389, NA.

400 *"We had men":* Richard H. Hoffman, *Stalag 17B* (Philadelphia: Xlibris, 1988), 120.

400 *Capt. Leslie Caplan:* Testimony, Dr. Leslie Caplan, for the War Crimes Office, Civil Affairs Division, Minnesota Military District," reproduced in O'Donnell, *Shoeleather,* 60–64; "Report of the International Committee of the Red Cross, Visit of October 5 & 6, 1944, NA.

401 *"packed in":* Quoted in Carrol F. Dillon, *A Domain of Heroes: An Airman's Life Behind Barbed Wire in Germany in WW II* (Sarasota: Palm Island, 1995), 137; William D. Henderson, "From Heydekrug to Hell, and Then Some," in Kenneth Nail, *Mississippians in the Mighty Eighth* (Tupelo, MS: Eighth Air Force Historical Society, 1999), 88.

401 *"in sickening slow motion"–"Go ahead"–"The men":* LaMore, *One Man's War,* 167.

401 *"These are the people":* Quoted in Richard L. Bing, *You're 19 . . . Welcome Home: A Story of the Air War over Europe and Its After-Effects* (Privately printed: 1992), 73.

401 *"As soon as we started":* Henderson, *Mississippians,* 89.

402 *Sgt. Edwin W. Hayes:* Edwin W. Hayes, MSS, 18–32, in ME; Henderson, *Mississippians,* 89.

402 *"It was a time of heroism":* Doherty quoted in documentary film, *Behind the Wire,* Air Force Historical Association.

402 *permanently disabled:* Caplan, "Testimony," in O'Donnell, *Shoeleather,* 63–64.

402 *"Like everyone else":* Carson, *Wing Ding,* 187.

402 *"bending to the will":* Wright Lee, *Not as Briefed: 445th Bombardment Group (H), Eighth Air Force; Memoirs of a B-24 Navigator/Prisoner of War, 1943–1945* (Spartanburg, SC: Honoribus, 1995), 153.

402 *"Each day":* Morris John Roy, *Behind Barbed Wire* (New York: R. R. Smith, 1946).

403 *"a silent, stern tyrant":* Francis Gerald, "A Wartime Log," in the possession of Gerald's daughter, Patricia Caruso.

403 *"demoralizing melancholia"–"captivity psychosis":* Walter A. Lunden, "Captivity Psychosis Among Prisoners of War," *Journal of Criminal Law and Criminology* 39 (April 1949): 721, 730.

403 *"A few seconds":* Vietor, *Time Out,* 113–14.

403 *"One night I heard":* Hoffman, *Stalag 17B,* 119.

404 *"I feel I'm on the verge":* Jostad interview, June 10, 2005.

404 *"and lost enough blood":* Oral history testimony in Lewis H. Carlson, *We Were Each Other's Prisoners: An Oral History of World War II American and German Prisoners of War* (NY: Basic Books, 1997), 84.

404 *suicides:* Plume interview, August 6, 2004. See also Bennett, *Parachute,* 192.

404 *"The most wonderful":* Clark interview, *Behind the Wire.*

404 *"I murmured":* Vietor, *Time Out,* 46.

404 *"Always the wire"–"Amazingly, in":* Halmos, *Wrong Side,* 25.

404 *"the best escape":* Westheimer, *Sitting It Out,* 217.

404 *"a mad rush":* Spivey, *Stalag Luft III,* 91.

405 *"What my father did":* John Katzenbach, "Author's Note," in *Hart's War* (NY: Ballantine, 1999), 489.

405   *"In the bag":* Westheimer, *Sitting It Out,* 218.

405   *"The Girl Kriegies":* Neary, *Stalag Luft III,* 3–6.

405   *"Sagan U":* Royal D. Fay, "Poets Laureate of Stalag I," *Aerospace Historian* 16 (Winter 1969): 17; Durand, *Stalag Luft III,* 224–26; Foy, *For You,* 100–101.

406   *"After we got":* Spivey, *POW Odyssey,* 69.

406   *"When it was our turn":* Westheimer, *Sitting It Out,* 225–26.

406   *One POW told his wife:* Spivey, *Stalag Luft III,* 73.

406   *"Good morning":* Interview in *Behind the Wire.*

407   *"I am sorry":* All quotes from letters in Bennett, *Parachute,* 214. These letters were published in Barth's camp newspaper.

407   *"impatient maidens":* Murphy, *Luck of the Draw,* 200–201.

407   *"There was a lot":* Loevsky interview, August 30, 2004; author interview with Hank Plume, August 17, 2004.

407   *Pow Wow—"the largest":* Bennett tells his story in *Parachute to Berlin.* He was later replaced as editor by Lt. Raymond A. Parker.

408   *Couriers delivered:* Westheimer, *Sitting It Out,* 208.

408   *Germans . . . secret radio:* Hubert Zemke and Roger A. Freeman, *Zemke's Stalag: The Final Days of World War II* (Washington, DC: Smithsonian Institution Press, 1991), 31–32.

408   *"Our guards":* Cleven interview, April 24, 2003.

408   *"hushed tones":* Lyman B. Burbank, "A History of the American Air Force Prisoners of War in Center Compound, Stalag Luft III, Germany" (Ph.D. diss., University of Chicago, March 1946), 6.

408   *"The day of deliverance":* Halmos, *Wrong Side,* 67, 70.

409   *"Slivers of cellophane":* Bennett, *Parachute,* 218.

409   *"empty show":* Halmos, *Wrong Side,* 81–83.

409   *John Vietor:* Vietor, *Time Out,* 154.

409   *"Forward":* Quoted in Antony Beevor, *The Fall of Berlin 1945* (NY: Viking, 2002), 17.

Chapter 15: Terror Without End

411   *It has been argued:* See for example, Lewis Mumford, "The Morals of Extermination," *Atlantic Monthly,* October 1959, 38–44; and Donald L. Miller, *Lewis Mumford, A Life* (NY: Weidenfeld & Nicolson, 1989), chap. 23.

411   *"that the time might":* A copy of the report is reproduced in a memorandum from Gen. Laurence Kuter to Hap Arnold, August 9, 1944, Spaatz MSS.

411   "coup de grâce": Webster and Frankland, *Strategic Air Offensive,* vol. 3, 98; memo to Air Staff, subject: Attack on German Civilian Morale, 22 July 1944, 20/3227, NA-UK.

411   *"Such an attack":* Quoted in Norman Longmate, *The Bombers: The RAF Offensive Against Germany, 1939–1945* (London: Hutchinson, 1983), 331.

411   *Thunderclap:* Air Staff paper, July 22, 1944, NA-UK.

412   *"psychological" moment:* Kuter to Arnold, August 9, 1944, Spaatz MSS.

412   *"revolting necessity":* Bishop C. Bromley Oxnam quoted in "A Revolting Necessity," *Nation,* 158 (March 1944): 324.

412 *It "[is] contrary":* Kuter to F. L. Anderson, August 15, 1944, and Kuter to Arnold, "Attack on German Civilian Morale," August 9, 1944, Spaatz MSS.

412 *"baby killing":* Charles Cabell to Richard Hughes, September 8, 1944, 168.7026-9, AFHRA. For Cabell's views on U.S. bombing policy, see Charles P. Cabell, *A Man of Intelligence: Memoirs of War, Peace, and the CIA* (Colorado Springs: Impavide Publications, 1997), 194–96.

412 *"It wasn't for religious":* Spaatz interview, conducted by Noel F. Parish and Alfred Goldberg, February 21, 1962, AFHRA; Davis, *Spaatz,* 434–35.

412 *"Our entire target policy":* Kuter to F. L. Anderson, August 15, 1944, Spaatz MSS; memo, Col. Charles G. Williamson to Maj. Gen. F. L. Anderson, September 12, 1944, Spaatz MSS.

412 *"There is no doubt":* Spaatz to Arnold, August 27, 1944, Spaatz MSS.

412 *"At the present moment":* Minute by the Prime Minister, August 23, 1944, NA-UK.

413 *"prepared to take part":* Eisenhower to Spaatz, August 28, 1944, Spaatz MSS; Conrad C. Crane, *Bombs, Cities, and Civilians: American Airpower Strategy in World War II* (Lawrence: University Press of Kansas, 1993), 106. This is the best work on U.S. terror bombing schemes.

413 *"very doubtful":* Air Marshal Sir Norman Bottomley to Air Chief Marshal Sir Arthur Harris, January 27, 1945, in Webster and Frankland, *Strategic Air Offensive,* vol. 4, 301.

413 *"would be bound"–"a political value":* Joint Intelligence Committee Report, January 25, 1945, NA-UK; Webster and Frankland, *Strategic Air Offensive,* vol. 3, 100.

414 *"whether Berlin":* Churchill to Sinclair, January 26, 1945, in Webster and Frankland, *Strategic Air Offensive,* vol. 3, 103.

414 *The prime minister's impatience:* Joint Intelligence Subcommittee report, January 21, 1945, NA-UK.

414 *Sinclair informed:* Sinclair to Churchill, January 27, 1945, in Webster and Frankland, *Strategic Air Offensive,* vol. 3, 104.

414 *The official records:* Hugh Lunghi, *Spectator,* 273 (August 6, 1994): 25; World War II Conferences, Yalta (Crimea), Box 4, Appendix RG 43, NA; Anderson to Spaatz, February 7, 1945, AFHRA.

414 *"The power of the Russian advance":* Spaatz to Arnold, February 18, 1945, Spaatz MSS.

414 *Spaatz and . . . Bottomley:* "Notes of the Allied Air Commanders' Conference Held at S.H.A.E.F. on 25 January, 1945," Spaatz MSS.

415 *"With [our] tremendous":* AAF, vol. 4, 71.

415 *Arnold . . . Aphrodite:* Spaatz to Arnold, December 10, 1944, Spaatz MSS. While not enthusiastic about robot planes, Spaatz was willing to use them against cities as long as the targets were military and economic installations.

415 *"as an irritant":* Arnold to Spaatz, November 23, 1944, Spaatz MSS.

415 *"terrorizing and intimidating":* Quotes in Perret, *Winged Victory,* 373.

415 *British . . . objected:* General F. L. Anderson to Spaatz, February 2, 1945, Spaatz MSS; Kuter to Arnold, February 5, 1945, Arnold MSS; *AAF,* vol. 4, 727.

415 *Truman . . . buried it:* AAF, vol. 4, 737. For more on the Weary Willies project, see Crane, *Bombs,* 78–85.

415 *Writing to a convalescing Arnold:* Spaatz to Arnold, February 5, 1945, Spaatz MSS.

416 *Albert Speer:* Albert C. Mierzejewski, "When Did Albert Speer Give Up?" *Historical Journal,* 31, no. 2 (June 1988): 391–97.

416 *"Attacks on Munich":* Marshall quoted in Anderson to Spaatz, February 1, 1945, Spaatz MSS; Minutes, Staff Meeting, USSAF, February 1, 1945, Spaatz MSS.

416 *"It is of the utmost":* Quoted in Robert Dallek, *Franklin D. Roosevelt and American Foreign Policy, 1932–1945* (NY: Oxford University Press, 1979), 472–73.

416 *"the inhumane barbarism":* Samuel I. Rosenman, ed., *The Public Papers and Addresses of Franklin D. Roosevelt,* vol. 8, *War–and Neutrality* (NY: Random House, 1939), 454.

416 *"from the air"–"bombed Warsaw":* Franklin D. Roosevelt, *The War Messages of Franklin D. Roosevelt, December 8, 1941, to October 12, 1942* (Washington, DC: United States of America, 1943), report to Congress, January 7, 1943, 32. For more on this theme, see George Hopkins, "Bombing and the American Conscience During World War II," *Historian,* 28, no. 3 (May 1966): 451–73.

417 *"Except possibly":* London *Times,* September 8, 1944.

417 *"No, man":* Quoted in Gregor Dallas, *1945: The War That Never Ended* (New Haven: Yale University Press, 2005), 210.

417 *"had raised the art":* "V-2 Weapons," *Newsweek,* November 20, 1944, 34.

417 *"If I'm going":* Quoted in Panter-Downes, *London War Notes,* 348.

418 *Mittelwerk:* Neufeld, *Rocket and the Reich,* 212.

418 *"the grandfather":* Ibid., 279.

418 *"about as far":* Quoted in Keegan, *Second World War,* 582.

418 *transatlantic rocket:* Joseph Warner Angell, "Guided Missiles Could Have Won," *Atlantic Monthly,* 189 (January 1952): 57–63.

419 *"There are no":* Doolittle to Spaatz, January 30, 1945, 520.422, AFHRA.

419 *"lower German morale":* Doolittle, *Lucky,* 402.

419 *"The chances of terrorizing"–"We will":* Doolittle to Spaatz, January 30, 1945, Spaatz MSS.

419 *"Hit Berlin whenever":* Spaatz to Doolittle, January 30, 1945, AFHRA. In sanctioning terror bombing, Spaatz, consciously or not, was acting in concord with the American Air Force's prewar planning report, AWPD/1. When the enemy is near collapse and "the morale of the people is already low because of sustained suffering and deprivation," this influential report noted, "heavy and sustained bombing of cities may crush morale entirely. . . . It is believed that the entire bombing effort might be applied toward this purpose when it becomes apparent that the proper psychological conditions exist"; AWPD/1, tab 2, Sec 2, pt. 3, App. 2, 6, NA. Even General Kuter had said earlier, in confidential deliberations, that "morale attacks including the killing of German civilians" might be employed when it was ascertained that they "will tip the scales causing the cessation of hostilities"; memo, Col. Charles G. Williamson to Kuter, September 4, 1944; September 6, Kuter endorsement; and memo to Anderson, September 12, 1944, Spaatz MSS.

419 *"women and children":* Freeman, *Mighty Eighth,* 209.

419 *"Is Berlin"–"Hit oil":* Doolittle to Spaatz, February 2, 1945, Spaatz MSS; Spaatz notes on telephone conversation of that day, Spaatz MSS.

420 *"stress"–"effort to disrupt":* Spaatz to Doolittle, February 2, 1945, AFHRA. For a different interpretation of Spaatz's motives, see Richard G. Davis, "Operation 'Thunderclap': The US Army Air Forces and the Bombing of Berlin," *Journal of Strategic Studies* 14 (March 1991): 90–111, Davis, *Spaatz,* 550.

420 *"We never had":* Interview, Gen. Carl A. Spaatz by Murray Green, August 8, 1968, Green Collection on Hap Arnold, U.S. Air Force Academy Archives, Colorado Springs, Colorado.

420 *"Gentlemen"–"There was no conversation"–"Big-Ass Berlin":* Charles Alling, *A Mighty Fortress: Lead Bomber over Europe* (Haverford, PA: Casemate, 2002), 71. I have also drawn on other accounts of the mission, including Robert A. Hand, "Last Raid," privately printed in 1996 and housed at ME.

421 *The men knew:* Diary of Maurice G. Westfall, in the possession of his family.

421 *"We were told":* Briol, *Dead Engine Kids,* 181.

421 *"If you go down"–"put it":* Quoted in Rice, *Wing and a Prayer,* 316.

421 *"Sometimes they look":* Quoted in Flower and Reeves, *The War,* 556.

422 *"aesthetic appeal":* J. Glenn Gay, *The Warriors: Reflections on Men in Battle* (1959; repr., Lincoln: University of Nebraska Press, 1970), 25–58; John Morris testimony, EC.

422 *"She's clear"–"a veritable"–"like a"–"It just doesn't":* Hand, "Last Raid," 19; Combat Mission Loading Lists, 360th Bombardment Squadron (H), 303rd Bombardment Group, February 3, 1945, NA; Mission Report, 303rd BG, February 3, 1945, NA.

422 *"Go home":* Saul Levitt, "The Rosenthal Legend," in *Contrails,* 247; Levitt, "U.S.–Berlin," *S&S,* March 26, 1944.

423 *"I had to do":* Author interview with Robert Rosenthal, August 8, 2005.

423 *"The smoke came"–"Before we left":* *S&S,* February 3, 1945, 3.

423 *"Rosie, the Indomitable":* Crosby, *Wing,* 363.

424 *"I could barely move":* Rosenthal interview, March 21, 2002.

424 *"Americanski":* Author interview with Robert Rosenthal, January 25, 2002.

424 *"the Rosenthal legend":* Levitt, "Rosenthal Legend," in *Contrails,* 246.

424 *"God, help them":* Briol, *Dead Engine Kids,* 187.

424 *"The ground heaved":* *S&S,* February 24, 1945; *Time,* March 5, 1945, 30–31.

425 *"carried along":* Ursula von Kardorff, *Diary of a Nightmare: Berlin, 1942–1945,* trans. Ewan Butler (NY: John Day, 1966), 191.

425 *Goebbels announced:* Hans-Georg von Studnitz, *While Berlin Burns: The Diary of Hans-Georg von Studnitz, 1943–1945* (Englewood Cliffs, NJ: Prentice Hall, 1963), 242.

425 *"If I had taken":* *S&S,* February 24, 1945, 1; *Time,* March 5, 1945, 30–31.

425 *"and there await":* Von Studnitz, *Berlin Burns,* 242.

425 *"After suffering":* Quoted in ibid.

425 *"Should a similar":* Joseph Goebbels, *The Diaries of Joseph Goebbels: Final Entries, 1945,* ed. Hugh Trevor-Roper; trans. Richard Barry (NY: Putnam, 1978), 1.

426 *Early estimates:* Olaf Groehler, *Der Bombenkrieg gegen Deutschland* (Berlin:

Akademie-Verlag, 1990), 398ff. See also Richard G. Davis, "German Rail Yards and Cities: U.S. Bombing Policy, 1944–1945," *Air Power History* 42, no. 2 (Summer 1995): 57–58.

426 *"Never was a target":* NYT, February 4, 1945, 5.

426 *"were smothered under":* S&S, February 1945, 3.

426 *Also destroyed:* "THUNDERCLAP Target List," Spaatz MSS; 3AD Mission Report of February 3, 1945, 8th Air Force Mission Reports, RG 18, NA; Westfall, "Diary."

426 *"Berlin, Saturday":* Quoted in Freeman, *Mighty Eighth,* 208.

426 *"I never saw":* Rice, *Wing and a Prayer,* 316.

427 *"The German people":* Brown, *Mighty Men,* 532.

427 *"It was a terrible":* Harry S. Mitchell, Jr., "Battle Diary," AHM.

427 *"This one":* Quoted in Rice, *Wing and a Prayer,* 316.

427 *"special decoration":* Transcript, German Overseas Service, February 17, 1945, Spaatz MSS.

427 *"Did Germany believe":* Quoted in Frederick Taylor, *Dresden, Tuesday, February 13, 1945* (NY: HarperCollins, 2004), 126.

428 *"The boxcar doors":* Kurt Vonnegut, *Slaughterhouse-Five or The Children's Crusade* (1969, repr., NY: Dell, 1999), 189.

428 *"Dresden was like":* Ibid., 227.

429 *Dresden . . . bombed only twice:* Photo Interpretation Report, Dresden, October 17, 1944, NA; 466th Bombardment Group, Mission Folder, Dresden, January 16, 1945, NA; Joseph W. Angell, "Historical Analysis of the 14–15 February 1945 Bombing of Dresden," USAF Historical Division, AFHRA.

429 *"We felt safe":* Steinhoff, *Voices,* 224–26.

429 *"It was as if":* Ibid., 228; Götz Bergander, *Dresden im Luftkrieg: Vorgeschichte, Zerstorung, Folgen* (1994; rev. ed., Würzburg: Böhlau, 1998).

429 *horrifyingly right:* Taylor, *Dresden,* 416.

430 *"one big flame":* Vonnegut, *Slaughterhouse-Five,* 227.

430 *"Coming out of":* Steinhoff, *Voices,* 229.

430 *Thermite-filled incendiaries:* USSBS, *Fire Raids on German Cities* (2nd ed., Washington, DC: U.S. Government Printing Office, 1947). Incendiaries were usually dropped in 500-pound clusters; on some raids the Eighth Air Force also used napalm-filled bombs, which became available in the summer of 1944. Until the development and use of the atomic bomb, the incendiary was the weapon that caused the greatest damage to property and life in German and Japanese cities; USSBS, *Physical Damage Report (ETO)* (Washington, DC: U.S. Government Printing Office, 1947), 23.

431 *carbon monoxide poisoning:* USSBS, *Fire Raids,* 1, 8, 35–38, 47, 50.

431 *"The heat was almost unbearable":* Anne Wahle and Roul Tunley, *Ordeal by Fire: An American Woman's Terror-Filled Trek Through War-Torn Germany* (NY: Dell, 1965), 34. For another powerful eyewitness account of the fire, see Alison Owings, *Frauen: German Women Recall the Third Reich* (New Brunswick: Rutgers University Press, 1993).

431 *"sitting bolt upright":* Wahle, *Ordeal,* 35–36, 40–41.

432   *"Where had everyone"–"The water":* Ibid., 35–36, 40–41.

432   *"accidental" releases:* PFF Bombing Report, Dresden, February 14, 1945, Low Squadron, 94th "A" Bomb Group, NA.

432   *"majority of bombs"–"8–10 miles":* Headquarters 1st Air Division, Office of the Director of Intelligence, Immediate Interpretation Report No. 232, February 15, 1945, Spaatz MSS; First Air Division Report, Dresden, for Lead Squadron, 94th "A" Group, February 15, 1945, NA.

432   *"bombed Prague":* 91st Bombardment Group, Mickey Operator's Narrative, February 17, 1945, NA; Supplemental Report to 91st Bomb Group, February 14, 1945, Spaatz MSS.

433   *"really felt as if":* Quoted in Taylor, *Dresden,* 332.

433   *"It was as if":* Taylor, *Dresden,* 332.

433   *P-51 Mustangs:* David Irving, *Apocalypse 1945: The Destruction of Dresden* (London: Focal Point, 1995), 191.

433   *20th Fighter Group was in Prague:* Taylor, *Dresden,* 435.

433   *"Not a single detached building": Time,* March 12, 1945, 33.

433   *35,000 and 40,000:* Olaf Groehler, "The Strategic Air War and Its Impact on the German Civilian Population," in Boog, *Conduct of the Air War,* 279–97; Bergander, *Dresden im Luftkrieg,* 157ff. In the 1940s, international law had not yet caught up with advances in aviation technology. Article 25 of the Hague Rules for Land Warfare (1907) prohibited indiscriminate bombing of inhabited areas by ground forces, but of course made no mention of air attacks. The long-range bomber became operational in "a kind of legal vacuum," in the words of a noted international lawyer, a vacuum that made area bombing legal under current rules of war. But as Air Force historian Richard G. Davis notes, the high proportion of incendiaries used by both British and American air forces in Europe against German cities "could be construed to violate the precept of 'proportionally' under the laws of war. In brief, if civilians are in jeopardy, the attacker may not use more force than necessary to destroy his legitimate military objectives." In 1948 the Red Cross Convention on the Protection of Civilians in Wartime finally made indiscriminate area bombing illegal under international law. See W. Hays Parks, "Air War and the Laws of War," in Boog, *Conduct of the Air War,* 354; Davis, "Rail Yards," 56.

433   *"dreadful stories"–"The British prided":* Von Kardorff, *Diary,* 202.

433   *"The fire kept burning":* Steinhoff, *Voices,* 226.

434   *"corpse mining":* Author interview with Kurt Vonnegut, January 10, 2000.

434   *POWs:* Joe Kleven and Art Kuespert, "Rainwater and Potato Peelings," unpublished personal testimony, EC.

434   *"The idea was to hasten":* Vonnegut, *Slaughterhouse-Five,* 230.

434   *"Only one person":* Vonnegut interview.

434   *"I'm not ashamed":* Morris testimony, EC.

435   *"The morning he"–"We couldn't get":* Quoted in Martin Chalmers's introduction to his edition of Victor Klemperer, *To the Bitter End: The Diaries of Victor Klemperer, 1942–1945* (London: Weidenfeld & Nicolson, 1999), xiii, 390–94.

435   *Doolittle . . . transportation center:* Notes from Allied Commanders' Conference, February 15, 1945, K239.046-38, AFHRA.

435 *Twenty-eight army trains:* Taylor, *Dresden,* 163.

435 *"For nearly twelve hours":* Quoted in Alan Cooper, *Target Dresden* (Bromley: Independent Books, 1995), 245.

435 *50,000 . . . workers:* Davis, *Spaatz,* 563.

436 *"It was like heaven":* Quoted in Robin Neillands, *The Bomber War: The Allied Air Offensive Against Nazi Germany* (Woodstock: Overlook, 2001), 359.

436 *John Morris:* Morris testimony.

436 *"the attack on Dresden":* Harris, *Bomber Offensive,* 242.

436 *"Even in war":* Quoted in Hastings, *Armageddon,* 335.

436 *nothing exceptional about the raid:* Throughout the war, the RAF conducted fire raids against at least forty German cities; USSBS, *Over-all Report (European War),* 71–72.

436 *"From our point of view":* Freeman Dyson, *Disturbing the Universe* (NY: Harper & Row, 1979), 20, 28.

437 *"business as usual":* Davis, *Spaatz,* 564.

437 *"Dresden was a mass":* Quoted in Probert, *Bomber Harris,* 322.

437 *Rail service was partially restored:* Air Ministry, RE, 8, Area Attack Assessment: Dresden, undated (filed 30 October 1945), NA-UK.

437 *March 2 and April 17:* Mission file, Intops Summary No. 352, 303rd Bomb Group, Dresden, April 17, 1945, NA.

437 *"The low squadron pattern":* "Photo Interpretation Report," October 7, 1944, sent to Assistant Chief of Staff, A-2, Headquarters, 41st Combat Wing, NA.

438 *"The unknown hand":* Davis, "German Rail Yards," 51; "Eighth Air Force Target Summary," n.d., probably drafted May 1945, AFHRA; "Eighth Air Force Statistical Summary of Operations, European Theater, August 17–May 8, 1945, June 10, 1945," AFHRA.

438 *"Public relations officers":* Anderson to Arnold, signed Spaatz, February 20, 1945, Spaatz MSS.

438 *the ratio of blast bombs:* Taylor, *Dresden,* 319.

438 *high percentage of incendiaries:* Davis, *Spaatz,* 568, 570.

438 *February 26, 1945:* Intops Summary No. 202, February 26, 1945; Mission Report, 303rd Bomb Group, Berlin, February 26, 1945, NA.

439 *"A common intervalometer":* Milt Groban, "To the Editor," 10.

439 *"industrial* coup de grâce*":* USSBS, *A Detailed Study of the Effects of Area Bombing on Darmstadt* (Washington, DC: U.S. Government Printing Office, 1947), 1–8.

440 *"It is soul destroying":* Wolff-Mönckeberg, *On the Other Side,* 68, 99, 112.

440 *wartime evacuations:* Elizabeth Heineman, "The Hour of the Woman: Memories of Germany's 'Crisis Years' and West German National Identity," *American Historical Review* 101, no. 2 (April 1996): 362.

440 *"The whole place":* Notes of the Allied Air Commanders' Conference, March 1, 1945, Spaatz MSS.

440 *Würzburg:* Hermann Knell, *To Destroy a City: Strategic Bombing and Its Human Consequences in World War II* (Cambridge, MA: Da Capo, 2003).

440 *"the wonder is that":* Richard Kohn, "Commentary," in Boog, *Conduct of the Air War,* 410.

440 *"hatred their leaders":* Hans Rumpf, *The Bombing of Germany,* trans. Edward Fitzgerald (NY: Holt, Rinehart & Winston, 1962), 150.

441 *"The majority of Germans today":* W. G. Sebald, *On the Natural History of Destruction,* trans. Anthea Bell (NY: Random House, 2003), 103.

441 *"widespread simultaneous"–"a crisis"–"As a result":* "General Plan for Maximum Effort Attack Against Transportation Objectives," December 11, 1944, Spaatz MSS; *AAF,* vol. 3, 639.

441 *"the hopelessness":* Kuter to Frederick Anderson, August 15, 1944, Spaatz MSS.

441 *"absolutely convince"–"for it would be":* Eaker to Spaatz, January 1, 1945, Spaatz MSS; Doolittle to Spaatz, December 27, 1944, Spaatz MSS.

442 *"This is the same old":* Cable's comment is in the folder at Maxwell Field that contains that archives's copy of the "General Plan for Maximum Attack Against Transportation Objectives," 168.7026-9, AFHRA.

442 *"We should never allow":* Eaker to Spaatz, January 1, 1945, Spaatz MSS.

442 *"from father to son":* Franklin D. Roosevelt to Henry Stimson, September 9, 1944, copy in Arnold MSS.

442 *"that this operation":* Spaatz to Eaker, Twining, Vandenberg, Daville, February 21, 1945, 520.3233-40, AFHRA.

442 *"spectacular success":* Clarion, "Summary," n.d., Spaatz MSS.

442 *follow-up intelligence:* USSBS, *Transportation,* 16.

442 *press briefing: AAF,* vol. 4, 735.

443 *"The Allied Air Commanders": Washington Star,* February 18, 1945, 1.

443 *"what morale there is":* A copy of the transcript of the press briefing is at the NA, RG 331. Selections of the briefing were sent to Spaatz; see Rex Smith to Spaatz, February 18, 1945, Spaatz MSS.

443 *Over Arnold's signature:* Arnold to Spaatz, February 18, 1945, Spaatz MSS.

443 *"several days":* Spaatz to Arnold, February 5, 1945, Spaatz MSS. Richard Davis, Spaatz's biographer, argues that Eisenhower's headquarters specifically requested Clarion to assist U.S. Ninth Army's crossing of the Rhine. That may be right, but there is nothing about the matter in the declassified document Davis uses to support his claim, i.e., "Notes of the Allied Air Commanders' Conference, February 1, 1945," Spaatz MSS.

444 *"absolute stupidity"–"as terror"–"locale":* Anderson to Spaatz, February 19, 1945, Spaatz MSS; Anderson to Kuter, February 27, 1945, 519.1611, AFHRA.

444 *"center of a new Germany":* Diary of Henry Stimson, March 5, 1945, Yale University Library, New Haven.

444 *"This directive puts":* All McDonald quotes in George C. McDonald to Anderson, February 21, 1945, Frederick Anderson Collection, Box 50, Folder 2, Hoover Institution Archives.

445 *new bombing directive on March 1:* March 1, 1945, Bombardment Policy, Papers of Nathan F. Twining, LC.

445 *"simply letting the aircraft":* Sebald, *Natural History,* 18. General Charles P. Cabell writes in his memoirs: "As the war ground on toward its visible end . . . we increasingly found ourselves in possession of a great Air Force 'all dressed up' but running out of places to go", Cabell, *Man of Intelligence,* 194.

446   *"We must not get soft"*: "Report on Air Attacks on Targets in Dresden," 519.523-6, AFHRA.

446   *"contributed in a fundamental way"*: Quoted in Taylor, *Dresden*, 413.

446   *"Everyone is so overcome"*: Lili Hahn quoted in Earl R. Beck, *Under the Bombs: The German Home Front, 1942–1945* (Lexington: University Press of Kentucky, 1986), 168.

446   *"when it will be our turn"*: Wolff-Mönckeberg, *On the Other Side*, 89.

Chapter 16: The Chimneys Hardly Ever Fall Down

447   *"whittled down"*: Air Ministry, 381–82.

447   *"sinister looking"*: Alling, *Mighty Fortress*, 95.

448   *The next day:* Boehme, *JG 7*, 107–9.

448   *"lanes of fire"*: Ibid., 112

448   *"Shattered fuselages"*: Quoted in ibid., 116.

448   *The Eighth lost six Mustangs:* Freeman et al., *Mighty Eighth War Diary*, 466.

448   *destroyed sixty-three bombers:* AAF Statistical Digest, World War II, 255, Table 159. For German claims, which were greater than sixty-three, see Boehme, *JG 7*, chap. 4. In the final months of the war an Eighth Air Force bomber crewman had an 80 percent chance of surviving thirty-five missions.

448   *Doolittle feared: AAF,* vol. 3, 744.

449   *"[They] never allowed"*: Quoted in Freeman, *Mighty Eighth*, 218; "Notes of the Allied Air Commanders' Conference," March 21, 1945, Spaatz MSS.

449   *"coaxed"–"without consent"*: All quotes in Galland, *First*, 273–74.

449   *Rat catching:* Boehme, *JG 7*, 136.

449   *"In a man against man"*: Quoted in ibid., 104.

450   *By April:* Price, *Last Year*, 177.

450   *"They didn't know"*: Quoted in Boehme, *JG 7*, 122.

450   *"But its introduction"*: Quoted in Price, *Last Year*, 146.

450   *Hermann's plan:* Adrian Weir, *The Last Flight of the Luftwaffe: The Fate of Schulungslehrgang Elbe* (London: Arms and Armour, 1997), 57.

451   *"It was in March"*: Hansen diary, USMHI.

451   *"the greatest air blitz"*: Sidney Gruson, "Role of Air Power in War Becomes Clearer," *NYT*, March 18, 1945, E5.

451   *"Germany's most valuable"*: AAF, vol. 4, 746.

452   *"dead wives"*: Quoted in Crosby, *Wing*, 360.

452   *"There can be"*: "Why a German Fights On," *Newsweek*, March 26, 1945, 35.

452   *The Luftwaffe paid dearly:* Freeman, *Mighty Eighth*, 226.

452   *"The first use"*: Goebbels, *Final Entries*, 323.

453   *Three days later: AAF,* vol. 3, 752.

453   *"the day of the"*: Boehme, *JG 7*, 161.

453   *On April 19:* Mission Report, 447th Bomb Group, April 19, 1945, NA; Doyle Shields, *History, 447th Bomb Group* (Privately printed, 1996), 317.

453   *"continuous operation"*: USSBS interview, Gen. Karl Koller, AFHRA.

454   *Technical setbacks:* Richard Suchenwirth, "Hitler's Last Opportunity," *Aerospace Historian* 8, no. 1 (Spring 1966): 31–33.

454 *high rates of fuel consumption:* Price, *Last Year,* 178.

454 *"If the Germans":* Col. Paul Tibbets, as told to Wesley Price, "How to Drop an Atomic Bomb," *Saturday Evening Post* (June 8, 1946), 136; author interview with Tibbets.

454 *"when the occasion":* Memo, "Incendiary Bombs," Arnold to assistant chief of air staff, Material, Maintenance and Distribution, April 26, 1943, Arnold MSS.

454 *Dugway Proving Ground:* Department of the Interior, Historic Properties, *Report: Dugway Proving Ground* (Washington, DC: U.S. Government Printing Office 1984), passim; Louis F. Fieser, *The Scientific Method: A Personal Account of Unusual Projects in War and in Peace* (NY: Reinhold, 1964), 129–30; Mike Davis, "Berlin's Skeleton in Utah's Closet," *Designer/Builder,* 11, no. 5 (January–February, 2005): 16–27.

455 *"If we are going":* Quoted in Ronald Schaffer, *Wings of Judgment: American Bombing in World War II* (NY: Oxford University Press, 1985), 93.

455 *"They obviously hoped":* Galland, *First,* 279–80. Luftwaffe jets destroyed about 150 Allied planes in the war, and the Germans lost approximately a hundred of their own jets in air combat; see Levine, *Strategic Bombing,* 185.

456 *"his targets":* All Hopper quotes are from Bruce C. Hopper, "Jeeping the Targets in the Country That Was," Spaatz MSS.

456 *"destruction and chaos":* Drew Middleton, *The Struggle for Germany* (Indianapolis: Bobbs-Merrill, 1949), 12.

456 *Leonard Mosley:* Leonard O. Mosley, *Report from Germany* (London: Victor Gollancz, 1945), 66. Only three cities in Germany were intact, and they more nearly resembled large towns: Heidelberg, with a population of 130,000; Celle, with 60,000, and Flensburg, with 62,000.

457 *Spearhead Teams:* Maj. James Beveridge, "History of the United States Strategic Bombing Survey (European) 1944–1945," 430, Record Group 243, Box 24, NA. A similar survey was made of the American bombing campaign against Japan.

457 *"among the most":* Brodie, *Strategy in the Missile Age,* 108.

457 *early discoveries:* Beveridge, "History," 270–75, 357.

457 *In Cologne:* Ibid., 399.

457 *Morale Division:* Ibid., passim; David MacIsaac, *Strategic Bombing in World War Two: The Story of the United States Strategic Bombing Survey* (NY: Garland, 1976), 89.

458 *Paul Baran:* John Kenneth Galbraith, *A Life in Our Times* (Boston: Houghton Mifflin, 1981), 222.

458 *"cast his lot":* Paul Nitze, Steven L. Rearden, and Ann M. Smith, *From Hiroshima to Glasnost: At the Center of Decision* (NY: Grove Weidenfeld, 1989), 34–35.

458 *"posse":* Galbraith, *Life,* 222; John Kenneth Galbraith, *Annals of an Abiding Liberal,* edited by Andrea D. Williams (Boston: Houghton Mifflin, 1979), 197–98.

458 *"leaders of industry"–"The answers":* Galbraith, *Annals,* 193; Galbraith, *Life,* 223.

458 *"a hideous thing":* Galbraith, *Life,* 195.

459 *"independent of the Air Force":* Ibid., 196.

459 *The idea for the survey:* Spaatz to Arnold, April 5, 1944, Arnold MSS.

459 *Arnold convinced Roosevelt:* Arnold to Spaatz, April 21, 1944, Spaatz MSS; Memorandum, "Organization of Machinery for Cooperation with British and Soviets in Survey of Results of Bomber Offensive," May 30, 1944, NA.

459 *"as others believed":* Galbraith, *Life,* 198.

459 *"economic warriors"–"a roster"–"unlikely warriors":* Galbraith, *Life,* 196, 199.

460 *"Probably for the first time":* Hanson Baldwin, "Civilians Gauge Air War," *NYT,* September 2, 1945, 18.

460 *"the first principle":* Interview with John Kenneth Galbraith, n.d., Imperial War Museum, Sound Archives.

460 *"a much decorated":* Galbraith, *Life,* 225.

460 *oil war had been won:* USSBS, *Oil Division Report,* vol. 2, 1–10; Webster and Frankland, *Strategic Air Offensive,* vol. 3, 110. Allied bombers made 555 attacks on 135 oil targets and unloaded 191,245 tons of bombs, about 15 percent of the total dropped on Germany; USSBS, *Oil Division Report,* vol. 2, 2.

461 *"clipped the wings":* USSBS, *German War Economy,* 82.

461 *Upper Silesian coalfields:* See the testimony of Col. Gen. Alfred Jodl and Albert Speer in USSBS, *German War Economy,* 81.

461 *"anyone using fuel":* USSBS, Supporting Document No. 10.A1, Record Group 243, Modern Military Record Division, NA.

461 *Edmund Geilenberg:* Speer to Martin Bormann, September 16, 1944, Spaatz MSS.

461 *"questioning the Reich's":* USSBS, *Underground and Dispersal Plants in Greater Germany* (Washington, DC: U.S. Government Printing Office, second edition, 1947), 1. Geilenberg also undertook a modest dispersal effort, building thirty-eight small distillation units, but less than 40 percent of the product reached the fighting fronts because of transportation difficulties; ibid., 60.

461 *"the German oil industry":* USSBS, *Underground,* 66.

461 *slow strangulation of rail:* USSBS, *German War Economy,* 13, 99. It was the marshaling yards, in my view, that were most crucial.

462 *"Even a first-class":* USSBS, *Over-all Report (European War),* 107.

462 *"industry"–"is to mistake":* Julian Bach, Jr., *America's Germany: An Account of the Occupation* (NY: Random House, 1946), 104. When the war ended, six million tons of coal were sitting at the Ruhr pitheads waiting for transportation; see Drew Middleton, "German Industry's Fate Studied," *NYT,* July 15, 1945, 40.

462 *"appalling slaughterings":* J. F. C. Fuller, *The Second World War, 1939–45: A Strategical and Tactical History* (London: Eyre & Spottiswoode, 1954), 228. Richard Overy challenges Fuller and other critics in "Air Power in the Second World War: Historical Themes and Theories," in Boog, *Conduct of the Air War.* The air war in Europe cost the United States over $43 billion; see USSBS, *Over-all Report (European War),* 1. Two giants of modern journalism, David Halberstam and I. F. Stone, have argued independently that the U.S. Strategic Bombing Survey "proved conclusively that the strategic bombing had not worked"; Halberstam, *The Best and the Brightest* (NY: Random House, 1972), 162; I. F. Stone, "Nixon's Blitzkrieg," *New York Review of Books,* January 25, 1973, 13–16. For more on this controversy, see David MacIsaac, "What the Bombing Survey Really Says," *Air Force Magazine,* June 1973, 60–63; and

Melden E. Smith, Jr., "The Strategic Bombing Debate: The Second World War and Vietnam," *Journal of Contemporary History* 12, no. 1 (January 1977): 175–91.

462 *"disastrous" failure:* Galbraith, *Life,* 226.

462 *"hadn't in fact":* Richard Parker, *John Kenneth Galbraith, His Life, His Politics, His Economics* (NY: Farrar, Straus & Giroux, 2005), 179–82.

463 *Galbraith's Spearhead team . . . found Speer:* John Kenneth Galbraith and George W. Ball, "The Interrogation of Albert Speer," *Life* (December 17, 1945), 57. In 1979, Galbraith published his notes of the final interview with Speer, notes, he says, his assistant had recently found; see Galbraith, "The Origin of the Document," *Atlantic Monthly* 244 (July 1979), 50–57. I have located a copy of Galbraith's interrogation at the AFHRA at Maxwell Field, Alabama.

463 *"miracle man":* Galbraith, *Life,* 207.

463 *"like stumbling on"–"bombing high school":* George Ball, *The Past Has Another Pattern: Memoirs* (NY: W. W. Norton, 1983), 54.

463 *youthful college professor:* Galbraith and Ball, "Interrogation," 57.

463 *"With charm":* Ball, *Past,* 63.

464 *Burton Klein:* Burton Klein, *German's Economic Preparations for War* (Cambridge: Harvard University Press, 1959). The blitzkrieg thesis is most persuasively argued in A. S. Milward, "The End of Blitzkreig," *Economic History Review* 16, no. 3 (1964), 499–518, and Milward, *German Economy.* The British bomb survey, which was not released for general publication until 1998, has a brilliant historical introduction by Sebastian Cox; see British Bombing Survey Unit, *The Strategic Air War Against Germany, 1939–1945* (London: Frank Cass, 1998).

464 *Blitzkrieg Economy:* Galbraith and Ball, "Interrogation," 57.

464 *"was for a long time":* Galbraith, *Life,* 204; Galbraith, "Germany Was Badly Run," *Fortune* 32, no. 6 (December 1945), 173.

464 *"cheap and easy"–"intentionally run down"–"no preparation":* Galbraith, "Germany Was Badly Run," 173; Werner Abelshauser, "Germany: Guns, Butter, and Economic Miracles," in Mark Harrison, ed., *The Economics of World War II: Six Great Powers in International Comparison* (Cambridge: Cambridge University Press, 1998), 151.

465 *"one of the greatest":* Galbraith, *Life,* 206.

465 *"most disastrous":* Ibid., 197.

465 *"a tightly stretched drum":* Ibid., 204.

465 *"fat and incompetent"–"astonishing luxury"–"unlimited graft":* Galbraith and Ball, "Interrogation," 58, 60, 63.

465 *undermobilized economy:* Ibid., 57.

465 *These measures allowed Speer:* Galbraith lays out his thesis in USSBS, *German War Economy,* 6–8; see also USSBS, *Area Studies Division Report* (Washington, DC: U.S. Government Printing Office, 2nd ed. 1947), 20–22, 69.

466 *"followed a path":* Mark Harrison, "The Economics of World War II: An Overview," in Harrison, *Economics,* 20.

466 *Beginning as early as 1939:* Richard J. Overy, *War and Economy in the Third Reich* (Oxford: Clarendon, 1994), 278, 270–74, 312; Abelshauser, "Germany," in Harrison, *Economics,* 145–64; Overy, "Hitler's War and the German Economy:

A Reinterpretation," *Economic History Review* 35, no. 2 (1982): 273; Jane Caplan and Carola Sachse, "Industrial Housewives: Women's Social Work in the Factories of Nazi Germany," trans. Heide Kiesling and Dorothy Rosenberg, *Women and History* 11–12 (1987); passim. In 1939, over 37 percent of the German workforce was made up of women, as opposed to 26 percent in Great Britain; see Overy, *War and Economy,* 707.

466 *Williamson Murray argued:* Williamson Murray, *The Change in the European Balance of Power, 1938–1939: The Path to Ruin* (Princeton: Princeton University Press, 1984), 4–15.

466 *Overy points out:* Overy, "Hitler's War," 273, 291.

466 *"did not depend":* Murray, *European Balance,* 13–14.

467 *Speer admitted this:* Overy, *War and Economy,* 27, 31, 312, 375.

467 *"much later":* Sebastian Cox, "The Overall Report in Retrospect," in *Report of the British Bombing Survey Unit,* xxviii; Speer, *Inside,* 214–16. Overy and other critics point out further that Wagenfuehr's statistics, when put under close scrutiny, fail to support his own thesis.

467 *at least two vital areas:* USSBS, Interview No. 60, Hans Kehrl, June 11, 1945, July 18, 1945, 137.315–60, AFHRA. After the war, Allied intelligence teams interviewed major department heads of the Ministry of Armaments. All of them testified that transportation bombing had seriously disrupted the gains achieved by economic rationalization; Imperial War Museum, Report 67, "Causes of the Decline in German Industrial Production, Autumn 1944," December 1945, 1–14; Overy, *War and Economy,* 362–74.

467 *"no appreciable effect":* USSBS, *German War Economy,* 10–11.

467 *"possible that production":* Ibid., 11–12.

467 *Speer's Ministry of Armaments assessed:* Albert Speer, "The Penalty of Overconfidence," in James Parton, ed., *Impact: The Army Air Forces' Confidential Picture History of World War II,* Vol. 3, *The Eve of Triumph* (Harrisburg: National Historical Society, 1989), x.

467 *"economic war":* "Interrogation of Albert Speer" by Lt. Sklarz and Sgt. Fassberg, May 15, 1945, AFHRA.

468 *"The losses inflicted":* Speer, "Overconfidence," xi.

468 *"The American attacks":* Interrogation of Speer, July 18, 1945, in Webster and Frankland, *Strategic Air Offensive,* vol. 4, 383.

468 *"The British inflicted":* Quoted in Alexandra Richie, *Faust's Metropolis: A History of Berlin* (NY: Carroll & Graf, 1998), 536.

468 *"mutual isolation":* Solly Zuckerman, "Strategic Bombing and the Defeat of Germany," *Royal United Service Institution* 130 (June 1985): 68–69.

468 *domination of the air and sea lanes:* Interrogation of Col. Gen. Alfred Jodl, 1945, 519.619-13, AFHRA; USSBS, Interview, Col. Gen. Alfred Jodl, June 29, 1945, 137.315-62, AFHRA.

468 *While American fighter boys:* Noble Frankland, "Some Reflections on the Strategic Air Offensive, 1939–1945," *Royal United Service Institution* 107 (May 1962): 102–3.

469 *Götterdämmerung:* Williamson Murray, "Reflections on the Combined Bomber Offensive," *Militageschtliche Mitteilungen* 51 (1992): 92.

469 *"to a complete standstill":* USSBS, *German War Economy,* 14.

470 *Hansell . . . electric power system:* Hansell, *Air Plan,* 259.

470 *"taut and vulnerable"–"all evidence":* Bombing survey quoted in ibid., 261; USSBS, *The Effects of Strategic Bombing on German Morale,* vol. 1 (Washington, DC: U.S. Government Printing Office, 1947), 18.

470 *too loose a leash:* British historians Max Hastings and Anthony Verrier are among the few critics who make this point.

470 *"decisive in the war":* Boog et al., *Germany and the Second World War,* vol. 6, 492.

470 *full strength:* USSBS, *Air Force Rate of Operations* (Washington, DC: U.S. Government Printing Office, 2nd ed., 1947), 4, 6.

471 *over two million tons:* Ibid., 31.

471 *The cost in lives lost:* USSBS, *Over-all Report (European War),* 1, 107; USSBS, *Statistical Appendix,* 1–3, Chart 1; United States Strategic Air Forces in Europe, "Statistical Summary of Operations, 1942–45," 519.308.9, AFHRA; Department of the Army, Statistical and Accounting Branch, Office of the Adjutant General, *Army Battle Casualties and Nonbattle Deaths in World War II, Final Report, 7 December 1941–31 December 1946* (Washington, DC: Department of the Army, 1953) 84–88; Wells, *Courage,* 115; Nanney, *Medical Services,* 20. There are no separate official casualty figures for the Eighth and Fifteenth Air Forces. The American Air Forces in the European and Mediterranean Theaters lost approximately 35,800 men dead, 13,700 wounded, 33,400 captured or interned, and 5,900 missing, i.e., killed. This figure includes fighter as well as bomber (twin-engine and four-engine) losses. There are no reliable figures for casualties in the Fifteenth Air Force, and even the more carefully documented Eighth Air Force casualties are subject to challenge; *Eighth Air Force Statistical Summary of Operations,* June 10, 1945; *Statistical Story of the Fifteenth Air Force,* n.d., AFHRA. A reliable and convenient source for the losses in men and machines suffered by the American Air Force in the ETO are the Statistical Appendices in Davis, *Spaatz.* For submarine losses, see Ronald H. Spector, *Eagle Against the Sun: The American War with Japan* (NY: Random House, 1985), 487; and San Francisco Maritime Natural Park Association, "United States Submarine Losses," www.maritime.org/subslost.htm.

471 *German losses:* Cooper, *German Air Force,* 377. The charts in Murray, *Luftwaffe,* indicate higher Luftwaffe loss rates in 1943–44 than those of the German submarine service.

471 *"suburban rings":* USSBS, *Over-all Report,* 91.

472 *25 million Germans:* In the absence of reliable records, all estimates of the number of Germans killed in the bombing are subject to challenge. The USSBS "estimate" was 305,000 killed, but this is impossibly low. I have arrived at my conclusions after examining scores of sources, including German historians of the bombing such as Olaf Groehler, who puts the total number of dead in the Third Reich, including Austria and the annexed areas, at around 406,000, which I also think is low; Olaf Groehler, "Strategic Air War," in Boog, *Conduct of the Air War,* 287–92. Among the most reliable yet ignored statistics are those provided by German wartime government officials. However odious the authors, they were in positions that made it important for them to know the facts.

Among them are Robert Ley, chief of the Nazi German Labor Front, which controlled German housing, and Dr. Karl Brandt, attending surgeon to Hitler and Reichskommissar of the führer for all German Military and Civilian Medical and Health Affairs. Brandt traveled extensively to bombed-out cities and met with local and district officials. Ley gave American interrogators a figure of 500,000 to 600,000 civilian deaths. Dr. Brandt gave a more precise estimate, up to 565,000. See USSBS Interview, No. 57, Dr. Robert Ley, June 27, 1945, 137.315-57, AFHRA; USSBS Interview, No. 61, Dr. Karl Brandt, AFHRA; USSBS, *Morale,* vol. 1, 7.

472   *At least three million dwelling units:* Groehler, "Strategic Air War," in Boog, *Conduct of the Air War,* 285, 290; Cooper, *German Air Force,* 377; Tony Judt, *Postwar: A History of Europe Since 1945* (NY: Penguin, 2005), 16–17; USSBS, *Over-all Report (European War),* 1.

472   *morale, which can be loosely defined:* Stanford Research Institute, *Impact of Air Attack in World War II: Selected Data for Civil Defense Planning,* vol. 1 (Washington, DC: Federal Civil Defense Administration, 1953), 4.

472   *"[You] underestimated . . . the powers":* Speer interview in Webster and Frankland, *Strategic Air Offensive,* vol. 4, 383.

472   *"Even after":* Ley interview.

472   *"there is overwhelming evidence":* Freeman Dyson, "The Bitter End," *New York Review of Books,* April 28, 2005, 6.

473   *"Bombing seriously depressed":* USSBS, *Morale,* 1; USSBS, *Over-all Report (European War),* 95–96.

473   *"is an invention":* Neil Gregor, "A *Schicksalsgemeinschaft?* Allied Bombing, Civilian Morale, and Social Dissolution in Nuremberg, 1942–1945," *Historical Journal* 43, no. 4 (2000): 1051.

473   *"In the coming war":* Quoted in USSBS, *Over-all Report (European War),* 95.

474   *"The organizations":* Barbara, Christina, and Sybilla Knauth, "The Chimneys of Leipzig," *Life,* May 15, 1944, 110.

474   *"This disaster":* Von Kardorff, *Diary,* 119–20. See also USSBS, *Cologne Field Report* (Washington, DC: U.S. Government Printing Office, 2nd ed. 1947), passim. The main party organ responsible for organized welfare was the National Socialist People's Welfare Organization (N.S. Volkswohlfahrt, NSV).

474   *"The most immediate thing":* Knauth, "Leipzig," 112.

474   *"The old dislike":* Ibid., 101.

475   *"the 'hell' ":* Seydewitz, *Civil Life,* 314.

475   *"penned more closely":* Ibid. See also USSBS, *Morale,* vol. 1, 67.

475   *"low ebb":* Quoted in USSBS, *A Brief Study of the Effects of Area Bombing on Berlin, Augsburg, Bochum, Leipzig, Hagen, Dortmund, Oberhausen, Schweinfurt, and Bremen* (Washington, DC: U.S. Government Printing Office, 2nd ed., 1947), 31.

475   *failed to report for work:* Von Kardorff, *Diary,* passim; Brodie, *Strategy,* 132. Total work absenteeism rates in Germany during the last year of the war more than doubled the wartime rates in Great Britain, approaching 20 percent of all scheduled hours during the final months of the war; see Stanford Research Institute, *Impact,* vol. 1, 175.

475   *"shelter deaths":* Stanford Research Institute, *Impact,* vol. 1, 237.

475 *A Berlin woman:* Richie, *Faust's Metropolis,* 532.

476 *"relatively permanent":* Irving L. Janis, *Air War and Emotional Stress: Psychological Studies of Bombing and Civilian Defense* (1951; repr., Westport, CT: Greenwood, 1976), 100.

476 *"adapt"–"getting used to it":* H. H. Garner, "Psychiatric Casualties in Combat," *War Medicine,* vol. 8 (1945), 343–57; Janis, *Air War,* 123.

476 *"I never became":* Quoted in USSBS, *Morale,* vol. 1, 20.

476 *"the greatest hardship":* USSBS, *Morale,* vol. 1, 3.

476 *"We have the Führer":* Quoted in Ian Kershaw, *The "Hitler Myth": Image and Reality in the Third Reich* (Oxford: Oxford University Press, 1987), 204.

476 *"easy"–"He doesn't have":* Quoted in ibid., 205–6.

476 *"flew out"–"The Führer is"–"inquired after":* Seydewitz, *Civil Life,* 313.

477 *"When this catastrophe":* Oberst Edgar Petersen quoted in Webster and Frankland, *Strategic Air Offensive,* vol. 3, 224.

477 *"Enjoy the war":* Von Kardorff, *Diary,* 119.

477 *"Many find themselves":* USSBS, *Morale,* vol. 1, 32.

477 *"defeat would be calamitous":* Ibid., 7.

477 *"essentials":* Quoted in Drew Middleton, "Apathy Dominates Ruined Brunswick," *NYT,* June 24, 1945, 11.

477 *"elementary problems":* USSBS, *Morale,* vol. 1, 32.

477 *"Everyone is concerned":* Von Kardorff, *Diary,* 119–20.

477 *"Our life in Berlin":* Wendel, *Hausfrau,* 200.

477 *"BU":* Jeremy Noakes, "Germany," in Jeremy Noakes, ed., *The Civilian in War: The Home Front in Europe, Japan and the USA in World War II* (Exeter, UK: University of Exeter Press, 1992), 56.

478 *"screaming and weeping":* Janis, *Air War,* 83.

478 *"staggered like"–"Those who lost":* Seydewitz, *Civil Life,* 311.

478 *"war of the vegetative neurosis":* USSBS, *The Effects of Bombing on Health and Medical Care in Germany* (Washington, DC: U.S. Government Printing Office, 1945), 3.

478 *"in a state of hysterics":* Von Kardorff, *Diary,* 119.

478 *"People are herding":* Ibid., 90.

478 *"Newspaper articles":* Quoted in USSBS, *Morale,* vol. 1, 51–52.

478 *"did irreparable harm":* Gerald Kirwin, "Allied Bombing and Nazi Domestic Propaganda," *European History Quarterly* 15 (1985): 357.

478 *"Why does nobody"–"One can only":* Von Kardorff, *Diary,* 201, 119.

479 *"As long as I am":* Quoted in Noakes, "Germany," in Noakes, *Civilian,* 56.

479 *the state stepped in:* USSBS, *Morale,* vol. 1, 60–61.

480 *French slave laborers:* Ibid., vol. 2, 1, 22.

480 *"Rather than":* Quoted in Noakes, "Germany," in Noakes, *Civilian,* 56.

480 *"counsel of despair":* Quoted in Overy, *Why the Allies,* 113.

480 *"soldiers of production":* Max Karant, "What Did the Air War Teach Us?" *Flying* 37 (October 1945): 130.

480 *"Tonight you go":* Quoted in Richie, *Faust's Metropolis,* 530.

481 *"all Nazism had":* Richard Bessel, *Nazism and War* (New York: Modern Library, 2004), 181.

481 *"all they":* Quoted in Williamson Murray, "Did Strategic Bombing Work?," in Robert Cowley, ed., *No End Save Victory: Perspectives on World War II* (New York: Putnam, 2001), 504.

481 *24,000 fighter planes:* USSBS, *V-Weapons (Crossbow) Campaign,* 1–3.

481 *"second front":* Roger Beaumont, "The Bomber Offensive as a Second Front," *Journal of Contemporary History* 22 (1987): 15.

481 *To defend the homeland:* USSBS, *German War Economy,* 39–40; interrogation of Speer, July 18, 1945, in Webster and Frankland, *Strategic Air Offensive,* vol. 4, 381; Overy, *Why the Allies,* 131.

482 *"home front army":* Overy, "Air Power," 25–26.

482 *quarter of a million:* Murray, "Reflections," 93.

482 *"in most lurid"–"a sea of flames":* USSBS, *The Effects of Strategic Bombing on German Morale,* vol. 2 (Washington, DC: U.S. Government Printing Office, 1946), 41.

482 *"psychological effect"–"While previously"–"fought well":* USSBS Interview, Col. Gen. Alfred Jodl, June 29, 1945, 137.315–62, AFHRA.

482 *"like something in a picture":* Von Kardorff, *Diary,* 201.

483 *"It's all a pack":* Ibid., 214–15, 225.

483 *"repugnant"–"hypocrisy":* Quoted in Antony Penrose, ed., *Lee Miller's War* (Boston: Little, Brown, 1992), 161, 166.

483 *"provoked by":* Raymond Daniell, "Disintegration of Germany Proceeds Rapidly," *NYT,* April 15, 1943, E3.

483 *"the world's vastest ruin":* Bach, *America's Germany,* 18.

483 *"for the denazification":* USSBS, *Over-all Report (European War),* 107.

484 *Approximately 1.5 million people:* Groehler, "Strategic," in Boog, *Conduct of the Air War,* 284–86.

484 *"total air war":* All Knauth quotes in Knauth, *Germany in Defeat* (NY: Alfred A. Knopf, 1946), chap. 7.

484 *"Massacre by Bombing":* Vera Brittain's "Massacre by Bombing" was first published in Great Britain in pamphlet form under the title *Seed of Chaos: What Mass Bombing Really Means* (London: New Vision Press, 1944). For a review of the opposition to bombing by American pacifists and the reaction of Shirer and the American press to Vera Brittain's courageous crusade against obliteration bombing, see James J. Martin, "The Bombing and Negotiated Peace—in 1944," in Martin, *Revisionist Viewpoints: Essays in a Dissident Historical Tradition* (Colorado Springs: Ralph Myles, 1971). See also Grayling, *Among the Dead Cities,* chap. 5.

484 *"there is something":* Sonia Orwell and Ian Angus, eds., *The Collected Essays, Journalism and Letters of George Orwell: As I Please, 1943–1945,* vol. 3 (NY: Harcourt Brace Jovanovich, 1968), 151.

484 *"Heaven knows":* Ibid.

485 *" 'Normal' or 'legitimate' ":* Ibid.

485 *"If we see":* Ibid., 152.

485 *"What he said":* Author interview with Paul Slawter, July 24, 1994.

Chapter 17: A Pageant of Misery

487 *"It seems to me":* Quoted in Webster and Frankland, *Strategic Air Offensive,* vol. 3, 112.

488 *"basting":* Churchill quoted in ibid., 101.

488 *"insult both"–"I do not":* Quoted in Dudley Saward, *Bomber Harris: The Story of Sir Arthur Harris, Marshall of the Royal Air Force* (Garden City: Doubleday, 1985), 292–94.

488 *"a milder one":* A copy of the directive is in Webster and Frankland, *Strategic Air Offensive,* vol. 3, 117.

488 *"The advances":* Msg. JD-117-CS (Redline), Spaatz to Doolittle, Spaatz MSS; on April 21, 1945, *Black Cat,* a B-24 Liberator of the 466th Bomb Group, was shot down by flak gunners over Regensburg. It was the last American bomber shot down over Germany itself, as opposed to German-occupied territory. Thomas Childers tells the story of *Black Cat* in his compelling book *Wings of Morning: The Story of the Last American Bomber Shot Down over Germany in World War II* (Reading, MA: Perseus, 1995). On April 25 and 26, the Fifteenth Air Force sent heavies against rail centers in the Austrian Alps, the last places in the Reich to feel the weight of American bombs.

489 *"I asked him":* Quoted in Freeman, *Mighty Eighth War Diary,* 499.

489 *died of starvation:* Weekly Intelligence Report, British Naval Intelligence Division, Naval Staff, Admiralty (May 4, 1945), No. 269, 63, copy at AFHRA. For Holland's travail, see Henri A. Van der Zee, *The Hunger Winter: Occupied Holland, 1944–45* (London: Jill Norman & Hobhouse, 1982); and Hastings, *Armageddon,* 407–17.

489 *"Unless a gift":* Quoted in Alling, *Mighty Fortress,* 147.

489 *"every officer":* Quoted in Van der Zee, *Hunger Winter,* 252.

490 *"In long, late-night"–"another kind of Air Force":* All Crosby quotes from *Wing,* 359–60, 365.

490 *"MANY THANKS YANKS":* Alling, *Mighty Fortress,* 148.

490 *"I felt better":* Crosby, *Wing,* 371.

490 *"to make aerial":* Doolittle, *Lucky,* 406.

490 *"One city was":* Anonymous, "Tour of the Ruhr–Personal Narrative, May 11, 1944, 100th Bombardment Group," AFHRA; Sgt. Kenneth R. Batten, "853rd Squadron History, May 1945," 491st Bomb Group, AFHRA.

491 *"There will never":* Interview with Danny Roy Moore, October 22, 1998, AHM.

491 *Kenneth "Deacon" Jones:* All Jones quotes in this section from Jones, "Diary."

491 *"European mankind":* London *Times,* June 27, 1943.

491 *Cologne: Daily Telegraph,* March 10, 1945. For an excellent account of the rebuilding of German cities, see Jeffry M. Diefendorf, *In the Wake of War: Reconstruction of German Cities After World War II* (NY: Oxford University Press, 1993).

491 *"Insolent and fat":* Hans Erich Nossack, *The End: Hamburg, 1943,* trans. Joel Agee (Chicago: University of Chicago Press, 2004), 44; Nossack's bomb-ruined Hamburg bears a striking resemblance to Cologne in 1945.

491 *The airmen were told:* Howard Katzander, "Allies Govern Cologne," *S&S,* May

4, 1945, 3–4; Earl E. Ziemke, *The U.S. Army in the Occupation of Germany, 1944–1946* (Washington, DC: Center of Military History, United States Army, 1975), 191.

491 *"fantastically impassable":* Sidney Olson, "Underground Cologne," *Life,* March 19, 1945, 28.

492 *"charred ruins":* Heinrich Böll, *The Silent Angel,* trans. Breon Mitchell (NY: Picador, 1995), 64–65.

492 *"a tacit agreement":* Sebald, *Natural History,* 10.

492 *"rocking explosives"–"the hammering":* Stephen Spender, *European Witness* (1946; repr., Westport, CT: Greenwood, 1971), 16.

493 *"I had rejoined":* Author interview with Robert Rosenthal, November 7, 2005.

493 *"We were waiting":* Loevsky interview, October 21, 2005.

493 *"What many of us":* Cleven interview, April 24, 2003.

494 *"The goons have":* Murphy, *Luck,* 233.

494 *Westheimer:* Westheimer, *Sitting It Out,* 261.

494 *"Prison life":* Cleven interview, April 24, 2003.

494 *"So off we went":* Loevsky interview, October 21, 2005.

495 *"There was lots":* Cleven interview, April 24, 2003.

495 *"It was hard":* Cleven interview, April 24, 2003.

496 *50,000 refugees:* Beevor, *Berlin,* 48.

496 *"[We pass] silent":* Halmos, *Wrong Side,* 94, 98.

496 *"Where are we going?":* Quoted in Childers, *Shadows,* 383.

497 *"to keep their chins up":* Spivey, *POW Odyssey,* 133.

497 *"Conditions inside the boxcars":* Murphy, *Luck,* 238.

497 *"The anger":* Wheeler, *Shootdown,* 137, 144.

498 *"I prayed":* William P. Maher, *Fated to Survive: Memoirs of a B-17 Flying Fortress Pilot/Prisoner of War,* ed. Ed Hall (Spartanburg, SC: Honoribus, 1992), 137; Paul E. Kennedy, *Adjutants Call* (Privately printed, n.d.), 54, in ME.

498 *"This ended the bombing":* Butts testimony in Harry Spiller, ed., *Prisoners of the Nazis: Accounts of American POWs in World War II* (Jefferson, NC: McFarland, 1998), 105.

498 *Red Cross parcels:* Butts, in Shapiro, *Prisoners,* 105; Wheeler, *Shootdown,* 157.

499 *"to murder"–"Acts of violence":* Churchill and Eisenhower quoted in John Nichol and Tony Rennell, *The Last Escape: The Untold Story of Allied Prisoners of War in Europe, 1944–45* (NY: Viking, 2003), 196.

499 *Special Forces units:* USSTAF, "Information on Current Problems Confronting the AAF in the ETO, 1944–45 . . ." 519.979, AFHRA; USSTAF, "ECLIPSE Memorandum No. 8: The Care and Evacuation of Prisoners of War in Greater Germany under ECLIPSE Conditions," May 19, 1945, 519.9731-13, AFHRA; USSTAF, "Minutes and Notes of Planning Meetings and Conference on Supply, Protection and Evacuation of Allied Prisoners of War, November 1944–May 1945, 519.973-3, AFHRA.

499 *"orderly and correct surrender":* Interview with Maj. Gen. Delmar T. Spivey, February 11, 1988, K239.0512-921, AFHRA; Spivey, *POW Odyssey,* 148.

499 *"Somebody sure pulled"–"a Great German"–"would be in":* Interview with Maj. Gen. Arthur Vanaman, January 18, 1967, K239.0521-1030, AFHRA.

500 *Spivey visited Berger:* Berger testimony, *Trials of War Criminals,* vol. 8, 57–75, 534–51, 1155–58; H. R. Trevor-Roper, *The Last Days of Hitler* (London: Macmillan, 1950), 134–35. As Trevor-Roper notes (p. 138), "Berger's accounts of his activities of these days are all characterized by indistinct and sometimes inconsistent loquacity." This issue is discussed in fascinating detail in Nichol and Rennell, *The Last Escape,* 357–71.

500 *Berger claimed:* Durand, *Stalag Luft III,* 360–61. In 1949, General Berger received a twenty-five-year sentence from the Nuremberg War Crimes Tribunal for his part in planning the Final Solution. Affidavits entered on his behalf by Spivey and Vanaman might have saved him from the hangman and led to his early release from prison in 1951.

500 *Red Cross representatives did inform:* Spivey, *POW Odyssey,* 148.

500 *"must be ready":* NYT, February 21, 1945.

501 *"a three-day hike":* Author interview with Joseph P. O'Donnell, May 7, 2003.

501 *Bataan Death March:* Approximately 750 Americans and 5,000 Filipinos died on the Bataan Death March.

501 *"It was obvious":* Caplan, "Testimony," in O'Donnell, *Shoeleather,* 66.

501 *"Men had rampaging":* Guderley interview, May 7, 2003.

501 *"littered by":* Caplan, "Testimony," in O'Donnell, *Shoeleather,* 66–67.

501 *"It was the worst night":* Guderley interview, May 7, 2003.

502 *"Day 35":* O'Donnell, *Shoeleather,* 12.

502 *"I saw":* Ibid.

502 *"But my top-turret gunner":* O'Donnell interview, May 7, 2003.

502 *"We wanted to":* Guderley interview, May 7, 2003.

503 *"Who are these people?"–"I wanted to . . . charge":* All Hoffman quotes from *Stalag 17B,* 184, 186–87. See also James M. Bloxom, *March to Eternity: Stalag 17B* (Privately printed, n.d.), in ME; and Richard H. Lewis, *Hell Above and Hell Below: The Real Life Story of an American Airman* (Wilmington: Delaware, 1985), 130–31.

504 *"It was Chanel No. 5":* Cleven interview, April 24, 1993; *Contrails,* 243–44.

504 *"Right now":* Quoted in *Contrails,* 245; "The Liberation of Moosburg," in *Splasher Six,* vol. 33, Summer 2002, at http://.100bg/spalser/moosburg .html, 3.

505 *freed his son:* Burbank, "Center Compound," 47.

505 *"FOR US":* Halmos, *Wrong Side,* 128.

505 *"We cheered":* Roger Burwell, "My War," 41, in ME.

505 *"I'm going to kill":* Quoted in Murphy, *Luck,* 245.

505 *"I figured"–"Men, you are":* Hoffman, *Stalag 17B,* 205–8.

506 *British Eighth Army:* O'Donnell interview, May 7, 2003.

506 *"directed to withhold news":* Eisenhower, *Crusade,* 22.

507 *"surveyed the room"–"Prussian and Nazi":* Butcher, *Three Years,* photograph caption, 843–44.

507 *"Marshal Zhukov himself":* Beevor, *Berlin,* 405.

507 *"I was glad to note":* Tedder, *With Prejudice,* 686; see also Butcher, *Three Years,* 846.

507 *"This is a city":* Harold King, dispatch for the Combined Allied Press, May 9,

1945, reproduced in Louis Snyder, ed., *Masterpieces of War Reporting: Great Moments of World War II* (NY: Julian Messner, 1962), 468–69.

507 *"the signal":* Quoted in Stephen E. Ambrose and C. L. Sulzberger, *American Heritage New History of World War II* (NY: Viking, 1997), 559.

507 *"Instantly":* Panter-Downes, *London War Notes,* 376–77.

508 *"London simply":* Rosenthal interview, November 7, 2005.

508 *"formed a conga line":* Panter-Downes, *London War Notes,* 374–77.

508 *"I can still see":* Carson, *Wing Ding,* 188.

508 *"My main feeling":* Quoted in R. Douglas Brown, *East Anglia, 1945* (Lavenham, UK: Terence Dalton, 1994), 63.

509 *"a fairyland":* Ibid., 61.

509 *"Spirits did not flag":* Longmate, *GI's,* 61.

509 *"As odd as it":* Alling, *Mighty Fortress,* 156.

509 *"It is midnight":* Von Kardorff, *Diary,* 220–21.

509 *"Suddenly, horns":* Hoffman, *Stalag 17B,* 224.

510 *"I was so skinny":* Cleven interview, April 24, 2003.

510 *"The fabulous Cleven"–"in the same":* Sheridan, *Never,* 149–50.

510 *"I begged to fly":* Cleven interview, April 24, 2003.

510 *"I'm just a baby":* Quoted in Sheridan, *Never,* 150.

510 *"Where's the ripcord?":* Cleven interview, April 24, 2003.

510 *"air aces":* Andy Rooney, "Nazi Camp Held Galaxy of U.S. Aces," *S&S,* May–June 1945, 1.

511 *Francis "Gabby" Gabreski:* Gabreski interview in Irv Broughton, ed., *Forever Remembered: The Fliers of World War II* (Spokane: Eastern Washington University Press, 2001), 29–30; Gabreski, *Gabby,* 170–71.

511 *John "Red" Morgan:* Lt. J. C. Morgan, "Disaster over Berlin," in Roy, *Behind;* "Congressional Medal Awarded Texas Flier," *S&S,* Dec. 20, 1943, 1; Rooney, "Flier Dropped with Arm Gone Is Safe in Reich," *S&S,* December 7, 1943, 1.

511 *"life had been":* Lowell Bennett, *Parachute,* 43.

511 *"to watch Berlin burn":* Ibid., 5; *NYT,* December 4, 1943, 4.

511 *"from somewhere inside"–"in the klink again":* *NYT,* January 22, 1944, 5; May 5, 1944, 7.

512 *"a discipline at least":* Bennett, *Parachute,* 228; author interview with Oscar Richard, March 1, 2003.

512 *"We are technically free":* Alan H. Newcomb, *Vacation with Pay* (Haverhill, MA: Destiny, 1947), 169.

512 *Zemke warned him:* Zemke and Freeman, *Zemke's Stalag,* 13–39, 79; Oscar G. Richard III, *Kriegie: An American POW in Germany* (Baton Rouge: Louisiana State University Press, 2000), 91.

513 *"The Russian nonchalantly":* Bennett, *Parachute,* 232–33.

513 *"Why are these men"–"the camp went stark":* Quoted in Richard interview; Carl W. Remy, Spiller, *Prisoners,* 118. For a different version of this incident, one not generally supported by prisoner testimony, see Zemke, *Zemke's Stalag,* 95–97.

513 *"This is something":* Forrest Howell, *Barbed Wire Horizons* (Tujunga, CA: C. L. Anderson, 1953), 198, in ME.

513 *"Hundreds of Jerries":* Newcomb, *Vacation,* 164.

513 *One American airman saw:* Howell, *Barbed Wire,* 201–2.

514 *"But most of us obeyed":* Richard interview.

514 frauleins: Vietor, *Time Out,* 168.

514 *"The Germans who dug":* Bennett, *Parachute,* 237–38.

514 *"This validated the war":* Gabreski, *Gabby,* 200–201.

514 *"Press—Pass Freely"–"Complete indescribable chaos":* All Bennett quotes in *Parachute,* 241, 244, 250–52.

515 *Col. Andrei Vlasov:* Patricia Louise Wadley, "Even One Is Too Many: An Examination of the Soviet Refusal to Repatriate Liberated American World War II Prisoners of War," Ph.D. diss., Texas Christian University, 1993, passim.

515 *6,250 freedom-starved men:* Edward Wenrich, testimony, in ME.

515 *"I grabbed"–"hitchhiked":* Richard interview.

516 *felt like a stranger:* Richard, *Kriegie,* 107; Richard interview.

516 *"big-ass birds":* Richard interview.

516 *"It was the saddest day":* Quoted in Stephen Bloomfield, "The Return of the Mighty Eighth," *Air and Space Smithsonian* 7, no. 5 (December 1992–January 1993): 62.

516 *"In those days":* Photo caption, 2nd Air Division Library, Norfolk, England.

516 *"I still remember":* Quoted in Gardiner, *Overpaid,* 213.

517 *"As I walked":* Carson, *Wing Ding,* 191; author unknown, "They Came to Madingley," reproduced in *Wing Ding,* 191–93.

Epilogue

518 *Eighth Air Force leaves England:* Forty-five men were killed in air accidents on the way home.

518 *"War is very screwy":* "Target Home," *S&S,* September 7, 1945, 3–4.

518 *45,000 or so British women:* Some historians put the number of GI brides as high as 100,000, but I have relied on David Reynolds's more conservative estimate. See Reynolds, *Rich Relations,* 422.

518 *immigration restrictions:* In late December 1945, the War Brides Act became U.S. law. It allowed "alien" spouses and "alien" children of U.S. citizens serving in or honorably discharged from the armed forces to bypass most existing immigration standards and quotas. By a 1924 law, the U.K. had been restricted to 6,000 entries per month. See Reynolds, *Rich Relations,* 418.

518 *"Operation Diaper Run":* Ibid., 418–19.

518 *"As we sailed":* Quoted in Elfrieda Berthiaume Shukert and Barbara Smith Scibetta, *War Brides of World War II* (Novato, CA: Presidio, 1988), 57.

519 *"Oh God":* Reynolds, *Rich Relations,* 422.

519 *"Some [women] were caught":* Interview with Ann O. Holmes De Vries, October 4, 1993, AHM.

519 *"a double dose":* S&S, May 25, 1945.

519 *"If the war's over":* Doolittle, *Lucky,* 423. Some of the Eighth's Mustangs had flown escort missions over Japan for the Twentieth Air Force.

519   *"you've had enough":* Author interview with Robert Rosenthal, March 25, 2003.

520   *"Throughout my war service":* All Rosenthal quotes in Rosenthal interviews, March 25, 2003; November 8, 2005.

520   *"91 percent dead":* William Shirer, *End of a Berlin Diary* (NY: Alfred A. Knopf, 1947), 287.

Bibliography

Manuscript Collections

Air Force Historical Research Agency, Maxwell Air Force Base, Alabama.
The most extensive repository of Eighth Air Force documents, it is also the world's largest collection on military aviation, with more than 1.5 million documents, approximately half of them on World War II. Among the collections' major resources are:

Operations summaries, combat mission reports, intelligence, weather, and medical reports, surveys of combat crews, and medical studies and statistical surveys of combat crews suffering from emotional disorders.

Flight Surgeon Reports

Prisoner of War Reports

Narratives of Operations

Escape and Evasion Reports

Interviews with Air Force leaders and personnel, among them: Frederick Anderson, Orvil Anderson, Albert P. Clark, James H. Doolittle, Ira C. Eaker, Barney M. Giles, Haywood S. Hansell, Jr., Gerald W. Johnson, William E. Kepner, Laurence S. Kuter, Elwood R. Quesada, Carl A. Spaatz, Arthur W. Vanaman, and Chuck Yeager.

Interrogations of combat crews

Transcripts of interrogations of leading German military, economic, and political figures, among them Hermann Göring, Alfred Jodl, Wilhelm Keitel, Karl Koller, Albert Speer, and Gerd von Rundstedt.

Eighth Air Force Fighter Command Reports

Unpublished reports, essays, and lectures by Luftwaffe leaders and combat fliers. Since the Luftwaffe records in Germany were destroyed, this is a particularly valuable source of information on the German fighter arm.

Records of the Central Medical Establishment

Miscellaneous records of the United States Strategic Bombing Survey

Miscellaneous records of the Committee of Operations Analysts

The papers of World War II air leaders, including Charles P. Cabell, William E. Kepner, and Guido R. Perera

Unit histories and records of the Eighth Air Force Bomb Groups

Records of the Air Corps Tactical School and the Air Service Tactical School

Records on Combat Crew Morale

Enemy Intelligence Summaries

The agency's collection is recorded on microfilm, with copies at the National Archives and Records Administration, College Park, Maryland, and the Air Force History Support Office, Bolling Air Force Base, Washington, DC.

Library of Congress, Manuscript Division, Washington, DC

Frank Andrews Papers

Henry H. Arnold Papers

James H. Doolittle Papers

Ira C. Eaker Papers

Muir S. Fairchild Papers

Curtis E. LeMay Papers

William "Billy" Mitchell Papers

Paul H. Nitze Papers

Elwood R. Quesada Papers

Carl Andrew Spaatz Papers

Nathan Twining Papers

Hoyt S. Vandenberg Papers

Of the above, the Spaatz Collection, comprising 379 boxes, is the best source on Eighth Air Force operations.

National Archives and Records Administration, College Park, Maryland

The repository of the official military records of the Army Air Forces during World War II (Record Group 18), including Headquarters Records, Combat Mission Reports, Intelligence Reports, Field Orders, Division, Wing, and Squadron Reports, and information on POWs and evaders. Also useful to this study were the records of:

Office of the Secretary of War

U.S. Joint Chiefs of Staff

Office of Strategic Services

Office of Scientific Research and Development

The United States Strategic Bombing Survey

Army Staff

SHAEF Public Relations Briefings
United States Theaters of War, World War II
Headquarters, Army Air Forces
Prisoners of War Records
Manuscript Collections: Robert Lovett Papers
Escape and Evasion Case Files
Records of the Swiss Legation of the United States
Records of Headquarters MIS-X (Military Intelligence Service, Escape and Evasion
Section)

Mass-Observation Archive, University of Sussex, Brighton, UK
The archive results from the work of the social research organization Mass-Observation, founded in 1937 and dedicated to the study of the everyday lives of ordinary people in Britain. It contains massive documentation—interviews, diaries, surveys, and so forth—of the attitudes of ordinary British civilians toward American servicemen stationed in England. The collection is especially rich on everyday life in Britain during the war.

U.S. Army Military History Institute, Carlisle Barracks, Pennsylvania
Chester Hansen Papers
Ira C. Eaker Papers
Omar Bradley Papers
Senior Officer Oral History Program

Mighty Eighth Air Force Heritage Museum, Savannah, Georgia
This fast-expanding library has a magnificent collection of unpublished memoirs, diaries, and letters of Eighth Air Force personnel.

U.S. Air Force Academy Library, Colorado Springs, Colorado
Laurence S. Kuter Papers
George C. M. McDonald Papers
Murray Green Collection on Hap Arnold

Eisenhower Presidential Library, Abilene, Kansas
Dwight David Eisenhower Papers

Lilly Library, Indiana University, Bloomington, Indiana
Ernie Pyle Papers

The National D-Day Museum, New Orleans, Louisiana
Unpublished memoirs by Eighth Air Force crewmen.

John F. Kennedy Library, Boston, Massachusetts
John Kenneth Galbraith Papers

The National Archives, Kew, UK (formerly called the Public Record Office)
Air Historical Branch Records, Series 1
Air Ministry Correspondence
Chief of Air Staff Papers
Air Publications and Records
Bomber Command Records
Air Ministry, Directorate of Intelligence
Air Historical Branch Narrative Histories

Royal Air Force Museum, Hendon, UK
Lord Tedder Papers
Sir Arthur Harris Papers

George C. Marshall Research Library, Lexington, Virginia
George C. Marshall Papers

Seely G. Mudd Library, Princeton University, Princeton, New Jersey
George W. Ball Papers

Yale University Library, New Haven, Connecticut
Diary of Henry Stimson (microfilm copy)

Hoover Institution on War, Revolution and Peace, Stanford University, Palo Alto, California
Frederick L. Anderson Collection

The Imperial War Museum, London
The Department of Documents has an extensive collection of diaries, private papers, and letters of Eighth Air Force personnel.

East Carolina University, Manuscript Collection, Greenville, North Carolina
Papers of Frank A. Armstrong

Swiss Internees Association Archives, Lakewood, New Jersey
Copies of official records pertaining to the Air Force internees in Switzerland, along with documentation dealing with internee life in the country.

Swiss Federal Archives, Bern, Switzerland
Houses the Final Report of the Federal Commission on Internment and Hospitalization of Foreign Military Personnel from 1940 to 1945.

Bundesarchiv/militararchic, Freiburg, Germany
Houses the Quartermaster General's Reports on Luftwaffe aircraft and crew losses, which are more accurate than the wartime records of enemy losses kept by the Eighth Air Force.

United States Holocaust Memorial Museum, Washington, DC
Records pertaining to the deportation of Hungarian Jews to Auschwitz and pressure exerted by Jewish groups to bomb the camp.

Oral History Collections

The Mighty Eighth Air Force Museum, Savannah, Georgia
This is the finest oral history collection on the Eighth Air Force.

American Airpower Heritage Museum, Midland, Texas
Houses a large collection of oral history interviews with Eighth Air Force veterans, most of them transcribed.

The National D-Day Museum, New Orleans, Louisiana
Houses a small but distinguished collection of oral histories of Air Force crewmen.

Columbia University Oral History Collection, Butler Library, Columbia University, New York City
This enormous collection contains oral history tapes and transcripts of Mrs. H. H. Arnold, Charles P. Cabell, James H. Doolittle, Ira C. Eaker, Robert A. Lovett, and Carl A. Spaatz.

Second Air Division Memorial Library, Norwich, UK
In addition to oral history transcripts and tapes, it houses unit histories and records of the Eighth Air Force's 2nd Division.

Imperial War Museum, Sound Archive, London, UK
Houses oral history interviews with World War II air leaders, including Ira C. Eaker, Sir Arthur Harris, and Jimmy Stewart.

United States Strategic Bombing Survey (European War)

A U.S. government field survey conducted in 1944–45 of the physical and psychological impact of strategic bombing on Germany. Several hundred plants and cities were examined and virtually all of the country's surviving political, economic, and military leaders were interviewed and interrogated. Over 200 detailed reports were published. Bibliographic information I have relied upon most heavily is in the notes.

Dissertations and Theses

Boylan, Bernard Lawrence. "The Development of the American Long-Range Escort Fighter." University of Missouri, 1955.
Bland, Edwin A., Jr. "German Methods of Interrogation of Captured Allied Aircrews." Maxwell Air Force Base, Montgomery, AL: Air University, 1948.

Burbank, Lyman B. "A History of the American Air Force Prisoners of War in Center Compound, Stalag Luft III, Germany." University of Chicago, 1946.

Wadley, Patricia Louise. "Even One Is Too Many: An Examination of the Soviet Refusal to Repatriate Liberated American World War II Prisoners of War." Texas Christian University, 1993.

U.S. Air Force Official History

Craven, Wesley Frank, and James Lea Cate, eds. *The Army Air Forces in World War II.* Although this history is dated and contains numerous errors, especially on enemy losses and casualties, it is indispensable. Five of the seven volumes deal with matters pertinent to the history of the Eighth Air Force.

Vol. 1: *Plans and Early Operations, January 1939 to August 1942.* Chicago: University of Chicago Press, 1948.

Vol. 2: *Europe: Torch to Pointblank, August 1942 to December 1943.* Chicago: University of Chicago Press, 1949.

Vol. 3: *Europe: Argument to V-E Day, January 1944 to May 1945.* Chicago: University of Chicago Press, 1951.

Vol. 6: *Men and Planes.* Chicago: University of Chicago Press, 1955.

Vol. 7: *Services Around the World.* Chicago: University of Chicago Press, 1958.

Books

Adams, Michael C. C. *The Best War Ever: America and World War II.* Baltimore: Johns Hopkins University Press, 1994.

Addison, Paul. *Firestorm: The Bombing of Dresden, 1945.* Chicago: Ivan R. Dee, 2006.

Alling, Charles. *A Mighty Fortress: Lead Bomber over Europe.* Haverford, PA: Casemate, 2002.

Ambrose, Stephen E. *Citizen Soldiers: The U.S. Army from the Normandy Beaches to the Bulge to the Surrender of Germany, June 7, 1944–May 7, 1945.* New York: Simon & Schuster, 1997.

——. *D-Day: June 6, 1944: The Climactic Battle of World War II.* New York: Simon & Schuster, 1994.

——. *The Wild Blue: The Men and Boys Who Flew the B-24s over Germany.* New York: Simon & Schuster, 2001.

Ambrose, Stephen E., and C. L. Sulzberger. *American Heritage New History of World War II.* New York: Viking, 1997.

Arbib, Robert S. *Here We Are Together: The Notebook of an American Soldier in Britain.* London: Longmans, Green, 1946.

Ardery, Philip. *Bomber Pilot: A Memoir of World War II.* Lexington: University Press of Kentucky, 1978.

Arnold, Henry H. *Global Mission.* London: Hutchinson, 1951.

Astor, Gerald. *The Mighty Eighth: The Air War in Europe as Told by the Men Who Fought It.* New York: Dell, 1997.

Atkinson, Rick. *An Army at Dawn: The War in North Africa, 1942–1943.* New York: Henry Holt, 2002.

Bach, Julian, Jr., *America's Germany: An Account of the Occupation*. New York: Random House, 1946.

Bailey, Ronald H. *The Air War in Europe*. Alexandria: Time-Life, 1979.

Ball, George W. *The Past Has Another Pattern: Memoirs*. New York: W. W. Norton, 1983.

Bard, Mitchell G. *Forgotten Victims: The Abandonment of the Americans in Hitler's Camps*. Boulder: Westview, 1994.

Beck, Earl R. *Under the Bombs: The German Home Front, 1942–1945*. Lexington: University Press of Kentucky, 1986.

Beevor, Antony. *The Fall of Berlin 1945*. New York: Viking, 2002.

Bekker, Cajus. *The Luftwaffe War Diaries*. Garden City: Doubleday, 1968.

Belenky, Gregory. *Contemporary Studies in Combat Psychiatry*. Westport, CT: Greenwood, 1987.

Bendiner, Elmer. *The Fall of Fortresses: A Personal Account of the Most Daring, and Deadly, American Air Battles of World War II*. New York: Putnam, 1980.

Bennett, John M. *Letters from England*. San Antonio: Privately printed, 1945.

Bennett, Lowell. *Parachute to Berlin*. New York: Vanguard, 1945.

Bergander, Götz. *Dresden im Luftkrieg: Vorgeschichte, Zerstorung, Folgen*. 1994. Revised edition, Würzburg: Böhlau, 1998.

Beschloss, Michael. *The Conquerors: Roosevelt, Truman and the Destruction of Hitler's Germany, 1941–1945*. New York: Simon & Schuster, 2002.

Bessel, Richard. *Nazism and War*. New York: Modern Library, 2004.

Biddle, Tami. *Rhetoric and Reality in Air Warfare: The Evolution of British and American Ideas About Strategic Bombing, 1914–1945*. Princeton: Princeton University Press, 2002.

Bidinian, Larry J. *The Combined Allied Bombing Offensive Against the German Civilian, 1942–1945*. Lawrence, KS: Coronado, 1976.

Bing, Richard L. *You're 19 . . . Welcome Home: A Story of the Air War over Europe and Its After-Effects*. Privately printed, 1992.

Boehme, Manfred. *JG 7: The World's First Jet Fighter Unit, 1944–1945*. Translated by David Johnston. Atglen, PA: Schiffer, 1992.

Böll, Heinrich. *The Silent Angel*. Translated by Breon Mitchell. New York: Picador, 1995.

Bond, Douglas D. *The Love and Fear of Flying*. New York: International Universities Press, 1952.

Boog, Horst, ed. *The Conduct of the Air War in the Second World War*. New York: Berg, 1992.

Boog, Horst, et al. *Germany and the Second World War*, vol. 6, *The Global War*. Edited by the Research Institute for Military History, Potsdam, Germany; translated by Ewald Osers et al. New York: Oxford University Press, 2001.

Borowski, Harry R., ed. *The Harmon Memorial Lectures in Military History, 1959–1987: A Collection of the First Thirty Harmon Lectures Given at the United States Air Force Academy*. Washington, DC: Office of Air Force History, 1988.

Bowman, Martin. *Castles in the Air*. Wellingborough, UK: Patrick Stephens, 1984.

——. *Great American Air Battles of World War II*. Shrewsbury, UK: Airlife, 1994.

Boyle, Andrew. *Trenchard*. London: Collins, 1962.

Boyne, Walter. *Aces in Command: Fighter Pilots as Combat Leaders*. Washington, DC: Brassey's, 2001.

Bradley, Omar. *A Soldier's Story*. New York: Henry Holt, 1951.

Bradley, Omar N., and Clay Blair. *A General's Life: An Autobiography*. New York: Simon & Schuster, 1983.

Brickhill, Paul. *The Great Escape*. 1950. Reprint. New York: Ballantine, 1961.

Bright, Charles, ed. *Historical Dictionary of the U.S. Air Force*. Westport, CT: Greenwood, 1992.

Briol, John J. *Dead Engine Kids: World War II Diary of John J. Briol*. Edited by John F. Welch. Rapid City, SD: Silver Wings Aviation, 1993.

British Bombing Survey Unit. *The Strategic Air War Against Germany, 1939–1945*. London: Frank Cass, 1998.

Brittain, Vera. *Seed of Chaos: What Mass Bombing Really Means*. London: New Vision Press, 1944.

Brodie, Bernard. *Strategy in the Missile Age*. Princeton: Princeton University Press, 1959.

Broughton, Irv, ed. *Forever Remembered: The Fliers of World War II*. Spokane: Eastern Washington University Press, 2001.

Brown, James Good. *The Mighty Men of the 381st, Heroes All: A Chaplain's Inside Story of the Men of the 381st Bomb Group*. Salt Lake City: Publishers Press, 1994.

Brown, R. Douglas. *East Anglia, 1939*. Lavenham, UK: Terence Dalton, 1980.

——. *East Anglia, 1941*. Lavenham, UK: Terence Dalton, 1986.

——. *East Anglia, 1942*. Lavenham, UK: Terence Dalton, 1988.

——. *East Anglia, 1943*. Lavenham, UK: Terence Dalton, 1990.

——. *East Anglia, 1944*. Lavenham, UK: Terence Dalton, 1992.

——. *East Anglia, 1945*. Lavenham, UK: Terence Dalton, 1994.

Budiansky, Stephen. *Air Power: The Men, Machines, and Ideas That Revolutionized War, from Kitty Hawk to Gulf War II*. New York: Viking, 2004.

Burgess, Alan. *The Longest Tunnel: The True Story of World War II's Great Escape*. New York: Weidenfeld, 1990.

Butcher, Geoffrey. *Next to a Letter from Home: Major Glenn Miller's Wartime Band*. Edinburgh: Mainstream, 1986.

Butcher, Harry. *My Three Years with Eisenhower: The Personal Diary of Captain Harry C. Butcher, USNR, Naval Aide to General Eisenhower, 1942 to 1945*. New York: Simon & Schuster, 1946.

Cabell, Charles P. *A Man of Intelligence: Memoirs of War, Peace, and the CIA*. Colorado Springs: Impavide, 1977.

Caidin, Mark. *Black Thursday*. New York: Bantam, 1981.

Calder, Angus. *The People's War: Britain, 1939–1945*. New York: Pantheon, 1969.

Caldwell, Donald L. *J. G. 26: Top Guns of the Luftwaffe*. New York: Orion, 1991.

Callahan, John Francis. ed. *Contrails, My War Record: A History of World War Two as Recorded at U.S. Army Air Force Station #139, Thorpe Abbotts, Near Diss, County of Norfolk, England*. New York: J. F. Callahan, 1947.

Carlson, Lewis H. *We Were Each Other's Prisoners: An Oral History of World War II American and German Prisoners of War*. New York: Basic, 1997.

Carson, Eugene T. *Wing Ding: Memories of a Tailgunner*. Privately printed, 2000.

Chandler, Alfred D., ed. *The Papers of Dwight David Eisenhower*. Vol. 3, *The War Years*. Baltimore: Johns Hopkins University Press, 1970.

——. *The Papers of Dwight David Eisenhower*. Vol. 4, *The War Years*. Baltimore: Johns Hopkins University Press, 1970.

Chennault, Claire Lee. *Way of a Fighter: The Memoirs of Claire Lee Chennault*. New York: Putnam, 1949.

Childers, Thomas. *In the Shadows of War: An American Pilot's Odyssey Through Occupied France and the Camps of Nazi Germany*. New York: Henry Holt, 2003.

——. *Wings of Morning: The Story of the Last American Bomber Shot Down over Germany in World War II*. Reading, MA: Perseus, 1995.

Churchill, Winston. *The Second World War*. Vol. 4, *The Hinge of Fate*. Boston: Houghton Mifflin, 1950.

——. *The Second World War*. Vol. 5, *Closing the Ring*. Boston: Houghton Mifflin, 1951.

Coffey, Thomas M. *Hap: The Story of the U.S. Air Force and the Man Who Built It, General Henry H. "Hap" Arnold*. New York: Viking, 1982.

——. *Iron Eagle: The Turbulent Life of General Curtis LeMay*. New York: Crown, 1986.

Cohen, Roger. *Soldiers and Slaves: American POWs Trapped in the Nazis' Final Gamble*. New York: Alfred A. Knopf, 2005.

Collins, J. Lawton. *Lightning Joe: An Autobiography*. Baton Rouge: Louisiana State University Press, 1979.

Comer, John. *Combat Crew*. Privately printed, 1986; repr., New York: Pocket Books, 1989.

Conley, Harry M. *No Foxholes in the Sky*. Trumbull, CT: FNP Military Division, 2002.

Cooke, Ronald C., and Ron Conyers Nesbit. *Target: Hitler's Oil: Allied Attacks on German Oil Supplies, 1939–1945*. London: William Kimber, 1985.

Cooper, Alan W. *Target Dresden*. Bromley: Independent Books, 1995.

Cooper, Matthew. *The German Air Force: 1933–1945, An Anatomy of Failure*. New York: Jane's, 1981.

Copp, DeWitt S. *A Few Great Captains*. Garden City: Doubleday, 1980.

——. *Forged in Fire*. Garden City: Doubleday, 1982.

Corn, Joseph J. *The Winged Gospel: America's Romance with Aviation, 1900–1950*. New York: Oxford University Press, 1983.

Corum, James S. *The Luftwaffe: Creating the Operational Air War, 1918–1940*. Lawrence: University Press of Kansas, 1997.

Corum, James S., and Richard R. Miller. *The Luftwaffe's Way of War: German Air Force Doctrine, 1911–1945*. Baltimore: Nautical & Aviation Publishing Company of America, 1998.

Cotterell, Robert. *POW*. Philadelphia: Xlibris, 2002.

Cowdrey, Albert E. *Fighting for Life: American Military Medicine in World War II*. New York: Free Press, 1994.

Cowley, Robert, ed. *No End Save Victory: Perspectives on World War II*. New York: Putnam, 2001.

Crane, Conrad C. *Bombs, Cities, and Civilians: American Airpower Strategy in World War II*. Lawrence: University Press of Kansas, 1993.

Cronkite, Walter. *A Reporter's Life*. New York: Alfred A. Knopf, 1996.

Crosby, Harry H. *A Wing and a Prayer: The "Bloody 100th" Bomb Group of the U.S.*

Eighth Air Force in Action over Europe in World War II. New York: HarperCollins, 1993.

Culler, Dan. *Black Hole of Wauwilermoos.* Green Valley, AZ: Circle of Thorns, 1995.

Dallas, Gregor. *1945: The War That Never Ended.* New Haven: Yale University Press, 2005.

Daley-Brusselmans, Yvonne. *Belgium Rendez-Vous 127 Revisited.* Manhattan, KS: Sunflower University Press, 2001.

Dallek, Robert. *Franklin D. Roosevelt and American Foreign Policy, 1932–1945.* New York: Oxford University Press, 1979.

——. *An Unfinished Life: John F. Kennedy, 1917–1963.* Boston: Little, Brown, 2003.

Daso, Dik Alan. *Doolittle: Aerospace Visionary.* Washington, DC: Potomac, 2003.

——. *Hap Arnold and the Evolution of American Airpower.* Washington, DC: Smithsonian Institution Press, 2000.

Datner, Szymon. *Crimes Against POWs: Responsibility of the Wehrmacht.* Warszawa: Zachodnia Agencja Prasowa, 1964.

Davies, Norman. *Rising '44: The Battle for Warsaw.* New York: Viking, 2004.

Davis, Richard G. *Carl A. Spaatz and the Air War in Europe.* Washington, DC: Center for Air Force History, 1993.

——. *Hap: Henry H. Arnold, Military Aviator.* Washington, DC: Air Force History and Museums Program, 1997.

Dear, Ian, and M. R. D. Foot, eds. *Oxford Companion to World War II.* Oxford: Oxford University Press, 2001.

D'Este, Carlo. *Decision in Normandy.* New York: Dutton, 1988.

Dewey, Donald. *James Stewart: A Biography.* Atlanta: Turner, 1996.

Diefendorf, Jeffry M. *In the Wake of War: Reconstruction of German Cities After World War II.* New York: Oxford University Press, 1993.

Dillon, Carrol F. *A Domain of Heroes: An Airman's Life Behind Barbed Wire in Germany in WW II.* Sarasota: Palm Island, 1995.

Dippel, John V. H. *Two Against Hitler: Stealing the Nazis' Best-Kept Secrets.* New York: Praeger, 1992.

Dolph, Harry A. *The Evader: An American Airman's Eight Months with the Dutch Underground.* Austin: Eaken, 1991.

Dönitz, Karl. *Memoirs: Ten Years and Twenty Days.* Translated by R. H. Stevens and David Woodward. New York: Leisure Books, 1959.

Doolittle, James H. "Jimmy," and Carroll V. Glines. *I Could Never Be So Lucky Again.* New York: Bantam, 1992.

Douhet, Giulio. *The Command of the Air.* Translated by Dino Farrari. 1942. Reprint, Washington, DC: Office of Air Force History, 1983.

Duerksen, Menno. *The Memphis Belle: Now the Real Story of World War II's Most Famous Warplane.* Memphis: Castle, 1987.

Dugan, James, and Carroll Stewart. *Ploesti: The Great Ground-Air Battle of 1 August 1943.* 1962. Reprint, Washington, DC: Brassey's, 2002.

Durand, Arthur A. *Stalag Luft III: The Secret Story.* Baton Rouge: Louisiana State University Press, 1988.

Dyson, Freeman. *Disturbing the Universe.* New York: Harper & Row, 1979.

Eisenhower, Dwight D. *Crusade in Europe.* Garden City: Doubleday, 1948.

Eliot, George F. *Bombs Bursting in Air: The Influence of Air Power on International Relations*. New York: Reynal & Hitchcock, 1939.

Ethell, Jeffrey, and Alfred Price. *Target Berlin: Mission 250: 6 March 1944*. London: Greenhill, 2002.

Feiling, Keith G. *The Life of Neville Chamberlain*. London: Macmillan, 1946.

Fest, Joachim C. *Speer: The Final Verdict*. San Diego: Harcourt, 2001.

Fieser, Louis F. *The Scientific Method: A Personal Account of Unusual Projects in War and in Peace*. New York: Reinhold, 1964.

Fifteenth Air Force. *The Air Battle of Ploesti*. Bari, Italy, 1944.

Fishbein, Morris, ed. *Doctors at War*. New York: Dutton, 1945.

Flower, Desmond, and James Reeves, eds. *The War: 1939–1945: A Documentary History*. New York: Da Capo, 1997.

Foot, M. R., and J. M. Langley. *MI9: Escape and Evasion, 1939–1945*. Boston: Little, Brown, 1980.

Foy, David A. *For You the War Is Over: American Prisoners of War in Nazi Germany*. New York: Stein & Day, 1984.

Franks, Norman L. R. *The Battle of the Airfields: 1st January 1945*. London: William Kimber, 1982.

Freeman, Roger A. *The Friendly Invasion*. Norwich, UK: East Anglia Tourist Board in conjunction with Terence Dalton, 1992.

——. *The Mighty Eighth: A History of the Units, Men and Machines of the US 8th Air Force*. 1970. Reprint, New York: Cassell, 2000.

——. *The Mighty Eighth War Manual*. London: Cassell, 2001.

Freeman, Roger A., Alan Crouchman, and Vic Maslen. *Mighty Eighth War Diary*. London: Jane's, 1981.

Freud, Sigmund. *Inhibitions, Symptoms, and Anxiety*. London: Hogarth, 1948.

Fuller, J. F. C. *The Second World War, 1939–45: A Strategical and Tactical History*. London: Eyre & Spottiswoode, 1954.

Furse, Anthony. *Wilfrid Freeman: The Genius Behind Allied Survival and Air Supremacy, 1939 to 1945*. Staplehurst, UK: Spellmount, 2000.

Futrell, Robert Frank. *Ideas, Concepts, Doctrine: Basic Thinking in the United States Air Force, 1907–1960*. 2 vols. Maxwell Air Force Base, AL: Air University Press, 1989.

Fyler, Carl. *Staying Alive: A B-17 Pilot's Experiences Flying Unescorted Bomber Missions by 8th Air Force Elements During World War II*. Leavenworth, KS: J. H. Johnston, 1995.

Gabreski, Francis, as told to Carl Molesworth. *Gabby: A Fighter Pilot's Life*. New York: Orion, 1991.

Gabriel, Richard A. *No More Heroes: Madness and Psychiatry in War*. New York: Hill & Wang, 1987.

Galbraith, John Kenneth. *Annals of an Abiding Liberal*. Edited by Andrea D. Williams. Boston: Houghton Mifflin, 1979.

——. *A Life in Our Times: Memoirs*. Boston: Houghton Mifflin, 1981.

Galland, Adolf. *The First and the Last: The Rise and Fall of the German Fighter Forces, 1938–1945*. 1954. Reprint, New York: Ballantine, 1973.

Gardiner, Juliet. *Overpaid, Oversexed, and Over Here: The American GI in World War II Britain*. New York: Abbeville, 1992.

Garrett, Stephen A. *Ethics and Airpower in World War II: The British Bombing of German Cities*. New York: St. Martin's, 1996.

Gaston, James C. *Planning the American Air War: Four Men and Nine Days in 1941*. Washington, DC: National Defense University Press, 1982.

Gay, Verbon F. *The Story of Rainbow Corner: The American Red Cross Club near Piccadilly Circus, London*. London: Fanfare, 1944.

Gentile, Don Salvatore, and Ira Wolfert. *One-Man Air Force*. New York: L. B. Fischer, 1944.

Gentile, Gian. *How Effective Is Strategic Bombing? Lessons Learned from World War II to Kosovo*. New York: New York University Press, 2001.

Gilbert, Martin. *Auschwitz and the Allies*. New York: Holt, Rinehart & Winston, 1981.

Gobrecht, Harry D. *Might in Flight: Daily Diary of the Eighth Air Force's Hell's Angels, 303rd Bombardment Group (H)*. San Clemente, CA: 303rd Bomb Group Association, 1997.

Goebbels, Joseph. *The Diaries of Joseph Goebbels: Final Entries, 1945*. Edited by Hugh Trevor-Roper. Translated by Richard Barry. New York: Putnam, 1978.

Goldberg, Alfred. "General Carl A. Spaatz." In *The War Lords: Military Commanders of the Twentieth Century*. Edited by Michael Carver. Boston: Little, Brown, 1976.

Gooderson, Ian. *Air Power at the Battlefront: Allied Close Air Support in Europe, 1943–45*. London: Frank Cass, 1998.

Gorham. Deborah. *Vera Brittain*. London: Blackwell, 1996.

Gray, J. Glenn. *The Warriors: Reflections on Men in Battle*. 1959. Reprint, Lincoln: University of Nebraska Press, 1970.

Grayling, A. C. *Among the Dead Cities: The History and Moral Legacy of the WWII Bombing of Civilians in Germany and Japan*. New York: Walker, 2006.

Great Britain, Air Ministry. *The Rise and Fall of the German Air Force, 1933–1945*. 1948. Reprint, New York: St. Martin's, 1983.

Greer, Thomas H. *The Development of Air Doctrine in the Army Air Arm, 1917–1941*. Maxwell Air Force Base, AL: United States Air Force Historical Study, Air University Press, 1955.

Grinker, Roy R., and John P. Spiegel. *Men Under Stress*. Philadelphia: Blakiston, 1945.

Groehler, Olaf. *Der Bombenkrieg gegen Deutschland*. Berlin: Akademie-Verlag, 1990.

Guderian, Heinz. *Panzer Leader*. Translated by Constantine Fitzgibbon. London: Michael Joseph, 1952.

Haines, William Wister. *Command Decision*. Boston: Little, Brown, 1947.

——. *ULTRA and the History of the United States in Europe vs. the German Air Force*. NSA Special Research History No. 13, June 1945. Reprint, Frederick, MD: University Publications of America, 1986.

Halberstam, David. *The Best and the Brightest*. New York: Random House, 1972.

Hale, Edwin R. W., and John Frayn Turner. *The Yanks Are Coming*. Turnbridge Wells, UK: Midas, 1983.

Hall, Grover C. *1000 Destroyed: The Life and Times of the 4th Fighter Group*. Montgomery, AL: Brown, 1946.

Halmos, Eugene E., Jr. *The Wrong Side of the Fence: A United States Army Air Corps POW in World War II*. Shippensburg, PA: White Mane, 1996.

Halpert, Sam. *A Real Good War*. London: Cassell, 1997.

Hamilton, Jim. *The Writing 69th: Civilian War Correspondents Accompany a U.S. Bombing Raid on Germany During World War II.* Marshfield, MA: Privately printed, 1999.

Hansell, Haywood S. *The Air Plan That Defeated Hitler.* Atlanta: Higgins-McArthur, 1972.

——. *The Strategic Air War Against Germany and Japan: A Memoir.* Washington, DC: Office of Air Force History, 1986.

Hanson, Victor Davis. *Carnage and Culture: Landmark Battles in the Rise of Western Power.* New York: Doubleday, 2001.

Harper, C. B. (Red). *Buffalo Gal.* Privately printed, n.d.

Harris, Arthur. *Bomber Offensive.* London: Collins, 1947.

Harrison, Gordon A. *Cross-Channel Attack.* Washington, DC: Office of the Chief of Military History, Department of the Army, 1951.

Harrison, Mark, ed. *The Economics of World War II: Six Great Powers in International Comparison.* Cambridge: Cambridge University Press, 1998.

Häsler, Alfred A. *The Lifeboat Is Full: Switzerland and the Refugees, 1933–1945.* New York: Funk & Wagnalls, 1969.

Hastings, Donald W., David G. Wright, and Bernard C. Glueck. *Psychiatric Experiences of the Eighth Air Force, First Year of Combat, July 4, 1942–July 4, 1943.* New York: Josiah Macy, Jr., Foundation, 1944.

Hastings, Max. *Bomber Command.* 1979. Reprint, New York: Simon & Schuster, 1989.

Hawkins Ian L., ed. *B-17s over Berlin: Personal Stories from the 95th Bomb Group (H).* 1987. Reprint, Washington, DC: Brassey's, 1990.

——. *The Munster Raid: Before and After.* Trumbull, CT: FNP Military Division, 1999.

Hawton, Hector. *Night Bombing.* London: Thomas Nelson, 1944.

Hedges, Chris. *War Is a Force That Gives Us Meaning.* New York: Public Affairs, 2002.

Herman, Jan. *A Talent for Trouble: The Life of Hollywood's Most Acclaimed Director, William Wyler.* New York: Putnam, 1995.

Hersey, John. *The War Lover.* New York: Bantam, 1960.

Higham, Robin, and Stephen J. Harris, eds. *Why Air Forces Fail: The Anatomy of Defeat.* Lexington: University Press of Kentucky, 2006.

Hinsley, Frances H. *British Intelligence in the Second World War.* London: Her Majesty's Stationery Office, 1988.

Hoffman, Richard H. *Stalag 17B.* Philadelphia: Xlibris, 1988.

Holley, Irving B., Jr., *Buying Aircraft: Matériel Procurement for the Army Air Forces.* Washington, DC: Office of the Chief of Military History, Department of the Army 1964.

Homze, Edward. *Arming the Luftwaffe.* Lincoln: University of Nebraska Press, 1976.

Hopewell, Clifford. *Combine 13.* Austin: Eakin, 2000.

Howell, Forrest W. *Barbed Wire Horizons.* Tujunga, CA: C. L. Anderson, 1953.

Hughes, Thomas Alexander. *Over Lord: General Pete Quesada and the Triumph of Tactical Air Power in World War II.* New York: Free Press, 1995.

Hurley, Alfred F. *Billy Mitchell: Crusader for Air Power.* New York: Franklin Watts, 1964.

Huston, John W., ed. *American Airpower Comes of Age: General Henry H. "Hap" Arnold's War Diaries.* Maxwell Air Force Base, AL: Air University Press, 2001.

Hutton, Oram C. [Bud], and Andy Rooney. *Air Gunner.* New York: Farrar & Rinehart, 1944.

———. *The Story of The Stars and Stripes.* New York: Farrar & Rinehart, 1946.

Infield, Glenn. *Big Week.* New York: Pinnacle, 1974.

International Committee of the Red Cross. *Report of the ICRC on Its Activities During the Second World War, September 1, 1939–June 30, 1947.* Geneva, 1948.

Irving, David. *Apocalypse 1945: The Destruction of Dresden.* London: Focal Point, 1995.

Jablonski, Edward. *America in the Air War.* Alexandria: Time-Life, 1982.

———. *Flying Fortress: The Illustrated Biography of the B-17s and the Men Who Flew Them.* Garden City: Doubleday, 1965.

Jackson, Julian. *France: The Dark Years, 1940–1944.* Oxford: Oxford University Press, 2001.

Janis, Irving L. *Air War and Emotional Stress: Psychological Studies of Bombing and Civilian Defense.* 1951. Reprint, Westport, CT: Greenwood, 1976.

Jennings, Hal B., ed. *Neuropsychiatry in World War II.* Vol. 2, *Overseas Theaters.* Washington, DC: Office of the Surgeon General, Department of the Army, 1973.

Judt, Tony. *Postwar: A History of Europe Since 1945.* New York: Penguin, 2005.

Kaplan, Philip, and Rex Alan Smith. *One Last Look.* New York: Charles Scribner's Sons, 1982.

Kardorff, Ursula von. *Diary of a Nightmare: Berlin, 1942–1945.* Translated by Ewan Butler. New York: John Day, 1966.

Katzenbach, John. *Hart's War.* New York: Ballantine, 1999.

Keegan, John. *The Second World War.* New York: Viking, 1989.

Kelsey, Benjamin S. *The Dragon's Teeth: The Creation of United States Air Power for World War II.* Washington, DC: Smithsonian Institution Press, 1982.

Kennedy, Paul E. *Adjutants Call.* Privately printed, n.d.

Kennett, Lee. *A History of Strategic Bombing.* New York: Scribner, 1982.

Kershaw, Ian. *Hitler, 1936–1945: Nemesis.* New York: W. W. Norton, 2000.

———. *The "Hitler Myth": Image and Reality in the Third Reich.* Oxford: Oxford University Press, 1987.

Klein, Burton. *Germany's Economic Preparations for War.* Cambridge: Harvard University Press, 1959.

Klemperer, Victor. *To the Bitter End: The Diaries of Victor Klemperer, 1942–1945.* Edited by Martin Chalmers. London: Weidenfeld & Nicolson, 1999.

Knauth, Percy. *Germany in Defeat.* New York: Alfred A. Knopf, 1946.

Knell, Hermann. *To Destroy a City: Strategic Bombing and Its Human Consequences in World War II.* Cambridge, MA: Da Capo, 2003.

Knoke, Heinz. *I Flew for the Führer.* 1953. Reprint, Mechanicsburg, PA: Stackpole, 1997.

Korson, George G. *At His Side: The Story of the American Red Cross Overseas in World War II.* New York: Coward-McCann, 1945.

LaMore, Tommy, and Dan A. Baker. *One Man's War: The WW II Saga of Tommy LaMore.* New York: Taylor, 2002.

Lande, D. A. *From Somewhere in England: The Life and Times of Air Force in World War II.* Osceola, WI: Motorbooks, 1991.

Landry, Tom, with Gregg Lewis. *Tom Landry: An Autobiography*. New York: Harper-Collins, 1991.

Langley, J. M. *Fight Another Day*. London: Collins, 1974.

Lay, Beirne, Jr. *Presumed Dead*. Originally published in 1945 as *I've Had It*. New York: Dodd, Mead, 1980.

Lay, Beirne, Jr., and Sy Bartlett. *Twelve O'Clock High!* 1948. Reprint, New York: Dodd, Mead, 1975.

Lee, Ulysses. *U.S. Army in World War II: The Employment of Negro Troops*. Washington, DC: Office of the Chief of Military History, Department of the Army, 1966.

Lee, Asher. *Goering, Air Leader*. London: Duckworth, 1972.

Lee, Wright. *Not as Briefed: 445th Bombardment Group (H), Eighth Air Force; Memoirs of a B-24 Navigator/Prisoner of War, 1943–1945*. Spartanburg, SC: Honoribus, 1995.

LeMay, Curtis E., and MacKinlay Kantor. *Mission with LeMay: My Story*. Garden City: Doubleday, 1965.

Lemmons, Ken, Cindy Goodman, and Jan Riddling. *The Forgotten Man: The Mechanic: The Kenneth A. Lemmons Story*. Little Rock: CinJan Productions, 1999.

Le Strange, Richard, and James R. Brown. *Century Bombers: The Story of the Bloody Hundredth*. Thorpe Abbotts, UK: 100th Bomb Group Memorial Museum, 1989.

Levine, Alan J. *The Strategic Bombing of Germany, 1940–1945*. New York: Praeger, 1992.

Levine, Isaac D. *Mitchell, Pioneer of Air Power*. New York: Duell, Sloan & Pearce, 1943.

Levitt, Saul. *The Sun Is Silent*. New York: Harper & Brothers, 1951.

Lewis, Richard H. *Hell Above and Hell Below: The Real Life Story of an American Airman*. Wilmington: Delapeake Publishing, 1985.

Link, Mae Mills, and Hubert A. Coleman. *Medical Support of the Army Air Forces in WW II*. Washington, DC: Office of the Surgeon General, 1955.

Longmate, Norman. *The Bombers: The RAF Offensive Against Germany, 1939–1945*. London: Hutchinson, 1983.

——. *The GI's: The Americans in Britain, 1942–1945*. New York: Scribner, 1975.

——. *How We Lived Then: A History of Everyday Life During the Second World War*. London: Hutchinson, 1971.

MacDonald, Charles B. *The Mighty Endeavor: The American War in Europe*. 1986. Reprint, New York: Da Capo, 1992.

MacIsaac, David. *Strategic Bombing in World War Two: The Story of the United States Strategic Bombing Survey*. New York: Garland, 1976.

MacKay, Ron. *Ridgewell's Flying Fortresses: The 381st Bombardment Group (H) in World War II*. Atglen, PA: Schiffer, 2000.

Madsen, Axel. *William Wyler: The Authorized Biography*. New York: Thomas Y. Crowell, 1973.

Maher, William P. *Fated to Survive: Memoirs of a B-17 Flying Fortress Pilot/Prisoner of War*. Edited by Ed Hall. Spartanburg, SC: Honoribus, 1992.

Man in the Street. *Meet the Americans*. London: Martin Secker & Warburg, 1943.

Martin, James J. *Revisionist Viewpoints: Essays in a Dissident Historical Tradition*. Colorado Springs: Ralph Myles, 1971.

Mason, Francis K. *Battle over Britain: A History of the German Air Assaults on Great*

Britain, 1917–18 and July–December 1940, and the Development of Britain's Air Defence Between World Wars. 1969. Reprint, Oscela, WI: Motorbooks International, 1980.

Maurer, Maurer. *Air Force Combat Units of World War II.* Washington, DC: Office of Air Force History, 1983.

McCarthy, David. *Fear No More: A B-17 Navigator's Journey.* Pittsburgh: Cottage Wordsmiths, 1991.

McCrary, John R. (Tex), and David E. Scherman. *First of the Many: A Journal of Action with the Men of the Eighth Air Force.* New York: Simon & Schuster, 1944.

McFarland, Stephen L. *America's Pursuit of Precision Bombing, 1910–1945.* Washington, DC: Smithsonian Institution Press, 1995.

McFarland, Stephen L., and Wesley Phillips Newton. *To Command the Sky: The Battle for Air Superiority over Germany, 1942–1944.* Washington, DC: Smithsonian Institution Press, 1991.

McKee, Alexander. *Dresden 1945: The Devil's Tinderbox.* New York: Dutton, 1984.

McLaughlin, J. Kemp. *The Mighty Eighth in WW II: A Memoir.* Lexington: University Press of Kentucky, 2000.

McManus, John C. *Deadly Sky: The American Combat Airman in World War II.* Novato, CA: Presidio, 2000.

Meilinger, Phillip S., ed. *The Paths of Heaven: The Evolution of Airpower Theory.* Maxwell Air Force Base, AL: Air University Press, 1997.

Mets, David. *Master of Airpower: General Carl A. Spaatz.* Novato, CA: Presidio, 1988.

Middlebrook, Martin. *The Battle of Hamburg: Allied Bomber Forces Against a German City in 1943.* London: Allan Lane, 1980.

——. *Schweinfurt-Regensburg Mission.* New York: Scribner, 1983.

Middleton, Drew. *The Struggle for Germany.* Indianapolis: Bobbs-Merrill, 1949.

Mierzejewski, Alfred C. *The Collapse of the German War Economy, 1944–1945: Allied Air Power and the German National Railway.* Chapel Hill: University of North Carolina Press, 1988.

Miller, Donald L. *Lewis Mumford, A Life.* New York: Weidenfeld & Nicolson, 1989.

——. *The Story of World War II.* New York: Simon & Schuster, 2001.

Miller, Nathan. *War at Sea: A Naval History of World War II.* New York: Oxford University Press, 1995.

Milward, Alan S. *The German Economy at War.* London: Athlone, 1965.

Mitchell, William. *Memoir of World War I: From Start to Finish of Our Greatest War.* New York: Random House, 1960.

——. *Skyways: A Book on Modern Aeronautics.* Philadelphia: J. B. Lippincott, 1930.

——. *Winged Defense: The Development and Possibilities of Modern Air Power—Economic and Military.* New York: Putnam, 1925.

Moran, Charles M. W. *The Anatomy of Courage.* Boston: Houghton Mifflin, 1967.

Morgan, Robert, with Ron Powers. *The Man Who Flew the Memphis Belle: Memoir of a WW II Bomber Pilot.* New York: Dutton, 2001.

Morison, Samuel Eliot. *Two-Ocean War: A Short History of the United States Navy in the Second World War.* Boston: Little, Brown, 1963.

Mosely, Leonard O. *Backs to the Wall: The Heroic Story of the People of London During WWII.* New York: Random House, 1971.

——. *Report from Germany.* London: Victor Gollancz, 1945.

Muirhead, John. *Those Who Fall.* New York: Random House, 1986.

Murphy, Frank D. *Luck of the Draw: Reflections on the Air War in Europe.* Trumbull, CT: FNP Military Division, 2001.

Murray, Williamson. *The Change in the European Balance of Power, 1938–1939: The Path to Ruin.* Princeton: Princeton University Press, 1984.

——. *Luftwaffe.* Baltimore: Nautical & Aviation Publishing, 1985.

——. *War in the Air, 1914–45.* London: Cassell, 1999.

Myers, Debs, Jonathan Kilbourn, and Richard Harrity, eds. *"Yank," the GI Story of the War.* New York: Duell, Sloan & Pearce, 1947.

Nail, Kenneth N., ed. *Mississippians and the Mighty Eighth.* Tupelo, MS: Eighth Air Force Historical Society, 1999.

Nanney, James S. *Army Air Forces Medical Services in World War II.* Washington, DC: Air Force History and Museums Program, 1998.

Neary, Bob. *Stalag Luft III.* Privately printed, 1946.

Neave, Airey. *Saturday at MI9: A History of Underground Escape Lines in North-West Europe in 1940–5 by a Leading Organiser at MI9.* London: Hodder & Stoughton, 1969.

Neillands, Robin. *The Bomber War: The Allied Air Offensive Against Nazi Germany.* Woodstock: Overlook, 2001.

Nelson, Craig. *The First Heroes: The Extraordinary Story of the Doolittle Raid—America's First World War II Victory.* New York: Penguin, 2003.

Neufeld, Michael J. *The Rocket and the Reich: Peenemünde and the Coming of the Ballistic Missile Era.* Cambridge: Harvard University Press, 1999.

Neufeld, Michael J., and Michael Berenbaum, eds. *The Bombing of Auschwitz: Should the Allies Have Attempted It?* New York: St. Martin's, in association with the United States Holocaust Memorial Museum, 2000.

Newcomb, Alan H. *Vacation with Pay.* Haverhill, MA: Destiny, 1947.

Nichol, John, and Tony Rennell. *The Last Escape: The Untold Story of Allied Prisoners of War in Europe, 1944–45.* New York: Viking, 2003.

——. *Tail End Charlies: The Last Battles of the Bomber War, 1944–1945.* New York: Viking, 2004.

Nilsson, John R. *The Story of the Century.* Beverly Hills: John R. Nilsson, 1946.

Nitze, Paul, Steven L. Rearden, and Ann M. Smith. *From Hiroshima to Glasnost: At the Center of Decision.* New York: Grove Weidenfeld, 1989.

Noakes, Jeremy, ed. *The Civilian in War: The Home Front in Europe, Japan and the USA in World War II.* Exeter, UK: University of Exeter Press, 1992.

Nolan, Bernard Thomas. *Isaiah's Eagles Rising: A Generation of Airmen.* Philadelphia: Xlibris, 2002.

Nossack, Hans Erich. *The End: Hamburg, 1943.* Translated by Joel Agee. Chicago: University of Chicago Press, 2004.

Novey, Jack. *The Cold Blue Sky: A B-17 Gunner in World War Two.* Charlottesville: Howell, 1997.

Nutter, Ralph H. *With the Possum and the Eagle: The Memoir of a Navigator's War over Germany and Japan.* Novato, CA: Presidio, 2002.

Odishaw, Hugh. *Radar Bombing in the Eighth Air Force.* Cambridge: Overseas Office, Radiation Laboratory, Massachusetts Institute of Technology, 1946.

O'Donnell, Joseph P. *The Shoeleather Express.* Privately printed, n.d.

Olsen, Jack. *Aphrodite: Desperate Mission*. New York: Putnam, 1970.

O'Neill, Brian D. *Half a Wing, Three Engines and a Prayer: B-17s over Germany*. New York: McGraw Hill, 1999.

Orwell, Sonia, and Ian Angus, eds. *The Collected Essays, Journalism and Letters of George Orwell: As I Please, 1943–1945*. Vol. 3. New York: Harcourt Brace Jovanovich, 1968.

Osur, Alan M. *Blacks in the Army Air Forces During World War II: The Problem of Race Relations*. Washington, DC: Office of Air Force History, 1977.

Ottis, Sherri Greene. *Silent Heroes: Downed Airmen and the French Underground*. Lexington: University of Kentucky Press, 2001.

Overy, Richard J. *The Air War*. New York: Stein & Day, 1981.

——. *Bomber Command, 1939–1945: Reaping the Whirlwind*. New York: HarperCollins, 1997.

——. *Goering: The "Iron Man."* London: Routledge & Kegan Paul, 1984.

——. *War and Economy in the Third Reich*. Oxford: Clarendon, 1994.

——. *Why the Allies Won*. 1995. Reprint, New York: W. W. Norton, 1997.

Owings, Alison. *Frauen: German Women Recall the Third Reich*. New Brunswick: Rutgers University Press, 1993.

Packard, Jerrold M. *Neither Friend nor Foe: The European Neutrals in World War II*. New York: Macmillan, 1992.

Panter-Downes, Mollie. *London War Notes: 1939–1945*. Edited by William Shawn. New York: Farrar, Straus & Giroux, 1971.

Pape, Robert A. *Bombing to Win: Air Power and Coercion in War*. Ithaca: Cornell University Press, 1999.

Parker, Danny S. *To Win the Winter Sky: The Air War over the Ardennes, 1944–1945*. New York: Da Capo, 1999.

Parker, Richard. *John Kenneth Galbraith, His Life, His Politics, His Economics*. New York: Farrar, Straus & Giroux, 2005.

Parnell, Ben. *Carpetbaggers: America's Secret War in Europe*. Austin: Eakin, 1987.

Parton, James. *"Air Force Spoken Here": General Ira Eaker and the Command of the Air*. Bethesda: Adler & Adler, 1986.

Parton, James, ed. *Impact: The Army Air Forces' Confidential Picture History of World War II*. Vol. 3, *The Eve of Triumph*. Harrisburg: National Historical Society, 1989.

——, ed. *Impact: The Army Air Forces' Confidential Picture History of World War II*. Vol. 6, *Bombing Fortress Europe*. Harrisburg: National Historical Society, 1989.

Peaslee, Budd J. *Heritage of Valor: The Eighth Air Force in World War II*. Philadelphia: J. B. Lippincott, 1964.

Penrose, Antony, ed. *Lee Miller's War*. Boston: Little, Brown, 1992.

Perera, Guido R. *Leaves from My Book of Life*. Boston: Stinehour, 1974.

Perret, Geoffrey. *Winged Victory: The Army Air Forces in World War II*. New York: Random House, 1993.

Pogue, Forrest C. *The Supreme Command*. Washington, DC: Office of the Chief of Military History, Department of the Army, 1954.

Price, Alfred. *The Last Year of the Luftwaffe: May 1944 to May 1945*. Osceola, WI: Motorbooks, 1991.

Prince, Cathryn J. *Shot from the Sky: American POWs in Switzerland*. Annapolis: Naval Institute Press, 2003.

Probert, Henry. *Bomber Harris, His Life and Times: The Biography of Marshal of the Royal Air Force, Sir Arthur Harris, Wartime Chief of Bomber Command*. London: Greenhill, 2001.

Puryear, Edgar F. *American Generalship: Character Is Everything: the Art of Command*. Novato, CA: Presidio, 2000.

Pyle, Ernie. *Brave Men*. New York: Henry Holt, 1944.

Reader's Digest True Stories of Great Escapes. Pleasantville, NY: Reader's Digest, 1977.

Reck-Malleczewen, Friedrich Percyval. *Diary of a Man in Despair*. Translated by Paul Rubens. New York: Macmillan, 1970.

Redding, John M. *Skyways to Berlin: With the American Flyers in England*. New York: Bobbs-Merrill, 1943.

Reynolds, David. *Rich Relations: The American Occupation of Britain, 1942–1945*. 1996. Reprint, London: Phoenix, 2000.

Reynolds, David, Warren K. Kimball, and A. O. Chubarian, eds. *Allies at War: The Soviet, American, and British Experience, 1939–1945*. New York: St. Martin's, 1994.

Rice, Curtis. *Coming In on a Wing and a Prayer: The World War II Life and Experiences of Lewis F. Welles*. Cambridge, MA: Acme Book Binding, 2000.

Richard, Oscar G., III. *Kriegie: An American POW in Germany*. Baton Rouge: Louisiana State University Press, 2000.

Richie, Alexandra. *Faust's Metropolis: A History of Berlin*. New York: Carroll & Graf, 1998.

Robinson, Douglas H. *The Dangerous Sky: A History of Aviation Medicine*. Henley-on-Thames, UK: G. T. Foulis, 1973.

Robinson, John Harold. *A Reason to Live: Moments of Love, Happiness and Sorrow*. Memphis: Castle, 1988.

Rooney, Andy. *My War*. New York: Times Books, 1995.

Roosevelt, Franklin D. *The War Messages of Franklin D. Roosevelt, December 8, 1941, to October 12, 1942*. Washington, DC: U.S. Government Printing Office, 1942.

Rosenman, Samuel I., ed. *The Public Papers and Addresses of Franklin D. Roosevelt*. Vol. 8, *War—and Neutrality*. New York: Random House, 1939.

Rossiter, Margaret. *Women in the Resistance*. New York: Praeger, 1986.

Rostow, W. W. *Pre-Invasion Bombing Strategy: General Eisenhower's Decision of March 25, 1944*. Austin: University of Texas Press, 1981.

Roy, Morris J. *Behind Barbed Wire*. New York: R. R. Smith, 1946.

Rumpf, Hans. *The Bombing of Germany*. Translated by Edward Fitzgerald. New York: Holt, Rinehart & Winston, 1962.

Salisbury, Harrison E. *Heroes of My Time*. New York: Walker, 1993.

——. *A Journey for Our Times: A Memoir*. New York: Carroll & Graf, 1983.

Saward, Dudley. *Bomber Harris: The Story of Marshal of the Royal Air Force, Sir Arthur Harris*. Garden City: Doubleday, 1985.

Schaffer, Ronald. *Wings of Judgment: American Bombing in World War II*. New York: Oxford University Press, 1985.

School, Rick, and Jeff Rogers. *Valor at Polebrook: The Last Flight of Ten Horsepower*. Kimberly, WI: Cross Roads, 2000.

Schwarz, Urs. *The Eye of the Hurricane: Switzerland in World War Two*. Boulder: West-view, 1980.

Sebald, W. G. *On the Natural History of Destruction*. Translated by Anthea Bell. New York: Random House, 2003.

Sevareid, Eric. *Not So Wild a Dream*. New York: Alfred A. Knopf, 1946.

Seydewitz, Max. *Civil Life in Wartime Germany: The Story of the Home Front*. New York: Viking, 1945.

Shaw, Irwin. *The Young Lions*. New York: Random House, 1948.

Sheridan, Jack W. *They Never Had It So Good: A Personal, Unofficial History of the 350th Bombardment Squadron (H) 100th Bombardment Group (H) USAAF, 1942–1945*. San Francisco: Stark-Rath, 1946.

Sherry, Michael. *The Rise of American Air Power: The Creation of Armageddon*. New Haven: Yale University Press, 1987.

Sherwood, Robert E. *Roosevelt and Hopkins, an Intimate History*. New York: Harper, 1950.

Shields, Doyle. *History, 447th Bomb Group*. Privately printed, 1996.

Shirer, William. *End of a Berlin Diary*. New York: Alfred A. Knopf, 1947.

Shukert, Elfrieda Berthiaume, and Barbara Smith Scibetta. *War Brides of World War II*. Novato, CA: Presidio, 1988.

Simmons, Kenneth. *Kriegie*. New York: Thomas Nelson, 1960.

Simpson, Brooks D., and Jean V. Berlin, eds. *Sherman's Civil War: Selected Correspondence of William T. Sherman, 1860–1865*. Chapel Hill: University of North Carolina Press, 1999.

Smith, Ben, Jr. *Chick's Crew: A Tale of the Eighth Air Force*. Privately printed, 1978.

Smith, Dale O. *Screaming Eagle: Memoirs of a B-17 Group Commander*. Chapel Hill: Algonquin, 1990.

Smith, Graham. *When Jim Crow Met John Bull: Black American Soldiers in World War II Britain*. New York: St. Martin's, 1987.

Smith, Starr. *Jimmy Stewart: Bomber Pilot*. St. Paul: Zenith, 2005.

Smith, Truman. *The Wrong Stuff: The Adventures and Misadventures of an 8th Air Force Aviator*. St. Petersburg: Southern Heritage Press, 1996.

Snyder, Louis, ed. *Masterpieces of War Reporting: The Great Moments of World War II*. New York: Julian Messner, 1962.

South, Oron P. *Medical Support in a Combat Air Force: A Study of Medical Leadership in WW II*. Maxwell Air Force Base, AL: Documentary Research Division, Research Studies Institute, Air University, 1956.

Spector, Ronald H. *Eagle Against the Sun: The American War with Japan*. New York: Random House, 1985.

Speer, Albert. *Inside the Third Reich: Memoirs*. 1970. Reprint, New York: Touchstone, 1977.

——. *The Slave State: Heinrich Himmler's Masterplan for SS Supremacy*. London: Weidenfeld & Nicholson, 1981.

Spender, Stephen. *European Witness*. 1946. Reprint, Westport, CT: Greenwood, 1971.

Spiller, Harry, ed. *Prisoners of the Nazis: Accounts of American POWs in World War II*. Jefferson, NC: McFarland, 1998.

Spivey, Delmar T. *POW Odyssey: Recollections of Center Compound, Stalag Luft III and the Secret German Peace Mission in WW II*. Attleboro, MA: Colonial Lithograph, 1984.

Stanford Research Institute. *Impact of Air Attack in World War II: Selected Data for Civil Defense Planning*. Vol. 1. Washington, DC: U.S. Government Printing Office, 1953.

Stapfer, Hans-Heiri, and Gino Künzle. *Strangers in a Strange Land*. Vol. 2, *Escape to Neutrality*. Carrollton, TX: Squadron/Signal, 1992.

Steinbeck, John. *Bombs Away: The Story of a Bomber Team*. New York: Paragon House, 1942.

Steinhoff, Johannes. *Voices from the Third Reich: An Oral History*. New York: Da Capo, 1994.

Stephens, Alan, ed. *The War in the Air, 1914–1994*. Maxwell Air Force Base, AL: Air University Press, 2001.

Stewart, John L. *The Forbidden Diary: A B-24 Navigator Remembers*. New York: McGraw-Hill, 1998.

Stiles, Bert. *Serenade to the Big Bird: A New Edition of the Classic B-17 Tribute*. Atglen, PA: Schiffer, 2001.

——. *Serenade to the World from 30,000: And Other Stories and Essays*. Edited by Roland Bishop Dickinson and Robert Floyd Cooper. Sacramento: Bishop, 1999.

Stouffer, Samuel A., et al. *The American Soldier: Adjustment During Army Life,* vol. 1. Princeton: Princeton University Press, 1949.

Stout, Jay A. *Fortress Ploesti: The Campaign to Destroy Hitler's Oil Supply*. Havertown, PA: Casemate, 2003.

Strong, Russell A. *First over Germany: A History of the 306th Bombardment Group*. Winston-Salem: Hunter, 1982.

Studnitz, Hans-Georg von. *While Berlin Burns: The Diary of Hans-Georg von Studnitz, 1943–1945*. Englewood Cliffs, NJ: Prentice Hall, 1963.

Tanner, Stephen. *Refuge from the Reich: American Airmen and Switzerland During World War II*. Rockville Center, New York: Sarpedon, 2000.

Taylor, Frederick. *Dresden, Tuesday, February 13, 1945*. New York: HarperCollins, 2004.

Tedder, Arthur William. *With Prejudice: The War Memoirs of Marshal of the Royal Air Force, Lord Tedder*. Boston: Little, Brown, 1966.

Terraine, John. *A Time for Courage: The Royal Air Force in the European War, 1939–1945*. New York: Macmillan, 1985.

Thixton, Marshall J., George E. Moffat, and John J. O'Neil. *Bombs Away by Pathfinders of the Eighth Air Force*. Trumbull, CT: FNP Military Division, 1998.

Tibbets, Paul W. *Return of the Enola Gay*. Columbus: Mid Coast Marketing, 1998.

Toliver, Raymond F., with Hanns J. Scharff. *The Interrogator: The Story of Hanns Scharff, Luftwaffe's Master Interrogator*. Fallbrook, CA: Aero, 1978.

Tornabene, Lyn. *Long Live the King: A Biography of Clark Gable*. New York: Putnam, 1976.

Trevor-Roper, H. R. *The Last Days of Hitler*. London: Macmillan, 1950.

Trial of the Major War Criminals Before the International Military Tribunal. Vol. 15. Nuremberg, Germany, 1948.

Trials of War Criminals Before the Nuremberg Military Tribunals. Washington, DC: U.S. Government Printing Office, 1949–1953.

Underwood, Jeffery S. *The Wings of Democracy: The Influence of Air Power on the Roosevelt Administration, 1933–1941.* College Station: Texas A&M University Press, 1991.

United States. *A Short Guide to Great Britain.* Washington, DC: War and Navy Departments, 1942.

United States Army Air Forces. *The Official Guide to the Army Air Forces: A Directory, Almanac and Chronicle of Achievement.* New York: Simon & Schuster, 1944.

——. *Target: Germany: The Army Air Forces' Official Story of the VIII Bomber Command's First Year over Europe.* New York: Simon & Schuster, 1943.

United States Office of the Adjutant General. *Army Battle Casualties and Nonbattle Deaths in World War II, Final Report, 7 December 1941–31 December 1946.* Washington, DC: Department of the Army, 1953.

United States War Department, Office of Statistical Control. *Army Air Forces Statistical Digest, World War II.* Washington, DC: U.S. Government Printing Office, 1945.

Van der Zee, Henri A. *The Hunger Winter: Occupied Holland, 1944–5.* London: Jill Norman & Hobhouse, 1982.

Verrier, Anthony. *The Bomber Offensive.* New York: MacMillan, 1969.

Vietor, John. *Time Out: American Airmen at Stalag Luft I.* New York: Richard R. Smith, 1951.

Vonnegut, Kurt. *Slaughterhouse-Five or The Children's Crusade.* 1969. Reprint, New York: Dell, 1999.

Wagner, Ray. *Mustang Designer: Edgar Schmued and the P-51.* Washington, DC: Smithsonian Institution Press, 1990.

Wahle, Anne, and Roul Tunley. *Ordeal by Fire: An American Woman's Terror-Filled Trek Through War-Torn Germany.* New York: Dell, 1965.

Walzer, Michael. *Just and Unjust Wars.* New York: Basic, 1977.

Way, Chris. *Glenn Miller in Britain: Then and Now.* London: Battle of Britain Prints, 1996.

Way, Frank, and Robert Sternfels. *Burning Hitler's Black Gold!* Privately printed, 2000.

Webster, Charles, and Noble Frankland. *The Strategic Air Offensive Against Germany, 1939–1945.* Vol. 3, *Victory.* London: Her Majesty's Stationery Office, 1961.

——. *The Strategic Air Offensive Against Germany, 1939–1945.* Vol. 4, *Annexes and Appendices.* London: Her Majesty's Stationery Office, 1961.

Weigley, Russell F. *The American Way of War: A History of United States Military Strategy and Policy.* New York: Macmillan, 1973.

——. *Eisenhower's Lieutenants: The Campaign of France and Germany, 1944–1945.* Bloomington: Indiana University Press, 1981.

Weinberg, Gerhard. *The World at Arms: A Global History of WWII.* Cambridge: Cambridge University Press, 1995.

Weir, Adrian. *The Last Flight of the Luftwaffe: The Fate of Schulungslehrgang Elbe, 7 April 1945.* London: Arms and Armour, 1997.

Wells, Mark K. *Courage and Air Warfare: The Allied Crew Experience in the Second World War.* Portland, Or.: Frank Cass, 1995.

——, ed. *Air Power: Promise and Reality.* Chicago: Imprint, 2000.

Wendel, Else. *Hausfrau at War: A German Woman's Account of Life in Hitler's Reich.* London: Odhams, 1957.

Werrell, Kenneth P. *Eighth Air Force Bibliography*. Manhattan, KS: MA/AH Publishers. 1981.

——. *The Evolution of the Cruise Missile*. Maxwell Air Force Base, AL: Air University Press, 1985.

——. *"Who Fears?" The 301st in War and Peace, 1942–1979*. Dallas: Taylor, 1991.

Westermann, Edward B. *Flak: German Anti-aircraft Defenses, 1914–1945*. Lawrence: University Press of Kansas, 2001.

Westheimer, David. *Sitting It Out: A World War II POW Memoir*. Houston: Rice University Press, 1992.

Wheeler, William H. *Shootdown: A World War II Bomber Pilot's Experience as a Prisoner of War in Germany*. Shippensburg, PA: Burd Street Press, 2002.

Wiesel, Elie. *Night*. Translated by Stella Rodway. New York: Hill & Wang, 1969.

Wilmont, Chester. *The Struggle for Europe*. New York: Harper, 1952.

Wolff-Mönckeberg, Mathilde. *On the Other Side: To My Children: From Germany, 1940–1945*. London: Mayflower, 1979.

Woodward, Ellis M. *Flying School: Combat Hell*. Baltimore: American Literary Press, 1998.

Wright, David G. *Notes on Men and Groups Under Stress of Combat: For the Use of Flight Surgeons in Operational Units*. New York: Josiah Macy, Jr., Foundation, 1945.

Wright, David, ed. *Observations on Combat Flying Personnel*. New York: Josiah Macy, Jr., Foundation, 1945.

Wylie, Philip. *Generation of Vipers*. New York: Holt, Rinehart & Winston, 1942.

Wyman, David S. *The Abandonment of the Jews: America and the Holocaust, 1941–1945*. New York: Pantheon, 1984.

Yeager, Chuck, and Leo Janos. *Yeager: An Autobiography*. New York: Bantam, 1985.

Yergin, Daniel. *The Prize: The Epic Quest for Oil, Money and Power*. New York: Simon & Schuster, 1991.

Zemke, Hubert, and Roger A. Freeman. *Zemke's Stalag: The Final Days of World War II*. Washington, DC: Smithsonian Institution Press, 1991.

——. *Zemke's Wolf Pack: The Story of Hub Zemke and the 56th Fighter Group in the Skies over Europe*. New York: Orion, 1989.

Ziegler, Philip. *London at War: 1939–45*. New York: Alfred A. Knopf, 1995.

Ziemke, Earl F. *The U.S. Army in the Occupation of Germany, 1944–1946*. Washington, DC: Center of Military History, United States Army, 1975.

Zuckerman, Solly. *From Apes to Warlords*. New York: Harper & Row, 1978.

Articles

Space considerations prevented the inclusion of most of the articles cited in the Notes that were published in mass circulation magazines and newspapers of the 1940s such as the *New York Times, Time, Life, Newsweek, Yank,* and *Stars and Stripes*. These articles are cited in full in the Notes.

"Aerial Gunnery." *Flying,* October 1943.

Agoratus, Steven. "Clark Gable in the Eighth Air Force." *Air Power History* 46, no. 1 (Spring 1999).

Amory, Cleveland. "The Man Everyone in Hollywood Liked," *Parade,* October 21, 1964.

Andrews, William F. "The Luftwaffe and the Battle for Air Superiority: Blueprint or Warning?" *Air Power Journal* 9 (Fall 1995).

Angell, Joseph Warner. "Guided Missiles Could Have Won." *Atlantic Monthly* 189 (January 1952).

Appel, John W., and G. W. Beebe. "Preventive Psychiatry." *Journal of the American Medical Association* 131 (1946).

Armstrong, W. R. "The Lifeline Called Comet." *Reader's Digest* 114 (June 1, 1979).

Ayers, Francis H., Jr., and Brent L. Gravatt. "The Fireman: Twelve O'Clock High Revisited." *Aerospace Historian* 35 (September 1988).

Bachrach, William H. "Combat Veterans Evaluate the Flight Surgeon." *Air Surgeon's Bulletin* 2 (September 1945).

Baldwin, Hanson W. "Air Warfare Review." *Skyways,* May 1944.

———. "Air Warfare Review." *Skyways,* December 1944.

———. "War in the Air: Strategic Air Bombardment of Germany–A Major Factor in Plan for All-Out Axis Defeat." *Skyways,* February 1944.

Barnes, Wyatt E. "Experience of War: My First Day in Combat." *Military History Quarterly* 11, no. 3 (Spring 1999).

Bayles, William D. "The Story Behind the Nazi Defeat: The Strategic Bombing Attack on Hitler's Oil Supply." *American Mercury* 6 (January 1946).

Beaman, John R., Jr. "The Unknown Ace." *American Aviation Historical Society,* Winter 1969.

Beaumont, Roger. "The Bomber Offensive as a Second Front." *Journal of Contemporary History* 22, no. 1 (January 1987).

Beck, Earl. "The Allied Bombing of Germany, 1942–1945, and the German Response: Dilemmas of Judgment." *German Studies Review* 5, no. 3 (October 1982).

Bednarek, Janet R. "Not Soldiers–Airmen: The Development of the USAF Enlisted Force." *Air Power History,* Summer 1992.

Beevor, Antony. "Stalingrad." *MHQ* 11, no. 1 (Fall 1998).

Bendiner, Elmer S. "The End of a Flying Fort: An Airman's Letter to His Wife." *Nation* 57 (December 11, 1943).

Biddle, Tami Davis. "British and American Approaches to Strategic Bombing: Their Origins and Implementation in the World War II Combined Bomber Offensive." *Journal of Strategic Studies* 18 (March 1995).

Bishop, John. "Swedish Stopover: Interned American Fliers." *Collier's,* August 26, 1944.

Bloomfield, Stephen. "The Return of the Mighty Eighth." *Air and Space Smithsonian* 7, no. 5 (December 1992–January 1993).

Blue, Allan G. "Fortress vs. Liberator." *American Aviation Historical Society Journal* 8 (Summer 1963).

"Bombardier: The Story of the 447th Bombardier Group." *Politics,* June 1944.

Bonney, Walter T. "Chiefs of the Army Air Forces, 1907–1957." *Air Power Historian* 7, no. 3 (July 1960).

Bright, Charles D. "Navigating in the Big League." *Aerospace Historian* 35 (December 1988).

Brodie, Bernard. "The Heritage of Douhet." *Air University Quarterly Review* 6 (1953).

Buckley, John. "Air Power and the Battle of the Atlantic, 1939–45." *Journal of Contemporary History* 28 (January 1993).

Callander, Bruce D. "Enlisted Pilots." *Air Force Magazine* 72 (June 1989).

——. "They Wanted Wings." *Air Force Magazine* 74 (January 1991).

Cameron, William R. "Ploesti." *Air Force Magazine* 54 (August 1971).

Caplan, Jane, and Carola Sachse. "Industrial Housewives: Women's Social Work in the Factories of Nazi Germany." Translated by Heide Kiesling and Dorothy Rosenberg. *Women and History* 2, nos. 11–12 (1987).

Carigan, William. "The B-24 Liberator—A Man's Airplane." *Aerospace Historian* 35 (Spring 1988).

Carlson, L. D. "Demand Oxygen System." *Air Surgeon's Bulletin* 1 (January 1944).

Carter, William R. "Air Battle in the Battle of the Bulge." *Air Power Journal* 3 (Winter 1989).

Christensen, Harold O. "The Last Flight." *American Aviation Historical Society* 30, no. 2 (1985).

Courtney, W. B. "Air Power, Today and Tomorrow." *Collier's,* September 8, 1945–September 15, 1945.

Crandell, Bernard W. "Angels Don't Shoot Guns." *Air Force,* June 1943.

Crane, Conrad C. "Evolution of US Strategic Bombing of Urban Areas." *Historian* 50, no. 1 (November 1987).

Creveld, Martin Van. "The Rise and Fall of Air Power." *MHQ* 8, no. 3 (Spring 1996).

Crossman, R. H. S. "Apocalypse at Dresden." *Esquire,* November 1963.

Davidson, Eugene. "Albert Speer and the Nazi War Plants." *Modern Age* 10 (1966).

Davis, Mike. "Berlin's Skeleton in Utah's Closet." *Designer/Builder* 11, no. 5 (January–February 2005).

Davis, Richard G. "General Carl Spaatz and D-Day." *Air Power Journal,* Winter 1997.

——. "German Rail Yards and Cities: U.S. Bombing Policy, 1944–1945." *Air Power History* 42, no. 2 (Summer 1995).

——. "Operation 'Thunderclap': The US Army Air Forces and the Bombing of Berlin." *Journal of Strategic Studies* 14 (March 1991).

"Death from the Stratosphere." *Popular Mechanics,* February 1945.

Denny-Brown, D. "Effects of Modern Warfare on Civil Population." *Journal of Laboratory and Clinical Medicine* 28 (1943).

DeNormann, J. R. C. "The Use of the Strategic Bomber Forces over Normandy." *British Army Review* 96 (December 1990).

Donnini, Frank P. "Douhet, Caproni, and Early Air Power." *Air Power History* 37, no. 4 (Summer 1990).

Dorr, Robert F. "B-24 Liberator: The Mostest." *Air Power History* 37 no. 4 (Summer 1990).

——. "Republic P-47 Thunderbolt." *Air Power History* 37, no. 3 (Fall 1990).

Drake, Francis V. "Victory Is in the Air." *Atlantic Monthly* 169 (March 1942).

Dyson, Freeman. "The Bitter End." *New York Review of Books,* April 28, 2005.

Eaker, Ira C. "The Flying Fortress and the Liberator." *Aerospace Historian* 26, no. 2 (1979).

——. "Hap Arnold: The Anatomy of Leadership." *Air Force Magazine* 60 (September 1977).

——. "Memories of Six Air Chiefs: Westover, Arnold, Spaatz: Part II." *Aerospace Historian* 20 (December 1973).

——. "Some Memories of Winston Churchill." *Aerospace Historian* 19 (September 1972).

Eaker, Ira C. and Arthur G. B. Metcalf. "Conversation with Albert Speer." *Air Force Magazine* 60, no. 4 (April 1977).

Ethell, Jeffrey L. "Nose Art." *MHQ* 8, no. 3 (Spring 1996).

Ethell, Jeffrey L., and Alfred Price. "Raid 250: Target Berlin." *Air Force Magazine* 63 (January 1980).

Farmer, James. "The Making of 12 O'Clock High." *American Aviation Historical Society Journal* 19 (Winter 1974).

Fay, Royal D. "Poets Laureate of Stalag I." *Aerospace Historian* 16 (December 1969).

"Flying Typewriters." *Newsweek,* (February 22, 1943).

Ford, Corey. "Tail-End Charlie." *Collier's,* December 25, 1943.

Ford, John C. "The Morality of Obliteration Bombing." *Theological Studies* 5 (1944).

Ford, Gervais W., and James J. Scanlon, "Double Duty Pilots in the 8th." *Air Power History* 42, no. 2 (1995).

Foregger, Richard. "The Bombing of Auschwitz." *Aerospace Historian* 34 (Summer 1987).

Frankland, Noble. "Some Reflections on the Strategic Air Offensive, 1939–1945." *Royal United Service Institution* 107 (May 1962).

Fraser, R., I. M. Leslie, and D. Phelps. "Psychiatric Effects of Severe Personal Experiences During Bombing." *Proceedings of the Royal Society of Medicine* 36 (1943).

Frey, Roagald. "The Master Interrogator." *8th Air Force News* 5, no. 2 (May 1979).

Friedheim, Eric. "Welcome to Dulag Luft." *Air Force* 28 (September 1945).

Frisbee, John L. "The Quiet Hero." *Air Force Magazine,* March 1988.

Fritz, Martin. "Swedish Ball-Bearings and the German War Economy." *Scandinavian Economic Review* 23, no. 1 (1975).

Futrell, Frank. "Air Power Lessons of World War 2." *Air Force and Space Digest* 48 (September 1965).

Gabay, John. "Diary of a Tailgunner." *MHQ* 8, no. 3 (1996).

Galbraith, John K. "Germany Was Badly Run." *Fortune* 32, no. 6 (December 1945).

——. "The Origin of the Document." *Atlantic Monthly* 244 (July 1979).

——. "The Speer Interrogation." *Atlantic Monthly* 244 (July 1979).

Galbraith, John K., and George W. Ball. "The Interrogation of Albert Speer." *Life,* December 17, 1945.

Gallagher, Charles. "Miller Magic." *8th Air Force News* 1, no. 3 (June 1975).

Galland, Adolf. "Defeat of the Luftwaffe: Fundamental Cause." *Air University Quarterly Review* 6 (Spring 1953).

Garner, H. H. "Psychiatric Casualties in Combat." *War Medicine* 8 (1945).

"General Mitchell's Daring Speech." *Aviation* 29 (October 29, 1924).

Gentile, Gian P. "General Arnold and the Historians." *Journal of Military History* 64, no. 1 (January 2000).

Gertsch, Darrell W. "The Strategic Air Offensive and the Mutation of American Values." *Rocky Mountain Social Science Journal* 11 (October 1974).

Gill, Brendan. "Young Man Behind Plexiglas." *New Yorker,* August 12, 1944.

Gittler, Lewis F. "Everyday Life in Germany Today." *American Mercury* 61 (October 1945).

Glaser, Daniel. "The Sentiments of American Soldiers Abroad Towards Europeans." *American Journal of Sociology* 51, no. 5 (March 1946).

Glass, Albert. "Combat Exhaustion." *United States Armed Forces Medical Journal* 2, no. 10 (1951).

Goodman, George W. "The Englishman Meets the Negro." *Common Ground* 5, no. 1 (Autumn 1944).

Gorn, Michael, and Charles J. Gross. "Published Air Force History: Still on the Runway." *Aerospace Historian* 31, no. 1 (July 1984).

Graham, Vickie. "Brother Bombardiers: Putting a Pickle in a Barrel." *Air Man* 31 (September 1987).

Grant, David. "The General Mission of Military Aviation Medicine." *Military Surgeon* (March 1942).

——. "Work of the Flight Surgeon." *Military Surgeon* (March 1944).

Green, D. M. "Aeroneuroses in a Bomb Training Unit." *Journal of Aviation Medicine* 14 (December 1943).

Gregor, Neil. "A *Schicksalsgemeinschaft*? Allied Bombing, Civilian Morale, and Social Dissolution in Nuremberg, 1942–1945." *Historical Journal* 43, no. 4 (2000).

Grob, Gerald N. "World War II and American Psychiatry." *Psychohistory Review* 19 (Fall 1990).

Groban, Milt. "To the Editor." *Commentary* 7 (July 1978).

Groh, John E. "Lively Experiment: A Summary History of the Air Force Chaplaincy." *Military Chaplains Review* 16 (Winter 1990).

Grow, Malcolm C., and Robert C. Lyons. "Body Armor, a Brief Study of Its Development." *Air Surgeon's Bulletin* 2, no. 1 (January 1945).

Gunzinger, Mark A. "Air Power as a Second Front." *Airpower Journal* 9 (Winter 1995).

Hall, E. T., Jr. "Race Prejudice and Negro-White Relations in the Army." *American Journal of Sociology* 52, no. 5 (March 1947).

Hallenbeck, G. A., et al. "Magnitude and Duration of Opening Parachute Shock." *Air Surgeon's Bulletin* 2, no. 3 (February 1945).

Hansell, Haywood S. "Strategic Air Warfare." *Aerospace Historian* 13, no. 4 (Winter 1966).

Hanson, Frederick R. "Combat Psychiatry: Experiences in the North Atlantic and Mediterranean Theaters of Operations, American Ground Forces, WWII." *Bulletin of the US Army Medical Department* 9 (1949).

Hanson, Victor Davis. "Not Strategic, Not Tactics." *MHQ* 1, no. 2 (1989).

——. "The Right Man." *MHQ* 8, no. 3 (Spring 1996).

Hastings, Max. "The Lonely Passion of Bomber Harris." *MHQ* 6, no. 2 (Winter 1994).

Heineman, Elizabeth. "The Hour of the Woman: Memories of Germany's 'Crisis Years' and West German National Identity." *American Historical Review* 101, no. 2 (April 1996).

Herf, Jeffrey. "The Nazi Extermination Camps and the Ally to the East: Could the Red Army and Air Force Have Stopped or Slowed the Final Solution?" *Kritika: Explorations in Russian and Eurasian History* 4 (Fall 2003).

Hess, William N., and Kenneth C. Rust. "The German Jets and the US Army Air Force." *American Aviation Historical Society Journal* 8 (Fall 1963).

Hodges, Robert H. "Auschwitz Revisited: Could the Soviets Have Bombed the Camp?" *Air Power History* (Winter 1997).

Holley, I. B. "Jr. Makers of the US Air Force." *Journal of Military History* 54, no. 1 (January 1990).

Hopkins, George E. "Bombing and the American Conscience During World War II." *Historian* 28, no. 3 (May 1966).

Jensen, Walters. "Today and Tomorrow in Aviation Medicine." *Military Surgeon* (February 1944).

Johnson, Leon W. "Why Ploesti?" *Air Force Magazine* 54 (August 1971).

Jones, David R., Jr., "Aeromedical Transportation of Psychiatric Patients: Historical Review and Present Management." *Aviation, Space, and Environmental Medicine* 51 (July 1980).

——. "The Macy Reports: Combat Fatigue in World War II Fliers." *Aviation Space and Environmental Medicine* 58 (August 1987).

Jones, F. D., and A. W. Johnson. "Medical and Psychiatric Treatment Policy and Practice in Vietnam." *Journal of Social Issues* 31, no. 4 (1975).

Julian, Thomas A. "The Role of the United States Army Air Forces in the Warsaw Uprising August–September 1944." *Air Power History* 42 (Summer 1995).

Karant, Max. "As I Saw It." *Flying* 36 (September 1945).

Keegan, John. "Britain and America." *Times Literary Supplement,* May 17, 1985.

——. "We Wanted Beady-Eyed Guys Just Absolutely Holding the Course." *Smithsonian Magazine* 14, no. 5 (1993).

Kelsey, Mavis P. "Flying Fatigue in Pilots Flying Long Range Single-Seater Fighter Missions." *Air Surgeon's Bulletin* 1, no. 6 (June 1944).

Kirwin, Gerald. "Allied Bombing and Nazi Domestic Propaganda." *European History Quarterly* 15 (1985).

Knauth, Barbara, Christina, and Sybilla. "The Chimneys of Leipzig." *Life,* May 15, 1944.

Koch, H. W. "The Strategic Air Offensive Against Germany: The Early Phase, May–September 1940." *Historical Journal* 34, no. 1 (March 1991).

Krammer, Arnold. "Fueling the Third Reich." *Technology and Culture* 19 (July 1978).

Kranskopf, Robert W. "The Army and the Strategic Bomber 1930–1939." *Military Affairs* 22, no. 4 (Winter 1958–1959).

Kuter, Laurence S. "The General vs. the Establishment: General H. H. Arnold and the Air Staff." *Aerospace Historian* 21 (December 1974).

——. "How Hap Arnold Built the AFF." *Air Force Magazine,* September 1973.

Laidlaw, William R. "Yankee Doodle Flies to War." *Air Power History,* Winter 1989.

Lay, Beirne, Jr. "I Saw Regensburg Destroyed." *Saturday Evening Post,* November 6, 1943.

LeMay, Curtis E. "Strategic Air Power: Destroying the Enemy's War Resources. 2. The Command Realities." *Aerospace Historian,* Spring 1980.

"Leviathan of the Air: The Boeing Flying Fortress." *Illustrated London News* 16 (August 1941).

"The Liberation of Moosburg." *Splasher Six* 33 (Summer 2002).

Liebling, A. J. "The Dixie Demo Jr." *New Yorker* (November 7, 1942).

Lindley, William. "Aircrew Over Kiel." *Air Power History,* Summer 1989.

Little, K. L. "A Note of Colour Prejudice Amongst the English Middle Class." *Man* 43 (September–October 1943).

Lunden, Walter A. "Captivity Psychosis Among Prisoners of War." *Journal of Criminal Law and Criminology* 39 (April 1949).

Lynch, Adam. "Kassel: Mission Disaster." *Military Heritage* 1, no. 4 (February 2000).

MacIsaac, David. "Reflections on Airpower in World War II." *Air Force Magazine,* September 1980.

——. "What the Bombing Survey Really Says." *Air Force Magazine,* June 1973.

MacKenzie, S. P. "The Treatment of Prisoners of War in World War II." *Journal of Modern History* 66 (September 1944).

Manzo, Louis A. "Morality in War Fighting and Strategic Bombing in World War II." *Air Power History* 39 (Fall 1992).

McFarland, Stephen L. "The Evolution of the American Strategic Fighter in Europe, 1942–44." *Journal of Strategic Studies,* 10 June 1987.

McGuire, Phillip. "Judge Hastie, World War II, and Army Racism." *Journal of Negro History* 62, no. 4 (October 1977).

Meiling, R. L. "The United States Air Force Medical Service: Tumultuous Years of Heritage and History." *Aviation Space Environmental Medicine* 55, no. 7. (July 1984).

Meilinger, Phillip S. "The Historiography of Air Power: Theory and Doctrine." *Journal of Military History* 64, no. 2 (2000).

Michie, Allan A. "Germany Was Bombed to Defeat." *Reader's Digest,* August 1945.

——. "Scarlet Pimpernels of the Air." *Reader's Digest,* November 1945.

Mierzejewski, Alfred C. "When Did Albert Speer Give Up?" *Historical Journal* 31, no. 2 (June 1988).

Mierzejewski, Alfred C., Ronald Schaffer, and Kenneth P. Werrell. "American Military Ethics in World War II: An Exchange." *Journal of American History* 68, no. 1 (1981).

Miller, Martin J. "The Armored Airmen: World War II U.S. Army Air Force Body Armor Program." *Aerospace Historian* 32 (March 1985).

Milton, T. R. "A Participant Remembers." *Air Force Magazine,* January 1980.

Milward, A. S. "The End of Blitzkrieg." *Economic History Review* 16, no. 3 (1964).

Moody, Walton S. "Big Week: Gaining Air Superiority over the Luftwaffe." *Air Power History* 41, no. 2 (Summer 1994).

Mulligan, Timothy P. "German U-Boat Crews in World War II: Sociology of an Elite." *Journal of Military History* 56, no. 2 (April 1992).

Mumford, Lewis. "The Morals of Extermination." *Atlantic Monthly,* October 1959.

Murphy, Charles J. V. "The Airmen and the Invasion." *Life,* April 10, 1944.

——. "The Unknown Battle." *Life,* October 16, 1944.

Murray, Williamson. "Attrition and the Luftwaffe." *Air University Review* 24 (March–April 1983).

——. "Did Strategic Bombing Work?" *MHQ* 8, no. 3 (Spring 1996).

——. "Overlord." *MHQ* 6, no. 3 (Spring 1994).

——. "Reflections on the Combined Bomber Offensive." *Militargeschichtliche Mitteilungen* 51 (1992).

——. "Why Air Forces Do Not Understand Strategy." *MHQ* 1, no. 3 (Spring 1989).

Newdeck, Ann. "Coombe House was a Flak Farm." *8th Air Force News* 4, no. 1 (February 1978).

Nisos, Michael J. "The Bombardier and His Bombsight." *Air Force Magazine,* September 1981.

"Now Terror, Truly." *Newsweek,* February 26, 1945.

Nufer, Harold F. "Operation Chowhound: A Precedent for Post-World War II Humanistic Airlift." *Aerospace Historian* 32, no. 1 (1985).

O'Connell, Robert L. "Arms and Men: The Gotha and the Origins of Strategic Bombing." *MHQ* 3, no. 1 (Fall 1990).

——. "Arms and Men: The Norden Bombsight." *MHQ* 2, no. 4 (Summer 1990).

O'Connor, Jerome M. "In the Lair of the Wolf Pack." *World War II,* July 2002.

Olmsted, Merle. "Down in the Drink." *Journal of the American Aviation Historical Society,* Fall 1998.

Olson, Sidney. "Underground Cologne." *Life,* March 19, 1945.

Overy, R. J. "Air Power and the Origins of Deterrence Theory Before 1939." *Journal of Strategic Studies* 15 no. 1 (March 1992).

——. "From 'Uralbomber' to 'Amerikabomber': The Luftwaffe and Strategic Bombing." *Journal of Strategic Studies* 1, no. 2 (September 1978).

——. "Germany," "Domestic Crisis," and "War in 1939: Reply." *Past and Present* 122 (February 1989).

——. "Hitler and Air Strategy." *Journal of Contemporary History* 15, no. 3 (July 1980).

——. "Hitler's War and the German Economy: A Reinterpretation." *Economic History Review* 35, no. 2 (1982).

——. "The Luftwaffe and the European Economy, 1939–1945." *Militargeschichtliche Mitteilungen* 26, no. 2 (1979).

——. "Mobilization for Total War in Germany." *English Historical Review* 103 (July 1988).

Parker, Steven A. "Targeting for Victory: The Rationale Behind Strategic Bombing Objectives in America's First Air War Plan." *Air Power Journal* 3 (Summer 1989).

Parks, W. Hayes. " 'Precision' and 'Area' Bombing: Who Did Which and When?" *Journal of Strategic Studies* 18, no. 1 (March 1995).

Parton, James. "General Ira Eaker, Creator of Eighth Air Force." *Air Force History* 39, no. 3 (1992).

——. "Lt. Gen. Ira C. Eaker–An Aide's Memoir." *Aerospace Historian* 34, no. 4 (1987).

Peaslee, Bud. "Blood in the Sky." *Aerospace Historian* 16, no. 2 (Summer 1969).

Petropoulos, Jonathan. "Co-Opting Nazi Germany: Neutrality in Europe During World War II." *Dimensions: A Journal of Holocaust Studies* 7, no. 1 (1997).

Postel, Claude. "The Air Attacks on Communications." *Military Review* 30, no. 10 (January 1951).

Prados, John. "The Prophet of Bomber War." *MHQ* 8, no. 3 (Spring 1996).

Quester, George. "Bargaining and Bombing During World War II in Europe." *World Politics* 15, no. 3 (April 1963).

Reese, Joscelyne. "Precision Bombing—Fact or Fiction." *Military Technology* 2 (April 1987).

Reinartz, Eugen G. "The School of Aviation Medicine—and the War." *Military Surgeon* 3 (March 1943).

Rentmeester, Lester F. "Big Brothers and Little Friends: A Memoir of the Air War Against Germany." *Wisconsin Magazine of History* 77 (Fall 1990).

"A Revolting Necessity." *Nation* 158 (March 1944).

Rice, Rondall. "Bombing Auschwitz: US 15th Air Force and the Military Aspects of a Possible Attack." *War in History* 6, no. 2 (1999).

Robbins, Michael. "The Third Reich and Its Railways." *Journal of Transport History* 5, no. 2 (September 1979).

Rose, Elihu. "The Court-Martial of Billy Mitchell." *MHQ* 8, no. 3 (Spring 1996).

Rust, Kenn C., and William N. Hess. "The German Jets and the U.S. Army Air Force." *American Aviation Historical Society Journal* 8 (Fall 1963).

Sachse, Carola. "Industrial Housewives: Women's Social Work in the Factories of Nazi Germany." Translated by Heide Kiesling and Dorothy Rosenberg. *Women & History* 11–12 (1987).

Saltsman, Ralph H., Jr. "Air Battle at Kiel." *Air Power History,* Summer 1989.

Schaffer, Ronald. "American Military Ethics in World War II: The Bombing of German Civilians." *Journal of American History* 67, no. 2 (1980).

Schaltz, Robert E. "The Impact of Allied Air Interdiction on German Strategy in Normandy." *Aerospace Historian* 17 (December 1970).

Scharff, Hanns Joachim. "Without Torture." *Argosy,* May 1950.

Schideberg, Melitta. "Some Observations on Individual Reactions to Air Raids." *International Journal of Psychoanalysis* 23 (1942).

Sears, Betty M. "Ira C. Eaker: The Military Career of Oklahoma's Greatest Aviator." *Red River Valley Historical Review* 3, no. 3 (1978).

Segre, Claudio G. "Giulio Douhet: Strategist, Theorist, Prophet?" *Journal of Strategic Studies* 15 (September 1992).

Shaw, Jon A. "Comments on the Individual Psychology of Combat Exhaustion." *Military Medicine* 148 (March 1983).

Sheeley, William F. "Frostbite in the 8th Air Force." *Air Surgeon's Bulletin* 2, no. 1 (January 1945).

Sherry, Michael S. "The Slide to Total War." *New Republic* 137 (December 16, 1981).

——. "War and Weapons: The New Cultural History." *Diplomatic History* 14 (1990).

Showalter, Dennis E. "The Birth of Blitzkrieg." *MHQ* 7, no. 1 (Fall 1994).

——. "The First Jet War." *MHQ* 8, no. 3 (Spring 1996).

Sitkoff, Harvard. "Racial Militance and Interracial Violence in the Second World War." *Journal of American History* 58, no. 3 (December 1971).

Skinner, Robert E. "The Making of the Air Surgeon: The Early Life and Career of David N. W. Grant." *Aviation Space and Environmental Medicine* (January 1983).

Smith, Dale O. "Was the Bombing of Germany Worth the Cost? Yes!" *American History Illustrated* 5 (April 1970).

Smith, Malcolm. "The Air War and Military History." *International History Review* 4 no. 3 (August 1982).

——. "The Allied Air Offensive." *Journal of Strategic Studies* 13, no. 1 (March 1990).

——. "Harris' Offensive in Historical Perspective." *Royal United Service Institute* 130, no. 2 (June 1985).

Smith, Melden E., Jr. "The Strategic Bombing Debate: The Second World War and Vietnam." *Journal of Contemporary History* 12, no. 1 (January 1977).

Smith, Myron J. "Novels of the Air War, 1939–1945: An Annotated List." *Aerospace Historian* 223 (Fall 1975).

Spaatz, Carl A. "Bombing Civilians." *Spectator* 170 (April 2, 1943).

——. "Strategic Air Power: Fulfillment of a Concept." *Foreign Affairs* 25 (April 1946).

Spivey, Delmar T. "Secret Mission to Berlin." *Air Force Magazine* 58 (September 1975).

Stokes, Raymond G. "The Oil Industry in Nazi Germany, 1936–1945" *Business History Review* 59 (Summer 1985).

Stone, I. F. "Nixon's Blitzkrieg." *New York Review of Books,* January 25, 1973.

Suchenwirth, Richard. "Hitler's Last Opportunity." *Aerospace Historian* 8, no. 1 (Spring 1966).

Sullivan, John T. "The Botched Air Support of Operation Cobra." *Parameters: Journal of the US Army War College* 18, no. 1 (March 1988).

Swan, Jon. "Apocalypse at Munster." *MHQ* 2, no. 3 (Spring 1990).

Swank, Roy L., and Walter E. Marchand. "Combat Neuroses: Development of Combat Exhaustion." *Archives of Neurology and Psychiatry* 55 (March 1946).

Taylor, Joe Gray. "They Taught Tactics!" *Aerospace Historian* 13 (Summer 1966).

Thouless, Robert H. "Psychological Effects of Air Raids." *Nature* 148, no. 3746 (August 1941).

Torrey, Volta. "The Nine Lives of Leuna." *Popular Science Monthly,* November 1945.

United States Army Air Forces, Assistant Chief of Air Staff. "What Happens When Bomber Crew Is Forced Down at Sea." *Impact* 1 (July 1943).

"24 Hours of a Bomber Pilot." *Harper's Magazine,* August 1944.

Vance, J. M. "The Politics of Camp Life: Bargaining Process in Two German Prison Camps." *War and Society* 10 (1992).

Vanden Heuvel, William J., and Rafael Medoff. "Should the Allies Have Bombed Auschwitz?" http://hnn.us/articles/4268.html.

Vernon, P. E. "Psychological Effects of Air Raids." *Journal of Abnormal and Social Psychology* 36 (1941).

Vonnegut, Kurt, Jr. "Memoirs." *Traces of Indiana and Midwestern History: A Publication of the Indiana Historical Society* 3, no. 4 (Fall 1991).

Watling, Geoffrey. "Mission to Gotha: The 445th Bomb Group, 24 February 1944, Part 1." *American Aviation Historical Society* 18, no. 2 (1973).

——. "Mission to Gotha: The 445th Bomb Group, 24 February 1944, Part 2." *American Aviation Historical Society* 19, no. 2 (1974).

Weers, Mozes W. A. "Why the Allies Won the Air War." *Air University Review,* January–February 1982.

Well, Mark K. "Human Element and Air Combat." *Airpower Journal* 2 (Spring 1988).

Werrell, Kenneth P. "A Case for a New History." *Air Power History* 39 (Spring 1992).

——. "Friendly Rivals: The Eighth and Fifteenth Air Force in World War II." *Air Power History,* Summer 1991.

——. "Mutiny at Army Air Force Station 569: Bamber Bridge, England, June 1943." *Aerospace Historian* (December 1975).

——. "The Strategic Bombing of Germany in World War II: Costs and Accomplishments." *Journal of American History* 73, no. 3 (December 1986).

——. "The USAAF Over Europe and Its Foes: A Selected, Subjective, and Critical Bibliography." *Aerospace Historian* 25, no. 4 (1978).

Wheeler, Gerald E. "Mitchell, Moffett, and Air Power." *Airpower Historian* 8, no. 2 (April 1961).

White, M. S. "Medical Problems of Air Warfare." *Military Surgeon,* May 1945.

"Why a German Fights On." *Newsweek,* March 26, 1945.

Williams, Kenneth D. "The Saga of 'Murder, Inc.' " *8th Air Force News* 12, no. 1 (January 1986).

Williams, Roger M. "Why Wasn't Auschwitz Bombed?" *Commonweal* 105 (November 24, 1978).

Wohl, Robert. "The Prophets of Air War." *MHQ* 7, no. 2 (Winter 1995).

Wolff, Harold G. "Every Man Has His Breaking Point: The Conduct of Prisoners of War." *Military Medicine* 125 (February 1960).

Wormley, Gordon W. "An Anoxia Accident in the 8th Air Force." *Air Surgeon's Bulletin* 1, no. 9 (September 1944).

Wolk, Herman S. "The Establishment of the United States Air Force." *Air Force Magazine,* September 1982.

Wyman, David S. "Why Auschwitz Was Never Bombed." *Commentary* 65 (May 1978).

Yurovich, Douglas P. "How Effective Is Strategic Bombing." *Parameters* 32, no. 1 (Spring 2002).

Zuckerman, Solly. "Strategic Bombing and the Defeat of Germany." *Royal United Service Institution,* 130 (June 1985).

Newspapers

London *Times*
London *Daily Telegraph*
Stars and Stripes
New York Times
Washington Star

Author Interviews

Much of this book is based on over 250 oral history interviews conducted in England, the Netherlands, France, Switzerland, Luxembourg, Belgium, Germany, and the United States. The testimonies used in the text are listed in the Notes.

Web Sites

Every Eighth Air Force Bomber and Fighter Group has a Web site that contains a history of the group, wartime records and diaries, oral history testimonies, photographs, mission reports, lists of crews and planes, and more. I have used these sites extensively.

Other Web Sites
www.aeroflight.co.uk/waf/switz/swisaf2.htm
www.wiesenthal.com/swiss/survey/noframes/indx.html
www.wissenthjal.com/swiss/survey/noframes/conclusions.htm
www.kaselmisson.com

Index

Page numbers in *italics* refer to illustrations, charts, and maps.